D1346792

The publisher gratefully acknowledges the generous support
of the Ahmanson Foundation Humanities Endowment
Fund of the University of California Press Foundation and
of James and Carlin Naify as members of the Literati Circle
of the University of California Press Foundation.

FRENCH
VOICES

This work, published as part of a program providing
publication assistance, received financial support from
the French Ministry of Foreign Affairs, the Cultural
Services of the French Embassy in the United States,
and FACE (French American Cultural Exchange).

Beirut

Samir Kassir

Translated by M. B. DeBevoise

Foreword by Robert Fisk

UNIVERSITY OF CALIFORNIA PRESS

Berkeley   Los Angeles   London

University of California Press, one of the most distinguished university presses in the United States, enriches lives around the world by advancing scholarship in the humanities, social sciences, and natural sciences. Its activities are supported by the UC Press Foundation and by philanthropic contributions from individuals and institutions. For more information, visit www.ucpress.edu.

University of California Press
Berkeley and Los Angeles, California

University of California Press, Ltd.
London, England
First paperback printing 2011
© 2010 by The Regents of the University of California

Originally published as *Histoire de Beyrouth* by Samir Kassir,
© Librairie Arthème Fayard, 2003.

Library of Congress Cataloging-in-Publication Data

Kassir, Samir.
 [Histoire de Beyrouth. English]
 Beirut / Samir Kassir ; foreword by Robert Fisk ; translated by
M.B. DeBevoise.
    p.   cm.
 Originally published: Paris : Fayard, c2003, under title Histoire
de Beyrouth.
 Includes bibliographical references and index.
 ISBN 978-0-520-27126-5 (pbk. : alk. paper)
 1. Beirut (Lebanon)—History.   I. Title.
 DS89.B4K3813   2010
 956.92′5—dc22   2009037305

19 18 17 16 15 14 13 12 11
10 9

For Gisèle,
Beyrouthine extra-muros

CONTENTS

ILLUSTRATIONS

MAPS

FIGURES

ix

FOREWORD TO THE ENGLISH-LANGUAGE EDITION

Robert Fisk

The story of Beirut is in many ways as tragic and as wonderful as Samir Kassir's life. Admired, exalted, free-spirited, dedicated to the intellect and to social progress, ancient Beirut with its Roman law school was as famous as Ottoman Beirut with its boulevards and flourishing academies and newspapers, and as renowned as the art deco Mandate capital of France's hopeless *Grand-Liban*. Yet it was destroyed by earthquakes, surrounded by armies, its people massacred from the Crusades to the 1975–90 civil war, in five Israeli invasions and in thirty-four years of Syrian military hegemony.

Samir Kassir flew like a moth through the last chapter of Lebanon's history, feted, admired, jealously despised, a beacon of freedom in a place without oxygen, his genius almost inevitably consumed by his country's violence. At forty-five, he was a journalist's dream: writer, philosopher, academic, intellectual, reporter. Yes, he was also what we would call a street reporter, fighting off threatening calls from the secret police while condemning the Syrian intelligence apparatus. And it ended in the Alfa Romeo, registration number 165670, so carelessly parked opposite his home in Beirut on the morning of 2 June 2005.

Now *I* was the reporter, filing to the London *Independent* as if my colleague were just another assassination target—which, in one sense, he was—the latest Beirut victim, and there I was interviewing the eyewitnesses like any crime reporter. " 'He always left home at 10:30 A.M. and I saw him walking across the street,' a female neighbour told me. 'He opened the door of his car, sat inside and started the engine. Then the car blew up.' Close inspection . . . showed clearly that the blast came from beneath the driver's seat. It tore open the roof, blasted out the driver's door, smashed the steering column and hurled Kassir onto the passenger seat. The ignition apparently detonated the bomb." It was a shock that no one in Beirut expected—except, of course, the assassins. After the Saint Valentine's Day murder of former prime minister Rafiq Hariri, we all thought Lebanon's assassins—with a UN international tribunal on their tail—were in their rabbit holes, fearful of arrest. But no, they were still on operational duty, still in killing mode. The moth had flown too close to the candle.

In retrospect, I think that Samir Kassir misunderstood his future killers. He had clearly identified them before he died. For him, they were the Syrian military-intelligence apparatus—apparently defeated after the outcry that followed Hariri's killing—and the Ba'thist power, which crushed any serious freedoms in Lebanon with the help of its Lebanese collaborators (who in Kassir's mind included the Syrian-supported President Émile Lahoud). As an internationalist, Kassir believed he had mortally offended these men—they were, inevitably, all men—because he broke the bounds of the narrow Arab nationalism which the Middle East dictatorships clung to so faithfully for their survival. He sought democracy in Syria—he was half-Syrian—as well as in Lebanon.

But because of his misunderstanding, Kassir broke one of the cardinal rules of journalism. As a reporter or columnist, you can take on governments or armies or corrupt politicians or secret policemen or clergymen or multinationals. But the one thing reporters must *never* attempt is to take on organized crime. They will never win. They will be eliminated, liquidated, murdered, burned without any compunction. You can take on the big city boss. But you cannot fight the mafia. Only states can do that, nations with powerful and uncorrupted police forces and armies, acting under national orders or UN instructions. Kassir saw his adversaries as political enemies—corrupt but amenable, in the end, to some kind of law—or as venal paramilitaries who could ultimately be brought to heel, humiliated in the face of rational argument and the force of law.

But Kassir's enemies were much bigger than that. They created and lived in a world of bribery and stolen wealth, which spread like a web over the Middle East, to Egypt, to Iraq, to Jordan, even to Israel. To offend Syria was to offend the Saudis. And the Iranians. And the party hacks who supported Syria—and were financially sustained by Syria—within Lebanon itself. This was not about individuals. I don't believe that the Arab kings and princes—nor President Bashar al-Assad of Syria—ever personally gave orders for the murder of prominent journalists or politicians (the slaughter of vast masses of rebellious citizens in the region—nationalist or Islamist—is quite another matter). We are talking about corporate crime.

This involves a multimillion-dollar nexus of wealth which defends itself against any assault. Money protects itself, ruthlessly and lethally. The pen is not mightier than the sword. The sword is far more powerful. Special pleading on behalf of Renaissance men—for the literary, historical, brave figures who should be able to cure the malaise of the Arab world—is useless. This was the reason for Kassir's death.

It is not difficult to see why this malaise—he often used the word—fascinated and appalled Kassir. He loved the way in which Western culture infused itself into the Arab world, through novels and French philosophy, in the nineteenth century, and he never forgot that this flowering occurred during the last years of the Ottoman Empire. Though no imperialist, Kassir saw the Ottomans as the key to both Arab hope and Arab tragedy, and it is no surprise that his chapters on Ottoman Beirut are by far the most revealing in this massive history of the city in which he lived—for most of his life—and in which he died. One of the great ironies of his death was that those who mourned him began their statistics of murdered writers with the journalists demanding Lebanese independence who were hanged by the Turks in Beirut during the First World War, in what—after them—is now called Place des Martyrs.

His Palestinian-Syrian origins, his Lebanese-French citizenship, made Kassir an internationalist. That the Lebanese security apparatus should have temporarily confiscated his passport at Beirut airport not long before his murder—to discover to what "use" it had been put—was an insult that the intelligence authorities probably did not fully comprehend. This, after all, was a journalist who began writing for a newspaper (the Lebanese Communist Party's *Al-Nida'*) at the age of seventeen, who had spent nineteen years writing for *Le Monde Diplomatique,* and who edited the frenetic *Le Liban en Lutte*—it supported Lebanese resistance movements during the initial Israeli invasion and occupation of 1982–83—and ran a political-cultural monthly, *L'Orient-Express,* until its advertisers turned against it in the late '90s. He wrote about Arabs rather than Arab nations; he explored the history of the Palestinians within the Arab world rather than within the narrow framework of Arafat's nationalism. Kassir's real passport was international.

There is little doubt that he was the bravest of those who spoke out against Syria. No sooner had he received a threatening phone call from the then-head of Lebanese security—who was imprisoned for four years on suspicion of complicity in Hariri's murder until suddenly released as the UN's investigation foundered—than he was telling his readers about it. Here is what he wrote about Syria in *Being Arab*:

> Suffocated for forty years under a dictatorship that, although less bloodthirsty than Iraq's, has still brutally run it into the ground, systematically bled dry by powerful mafias, and weakened by a culture of fear, Syria is now in a position almost without equivalent in the Arab world—apart perhaps from Libya, although it doesn't have Libya's oil—in that it combines the corruption of the Soviet republics with a Chinese-styled closed police state. (Trans. Will Hobson [London: Verso, 2006], 20)

Lebanon—one of "the laboratories of modernity," as he called it—could take pride in the resistance which forced Israel from its territory, but its achievement had been appropriated by "Syrian obstructiveness and Islamist activism." Islamism of the bin Laden, Wahabi type was treated with contempt by a man who could always be described with that old journalistic cliché "leftist." A belief in a mere forty years of "golden" Islam—after which the rest of Islamic-Arab history had gone to pot—was a nonsense that Kassir scarcely bothered to dispute. This was a man, therefore, who would generate as many enemies as admirers. The use of that one word "mafias" touched, of course, on the reason for his own demise.

In *Beirut,* Kassir describes lovingly how the Ottoman rulers of the city paved its roads, laid down water mains, administered the law, encouraged higher education. "In its imperial phase," he was to write elsewhere of the Ottomans, "Arab history reads like an accumulation of cultural experiments or, more precisely, as an accumulation of cultural diversity. This is hardly surprising, given that its legacy is still the basic point of reference—and legitimization—for the most divergent systems of thought. Primacy of the profane over the sacred for some, of the sacred over the profane for others, philosophical rationalism, theocratic authoritarianism, dissenting mysticism, even utopianism—nothing human is alien to the Ottoman Empire's cultural universe" (*Being Arab,* 37). The Ottomans, he says, could embrace the Aristotelian rationalism of Averroës, the theology of Ghazali, the sociology of Ibn Khaldun.

I'm not sure if Kassir wasn't a little too generous to the Ottomans. Theirs was not an inclusive society, although it did attempt—faithfully or unfaithfully, depending on whether you lived inside or outside the empire—to live like "us." The Ottomans commissioned the greatest engineering feat of its time, the Suez Canal; they introduced state-of-the-art Swiss rack-and-pinion steam locomotives to haul Lebanon's passenger trains over the mountains to Damascus—the locos still rot beside the east Beirut highway opposite the old Phalangist militia headquarters; and the sultans of Constantinople learned to paint and to play the piano. "They wanted to be like you," Professor Kamal Salibi once told me. "So you destroyed them." And he was right. How easily we forget that one of the successful Allied war aims in the First World War was to destroy the Ottoman Empire.

Salibi, a Protestant, is of a previous generation, although his *A House of Many Mansions* remains the prime de-mythology of the Lebanese Phoenician story, a narrative to which Kassir grants due if ritual prominence. Kassir's classical Beirut is pompous—if slightly heavy—and his post-Crusader Beirut heavy in irony. Much as obituaries should avoid perfecting the dead, forewords should be frank about the books they introduce: Kassir recalls post-independence Beirut, with its tawdry corruptions and call girls and tatty cinemas, in accurate if bawdy and cheap detail. He treats the 1975–90 civil war with near-contempt.

Kassir's academic background—his Sorbonne doctorate in modern history and his lectureship at the Université Saint-Joseph in Beirut—sits lightly on his work. "Arab victimhood goes beyond the 'Why do they hate us?' question, which Arabs would be as entitled to ask as the Americans were on the morning of September 11," he writes with simplicity. "Inflamed by the West's attitude to the Palestinian question, it has incorporated other elements, notably the feeling of powerlessness and also a certain crime-novel vision of history" (*Being Arab,* 80).

Kassir's touch with practical politics was equally light. He was a founder of Lebanon's Democratic Left Movement, which won a seat in the 2005 elections, but which was infinitely more important as a catalyst of the protests that followed Hariri's murder. Kassir's party colleagues were to elevate him to martyr status after his murder—somehow "Comrade Kassir" did not suit his bon vivant lifestyle, and naming a square after him blunted his status as a historian of Beirut. He was part of the city and would surely have known how easily streets change their names in Beirut. Until 1941, there was even a Rue Pétain.

His second wife, Gisèle Khoury (Kassir was an Orthodox Christian), works for Al-ʿArabiyya television, and he left two daughters, Mayssa and Liana, by an earlier marriage. A host of Kassir journalism prizes and festivals now make his name sacred. A Samir Kassir Foundation oversees the translation of his work into English, Norwegian, and Italian.

But the Samir Kassir who lived—rather than the one who died and immediately entered the gloomy portals of Lebanon's assassinated nobility—would be fighting for more than just political freedom. The continuing demise of the city about which he writes—with varying eloquence, to be sure—would have engaged his wrath today. For developers and the billion-dollar Solidere company, which rebuilt the center of the city—tearing down ruined Ottoman streets while carefully restoring the colonial French Mandate piles that survived the civil war—are now eating into the wreckage of the empire's homes and villas that Kassir so admired.

Two weeks before writing this foreword, I took a walk through Kassir's old Beirut—the streets bathed in purple and crimson bougainvillea, ancient yellow stones glowing with warmth, but their Ottoman keeps now in a state of ruin, their roofs collapsing, their marble balconies cracked, their staircases propped up with wood, their frescoed windows shaking in the wind because war-shattered glass was long ago replaced with plastic sheeting, now torn. In Lebanon, only land has value, property none. Thus it is more profitable to tear down yet more of the pride of the Sublime Porte and build another high-rise suburb. After the murder of Kassir comes the murder of the city he loved.

For thirty-four years, I have looked at these buildings as a foreigner, driving past them in the war, queued behind traffic in their canyon streets as my driver Abed—whose father was taken by the Ottomans, only days after his marriage, to fight Allenby's army in Palestine—recalled a Beirut of cream-and-brown streetcars and cobbled streets. This, he would tell me, was the Palais Heneiné—built in 1880 by a Russian count and once the U.S. Beirut Consulate to the Ottoman Empire. And that used to be the Bustani School . . .

And indeed, there it is, the collapsing vestibule of this most famous and challenging of Beirut's educational institutions, the first secular school of Beirut (1863) for children of every religion, its classrooms now decayed into run-down Pepsi parlors, its great goitered arches crumbling behind a concrete wall, the home now to stringy cats and garbage. Butrus Bustani, a Christian, was one of the great intellectuals of late nineteenth-century Lebanon, editor of a famous Arabic dictionary and encyclopedia. His schoolteachers' homes now sprout trees. Around the corner is the home (1880) of Selim Dahesh, author of 150 books—now commemorated in the Dahesh Museum of Art in Manhattan—where eighty-eight-year-old Zeina, daughter of one of Lebanon's most famous painters, sits by cracked windows, looked after by neighbors, living most of her time in a marble kitchen that should be in a ghost story, and greets each of her visitors with mesmeric eyes and arthritic hands.

Kassir is no longer here to defend this history. Nor what is left of the post-Ottoman frenzy for knowledge. Only three hundred meters from the Bustani school a gaunt concrete gateway leads to the American Printing School, the first Western publishing center in Beirut—every metal wall sheet imported from America in 1920, its three stories of shelving a Meccano-set of stairs, and a single iron elevator grinding to the top floor, where a dead pigeon lies beneath an iron printing press made by Mensfeld of Leipzig in 1929. The staff still pack books for distribution—children's fairy stories, a dictionary of pharmacology. On top of the dictionary I found a pocket edition of Pascal's *Pensées*.

I am suspicious of foreigners who tell me they love Beirut. I love the life I live in Beirut, but I think you have to be homegrown—or at least Arab-grown—to claim a city like Beirut as an *amour*. I've climbed down excavated Canaanite walls in the city center, been the first to cup in my hands a tiny iron animal brooch that had not seen the sunlight for two thousand years, in Roman Berytus. I've watched Beirut burn. Kassir's massive work is not unsurpassable, although his ability to look sideways into the city's history rather than downwards is almost unique. Perhaps it is less violent.

That he should die there was perhaps inevitable. "Why don't they leave us alone now?" one of his young neighbors asked me before the cops towed Kassir's Alfa Romeo away and his followers spread a sea of candles across the road. "Why must they go on using this methodology of murder? We have to stop this. Are they trying to drive all the young people out of Lebanon?" Not long after Kassir's killing, his colleague and editor at *An-Nahar* was atomized by a car bomb in eastern Beirut. There were twelve political murders at this time—a dozen in just three years, including that of Kassir. No arrests, of course. There never are in Beirut. Warm and gentle Beirut may be. But tough and cruel.

Beirut
June 2010

TRANSLATOR'S NOTE

Samir Kassir's untimely death deprived him of the opportunity to make corrections to the original French edition. With the encouragement of University of California Press and the approval of the Kassir Foundation I have silently corrected minor errors of fact in the French text, while also in places adding elements of historical detail that American and other English-speaking readers may find helpful in following the narrative of events, particularly in the twentieth century. The organization of the French text has been slightly modified as well, and a very small amount of extraneous detail deleted.

The use of gallicized versions of many personal and proper names, as well as toponyms, is difficult to avoid, as Kassir rightly says, in recounting the history of an Arab city where the French language has been a formidable presence for almost two centuries now. In the case of place names the ʿayn has been retained, in keeping with standard Arabic pronunciation, except for very well known places; long vowels are indicated only where there is a risk of ambiguity. With regard to the transliteration of Arabic personal names, I have respected English rather than French orthographic conventions, while making an exception for political and other figures who are known to history by the French spelling of their names; and on the whole I have followed the author in adopting the simplified system of transliteration favored by most Western Arabists, dispensing with vowel markings in the text. Full diacritical form is nevertheless given not only for Arabic words and phrases but also for all classical authors and most other figures up through the early modern period. Complete transcriptions of Western borrowings from the Arabic may be found in the glossary.

On behalf of the Press, I thank Ilham Khuri-Makdisi for reviewing and revising the transliterations.

ACKNOWLEDGMENTS

This book owes its existence to the faith shown by Agnès Fontaine a long while ago, when Beirut lay still in ruins, that the city would rise again and take its rightful place alongside the other great cities of the world as part of a series of urban histories she was about to launch at Éditions Fayard in Paris. I thank her for this faith here, as well as her successor, Denis Maraval, and dare to hope that this book will go some ways toward repaying their immense patience.

The historian rarely stands before his work alone—still less the historian of current events, especially when he has taken so long to finish. In the meantime a thousand and one ideas have come to me from conversations with teachers and friends who have by now perhaps forgotten my debt to them. My gratitude extends to all those scholars of Beirut whom I have had the occasion to meet in the course of the last ten years, to the many writers and artists who continue to portray the city in their own work, and also to citizens of Beirut from other walks of life who have helped me to see the history of our city in new ways.

Among all those to whom I owe thanks, I find myself under special obligation to a few friends in particular. Fawaz Traboulsi brought to bear the critical scrutiny of a fellow historian, and Melhem Chaoul looked at the manuscript from the point of view of a sociologist. Both prompted me to sharpen my arguments and to give them a nuance they lacked. Nawaf Salam read large parts of it as well, ready always to clarify a point of detail, to enrich the bibliography, and to share insights gained from writing his own history of Beirut.

Jade Tabet helped me find my way through the architectural strata of the city. Rasha Salti continually urged me to think more incisively about its social culture. Alexandre Medawar allowed me to look upon Beirut from the aerial perspective of a cartographer. Maïssa Kassir did me the favor of casting a skeptical eye on the result.

Henri Laurens, intermittent resident of Beirut, eminent Ottomanist and head of the former Centre d'Études et de Recherches sur le Moyen-Orient Contemporain (CERMOC), now the Institut Français du Proche-Orient, kindly found time in a busy schedule to corroborate or challenge my judgments. Dominique Chevallier's seminar at the Sorbonne continues still to stimulate my thinking, at a distance of some two decades, no less than the conversation of my learned friend Farouk Mardam-Bey.

Any faults that may yet remain, despite so much generous assistance from so many, are obviously my own.

ALBA	Académie Libanaise des Beaux-Arts (Fine Arts Academy of Lebanon)
ANM	Arab Nationalist Movement
APUR	Atelier Parisien d'Urbanisme (Paris Urbanism Workshop)
ATCL	Automobile and Touring Club of Lebanon
AUB	American University of Beirut
BCD	Beirut Central District
BSL	Banque de Syrie et du Liban (Bank of Syria and Lebanon)
BSR	Bureau of Studies and Research
BTA	Beirut Traders Association
CAOL	Communist Action Organization in Lebanon
CLT	Compagnie Libanaise de Télévision (Lebanese Television Company)
CPF	Collège Protestant Français (French Protestant College)
CPSL	Communist Party of Syria and Lebanon
CUP	Committee of Union and Progress
DFLP	Democratic Front for the Liberation of Palestine
DGU	Direction Générale de l'Urbanisme (Directorate-General of Urban Planning)
FFM	Faculté Française de Médecine (French Faculty of Medicine)
IAURIF	Institut d'Aménagement et d'Urbanisme de la Région Île-de-France (Institute for Development and Urbanism of the Île-de-France Region)
ICRC	International Committee of the Red Cross
IDHEC	Institut des Hautes Études Cinématographiques (Institute of Advanced Film Studies)

IRFED	Institut de Recherche et de Formation en Vue du Développement (Institute of Research and Training for Development; later, the International Training and Research Institute for Education and Development)
LCP	Lebanese Communist Party
LNM	Lebanese National Movement (al-Haraka al-wataniyya); originally the Front for Progressive Parties and National Forces
LNRF	Lebanese National Resistance Front
MEA	Middle East Airlines
MLF	Mission Laïque Française (French Secular Mission)
NLP	National Liberal Party
OEG	Office de l'Économie de Guerre (War Economy Board)
PASC	Palestinian Armed Struggle Command
PFLP	Popular Front for the Liberation of Palestine
PLO	Palestine Liberation Organization
PSP	Progressive Socialist Party
SERIAC	Société d'Études et de Réalisations Industrielles, Agricoles et Commerciales (Industrial, Agricultural, and Commercial Design and Construction Corporation)
SPC	Syrian Protestant College
SSNP	Syrian Social Nationalist Party
TFL	Troupes Françaises du Levant (French Troops of the Levant)
TMA	Trans Mediterranean Airways
UAR	United Arab Republic
UL	Université Libanaise (Lebanese University)
UNESCO	United Nations Educational, Scientific, and Cultural Organization
UNIFL	United Nations Interim Force in Lebanon
UNRWA	United Nations Relief and Works Agency for Palestine Refugees in the Near East
USJ	Université Saint-Joseph (Saint Joseph University)
USMF	United States Multilateral Force

Prologue

FIGURE 1 *(preceding page)*. The promontory seen from the sea, ca. 1970. Reproduced by permission of the Beirut Ministry of Tourism.

The Eyes of the Mind

Your adolescence was followed
By a long chain of mountains
You love abandoning yourself to the din of sleeping cities
You love exposing yourself to the miracle of the air.
You saw the young girl who comes from the sea
She wears the roses of Alexandria in her hair
The dreams of madness start out through the gardens.

GEORGES SCHÉHADÉ

"*Do you know the Lebanon?*"
I shook my head.
"*In the evenings the sky is like wine and the shadows falling across the terraces have purple edges to them. Overhead, vines—grape and other things with big flowers and a wonderful smell. Everything is very still and warm and soft. It's the kind of atmosphere in which myths are born and the pictures in your mind's eye seem more real than the chair you're sitting on. I wax lyrical, you see.*"

ERIC AMBLER, *JUDGMENT ON DELTCHEV*

There are places that inspire lyricism. Lying in the shadow of a mountain, streaked by riverbeds aligned with one another by some unknown Providence or hand of fate, set alongside coves and shores of rock, pebble, and sand and endowed with natural harbors that for centuries have witnessed the ceaseless labors of mankind, the long and narrow plain that runs along the Mediterranean littoral has captured the imagination of travelers since ancient times, whether they first set eyes upon it from the sea or from the heights of Mount Lebanon. Here, bathed in color night and day, its line broken only by two great cliffs, not quite twenty miles apart, that seem to still the flow of the water, and by a promontory a little further to the south that stands sentinel over the sea, the coast of the Mediterranean has given more than one author the impression of enfolding the heavens in its embrace. "It is indeed

3

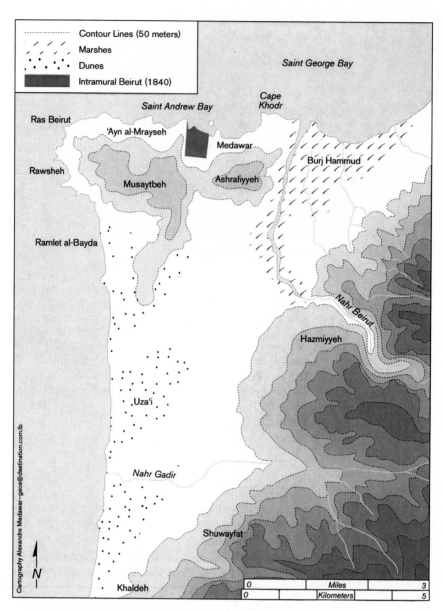

MAP 1. Beirut and Its Physical Site

the happy shore," the French geographer and anarchist Élisée Reclus wrote about the coast of Byblos, "where voluptuousness was deified."[1]

Lying a few leagues from that ancient city and, according to a legend cited by Reclus, founded on the same day, Beirut has fewer claims to immemorial glory. But seen from the broad promontory that looks out upon the open sea, practically at the midpoint of the eastern shore of the Mediterranean, halfway between Antioch to the north and Gaza to the south, at the center of the western edge of the coastal plain that for some hundred twenty miles constitutes the border of the Lebanese Republic with Syria, Beirut can no more be depicted in neutral terms than Byblos itself. Even if one were to try only to situate it geographically, the alchemy of words could not be avoided. Inevitably one is forced to resort to a formula that was destined to appear in every tourist guide: between sea and mountain. An indispensable phrase—how else can one describe a city built on a cape and dominated over its full extent by a steep and commanding barrier?

From whichever side one considers it, Beirut depends for its effects on the dramatic juncture of the land, at varying elevations, with the Mediterranean. Not only is it overhung to the east by the Mount Lebanon range—even more abruptly today than in ancient times, when it rose to a height of more than fifteen hundred feet some four miles from the city limits and more than three thousand feet scarcely two-and-a-half miles further (today the urban footprint climbs up to the line of the mountain and in some places goes beyond it); the uneven relief of the promontory on which the city is built was to determine its contours and often its toponyms. The old town occupied the gap between the two hills that form this headland. In the nineteenth and twentieth centuries the metropolitan area expanded with astonishing rapidity, taking possession of the slopes and finally, in the disarray of the war that lasted from 1975 to 1990, spilling over along the northern littoral and, to the south and east, onto the mountainside itself. Nearer to the coast, again to the east, overlooking the modern port and bordered by a river that bears the city's name, Nahr Beirut (known to the ancient Romans as Magoras), the hill of Ashrafiyyeh rises to a height of more than three hundred feet. To the west, the hill of Musaytbeh—broader though more modest, only some two hundred fifty feet high—plunges vertically almost into the sea, looming over the island-cliffs known to Western visitors as La Grotte aux Pigeons or the Pigeon Rocks, and to natives of Beirut as Rawsheh (or Raouché, from the French word for rock, *rocher*), and, on its northern face, descending more gently to the fishing port of 'Ayn al-Mrayseh.

All these things combine to give Beirut a striking and altogether pleasing eminence, readily perceived by the visitor who catches sight of it from a distance, whether arriving by sea or coming overland from Damascus. Even the insistent erosion of the native vegetation, which in the second half of the twentieth century was to impoverish the landscape by eradicating the pine forests on the foothills of Mount Lebanon that succeed the olive and banana trees of the plain, and before

FIGURE 2. A bank note showing the Pigeon Rocks across from the cliffs of Rawsheh.

them the cypress and sycamores of the city, has not entirely dispelled the sense of wonder that is summoned up by the sudden appearance of a peninsula that seems to have fallen to earth from the heavens. The arresting natural contrasts of this triangle of land, at once darkened by the shadow of the mountain and bathed in an iridescent light by the shimmering reflections of the sea, are further accentuated by a secondary layer of relief composed of a dense mass of buildings of unequal height, set next to one another like the flowers of a bouquet. No less than the charming small town of the nineteenth century had done, with its reddish orange roofs staggered in tiers against a green background, the modern city captivates and delights.

But does the visitor therefore have to stand back a step or two in order to appreciate the beauties of Beirut? Today there is no choice, because the nearer one comes to the city the more clearly the consequences of uncontrolled growth, and of a corresponding lack of intelligent urban planning, can be seen. One must resign oneself instead to snatching occasional glimpses of Beirut's architectural heritage and panoramic perspectives—here a triple arcade, there a stained-glass window, elsewhere a fragment of a larger view taking in mountain or sea, sometimes both. One thinks of the surprise that greets travelers on reaching Ras Beirut, at the western end of the corniche, where they see suddenly rise up across the water to the northeast, as though it had been thrust up from the deep, the snow-capped crest of Mount Sannīn. Another classic scene, perhaps even more intrinsic to the idea of Beirut since it does not require the intercession of a mountain, is presented by the Pigeon Rocks themselves, anchored in the small bay that lies next to the western flank of the promontory. There they stand, clad in walls of limestone, as though some supernatural power had wrested them out of the bowels of the earth: two almost perfectly vertical monoliths, nearly one hundred fifty feet high, long the reward of carefree rock climbers seeking enchantment and the refuge of unhappy souls seeking to take their own lives.

Small consolation, even so, for a city that announces itself from such a distance. The full extent of the architectural wasteland that began to take shape during the 1960s was able to be judged only after the war, with the spectacular renovation of long-neglected masterpieces. It arose from monumental failures of urban planning—failures on such a scale that the attractions of the physical site itself had come to be neutralized. Beginning in the 1950s, and then ever more quickly during the following decade, concrete began to crowd out gardens. Apartment blocks, soon followed by towers devoid of charm, or indeed of any real utility, now dwarfed their neighbors; inexorably they displaced the low houses built out of *ramleh,* the reddish sandstone that helped to give the traditional domestic architecture of Beirut its distinctive character. The negligence of public administration, reinforced by sharply accelerating rates of demographic growth, erased all memory of the fact that intelligent efforts at managing the expansion of the city had been made during the last years of the Ottoman Empire, and afterward during the French Mandate, often with picturesque results. Still less could the secret rationality of the old suqs inherited from the nineteenth century any longer be suspected.

The very form and shape of the city had been hidden from view by concrete. Albums of postcards and of old photographs of Beirut from the 1930s and 1940s—wildly popular since the war a half-century later—plainly show that during the late Ottoman period and the French Mandate the city outgrew its former boundaries, the original port and the walls of the old town, which occupy the flat land lying between the two hills that form the promontory to the south. Neighborhoods began to spread out on all sides, but private gardens and empty lots still allowed the urban tissue to breathe: the hills themselves preserved an almost cavelike appearance, dotted with two- and three-story buildings whose roofs, covered by Marseille tile, descended gradually from the campus of the American University of Beirut on Musaytbeh and, to the east from the heights of Ashrafiyyeh, down to the modern port. Since then the promontory has been filled up by buildings of miscellaneous design and sometimes disproportionate size, without any effort having been made to integrate them with their natural situation; to the contrary, one detects an ambition—sometimes openly acknowledged—to remodel the headland, if not actually to efface it after the manner of the embankments along the shore, which were replaced by new construction. However this may be, the contempt for common sense and anything approximating a rational street plan has been total. It is a paradox of modernity that as the city grew, the more it came to resemble the labyrinth of the old walled town before the first attempts to untangle the maze of alleys and side streets momentarily gave it an air of harmony. And no matter how much wider the city's thoroughfares became, the congestion of pedestrian and automobile traffic and the increased stress placed on sidewalks and streets only amplified the sense of dislocation and alienation, and deepened the impression of a great many people crammed together in a small space.

1974: SCENIC ESCAPE FROM THE FAMILIAR

If Beirut in its golden age was no longer a beautiful city, it left no one indifferent—least of all those who did not live there year-round. The perspective that outsiders bring to a place nourishes myths more surely than the routine experience of its native population. Beirut, more than most cities, naturally lent itself to this kind of idealization. Just as one must stand back a ways to appreciate the allure of the city's setting, so too one needs to keep a certain distance in order to let the eyes of the mind perceive the exhilarating fascination that Beirut once exerted upon occasional or seasonal residents, many of them from the other side of the Mediterranean, or even of the Atlantic. For these distant travelers, as for those visiting from neighboring countries, Beirut's many masks converged to create the image of an idyllic place—an image now converted by nostalgia into the memory of a lost golden age.

This age reached its apogee on the eve of a chain reaction of violence that between the spring of 1975 and the fall of 1990 came close to sweeping away the city, and along with it the country itself. In 1974, Beirut ranked among the greatest metropolises of the Near East. With a population of only slightly more than a million, its demographic weight was modest by comparison with Cairo, even with Damascus; and as the capital of one of the smallest Arab states, it could scarcely claim to be a major international center of decision making or diplomacy, even if the welcome Beirut granted to the leadership of the Palestinian resistance placed it at the heart of a political dynamic that transcended regional boundaries. No matter. And yet since the early 1960s it had incontestably been one of the premier poles of cultural and economic attraction in the Arab world. Among all the cities of this world, it yielded perhaps only to Cairo—and even then, not in every domain.

As a university seat and medical center, as the capital of Arab publishing and journalism, as a transit port and airline hub, and as a market and clearinghouse for every kind of commercial and banking transaction, from the most ordinary to the most dubious, Beirut fulfilled a great many functions that went beyond the frontiers of the Republic of Lebanon. In exchange for these services it was paid in the form of currency—every currency in the world. Though it was not a wealthy city, it gave every appearance of being one; and because money begets more money, it exhibited the same insouciance one finds in wealthy cities everywhere, serenely confident that its sources of revenue would never dry up.

Extrovert by virtue of the many roles that it played, Beirut was outgoing also by virtue of its very personality. What made its reputation, and in large measure accounted for its charm, was not only the variety of services that it rendered; it was also, and perhaps especially, the fact that it was a bustling metropolis—the like of which could not be found within a radius of several hundreds of miles. If the range of purposes Beirut served can be described in a sentence or two, a whole kaleidoscope of images must be conjured up to capture the sparkling effervescence of this golden age, which fell between the Palestine war of 1948 and the interminable conflict that began not quite thirty years later. Even conceding that the dizzying pace of life that accompanies every recollection of this period is, yet again, only an effect of nostalgia, it is nonetheless true that Beirut was then a remarkably vibrant city, more vibrant than any other in the entire region, at least to judge from its unrivaled power of attraction.

Lebanon's Arab neighbors flocked to Beirut in great numbers. Whether they came from the oil states of the Arabian Peninsula, not yet equipped with the amenities of modern cities, or from highly urbanized countries elsewhere, Arab visitors had every reason to be enchanted—in the first place, by the natural environment. With the exception of Syria, which in its exposure to the Mediterranean shares with Lebanon much the same coastal panorama (apart from the Aleppo pines [*Pinus halipensis]* one finds to the north, more similar to the pines on the upper slopes of Slunfeh and Kassib than to the cedars and parasol pines of Lebanon), and where, on its border with Lebanon, Mount Hermon is crowned by snow year-round, the Near East knows no comparable line of mountainous relief and adjacent sea, and so none of the flora and microclimates found in these two countries. The change of scenery is dramatic: suddenly the monochromatic shades of sand of the Arab steppes give way to a palette of greens and blues, augmented by white during the winter. Even by comparison with the Ghuta, the fertile plain around Damascus that preserves something of the aspect of the Garden of Eden that may once have flowered there, or with the towns of the Orontes Valley, sparkling with water and foliage, Beirut presents a richness of color combined with a softness in the tones of the surrounding landscape that neither of these places can match. Indeed it is this fact, and more precisely the presence of a mountainous terrain, that led the French poet and historian Alphonse de Lamartine to call Beirut the Switzerland of the Levant, long before the law on banking secrecy enacted in 1956 gave another dimension to the analogy.

Already agreeably disoriented by the novelty of its vistas, travelers who arrived in Beirut from the Persian Gulf for the first time in the 1960s and 1970s were all the more disconcerted for having come upon a city built on hills where nothing resembled what they knew—neither the jumble of streets and boulevards nor the lavish window displays in the stores, nor the ample supply of leisure activities nor the orgy of neon signs advertising them, nor the hectic life of the city (both day and night), nor the freedom of appearance enjoyed by the men (and even more so by the women) they passed on the sidewalks. Europe during this period was not yet the familiar destination that it was to become after the oil boom. By default, Beirut was the nearest city of the West. But it was a Western city that spoke the same Arabic

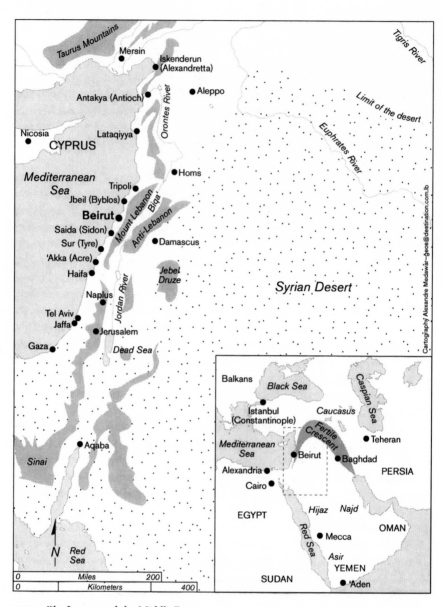

MAP 2. The Levant and the Middle East

they did, albeit with a more relaxed accent. Syrians, Iraqis, and even Egyptians, though they were better prepared for such an encounter than visitors from the Gulf states, were no less apt to find themselves caught up in the pulsating life of the city, no less vulnerable to its promptings and solicitations, no less beguiled by its exuberance; and finding themselves reassured at the same time by the many similarities between Beirut and their own capitals, some of which had preceded Beirut on the road to modernity, they were eager to explore a city that they had embraced from the very first moment they set foot in it as their home away from home, neither entirely different from where they came from nor quite the same.

To get to Beirut one had to cross a border, of course, which for everyone but the Syrians meant holding a passport and obtaining a visa. For those who could afford to make the trip, Beirut was the least foreign international destination imaginable, and yet also the most stimulating. There were any number of reasons to go there: to sign a contract, withdraw money from a bank account, meet a business associate, or collect a merchandise sample; to do a bit of shopping, with an obligatory pause to admire the cliffs of Rawsheh before adjourning for lunch in a mountain *guinguette* or in a seaside café; or else simply to spend a weekend, perhaps only a night—as in those Egyptian films of the period where a map of Cairo suddenly dissolves into a tracking shot of the streets of Beirut. With the decline of Alexandria, Beirut became the favorite set of Egyptian directors filming tales of escape from everyday life. There was nothing very surprising in that, for if life in the Lebanese capital was not always as splendid as the honeymoons in the movies filmed there, it had long served also as the backdrop for the escapes of quite real men and women—as if, when talents were distributed among Arab cities, the fairies decided that Beirut was to be the capital of relaxation and easy living.

This was a rather conventional role, of course, and one in which Beirut could revel without having to pretend. Yet without always knowing it, the city played against type—to the point of making a seaside café called La Dolce Vita a theater of subversion. Named after Federico Fellini's famous film, it was the toniest café in Beirut in the early 1960s and the meeting place for exiles from every country, from Iraq to Morocco. Not content simply to talk about changing the world or to fill the air with their quarrels, politicians, journalists, and writers gathered there under a cloak of seemingly idle banter to establish contacts, enter into negotiations, and initiate conspiracies—so many plans concocted in the early hours of the morning, whispers of which filled the columns of local papers the next day and gave chiefs of police in more than one Arab country recurrent nightmares.

The appeal of nocturnal plotting, together with the possibility of catching echoes of it through the ears of the only pluralist press then in existence between the Gulf and the Atlantic, constituted a further inducement for the Arab intelligentsia and all those who dreamed of belonging to it—exiles (not all of them involuntary) as well as visitors who came so often that they spent more time in Beirut than in their own countries. The city's charms attracted minds no less than money, and from the 1940s onward it was the preferred place of refuge for a number of eminent Syrian scholars and intellectuals, some of them enthralled by the rustic campus of the American University, others hypnotized by the chance of finding a wife or simply by the ease of living in Beirut. The trickle became a flood after the Arab defeat of 1948. In addition to tens of thousands of refugees, the exodus from Palestine brought to Lebanon the spirit of modernity, both in the sphere of banking and in cultural life. Immigration from abroad reached its peak in the 1950s with the advent of authoritarian regimes in the majority of the Arab countries. During this time the Lebanese economy absorbed the traffic that formerly had passed through the port of Haifa, recycled the fortunes fleeing Aleppo, Baghdad, Cairo, and Damascus, and captured additional investment in the form of the first petrodollars. The prosperity created in this way was deceptive to the extent that it benefited only a small part of the population; nonetheless it was sufficient to grease the wheels that turned behind the stage on which a vast human comedy was about to turn into tragedy.

Standing at the center of this age of gold and glitter, Beirut was at last in a position to pursue the vocation it had selected for itself during the Awakening (al-Nahda) of the nineteenth century. As a city of culture—one among its many masks—where the inflow of foreign writers and capital caused publishing houses to grow like mushrooms, it became intoxicated with ideas, while yet retaining an ineffably light touch that blunted the edge of the fiercest debates and the most tempestuous controversies: literary quarrels between ancients and moderns; philosophical quarrels between existentialists and Marxists; doctrinal quarrels between Nasserites and Ba'thists (which is to say between Arab nationalists who had converted to socialism and socialists newly alert to the mobilizing virtues of nationalism). These feuds were all the more furiously conducted since for many of the participants, whether they were citizens of Beirut by adoption or by birth, the stakes were really rather small. The level of intellectual pretension, on the other hand, much of it stimulated by the latest fashions from Paris, was quite high.

Although the actors of this theater of shadows and light did not appreciate it at the time, the atmosphere surrounding their performances enriched Arab culture more lastingly than the performances themselves. For the most precious of the many things that Beirut gave artists and writers was a calm and peaceful setting in which an extraordinarily exhilarating range of ideas could be exchanged. For Arab intellectuals, cruelly dispossessed of their freedoms and subject to increasingly repressive prohibitions in their native lands, Beirut was a veritable paradise—so distant and yet so near. Owing in large part to the Westernization of customs and attitudes encouraged by Lebanon's role as a financial intermediary, the capital offered its exiled guests, as well as its own intellectuals, the most diverting and at the same time the least disorienting stage on which to play: an Arab city that was nonetheless foreign; a foreign city that was nonetheless Arab.

There was no happy medium, at least not yet. The seduction was immediate. Only a few were offended—by the kitsch, by the display (sometimes the indecent display) of wealth, by the absence of seriousness, by an excess of frivolity, ostentation, and affectation. But even if Beirut was capable of arousing hostility, this was only among a minority who mostly refrained from expressing their displeasure. Beirut held out to everyone, even the most hesitant, the prospect of enjoying a comfortable life; but it offered this opportunity more willingly to those who came from far away than to the outcasts camped out on its own outskirts. No failing, no vice was damning enough to ruin the image of Beirut as an oasis of liberty that its Arab consumers—political and economic refugees, persecuted intellectuals, even ordinary tourists—had constructed for themselves; still less did these vices have the power to undermine the legend that the funerary remembrances of a later time were to fix in the popular mind.

Lightness, kitsch, operatic ostentation, easy money—all these things were regarded as virtues by the other image of itself that Beirut was keen to promote during this same period: for Arabs, a playground by the sea; for Westerners, the nearest part of Arabia. All the *levantineries* that exasperated Colonel Lawrence in his search for "pure" Arabs—the exoticism in miniature, the pleasures of luxury (or its pastiche), the simplification of oriental complexities made possible by the natives' fluency in Western languages and customs—combined to make Beirut a convenient stopover on the road to the romance of the East, far enough from home that travelers could claim to have penetrated a remote world, but one that at the same time was agreeable enough to dissuade them from pressing on into the interior. Many who imagined that they were only passing through ended up settling in Beirut for good.

Among these newcomers, however, there was no Lawrence Durrell to write about it—still less a Michael Curtiz to set a legendary film there. Elements of the city's magic are perceptible in the Arabic literature of which Beirut was then the publishing capital, but following the appearance of Pierre Benoît's *La châtelaine du Liban* (1924), under the French Mandate, Western appreciations of Beirut were few, apart from a small number of unmemorable action movies—as if the exoticism of the place had become too prosaic, too ordinary to stimulate the imagination. Beirut's cosmopolitanism, though it was an essential ingredient of its charm, could not by itself inspire literary activity. Indeed, because this cosmopolitanism was taken for granted, it may have had the effect of separating the city from its own skin.

Mass tourism was only in its early stages then, and Lebanon did not yet know the summer invasions of the blond-haired Scandinavians and Germans who had begun to pour money into Spain and Greece, and soon afterward Tunisia. But of all the Arab cities, it was Beirut where Europeans and Americans most often met one another for business and pleasure, not only on the beaches and in the seaside resorts, in the bars and the grand hotels, but also in the schools and universities, in corporate offices, and in banks and publishing houses, to say nothing of diplomatic chancelleries that were staffed to a much greater extent than the country's size or its political influence would have seemed to justify.

The functions of all these places, except for the institutions devoted to teaching and research, were conveniently concentrated in a single location: the bar of the Hôtel Saint-Georges. Together with the Normandy, it was the Saint-Georges that gave Beirut its reputation for freewheeling skullduggery and conspiracy. Already in the 1950s it served as the rear base of operations for Kermit Roosevelt Jr. and his fellow apprentice sorcerers, sent out by the CIA to play "the game of nations," as one of them was later to call the panoply of manipulations that were deployed in the region during the cold war, from Mossadegh's Teheran to Nasser's Cairo.[2] Despite Lebanon's official alignment with the United States, reaffirmed by the landing of the Marines on its shores in 1958 (though later counterbalanced to some degree by close cooperation with Egypt), Beirut was one of the soft underbellies of the cold war, a neutral territory for secret services where every sort of contact could be made, discreetly or with some degree of publicity, according to the client's wish.

Except in 1958 (and perhaps later on the eve of the war of 1975–1990), military maneuvers and espionage missions were very seldom directed at Lebanon itself. Rather in the fashion of those American and European "B" movies of the period that edited out the surrounding mountain and coastal plain (and sometimes Damascus as well), so that Beirut appeared to be a desert port peopled by Bedouins, a parallel world was created in order to erase the boundaries that separated it not only from Syria but also from Iraq, Jordan, and Egypt, even Iran—all countries very well represented in the Lebanese capital by cohorts of more or less secret agents, in addition to groups of political exiles, whose presence could not help but multiply the number of missions assigned by the spymasters of these nations to their respective stations in Beirut.

Beirut did not limit its hospitality to oriental intrigues, as the history and literature of Western espionage shows. It was there that Kim Philby, a very real British master spy, chose to disappear and then reappear before being spirited out for good by the KGB in January 1963. And although James Bond was never spotted at the bar of the Saint-Georges, where Philby himself was a familiar figure, he did make a brief appearance in a Beirut nightclub in *The Man with the Golden Gun* (1965), having been sent to avenge the assassination of his colleague 002; and it was in Beirut that he was to find the golden bullet that would take him to the Far East. Philby's favorite author, the great Eric Ambler, more than once had occasion to resort to the services of Beirut, whether to illuminate the subtleties of a character perplexed by the provinciality of Sofia, as in *The Mask of Dimitrios* (1939), or to give the order for funds to be transferred to Geneva. In the genre of pulp fiction, less sophisticated but no less revelatory of the city's talent for extroversion, the first incursion of the

British Special Air Service (SAS) in Beirut, in 1972, was aimed at discovering a dark plot linked once again to the Far East—in the event, to China.

Tintin, the hero of Hergé's famous comic books, did not seek adventure in Beirut any more than James Bond did. But the boy detective made a stopover there at least once, en route to the imaginary Arab emirate of Khemed in *Coke en stock* (1958). As a good reporter who follows a story wherever it may lead, Tintin prefers the arid expanses of the desert to the city. Beirut appeared to be no more than the antechamber to these expanses, a place where nothing was destined to happen apart from secret machinations and dark plotting; a place where soldiers fighting in nearby theaters of war came for rest and relaxation and where grand dukes stopped to visit on their tours; a place where newspaper correspondents could eavesdrop on the conversations of diplomats and gather information that would help them to understand the societies of the Near East. The first step to understanding, for a correspondent passing through Beirut, was to ignore his immediate environment. Just so, as the American journalist Jonathan Randal was later to note about the reporting of the war in Lebanon,[3] the first reaction to the onset of hostilities was disbelief that such things could happen in Beirut.

But they could. Indeed, more was to take place there than anyone could have imagined.

1975–1990: OUTSIDE OF LIFE

An entire city obscured by smoke from explosions and fires, turned red by the flickering of flares, a vast blood stain satisfying the world's appetite for scenes of violence on a daily basis. Empty streets—empty except for disheveled combatants and unlucky passersby desperately running for safety. Buildings disemboweled by shells, others perforated by their shrapnel. Rockets leveling high-rise apartment buildings, booby-trapped cars cratering intersections. Men and women, old people and children throwing themselves to the ground—none of them trained to endure the violence that surrounded them, but always there to submit to it. Blood running in the streets; blood drying on corpses strewn here and there, in some places piled up on top of one another . . .

Death, and more death—all of it in prime time. No one anywhere in the world who tuned into the evening news during the fifteen-year conflagration that consumed thousands and thousands of lives was able to escape these familiar images of Beirut and Lebanon. No one who wished to produce a documentary based on current events during this time could have failed to sample these images; despite having been reproduced ad nauseam, they had lost none of their power to shock. No one who opened up a newspaper at one moment or another during these fifteen years could avoid being assaulted by the accounts of the violence in which Lebanon seemed to wallow. No one searching for a metaphor for chaos, for the folly of mankind, for the incomprehensibility of politics, had any need to rely upon his imagination in the course of these fifteen years: Beirut, now synonymous with war, came to mind at once.

Other conflicts, some of them civil wars as well, were taking place elsewhere during the same period, in Nicaragua, Angola, Afghanistan, and Sudan. And if one limits oneself to the cold cruelty of statistics, even taking into account the devastating number of fatalities (some 130,000 dead in fifteen years) as a share of the country's population—roughly the equivalent of two million dead in a country the size of France—the butchery of the Lebanese war was modest by comparison with the genocide in Cambodia. No matter. The Lebanese conflict stands out as one of the most prominent events in the journalistic historiography of the second half of the twentieth century, having taken over from Vietnam as the lead story of the world's newspapers and broadcasts before being supplanted in its turn by the conflicts that drenched the Yugoslav Federation in blood in the 1990s.

The timing could hardly have been better. When Saigon fell, on 30 April 1975, a few leftist students in the École Supérieure des Lettres in Beirut celebrated by cracking open bottles of champagne; but already for seventeen days the city's attention had been concentrated on events closer to home. On 13 April, hostilities had erupted on the outskirts of the Lebanese capital—a brief spasm of violence that served as a sort of trial run for the war that was to follow. In early May, a second round of attacks escalated along what was later to be called the "line of demarcation." Almost four months later, on 17 September, the fighting had taken over the whole of the historic heart of Beirut, which was to remain under siege practically without interruption for the next fifteen years. When at last the guns fell silent for good in Beirut in the autumn of 1990, and the militias were obliged to give up their arms, some of these same weapons quickly found other purposes in Yugoslavia.

Only accidents of history and technology can explain the extraordinary publicity that surrounded the civil war in Lebanon for so many years. If the fall of Saigon had in some perverse sense benefited the Lebanese conflict, by freeing up headlines and war correspondents, another coincidence had helped spread images of the war throughout the world: the transformation of television journalism through the widespread use of videotape in the second half of the 1970s, and thereafter the growing availability of satellite links. Almost at once Beirut became a global theater of death, whose scenes were broadcast, if not live, then with only a slight delay—a form of theater that was all the more riveting when death touched the media itself, as it did during the Israeli bombardment on the eve of the great invasion of 1982, which cut down a French television cameraman as he was filming it.

Neither the international press nor television waited for these advances in communications technology before rushing off to Beirut, however. By late summer of 1975 special correspondents had taken up permanent residence there, and all the more naturally as many of them knew the city well from having made it their usual stopover on the way to cover the latest convulsion in the Near East. Scarcely had the fighting even begun than several hastily written books appeared. Over time a considerable literature came to be produced—very uneven, to be sure, and in many cases rapidly overtaken by events—in French, English, and Arabic. The country, and still more the city, continued to feed the curiosity of foreign reporters; for them, at least, the golden age would survive even after it had disappeared for everyone else.

The convenience of three commonly spoken languages, until recently the guarantee of a comfortably familiar exoticism, now ensured access to a complicated and perilous world. Just as Beirut's trilingualism had once served to mitigate the tourist's sense of disorientation, now it did much of the journalist's work for him, even when he was new to the city: from warlord to man in the street, interviews could be conducted in either of the two Western tongues; translators could be readily engaged if necessary, and taxi drivers were eager to hire themselves out as advisors, offering to guide their clients, in addition to driving them around, through the maze of local politics and foreign influence. Seldom has cannon fodder been more sought after or more voluble. Someone could always be found to explain, as though it were perfectly obvious, that things were not as complex as they seemed; or, conversely, that they were far more complicated than most people realized. And when all arguments had been exhausted, the conversation could still be prolonged in good conscience: make no mistake, native sources would tell foreign journalists (especially inexperienced ones), it is all a plot—*the* plot, the Grand Conspiracy. And that worked, at least in the beginning: even though these people may well exaggerate, editors in London and Paris and New York told each other, they are too well informed, too smart for us to deprive our readers (or listeners or television viewers) of their insights. War was more accessible than ever before, only now with the human element as an added bonus to give color and credibility to political analysis of every variety.

Extrovert in its prosperity, the city was still more open in its time of ruin. Its residents, normally so reserved in their dealings with one another, continued to extend a warm welcome to foreigners, as long as they came from far away. But still more than by its way of life, it was through the many meanings the war held for those taking sides in it that Beirut affirmed its continuity. Every day that passed, every new controversy that arose, every fresh hatred that erupted brought undeniable proof of an internal rift having deep roots in scores from the past, some of them more than a century old, none of them ever really settled. The war of Lebanon was unquestionably a war between Lebanese, and in particular, between the residents of Beirut, even if some of them refused—and were always to refuse—to resort to violence. But it was nevertheless a war in which many others came to take part as well, more or less distant strangers who both protracted and aggravated the national dissensus by arming the protagonists, by manipulating them and being manipulated by them in turn. In war as in peace, the city was regionalized; indeed, it was internationalized. This much is evident. There is no need for analysis to establish the point. The diversity of the human element that had always shaped it was still present.

Nationals of almost three dozen countries participated in the hostilities; many of them were killed there. Apart from a permanent corps of Lebanese belligerents, supplemented by Palestinians, Syrians, and Israelis, Beirut saw a great many others come and go: Iraqis and Libyans sent by their governments in the name of Arab solidarity to support the Palestinian cause (the same governments that a few years later were to provide diplomatic aid, and even arms, to the Palestinians' former adversaries); Saudis, Emirati, Yemenites, and Sudanese, who for two years served as peacekeepers within a larger Arab Deterrent Force, subsequently manned by Syrians alone; Americans, French, Italians, and British, who composed a short-lived U.S. Multinational Force (USMF); Iranian Revolutionary Guards who trained new Hizbullah recruits in the suburbs. Further emphasizing the cosmopolitan character of the war, the United Nations Interim Force in Lebanon (UNIFL), formed in 1978 and still in place more than twenty-five years later (its mandate having been renewed again in 2003), mobilized contingents of French, Italians, Nepalese, Irish, Indians, Norwegians, Swedes, Iranians (among the latter, soldiers who had helped to bring about the Shah's downfall), and Ghanaians—none of whom were averse to spending a few days in Beirut when a pause in the violence allowed them to leave their bases in the southern part of the country.

And then there were those who came in a private capacity: French fascist mercenaries, lately associated with the Occident group, who fought alongside Christian militias in 1976; Egyptian, Moroccan, and Tunisian fighters supporting the Palestinian resistance as well as representatives of liberation movements allied to it; Eritreans, Sahrawis, and Kurds affiliated with the Kurdistan Workers Party, not to mention Iraqi Communists; extreme left-wing militants from Europe and South America grouped together within radical Palestinian formations (including Argentinean Montoneros and members of German, Swiss, and Italian offshoots of the clandestine French group Action Directe); a handful of Japanese Red Army members; and a certain Venezuelan terrorist nicknamed Carlos. In addition to these combatants there were journalists of every nationality, Swiss delegates of the International Committee of the Red Cross (ICRC), French and Belgian representatives of Médecins sans Frontières (Doctors without Borders), and envoys of other international organizations for which Lebanon was, after Biafra, the primary site of humanitarian intervention.

Finally, there were those who had chosen to make Beirut their home and who continued to live there. Among them were rival intellectuals from every Arab country, who, in addition to Lebanese hospitality, often enjoyed the protection of the

Palestinian resistance; with the exception of Syrians who had gone elsewhere in order to avoid being arrested by the regime they had fled, the majority were to remain in Beirut so long as the Palestinians held the upper hand, which is to say until 1982. There were also citizens of French descent. Thanks to the privileged relations
that had long united these Christians with their motherland, on the one hand, and
to the Arab policy inherited from Charles de Gaulle, on the other, they suffered fewer
atrocities, at least at the outset, than other Lebanese; and even after these advantages no longer guaranteed their safety, some chose to stay, while taking care to
change neighborhoods. Unskilled foreign immigrant workers hired to do the most
menial jobs—Egyptians, Indians, Sri Lankans (especially the women), Filipinos and
Filipinas—were sometimes requisitioned by the militias themselves to fill sandbags.
Despite the dangers of bombardment, they somehow seemed to find life in Beirut
more promising than the poverty of their native villages.

Never more than during these fifteen dark years did Beirut deserve its reputation as a microcosm. Many of the people who were exposed to the dehumanizing
effects of the war had come to Beirut only as official observers, of course; but even
as spectators they were potential—and all too frequently, alas, actual—victims.
Others, as we have just seen, took a more active part in the escalating violence. But
it was not only the fact that the fighters came from so many parts of the world that
gave the conflict a global dimension. For it was here, in Lebanon, that the ancient
hatreds of the East intersected with the most modern forms of armed antagonism;
here that all the quarrels of the world became condensed and concentrated.

The first of these quarrels—the one that was obvious to everyone, even if no one
was prepared to admit it—might appear to have been peculiar to the country itself.
Christians and Muslims, represented by practically all the denominations arising
from the genesis of both Christianity and Islam in the Levant and the source, as it
used to be said, of contemporary Lebanon's richness, now and henceforth were the
source of its misfortunes and troubles. But perhaps the enmity between Christians
and Muslims was not really a distinguishing feature of the Lebanese predicament.
No one here was arguing about the superiority of one faith over the other; and the
existence of various persuasions on either side amounted to nothing more than a
reassertion of mankind's ancient habits of tribal allegiance, intensified by the failure of the European nation-state to export itself to the East. In recent years much
the same thing had been witnessed in Africa, and it was soon to be seen yet more
clearly in Yugoslavia, another former Ottoman land. No matter how lethally effective communal division may have been, it can hardly account for the war in Lebanon by itself: at no moment did it appear in its pure form; it was constantly refracted
and distorted through the lenses of other, more far-reaching conflicts. It is probably this fact, more than any other, that throws light on the special character of the
Lebanese war. Beirut, and the country of which it was the capital, were at one and
the same time the site of conflicts between left and right, between Israelis and Arabs,

among Arabs themselves, between the United States and the Soviet Union, and, last but not least, between the "Great Satan" embodied by the United States and its scarcely less demonized counterpart, "Islamic terrorism."

Indeed, the variety of the conflicts that constituted the war in Lebanon was so rich that it favored the most improbable reversals of alliance. After a while, one-hundred-eighty-degree turns no longer aroused surprise, or even disgust; only indifference. And although reconciliations could occur as suddenly as ruptures, there was seldom much reason for hope: because the worst came to pass so often, it was always expected, and left no one unscathed. Massacres and atrocities were so habitual on all sides that no faction, no protagonist, native or foreign, could escape their fury; no one any longer was able or willing to take off the executioner's mask. "Even Killers Have a Mother"—thus proclaimed the title of one of these hastily written attempts to capitalize on current headlines by journalists who had no scruples about posing as anthropologists of violence.

But it hardly mattered. Everything could be said and written about this war, because anything could happen in a country that appeared to be at once the victim, the perpetrator, and the incubator of a generalized—and, more disturbingly still, a contagious—madness. By the mid-1980s, possession of a Lebanese passport had become a curse in airports, and the simple mention of travel to or from Beirut on a foreign passport was enough to draw the attention of customs officers and delay the holder's passage. Pulp novels exported the image of terrorist and spontaneously violent Lebanese to the four corners of the earth. Even in the works of the most serious authors, "Lebanonization" gradually came to supersede "Balkanization"—the very word that so frightened the Lebanese at the beginning of their war—and Beirut found its name converted into a shorthand for the fascination with death. In the major capitals of the world, embassies and government buildings were now equipped on their perimeters with concrete stanchions meant to prevent suicide bombings like the ones that in 1983 destroyed the American embassy in Beirut, the U.S. Marine barracks there, and the Drakkar post of the French Foreign Legion—three landmark events in the political imagination of the late twentieth century.

The clamor of the world is unkind. For some two centuries the city had assiduously cultivated a claim to universality, and now this ambition had at last been achieved—by means of war; worse still, by the rejection of universality. For the first time in its modern history, Beirut closed itself to outsiders. The attraction of the West led to its opposite: unfortunate foreign nationals were taken hostage, some for many years. In keeping with the cold rationality of state interests, the madness in Beirut caused the geopolitical calculations of the war that at the same moment was being fought by Iraq and Iran to migrate westward, with the result that those who sought to import the Iranian Revolution to Lebanon succeeded in substituting an illiberal and aggressive hatred of difference for the civilized tolerance of otherness that for so long had been the hallmark of the capital. Weary of war, Beirut submitted to it, unwillingly. And in doing this it lost its soul: having first witnessed the assassination of Malcolm Kerr—scholar and devoted friend of the Arab world, a native of Lebanon who went on to become president of the American University of Beirut, an institution so closely associated with the city's reputation and prosperity that its origins are apt to be forgotten—Beirut then, to its shame, allowed Michel Seurat—a French Arabist specializing in the study of Islam who had taken up permanent residence in Beirut, where he passed as a native, a tireless campaigner for the Palestinian cause and brave herald of the rebirth of civil society in Syria, crushed by its own government—to die in a jail in one of its suburbs.

The Western hostages were not the only ones who found themselves outside of life, standing apart from it, as it were—thus the title *(Hors-la-vie)* of a fine film by Maroun Bagdadi, whose work is perhaps more closely identified with Beirut than that of any Lebanese filmmaker, chronicling the ordeal of a kidnapped French journalist. The whole of Lebanon stood outside of life during this era in its history. To be sure, the war was not continuous, either in time or in space: more or less long periods of calm interposed themselves between the cycles of violence, creating a semblance of normality; a few regions, better protected than others, were spared much of the worst fighting. Nonetheless these fifteen years formed a continuum in which life, though it went on, seemed to be suspended in time—something that was better measured in Beirut than elsewhere.

The war did not take place in Beirut alone, and there were very few places it did not touch at one moment or another, in one way or another. Yet Beirut was incontestably the center of it. Against the backdrop of a modern metropolis, the immemorial atavism of the violence spoke even more forcefully to contemporaries than it might have done elsewhere. A city at war is incomparably telegenic, as viewers were to discover again a few years later in Sarajevo; all the more so when, as in Beirut, the urban landscape presents so many scenes of striking contrast: dozens of acres, deserted, where ghostly buildings overrun by weeds whispered the death of civility; a clear, clean, and precise line of demarcation, barricaded by sandbags, with bunkers haphazardly installed on the ground floor of what remained of buildings, sometimes higher up, manned by fighters exchanging insults and gunfire; on both sides of this line, militarized neighborhoods where the roads had been turned into cul-de-sacs, sealed off by improvised barriers—the bombed-out shells of buses, mountains of red sand, containers stolen from the port—to protect residents who were trying desperately to preserve something of their normal daily routine; neighborhoods that swarmed with activity until a rain of shells or a car bomb emptied it for a few hours or a few days, smashing windows and knocking down walls; and neighborhoods lying further out where cinemas and restaurants sought to maintain the illusion of peace, inevitably undermined by the sight of uniformed militia members and military vehicles, and sometimes completely shattered without warning by a long-range artillery barrage, an assassination attempt, or some other form of violent revenge.

There were many ways of waging war in Beirut: indiscriminate heavy artillery bombardment of residential neighborhoods, the most common phenomenon of the conflict; lone gunmen (wrongly called snipers) who were responsible for holding enemy fire from the next street at bay or for blocking intersections; kidnappings carried out on the basis of denominational affiliation, particularly frequent at the beginning of the war, when the city was not yet completely divided up, and culminating in the Black Saturday attack of 6 December 1975 in which hundreds of Muslims were taken hostage (a strategy that was to be revived in the 1980s); small wars-within-a-war between militias nominally fighting on the same side, in which automatic weapons were predominant; nocturnal dynamiting of vehicles and stores; car bombs set off by remote triggering devices, the outstanding technique of political assassination aimed at destabilizing the region; and the commandeering of private apartments, with little or no warning, to house civilians forced out of their own homes.

As if that were not enough, Beirut was destined to absorb the crushing blows of conventional warfare, massively delivered against it by Israel in the summer of 1982. While Israeli armor and ships imposed on the western part of the city—West Beirut, as it was now known—a siege from another age, cutting off the water supply and blocking shipments of food, the Israeli air force, whose pilots had been trained at a cost of millions of dollars and equipped with the latest American technology (and therefore assured of mastery of the skies), calmly set about destroying the Sports City stadium, razing residential buildings, and, by a remarkable and sad irony, bombing the synagogue of the city's Jewish neighborhood, guarded by Palestinian soldiers. The devastating loss of human life that accompanied this apocalyptic sequence of events was incommensurate with anything that had gone before. Yet it was at this moment that the people of Beirut, at least those who had endured the siege in June and July, were to show the greatest dignity in adversity—until shortly afterward, in September, when other Beiruti, and other Lebanese, inflicted a terrible stain upon the city's honor: the massacre at the Sabra and Shatila refugee camps. There, in the space of forty-eight hours, more than a thousand Palestinian and Lebanese civilians perished as the Israeli occupiers turned a blind eye to the slaughter. Beirut tolerated the occupation for not more than two days. Thereafter, from its streets, resistance began to grow. And, as it was to do after each ordeal, Beirut tried to breathe. To breathe life—so near to death.

Twice, in November 1976 and then in October 1982, Beirut believed that reunification was possible. Plans were drawn up for reconstructing the center of the city. But in each case the lull in the fighting turned out to be only an interlude, lasting scarcely more than a year and a half at most; in the meantime the war continued elsewhere, and the line of demarcation eventually came to be reinstated. The violence ceased on other occasions as well, more briefly but not less hopefully. And then there were periods of neither war nor peace, or, more exactly, of semi-war and semi-peace—periods that, taken together, probably accounted for the better part of the fifteen years of the conflict.

And yet never, not even during the most promising intermissions, did the city live in any normal way. Despite the attempts at reunification, it was no longer capable of seeing itself whole. In the place of Beirut there were now West Beirut and East Beirut, two hemispheres, two separate worlds that turned their backs on each other. If it was still sometimes possible to go back and forth between them, albeit rarely without risk, the everyday workings of the city were split in two; with the forced relocation of businesses and government offices, vehicular traffic in one part of the city was now sealed off from traffic in the other. Even during lulls in the fighting, the cityscape bore the marks of war: one-way streets, redirected to accommodate the new geography of violence; metal stakes driven into the pavement to prevent unknown drivers from stopping and planting bombs in parked cars; streets closed off to shield party offices and the residences of their leaders from attack.

More striking still, in the face of so much abnormality, was the stubborn determination of the inhabitants to go on living as normally as possible. Year in and year out, children went to school, even though they were never sure of being able to finish an entire year of classes. Marriages were celebrated, sometimes with great pomp. Plays were put on in the theaters. Shows were mounted in the galleries. Other forms of leisure and entertainment were adapted to changed conditions: new cinemas and restaurants opened, and all the more readily as East Beirut expanded toward the suburbs of the north shore and the old summer encampments on the mountainside. With the arrival of spring, the familiar rituals of sunbathing and swimming filled the beaches and seaside resorts, or at least as far as security permitted.

Was the war therefore forgotten? It was forgotten every day, without for a moment ever being absent from anyone's mind. There was always the chance of being shot at by a lone gunman while taking a detour along an unsafe street in order to get to a concert on time; of seeing a boobytrapped car explode on the way to the supermarket; of being shelled coming back from the beach. Even knowing that one might never come back from this or that place, one went just the same. And even for those who did not want to fight, there was no choice but to approach daily life as though it were an assault course—knowing when to take cover, constantly listening, straining to separate the background noise of random gunfire from the sound of shots that were meant to kill. Many innocent bystanders lost their lives; others sustained permanent injuries. It is perhaps for this very reason that Beirut was so gruesomely fascinating—because life went on despite the onslaught, and because the city, in its decline and decay, nevertheless remained a city.

And yet the moment finally came when the city no longer resembled itself. West

Beirut, where most of the shrines of the golden age were concentrated, somehow or other managed to keep up appearances until 1982. But all attempts at pretense suddenly evaporated after the tranquil hiatus of the first months of 1983. The Palestinians having been forced to withdraw, purely Lebanese animosities once more reasserted themselves as the focus of American attention began to shift to other theaters of the cold war. The militias no longer even bothered to try to conceal their motives. It was now war for the sake of war—for the sake of adding this or that side street to one's territory, of lining one's pockets with profits from rackets and trafficking of all kinds. Sectarian fighters who had been forced to leave their homes in the countryside looked to settle accounts with a city that had long relegated them to its margins. The newcomers had come to rule, not to create a place for themselves in the life of the city; and having failed to tame Beirut, they sought to make a martyr of it. Outsiders hoping to mediate between the contending factions were now denied access to it. The few foreigners who still dared to enter the city found that they were welcome only as hostages.

Though it still appeared as a headline of the international news, Beirut had now been forgotten by the world. Many of its own inhabitants no longer thought of anything but getting out. By the tens of thousands they began to leave—for Paris and London in the case of the social elites and the most Westernized segments of the middle class, followed by many less affluent residents who met up again in Germany, Sweden, Australia, and Canada. East Beirut, which seemed to expand to the extent that West Beirut contracted, proved incapable of preserving the city in its old image. The war left its scars there as well: no matter that the leisure and entertainment industry found some measure of compensation in the extramural outgrowth to the east, the inhabitants of this sector had likewise begun to leave en masse; those who remained had to make their way through a wasteland. But the real problem lay deeper. The ideology of occupation and urban warfare scarcely lent itself to the mixing of peoples and the exchange of ideas that used to be Beirut's hallmark. Westerners, who once had been warmly welcomed, were now shunned. The same was true of wealthy visitors from the Persian Gulf. As for the Arab intellectuals who had so proudly boasted of the city during its three glorious decades, and who for the most part held on in West Beirut until 1982, there was nothing in East Beirut to tempt them.

Beirut had lost its old spirit, which now had to be sought much further afield. Paris and London welcomed journalists and writers from the Gulf to the Atlantic, and gave a home to pan-Arab magazines and advertising agencies; but together even these two cities could not quite replace Beirut as the intellectual capital of the Arab world. The old spirit of the city survived above all in the legend composed by its elegists. If Western authors, with one or two exceptions, did not notice the death of Beirut, Arab writers well recognized its grief and suffering. "We have been unjust to you, O Beirut, this we confess," proclaimed the Damascene poet Nizar Qabbani, bard of women and romance and long a resident of the city, where his collections had been published in print runs of millions of copies. "Beirut, our tent," sighed the Palestinian poet Mahmud Darwish on leaving his home of ten years, "Andalusian and Syrian Beirut." And while the city became congealed in myth, it found consolation in the confidence that one day it would exist again: in the words of the Lebanese poet Nadia Tuwayni, "a thousand times died, a thousand times reborn."

WHICH CITY? WHICH HISTORY?

Poetic license cannot by itself account for the idea of a city that is always reborn. In the event, Tuwayni's hyperbole only repeated the widespread popular belief that Beirut had survived destruction seven times over the course of its long history, while at the same time amplifying this belief. Well before the most recent of these ruinations, Élisée Reclus, the father of modern geography, had handed down the legend to succeeding generations: "This city is one of those that must live and relive, come what may: the conquerors pass on and the city is reborn behind them."[4]

Can we be so sure? If it is reborn, is it then the same city? Is its history the same history? The historian of Beirut cannot evade these questions. At the very outset he finds himself confronted with the problem of choosing a starting point for his inquiry and, by virtue of that, a point of view. Are Beirut's many lives and deaths in need of rediscovery? If so, how far back must the historian go? All the way to remotest antiquity, on the ground that continuous human settlement at this site is attested long before the Neolithic revolution, perhaps as early as 5000 B.C.E.? Is he obliged to search for evidence of a linear progression linking the ages of the ancient city and the metropolis of the twentieth century, by turns proud, battered and bruised, convalescent? Should he conflate Berytus, the mother of Roman law, and Bayrūt, the capital of Arab letters, in a single unbroken span of time? Or, admitting the existence of distinct stages, should he lay emphasis instead on more recent ones, because they alone have built the city as it now stands before our eyes and resides in our imagination?

These difficulties arise in part from the fact that Beirut's past was long the poor relation of both Lebanese national history and the ancient and medieval history of the Levant. But they occur also because in Lebanon, more than elsewhere, whatever choice the historian makes amounts to an assertion of identity,[5] and because within Lebanon this is nowhere more true than in Beirut itself. For in trying to reconstruct the urban history of the eastern coast of the Mediterranean, from the earliest times to the present, scholars have traditionally distinguished places such as Byblos and Tyre, modest today, whose historiography is almost exclusively centered on an unfading ancient glory, from places such as Damascus and Aleppo, which, though each claims to be the oldest inhabited city on earth, are of interest to historians mainly in their relation to the Arab and Ottoman past. Beirut belongs to both of these classes, however. It is therefore an object of inquiry for two groups of specialists who have nothing to say to each other, on the one hand Phoenicianists, Latinists, and Hellenists, and on the other Ottomanists and students of twentieth-century history. In this regard Beirut can be compared only to Alexandria, where an interval of fifteen centuries separates the Ptolemean golden age from the time of Durrell. Even so, Alexandrian studies do not encounter the difficulty posed by Beirut—as the capital of a state that is itself recent and, for much of its history, problematic—of giving a coherent historical account of a national community.

What is more, since the prospect of yet another rebirth of Beirut, after fifteen years of war, at once calls to mind all the other, more ancient rebirths, there is a risk that the continuity, if not of the city's buildings and streets, then in any case of the myth that has grown up around the city will harden into dogma. On this view Beirut is like the phoenix, forever reborn from its ashes, and therefore eternally one, if only by virtue of the ceaseless combat of life against death that has taken place there through the ages. "An ancient city for the future"—as the slogan of the corporation responsible for rebuilding and developing the center of the city after the civil war was to put it.

Legend and advertising apart, the notion of an abrupt break with the past became more difficult to defend once the first tangible signs of reconstruction strengthened a growing concern for conservation, based on both archeological research into the vestiges of antiquity and restoration of the architectural monuments of two more recent eras, the later Ottoman Empire and the French Mandate. Such evidence of the unity of the physical site is all the more compelling since no straightforward linearity links the old and the new in Beirut. But even if the city exerted comparatively little influence on the course of history until the modern period, one cannot ignore the fact that it has been honored by the presence of heroic figures since ancient times: Pompey, Saladin, and Jazzār, who defeated Napoleon Bonaparte at Acre; probably also Muʿāwiya, the brilliant founder of the Umayyad Dynasty; perhaps even Rameses II and Jesus of Nazareth.

The obligation to choose does not vanish for all of that. Neither the unity of the site, nor the stability of its names from Phoenician to Arabic via Greek and Latin (Birūta, Berytus, Bayrūt), nor the frequency of the visits paid to the city over the centuries by illustrious conquerors disposes of the need to attach relative priority to the various stages that jointly constitute the city's history. If the historian cannot wholly escape taking a slightly romanticized view of Beirut, owing to its several rebirths, neither can he avoid what *today* constitutes the memory of the city in its two most familiar images, as contradictory as they are complementary: crucible of Arab modernity and scene of self-destruction. These twin images, each of which resides in the imagination rather than in relics, cannot help but form the starting point for subsequent research. Unlike Byblos, Tyre, and Sidon, Beirut emerged as a great metropolis only toward the middle of the nineteenth century. From then on, however, it was to occupy a place in the Arab and the Mediterranean world that transcended its physical boundaries no less than the size of its population.

I therefore propose to consider the history of Beirut from the moment when its rise as a major city calls for an explanation. If I have chosen also to give an account, in the long first chapter that follows, of the different periods that its site has known from ancient times until the moment when the East once again assumed prominence in Western thinking, at the end of the eighteenth century, this is not out of any desire to demonstrate my command of the relevant scholarly literature nor to disarm my critics in advance, but rather because modern ideas of Beirut, as of Lebanon in general, are so often apt to suffer from misconceptions about this past or from doubtful conclusions drawn from it, such as the belief in a permanent renaissance. At the same time, I am mindful that the city's claim to historical continuity must be balanced by a recognition of the discontinuity of its settlement over the centuries. Having died and then been reborn, the city inevitably had to replace the people it had lost. The extraordinary demographic growth recorded from the beginning of the nineteenth century, on the eve of Beirut's boom, until the beginning of the twentieth suffices by itself to establish the reality of the break from the past. This has the consequence, among others, of diminishing the need to rely on genealogical history, except in connection with certain developments that accompanied Beirut's rapid expansion.

The demographic growth of the nineteenth century cannot be judged in quantitative terms alone. If the population was renewed, the same is true of the hearts and minds of the people who composed it. Surely all of them, newcomers no less than the increasingly small minority of old families, remained attached to at least some of the particular customs and beliefs with which they had been brought up; nonetheless each of them was changed by the experience of living in a city that itself had been transformed. This observation, the truth of which will become evident in the pages that follow, led me in turn to reject a microsociological approach— in part, too, because excellent work of this type has already been done. While not neglecting the narcissism of small differences, I have chosen to examine subcultures only to the extent that they contributed to the formation of the city's modern identity.

Just as Beirut is obviously plural by nature, so too any satisfactory history must take into account the various political, economic, and above all cultural dimensions of the city's life during the past two centuries. It should not be supposed that plurality resists definition. The character of Beirut during this period can indeed be defined, which is to say that it can be given a context and framework in which its history can be written. In seeking to formulate the most expansive definition possible, and one that will also be of greatest interest to the historian, it will be useful to think of Beirut as a *Westernized Mediterranean Arab metropolis*. Let us take these terms in reverse order. Beirut was indisputably a metropolis from an early date, no matter that simple numbers might seem to suggest otherwise. Even when its demographic profile was unimposing by comparison with the other major cities of the Middle East, it belonged among them by virtue of the various functions it fulfilled in the regional economy. That the city is also Arab goes without saying. Nevertheless it should be kept in mind that, above and beyond the economic and cultural place that Beirut occupies in the modern Arab world, this aspect of its character has also made itself felt in the domain of religion; and that, despite the city's minor importance until the Tanzimat of the mid-nineteenth century, its development cannot be understood in isolation from the social and urban history of Ottoman Syria and, more generally, of Arab Islam.

Beirut is Mediterranean in a dual sense. First, before becoming a great city it was for a long time one of the chief commercial ports of the Levant, and therefore intimately associated with the development of trade along the rim of the inland sea. Other cities of the eastern littoral had welcomed European merchants (notably Genoans and Venetians) over the centuries, but few contested Beirut's primacy as a point of entry into the Islamic world for not only the manufactures, but also the ideas, of Christian nations. With the growth of the city's port in the late nineteenth century this role was reaffirmed and at the same time modernized, so that Beirut became a vital transit hub for the outflow of goods and materials produced in response to rising demand from Europe after the Industrial Revolution. But the city was Mediterranean for another reason as well. In orienting its development toward commercial expansion, it came to participate in an international style of urbanism, itself in the process of formation, that was shaping the growth of cities on both sides of the sea, from Marseille to Alexandria and from Algiers to Smyrna. While conserving elements of a Levantine architectural syntax, the majority of the buildings recently completed or under construction in Beirut at the turn of the twentieth century displayed European influences, for the most part French and Italian. Some of these influences were transformed directly, others were taken over from Ottoman models or annexed from contemporary Egyptian sources.

Finally, and most plainly of all, Beirut is Westernized; indeed, this is perhaps the most striking element of the standard image that has grown up around the city. Among both Arabs and Westerners themselves, Beirut's reputation derives chiefly from its cosmopolitanism and its talent for acculturation. For at least a century its prosperity depended on the ease with which Western consumer goods could be acquired there and with which European (and, later, American) leisure activities could be enjoyed, as well as on the relaxed style of life that Arab visitors, in particular, found so seductive. To reduce Westernization to these things alone would surely be a mistake; but to overlook them would be still more misleading, not only with regard to the history of Beirut and of Lebanon, but also for the history of Arab

FIGURE 3. Aerial view of the city and its environs, ca. 1993: in the foreground the promontory of Beirut; behind it Mount Lebanon, the Biqa' Valley, the Anti-Lebanon, and, in the far distance, the fertile plain of the Ghuta, near Damascus.

modernity as a whole. The tendency to ignore Western influence—perhaps the greatest weakness of contemporary Arab historiography—is the result of an absence of critical analysis that, paradoxically, varies in proportion to the strength of the spell that so many intellectuals, now scattered over the face of the earth, nostalgically ascribe to the lost *dolce vita* of Beirut, the memory of which unites them despite their mutual antagonisms. In much the same way, Egyptian cinema—so highly regarded by the most serious-minded critics—has so far escaped examination by historians of *mentalités* in the Arab world.

In acknowledging this dimension of the city's experience, of course, one runs the risk of seeming to credit the disparaging image summed up by the catchphrase "Beirut-Banks-Brothels." Not that this image is totally false; to the contrary, it has long been an essential part of the city's identity. But reductionism of this sort prevents us from fully understanding its past. The history of Beirut has four main branches: social history, something infinitely more subtle than a simple catalogue of the services Beirut rendered to its visitors would suggest; urban history, which in a thousand and one baroque ways reflects the city's constant determination, not always well appreciated, to embrace a hybrid cosmopolitanism; the history of mentalities, which cannot be abridged so that it reads as a mere chronicle of the city's wealthiest inhabitants; and, finally, the history of ideas, eclipsed until now by the obsession with profit and pleasure. Beirut in its golden age cannot be likened either to a sort of floating casino moored off the coast of the Near East or to a free city, of which there were many in the colonial world. Distant though its horizons may have seemed to visitors from lands of sand and oil, life in Beirut was not an off-shore operation.

Beirut was, and is, a very real place, whose playfulness and love of show and spectacle fail to conceal its inner seriousness. It is perhaps in just this that the true modernity of Beirut resides, that its value must ultimately be weighed in relation to its place in the history of mentalities and in the history of ideas. For Beirut stands out among the cities of its age not only for having helped to formulate the concept of Arab modernity, but also, and still more importantly, for having helped to make it a living thing—even if, in doing so, Beirut lured itself into a dead end.

In proposing a history along these lines, I have no intention of idealizing my subject; nor do I forget that the city exhausted itself as a consequence of its own violence. No inquiry into the fate of Beirut can avoid asking why it failed. Nonetheless I have not wished to consider the history of Beirut solely in the light of its most recent and most tragic episode. The reader will see that nothing, or very little, of what led to the war has been ignored; but the war itself is treated only as the culmination of the events that went before, no matter that this outcome was not inevitable. The temptation was great to speak of the city under siege, and of the ways in which it adapted to catastrophe. But to have given in to that temptation would have distorted my fundamental purpose in writing this book, which as the history of a city must be a tale of civility—even if this remains to be reinvented—and not a tale of its death.

Beirut
August 2003

PART ONE

From the Ancient to the Modern World

FIGURE 4 *(preceding page)*. Roman columns in the city center.

1

Beirut before Beirut

Humankind has left its mark on the Near East since the remotest prehistory. The site on which Beirut grew up is no exception. Acheulean bifacial tools, exhumed at Ras Beirut in the northwest part of the promontory, date back to approximately 600,000 B.C.E.[1] During this epoch, toward the end of the Lower Paleolithic, the two largest hills of the present-day city were islands, and the mouth of the river that empties into the Mediterranean was situated at Furn al-Shubbak, on the south-eastern periphery. The promontory as we know it today, with its sand dunes and its substrate of sandstone, took shape in the Middle Paleolithic.[2] But despite the fluctuations of the river and other modifications of the site, the human imprint is found in every stage of prehistory. In addition to the dozen or so settlements discovered at Ras Beirut, others have been inventoried at Furn al-Shubbak, Sinn al-Fil, and Antelias, where human skeletons were found in the layers of the Upper Paleolithic.[3]

Since that time the region seems never to have been uninhabited. At the end of the Paleolithic, the transition to the Natufian culture of the Mesolithic (ca. 10,000–8,000 B.C.E.) in the Levant left traces of a great many open-air settlements in the sands to the south of Beirut, identified by a mass of flint artifacts and splintered remains.[4] Agriculture was not yet practiced, and the sickle was used to gather wild cereals. But the Neolithic revolution was not far off. From its origin in the lands of the Euphrates basin, it quickly spread to the Mediterranean coast. In Beirut, evidence of a Neolithic village was found beneath a Roman settlement on land where Beirut International Airport was built in the late 1940s. Other Neolithic vestiges have been discovered in the heart of the modern city as well, between Place des Martyrs and the sea.[5] Across from the Pigeon Rocks, on the cliffs of Rawsheh, flint stylets attest a Chalcolithic Age settlement (fourth millennium B.C.E.), contemporary with the site inventoried at Byblos.[6]

Soon thereafter, toward the end of the fourth millennium and the beginning of the third, the Fertile Crescent saw the appearance of writing—and, with it, of history. At the same time this second revolution was taking place, cities arose on the eastern coast of the Mediterranean, thereafter known as the land of Canaan.

WATER AND SEA

The physical continuity of a site does not necessarily imply continuous human habitation. The Canaanites, who gave their name to this littoral, probably came from elsewhere. Today they are generally believed to have originated in the Arabian Peninsula. Nonetheless, they were able to take advantage of a new and qualitatively different environment, facing the sea, and the city-states they founded in succession on this coastal strip were soon distinguished by the daring of their sailors and the skill of their merchants. Hugging the coast at first, then venturing further into open water, Canaanite seafarers established trading posts along the Mediterranean rim and beyond, going as far as the west coast of Africa. The Greeks whom they met in their travels later called them Phoenicians, in reference to the myth of the phoenix that rose up from its ashes. In time the name Phoenicia came to supplant Canaan, designating the narrow coastal plain of the eastern Mediterranean, and more specifically that part of the coast lying between Acre and Ugarit beneath the peaks of the Lebanon range, known collectively as Mount Lebanon—itself mentioned in the Bible.

The Phoenicians should have had no reason to regret this change of name, for it was owing to the Greeks that their civilization came to be well remembered by those who came after them. It was also through their contact with Greek mythology that the Phoenicians were able in turn to make the gift of a name—Europe, which first belonged to the unfortunate heroine of a Greco-Phoenician myth, princess of Tyre, sister of Cadmos, raised by Zeus. Cadmos, having set off in search of Europa, founded Thebes, the homeland of Oedipus and his tragic lineage, bringing with him the most precious invention of all: the alphabet. Herodotus later lent credence to the myth, ascribing the creation of the first known alphabet, composed of twenty-two phonetic letters, to the Phoenicians.[7] Older systems of proto-alphabetical writing have subsequently been identified in the Near East, notably the so-called Sinai script of the early second millennium, but the Phoenicians may yet claim to have sufficiently improved this system to allow it to be generally used, and, in particular, to take credit for having transmitted it to the Greeks.

Canaanite-Phoenician civilization cannot be reduced to this contribution, however, nor to the development of commerce. Although still largely unknown, this civilization seems to have been more complex than scholars long believed. Modern discoveries in the ancient cities of the Lebanese littoral, particularly Byblos (Gubla or Gubal in its Phoenician form, later arabicized as Jbeil), Sidon (Saida), and Tyre (Sur), testify to original advances in metalworking, textiles, and glass. These city-states seem also to have played an intermediary role, both economic and cultural, between various ancient civilizations, and especially between the Nile Valley and Mesopotamia; though independent for long periods, they were at other times dominated by one or another of the great empires.

The historical record of the Canaanite city-states mentions these three places— Byblos, Sidon, and Tyre, all of them today part of the Lebanese Republic—most prominently, in addition to Arados (present-day Arwad) and Ugarit, now in Syrian territory. But archeology indicates the existence of others as well, such as Botrys (present-day Batrun), where an impressive jetty can still be seen, and Tripolis, whose hellenized name refers to a joint settlement by three communities (Sidon, Tyre, and Arados), and where ambassadors of the Phoenician city-states met from time to time. Emergency excavations undertaken in the downtown commercial district in the 1990s confirmed the antiquity of the Canaanite presence in Beirut, exposed at a depth of only eight inches or so on the ancient tell and in the area of the suqs. Vestiges of a low wall and of earthenware jars from the Early Bronze Age (2400– 2000 B.C.E.) have been uncovered, together with a high defensive wall dating from between 1900 and 1800, and a funerary jar containing the skeleton of a little girl, dated to the eighteenth century.[8] Nonetheless it was not until the fourteenth century that the name of the city appeared in a written document.

Geography suggests that the origins of Beirut are to be located in the earliest days of seafaring. As Élisée Reclus observed:

> The coast [of the eastern Mediterranean], which, taken in its entirety, seems to be almost perfectly straight, with scarcely any indentation, and which is in fact completely inhospitable in its southern part, along the whole of the littoral of ancient Philistia, is broken to the north of Mount Carmel into a certain number of semicircular coves where large boats were accustomed to take refuge before man-made harbors existed. The shoreline of Syria, like that of Mauritania in Africa, of Chile in the New World, and of other mountainous regions, exhibits, apart from the principal peaks of the coastal chain, a series of promontories arranged stepwise and set back from one another, so as to form places of shelter that are greatly valued against certain winds: thus were born on this coast, well protected against the surge of the sea from the south and west, the towns of Berytus (Beirut) and Tripoli.[9]

Reclus went on to claim that Beirut, whose situation was no less favorable than that of Byblos, being a "site of cultivation and a market for the people who had come down from the mountains," had the additional advantage of offering ships far superior protection with its "long peninsula, thrown off from the shore into the sea." And whereas "the little port of Byblos had room only for a fleet of small boats, . . . all the seagoing vessels of Phoenicia and Greece could find shelter against the winds from the south and the southwest near the springs of Beeroth, at the foot of its dunes of red sand amid the rustling of the tall pines."[10]

There can be no doubt that Beirut offered both a haven for seafarers on the Mediterranean side and, thanks to the many freshwater wells of its tell, a watering place.[11] Not the least of the advantages of the site was that the narrow coastal plain at the foot of Mount Lebanon became wider around the promontory. Another was that the roadstead—a natural basin where ships could safely ride at anchor near the shore, in the absence of a true harbor—was protected against the prevailing south-westerly winds by the cape of Ras Beirut and the hills of the promontory, a rare east-west projection on a coast that otherwise lies on a north-south axis. Furthermore, the roadstead was at that time protected against winds from the north by islands, some of which were still visible at the beginning of the twentieth century.[12] Notwithstanding these natural assets, Beirut does not occupy a large place in Phoenician historiography, which for the most part remembers the residents of Tyre as the great sailors of the age. Moreover, even during the Roman period, the roadstead of Beirut was little used,[13] and it was not until the modern era that its suitability as a port was to be fully exploited.

None of this, however, tells us how Beirut came into existence. History has recorded that Tyre was founded by Sidon; it gives no information about Beirut beyond a few hints that it enjoyed privileged relations with Byblos, its great neighbor to the north. Nor has any foundation myth survived in the collective memory of the city. The two accounts that have come down to us from the ancient period are too hellenized to provide original insight, even if they both confirm the city's maritime vocation. The first account, which goes back to Sanchuniathon, a Phoenician priest of uncertain date who may already have been hellenized himself,[14] has in any case come down to us through two much later authors, Philo of Byblos in the second century C.E. and Eusebius of Caesarea, at the end of the third. The second narrative was related by Nonnos of Panopolis, a fifth-century pagan who converted to Christianity, in the epic poem *Dionysiaca*. A third legend, this one Christianized, came from William of Tyre, the twelfth-century chronicler of the Crusades, who claimed that the city had been founded by Gergesus, a son of Canaan (himself a nephew of Noah), from whom the city took the name of Gerisa. Apart from this reference to Canaan, William of Tyre tells us nothing of value. By contrast, the legends associated with Philo and Eusebius have the merit of bringing out a symbolism that is found in other accounts.

In the cosmogony ascribed to Sanchuniathon, Beirut figures only in the oldest part, the "divine history of the Uranids," which is to say the family of Uranus, son of Helion, and a woman named Beyrut. From Uranus's union with his sister Ge came Ilus (in Semitic, El), who is identified with Cronus—an exceptional association since, apart from Philo's account, Cronus is assigned all the attributes of Baalshamin.[15]

After battling Uranus, Ilus/Cronus gave Byblos, which he had founded, to the goddess Baaltis and Beirut to Poseidon and the Cabiri, who divinized the remains of Pontus (the Sea) there. This Pontus was none other than the father of Poseidon, as well as of Sidon, who was endowed with a marvelous voice. As for the Cabiri, sons of the god Sydyc (Zedec) and protectors of sailors, Herodotus tells us their image was found in the form of figureheads on the prow of Phoenician ships.[16] This myth must have been widespread, since echoes of it may be detected in contemporary numismatics: the god of the sea appears on coins either driving a chariot drawn by sea horses or else naked, leaning on his left elbow and holding up a trident around which is coiled a dolphin—the same attitude given him by a statue attributed to Lycippus. The trident with its dolphin seems to have been a symbol of prosperity, and also figures on weights from the Seleucid period in Beirut. The Cabiri, eight in number, are likewise depicted on the money of the city during the time of the Syrian-born Roman emperor Elagabalus.[17]

The sea, again in the person of Poseidon, was no less present in the myth transmitted by Nonnos of Panopolis. To win Beroë, the eponymous goddess of the city (said by some to be the daughter of Oceanus and Thetis, by others the offspring of Aphrodite and Adonis), Poseidon had to triumph over Dionysus, Eros having aimed his arrows of love at both of them. But beyond what it tells us about the city's founding, his version continues to be of interest for its description of the Byzantine city of Nonnos's own time.

> There is a city, Beroë, the keel of human life, harbor of the Loves, firmbased on the sea, with fine islands and fine verdure, with a ridge of isthmus narrow and long. . . . On one side it spreads under the deep-wooded ridge of Assyrian Lebanon in the blazing East. . . . O Beroë, root of life, nurse of cities, the boast of princes, the first city seen, twin sister of Time, coeval with the universe, seat of Hermes, land of justice, city of laws, abode of Euphrosyne, house of [Aphrodite of Paphos], hall of the Loves . . . star of the Lebanon country.[18]

Much more revealing than these foundation myths is the city's name. The first known appellation, Birūta, refers in all probability to the rich hydrographic endowment of the site, whose settled area, overlooking the coastline, was pierced by many wells. The words for "well" in other Semitic languages exhibit a striking similarity to Birūta: *burtu* in Akkadian, *be'er* in Hebrew, and *bīr* in Arabic. The Greeks called it Berytos, the Romans Berytus, and the Arabs Bayrūt. A rival interpretation asserts a resemblance with the Hebrew *b'rôth*, meaning "cypress."[19] But the reference to freshwater springs is supported by evidence from the Egyptian royal archives of Tel el-Amarna: in official correspondence of the Eighteenth Dynasty, dating to the fifteenth century B.C.E, Akkadian scribes sometimes substituted for the name Birūta the cuneiform ideogram denoting "well."[20]

FROM THE EGYPTIANS TO THE ROMANS

The oldest inscription discovered in Beirut dates back to the early part of the second millennium, to the time of the great conquests of the Twelfth Dynasty, when the city was under the rule of the pharaohs. Three monuments found there attest to its relations with Egypt. The most important of them is a sphinx with a human head in black and white marble, between whose forelegs, engraved in hieroglyphs, is the name of Amenemhat IV, the last pharaoh of the dynasty (1786–1777 B.C.E.). The cartouche indicates that the sphinx had been sent to the native "king" as a token of esteem; found in 1926, just north of the present-day Place des Martyrs, the statue was subsequently acquired by the British Museum. The name of this pharaoh has also been found at Byblos in an obsidian casket from the same period.[21]

It was not until the fourteenth century that the first known mention of Beirut occurs in an ancient text. This evidence, from the famous tablets of Tel el-Amarna, which constitutes the main part of what has come down to us from early antiquity about the city, consists of three letters addressed by "the man of Birūta," Ammunira (or Am Nūr), to the "king, my Sun, the gods, the breath of my life," otherwise known as Akhenaten, the Eighteenth Dynasty ruler who placed himself at the center of a monotheistic cult. Beirut, then the seat of a small kingdom that was vassal to the pharaoh, found itself in a difficult situation. Internal dissension in the aftermath of the religious reforms instituted by Akhenaten had strained his empire, and the city was torn between its duties of vassalage and fears for its safety arising from the aggressive behavior of neighboring peoples. These letters, written in the more general context of the Hittite menace, described the distressing predicament of the coastal cities in the face of incursions by the Amorites, a mountain people whose princes were engaged in a double game aimed at playing off their Egyptian suzerains against the Hittites, and by the nomadic Hapiru. They also mention the asylum given by Ammunira to another vassal of the pharaoh, Ribaddi ("the man of Gubal"), who had been supplanted by his own brother in the wake of a palace revolt fomented in conjunction with the Amorite besiegers. The Amarna letters also include a message from the same Gubal king, in exile in Birūta, imploring the pharaoh to intercede on his behalf. In the event, Ammunira, who had long remained faithful to Egypt, ended up delivering Ribaddi to his enemies.[22]

The Hittites managed to hold the whole of the region in subjection for almost a century, before the campaign of Rameses II in Asia succeeded in reestablishing the pharaonic empire. There is no mention of Beirut in the annals of the Egyptian campaign, which brought victory over the Hittites at Qadesh on the Orontes River in approximately 1285 B.C.E., but it may reasonably be supposed that Rameses did pass through there because he commanded three steles to be erected on the cliff that guards the mouth of Nahr al-Kalb (the Lycus River of the Romans), not quite ten miles outside the city. The relations between Beirut and Egypt under Rameses II are also attested by a stone vase fragment bearing the pharaoh's name, found near Place des Martyrs in a late Bronze Age tomb. A final mention of Birūta occurs toward the end of the Nineteenth Dynasty in a letter from a court official to a young scribe who, it seems, had applied for a position: the official asks him, in a rather sarcastic tone, to provide information about Birūta, among other things. It is impossible, however, to conclude anything whatsoever about the reasons for this request.[23]

Outside Egypt, references to Birūta from the time of the Eighteenth and Nineteenth Dynasties have been found in the palace archives of Ugarit, another city on the coast of Canaan, some one hundred twenty miles to the north, near the present-day city of Lataqiyya in Syria. A letter of accreditation written in Akkadian introduces the messenger of the "king of the country of Birūta to the prefect of the country of Ugarit." Another document presents the city as a commercial partner of Ugarit. This was not enough to forestall disputes, however, to judge from the account of negotiations for the release of a Ugarit subject, held hostage in Birūta, and from two other texts that describe incidents involving residents of Birūta who had dishonestly posed as traders in wine. Ugarit was probably a more important power than Birūta during this period; along with Alalakh it controlled the commerce with the Aegean world. But fragments of Mycenaean pottery discovered at Beirut may indicate that it too had direct contact with this world.[24] Other archeological traces point to a continuous pattern of urban settlement: several walls of the Middle and Late Bronze Age, steps of a stairway between the tell and the port, parts of dwellings, and a glacis from the thirteenth century B.C.E. or so have been uncovered by recent excavations.[25]

After the tablets of Tel el-Amarna and the letters of Ugarit, centuries passed without any mention of Birūta in a written text. If the mouth of Nahr Kalb saw the erection of steles by the Mesopotamian conquerors Shalmanesar III, in the ninth century, Asarhaddon in the seventh, and Nebuchadnezzar in the sixth, in addition to those of Rameses II, none mentions the city by name. And yet the other coastal cities figure in the lists of tribute paid to the kings of Assyria and Babylonia. Two possible explanations have been advanced in this regard: either Birūta was destroyed in the course of the invasion by the Sea Peoples in the twelfth century, or it was annexed by a neighboring city, perhaps Byblos or Sidon.

Archeology alone cannot settle the matter with certainty. It does appear that the Phoenician embankment remained undamaged until the late Iron Age (roughly 700 B.C.E.), and the pattern of urban settlement, so far as the recent excavations in the area of the old suqs permit this to be reconstructed, likewise suggests some degree of continuity up through the arrival of the Persian Achaemenids in the fourth century.[26] With regard to this latter period, earlier discoveries had already shed some light; in particular, small terracotta horsemen wearing the conical cap of the Phoenicians were found around 1930 in a ditch dug into a mound on the eastern side of the Sérail. Other vestiges from the Achaemenid period have recently been uncovered as well,[27] notably a canine cemetery near the thirteenth-century glacis.[28] But these vestiges do not allow us to conclude either the continuing existence of the city during the Phoenician period or its destruction by the Sea Peoples. Even on the latter assumption, it might have recovered very slowly without resuming its former place in the geography of commerce and politics. Herodotus does not mention Beirut, though he does refer to Tyre and Sidon.[29] Recent excavations have nevertheless confirmed that there was no rupture between the Achaemenid era and the Hellenistic city. A fourth-century inscription at Delphi also speaks of a man from Sidon who was born in Berytos.[30] And shortly before the time of Alexander, a list of the cities of the littoral given by the *Periplus Scylacis* (erroneously attributed to the explorer Scylax of Caryanda) includes Berytos, noting its "north-facing port."[31]

It is only in the aftermath of Alexander's conquest of the Levant that Beirut clearly stands out in the historical record. Even though the city goes unmentioned in the annals of the Macedonian campaign, which had nonetheless long been stalled before the gates of Tyre, it is known that coins were struck in Birūta in the name of the conqueror.[32] Alexander's death inaugurated a period of mixed rule, for both the city and the entire surrounding region. Whereas Syria was shared in the first instance between the two great rival Macedonian dynasties in the Near East, Birūta fell to Ptolemy I, the governor (and later king) of Egypt. The city was conquered shortly afterward by Seleucus I, and then retaken by the Egyptian dynasty, as coins struck in honor of Ptolemy III and Ptolemy V attest, before finally reverting in the early second century B.C.E. to the control of the Seleucids, who in the meantime had extended their hold over all of Syria. Like other cities of Phoenicia, Birūta enjoyed a certain degree of autonomy, as confirmed by various coins, while at the same time profiting from the extension of Hellenistic influence. Birūta was now called Berytos or Berytion,[33] and possessed an agora, which seems to have been located near the present-day Rue Foch.[34]

Although the turmoil of the civil war that shook the Seleucid kingdom toward the middle of the century did not long interrupt this first moment of prosperity, the city, having retained its legitimist loyalties, was destroyed soon afterward by the usurper Diodotus Tryphon, who set fire to it and razed its buildings between 143 and 138 B.C.E.[35] An inaccurate translation of Strabo gave rise to the belief that the city lay in ruins until the time of Octavian, which is to say for more than a century; but in fact it seems to have overcome this ordeal much sooner.[36] Its inhabitants very quickly returned and restored the city under the name of Laodicea in Phoenicia or, alternatively, Laodicea in Canaan—names that were already in common use by the time of the Seleucid civil war. Under the reign of Seleucus IV Philopater (187–175 B.C.E.), coins bore the legend (in Phoenician script) "Laodicea which is in Canaan," and a minister of the sovereign, one Heliodorus, was honored around 178 at Delos by a dedication to Apollo made by "merchants and shipowners from Laodicea in Phoenicia." Coins that seem to have been in circulation between 176

FIGURE 5. Hellenistic vestiges uncovered near Place des Martyrs, just south of the tell.

and 123 show the prow of a ship on which the Greek initials of Laodicea in Phoenicia are inscribed together with the symbol of Berytos (also called Astarte, after the Semitic goddess of fertility, sexuality, and war worshiped by the Syrians). A weight dating from 128, which is to say during the period that immediately followed the devastation wrought by Tryphon, on which the symbols of the city appear together with the name of the magistrate Nikon, tends to support the theory of a rapid recovery, either on the same site or (this is disputed) further to the south, near the valley of Shuwayfat.[37] A number of buildings, among them fine houses, have been dated to the period 150–125, not only in Berytos but also in other towns of Seleucid Syria that experienced comparable economic and demographic growth. But in the absence of more precise dating that could place such construction before or after Tryphon, this last piece of evidence does not tell us how long the city lay in ruins.[38]

The rebirth of Berytos is better attested by the prosperity of its merchants at Delos, the great commercial center of the age. As the dedication to Apollo in honor of Heliodorus shows, Berytians had been resident there at least since the consolidation of Seleucid rule over Syria. At the end of the second century B.C.E. they seem to have formed an "association of worshipers of Poseidon, merchants, shipowners, and warehousemen" at Delos. One finds mention of its existence in 110–109, some thirty years after the destruction of their native city. The text of a dedication stele at the site of their trading post ("The association of Poseidoniast merchants, shipowners, and warehousemen from Berytos has devoted to their ancestral gods this building, the portico, and outbuildings") indicates that they occupied spacious and well-ordered premises.[39]

The Seleucid era drew to a close. At the beginning of the first century B.C.E. the weakening of the dynasty led to unrest in the cities of the Phoenician coast, and eventually to its suppression by Tigranes the Great, king of Armenia and son-in-law of Mithradates VI, king of Pontus, to whom the Seleucids had appealed for help in regaining control of Syria (84–69). Neither Berytos nor any of the other coastal cities of the coast was punished for insubordination; indeed, Berytos was able to enlarge its autonomy.[40] The Armenian intervention did not succeed in neutralizing another threat, however, this time from the Itureans, a people of Arab origin whose primary settlement in the Lebanon mountains now extended into the central Biqaʿ Valley, from which they launched raids on the cities of the littoral, from Beirut to Tripoli. The Armenian intervention did, however, have the effect of drawing Syria to the attention of Rome, which until then had been focused on Pontus. Roman victories momentarily enabled the Seleucids under Antiochus XIII to shore up their waning authority, but soon they were forced to step aside before the advance of Pompey's legions, which in 64 B.C.E. conquered Syria.

THE ROMAN COLONY

Next to the modern period, the Roman era remains the best-known and the richest chapter in the history of Beirut, whose new status as a colony, conferred by the *ius italicum,* made it one of the major urban centers of the eastern empire. Its rise was not immediate, and we have little information about the development of the city during the first three decades of Roman rule. From Strabo we know that the Romans moved swiftly to put an end to the raids of the Itureans: Pompey, he says, destroyed their strongholds, spread over the coast and the slopes of Mount Lebanon, and in the Massyas Plain (the Biqaʿ Valley, now their seat), because "from them the robbers [were accustomed to overrun] both Byblus and the city that comes next after Byblus, I mean the city of Berytus."[41] Whether or not the city profited from this pacification, as one might suppose, there is no doubt that Berytus existed as an urban entity. Contrary to the suggestion of enduring ruin after its destruction by Tryphon, the city seems to have been involved in the civil war between Octavian and Antony. It was part of the Roman territory handed over in dower to Cleopatra by Antony, and indeed sheltered part of Antony's fleet; coins were struck there in the queen's likeness in 31 B.C.E., the year of the Battle of Actium. Other coins struck the same year suggest, however, that the city rose up in revolt against Cleopatra.[42]

Things became somewhat clearer after Actium. Berytus, now known as "Colonia Iulia Augusta Felix Berytus" (in honor of Octavian's daughter, Julia), benefited more than most cities from the Roman peace. The colony was endowed with a vast territory, which divided the land of the Itureans,[43] now subdued, into two parts and, according to Strabo, covered much of the Massyas Plain, "as far as the sources of the Orontes River [which] are near M[ount] Libanus,"[44] which is to say north of the Biqaʿ Valley, around Heliopolis (Baalbek). This latter city was later withdrawn by Claudius and seems to have been reconstituted as a separate colony.[45]

It has long been supposed that the founding of Berytus as a colony dates to the tour of the eastern provinces made by Marcus Agrippa, Octavian's admiral at Actium, also his friend and son-in-law, in 15–14 B.C.E. This view depends once again on the testimony of Strabo, who, recalling that the city "has now been restored by the Romans," notes that Agrippa settled the veterans of two legions there, and "added to it much of the territory of Massyas."[46] It is nonetheless contradicted by Pliny the Elder's reference to Colonia Iulia Augusta Felix Berytus (whose wine he praised), since his information about Syria derived from the decade 30–20 B.C.E.[47] It may be possible, then, to push back the founding of the colony to just after the Battle of Actium, or indeed to the time of Julius Caesar, whose desire to extend Roman dominion eastward may have led him to establish the first Roman colony in Syria at Berytus. But while it is true that the first legions to be based there, the Legio V Macedonica and the Legio VIII Gallica, had both fought with Caesar, they had also contributed to Octavian's war effort; and it was Octavian who, after Actium, set about developing colonies from Spain to Lydia, populating these outposts with some one hundred thousand veterans discharged from his armed forces. If, as recent scholarship suggests, men from V Macedonica and VIII Gallica (now Augusta) were settled in both Berytus and Heliopolis in 27 B.C.E.,[48] the colony would have been established well before 14 B.C.E., and the role of Marcus Agrippa, if indeed it can be proven at that point, may have been limited to introducing new contingents of veterans and to enlarging the colony's territory, together perhaps with an extension of the right of Roman citizenship.

While the debate over the date of the founding of the colony has proceeded on the basis of only a few pieces of historical evidence,[49] not even this much is available regarding the choice of Berytus as its site—a decision that was all the more bold in view of the rarity of colonial foundations during this period in Syria.[50] One is confined instead to conjectures. Was it due to the ties that had been established at Delos between the Romans and the Berytian traders there? Or, if in fact the city did rise up against Antony and Cleopatra, was it a reward for this? Or was it because Berytus's geographical situation, at the midpoint of the eastern coast of the Mediterranean, recommended it as a potential point of transit between Italy and the Syrian provinces, despite the difficulties of the surrounding terrain? Or was it quite simply because the city existed, and, lacking a glorious past and a well-developed system of indigenous administration, presented fewer obstacles to Romanization than other urban centers?

Together with the *ius italicum,* by which it was exempted from all personal tax, or capitation, the colony was given its own system of administration, modeled on

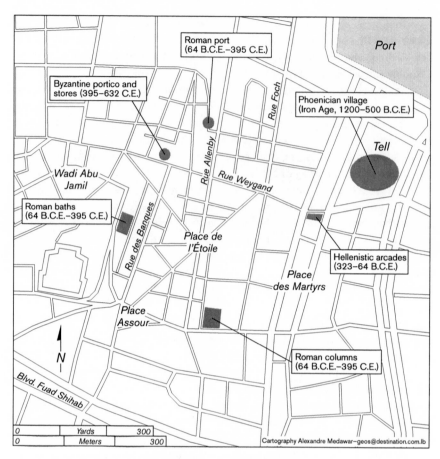

MAP 3. Phoenician, Roman, and Byzantine Remains in Beirut

that of Rome itself. Corresponding to the Roman Senate was a curia composed of one hundred local councilors chosen from the *ordo decurionum,* the class of the wealthiest inhabitants; and, as at Rome, the highest magistrates were appointed in pairs, the *duoviri iuri dicundo* (for the administration of justice) and the *duoviri aediles* (for the conduct of municipal affairs). Every five years, these magistrates were transformed into *duoviri* (sometimes *quattuorviri*) *quinquennales,* known also as *censoria potestate,* which is to say that they carried out a census of the population, inspected the colony's finances, and drew up a budget for the next five years. Thanks to this duoviral system of administration, the colony enjoyed a large degree of autonomy, with the Roman governors intervening only in the event of conflict.[51]

The model of the imperial capital was reproduced also in the layout of the city, which comprised a forum and a capitol where the Roman triad of divinities (Jupiter, Juno, and Minerva) was venerated, together later with images of Rome and the emperor. The forum in Berytus, represented on the local coinage, was not superimposed on the agora of the Hellenistic city. The practice of creating a separate public space was not unusual: one finds examples of it at Ostia, Capua, and Pompeii, and in general where a city preexisted the colony, which had to be settled on adjacent land. This was long supposed to have been the case in Berytus, even if the typical colonial plan was not always respected there. Colonies were usually laid out on the model of the Roman camp familiar to military veterans, a large square traversed by two main arteries, the *cardo maximus,* along a north-south axis, and the *decumanus,* running from east to west, with the forum situated at the intersection of the two.[52] In the 1940s, assuming that this rule obtained in Berytus, the French archeologist Jean Lauffray situated the *decumanus* on the axis of the present-day Rue Weygand, and the *cardo maximus* along a line passing through Cathédrale Saint-Georges, parallel to Rue Maʿrad. The emergency excavations undertaken fifty years later did not unambiguously confirm this theory, however. Although their results were greeted in the press as confirming Lauffray's intuition, another interpretation of these findings instead favors a plan more in keeping with the tradition, common in Roman Syria, of a single axis (in this case north-south), along which columns were found and vestiges of a Roman road between the present-day Maronite and Orthodox cathedrals.[53]

Whatever its initial plan may have been, some of the colony's facilities, such as the vast thermal baths uncovered at the foot of the Grand Sérail and the necropolises built outside the walls of the Roman city, both on Qantari Hill in front of al-Murr Tower,[54] and on the hill of Ashrafiyyeh,[55] where two have been found (the most recent discovery was made in 2001, next to the Orthodox cemetery), clearly show that it had grown in size.[56] Traces of a hippodrome, likewise located on the outskirts of the Roman city (at Wadi Abu Jamil, the Jewish quarter of the modern city), with its long parallel sides and its two hemicycles, can be seen in older aerial views of the city.[57] Roman villas have also been found at Jnah, on the southern periphery of modern Beirut.[58]

Still more impressive evidence of the city's expansion comes from the aqueduct that brought water from the Magoras, as the Romans called Nahr Beirut. Its surviving elements, known by the name of Qanatir Zubayda (the Zubayda Arches), give some idea of the scale of the original structure. With its three levels of arcades carried over a distance of 240 meters (nearly 800 feet) above the river, it may be compared to the aqueduct at Segovia in Spain, or to the one at Gard in southern France.[59] The aqueduct in Beirut, like those at Apamea in the north of Syria and at Bostra in the south, was meant to supply water to the city rather than for irrigation,[60] although mention is made in ancient sources of land under vines nearby, and the wines of Berytus, first praised by Pliny, were renowned.[61]

FIGURE 6. Roman columns
on an ancient thoroughfare
thought to have been the
cardo maximus.

Berytus's very status as a colony appears also to have contributed to its improvement and development, the result of a tradition of civic giving known as euergetism, by which it received donations from local princes allied with Rome. The fact that the city bore the name of Augustus's daughter was probably not unimportant, at least at first. Flavius Josephus tells us that under the reign of Augustus, Herod the Great, always attentive to what was done and said in Rome, had built in Berytus "halls, porticoes, temples, and market-places"[62]—the use of this latter term in the plural may refer to the construction of a second forum. Even if it is true that Herod also took an interest in the improvement of Tyre,[63] which was not a colony, and that euergetism benefited various cities in Syria,[64] Berytus seems to have been the object of sustained attention from the Herodians. Agrippa I, Herod's grandson and a friend of Caligula, made the city a gift in his turn of "statues and copies of ancient works of sculpture," and caused to be built a "theater that, by its elegance

FIGURE 7. Roman baths discovered on the slope leading up to the Grand Sérail.

FIGURE 8. The Zubayda Arches, vestiges of the aqueduct over the Magoras.

and its beauty, surpassed many others," together with a circus, baths, and porticoes.[65] At the inauguration of the circus, vestiges of which have survived near the sea, in the modern district of Minet al-Hosn, great festivals were held, crowned by a gigantic combat of gladiators that featured fourteen hundred criminals, arrested in the lands under Agrippa's rule, fighting each other in pairs.[66] His son, Agrippa II, to whom the Romans had confided the administration of Coele-Syria in making him tetrarch of Chalcis (modern 'Anjar) from 50 to 100 C.E., endowed the city in his turn with "annual spectacles," in violation of Jewish proscriptions, that were held in a theater built at great cost.[67]

For the majority of the monuments granite was imported from Egypt, but some were built from marble extracted from quarries in the Lebanon mountains.[68] The same was true of the facilities built by the Romans themselves. These probably included a civil basilica housing law courts, though the structure that had been identified with it, and which was thought to have stood next to a second forum during the Flavian period,[69] was revealed by recent excavations to have been either a palaestra or a portico.[70] However this may be, innumerable vestiges of Roman constructions and Herodian gifts, to say nothing of military buildings, long remained exposed to view: many were visible until the construction of the modern city covered them over; some have recently been disinterred, in the last decade of the twentieth century. Beneath the ground, which presently lies on a level with the entablature of the forum's columns,[71] many others still lie concealed.

The importance of Berytus as an urban center, suggested by the donations, is attested by several events whose extramural significance was connected with the political life of the Roman East, indeed of the empire itself. In 8 B.C.E., for example, Herod the Great obtained permission from Augustus to set up a tribunal there in order to try his sons Alexander and Aristobulus for high treason, but with the indulgence of a Roman court he was able to bring them back directly to Galilee to be executed. It was also in Berytus, in the circus donated by Agrippa I, that Vespasian was proclaimed emperor by his legionnaires in July 69 C.E., after the death of Nero. A year later, his eldest son, Titus Flavius Vespasianus, to whom it had fallen to prosecute the war against the Jews, celebrated Vespasian's birthday in the same arena with festivities that were crowned by the execution of Jewish rebels taken prisoner in Jerusalem.[72]

The integration of Berytus into the Roman world is perhaps best illustrated by the careers of some of its native men of letters. They include the grammarian Lupercus, author of works on Greek rhetoric in the time of Claudius; Publius Egnatius Celer, a Peripatetic philosopher who lived in Rome under Nero; the physician Strato, author of works praised by Galen; the grammarian Marcus Valerius Probus, a celebrated scholar of the first century C.E. and the author of commentaries on Virgil and Horace as well as a treatise of Latin rhetoric mentioned by Suetonius and also, in 57, by Saint Jerome in his Latin version of Eusebius's *Chronika;* the Platonist philosopher Hermippus, a pupil of Philo of Byblos who composed works on astrology and the interpretation of dreams under Trajan and Hadrian, in the late first and early second centuries; Theodorus, also a Platonist, who flourished in the middle of the second century; and Lucius Cavenus Taurus, a Platonist as well, author of a treatise comparing Plato and Aristotle, and the first of three philosophers honored with the right of citizenship by the people of Delphi, in about 163.[73]

Like all other colonies, which were expected to serve as centers of Romanizing influence,[74] Berytus dutifully played the role assigned to it. Over time, however, its initial prestige was severely diminished. From the second century onward, the colonies and municipalities created in the East tended no longer to be distinguished from neighboring cities, unless by virtue of their fiscal prerogatives and the names of their magistrates.[75] The grant of colonial status to several Syrian cities under the Severan emperors attenuated differences still further.[76] The city's economy no longer displayed a distinctive character, all the less since its promise as a port seems not to have been fully realized. Its industries were found in other cities of the region, notably metalworking and the manufacture of quality textiles, which, as in Byblos, Laodicea, and Gerasa, was now giving way to the royal purple dye works of Tyre and Sidon.[77] Nor did the practice of religion in Berytus any longer differ markedly from that of its neighbors. Despite the origin of the colony's founders, Roman gods were seldom honored.[78] And yet if a pair of local gods replaced the familiar Roman triad of the cities of Syria in Berytus,[79] this was only further evidence of the syncretism that had been the mark of the East since the triumph of Hellenism. Similarly, temples in Heliopolis dedicated to Jupiter and Bacchus did not erase the name of Baal, which has been conserved in the indigenous toponym of Baalbek; and overlooking the Roman city of Berytus, and very probably on its territory, the temple of Deir al-Qal'a in the present-day village of Beit Mery, to the north, perpetuated the cult of Baal-Marqod.[80] But already a new faith had begun to make its presence felt in the life of the city.

THE CHRISTIAN CITY

Unavoidably, being only one or two days distant from the places that saw the birth of Christianity, Beirut was a point of departure in its expansion and, if one considers the Holy Land in the broad sense, actually a part of this land. Many rituals still commonly practiced today go back to the first age of Christian revelation. According to the gospels of Matthew (15:21) and Mark (7:24), Jesus preached in the region of Tyre and Sidon. Did he also come to Berytus? In a late work titled *Descriptio Terrae Sanctae* (1285), editions of which were published by both Jesuit and Protestant scholars in the early twentieth century, a German Dominican named Burchardus de Monte Sion claimed that he did.[81] Saint Peter, for his part, is said to have stayed in Berytus and to have appointed a bishop in the person of Quartus, who is mentioned in Paul's Epistle to the Romans (16:25). Another apostle, Jude, is said to have been martyred there, and a church described in the fifth century was dedicated to him.

Tradition also situates the death of Saint Barbara in Berytus. Another legend places the scene of her martyrdom at Nicomedea, on the sea of Marmara, but the memory of the saint in modern Beirut, preserved first in a church bearing her name that stood until the fifteenth century, when it was transformed into a mosque,[82] is perpetuated in the Christian communities of the city, on the evening of 3 December every year, by the wearing of masks and the eating of a sweet dish of grains and raisins called *birbara,* from the Arabic version of her name.[83] More than these things, however, the city claims the privilege of having been the theater of Saint George's combat against the dragon, even if here too Nicomedea cultivates a similar tradition, as does Ludd in Palestine.[84] In Beirut, Saint George was in any case to bequeath his name to the bay that bathes the northeastern face of the promontory, and to the adjacent cape—named Khodr, again after the common Arabic form of the saint's name—just west of the mouth of Nahr Beirut. The cult of Khodr endured among the city's Muslims until the twentieth century, and there is still today a mosque that bears his name. The discovery of the True Cross in Jerusalem during the pilgrimage of Saint Helena, mother of Emperor Constantine, whose route had been illuminated by a succession of flaming logs on the high ridges overlooking the city, is still commemorated in the Christian villages of Mount Lebanon, on 14 September, by bonfires *(abboulehs).*

The origin of popular traditions can never be dated with precision, and in this case it may well be that the rituals associated with the lives, real or imagined, of the saints gained currency only once Christianity had succeeded in establishing itself. But it is true that in the Roman East the new faith triumphed rather quickly. Already before the Edict of Milan in 313, handed down after the conversion of Constantine, and so well before the consecration of Christianity as the state religion under Theodosius in 392, there were tangible proofs of the advance of the faith in Berytus. The presence of a bishop there is attested by the middle of the third century.[85] Apphianus, martyr of the church and a native of Asia Minor, was converted during the time of his law studies in Berytus before meeting a cruel death in Caesarea. Saint Gregory Thaumaturge, a future bishop of Caesarea, may also have lived there for a time in the third century, though he probably was not a student.[86] Pamphillus of Berytus, who bore this name in honor of his education there, went on to found a celebrated school of biblical studies with his disciple Eusebius, the father of religious history, in another Caesarea, in Palestine.[87] Many inscriptions from the Roman period, in both Latin and Greek, contain the Christian symbols of cross and palms. By the fourth century, Berytus was unquestionably a Christian city, notwithstanding the survival of paganism.

The domination of Christianity brought with it theological quarrels, and the city was inevitably drawn into the turmoil stirred up by charges of heresy. Its successive bishops generally took the side of Arius, condemned by the first Council of Nicaea in 325, then triumphant at Sermium and Rimini before being condemned once again, with the advent of Theodosius, by the first Council of Constantinople in 381. Others, in the fifth century, rallied in support of the heretical monophysism of Eutyches, condemned at Chalcedon in 451. A few bishops nonetheless distinguished themselves by their defense of orthodoxy, such as Timotheus, one of the fathers of the Council of Constantinople, and, in the fifth century, John, who was to take his place in the Greek martyrology, his feast day thereafter being celebrated on 19 February.[88]

The consolidation of orthodoxy in Constantinople in the middle of the fifth century resulted in the elevation of the bishopric of Berytus, which until then had been a dependency of the metropolitan see of Tyre. Under Theodosius II, the church recognized the city as an ecclesiastical province in its own right, attaching to it the dioceses of Byblos, Botrys (modern Batrun), Tripoli, 'Arqa, and Tartus.[89] The expansion of Christianity in the city is also illustrated by the number of churches. According to Severus of Antioch, who had studied law there in the late fifth century before going on to become, at the turn of the sixth, the moderate leader of the Monophysite party, and whose testimony is reported by his friend and hagiographer Zacharias Scholasticus, there were no fewer than six churches in Berytus, among them one devoted to Saint Jude. Another had been built to commemorate a miraculous phenomenon, the oozing of blood by an icon that had been repeatedly stabbed by Jews; later, in the thirteenth century, during the time of the Crusades, it was occupied by the Franciscan order. The record of the second Council of Nicaea, which condemned the iconoclasts in 787, referred to this "miracle of Berytus," noting its celebration by both the Eastern and the Western churches (9 November in the schedule of liturgical chants of the Roman synaxarion).[90] The tradition must have long been perpetuated since it is mentioned by the fifteenth-century Arab annalist Sālih bin Yahya, who locates its origin in the fifth century.[91]

THE SCHOOL OF LAW

If Beirut can claim to occupy a place in the history of Christianity, it is yet less owing to its miraculous traditions or to its part in the theological controversies of the early church than to the contribution made by its school of law to the juridical corpus that was to serve as the basis for the civil institutions of Christian Europe, the *Corpus Juris Civilis* of Justinian in the sixth century. The first reference to this school is found in Gregory Thaumaturge, in his panegyric on Origen, delivered in 239. Some authors claim that it was founded during the reign of Septimus Severus in the late second century.[92] It was not the only such school in the empire, others having been established in Rome, Alexandria, Caesarea, and Athens—and there was to be yet another later, at Constantinople. Others hold that the teaching of law in Berytus was dispensed initially in an informal setting,[93] and that the city attracted jurists because it was a depository for imperial constitutions, which is to say a center for the translation of edicts into Greek and their subsequent publication. This function, first attested only in 196, nonetheless may have been exercised previously by virtue of Berytus's status as a colony.[94] Certainly by the beginning of the third century the great Syrian jurists were found at Berytus, men such as Ulpian of Tyre, Papinian (brother-in-law of Septimus Severus), Julius Paulus of Emesa, and Claudius Tryphonius,[95] and it may well be that the school owes its existence to them.[96] Its success is suggested by Diocletian's decision at the end of the third century to exempt students of law in Berytus from taxation. Later, probably in the mid-fifth century, the school was endowed with a formal charter (privilegium studii), granted by imperial favor, stipulating the terms of its operation as a state institution.[97]

By the middle of the fourth century, the school's reputation was already secure, and the familiar image of the city as the mother and nurse of laws had made its appearance. An early mention of this formula occurs in the Vitae Sophistarum (399/400) of the philosopher Eunapius, a partisan of Julian the Apostate. Referring to a high official named Anatolius, Eunapius writes: "He attained the heights of the science of law. There is nothing surprising about this, for Berytus, his homeland, is the mother and nurse of these studies."[98] Libanius, the famous rhetor of Antioch, had anticipated the idea in a letter of 361, in which he used the phrase legum mater.[99] Libanius did much to advance the reputation of the school from afar; while lamenting their decision to give up Greek literature and philosophy in favor of Roman law, he gladly wrote recommendations for the many young patricians who wished to study at Berytus. The school's students came from all over, not only from Antioch, but also from Palestine, Alexandria, the cities of Roman Arabia, even from Constantinople.[100]

Berytus reached the height of its fame in the fifth century, when it was known as the school of the "ecumenical masters." While not abandoning the use of Latin, these masters (or universal doctors) taught in Greek. The founder of their line was Cyrillus, author of a treatise on legal definitions that was prized by students, and their most illustrious representative his younger son, Patricius, a great teacher described by contemporary historians as the "king of the school," and later cited as an authority in the prefaces of the Justinianic Code. Cyrillus's eminent successors as head of the school at Berytus included Domninos, Demosthenes, and Eudoxius.[101] Eudoxius's son, Leontius, had a lengthy and distinguished career as a professor of law before entering the service of the state, occupying the high offices of pretorian prefect of the East under Anastasius I (491–518) and then of commander-in-chief (magister militium) in 528–29; subsequently he was raised to the dignity of patriarch.

Justinian's decision to keep the school of Berytus open, while closing those of Caesarea, Athens, and Alexandria, suggests that its position was unassailable. Outside Rome and Constantinople, Berytus was now the only city to offer training in law. But the supreme recognition of its preeminence was to be found in the part played by its professors in composing the Code of Justinian. Leontius was associated with the enterprise from the beginning. His son Anatolius, grandson of Eudoxius, served as one of the compilers of the *Digesta,* together with his colleague Dorotheus.[102] The second preface to this digest, called *Constitutio Omnem,* gave official sanction to the city's reputation as the mother and nurse of laws by requiring that all three volumes of Justinian's codification be transmitted upon its completion in 533, not only to the two imperial capitals, but also "in the most fair city of Berytus, which may well be called the nurse of laws."[103]

The contribution of the law school at Berytus was not limited to jurisprudence. Beginning in the third century, the school seems to have combined the teaching of Roman law with tolerance for the Christian faith, even if it did not at first explicitly endorse the precepts of this faith. Pamphillus was a student there, and both the martyr Apphianus and his brother Aedesius converted to Christianity during the course of their studies. The enrollment of Severus of Antioch, in the late fifth century, gives further evidence that the school of Berytus had succeeded in adapting to the religious transformation of the empire. Indeed, Cyrillus, the first of the ecumenical masters, appears to have resolutely incorporated Christianity as an element of the school's teaching during this period.[104]

The renown of Berytus was largely forgotten in the centuries that followed, except among legal scholars.[105] It was not until Beirut's renaissance in the modern period that the image of *Berytus nutrix legum* was to reemerge, notably as the motto of the society of lawyers founded in 1919. Six years earlier, hoping to confer greater legitimacy on the law faculty that had been created at the Jesuit Université Saint-Joseph on the eve of the First World War, its first dean, the French scholar Paul Huvelin, devoted his inaugural lecture in 1913 to the school of Berytus. Three-quarters of a century later, the excavations conducted in the aftermath of the civil war once again awakened memories of the school and aroused hopes of uncovering vestiges of it. But no archeological trace was found. It is quite possible, moreover, that no trace ever will be found, for the system of instruction in Roman antiquity, unlike that of modern or even medieval universities, did not require its own buildings. Lectures—by five professors, one for each year of study—might perfectly well have been given in a more or less open space, perhaps in the vicinity of a religious edifice such as the Byzantine basilica, which itself succeeded a Roman temple, on whose site a cathedral dedicated to Saint George was erected by the Greek Orthodox community in the eighteenth century.

If the actual location of the school of Berytus has not been identified, we do know something about the atmosphere of the place from the outraged testimony of Eusebius, who condemned Berytus as a den of iniquity and a perilous trap for virtuous students. Gregory Thaumaturge, also writing in the third century, likened the city to a magician who cast a spell over the minds of the young, the better to corrupt them.[106] Student life was enlivened by regular visits to gardens, baths, and restaurants—rather like today. Nonnos of Panopolis, in the fifth century, reproached

Berytus as the brothel and kingdom of Astarte. We know, too, that a tradition of hazing aroused apprehension among new students, such as Zacharias Scholasticus, who on arriving from Gaza managed to escape harm thanks to the watchful protection of Severus. Zacharias also mentions the practice of black magic and satanism, as well as cults of malediction, encouraged by the local pastime of betting on horse races.

No matter that the city had been conquered by Christianity, pagan influence long survived and nourished the atmosphere of liberty—indeed, license—that prevailed there. Temples dedicated to Astarte and to Bacchus were still frequented in Nonnos's time, and an altar from the sixth century dedicated to Venus/Astarte has been clearly identified.[107] Berytus's image as a Christian city needs to be qualified further in order to take into account the presence of a substantial Jewish population, attested by funerary inscriptions in necropolises both there and in some cities of Palestine,[108] and by references to the collapse of a synagogue during the earthquake of 502. But this religious diversity is probably also a sign of the size of the city during the Byzantine period, and of its place in the commercial life of the empire.

Beirut in late antiquity, so far as we are able to imagine it, assuredly had the unmistakable appearance of prosperity. Already in the mid-fourth century, the anonymous *Expositio totius mundi et gentium* described it as "charming" *(valde deliciosa)*. Libanius, in a letter of the same period, refers to "very beautiful Berytus," and elsewhere speaks of "the most elegant city in Phoenicia."[109] We have also noticed the description given by Nonnos in the fifth century. But the highest compliment came once again from Justinian himself. In addition to the mention of "most fair city of Berytus" in the second preface of the *Digesta,* the third preface, called *Constitutio Tanta,* indicated, in introducing Dorotheus, that he taught "in the most splendid city of Berytus."[110]

The city was surrounded by islands at that time, and embellished by a great many gardens, planted with cypress and palm, as well as forests of pine.[111] The Magoras aqueduct continued to supply it with water, but population growth had forced the city to look for additional sources in the mountain springs that lie beneath the present-day village of Dhur Shuwair—this according to Sālih bin Yahya, whose account is corroborated by the vestiges of canals and fountains discovered at Baʿabdat, Brummana, and Beit Mery.[112] As in earlier centuries when it was a Roman colony, Berytus drew its livelihood from metalworking, for which iron ore was extracted in the surrounding area, as well as from the manufacture of textiles, wool, linen, and silk.[113] The rich soil of nearby farmland, particularly the part of it that was planted with vines, naturally favored agriculture; four centuries after Pliny, its wine brought it the praises of Nonnos. But commerce seems to have acquired a growing place in its economy. Merchants born in Berytus were found throughout the Roman world, and trade-related facilities were built in the city itself. Already under Justinian, Berytus's reputation as a center of the silk trade was secure.

It was precisely at this moment, in the middle of the sixth century, when it was at its height, in both the economic and the cultural spheres, and at a time when it was beginning to become accustomed to natural catastrophes, that Berytus was to suffer complete ruin. Two centuries earlier, around 334, Berytus and neighboring cities had been struck by an earthquake, but it recovered rapidly. Later it was left mostly untouched by a seismic event that rocked the coast, in 494, and shortly thereafter by another, in 502, that devastated Sidon and Tyre while causing only minor damage in Berytus, apart from the collapse of the synagogue. But the cataclysm of 551 was something altogether different. The sea receded a mile from the coast, and the tidal wave that followed, after smashing the ships riding at anchor in the roadstead, swept away virtually the entire city, causing thousands of deaths (as many as thirty thousand according to one account).[114] Agathias, passing through in 565, after the death of Justinian, wrote: "Berytus, then the most beautiful sight of Phoenicia, was stripped of all its splendor. Its superb buildings, so renowned, adorned with so much art, crumbled. No one was spared; there remained only heaps of rubble."[115]

Undaunted by the extent of such devastation, Berytus struggled to rise up again. The school of law was temporarily relocated to Sidon and, despite another earthquake three years later, in 554, the survivors of the tidal wave rebuilt their homes. Alas, this brave attempt was to have no future. In 560, a great fire completed the destruction of what remained of the city and of what had been rebuilt. After this latest catastrophe the will to start over again had finally been crushed: "Do ye who pass me by bewail my fate and shed a tear in honor of Berytus that is no more. . . . Inscribe upon a single stone above us, dear mortals who survive: 'Here lies Berytus, lamented city, buried above ground. Sailor, stay not thy vessel's course for me, nor lower thy sails, dry land is the port you see. I am become one tomb.'"[116]

The city was long to remain covered by ashes. At the end of the sixth century a Christian traveler, Antonine of Placentia, found it still devastated.[117] The Byzantine authorities actively supported reconstruction efforts, and coins struck there in honor of the emperors Maurice (reigned 582–602) and Constans II (641–68) suggest that commercial activity gradually resumed.[118] Progress was slowed, however, by internal dissension at Constantinople and by the military campaign of Chosroes II in Syria, whose inland cities were subjected to Persian domination until being reclaimed for Byzantium by the emperor, Heraclius, on the eve of the Arab conquest. Although the littoral escaped annihilation by the Persian armies, the long confrontation between the two empires scarcely helped in restoring Berytus to its former glory. And so, when the Arab conquerors appeared in Syria, it did not tempt them.

IN THE SHADOW OF ISLAM

For the armies of Islam that suddenly swept out of the Arabian Peninsula to challenge the two great empires of Byzantium and Persia shortly after the death of the

Prophet, in about year 12 of the Hegira (634 C.E.), the Mediterranean littoral was not an object of immediate concern. Their extraordinary campaigns were aimed primarily at taking Damascus, Jerusalem, and Ctesiphon, all of them places that figured far more prominently in the imagination of the age. No coastal city, unless perhaps Caesarea in Palestine, appeared to warrant any special exertion. Indeed the cities of the Levantine seaboard are typically mentioned by the Arab chronicles of the Conquest only in a list of places captured.

Beirut was not alone, then, in its virtual anonymity. At most one notes a passing reference here and there, never a separate discussion. The ninth-century Persian historian al-Balādhurī contents himself in *Futūh al-buldān* (On the Conquests of Countries), for example, with citing Beirut among a list of coastal cities subjugated by Yazid ibn Abi Sufyān in the aftermath of the conquest of Damascus, in 14/635. Directing the advance guard of the army, Balādhurī adds, was Yazid's brother, Caliph Muʿāwiya ibn Abi Sufyān, as the founder of the Umayyad dynasty was later to be styled; but we do not know whether he passed through Beirut at this time. Balādhurī is still less forthcoming in describing subsequent events. Although he mentions the retaking by the Byzantines of some of these places toward the end of ʿUmar's caliphate (13–23/634–44), he does not indicate which ones. Nor does he say anything more about Muʿāwiya's campaign at the beginning of ʿUthmān's caliphate to regain control of the littoral, except that he repaired its fortifications and stationed troops *(muqātila)* there. The eighth-century Arab historian al-Wāqidi, in his *Futūh al-Shām* (Conquests of Syria), gives another, though not more specific, version that situates the capture of Beirut (here again mentioned only in the company of other cities) in the context of the occupation of Caesarea in 19/640 by ʿAmr, the conqueror of Egypt. The modesty of Beirut's reputation at this time is confirmed by the administrative reorganization of al-Shām (the Arabic name for Syria), which was divided into five *ajnād* (singular *jund*), or military districts, with Beirut coming under the authority of Damascus.

Neither in Wāqidi nor Balādhurī, nor in any other early source, do we find any information about the way in which the city fell and, as a result, about the sort of treatment it received, though the Arab chronicles go to great lengths to describe the pacts of protection *(dhimma)* that spared the majority of the cities of Syria from being sacked and permitted their inhabitants to preserve their Christian (or Jewish) faith in exchange for payment of a head tax. The only indication, a very late one, is furnished in the fifteenth century by Sālih bin Yahya, who states that there were still many Christians in Beirut after the Arab conquest; he adds, however, that their number later diminished, whereas that of the Muslims continued to grow until they represented a majority of the population.[119] This was a common phenomenon in all the cities of Syria, where garrisons of Islamic soldiers fairly rapidly became integrated into the urban fabric. In the case of Beirut and its neighbors along the coast, one must not forget Muʿāwiya's attempt, reported by the ninth-century

Arab historian and geographer al-Yaʿqūbī, in *Kitāb al-buldān* (Book of Countries), to settle Islamized Persians there; but we do not know whether these were the *muqātila* mentioned by Balādhurī in connection with the second conquest of the coastal cities, or whether other groups of foreigners were settled there as a consequence of a later decision by Muʿāwiya after he became governor of Damascus, or indeed during his caliphate.

AN ISLAMIC OUTPOST

Once incorporated into the Muslim state, the cities of the Mediterranean littoral theoretically constituted a *ribāt,* the term used by the Arabs to designate the extreme outer reaches of their sphere of control, which were meant to guard the Dār al-Islam (Abode of Islam) and serve as a base for new conquests. But although this idea of a frontier outpost is very much present in the works of most contemporary Arab travelers and geographers, events along the Mediterranean boundary of the early caliphate aroused scarcely any interest among historians. Tradition has it that Muʿāwiya had asked the craftsmen of Beirut to build a fleet that would enable him to take Cyprus; but until the tenth century there is no mention of attacks by Byzantine ships against coastal strongholds in the Levant or of other military preparations in their roadsteads. Only a few documents, conserved in family archives, mention episodes of belligerent behavior: skirmishes with the Mardaites, Christian warriors from the northern Lebanon mountains, one of which ended with the death of the head of the Arslān family, a branch of the Lakhmid line, at Sinn al-Fil on the eastern outskirts of Beirut in about 171/787; and a Byzantine raid in 185/801, in the course of which another member of the Arslān family was carried off and then freed after the payment of a ransom by one of the sons of the caliph Harun al-Rashīd.[120] These accounts are not corroborated by any official source, however.

Beirut is well remembered, on the other hand, for the welcome it gave to a more peaceable holy warrior *(murābit),* the imam ʿAbd al-Rahmān bin ʿAmr al-Awzāʿi (or, following the local pronunciation, al-Uzāʿi). According to the ninth-century historian al-Tabarī, Uzāʿi was born in Damascus and held an administrative post there before coming to Beirut, where he died at the age of seventy or so in 157/774.[121] Sālih bin Yahya, for his part, says Uzāʿi was born at Baalbek in 88/707 or 93/712, adding that as a child in the Biqāʿ he was brought by his mother to Beirut, where he lived—*rābata,* Sālih writes, with reference to the *ribāt*—until his death.[122] While holding the office of mufti, Tabarī tells us, Uzāʿi's fame as a jurisconsult went far beyond the confines of the city. The esteem in which he was held is suggested by the appeals that he addressed to the highest officials of the state, even after the advent of the ʿAbbasids and the transfer of the capital to Baghdad; indeed, he was said to be able to intervene directly with the caliph, al-Mansūr. Beyond his political connections, his rulings regarding the application of religious law *(shariʿa)* were the first to be generally adopted by Islamic jurisprudence, and his school was predominant not only in Syria—for two hundred years, according to Sālih—but also in the Maghrib, where its authority extended as far as Andalusia before being supplanted by that of Mālik ibn Anas.[123] Uzāʿi left his name to two places in Beirut: the *zāwiya*, where he dispensed opinions, to the south of what was to become Suq al-Tawileh, site of a now-vanished fountain that was dedicated to him in 1528; and the village of Hantus (or Hantush) where he was buried, in the distant southern suburbs of the modern city, known since by the name Uzāʿi (or Ouzaï in its gallicized version). The imam's reputation for holiness, inherited by his son Muhammad and a certain number of disciples, was to give Beirut a distinctive place in the mental geography of Muslims, and for centuries afterward it was customary for Arab visitors to the city to honor his memory.

However great Uzāʿi's prestige may have been, Beirut nonetheless occupies an extremely modest place in classical Arab literature. Abū Nuwās, the bacchic poet of the golden ʿAbbasid era, refers to the apples of Lebanon, but the praises of Pliny and Nonnos for the vineyards of Beirut evidently never reached his ears; and though al-Mutanabbī, the towering figure of classical Arab poetry, mentions the steep roads of Lebanon, he seems not to have passed through Beirut either. Two of his contemporaries, the tenth-century geographers al-Istakhrī and ibn Hawqal, nevertheless do mention the city. The first, in *Kitāb al-Masālik waʾl-mamālik* (Book of Routes and Realms), makes reference to its fortifications; the second, in a work of the same title, to a strong garrison of Damascene soldiers, while emphasizing a difference of temperament between the inhabitants of Damascus and those of Beirut, whom he found more affable. Ibn Hawqal also speaks of Beirut's port and maritime commerce, and describes the surrounding vegetation, notably palms, sugar cane, and various kinds of fruit tree. A few decades later, in 1047, the Persian traveler Nāsir-i-Khosrau was struck by the sight of a triumphal arch from the Roman period, described in his *Safarnameh*.[124]

Beirut seems to have played no role in the political life of the Islamic world until the tenth century. It had passed from the Umayyad to the ʿAbbasid state without notable incident, and with the decline of the ʿAbbasids fell along with the rest of Syria into the lap of the Tulunid sultanate, established at Cairo in 264/877, and then into that of the Ikhshidids in 323/935. In the interval its population remained mixed, though in what proportions is unknown. History has preserved the names of two eminent Christians. Prior to the advent of Islam, the great Byzantine hymn writer Saint Romanos, whose canticles won him fame in Beirut, was brought to Constantinople by Anastasius I (491–518). Three centuries later the bishop of Beirut, Thuma, was summoned to take part in the Council of Constantinople, in 869.[125]

Gradually the stability ushered in by Islam in its first age of greatness came to be undermined. With the weakening of the ʿAbbasid state and the quarrels between the various sultanates, the Byzantines grew bolder, and Emperor John Tzimiskes

(969–76), whom the Arabs called al-Shāmshaqīq, seized a large part of Palestine in the tenth century. In doing so he took Beirut by force, in 364/974, and, according to ibn al-Qalānisī, allowed it to be looted while deporting many of its inhabitants. The city was retaken only two years later by the governor of Damascus, who entrusted its administration to Darwish bin ʿUmar al-Arslāni. Shortly thereafter, in 384/994, Syria and Palestine came under the control of the Fatimid caliphate, and Beirut seems to have prospered more than most of its coastal neighbors, although here again we have scarcely any information apart from the names of the two Fatimid governors of the city: Fath, a protégé of the government of Aleppo appointed in 405/1014, and Abu Saʿīd Qabūs, appointed in 435/1043. The annals do nevertheless mention a revealing episode that took place in 448/1056, when along with Acre and Byblos the city was given by way of compensation to the dismissed governor of Aleppo, Sālih ibn Mirdās. Small consolation, as it turned out: allies of ibn Mirdās soon recaptured Aleppo, and the Fatimid caliph subsequently took Beirut away from him.

With regard to the main point, whether the wave of conversions to Shiʿism that had been set in motion by the Fatimids spread to Beirut, no evidence has come down to us. We know that in Egypt, for example, where the dynasty had built a new capital at Cairo, the Shiʿi imprint was so profound that a century later it would require the resolute efforts of Saladin and his Ayyubid successors, and then of the Mamluks, to eradicate all traces of it. Nothing similar is indicated in the case of Beirut. It is true that the Fatimid hold over Syria was weakened in the second half of the eleventh century by the advance of the Seljuk Turks, who, upon reaching Iraq, went on to establish themselves in Aleppo and Damascus and, from there, in the cities of the coast. In Beirut, their power was exercised in the name of the atabeg of Damascus by an Arab governor from the Tanukh family. But not for long: seizing on the obstacles placed by the Seljuks in the way of Christian pilgrims in the Holy Land as a pretext for intervention, and advancing at first under the indulgent eye of the Fatimids, Catholic Europe involved the East in a war of religion that was to last for two centuries—and that managed, for the first time since the Arab Conquest, to sever the bond that had joined Damascus and Beirut.

A FRANKISH SEIGNEURY

If Beirut did not fall immediately into the hands of the Crusaders, it was yet one of the cities that remained longest in their possession: one hundred seventy-one years in all, with a brief interlude of nine years. Damascus, by contrast, escaped capture by the Franks throughout this period and became, in alternation with Aleppo, under its atabeg Zanki, and Cairo, under the Ayyubids and Mamluks, one of the centers of Islamic resistance to the European invasion.

Following the failure of the People's Crusade of Peter the Hermit, the armies of the First Crusade had started out by taking Antioch in 1098 and then entered the Orontes Valley, advancing as far as the Biqa' Plateau. But instead of proceeding southward along the road to Jerusalem, the Crusaders veered off toward the coast, where they passed through Tripoli before reaching Beirut. They did not long linger there. At this stage in its history the city remained a prize of little interest and its Seljuk governor, a Tanukh emir, had scarcely any difficulty in purchasing his own safety and that of its inhabitants by providing the attackers with fresh supplies. The Crusaders lifted the siege and continued on their way to Jerusalem, which fell in 1099. Three years later, Baldwin of Boulogne—count of Edessa, brother of Godfrey of Bouillon, and the first titled king of Jerusalem—made a new, though rather half-hearted incursion into Palestine. Once again, the governor of Beirut managed to fend off assault by agreeing to reprovision the Christian forces. Baldwin returned to the charge with greater determination in 1110, however, and with the assistance of Bertrand of Toulouse, count of Tripoli, he laid siege to the city. The battle lasted two months. The siege towers, made from wood cut in the forests of the promontory, were destroyed at the outset by the defenders but rapidly rebuilt. Then the appearance of an Egyptian flotilla obliged the Crusaders to retreat. Returning at the head of a fleet of forty ships, Baldwin finally succeeded in taking the city. Ibn al-Qalānisī recounts that it was sacked at once, and its inhabitants deported.

Bequeathed to Baldwin's second son, Fulk of Guînes, Baruth (as the city's name was spelled by the Crusaders) gave signs of recovering from the ordeals of the siege. Baldwin had inaugurated the period of Frankish domination by ordering that a basilica be erected there on the cross-shaped plan customary in Latin Christianity. This church, dedicated to Saint John the Baptist, was to be transformed into a mosque (the present-day al-'Umari Mosque) in the late thirteenth century. In the meantime the Crusaders sought to strengthen the city's defenses, hastening to repair the surrounding wall, damaged by the siege, and to construct two new guard towers. The result seems to have been convincing, to judge from the favorable description given by the twelfth-century geographer al-Idrīsī in *Nuzhat al-mushtāq fī ikhtirāq al-āfāq* (The Delight of Him Who Desires to Journey through the Climates), which says that the wall was rebuilt with large stones. Idrīsī also mentions the proximity of the mountains, which were said to furnish all of Syria with high-grade iron ore, as well as the density of the pine forest to the south of the city, which the Franks called "la Pinoie." Another traveler, the Byzantine John Phocas, described a "large and populous city, set round about with spacious meadows," while laying emphasis on its "fair harbor." It was not, however, a natural harbor; it "has been wrought by art, and is embosomed in the city in the form of a half-moon, and at the two extremities of the half-moon are placed, as horns, two great towers, from one of which a chain is drawn across to the other, and shuts the ships within the harbor."[126]

Despite the deportations that followed the siege, the Muslim presence did not entirely disappear during this long first period of seventy-seven years. Apart from

FIGURE 9. The al-ʿUmari Mosque, formerly the Church of Saint John the Baptist during the Crusades.

the visit by Idrīsī, we have some evidence of it from an account of a bloody quarrel between two families, the Talhūqs and the Banū Hamra, in 1144. The Talhūqs were settled in Ras Beirut, outside the city walls, whereas the Banū Hamra, a clan of either Bedouin or Persian descent that had come from the Biqaʿ at an earlier date, lived within. Following a brawl, the reason for which is now forgotten, the Talhūqs retreated to al-Gharb, a mountainous district that overlooks the Shuwafat plain to the southeast of Beirut. But with the assassination of one of their members who had ventured into the city, a powerful Talhūq force swept down and broke through the gates, killing several inhabitants.[127] The annals of the period have also recorded certain events related more closely to the military maneuvers that formed the heart of the Crusades over two centuries. Thus, for example, a raid launched in 1151 by an Egyptian fleet against Beirut and other neighboring ports, reported by ibn al-Qalānisī and by al-Maqdisī in *Kitāb al-Rawdatayn fī akhbār al-Dawlatayn* (Book of the Two Gardens on the Reports of the Two Reigns [of Nur al-Dīn and Saladin], edited and augmented by Shīhab al-Dīn Abū Shāma in the mid-thirteenth century); another raid, described by ibn al-Muyassar in *Akhbār Misr* (Annals of Egypt, published in 1157—a year marked by a devastating earthquake); and the death in Beirut on his return from Antioch of Baldwin III, king of Jerusalem, probably poisoned by one of his rivals.

Beirut was in the hands of Jocelyn, count of Edessa, when Salāh al-dīn al-Ayyūbī, the famous Saladin of the literature of the Crusades, took the city in 1187.[128] Saladin, the sultan of Egypt and Syria, had tried earlier to subdue the city, in 1181. Coming overland from Damascus, while his fleet set sail from Egypt, he had begun by laying waste to the hinterland before instituting the siege. He nonetheless was obliged to raise it after a few days. According to the historian ibn al-Athīr, the news that a Crusader ship had reached Damietta caused him to abandon his efforts; Saladin's biographer, ibn Shaddād, speaks only of the failure of the siege. Be that as it may, Saladin came back to Beirut only in the aftermath of his great victory at Hittīn, in 1187, which was crowned by the capture of Jerusalem and several other cities. After a week-long siege the Crusaders capitulated and were given permission to retreat to Tyre. Later, after taking Acre, Saladin chose to spend several days in Beirut, where he received Bohemund III, the Frankish governor of Antioch and Tripoli.

Notwithstanding its preeminent place in the memory of Arabs and Europeans alike, Saladin's exploit represented only an interlude in the history of the Crusades. The treaty signed in 1192, a year before the sultan's death, after the recapture of Acre by the Third Crusade, left the Palestinian littoral to the Franks. It was not long before Beirut fell once again under the domination of the Crusaders. In 1197, alarmed by rumors that an attack by the Crusaders' fleet was imminent, the sultan's brother and successor al-ʿĀdil rushed to Beirut and there, seeking to rob the city of all strategic importance, ordered that its walls and citadel be destroyed. The governor, ʿIzz al-dīn Usama, persuaded him to rescind the order, however, promising to resist to the end. But Usama did nothing of the kind. Instead, ibn al-Athīr reports, he surrendered without a fight on the fleet's arrival in the roadstead. A truce concluded the following year, in 1198, between the Franks and al-ʿAzīz, Saladin's son and now sultan in his turn, formalized the new state of affairs.

This second chapter in the Latin history of Beirut was to last ninety-four years. More than a third of it was passed under the rule of a single lord, John of Ibelin, who rebuilt the city's walls, restored the citadel, and constructed new towers. For the thirty-five years of his reign, during which time he also inherited the seigneury of Jaffa and acted briefly as regent of the kingdom of Cyprus, John encouraged industry and commerce. In particular, he promoted trade with merchants from Venice, Genoa, and Pisa, who were to enjoy an enduring presence in the Levant, long after the Crusades. Another lasting settlement was made by the Franciscans. But if Frankish domination appeared to be permanently established in Beirut, its days elsewhere in the Near East were numbered. The Mamluk state in Egypt, founded by pretorian slaves who came to power after a revolt against the Ayyubid dynasty in 1250, now rose up against the Crusaders while at the same time moving to dispose of another threat that had emerged with the appearance of the Mongol forces led by Hulagu, khan of the Ilkhanate, potentially allies of the Christian host. Under pressure first from the Mamluk sultan Baybars, and then from his successor Qalāʾūn, the Latin domains shrank and finally disappeared, surviving only on Cyprus. Outside Beirut, now ruled by a fifth-generation descendant of John of Ibelin, Qalā'ūn's son Ashraf directed the siege in 690/1291. The Crusaders saw advantages in capitulation; but the Mamluks were not in a mood for compromise. The general charged with taking possession of the city, Sanjar al-Shujā'ī, put the Frankish lords to death and then, having demolished the ramparts and the citadel, sent their subjects to Egypt, where eventually they were freed by the sultan, who gave them the choice either of settling in Cyprus or of returning to Beirut.[129] This may have been an empty promise, since there is no evidence that any Franks ever came back to the city.

THE MUSLIM RESTORATION

By the end of the thirteenth century, the Crusades were all but over in the East. One finds mention made repeatedly during the fourteenth century of raids undertaken against coastal cities, even of the capture for a brief time of a port, such as Sidon. But organized campaigns involving whole armies were henceforth a thing of the past, at least in the Levant. Jerusalem, having been taken and retaken, was now firmly in Muslim hands, diminishing the enemy's prospects for establishing new bridgeheads. Muslim strategists, for their part, had drawn the conclusion that, on balance, it was better actually not to defend coastal cities, lest the Crusaders become entrenched there. The Ayyubids were the first to recognize this, as we have seen with 'Ādil's thwarted attempt to destroy its ramparts. The Mamluks were more systematic, resolutely setting about to demolish the ports and coastal fortifications of Syria and Palestine. None of the coast's many fortresses was spared, except the citadel overlooking Tripoli, though here and there watchtowers were built on the ruins of the destroyed fortifications in order to detect the approach of enemy forces and thereby turn back a first wave of attack. Whereas the Palestinian littoral was to suffer from the crippling effects of this policy for almost six centuries, Tripoli and Beirut, and later Sidon, recovered more rapidly. Syrian commerce had need of ports, and ports had to be defended, albeit by means that bore no relation to those of the past.

In Beirut, the Mamluks were determined from the middle of the fourteenth century to reconstruct the fortifications looking out upon the sea and to rebuild the western wall, using the vestiges of the Crusaders' ramparts. The governor of Damascus, Tinkiz, raised a tower there called al-Ba'albakiyya, in reference to the soldiers from Baalbek that guarded it. His successor, Baydamar, transformed the roadstead into a port and revived the use of a long chain—already mentioned by John Phocas—to block access to it. Suspended between the tower built by Tinkiz and the end of the western wall, rebuilt by Baydamar, this chain (silsila) was to give the new port the name of Bāb al-Silsila.[130] The Mamluk defenses were completed with the establishment of a system of communication that, by means of fires lit in the mountains, made it possible very quickly to sound the alarm in Damascus, from which reinforcements could be dispatched in less than a day.[131]

If the absence of fortifications served to deter landings by regular armies, it also encouraged the launching of raids against the city, generally from Cyprus, where for a time the crusading spirit survived. Genoese, Venetian, Pisan, and Catalan corsairs harried the coast as well, usually in an attempt to settle accounts among themselves. Thus in 734/1334, Sālih reports, a band of Genoese attacked Beirut to lay their hands on a Catalan ship. The city's Muslim defenders, who had taken the side of the Catalans, failed to prevent the ship from being taken, and many lives were lost in two days of fighting. Thirty years later, in the face of repeated attacks against Beirut and Sidon, and even Alexandria, which was the target of a raid by Hugh IV of Lusignan, who then pillaged the city in 767/1365, the Mamluks resolved to retaliate by invading Cyprus. The order was given to construct a fleet in Beirut, where wood was available in ample quantities, but, according to Sālih, though the enterprise was diligently planned by Baydamar it miscarried after his death, and the only two ships that had been finished soon rotted in their slips.[132] A dispute between the king of Cyprus and the Genoese, who took Famagusta in 1372, had the effect only of raising the stakes and aggravating tensions further. Additional attacks by the Genoese followed, especially in 1382 and 1403. The merchandise plundered at Beirut during this last raid included a large cargo of spices belonging to the Venetians, who nonetheless succeeded in forcing their competitors to make good their losses.[133]

Neither the boldness of such attacks nor their recurrence meant that Mamluk authority was in any way threatened. While the raids often caused many casualties among both the civilian population of the coastal cities and the Muslim forces stationed there, the attackers were sometimes slaughtered, as in 1403. The Burgi Mamluks, who had supplanted the Bahri Mamluks in 1382,[134] succeeded even in taking Cyprus in 1424, holding it for two years before the restoration of the Lusignan dynasty, which was finally ousted in its turn by Venice in 1489. Beirut played a role in this fleeting conquest, through the help given by the emirs of the Gharb, south of the city, who had settled there. But the strategic importance of the city for the Mamluks did not derive solely from its geographic situation. Apart from the wood that it furnished for naval construction, it also produced iron ore, indispensable for the manufacture of armaments and war ships; in all of the sultanate no ore was to be had other than that which was extracted from a small mine near Beirut.[135]

The traffic of its port also generated substantial customs revenue, claimed on the authority of the governor of Damascus. The self-assurance of Mamluk rule is furthermore suggested by the tolerance it displayed toward Venetian merchants, who had a church there, as well as toward caravanserais *(khans)* and Turkish baths.[136] The Bahri Mamluks took a less indulgent view of the Shi'a settled not far from there, in the Kisrawan district, beyond the Kalb River. It is not known whether their policy of de-Shi'itization, as it might be called, begun already by Saladin, had direct repercussions on Beirut. But the devastation visited upon Kisrawan by this campaign in the early fourteenth century unquestionably had a decisive impact on the subsequent history of the Lebanon mountains, and therefore indirectly on Beirut itself, since it created a demographic void that attracted the Maronite Christians of the north, who began a long migration southward, lasting several centuries, to the disadvantage of the Druze who had preceded them there.

Paradoxically, the Mamluks' intolerance toward the Shi'a did not prevent them from calling upon the services of the Druze, a sect that had its origins in Shi'ism and that went back to the reviled era of the Fatimids. Under both the Bahri and the Burgi Mamluks, the authority of the governor of Damascus was given effect in Beirut through the Buhtur emirs. The history of this family is known to us through the writings of one of its descendants, Sālih bin Yahya himself, who traced his lineage back to the Tanukhs, and thence to the Manadhiras, the Lakhmid kings of Hira who were themselves related to Qahtān, the legendary ancestor of the Arabs, through Zayd bin Kahlān. The Tanukhs were Islamized Christians who had dispersed after the Conquest through the region of the Euphrates, where one of them became emir of Hira during the Fatimid period. His son 'Ali, called Majd al-Dawla, had settled in Lebanon and received from the Fatimid caliph responsibility for the Gharb and the Syrian coast, a charge that was later renewed by the Seljuk atabeg of Damascus. It may have been a Tanukh emir who saved Beirut from siege when the First Crusade passed before its walls. After the conquest of the city by the Franks, the Tanukhs preserved their authority in the Gharb, where, according to Sālih, 'Ali's son, Buhtur, was confirmed as emir by the atabeg of Damascus. Sālih goes on to say that Saladin personally invested one of Buhtur's descendants in this office in Beirut. But while they took part in the struggle against the Crusaders, the Tanukhs, along with 'Ali and his line, who had converted to Druzism at an undetermined moment during the eleventh or twelfth century, maintained ambivalent relations with the Frankish lords of Beirut both before and after Saladin's conquest—so ambivalent that they aroused the suspicions of the Mamluk sultan Baybars, who arrested three emirs of the family. Yet these same men were to be encountered again, now freed after Baybars's death and returned to good graces under Ashraf, during the capture of Beirut by the Mamluks. They contributed thereafter to the upkeep of the garrison stationed in the city, and one of them had the walls of the Church of Saint John the Baptist painted white as part of its transformation into a mosque.[137] Their descendants distinguished themselves in the defense of Beirut against the Genoese raids, despite fresh setbacks during Baydamar's tenure in Damascus. Sālih himself commanded a unit of one hundred men in the Mamluk campaign against Cyprus.

The power of the emirs of the Gharb, still exercised in the name of the governor of Damascus, manifested itself through the construction of palaces and baths, especially after the repair of the seaward ramparts. One of these palaces is mentioned by ibn Sibāt in his history of the house of Buhtur, which brought Sālih's account up

FIGURE 10. The interior of the al-ʿUmari Mosque, whose walls, formerly decorated with frescoes, were whitewashed after the Mamluk capture of the city.

to 1523.[138] But however great may have been the Buhturs' support of public works, described in great detail by Sālih, Beirut seems still far from having regained its former eminence. A few vestiges have been found from this period, as a result of the emergency excavations of the 1990s, but there is nothing comparable to what may be seen in the old city of Tripoli, a veritable conservatory of Mamluk architecture. The only identifiable edifice is the mausoleum *(zāwiya)* of the Syrian cosmographer ibn ʿUraq al-Dimashqī along Rue Weygand, not far from that of Uzāʿi. The fifteenth century had not been an auspicious period for the Levant. Epidemics and famines only worsened the baleful consequences of the campaign waged by Tamerlane (Tīmūr), who threatened Damascus and devastated the north of Syria, and the rise of piracy against ships engaged in commerce with Europe soon made Beirut a dangerous destination. It was not until the fall of the Mamluk state, vanquished by the Ottomans on the plain of Marj Dābiq, north of Aleppo, in August 1516, and then outside Cairo in January 1517, that the balance of power decisively shifted.

In the meantime Saladin had managed to mobilize and reinvigorate the moral forces of the Muslim East, while the Mamluks triumphantly led the resistance to the Crusaders, first by repulsing the Franks and then by parrying the Mongols' thrusts. But these successes came at the price of political instability, marked by the militarization of the Mamluk state and an endless succession of conspiracies that enduringly linked their name in Arab history with decadence. It fell to the Ottoman

FIGURE 11. Mausoleum of ibn ʿUraq al-Dimashqī.

dynasty to bring about the true restoration of Muslim power in the geopolitical balance of the early modern world. The subsequent decline of its empire, in the late eighteenth century, must not cause us to forget that the Ottomans constituted a power of the first order; indeed, had the term held any meaning at the time, one might even speak of a world power. Never since the apogee of the Umayyad and ʿAbbasid dynasties had the glory of Islam been raised up so high or extended so far.

THE GREAT OTTOMAN MARKET

The Byzantine Empire was but a shadow of its former self when Mehmet II conquered Constantinople in 1453. Nonetheless it was the first enemy of ancient reputation that the Muslim armies had encountered since breaking out from the Arabian Peninsula eight centuries earlier. The longing to confront the second Rome had inhabited the Arab mind for centuries—and inspired some of the best-known epic poems of Arabic literature. The Ottoman expansion coincided also with the end of Arab rule in Andalusia; expelled from Spain, Islam reappeared on European soil from the southeast, gradually gaining control over the Balkans and a large part of the Danube basin. The Ottomans were finally halted at the gates of Vienna, of course, not once but twice. In the interval they had rid themselves of the Mamluk state, though not of the Mamluks themselves, and extended their dominion over the entire eastern and southern rim of the Mediterranean, as far as Algeria. Now that it stood astride three continents, with Byzantium no longer blocking expansion to the north and west, the enlarged empire effectively deprived the Levantine littoral of its old function as *ribāt*, all the more so once the Venetians were thrown out of Cyprus in 1571. Despite the defeat the same year of Ali Pasha's fleet by the Holy League at the Battle of Lepanto, the Levant no longer had to fear the maritime threat embodied first by the Byzantines, and then by the Crusaders and their Genoese successors. In the place of warships, merchant vessels began to call upon what were henceforth known to Europeans as the *Échelles du Levant*—the Ports of the Levant, which included the port of Beirut.

The nature of Ottoman supremacy in the Levant, which was to last four full centuries after the victory of Sultan Salim I over the Mamluks in 1516–17, until the end of the First World War, was long obscured by the orientalist perspective of European travelers, and after them by Arab nationalist ideologies. In the late twentieth century, however, the failure of the nation-state in the Near East (thrown into particularly vivid relief by the Lebanese civil war) and in a part of the Balkans, on the one hand, and the opening of the imperial archives in Istanbul, on the other, led to a reevaluation of the Ottoman heritage. The familiar image of arbitrary rule exercised solely by coercion has now given way to a much more complex picture, of a vast territory (three-quarter million square miles at its height) that nonetheless constituted a cohesive entity, at least until the end of the eighteenth century, despite the remarkable ethnic and cultural diversity of the peoples living under Ottoman sovereignty—Turks, Greeks, Arabs, Serbs, Armenians, and Bulgarians among others. This diversity was counterbalanced by powerful forces of attraction. One of them indisputably was Islam. But there were others. The tradition of efficient administration upheld by the Ottomans in all their domains, not only with regard to taxation but in the juridical and religious spheres as well, did much to ensure the longevity of the empire, not least by compensating for the chronic political instability that accompanied the frequent, indeed almost annual, replacement of provincial governors. Conversely, the system served also to limit the autonomy that many *vilayets* came to enjoy during the eighteenth century, with the appearance of quasi-dynastic rule by provincial governors, even forms of local monarchy. For four centuries tribute continued to be paid, and Friday prayers continued to be said, in the name of the sultan. At no time were political disturbances so great as to create internal barriers to movement within the imperial territory. This freedom of circulation, sometimes hampered by unrest but never interrupted, combined with the immense needs of a population spread over three continents to sustain an enormous domestic market that, in its turn, strengthened the cohesion of the empire as a whole.[139]

Syria—Bilād al-Shām, to give it its customary Arabic name—seems to have occupied a privileged place, to judge from the quality of the governors who succeeded

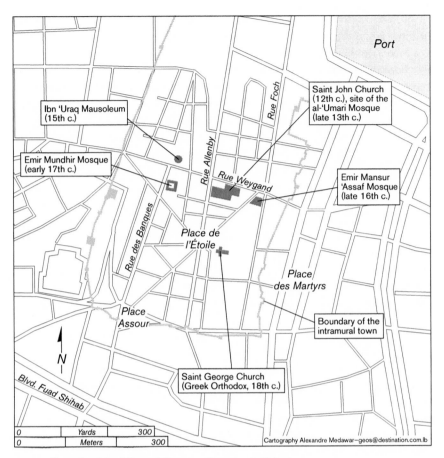

MAP 4. Crusader, Mamluk, and Ottoman Remains in Beirut

one another in the country's provinces (Aleppo, Damascus, Tripoli, and later Sidon), several of whom succeeded in climbing to the pinnacle of power, the post of grand vizier in Istanbul. Far from the fronts of war in Danubian Europe and sheltered from the Safavid threat that made itself felt in Ottoman Iraq from time to time, while lying along the routes of commercial traffic originating in more distant parts of Asia, Syria particularly benefited from access to the great Ottoman market as a manufacturer of textiles and metal products and as a major supplier of grain and timber. For the most part these benefits accrued to the inland towns and cities; the economy of the coastal ports, which so attracted the attention of European travelers, remained insignificant by comparison with the scale of overland commerce. Moreover, the merchants who frequented these ports did not devote themselves exclusively to trade with Europe; coastal shipping also helped to promote the exchange of goods and products among the provinces. Indeed, no city of the Syrian littoral—not even Tripoli, the seat of a vilayet since the beginning of Ottoman domination, nor Sidon, which had been elevated to the status of a province in the mid-eighteenth century and which was to grow in size considerably during the following century, and certainly not Beirut—could stand comparison with the cities of the interior, foremost among them the two great metropolises of Aleppo and Damascus.[140] Aleppo had acted for centuries as a transshipment point for cargo traveling by camel and mule, and the demand of the Ottoman market only increased the value of its position between the steppes of the hinterland and the coastal plain. The economic importance of Damascus, which commanded other commercial routes and presided over the agriculture of the Ghuta Plain and the Biqaʿ Valley, was strengthened by the political influence inherited from its past as capital of the Umayyad dynasty and citadel of Muslim resistance to the Franks. Its prestige was to be further augmented under the Ottomans, not only through the de facto control that its governors exercised over the other provinces of Syria, Aleppo excepted, but also, and especially, through their role in organizing the pilgrimage to Mecca, that annual "Islamic congress" (in the French historian André Raymond's phrase) which was to become one of the foremost emblems of Ottoman unity.[141]

The Ottoman Empire was not only a Muslim power. Notwithstanding the reductive arguments pressed by various nationalist and Christian historiographers—Greek, Serbian, and Lebanese alike—it was also the successor to Byzantium. Christian Greeks were legion in the ranks of its administration. Despite the conversion of Hagia Sophia into a mosque, the Greek Church itself was more often allied with the government than suppressed by it, and the patriarch of the Phanar was regarded as one of the leading figures of Istanbul. When Lala Mustafa Pasha conquered Cyprus in the name of Sultan Salim II in 1571, it signified not the Islamization of the island, but rather a restoration of the Greek Church. Similar nuances may be detected elsewhere in the geopolitical outlook of the Sublime Porte. The alliance concluded by Süleyman the Magnificent and François I of France against the Holy Roman Emperor Charles V recommended itself not only by the increased room for maneuver it gave both parties against Austria, but also, from the French point of view, for its grant of commercial concessions and recognition of France's status as protector of the Catholics in the Ottoman Empire. "Except for Venice and a few Frenchmen," the historian Jules Michelet was later to remark, "no one in Europe understood anything about the Eastern Question." Strictly speaking, the Eastern Question had not yet arisen, since here Michelet was referring to the sixteenth century. When it did arise, however, at the end of the eighteenth century, one of its principal elements was the dynamism of the Christian minorities, reinforced by their right to self-rule and, in the case of the Uniate churches, by French protection.

The Ottoman *millet* regime, governing those non-Islamic religious communities that enjoyed official recognition, took root in Qur'anic prescriptions relating to protection of the people of the Book (*dhimmīs*) in exchange for payment of a head tax (*jizya*). The originality of the sultans' policy consisted in systematizing these prescriptions so as to allow Christians and Jews nearly total autonomy, supplemented in certain cases by foreign protection. To be sure, this did not amount to full equality before the law; a great many restrictions, more or less faithfully observed depending on the period, weighed on the social life of non-Muslims. But nor did it resemble the state of subjugation that the French word *dhimmitude* has often, and wrongly, been supposed to imply. Throughout most of the empire, Christians and Jews had, in addition to freedom of worship, the right to manage their own affairs. By and large this was the case in Beirut, where the Greek Orthodox community also profited from the sympathetic feeling that had long existed between the Ottomans and the Greeks, although the Church of Antioch, which had its seat at Damascus, remained without any attachment to the Phanar. In the mountains above Beirut, the imperial system chiefly benefited the Maronites, and all the more as religious autonomy was conjoined there with the political effects of tax farming, an administrative arrangement under which taxes were collected by private individuals rather than state officials.

Mount Lebanon had never been considered a province before 1861. In principle it belonged jointly to the pashaliks of Damascus and Tripoli, and later of Sidon and Tripoli, but as a practical matter it fell under the jurisdiction of the governor (*wālī*) of Damascus, and so was subject to the fiscal regime known as *iltizām*, comparable in many ways to the system of tax farming under the ancien régime in France. The application of this regime in Mount Lebanon did not differ in any important respect from that in other provinces, except for the use of the term *muqāti'ji* to designate the chief tax collector, or farmer general.[142] What set this region apart from its neighbors was the mixture of denominations found there and the distinctive social dynamics arising from the interaction of its two principal groups, the Druze and the Maronites.[143] Neither group was represented in significant numbers in other parts of the empire: a few were found in the Wādi al-Taym at the foot of Mount Hermon, in the southeastern Biqaʿ, in the confines of the Hauran region (in the case of the Druze), and in northern Syria (in the case of the Maronites), but the majority of their members lived in the Lebanon mountains.

Certain religious particularities gave these groups the appearance of being protonational minorities. Druzism, as an offshoot of Fatimid Shiʿism, incorporated elements of ancient Eastern wisdom and cultivated esotericism while strictly forbidding proselytism. The Maronite Church, founded by Saint John Maron, a fifth-century monk who initially was venerated by the Orthodox Church, had forsworn its monothelitic origins and, by allying itself with Rome, managed to preserve a distinctive identity in relation to the other Christians of the Near East, who observed the Greek and Armenian rites in Syria, the West Syrian in Syria and the Assyrian in Iraq, and the Coptic in Egypt. At the same time it succeeded in resisting the tide of Uniatism, encouraged by European missionaries, which in the early eighteenth century split the Eastern Orthodox communities in two by stimulating the creation of Greek Catholic, Armenian Catholic, Syrian Catholic, Chaldean (Assyrian Catholic), and Coptic Catholic churches. Although it had come from northern Syria, the Maronite community was also shaped by the topography of Mount Lebanon, especially by the rugged relief of its northern part, flanking the Qadisha Valley beneath the forest of the Cedars, where Maron's church had first been established. Later, under the Mamluks and, still more so, under the Ottomans, the promise of lands in the south that were easier to work caused its adherents, mostly poor farmers, to populate the entire mountain chain, filling it with terraced agriculture. In return the Maronites and the Druze jointly gave the Mountain its peculiar identity—and its capital letter. This identity was recognized by a system of tax collection that, without being the special prerogative of the Mountain, underscored its particular status as a result of the central government's willingness to confide responsibility for administering fiscal policy to prominent families belonging to these two minorities, among others.

Acting on behalf of the imperial treasury, these families of *muqāti'jiyya*, some of whom had held office since the Mamluk period, came to constitute local powers allied to the provincial capitals, or else in rivalry with them. The Ottomans, who had cast aside the Tanukh emirs by reason of their prior association with the Mamluks, proceeded to coopt the three most powerful families of the region: the Kurdish Sayfas in the north, the Turcoman 'Assafs in Kisrawan, and the Druze Ma'ns in the Shuf Mountains. By the early seventeenth century, in the wake of violent quarrels arising from a desire to settle old scores, there remained only the Ma'ns. Notwithstanding repeated tests of strength between Fakhr al-Dīn II al-Ma'ni and the governors of Damascus, the Ottoman authorities expanded the authority of the family two years after Fakhr al-Dīn's death, in 1637. But with the interruption of the Ma'nid line, the central role in ensuring the stability of the Mountain fell in 1690 to a Sunni Muslim family, the Shihabs, the leading figure of which at the end of the eighteenth century was to be Bashir II Shihab.

The dynastic principle is nonetheless misleading. The Emirate—as the Mountain was known during this period of Lebanese history—was in no way equivalent to a principality, contrary to the Eurocentric view readily adopted by certain historians in the early twentieth century. Similarly, the titles of *emir, bey,* and *shaykh* conferred by the Ottomans upon the *muqāti'jiyya* of the Mountain were not in the least aristocratic attributes.[144] Whereas European travelers often spoke of the Druze Government (although the Shihabs who had assumed its leadership in succession to the Druze Ma'ns were Sunni, and Bashir II himself had left open the possibility that he might convert to Christianity), the term "Emirate" served the Porte as a con-

venient formula for referring to the collection of tax and the political management
of the diverse communities of the Mountain—so convenient, in fact, that it was
content to accept the de facto hereditary devolution of the post of governor–farmer
general, even if by law the person holding this office held only a renewable mandate. The Ottomans' chief concern, here as in their other domains, was that tribute
be regularly received by the imperial treasury and that any extension of the emirs'
claims to authority not be allowed to upset the regional balance of power. If necessary, the governors of Damascus and Sidon could be called upon to restore equilibrium through the exercise of selective violence.

The first recalibration of this balance was directed at Fakhr al-Dīn II, who, having expanded his territorial control to encompass the area of Homs (anciently the
city of Edessa), in northern Syria, found himself in conflict with his administrative
superior, the wālī of Damascus. Profiting from the fact that the Sublime Porte was
preoccupied by its war against Persia, Fakhr al-Dīn established relations with the
grand duke of Tuscany. Exiled a first time in 1613, Fakhr al-Dīn took up residence
in Florence, where his presence attracted the attention of European diplomats,
though no offers of practical assistance were forthcoming. After his return to grace,
new conflicts with the Ottoman governors led to his arrest and deportation to Istanbul, where he died in 1635. These events, though they occurred prior to the formation of a national consciousness, later caused Fakhr al-Dīn to be seen as the pioneer of Lebanese nationalism (indeed, in the view of some, as the founder of the
Lebanese state), whereas in fact he was no more than a skillful politician looking
to enlarge his tax base, like so many other provincial officials in the empire. The
idealized image of Fakhr al-Dīn is also due to the fact that the Mountain now found
itself home to a growing number of communities with the southward migration
during this period of the Maronites, upon whose services Fakhr al-Dīn came to rely
for military and other purposes. The increase in trade with Europe, in which the
many Italian merchants resident in the ports of the Levant played a prominent role,
also had begun to affect the daily lives of the inhabitants of the Mountain.

The rise of Lebanon in the Ottoman system of provincial administration under
Fakhr al-Dīn had repercussions on the development of Beirut, which later authors
have become accustomed to describe as the capital of a state during this period. But
despite the works that he sponsored there, the city's actual status was much more
ambiguous. At the beginning of Ottoman rule Beirut had been attached to the province of Damascus as one of its ten districts *(sanjaks)*. This did not prevent the Ottomans, like the Mamluks before them, from accepting that it was under the immediate control of a prominent local family. In the event this was the house of 'Assaf,
from Kisrawan, whose impact upon the history of Beirut is indicated by the sixteenth-
century mosque that bears the name of Emir Mansur 'Assaf, near the former basilica of Saint John, now the al-'Umari Mosque. After a brief interlude under the Sayfas

FIGURE 12. Mosque
of Emir Mansur ʿAssaf
(sixteenth century).

toward the end of the century, Fakhr al-Dīn gained the upper hand in 1598. Although he spent most of the year in Dayr al-Qamar, in the heart of the Shuf Mountains, or else in Sidon, he took a special interest in Beirut and carried out a systematic program of improvements there. He replanted the pine grove beyond the
city's walls, laid out gardens, and constructed a great palace as a winter residence—
all of this under the direction of two Italian architects, Francesco Cioli and Francesco
Fagni.[145] One tower, the Burj al-Kashāf, stood until the mid-nineteenth century,
and survives still in the name of the esplanade that once looked out above the old
wall to the east, and subsequently became the heart of the modern city: al-Burj. But
the principal architectural legacy of Fakhr al-Dīn's era is not due to him; it is a small
jewel of a mosque built in 1620 by Emir Mundhir, a descendant of the Tanukh emirs
of the Gharb, to the west of the old wall.

After Fakhr al-Dīn's death, his family remained in charge of tax collection in the
Mountain and beyond, its reach now extending as far as the outskirts of Tripoli.
The Maʿns continued to keep a residence in Beirut, even if with the establishment
of the vilayet of Sidon, in 1660,[146] the wālī's seat was now only three hours away—
near enough for him directly to exercise authority. Beirut later had its own governor, though this did not put an end to the unsettled state of its relations with the

FIGURE 13. Mosque
of Emir Mundhir
(seventeenth century).

Mountain, as the construction of buildings by Emir Mansur Shihab shows. Beirut remained in any case a modest town, whose population did not exceed a few thousand at a time when Damascus numbered a hundred thousand. Even so, the Greek Orthodox community was able to provide itself with a cathedral of impressive proportions, dedicated in 1767.

Populated for the most part by Sunni Muslims and Greek Orthodox, the city was home also to a few Druze families and probably a small Maronite minority. The Maronite patriarch and historian Istifan al-Duwayhi mentions the names of three Maronite bishops between the sixteenth and eighteenth centuries; beyond this we know only that these prelates did not sit in the city, but resided instead with the head of their church in Dimān.[147] About the activities of this population very little information has come down to us. Apart from the weaving of white silk, Beirut does not stand out in early Ottoman history on account of a particular artisanal trade. Its commercial function was limited as well: the city served mainly as an intermediary, supplying Damascus with silk from the Shuf;[148] and if it welcomed Venetian merchants, its roadstead could not handle more than small-scale coastal shipping, a part of it having been filled in by Fakhr al-Dīn in order to discourage the Ottoman fleet from dropping anchor there.[149] The Chevalier d'Arvieux, visiting Beirut in 1660,

FIGURE 14. The Greek Orthodox Cathedral of Saint George, dedicated in 1767.

observed that sand washed in by the sea had congested traffic still further.[150] The port of Sidon was to capture the better part of Syrian commerce with the West until the end of the following century.[151]

THE ORIGINS OF THE EASTERN QUESTION

It was at this point, in the late eighteenth century, when the Eastern Question first emerged as a consequence of the Russian thrust southward in search of warm-water ports, that the province of Sidon, and with it the city of Beirut, made their entrance on the stage of international politics. The first Crimean War, which ended with the treaty of Küçük Kaynarca (Kuchuk Qaynardji) in 1774, marked the beginning of the Ottoman retreat.[152] Now that the Black Sea had ceased to be an Ottoman lake, the eastern Mediterranean was once again a theater of confrontation, with the Russian fleet aggressively asserting itself along the coast, particularly at Beirut, with the aid of Greek corsairs. From the beginning it was clear that the Eastern Question promised to amalgamate and sharpen all existing antagonisms. Apart from the war in the Crimea, the Ottomans found their rule violently challenged in Palestine and Syria by the expansionary ambitions of the Mamluk sultan of Egypt, ʿAli Bey al-Kabīr.[153] Additionally, vague longings for independence had been stirred up in Galilee by ʿAli Bey's momentary ally, Dāhir al-ʿUmar al-Zaydānī, who promptly joined him in taking the side of the Russians, further attracting the notice of the Porte.

The instrument of this attention soon appeared in the person of the Bosnian-born Ahmad Pasha al-Jazzār, who managed to give the vilayet of Sidon an unprecedented degree of influence before going on to redirect the course of European—and world—history by his defeat of Napoleon Bonaparte before the gates of Acre in 1799. An exceptionally shrewd judge of events who had anticipated the disruptive effects of the new and unequal balance of power in the region, a master of political intrigue, and a member of the sultan's inner circle in Cairo until he betrayed ʿAli Bey and joined forces with Dāhir (soon abandoned in his turn in exchange for the favors of the Porte), Jazzār succeeded so well in strengthening Ottoman authority that in addition to the pashalik of Sidon he was granted that of Damascus as well.[154]

Jazzār found himself faced with a particularly tricky situation in Beirut, the site of intense maneuvering throughout the 1770s. At the beginning of this decade it was subject to the de facto control of the Shihabs, considered loyal by the Porte. In 1772, the Russian fleet, which had already intervened against Sidon at the request of ʿAli and Dāhir, attempted a first landing at Beirut, unsuccessfully. There followed five days of violent bombardment. The Russians then came ashore and pillaged the city, before finally being hurled back into the sea. In answer to the appeal of Emir Yusuf Shihab, Jazzār (who had not yet been appointed governor of Sidon) was then sent out at the head of an expeditionary force of North African soldiers.[155] No sooner had he set to work reinforcing the city's garrison and consolidating its fortifications than Yusuf came to suspect Jazzār's intentions and requested the intercession of the governor of Damascus. This call went unanswered, however, even though the sanjak of Beirut had now assumed great importance for the wālī: not only was its geographic position essential in the event that the Ottoman army sought to tighten the net around Dāhir, but as the only port controlled by the Ottomans along the entire coast from Egypt to Tripoli, expedited communications between Istanbul and Damascus had to pass through it.[156] Yusuf Shihab therefore decided to change sides, embracing Dāhir and his Shiʿi allies from Jabal ʿAmil, on the border of Galilee, the Matawilas. A new round of Russian bombardment was unleashed against Beirut, in August 1773, at the request of Dāhir and Yusuf. This failed to provoke any reaction on the part of the Ottomans, however, giving rise to public protests in Damascus against the inertia of the governor and his commander-in-chief.

After several weeks of siege, a combined assault was launched against Beirut, where Jazzār's troops remained dug in, by the Russian fleet from the sea and Yusuf's forces on the ground. Jazzār was forced to surrender, and found asylum with Dāhir before returning to the service of the Porte.[157] The Russians entered the city in October and held it until February 1774. During that time the Muscovite flag replaced the Ottoman standard and the main gate of the city was adorned with a portrait of Empress Catherine, before which passersby were obliged to bow and cavalrymen to dismount, according to the testimony of the French consul in Tripoli.[158] For the term of their occupation the Russians installed artillery, which included a great cannon, before the east wall of the city. This may be why the esplanade was later to bear the name Place du Canon (or Place des Canons)—an expression that is not commonly used by the city's Arab speakers today, however, who refer instead to El Burj.

Neither the peace of Küçük Kaynarca nor Dāhir's death the following year, in 1775, put an end to the unrest. The Russian fleet remained in the vicinity, and not only out of strategic considerations: having received payment from Dāhir and Yusuf for its two previous interventions,[159] it was still prepared to be of service. The occasion presented itself in 1777. The previous year Jazzār, who in the meantime had become governor of Sidon, went to Beirut to demand payment from Yusuf of the city's arrears in tribute. Yusuf was obliged to hand over Beirut to the wālī, while yet managing to obtain recognition of his authority over the Shuf, the hinterland of Byblos, and the Biqaʿ.[160] But the maneuvering was not over. Yusuf returned to the charge the next year, and the Russians with him. In 1777, Beirut endured another two Russian attacks in addition to blockade by the emir's troops. The ensuing instability severely disrupted commercial activity, and triggered the exodus to Tripoli of the European merchants who were resident there.[161] Jazzār, who now was governor of both Damascus and Sidon, succeeded at last in completely restoring Ottoman authority in Palestine and Mount Lebanon, and in taking Beirut back from the Shihabs. He then gave his support to the new emir of this family, Bashir II, who was thereby able to inaugurate a long stable period that was to mark the high point of Ottoman suzerainty in the Mountain.

Skillfully navigating a safe course through the turbulent time that followed, marked by Bonaparte's Egyptian expedition and the failure of his siege of Acre in the spring of 1799, then by the Ottoman reconquest and British intervention, Bashir succeeded in sheltering Mount Lebanon from turmoil. After Jazzār's death in 1804, which led on to a period of unrest in the pashalik of Sidon, he managed to find another ally of stature in the person of the governor of Egypt, Muhammad ʿAli, a great reformer and the new strongman of the region, who was scarcely able to conceal a desire to extend his power to Syria. In the Mountain itself, Bashir profited from this new round of maneuvering in order to reduce the influence of the other leading families, Druze in particular, and consolidated his authority there still further. But he also distinguished himself, and more peaceably in this respect, by his architectural achievements. Having moved the seat of government to Beiteddin in the Shuf, Bashir built a remarkable palace there, in addition to four other residences for his wife and children, which in combining the heritage of Damascene architecture with Italian chiaroscuro technique remains one of the jewels of the Lebanese patrimony.[162] This was a time of major socioeconomic changes as well. The increasing predominance of the Maronite peasantry in the southern part of Mount Lebanon did not fail to arouse communal frictions, as we shall soon see. The economy of the Mountain as a whole was affected particularly by the expansion of sericulture, now poised to enter its golden age. But unequal terms of trade gradually made their influence felt, and soon French silk manufacturers in Lyon directly controlled silk-worm cultivation.

Prosperity was slower to come to Beirut. Up to that point nothing in the life of the city, whose population scarcely exceeded four thousand after these convulsions, suggested that it would come to play a major role in the growth of the regional economy. After some twenty years of troubles, the city was content simply to breathe freely once again. The European merchants who had fled it for Tripoli returned after the restoration of Ottoman authority there, and Beirut was able to renew its old contacts, still intermediated by Sidon, with Marseille, Genoa, Livorno, and Venice.

Sidon's prosperity belonged to the past, however. The great port of the eighteenth century proved incapable of recovering from its demotion by Jazzār. By moving the seat of the pashalik to Acre, whose fortifications he reinforced, Jazzār not only determined the future course of history in Europe by forcing Bonaparte to give up his dreams of oriental domination; he also prepared the way, obviously without knowing it, for the rise of Beirut—all the more so as he also made room for it, literally, by pushing back a part of the city's wall, which as a master of siegecraft he judged to be too close, and then by clearing the surrounding area.

The curtain was about to rise on an entirely different history. It is ironic, to say the least, that a cruel opportunist should have been working behind the scenes, a man so universally despised that popular memory has wished to retain only the bloody image conjured up by his nickname, al-Jazzār—the butcher. Contrary to the usual belief, this name had come with him from Egypt, where he acquired it as an executioner in the service of 'Ali Bey. The people of Beirut and all those who profited from the economic boom whose foundations were laid later, during the decisive decade of the 1830s, should perhaps summon the courage to ask themselves whether their city, before its rise to power with the emergence of Ibrahim Pasha, did not in fact have an improbable guardian angel in that dreaded figure of Lebanese history, Ahmad Pasha al-Jazzār. By diminishing Sidon's position among its rivals on the coast and protecting Beirut against the arbitrary authority of the government of the Mountain, and also for having made possible its future expansion by pushing back a section of its wall, the same man who vanquished Bonaparte did more than many figures reckoned to have been among the city's chief benefactors to provide a first, tentative answer to the great question that the rebirth of Beirut was soon to pose.

2

The Great Transformation

The immensity of the city's metamorphosis in the space of a few decades can be appreciated by considering the following numbers. Beirut had between four and six thousand inhabitants at the beginning of the nineteenth century, more than one hundred thousand by the end. In geographical extent it had grown many times over, already by fifteen times in just a quarter century, between 1841 and 1876, and after that by still more. Port traffic increased twelve-fold in fifteen years, even before the construction of the new port, which by the beginning of the twentieth century was to account for almost a third of Syria's total. A new highway had shortened the trip to Damascus from three days to thirteen hours. And then there were all those things that seemed to have come out of nowhere, whose civic significance cannot be measured in quantitative terms: paved streets and public squares; banks and hotels; a network of schools, two universities, hospitals; newspapers, learned societies, political parties—in short, all the characteristic elements of modernity that came into existence during this period in many cities along the shores of the Mediterranean, but that, because of the speed with which they emerged in Beirut, made its transformation in the nineteenth century an unrivaled phenomenon.

The metamorphosis that unfolded during this period was at once demographic, urbanistic, and cultural; indeed, it would not be an exaggeration to speak of a second birth. Beirut had already existed for centuries. But only now, in this very brief lapse of time—brief by comparison with a history measured in millennia—did it come to take its place as a great city on the maps of the world—a "rare jewel in the sultan's crown," as Kaiser Wilhelm II called it during a visit at the height of this extraordinary transformation. It was all the more remarkable for being wholly unexpected. The French linguist and philosopher Count Volney, visiting in 1784, found little reason for optimism in contemplating Beirut's future. Limited in its supply of water, and bounded by the hills of the promontory in which a small rectangular settlement of scarcely fifty acres was nestled, this "unpleasant place" seemed to him destined never to acquire any importance.[1] The prospect of prosperity appeared all the more remote since the rugged mountain barrier of the Lebanon restricted overland access to it, and the Anti-Lebanon, by reinforcing this barrier, had the effect of isolating Beirut from the interior of Syria, and above all from Damascus, the ancient capital of the region.

In the event, such forecasts were able to be confounded, and the designs of nature thwarted, only by a vast expansion of foreign influence unleashed by the development of capitalism in Europe and the beginnings of the Industrial Revolution there, and then continually fueled by rivalries between the Western powers and competition between their economies. Modern Beirut was in large part the product of this expansion, which, in disrupting the stability of the Ottoman geopolitical system, brought about rapid economic development over the entire littoral of the eastern Mediterranean. Probably the advantage that Beirut derived from such development was not as great, at least in the near term, as in Alexandria, but it nonetheless exceeded that of all the other ports of the Syrian coast.

EUROPEAN EXPANSION AND THE EASTERN QUESTION

The Levant's relative proximity to Europe made it likely that the transformation of the world economy would make itself felt there more quickly than elsewhere. Since the last quarter of the eighteenth century, commercial relations between the two regions had been changing rapidly. Although the great internal market of the Ottoman Empire gave the Mediterranean as a whole the appearance of stability, increasingly unequal terms of trade had significantly modified the comparative status of its northern and southern shores, as a consequence first of the rising power of European merchants and shipowners, who now controlled long-distance maritime commerce, and second of the relative decline of overland commerce and coastal shipping.

French textiles had made a decisive entry into the markets of the Levant—a local sign of the universal triumph of manufacturing. More generally, products from Europe (and from plantations in the Americas and Asia controlled by Europeans) had gradually supplanted those from Ottoman lands, not only in Europe but in the Sublime Porte's own markets. The flow of imports that resulted from this change of preferences was still limited, but by the late eighteenth century coffee from Yemen— the famous mocha—faced competition in both Istanbul and Cairo from that of Martinique, having already practically disappeared in the capitals of Europe. Egyptian sugar found itself challenged by sugar from the Caribbean, refined in Marseille. But if the opening up of Ottoman markets to European trade reduced the value of certain goods, more cheaply produced in the New World, it increased the value of others: cotton from Egypt and Palestine, silk from Lebanon and Syria. Increasingly the countries of the Levant, like those of the Maghrib at the same moment, were becoming suppliers of raw materials and consumers of finished products.[2]

The bases of European power in the Near East were laid after the French Revolution, with the end of the Napoleonic wars. As a result of the technological advances of the early nineteenth century, sometimes stimulated by the needs of armies, and the new techniques of production that were able to develop without interruption after 1815, the gap between Western Europe and the rest of the world widened. Above all, the European balance of power created by the Congress of Vienna that year liberated commerce from the dread of violence. Rid of the hindrances of naval warfare and maritime blockade, European shipowners and merchants once again enjoyed virtually complete freedom of movement, hampered only in the western Mediterranean by Barbary corsairs—and this not for much longer. In the eastern Mediterranean, by contrast, no obstacle interfered apart from distance. But this constraint was to disappear in its turn with the appearance of the steamship in the 1830s and the establishment of regular commercial service from various European ports, marking the end of an era for the ports of the Levant.[3]

Falling shipping costs—accelerated by the advent of the railroad, which cut transportation time between factories and ports—considerably enlarged the export capacity of European industry. To take only one example, British exports to the cities of the eastern Mediterranean increased by a factor of eight between 1815 and 1850. By the mid-nineteenth century, the Bedouin of the Syrian desert was accustomed to wearing shirts made of cotton from Lancashire,[4] whereas to make coffee he had to provide himself with something other than mocha, very rare in his part of the world since the 1820s. In Beirut, according to the French consul Henri Guys, people were now in the habit of drinking coffee from Brazil.[5]

The commercial expansion of Western Europe in the Levant was supported by an increasingly ramified network of diplomatic contacts. Already for quite a while foreign consuls and consular representatives had resided in the principal Ottoman cities, but now, invested with greater authority by the growing political and military power of their countries, they displayed a permanent inclination to meddle in local affairs. With the exception of Russia, this power was not directly used against the heart of the Ottoman Empire; instead, in the aftermath of Bonaparte's failure in Egypt, and now for quite different purposes, it was brought to bear in the Arab provinces, repeatedly, with the French conquest of Algeria in 1830, the capture of the port of Aden by the British in 1839, and the institution of a French protectorate over Tunisia, in 1881, and of a British protectorate over Egypt the following year.

In the interval, the eastern shore of the Mediterranean was the site of rather more sophisticated European military interventions than in the past—evidence of the incipient complexities of the Eastern Question—beginning with the conflict between

FIGURE 15. The port of Beirut in the early nineteenth century (after Bartlett).

the Sublime Porte and its Egyptian viceroy, Muhammad ʿAli, who had sent his son Ibrahim Pasha to conquer Syria in the fall of 1831, and culminating nine years later in the Turkish-Egyptian Crisis. An alliance among Great Britain, Austria, and Russia, hastily assembled in support of Ottoman authority in the region, finally put an end to the threat of further conquest. Ibrahim, having taken Damascus in June 1832, had in the meantime already twice threatened Istanbul, with the more or less tacit support of France. Beirut was now subjected to bombardment by the allied navy, while agents of British influence undermined the foundations of Egyptian power in the Lebanon mountains. Rather than incur the risks that would follow from a breakdown of the Congress System, France chose to fall in line with its partners and bring diplomatic pressure on Muhammad ʿAli to withdraw his troops. In exchange the viceroy obtained for himself and his family a guarantee of hereditary devolution of power in Egypt, accompanied by the title of khedive.

Twenty years later it was France's turn to intervene militarily, this time with the aim of protecting the Christians of Mount Lebanon after the bloody civil war of the summer of 1860. The Porte, overwhelmed and in any case indebted to Paris (and to London) for its victory against Russia a few years earlier, in the second Crimean War, could only acquiesce. As a practical matter, however, the autonomous status granted the Christians of the region, under multilateral international guarantee, amounted to a relinquishment of Ottoman sovereignty.

Notwithstanding colonial encroachment in the Maghrib and the establishment of a belt of British protectorates around the Arabian Peninsula—from Aden in the south to Kuwait in the north, passing through the Pirate Coast (called the Trucial Coast after 1820) on the Persian Gulf—and in spite of Russian penetration in the vicinity of the Black Sea and gathering storms in the Balkans, it was in the Levant that the interplay of European rivalries, unspoken or declared, most vividly exposed the dysfunctional character of Ottoman rule during the course of the nineteenth century. In the wake of Bonaparte's Egyptian expedition, the ascendancy of Muhammad 'Ali—whose enlightened rule and territorial ambitions encouraged French hopes for an "Arab kingdom"[6] while at the same time arousing fears of a premature dismantling of the Ottoman Empire, and also of the grave threat to European stability that this implied—made it clear that the Eastern Question was first and foremost a question of European interference in eastern affairs.

As a sick man who nonetheless could not be allowed to die too soon (in the phrase usually attributed to Tsar Nicholas I of Russia),[7] the Porte saw its efforts at reform constantly frustrated by the contradictions of Great Power policy, concerned not only to encourage legislative and economic modernization but also to preserve the privileges previously granted by diplomatic favor, which with the shift in the balance of global power had become emblems of domination. Even the equality of the Empire's subjects proclaimed in the Gülhane imperial edict (the *Hatt-i sherif* of 1839)—the point of departure for the grand scheme of administrative reorganization known as the Tanzimat—was to be undercut by the reestablishment of privileges for non-Muslim communities, negotiated by the European powers at the time of the Porte's second round of reforms (the *Hatt-i hümayun* of 1856) in the aftermath of the second Crimean War.

With the return of the old millet system, some subjects now found themselves more equal than others. That de facto inequality should now benefit Christians, rather than Muslims, represented the height of paradox for a state that had devoted itself above all other things to the glory of Islam, and the tensions that resulted from this strange reversal were nowhere felt more keenly than in Syria, where communal diversity was particularly rich.[8] With the spread of the civil war that broke out in Mount Lebanon between Druze and Maronites in January 1859, the massacre in July of the following year of several thousand Christians in Damascus, a unique event in the long history of that city, translated these tensions into blood and sent down into Beirut, long hallowed as a place of shelter, streams of refugees who soon settled there for good.[9]

The Ottoman Empire nonetheless remained committed to modernization, and did nothing to interrupt the passage of reforms, even if during the last quarter of the century the despotic Abdülhamid II, the last sultan to enjoy absolute power, sought to deprive them of their intended effect. Nor did it attempt to distance itself from the Great Powers, other than by occasionally placing its hopes in one of them rather than another, and then, with characteristic suddenness, abandoning its French and British tutors for the Prussian model of government, whose success since 1870 had made a great impression on Abdülhamid. From the inauguration of the Tanzimat and throughout the rest of the century, the Porte showed an inclination to accept European interference in its internal affairs that seemed to border on complacency. Although less spectacular than the meddling in political and military matters occasioned by great conflicts such as the Turkish-Egyptian Crisis, the Crimean War, and the Balkan Crisis of the 1870s, European interventionism in the functioning of the Ottoman economy and justice system came to constitute the heart of the Eastern Question, with increasingly pronounced and far-reaching effects on life both in Istanbul and throughout the empire, which now more nearly resembled a semicolonial state than a great power.

Unlike China during this period, however, Turkey could still rely on a strong central government, administered by a new bureaucratic elite that continued to believe in the possibility of reversing the tide of decline. Evidence of this faith was also to be found in Beirut, right up until the end of the empire. Thus in the spring of 1915, for example, in the middle of a world war and just as Istanbul was preparing to join in the grand butchery alongside the Central Powers, its governor, Bakr Sami Bey, and his successor, 'Azmi Bey, attached the highest priority to building new main roads as part of a program of urban planning that in their view had too long been delayed by indecision and local difficulties.

THE REBIRTH OF THE LITTORAL

From the new geopolitical situation created by the Eastern Question two things followed that in combination were to determine Beirut's future development. The first was the transfer, under the stimulus of European expansion, of commercial activity from inner Syria to the coastal districts at the expense of Aleppo, the traditional crossroads of continental traffic. Of all the ports of the eastern Mediterranean, Beirut profited most from the economic rebirth of the coast, having become the bridgehead for what might be called a colonial axis connecting Europe with Damascus. A second consequence, similar in its effect but on a smaller scale, was the transformation of that part of the Mountain that lay nearest Beirut, whose political landscape could not help but be affected by profound changes in its immediate environment.

In both cases, however, geopolitical shifts were a necessary, but not a sufficient, condition for urban development, and Beirut was not obviously better suited than its neighbors on the coast to take advantage of them. Quite to the contrary, nothing seemed to prepare the city to assume a central role in the affairs of the region, not even its ancient glory, which in any case was far inferior to that of Sidon. Apart from the Roman episode of its long history, it had never been a major city. And during the thirteen centuries that had elapsed since the ruin of Berytus, it found itself consigned to a lower rank not only than Sidon, but also Tripoli, to say nothing of Damascus.

As Count Volney had already observed, Beirut's natural endowments were not promising. If Saint George Bay was a particularly favorable site for anchoring ships, with its deep waters and its orientation along an east-west axis rare in the eastern Mediterranean,[10] the peninsula, punctuated by escarpments, cliffs, and sand dunes, and bounded by a river to the east, presented barriers to development. More than this, the traditional maritime outlet for products coming from the Syrian interior lay elsewhere, and the obstacle represented by Mount Lebanon was all the more formidable at a time when speed and convenience were the chief considerations in calculating the economic profitability of shipping cargo. Moreover, the barrier was not only physical. Beirut had no means of exerting political control over its near hinterland: when the city was not under the sway of the Shihab emirs, the relocation of administrative authority elsewhere on the coast had the effect of isolating its port in the shadow of the promontory that loomed above it.

Quite naturally, then, anyone who inquires into the rise of the city during the nineteenth century immediately runs up against the question why Beirut should have prospered, and not one of the other ports of the Levant. To this question history offers a response that is unlikely to satisfy either defenders of deterministic explanations of urban development or those who uphold the primacy of individual and corporate initiative in the growth of cities. Why Beirut? Perhaps quite simply because it was too late for Tripoli and Sidon, and too early for Haifa.

No matter that Tripoli could boast of a fine urban tradition since the Mamluk period, it was hurt by the decline of trade through Aleppo. Additionally, it was further removed than Beirut from the centers of silk manufacture in the Mountain. Sidon, on the other hand, seemed to enjoy a great many advantages. Near to Dayr al-Qamar and Beiteddin, respectively the economic and administrative centers of the Mountain, it lay on the same latitude as Damascus. Its position to the south of Beirut, where the steep slopes of the Lebanon ridge gradually became gentler, made it possible to traverse the rugged terrain more easily, or indeed to circumvent it altogether by passing through the Marjaʿuyun Plain. And throughout the preceding century, in fact, the port of Sidon had captured the better part of the trade with Europe. Beyond the city, the vilayet of Sidon had also benefited from the attentions of the Sublime Porte, renewed at the end of the eighteenth century by its governor, Jazzār Pasha. Even so, as a consequence of his decision to transfer the seat of the province to Acre, the glory of Jazzār's tenure signified the beginning of the end for the city of Sidon, which never recovered from this demotion, even if the province managed to preserve its name until 1864. The interruption of maritime trade during the Napoleonic wars prevented it from profiting from the more tranquil reign of Süleyman Pasha (1804–18), who remained in Acre; and when peace in Europe restored the freedom of commerce in the Mediterranean, the vilayet found itself once again in the grip of turmoil, this time aroused by the arbitrary rule of Süleyman's successor, 'Abdallah Pasha.

Having abandoned Sidon, international commerce was obliged to turn north. To the south, the Palestinian littoral had remained undeveloped since the fourteenth century, when the Mamluk state dismantled the fortifications of its cities in order to forestall a return of the Crusaders. Bonaparte's campaign had not helped matters. Only Acre, whose defenses had in part escaped the Mamluk destruction and now had been rebuilt and extended by Jazzār, constituted an exception to this situation. Like Sidon, however, it felt the effects of war in Europe and of the unrest in the Levant, and was not immediately able to recover the momentum that Bonaparte's conqueror had given it. Indeed, it was not until their conquest by Ibrahim Pasha that the cities of the Palestinian coast began to revive. And yet commerce there lagged until after the Crimean War.[11] By this time Beirut had already taken off. And while the three Palestinian ports of Jaffa, Haifa, and Acre actively contributed in the years that followed to reducing the Syrian trade deficit with Europe,[12] they were not in a position to challenge Beirut. Jaffa lay too far away from the inland cities of Syria, and mainly served southern Palestine, exporting its own oranges; Acre specialized in the shipment of grain from the district of Hawran.

The port of Haifa, on the other hand, situated like that of Beirut on an east-west axis, offered fine possibilities and underwent expansion as a result. In the 1880s a plan was drawn up for linking the city with Damascus by railroad. Ultimately it was thwarted by Beirut, whose business leaders, anxious at the prospect of competition from this quarter and alert to the larger implications of such a rivalry, hastily devised a railroad scheme of their own that for the moment robbed the Haifa route of its appeal. It was not until the end of the First World War and the British Mandate in Palestine that the port of Haifa rose to prominence. So great was its success that later, following the disappearance of Palestine with the creation of the state of Israel in 1948 and the closing of its borders with the surrounding Arab states to trade, the chief beneficiary proved to be Beirut itself.

However much it may have profited from competition in the meantime, by the middle of the nineteenth century Beirut enjoyed one advantage that proved to be decisive: its head start over neighboring cities had grown exponentially in value by virtue of the fact that the initial expansion of its port coincided with the arrival of the first steamship there in 1836.[13] Within a few years the rapid growth in the number of lines serving Beirut had succeeded in giving it the air of a familiar destination.

CHANCE INTERVENES

Beirut owed this impetus—so opportune in its timing as to seem providential—to Muhammad 'Ali's son Ibrahim Pasha. On setting foot in Bilād al-Shām in 1832,

Ibrahim undertook to reform the administration of the cities under his rule. But this twist of fate would not have had its full effect had he not also resolved to enlarge Beirut's port, whose reconstructed pier now reduced somewhat the difficulties described by travelers in the past and, more important, lent itself to the docking of steamships. These improvements were strengthened by the construction of a lazaretto, which soon came to serve as a central quarantine ward for all of the Syrian ports.

If the spectacularly rapid development of a major city from almost nothing—and not for the first time—prompts the historian to search for an explanation, all the more, then, does Ibrahim Pasha's decision to build a genuine port arouse curiosity. On the reasons for this decision (if in fact a decision was ever made) we have no real information, and so speculation is in order. It seems reasonable to suppose that Ibrahim—an inspired reformer in the manner of his father—anticipated the transformation of international trade brought about by the steamship. Even so, did he have in mind a definite function for Beirut, equivalent to the one performed by Alexandria, as part of a coherent overall plan? This assumes that his ideas for Syria had been settled at once, which is by no means clear, at least not at the beginning of the occupation when none of the protagonists, not even Muhammad ʿAli and his son, could say what was actually being demanded. Was it compensation for all services rendered to the Porte, and dearly paid for by the loss of the Egyptian fleet in the Peloponnese during the war of Greek independence? Independence for a greater Egypt that now encompassed Syria—and also extended as far west as the region of Tripolitania, in Libya, and Tunisia—in the name of the Arab identity that Ibrahim Pasha, an Albanian by birth, claimed to cultivate? Substitution of an Arab kingdom allied with the July Monarchy in France for an Ottoman Empire awaiting the final blow that Ibrahim himself had twice failed to deliver? Or, as it would finally turn out, the willingness of the Ottomans to guarantee Muhammad ʿAli's family hereditary transmission of power and a free hand in Egypt?

The changing appearance of what was at stake[14] leads us, if not to deny the importance of Ibrahim's own will, then at least to doubt how far it was calculated; and, with regard to Beirut in particular, to detect the workings of a policy of expedience, which nonetheless was informed by a broad reformist vision. Some historians of the city see in the public works of the Egyptian era evidence of Beirut's favored status (ignoring the fact that the reorganization contemplated by Ibrahim involved all of Syria) and regard the conquest of the city as an attempt both to maximize the scope of the reforms to be put into effect there (though the same reforms were to be instituted everywhere the Egyptian flag waved) and to prepare it to meet the challenges posed by the expansion of European commerce. But prior to this, before a deliberate program of reform could be acted upon, it is hard to see what, apart from the accidents of circumstance, might have especially recommended Beirut as a site for experimentation.

The small city of 1832 offered Ibrahim Pasha no obvious strategic advantages, any more than it did to European traders. Situated at the midpoint of the Syrian coast, halfway between the Taurus Mountains in the north and the Sinai Peninsula in the south, it nonetheless exhibited a degree of geographic convenience that perhaps was not unrelated to the decision to make it a central isolation ward for infected travelers and cargo arriving by sea, even if the relative decline of Tripoli seems to have been a more decisive factor. Another contingency favoring the emergence of Beirut as a metropolitan center was its administrative status when it fell under Egyptian rule, having already during the time of Jazzār forty-five years earlier been withdrawn from the jurisdiction of the governor of the Mountain. Had it still come under his authority, Beirut would have been excluded from the program of public works undertaken by Ibrahim Pasha, notwithstanding that Ibrahim was unwavering in his support for Emir Bashir II Shihab, a faithful ally, going so far as to offer Bashir control over Syria. With the departure of the Egyptians and the restoration of Ottoman rule, this independence from the Mountain came to assume still greater consequence. There is no doubt that if Beirut had been an element of imperial dealings with the Mountain, Istanbul would have hesitated to approve Ibrahim Pasha's scheme of urban revitalization there.

The puzzle of Beirut's sudden rise presents itself only in retrospect. To contemporary observers it was clear that the city was on the move; nothing seemed capable of slowing its progress, not even bombardment by the fleet of the Anglo-Russian-Austrian alliance sent to drive out Ibrahim Pasha. Indeed, by destroying a part of the city's walls with his guns, Commodore Charles Napier of the Royal Navy unwittingly rendered a signal service to Beirut by opening the way for the city to expand beyond its old boundaries.[15]

The Egyptian occupation having been brought to an end, and its legacy blessed by the restored Ottoman power, determinism reasserted itself. Henceforth the development of Beirut obeyed the structural logic of European commercial expansion, which created an environment within which the city could only grow. And yet the geopolitical implications of this expansion at once placed Beirut in an awkward position, aggravated by events in Mount Lebanon. Here, too, Ibrahim Pasha's sudden appearance in Bilād al-Shām in the fall of 1831 and, still more so, his forcible eviction in 1840 had dramatic and unforeseen consequences, in this case by abruptly accelerating social—and denominational—changes that had long been underway.[16]

THE GROWTH OF COMMUNAL TENSIONS

Egyptian reforms, carried out in imitation of the ones that Muhammad ʿAli had instituted in the Nile Valley, were at first favorably received in the Mountain. But fiscal restructuring and military conscription quickly aroused opposition, intensified by Ibrahim Pasha's move to disarm the population. British agents were well placed to stir up discontent, increasing the pressure on the occupier. And yet when the Egyptians finally departed, the situation did not therefore revert to its former state. The old governor of the Mountain, Bashir II Shihab, had joined his fate to that of Ibrahim Pasha, abandoning a lifelong habit of prudence that, at Acre in the last year of the previous century, had left him a way out with both Bonaparte and Jazzār. Indeed he had tried to repeat this double game with Ibrahim, and delayed in bringing up his forces, again in support of a siege at Acre, until an imperious demand by Muhammad 'Ali convinced him to move quickly.[17] So effectively did he assist the advance of Egyptian troops northward along the coast[18] that he was to be found at Ibrahim's side during the taking of Damascus in July 1832, and for a time the conqueror thought of entrusting him with the government of Syria eight years later. But Bashir could not avoid being swept from power by an insurgency in his own stronghold. Exiled first to Malta, he ended his days in Istanbul, where he is said to have been strangled. However one regards the unhappy fate of the elderly man with the white beard who for so many years ruled the Mountain from his magnificent palace at Beiteddin—a man who, rightly or wrongly, was to become one of the symbols of the Lebanese national imagination in the twentieth century, with the result that in 1947, four years after the Republic achieved its independence, Bashir's remains were repatriated and a national funeral held—the disintegration of the political system over which he presided in the wake of the resolution of the Turkish-Egyptian crisis was cataclysmic in its effects. Nowhere were the repercussions of this upheaval more lastingly felt than in Beirut, cascading down the decades to come and crowned by the city's election in 1920 as the capital of the state of Greater Lebanon, whose core—the Mountain—had been reconstructed by the trials of the two decades that followed Ibrahim's ouster, from 1840 to 1860.

Called upon to replace his cousin, Emir Bashir III Shihab fell from power after a few months. The Egyptian occupation had fatally disrupted the stability of the Mountain, and the emirate system was no longer able to contain communal tensions. Not only did the growing assertiveness of the Maronites and their slow migration southward[19] create among the Druze a sense of irresistible decline, and on both sides sustain a spirit of defiance that was increasingly difficult to control, but as a consequence of the imperial decree of 1839 the practice of tax farming had been abandoned. The return to direct administration in all the provinces of the empire, reversing the tendency to local autonomy tolerated since the eighteenth century, was made all the more necessary in Mount Lebanon by an alarming increase in sectarian animosity. The policy finally imposed by the Ottoman foreign minister, Shakib Effendi, at the end of three years of turmoil, attempted to resolve the problem by dividing the Mountain into two qā'imaqāmat, or administrative regions, one in the north directed by Maronites, the other in the south by Druze. Additionally, the principle of power-sharing along confessional lines was adopted in the administrative departments of the two regions. Far from reducing tensions, this dual qā'imaqāmat system had the effect only of crystallizing them in the southern region, originally placed under Druze control, which nonetheless had a very large Maronite population, perhaps even a majority. There followed fifteen years of unrest, known by the name of *harakat* (literally, movements), an amalgamation of local uprisings and denominational conflicts. These culminated in the bloodbath of the summer of 1860, when a peasant revolt sparked eighteen months earlier in the exclusively Maronite district of Kisrawan, under the leadership of a village blacksmith named Taniyus Shahin, degenerated into a civil war in the mixed districts, a little further to the south, before finally reaching Damascus. The conflict, though it did not last long, was punctuated by several massacres in which Christian peasants were the principal victims, often with the permissive (if not actually collusive) neutrality of Ottoman garrison commanders. The violence triggered a large exodus of Christians from the Mountain, joined shortly thereafter by their coreligionists from Damascus, who took refuge by the thousands in Beirut, abruptly swelling its population.

The time when conflict in the Levant unfolded in isolation from the outside world was now past. Although the telegraph had not yet arrived in Syria (it was to come to Beirut only in 1863), information traveled more rapidly than before thanks to steamships. As during the Crimean War a few years earlier, European public opinion was able to follow the course of events at the other end of the Mediterranean with only a slight delay. Karl Marx took a personal interest in the saga of Taniyus Shahin, and the massacres in the Mountain aroused such emotion in France that Napoleon III used them as a pretext for reasserting his country's status as the protector of Eastern Christians, inherited from the first Capitulations of the Ottoman Empire in the early seventeenth century. The dispatch of a French expeditionary corps—a convenient diversion meant to reassure Catholic opinion at home, unsettled by the prospect of conflict with Garibaldi's forces in Italy—also allowed the emperor to take the first steps toward carrying out the plan, urged by his foreign minister, François Guizot, of encouraging the formation of an Arab kingdom under the Algerian emir 'Abd al-Qādir.[20] Qādir, though he had distinguished himself in the emperor's eyes by the aid and protection he had given to the Christians of Damascus, where he was living in exile, never showed any real interest in the role that the French now assigned him,[21] and Napoleon III himself made no serious effort to pursue his own grand oriental ambitions. In the meantime, the French expedition, commanded by General Charles de Beaufort d'Hautpoul, laid the groundwork for another policy, which, as we shall see later, utterly contradicted the Arabist designs of the Second Empire. Instead it prepared the way for the transition some twenty years later, under the influence of intellectuals such as Ernest Renan, from a policy of support for an Arab kingdom to one that asserted the rights of minorities in the Near East and, still more paradoxically, legitimized the colonial appetites of the anticlerical Third Republic.[22]

FIGURE 16. Landing of the French Expeditionary Corps in Beirut, 1860. Reproduced by permission of the Nadia Tueni Foundation.

For the moment, however, the age of the French protectorate lay some ways yet in the future. Having arrived after hostilities had ended, the emperor's soldiers were confined to the outskirts of Beirut. There they occupied themselves chiefly with giving aid to refugees, without any real military tasks apart from conducting topographical surveys of the surrounding area. Even if it was mainly intended for domestic French consumption, this intervention was nonetheless not wholly without international implications. In addition to stating, for the first time on such a scale, France's claim to protect the Christians of the East, and thereby appearing to give hope to protonationalist aspirations among the Maronites of the Mountain, General de Beaufort's expedition immediately aroused apprehension among the other powers. Once again, however, jealousies and rivalries on the European side gave the Porte an opportunity to limit the damage to its position. Unable to forbid the French campaign, Fuad Pasha, the foreign minister, hastened to make his way to Beirut in the hope at least of preempting it, which after considerable exertions he succeeded in doing. Fuad proceeded at once to convene a tribunal in the countryside and, with implacable rigor, sentenced to death the Druze chieftains responsible for the massacres as well as the Ottoman officers convicted of having turned a blind eye to them. In the meantime reinforcements from Istanbul pacified the Mountain, depriving the French intervention of its purpose.

If the Porte was obliged to resign itself to the inevitability of a diplomatic solution that would involve the loss of its sovereignty over the region, at least it could prevent France, despite the advantage conferred by the presence of French troops on the ground, from dictating the terms of the Mountain's new status. The result of all this maneuvering was a conference of the Great Powers held in Beirut in the spring 1861, with Fuad Pasha presiding, which produced a protocol between the Ottoman Empire and five European nations (France, Great Britain, Russia, Austria, and Prussia). By the terms of this organic statute, ratified and amended in 1864, the dual qā'imaqāmat system gave way to a new administrative arrangement that made the entire Mountain a single autonomous district (or *mutasarrifiyya,* to give it its Arabic name). Two features of the agreement deserve to be noted: the governor named by the sultan was to be a Christian Ottoman subject, with the sole condition that he was not a native of the Mountain; and an administrative council was to be elected on a denominational basis, but in such proportions as to assure the primacy of the Maronite community.

Its autonomy now statutorily guaranteed by the Great Powers, Mount Lebanon entered upon a long period of peace during which the institutional foundations of a national consciousness embracing all its various groups were laid; and very quickly also upon a continuing campaign of territorial expansion, one of whose chief aims was the incorporation of the city that represented its natural commercial outlet to the world. Even before this protonational impulse, originating in the Maronite community, gave rise to dreams of a Greater Lebanon—an entity that, in conformity with what were now regarded as historical boundaries, laid down by Fakhr al-Dīn, would include the entire Syrian littoral (as well as the inland plain of the Biqaʿ and the whole western face of the Anti-Lebanon)—Beirut was to find itself an object of covetous desire on the part of the Mutasarrifate; indeed, the first governor, the Armenian Dawud Pasha, had his sights trained on Beirut from the outset. The question arose more seriously in the 1890s, when the annexation of the city was first publicly demanded by leading figures of the Maronite Church, now the principal actor in the political life of the Mountain,[23] and by the most militant ideologues of the nascent movement to construct a Greater Lebanon.

Beirut held itself aloof from this current of opinion in its near hinterland. While the population of the metropolitan area continued to grow with the influx of a large number of Lebanese (as the inhabitants of Mount Lebanon were then known, uniquely among the peoples of the region), it attracted just as many immigrants from the interior of Syria. By the end of the century Beirut served as a port not only for Mount Lebanon, but also for Damascus. Its economic elites furthermore resisted the idea of being absorbed into the Mutasarrifate, no matter that the sultan

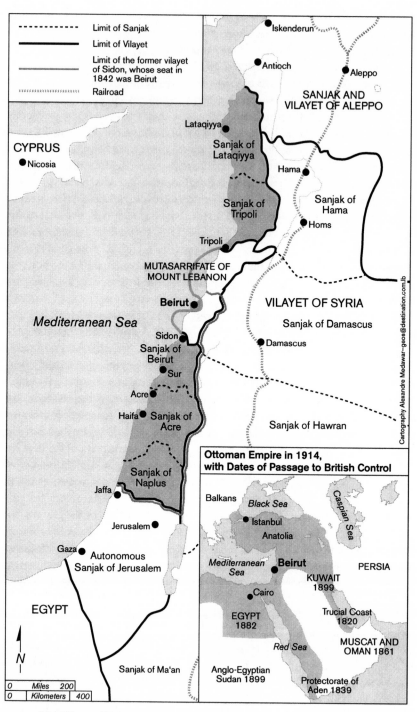

Limit of Sanjak

Limit of Vilayet

Limit of the former vilayet of Sidon, whose seat in 1842 was Beirut

Railroad

Iskenderun

Antioch

Aleppo

SANJAK AND VILAYET OF ALEPPO

Lataqiyya

Sanjak of Lataqiyya

Hama

CYPRUS

Nicosia

Sanjak of Hama

Sanjak of Tripoli

Homs

Tripoli

MUTASARRIFATE OF MOUNT LEBANON

VILAYET OF SYRIA

Beirut

Sanjak of Damascus

Mediterranean Sea

Sidon

Damascus

Sanjak of Beirut

Sur

Acre

Haifa

Sanjak of Acre

Sanjak of Hawran

Sanjak of Naplus

Jaffa

Ottoman Empire in 1914, with Dates of Passage to British Control

Jerusalem

Balkans

Black Sea

Caspian Sea

Gaza

Autonomous Sanjak of Jerusalem

Istanbul

Anatolia

Mediterranean Sea

Beirut

PERSIA

EGYPT

Cairo

KUWAIT 1899

EGYPT 1882

Trucial Coast 1820

N

Red Sea

MUSCAT AND OMAN 1861

0   Miles   200

0   Kilometers   400

Sanjak of Ma'an

Anglo-Egyptian Sudan 1899

Protectorate of Aden 1839

Cartography Alexandre Medawar—geos@destination.com.lb

MAP 5. The Vilayet of Beirut in 1888

was known to approve of such an outcome—a puzzling thing in view of the fact that quite recently, in 1887–88, he had raised Beirut to the status of a vilayet, extending from Lataqiyya in the north to Naplus in the south.

Nothing disposed Beirut, the commercial center of an area stretching over almost 12,000 square miles (three times the area of the future Greater Lebanon), to submit to a popular will that existed outside of it, if only a few miles beyond its suburbs. On the contrary, despite the unbroken contact assured by a seemingly inexhaustible stream of new residents from the villages of the Mountain, the city was determined to disseminate its own ideology.[24] It was an ideology destined to triumph at a time when urban life in all Ottoman lands, already strongly rooted in the traditions of Islam, was further strengthened by the appeal of modernism. Beirut, a city reborn in the declining years of an empire, welcomed its diversity and cultivated its ambiguities—as it would continue to do even after the age of empires had passed, and always with a view to drawing from it the greatest possible profit.

3

The Ibrahim Pasha Era

O nature! Beauty, ineffable grace of the cities of the East built on the shores of seas, scenes shimmering with life, spectacles of the finest human races, of costumes, of barques and vessels passing one another on waves of azure—how to paint the impression you inspire in every dreamer, which yet is only the reality of a sentiment foretold? One has already read about it in books, admired it in pictures, especially in those old Italian paintings that recall the era of the maritime power of the Venetians and the Genoese; but what surprises today is finding it still so similar to the idea that one has formed of it. . . .

These lines that the port of Beirut inspired in Gérard de Nerval on the occasion of his visit there in 1843 would more fittingly perhaps be quoted in an anthology of literary travel than in a work of history. The poet had found it amusing to make his way first through the "immense" bazaar with its "long aisles of stalls protected by drapes of various colors, which do not prevent a few rays of sun from falling upon the brightly colored fruits and vegetables, or from traveling farther, so that the richly embroidered clothes hanging in front of the second-hand shops sparkle." But he was especially anxious to discover for himself the sensations that earlier visitors had recorded in their narratives and pictures. Put off by the tall houses, which seemed to resemble "fortresses," he hastily went through the suqs. "I was eager to get to the port," he confessed, "and to give myself up entirely to the impression of the splendid spectacle that awaited me there"[1]—as though to acknowledge that nothing in the city itself was capable of diverting him from the task of producing a variation on a theme that had already been developed by Western painters.[2]

Though it may only have been the foible of a man of letters, Nerval's feeling was

FIGURE 17. The walls of the city in the 1820s, before it began to expand beyond them.

surely also a response to the city's unimposing appearance at the time, notwith-standing the first signs of prosperity he noted, referring to the port's busy traffic and the affluence of the bazaar—in reality not nearly so large as he claimed—as well as to the street "devoted to French commerce," where he was delighted to find that "Marseille contends rather successfully with the trade of London."[3] A few years ear-lier, in 1838, Édouard Blondel, a French merchant with an eye for detail whose opin-ion was informed by a longer stay in the city, had warned his readers: "Despite the pleasing aspect that Beirut presents from the sea, one must not expect, as do the majority of travelers who visit the East for the first time, to find that the inside matches what the view from outside seems to promise."[4] Both Nerval and Blondel wrote after the public works projects planned under the Egyptian occupation had been begun; some of these are mentioned by Blondel.

If the city at this juncture failed to capture the attention of the European visitor, except as an excuse for extolling the virtues of travel, still less when Ibrahim Pasha arrived there did it offer anything, apart from its physical situation, that could have impressed someone en route to Damascus from Cairo. Its ramparts, reconstructed by Jazzār after their bombardment by the Russian fleet, bore no comparison with those of Acre, which had so recently taunted the Egyptian general, even if Alphonse de Lamartine, who visited Beirut a few years before Blondel, had remarked upon its "most picturesque Turkish fortifications."[5]

A SMALL AND OVERCROWDED SITE

Beirut was then built, as it had been for centuries, upon a quadrilateral site defined by the meeting of the coast with the walls of the city. From the port to the southern gate it extended some 625 yards, and measured 400 yards at the point of its greatest width between the eastern and western gates.[6] At its northeastern extremity the wall was adjoined by a Tower of the Sea (Burj al-Bahr), overlooking the port. Also known as the Armed Tower (al-Burj al-Musallah), this structure dated back to the Crusades; impressive though its dimensions were, the photographs that have come down to us show it to have been smaller than the "immense shadow" cast by Nerval's "seaside castle" seems to suggest.[7] The port proper, although it had appeared on maps used by small coastal traders for centuries and was regularly frequented by foreign merchants, remained very narrow and poorly equipped. It was bordered on the west by the Fanal Tower (Burj al-Fanal), and on the east by the Chain Tower (Burj al-Silsila—so named, as we have already had occasion to note, on account of the device inherited from the Crusader and Mamluk periods that made it possible to bar access to the port, itself called Bāb al-Silsila).

Within this guarded place (Bayrūt al-mahrūsa), roughly in the shape of a square, several religious edifices bore testimony to an apparently uneventful history. Blondel reported seeing "five or six mosques" and "various Christian churches," none of them worthy of closer inspection. Like the administrative buildings, they seemed to him "shabby and devoid of interest."[8] The rest of the city was no more inviting, to judge from the description given by the French traveler Jean-Joseph-François Poujoulat on the eve of Ibrahim Pasha's sudden appearance there: "I have seen nothing so bizarre, irregular, and extraordinary as the construction of the Arab town of Beirut; the houses, built of stone, are higher there than in any other town of Syria; archways, secret outlets, dark alleys; narrow and winding streets inspire at first a kind of fright in the traveler who wishes to walk through the town; each house stands as a sort of great inaccessible dungeon."[9] Blondel, noting the first transformations of the Egyptian era, preferred understatement: "The streets nearest to the sea, inhabited almost exclusively by Europeans, consuls and merchants, are of medium breadth. The houses that line them are not disagreeable in appearance; they are highly irregular, but built entirely of stone. It is true that, in penetrating further, the streets become narrower and more winding. They pass under a considerable number of low and dark archways that do not improve their attractiveness."[10]

If the irregular layout that disconcerted foreign visitors was typical of Arab cities of the period, Beirut's fondness for tall buildings was not. Many houses there were three stories high, even four, and their massing sharpened the sense of disorder and overcrowding, by contrast with the rest of the promontory; beyond the city's walls, cemeteries alternated with sand dunes and gardens, though scattered groupings of houses were beginning to form.[11] Within the enceinte, the dense concentration

FIGURE 18. The port of Beirut: in the foreground the fort and, to the right, the bridge connecting it to the shore; in the background the Burj al-Kashāf.

FIGURE 19. The view of the citadel from the port, ca. 1870.

FIGURE 20. The enceinte as it appeared before the arrival of Ibrahim Pasha.

of buildings was a sign of urbanism. Despite its modest dimensions, which made it seem more like a large market town, Beirut had many of the characteristics of a city: besides its ramparts and Christian and Muslim houses of worship, it had public buildings (including a seraglio), inns, two hotels for foreigners,[12] and, above all, a native population and a great variety of religious denominations.[13]

How many people lived inside these walls? The historian Dominique Chevallier has shown that throughout the nineteenth century official figures were usually the result of little more than guesswork,[14] and can be regarded only as rough estimates, especially at this early stage. In the last quarter of the eighteenth century, the city may have numbered four to five thousand souls, perhaps six thousand.[15] For the first decades of the nineteenth century the figure of six thousand is generally given. This same figure is reported by the French diplomat and traveler Léon de Laborde for the year 1827,[16] whereas Poujoulat and Joseph-François Michaud in their account of the city several years later speak of nine thousand inhabitants.[17] Even though we have no reliable way of evaluating such anecdotal evidence, the implied progression seems incontestable, and we may reasonably follow Chevallier in placing the population at ten thousand for the intramural city and its immediate environs in 1834. In other words, the first increase in population preceded the Egyptian era. If Syria as a whole was then entering into a period of demographic growth, the advance registered by Beirut—like all later ones—came mainly from immigration, itself generated by instability in other more or less nearby regions. The unrest that shook the pashalik of Sidon under ʿAbdallah Pasha may have contributed to this situation, and before that the unrestrained violence of the Wahhabi revolt outside the Arabian Peninsula, which around 1810 brought a slight influx of refugees to the vilayets of Aleppo and Damascus. Mount Lebanon, from which a visitor in 1812 came away with an impression of extreme poverty,[18] may also have furnished a first wave of Christian immigrants. Beirut, where Christians in the 1830s represented, if not a majority, at least a sizable proportion of the population, larger than in any other port along the Syrian coast,[19] seems already to have had a reputation as a haven for persons displaced by war and famine.

This demographic inflation accounts for the overcrowding in the intramural city noted by both Poujoulat and Blondel. The wall reconstructed by Jazzār, set a bit beyond the original line of the enceinte to give defenders greater freedom of action, represented a first extension of the city's limits. Already settlements were taking shape outside the ramparts, where the orchards destroyed by Jazzār to prevent a surprise attack were promptly recolonized; higher up on the promontory, summer residences built by wealthy residents were interspersed with a few hamlets.[20]

In parallel with this first and still limited phase of expansion, the return of peace in Europe revitalized international commerce, to the advantage of the entire Syrian coast. Encouraged by the decline of Sidon and by the appearance in the 1820s of the first resident foreign consuls, Beirut's hopes of claiming a share of this trade were rewarded by the opportune emergence of Ibrahim Pasha, which, in enabling the city to capture the better part of it, stimulated further expansion.

THE EGYPTIAN MODERNIZATION

The Egyptian campaign got underway on 29 October 1831. Having subdued Gaza, Jaffa, and Haifa without fighting, Ibrahim Pasha laid siege to Acre on 26 November. Meeting with no success after three months, he detached a part of his forces and marched north to Tyre, and thence to Sidon, Beirut, Tripoli, and Lataqiyya. It was only on 27 May 1832, at the end of the sixth month of the siege, that Acre fell. Ibrahim then rode on to Damascus, conquering it on 16 June. By the end of July the whole of Syria was under his control, enabling him to carry the attack forward into Anatolia, where a great victory at Konya, on 27 December, placed him in a position to attack Istanbul itself. In the face of demands by the powers that he withdraw, Ibrahim retreated beyond the Taurus Mountains and devoted himself to the administration of Syria, which by the Treaty of Kütahya, signed on 8 April 1833, the Sublime Porte conceded to Muhammad ʿAli while at the same time retaining nominal sovereignty over it. Yet the sultan could not resign himself to this loss. After six years of tolerating the state of affairs created by the treaty, he directed his armies to launch a counteroffensive. It had no immediate effect, however, and after the Battle of Nisip in northern Syria, in June 1839, Ibrahim saw the gates of Istanbul open before him a second time. But in fact this was the beginning of the end: the empire's occasional allies among the Concert Powers were now willing to intervene militarily, and in the event effectively, following the spread of unrest in several parts of Syria that distracted the attention of the Egyptian army. On 11 September 1840 the British fleet bombarded Beirut, in preparation for a landing further to the north, and soon Ibrahim Pasha was obliged once again to contemplate withdrawal. By the beginning of 1841, his army had entirely departed from Syria.

This troubled decade was notable not only for violent conflict and the often authoritarian behavior of the foreign occupiers. More long-lasting, and ultimately no less disruptive, were the consequences of the changes that the Egyptians made in the administration of Syria, and especially of its cities, during the armed peace that followed the conquest of Damascus. In this regard the personal involvement of Muhammad 'Ali and Ibrahim Pasha was decisive. Without setting foot in Syria the whole time his army occupied it, the sultan's insubordinate viceroy nonetheless was determined to impose there the modernizing reforms that had already been tried and tested in Egypt, keeping himself abreast of events down to the least detail, as the Egyptian archives attest. In permanent correspondence with Ibrahim Pasha and the officials of his government, Muhammad 'Ali took it upon himself to fill the posts that his son had created for the smooth running of the territory's affairs. Ibrahim Pasha, for his part, quickly understood that the demands of the military campaign would long have the greatest claim upon his attention and that, despite the efficiency of his lieutenants (among them the famous Colonel Sève, a former officer of Napoleon's Grande Armée who under the name Soliman Pasha became chief of staff of the Egyptian army), he could not direct the government of Syria by himself. Ibrahim recommended to his father that a governor be appointed. Emir Bashir II Shihab turned down the offer, but Muhammad Sharif Bey, an official who had won favor for his conduct of affairs in Upper Egypt, accepted. The supervision of finances was confided to Hanna Bahri, a Christian Syrian who had long been a trusted advisor to the Egyptian government.[21]

Even so, Ibrahim did not cease to closely monitor the various matters constantly brought to his attention. The Egyptian archives bear witness to his tireless arbitration of disputes and his unflagging interest in the smallest questions of local administration. In Beirut, for example, Ibrahim personally expedited a police inquiry into a murder committed outside a tavern beyond the city walls.[22] More striking still was his determination to carry out reforms and extend their reach throughout the conquered territory, as if he were sure of holding it forever. And though the needs of the army often kept him in the north of Syria, and while Damascus, owing to its symbolic value, may well have warranted special consideration, he nevertheless showed equal curiosity about the various regions under his authority. The littoral was thus in no way neglected, and the pashalik of Sidon enjoyed the same importance in his eyes as that of Damascus.[23]

Urban reforms were the object of the most sustained effort, in keeping with Syria's long tradition in this regard. Unlike Egypt, still a mostly peasant society despite Cairo's preeminence since medieval times, the history of Syria had for thousands of years been one of cities. Modernization could only be undertaken on this basis, then, seeking to bring together local elites as far as possible. Ever since the taking of Jaffa, Ibrahim Pasha had chosen to leave the daily management of affairs in the hands of natives.[24] He went further after the conquest of Damascus, where he installed an advisory council *(Majlis al-Shūra)* of twenty-two members, including not only beys and effendis but also merchants, among them a Christian and a Jew.[25] This model was soon generally adopted,[26] and every city of more than twenty thousand inhabitants was endowed with a similar authority, distinct from the traditional Ottoman provincial diwan. Charged with responsibility for assisting the governor *(mutasallim),* and consisting of between twelve and twenty-one members, depending on the case, the council everywhere provided for the representation of non-Muslim communities.[27] Over time a hierarchy of advisory councils emerged, with two of them acquiring supervisory authority over the others: Damascus, the central seat of administration in Syria under the direction of Sharif Bey, and Acre. In the case of dispute between these two Majlis, the final decision fell to Cairo, where Muhammad 'Ali had reports sent to him daily.[28] Anticipating the reforms instituted a few years later by Istanbul, the new system of regulation set in motion a long process that was to give ancient cities a new look. And among these cities, each one more ancient than the last, Beirut was not the least favored.

CLEANING UP THE CITY

Beirut was subdued without resistance by the Egyptian army on 2 April 1832. As at Sidon and Tyre, Ibrahim Pasha initially gave the post of mutasallim to a close relative of Bashir II, Emir Melhem Shihab, but he was soon replaced.[29] Although the city's population was well below twenty thousand, a council of twelve members was appointed by Ibrahim's order on 25 January 1834.[30] It was unique among such bodies in upholding the principle of sectarian representation, having both Muslim and Christian members—a sign of Beirut's singular denominational character as the only city on the entire coast with a large Christian community.

Beirut was not subject to the influence of the notables *(ashrāf)* who elsewhere constituted the urban aristocracy, although some members of this class were to be found in the city, and even a *naqīb al-ashrāf,* the syndic of the descendants of the Prophet (at this time Shaykh Ahmad al-Agharr). The beys, members of the Ottoman pretorian elite who had come to Beirut seeking asylum in the wake of the Egyptian advance, were likewise unrepresented on the council. The councilors appointed by Ibrahim Pasha were instead recruited from the ranks of the merchant class. This peculiarity may explain another, namely, that the Majlis of Beirut was sometimes called upon to settle commercial disputes, a function that went beyond its initial remit.[31] As the source of the power, whether tacit or openly acknowledged, that the merchants were to exercise over the life of the city for the rest of the nineteenth century and beyond, the council distinguished itself more generally by its efficiency and its diligence, attested by a daily schedule of meetings.[32] New departments of public health and commerce were formed in addition to a police force, whose creation signaled a new concern for public safety.

Even more important in reforming municipal affairs than the Majlis and its dependent administrative authorities was the personality of the governor appointed in 1835. Mahmud Nāmi Bey, an Egyptian officer of Circassian origin, had been trained in France, where he was one of the first scholarship students sent nine years earlier by Muhammad ʿAli to learn about the latest industrial technologies.[33] As head of the council he displayed great drive and determination, and a sense of public service that attracted the attention of contemporaries. Blondel, for example, described him as someone "who is much concerned with improving Beirut and making it more attractive, and who from this point of view has already rendered great service to its inhabitants."[34] Three decades later his son, Ibrahim Fakhrī Bey, carried on his efforts at reform as president of the new municipal council established in Beirut by the Ottoman authorities in 1868.[35]

It goes without saying that the works undertaken by Mahmud Nāmi Bey and the first Majlis of Beirut were not nearly as spectacular as those of the Ottoman governors at the end of the century. The city was starting from next to nothing; infrastructure was rudimentary. Particular emphasis was placed on public hygiene and development of the road network. In line with the general objectives of the Egyptian government in Syria as a whole, sanitary measures were given highest priority: drainage works, installation of water mains, and relocation of cemeteries beyond the city walls.[36] According to uncorroborated accounts, Ibrahim Pasha also had trees planted in the nearby Pine Forest with the doubtful purpose of purifying the air and preventing the spread of fevers.[37]

Scarcely less pressing was the need to mend existing roads and to build new ones—a task that remained unfinished at the end of the Egyptian occupation. Blondel reported in 1838 that Mahmud Nāmi Bey had "obtained authorization from his government to pave the city, and the work was energetically pursued," going on to add that "advantage was taken of the occasion to restore the streets to their original breadth, by removing everything that stood in the way, many individuals [having] not hesitat[ed] to trespass upon them in order to establish small shops, construct stairways, and a thousand other things as it pleases them."[38] Two years later, Frédéric Goupil-Fesquet, the first daguerreotypist to have taken pictures of Beirut, noted in his turn the "cleanliness of the streets recently paved by the governor Mahmud Nāmi Bey," and confessed that to his mind this was "a source of astonishment and admiration, for ordinarily all the cities of Syria are remarkable for their filth."[39]

The work on the road system was even pursued outside the walls with the laying of cobblestones in a street that led from the southwest corner of the wall to the new neighborhoods that had begun to spring up on the hillside. This area, later brought within the city's limits, was to keep the name of Zuqaq al-Blat (Rue Pavée, in its French translation): the paved street.

THE AGE OF STEAM

In addition to the city proper, the government paid particular attention to the development of the port. In 1834 construction began on a lazaretto, a mile or two from the port. Once again the role of luck is undeniable; in this case, a fortuitous combination of circumstances allowed Beirut to benefit from the Egyptian concern for public hygiene while at the same time promoting commercial expansion. Ibrahim Pasha's resolve, seconded by the foreign consuls, to establish a network of quarantine centers throughout Syria to slow the spread of epidemics had nonetheless aroused the hostility of religious leaders. In Damascus the ʿulama protested against the idea, arguing that coercive detention of individuals without evidence of criminal wrongdoing was contrary to the precepts of Islam,[40] and notables in Tripoli opposed the establishment of a maritime quarantine there on the same ground. It was therefore decided to install the lazaretto near Beirut, where the ʿulama's influence was less great; a site was chosen that lay outside the city, but not too far, at Cape Khodr along Saint George Bay. This area, later incorporated into municipal Beirut, was to keep the name of Qarantina.

The period of quarantine was twelve days, and in principle it was obligatory for all visitors, but difficulties were not slow in emerging. According to the French consul, Henri Guys, Ibrahim Pasha had initially charged him with responsibility for devising a system of sanitary regulations, aided by the other consuls. In addition to advancing the funds for the construction of barracks, the consuls of France, Austria, Denmark, Spain, and Greece formed a supervisory committee.[41] To run the center Ibrahim appointed Baron d'Armagnac,[42] another Frenchman who had sided with Muhammad ʿAli, following the example of Soliman Pasha, whom d'Armagnac had served as aide-de-camp. But the consular management of the quarantine caused such chaos that Ibrahim was obliged to instruct Hanna Bahri, his intendant of finance, to conduct a formal administrative inquiry, at the conclusion of which Bahri recommended that its functions be reassigned to the quarantine of Alexandria.[43] Before this step could be taken, however, the Egyptians had quit Beirut.

However limited the effectiveness of the quarantine may have been from a medical point of view, it undeniably benefited the economic development of Beirut, which from now on was an obligatory port of call for ships in the eastern Mediterranean.[44] To accommodate the increase in traffic the port itself had to be adapted, and Mahmud Nāmi Bey directed that warehouses be built and the wharves enlarged

FIGURE 21. The lazaretto (in a late photograph by Louis Vignes [1831–96]).

in the wake of complaints by foreign merchants to Ibrahim Pasha regarding the inadequacy of the facilities.[45] Particular attention was also paid to regularizing port and customs procedures, which helped to consolidate Beirut's advantages in seeking to capture a larger share of the trade with Europe. Henceforth the silk of Mount Lebanon and the products of Damascus were exported mainly through Beirut, and the rising flow of imports made it the gateway to the Levant for European industry. The decline of Sidon had already promised a more prosperous future for local merchants and, even if no "brilliant fortunes" had yet been amassed there,[46] caused French merchants to look favorably on Beirut in considering where they ought to reestablish themselves in the wake of Ibrahim Pasha's campaign on the coast, which had paralyzed commercial activity in its southern part.[47] This inclination was strengthened with the development of the port under Egyptian auspices, and the number of local companies doing business there rose during the 1830s from twenty to thirty-four. An equivalent number of European firms set up operations in Beirut during this decade as well.[48] "Truly, it has become the port of this Orient," a Jesuit missionary wrote in 1836. "It is expanding and the Christians of the country are growing in number at a most remarkable rate."[49] The arrival of the first steamships accelerated the pace of activity, facilitating not only commerce but also the exchange of news and information. "Oh! What a comfort it is to be able now to communicate with such ease and promptness by the means of the steamships," confided the superior general of the Jesuits in a letter to one of his missionaries in Mount Lebanon.[50]

Encouraged by the course of events and encouraging it in their turn, Western diplomatic services lost no time in ratifying the merchants' choice of Beirut. The first consular offices there went back to the early 1820s and the revival of Mediterranean commerce following the Napoleonic wars, but it was not until the next decade that a posting to Beirut acquired any real importance. The career of Henri Guys well illustrates the point. Guys was named vice-consul in Beirut in 1824, three years after French consular representation had first been established. Four years later, in 1828, he became "consul of France at Saint-Jean-d'Acre and dependencies, residing at Beirut," and then consul of the first grade in 1833. Finally, in 1837, the French consulate at Acre was officially transferred to Beirut—though Guys himself, considered unsympathetic to the Egyptian government and overly attached to an outdated conception of Western commerce, was transferred to Aleppo the following year.[51] The consulate in Beirut absorbed the office in Tripoli at this time as well, leaving only a single agent in that city. Similar developments could be observed in the case of other countries, albeit on a smaller scale. The United States, for example, which had maintained consular representation in Beirut since 1832, raised its agent to the rank of consul in 1836.[52]

Beirut further profited from the broad scope of Egyptian reforms, which were instituted there, as in other cities, by means of a great many novel measures. In addition to the formation of a police force,[53] already mentioned, smallpox was combated by the introduction of a vaccine,[54] which the Egyptian government was able to distribute more widely by turning to its advantage the competition between the French, English, and American missionaries who were coming to the Levant in growing numbers to open new schools, or at least to offer classes.[55] Communications between the various administrative centers of Syria were improved as well with the inauguration of a government postal service that enabled mail to reach Acre from Antioch in two days, and Alexandria from Acre in three.[56] In this case, however, the commitment to reform came into conflict with European interests. Created to fulfill Muhammad ʿAli's desire that he be kept informed of events on a daily basis, the postal service was initially reserved for the internal correspondence of the Egyptian administration. But the plan to open it up for use by private individuals everywhere in the country encountered opposition from the British consul in Damascus because it threatened to take business away from British couriers operating between the Syrian capital and Beirut.[57]

Such an objection, minor though it was, even trivial, speaks volumes about the ambiguity of the Great Powers' position, both with regard to Muhammad ʿAli and to the Ottoman Empire: promoting modernization while seeking to prevent it from ever being carried out, or, in the event that this could not be done, moving to thwart it by all possible means. In 1840, another intervention, this one much more serious, proved the point—and in a particularly violent way in Beirut. While insurgent forces from the Mountain led by Shaykh Francis al-Khazin were still camped in the pine grove south of the city, the British navy bombarded the ramparts on 11 September, provoking an intense panic that was followed by the exodus of several thousand inhabitants. A few weeks later, the troops sent by the Porte landed a few miles to the north. Thus did Beirut fall back into the Ottoman lap.

THE FIRST SIGNS OF PROSPERITY

Fewer than nine years had elapsed since the arrival of the Egyptian army, but the city that emerged from this episode had been transformed no less surely than if it had lasted a century. The record of the occupation was mixed, however, and many of the government's methods had provoked animosity—more perhaps in the Mountain than in Beirut itself—with the result that a rather unfavorable impression of the period began to take shape in the popular mind. This view was also endorsed by the French consul, who accused the Egyptians of acts of cruelty and wrongful use of forced labor. Nonetheless, having first known Beirut at the beginning of the century before taking up his duties there between 1824 and 1838, Guys later conceded that it was during this period, which coincided with the Egyptian occupation, that its economic development and prosperity took root.[58]

As knowledgeable observers such as Blondel and Goupil-Fesquet were well aware, and as Nerval's description of the city in 1843 illustrates, the transformation was still only very slightly visible in the streets of the city. Sanitary conditions were unquestionably improved, but they remained inadequate to support a natural increase in population to any significant degree; indeed, they were probably comparable to those that prevailed in preindustrial Europe.[59] There were some indications, however, that the occupation had had profound and far-reaching consequences, going beyond the isolated signs of metamorphosis that immediately presented themselves to view. Population was in fact growing, and though this growth was not yet self-sustaining, it would soon exceed that of all the other cities of the coast—underscoring Beirut's power of attraction in the region.

Construction had also increased outside the city walls, where demand for stones and masons now outstripped supply.[60] The scene was well captured by Goupil-Fesquet: "In the distance one perceives country houses that make this a delightful place to visit. On leaving the city more than three hundred of them come into view, stretching quite far up into the mountain in the midst of the most charming countryside. The majority of these handsome villas, inhabited by American missionaries and by European families, have been embellished by orchards filled with orange and pear and olive trees and the like."[61] But foreigners were not the only ones to populate this countryside. Already by the late 1830s, as other travelers observed, perhaps with some exaggeration but nonetheless tellingly, half of the population lived among the gardens surrounding the city.[62]

Less and less could life in Beirut be confined within its walls.

4

The Roads from Damascus

"Beirut is now in the running to position itself after Smyrna and Alexandria," Henri Guys observed in 1847. Coming from the former French consul—who begins his account of the city during his long stay between 1824 and 1838 by saying that there is "nothing odd about it, at first sight," and who devotes several pages to describing in some detail the modest character of a "place very recently become commercial"— the remark is doubly revealing. It seems to have been a last-minute addition to a narrative that ended almost ten years earlier (Guys had in the meantime been transferred to Aleppo), updated with information collected during a more recent visit. Beirut was now equipped, he reports, "with consulates from almost every nation, commercial establishments, hotels, well-stocked stores, a European pharmacy, and finally a casino—a luxury that only ports of the first rank can permit themselves."[1]

Unfavorably though he had once rated Beirut's prospects, the former consul remained attentive to the changes it was undergoing—changes that his long experience of the city permitted him to appreciate in a way that casual visitors could not. Thus, for example, the French writer and photographer Maxime du Camp, coming from Alexandria in 1850 in the company of Gustave Flaubert, gave an impressionistic but nonetheless incisive sketch: "Beirut is incomparable; not the city itself, which is pitiful and lacking in grandeur, but the country that surrounds it, the forest of parasol pines, the roads bordered with nopals, myrtle, and pomegranate trees in which chameleons run; the view of the Mediterranean and the aspect of the wooded summits of the Lebanon that draw the purity of their lines on the sky. It is a retreat made for the contemplative, for the disillusioned, for those who have been wounded by existence; it seems to me that one can live happily there doing nothing but looking at the mountains and the sea."[2]

THE PREMIER PORT OF SYRIA

The postcard landscape limned by du Camp, though it no longer gave a true picture of the place at this time, was nonetheless one of the things that contributed, if
not to its development, in any case to its rising fame as a tourist attraction. "Thanks
to the steamship," another traveler, Charles Auberive, wrote in the 1850s, "Beirut
has become a city where before long one will hasten to go in search of perpetual
springtime at the foot of the Lebanon, as formerly one went to Nice and the Mediterranean coast. . . . The crossing is not difficult. A week's sail, and the service is admirably good. In the eighteenth century, it was a much more difficult matter to go
from Paris to Provence."[3] In fact, Beirut was on its way to becoming a fashionable
destination—within the limits of the tourist trade of the period. Paradoxically, it
was to be still more highly esteemed after the bloody events of 1860, when French
military intervention made the Levant part of the mental world of every European
citizen, however poorly educated or impecunious.

Already in the 1840s, a variety of accounts anticipated Beirut's irrepressible rise,
on grounds that went beyond mere orientalist sentimentality. Writing to Lamartine in 1842, the Jesuit father Benoît Planchet observed: "Even though Aleppo is a
more considerable city than Beirut, it has no importance. Beirut is the premier port
of Syria, its population can only increase from day to day, communications with
Europe are easier there, European protection more effective, the cost of living less."[4]
Eleven years later another missionary, Father Jean-François Badour, pointed out to
the new superior general of the Jesuits that "the city of Beirut has become in only
a few years one of the principal ones of this part of the East."[5] In the interval, a French
consular report of 1846 noted that "Tripoli, like the other ports of Syria, has lost its
importance since Beirut took possession of the commerce of the entire coast."[6]
Sidon, having lost its prosperity, was described in 1855 as having been crushed by
Beirut.[7]

The basis for these comparisons, of course, was the development of the port under Ibrahim Pasha, when the first steamships began to bring cargo, passengers, and
mail, even if it took some time for all the effects of this change to be felt. The first
generation of wooden-paddle steamships had limited capacity, not exceeding 1,500
tons.[8] This was nonetheless a considerable advance, if only because of the increase
in traffic it automatically permitted by adding to the number of months open to
shipping; in the age of sail, insurers covered risks at sea to and from Beirut only for
one hundred thirty days per year (from 3 May to 13 September) on account of the
vulnerability of its outer harbor to storms in the fall and winter months.[9] The revolution in maritime transport gained further impetus with the advent of iron-hull
steamships equipped with screw propellers in the 1840s and their general adoption
in the next decade.[10] Ships under sail were still to be seen in Beirut for a short time.
A Jesuit father mentioned one leaving for Alexandria in a letter of 1850,[11] and the

French consul counted as many as ten being loaded with bales of silk in 1852, but these, he added, were the last.[12]

Apart from technological advances, the rising tide of capitalism allowed trade to be conducted more efficiently. Shipping could now operate on an industrial scale as well, with the establishment of regular service. The first steamship line to serve the Syrian ports in the 1830s and 1840s was British, soon joined by a French line, and then an Austrian one. By mid-century, British lines were the most common in the Mediterranean; among French lines the Compagnie des Messageries Impériales (renamed Messageries Maritimes in 1871) led the way. But ships belonging to the Great Powers were not the only ones that called on Beirut. In addition to the Italians, heirs to the oldest Levantine merchant tradition, and the Greeks, still a familiar presence on Ottoman shores, there were ships flying the Belgian, Danish, Spanish, Swedish, and Norwegian flags. Turkish and Egyptian vessels also made port in Beirut.[13]

As the increasing rate of cargo traffic since the 1830s showed, there had been no break in continuity after the departure of the Egyptians. To the contrary, the Ottoman restoration acknowledged the central role acquired by the port and, as a consequence of this, by the city. With the end of the Egyptian interlude, Beirut advanced in rank within the Ottoman system of administration, and immediately found itself an object of the first round of reforms, decreed in 1839. In 1842, Beirut replaced Acre as the official seat of the vilayet of Sidon, which itself had been enlarged. The city's promotion was nonetheless qualified by the Provincial Law of 1864, which in redrawing administrative boundaries united the vilayets of Damascus and Sidon to form a single province, now called Syria, with Damascus as its capital (attracting protests from some notables in Beirut—a sign of the change of attitude aroused by the city's first spurt of economic growth). In this new province Beirut was one of five sanjaks, along with Acre, Tripoli, Lataqiyya, and Nablus. Just the same, the chamber of commerce remained in Beirut.

Istanbul's recognition of the city's growing importance was also ratified by the European powers. In the 1840s, several countries upgraded their consular representation. Apart from France and Great Britain, Russia and Austria maintained consulates general, soon followed by Prussia, Sardinia, Tuscany, Spain, the Kingdom of Naples, the Netherlands, and Greece.[14]

AN URBAN EXPLOSION

The administrative promotion of Beirut was accompanied by increasing rates of immigration that fueled spectacular demographic growth. Throughout the 1820s, as we have seen, the city's population was still small, probably no more than eight thousand. The first striking jump occurred in the next decade, so that by 1840 there were about fifteen thousand people living there. Come the 1850s this number exceeded forty thousand. "In the last ten years the population has doubled," Father Badour wrote in 1853.[15] The figures themselves are modest, compared with other cities in the region, but the rate of increase was explosive: in only two decades, between 1830 and 1850, it is likely that the population quadrupled.

This increase, like the ones that followed during the rest of the century, is not attributable to natural growth, even if such growth can be observed in the population of Syria as a whole and if, in Mount Lebanon in particular, natural and cultural factors (notably the Maronite migration to the south) combined to produce demographic saturation. Even so, the pattern of growth was irregular since mortality rates had not yet been brought down. Hospital facilities remained poor throughout Syria—indeed, nonexistent, as in Beirut until the opening of an Ottoman military hospital in 1846. Hygiene was no less problematic in the middle of the century. During one cholera epidemic the foreign consuls intervened to remove the manure heaps from Ras Beirut.[16] As for the quarantine system, it could no longer assure the protection against epidemics it was intended to provide; the lazaretto itself constituted a danger to public health two decades after its creation, since with the expansion of the city eastward along the seafront in the interval it had become a source of infection. Moreover, it was now too crowded to serve its purpose. Built to accommodate at most a few hundred people, it sometimes found itself overwhelmed by as many as two thousand at a time. In times of political crisis it was used as a shelter for refugees, many of whom died owing to the negligence of the authorities.[17] Cholera and plague continued therefore to be rife, with the result that each new outbreak triggered an exodus of the population from Beirut to the more salubrious environs of the Mountain.[18]

The movement in the other direction, from mountain villages to the city, was much more considerable—and longer lasting in its effects. Certainly demographic overconcentration played a part, but it was more a result of the sectarian unrest that, following the Egyptian occupation, shook Mount Lebanon for twenty years. Safe from this turmoil, Beirut offered a home to Christian refugees, just as it had welcomed Christians fleeing inner Syria in the wake of the Wahhabi incursions of 1810 and the chronic internal quarrels of the Melkite community, divided since the defection of the Uniate churches in the late seventeenth and early eighteenth centuries into Greek Orthodox and Greek Catholic. This pattern of migration reached its height in 1860 following the sectarian massacres in Mount Lebanon and Damascus. The city was not yet prepared to absorb an influx on this scale, and many refugees from the Mountain, crammed together in appalling conditions at the lazaretto, died from exposure, malnutrition, and diseases contracted from the quarantined population.[19] The rise in mortality due to such events did nothing to slow the demographic growth associated with the exodus of 1860, however. For Beirut was not only a place of asylum. Its economic dynamism attracted inhabitants of the Mountain as well as those of the Syrian interior, and even merchants from Sidon and Tripoli came to settle there.

FIGURE 22. The beginnings of expansion beyond the city's walls (in a print from the first known series of photographs of Beirut).

As a result of the increase in population, but also of its booming economy and its new place as a center of administration within the empire, the face of the city was palpably changing. To be sure, the maze of old alleys that had perplexed Poujoulat still survived, leading Henriette Renan to remark in 1861: "To know where one is in Beirut seems to me an impossible problem."[20] The difficulty had in fact been aggravated in recent years as immigration and new businesses filled up whatever space was left in the old town, already packed with three-story houses. Fewer and fewer gardens remained, and the city now began to take on a very dense appearance, above all in its southern part, where commerce was chiefly concentrated.

And yet Beirut could no longer be reduced to the disagreeably compact world within its walls. The openness of the residential areas that were growing up beyond them gave the city a new look. The medieval enceinte could still be seen, but it was all the less capable of containing further expansion as it was now battered and breached. The bombardment of September 1840 had damaged both the walls and the towers of the port, and destroyed the bridge that connected the towers to the shore.[21] What is more, the old fortifications were never rebuilt—proof that the city no longer had any use for them. Very symbolically, a high fortress that formed part of the ramparts not far from the port was reconverted for peaceful purposes and then transformed into a mosque called al-Majidiyyeh, after the reigning sultan,

Abdül Majid.[22] New openings were made in the wall as well with the construction of two gates, Bāb Abu al-Nasr, near the southeast corner, and Bāb Idris (named for a local family), in the western wall.

From the accounts of a good many visitors we know that the city's extramural expansion, under the impetus of a rapidly growing population, began to be visible in the late 1840s. Foreign governments had set an example that was to be widely imitated by installing their consulates on Qantari Hill in the neighborhood of Zuqaq al-Blat—the street famously paved by Mahmud Nāmi Bey—and above all in Santiyyeh, closer to the coast, an area that until then was home only to a cemetery, which became known as the "Consuls' Quarter." Their lead was followed by wealthy citizens—notables and merchants, Muslim and Christian alike—looking to flee the desperately cramped conditions of the old town. To the east of the wall as well, on a line with Place des Canons, the construction of the first residence of the Jesuits and of the Apostolic Delegation,[23] and then of the Greek Orthodox School of the Three Doctors, encouraged many Christian families to settle there. Stylish homes also suddenly appeared further out, in the Qirat neighborhood to the south of the enceinte—near the future Jesuit university—and especially on the Medawar cliff, nearer the sea,[24] where the new Christian bourgeoisie chose to build their homes. There also appeared the first suburbs, further out still, populated by recent immigrants. The entire countryside around the old town was now effectively a part of the urban core. Improved security during this period provided additional incentive to take up permanent residence outside the walls. By 1845, three hundred forty-five houses had been built outside the old town, and five years later all sources agree that the countryside was extensively populated.[25]

The morphology of the city, now more spread out, was becoming more varied as well. The old town itself, though no less compact than before, was gradually changing. The function and often the outward appearance of houses built around an open courtyard (sold or leased out by notables who had left them for the open spaces beyond the walls) were now different. The buildings themselves had been enlarged in area and height by successive additions. The upper floors—often modest in size, one or two rooms—were typically occupied by several families, while the bottom floor was reserved for commercial use or otherwise converted into warehouse space. Outside the walls, new facilities appeared. In 1853 the governor, Salim Pasha, constructed a large barracks (qichla) on Qantari Hill that seems to have helped make the area beyond the enceinte safer, even though several barracks, intramural and extramural alike, already existed. This huge compound was completed eight years later, in 1861, by the addition of a military hospital.

The development of port activity and the influx of foreigners stimulated the construction of other private facilities. The old boarding houses no longer sufficed to put up travelers. The Hôtel de l'Europe, the first hotel to be built near the port, by an Italian named Battista in 1849, welcomed large numbers of tourists, among whom

Beyrouth,
Hôtel d'Orient.

FIGURE 23. One of the first seaside hotels, on the bay of Minet al-Hosn.

Flaubert and du Camp (who visited the following year) were the most famous.[26] Soon other Italian hoteliers opened establishments to the west of the ramparts, along the coast and in the gardens above it. During the twentieth century this movement toward the bay of Minet al-Hosn culminated in the area's emergence as the quarter of the grand Western-style hotels.

One of the landmarks of this westward expansion was the opening in 1853 of the Antun Bey Inn, named for its developer. The largest hotel in the city, built right on the water's edge, it housed the majority of the foreign consulates and their postal services. But it was already more than a traditional inn, and more than a center of business: when the Imperial Ottoman Bank opened a branch in Beirut in 1856, it was there that it chose to install its offices. In this sense, the Antun Bey Inn represented a transitional stage between the old caravanserai economy of the ports and the modern city beyond the harbor that the Beirut-Damascus road, the great public works project of the nineteenth century, was to bring into being.

THE ROAD TO THE FUTURE

If the arrival of Ibrahim Pasha represented the first major turning point in the modern history of Beirut, the second decisive moment indisputably occurred in the early 1860s, when the gradual opening of a carriage road serving the hinterland of Mount Lebanon, and beyond that the Biqa' and the Anti-Lebanon, coincided with the civil war in the Mountain and its spread toward Damascus. In a single stroke this new artery of commerce confirmed Beirut's new stature while at the same time encouraging the immigration that was to dramatically enrich its demography.

The idea of building a military transport route between Beirut and Damascus had already been contemplated under Egyptian rule. But it was really only with the spectacular boom in trade of the intervening years that the necessity of a new road linking the coast to Damascus made itself felt. Its chief proponent was a representative of the Messageries Impériales, Count Edmond de Perthuis, a former Orleanist naval officer who had settled in Syria after the revolution of 1848. Until then merchandise was carried over the mountains by pack-saddle animals, following a steep and dangerous road—a journey of at least two days and one night for well-equipped travelers, and more often three to four days in the case of a slow caravan. Perthuis considered two alternatives: a direct connection between Beirut and Damascus, or a longer but safer route via Sidon. The first would be difficult to build owing to the elevation of the Lebanon ridge, almost 5,000 feet (1,500 meters) high at this latitude, and liable to be plagued by bandits, who readily found refuge there; the second was apt to deal a blow to Beirut's ascendant economy by revitalizing the port of Sidon. Fearing the loss of everything they had achieved over the past quarter century, local entrepreneurs did their utmost to ensure that a direct route would be chosen—successfully, in the event.[27] In July 1857, the Porte granted the concession for a carriage road to Perthuis, who the following year set up a joint share company under Ottoman law, the Compagnie Impériale Ottomane de la Route Beyrouth à Damas, having offices in Paris and Beirut. The company raised a total of three million francs from its shareholders (among them the Paris-Orleans Railway Company and the Paris-Lyon-Mediterranean Railway of Crédit Lyonnais), selling six thousand shares at five hundred francs apiece.[28]

Construction began on 3 January 1859, following a formal ceremony presided over by the governor, Khorshid Pasha, in the presence of the foreign consuls and to the accompaniment of cannon fire. In less than a year the section of the road between the city and the Pine Forest was completed. A few months later, however, work was interrupted by the civil war in the Mountain. In the meantime stretches of the road had been opened up to passenger and freight traffic as they were finished, just in time to assist the exodus of at least some of the inhabitants of adjacent regions. Finally, on 1 January 1863, almost four years to the day after construction began, the first convoy of merchandise arrived in Damascus, and shortly thereafter daily stagecoach service was available along the entire road.

The distance of 70 miles (112 kilometers) between Beirut and Damascus could now be covered in twelve to fifteen hours, depending on the nature of the convoy, and thirteen by stagecoach.[29] To meet demand, the company used three hundred forty-eight horses and mules, fourteen omnibuses, and one stagecoach to begin with, later two. Ten relay stations permitted rapid and regularly scheduled passenger service: every day of the year, except when there was snow in the mountains, one stagecoach departed from Beirut and the other from Damascus.

The Beirut-Damascus road changed the lives of the people of the region to an even greater degree than the steamship modified the travel habits of Europeans. So great was the road's success, and particularly that of the stagecoach, that from the beginning places had to be reserved in advance for the summer season. Fares were high, but evidently not exorbitant in the minds of the some eleven thousand passengers that the Compagnie Impériale Ottomane transported per year. Freight traffic grew rapidly, from not quite 5,000 tons in 1863 to more than 21,000 in 1890. Nonetheless the company was slow to make a profit. Technical and political problems delayed construction and, together with difficulties arising from robbery and floods in the early years of operation, increased its expenses. Despite the quality of its management and service, it was not until almost ten years after construction was completed that the company managed to recover its costs. In 1872 it began to pay out dividends, forty-two francs per share initially, rising ten years later to eighty francs.[30]

In addition to rewarding its backers and justifying their faith in the economic feasibility of such an undertaking, the Beirut-Damascus road had an enormous effect on the two cities and on the whole region that lay between them.[31] Separated by less than a day's travel from its port, Damascus was now linked to large-scale international commerce and, as a consequence, saw its supremacy over Aleppo further strengthened. Zahleh, midway between the two, also benefited from the new axis of trade, which helped to transform the fertile lands of the surrounding Biqaʿ Plateau into an agricultural area, and the villages that lined the road on the western side of the Lebanon ridge, notably ʿAley and Sofar, entered upon a course of development that was to make them popular holiday resorts among the new middle class of Beirut and even beyond. As for Beirut itself, the road confirmed its position as the principal port of Syria.

Paradoxically, the economic centrality of Beirut came to be recognized at just the moment when it ceased to be a provincial capital, the vilayet of Sidon having been united with Damascus in 1864 to form the province henceforth known as Syria. Eight years later, in 1872, the creation of the autonomous administrative district of Jerusalem furnished the occasion for prominent citizens in Beirut to demand a similar status for themselves, much to the annoyance of the Porte. Its displeasure did not last long: in 1888, reversing its preference for a consolidated province of Syria, chiefly out of a fear of encouraging the political demands of the Arab population (given expression at the beginning of the decade by the many posters that went up on the walls of Damascus and Beirut), Abdülhamid created a new vilayet having its capital at Beirut and bearing its name.[32]

All this came at a time when the Ottoman authorities were beginning to formalize the hitherto ad hoc urbanism of the new province by drawing up plans for coordinated development. Various improvements had been made in response to the needs of a rapidly expanding port, but—paradoxically, again—the facilities of the port itself were slow in being modernized.

A NEW PORT

Plans for a new port had been under consideration since 1860. A first proposal had been prepared by a naval officer attached to the French Expeditionary Corps named Émile-Charles Guépratte.[33] Perthuis, anticipating the completion of his road project, now devoted himself to the task of convincing the Messageries Impériales to commit itself to this new enterprise. In 1863, the French civil engineer Auguste Stoecklin was dispatched to Beirut from Paris to examine Guépratte's plan. His report was favorable. The plan was then adopted by the Messageries and submitted for approval to Istanbul, which, having given its agreement in principle, now temporized: rather than endorse the concessional arrangement that had been suggested, the Porte insisted on taking direct control of the project, since to grant a license to build and operate the port to a foreign company at a moment when the Great Powers had become guarantors of the autonomy of Mount Lebanon would only further emphasize the empire's dependence on them.

Nonetheless there were pressing needs that called for immediate attention. The embankment in front of the old customs house, envisioned since the time of the Egyptian occupation, was finally completed. A new customs house was constructed, on the same site, with room for a court dealing with trade disputes in addition to more spacious customs sheds. The wharf on which the offices of the public health department stood was enlarged, and on the renovated pier an awning now protected departing passengers against the elements. A docking basin for barges was also built. At the same time a lighthouse was erected with the help of French engineers on the cape of Ras Beirut, at the northwestern corner of the promontory.[34] There was talk of reclaiming additional land from the sea, but nothing came of the idea.[35] And so despite these profound transformations, the port remained incapable of managing a volume of traffic that was increasing at a spectacular rate: from fewer than 50,000 tons per year in the 1830s, it rose to more than 600,000 in 1886.[36] Yet ships could not discharge their cargo on the docks, making the costly and time-consuming business of loading and unloading barges unavoidable.

The question of building a new port was brought up again in 1879, when local business leaders petitioned Istanbul, asking that the concession be granted instead to the municipality of Beirut.[37] This approach turned out to be no more productive than the earlier one. Behind the scenes, negotiations resumed between the original group of prospective investors and the Porte. Finally, in June 1887, a company was formed that brought together the Compagnie Impériale Ottomane de la Route

Beyrouth à Damas, the Ottoman Bank, the Comptoir d'Escompte de Paris, the Banque de Paris et des Pays-Bas, and the Compagnie des Messageries Maritimes. The concession was then granted at once to a Christian businessman from Baalbek, Joseph Moutran, who shortly thereafter obtained permission to operate a railroad between Damascus and the district of Hawran. Moutran was in fact a front man for the French group, and the "coup de théâtre" (as it was called by Maxime de Dumast, one of the investors) was meticulously prepared. Moutran turned around and transferred the concession to the French consortium, which on 20 June 1888 was reincorporated as the Compagnie Impériale Ottomane du Port, des Quais et des Entrepôts de Beyrouth (an entity that preserved its exclusive prerogatives until 1990, becoming a wholly French-owned enterprise under the Mandate and later, in 1960, coming under Lebanese control). Based in Paris, with a permanent representative in Beirut, it disposed of capital reserves amounting to some five million francs, raised by its partners and a few local entrepreneurs. Perthuis served as its first president, and Salim Malhama, a Maronite notable from Beirut who held a ministerial portfolio under Abdülhamid, sat on the board of directors. In addition to the right to build and operate the port, the company acquired in May 1890 a concession to manage the customs sheds, the primary beneficiary of which was the Ottoman Public Debt Administration.[38]

The new plans, more or less inspired by Guépratte's initial scheme, were drawn up in early 1889 by Stoecklin's son-in-law, Henri Garetta, and work began at once in May of the same year. Hampered by two bad winters and interrupted by a serious epidemic, construction was not completed until October 1895. But beginning in June 1893 the port was able to handle traffic on a limited basis. The old harbor was 150 meters long and 100 meters wide, with a depth of two meters. The new harbor, located further to the east, provided deeper anchorage (two to six meters) next to an 800-meter-long pier running almost parallel to the coast and protected by a breakwater 350 meters long. The dock area covered twenty-one hectares (fifty-two acres), with vast warehouses whose metal cladding had been designed by Gustave Eiffel.[39] Additional buildings were erected on land reclaimed from the sea to house quarantine facilities, harbor police, and customs authorities.[40] Passengers now disembarked at the pier onto covered barges; until then, small boats had gone out to fetch them, equipped only with an awning as protection against the sun.[41]

With the completion of this project, the face of the seafront was utterly changed. The old port was filled in, and the old towers and fortress pulled down. The wharves reserved for the loading and unloading of bulk cargo, such as wood and wheat, were relocated within the harbor's main docking basin. The passenger wharf became a street (later named Rue de la Marseillaise), and the Antun Bey Inn lost its private dock (subsequently known as Rue du Quai). Later, in 1903, the new port was provided with its own railway station, constructed by the Compagnie Impériale Ottomane, which became the terminus of the Beirut-Damascus line as well as of the railway (known by its French name, Tramway Libanais) that since 1893 had served the northern coast as far as Ma'ameltein, the boundary between the former vilayets of Sidon and Tripoli.[42]

For Beirut, the beginning of the railroad era coincided with the construction of its new port. By the 1880s it had become clear that the route built by Perthuis was no longer adequate: the number of relay stations could not be indefinitely increased, and although the stable of horses and mules had been enlarged, forage and shelter could not be supplied for more than a thousand animals. Moreover, the refusal of the Ottoman government to guarantee the extension of the company's concession led it to defer investment in new facilities. The idea therefore presented itself of transforming the carriage road into a railway. A British plan then being considered for building a railroad between Damascus and Haifa provided additional incentive. The chance that port traffic might be diverted from Beirut to its Galilean competitor disturbed the French investors and, to an even greater degree, local businessmen— all the more since a new port was now in the planning stages.[43]

A race against the clock therefore began to obtain the Porte's approval of a railway concession. After the failure of a plan that would have connected Beirut with Damascus via Tripoli, Aleppo, Hama, and Homs, thus going around the Mountain,[44] the Compagnie de la Route Beyrouth-Damas created the Société Ottomane de la Voie Ferrée Économique de Beyrouth à Damas in early 1891 and began to study alternative routes. The engineers were ordered to draw up plans that could be carried out as quickly as possible, with a view to preventing Haifa from overtaking Beirut as the economic center of the Syrian coast. In June of the same year, a prominent Sunni Muslim from Beirut named Hasan Beyhum was granted permission to construct a railroad along the route proposed by the Société Ottomane de la Voie Ferrée Économique. This company was merged with the Société des Tramways de Damas et Voies Ferrées Économiques de Syrie, which, in the meantime, had acquired from Joseph Moutran, the front man in the business concerning the new port of Beirut, the concession for a railway line between Damascus and Muzayrib, in the Hawran. The new company, formed with French and Belgian capital, bore the name Société des Chemins de Fer Ottomans Économiques de Beyrouth-Damas-Hauran en Syrie. It then moved quickly to purchase Beyhum's concession for the remainder of the route, and construction began at once. Four years later, in 1895— the year in which the new port was completed—the Beirut-Damascus line was inaugurated. The Haifa-Damascus line, begun in 1892, was temporarily abandoned six years later, with only about five miles of track having been laid in the interval.[45] Only under the British Mandate for Palestine was it to begin to fulfill its early promise, more than twenty years later.

The roughly eighty-five miles (one hundred forty kilometers) of track of the Beirut-Damascus line—twenty of them in the form of a cog railway that crossed Mount Lebanon at a height of 4,875 feet (1,486 meters), and then the Anti-Lebanon[46]—

BEYROUTH · Gare de chemin de fer.

FIGURE 24. The dedication of the harbor railway station in 1903.

could be covered in only nine hours. In real time Beirut was now closer to Damascus than either Haifa or Tripoli, guaranteeing its preeminence for the foreseeable future. Nonetheless, the railway company was slow to achieve the financial success that the route seemed to assure. It continued to lose money until just before the First World War, and it was not until the 1920s that the railroad came to play a preponderant role in the economy of Beirut.[47]

Lying at the intersection of sea, land, and rail routes, Beirut was bound to become a node of the new air routes between Europe and the Near East. In 1913, four years after Louis Blériot's successful crossing of the English Channel, his compatriot Jules Védrine became the first pilot to land in Beirut, followed two months later by a pair of Ottoman aviators in a two-seater plane. Here as elsewhere, however, the development of airborne commerce was yet a few decades away.

In the meantime, Beirut's new port facilities had allowed it finally to absorb the annual growth in shipping traffic. This had already reached a new peak in 1891–92, prior even to the completion of the new harbor. There was a drop in 1895 owing to a disappointing silk harvest in the Mountain, the Ottoman massacre of Armenians in Anatolia, and business failures associated with gold speculation in the Transvaal. Trade subsequently resumed its upward course, registering continual growth in both imports and exports until 1913.[48] It fell only during years of international conflict: the Greek-Turkish War of 1897, the Italian-Turkish War of 1911–12 (marked by the bombardment of Beirut), and the two Balkan wars of 1913. When the First World War broke out the following year, nine companies served the Syrian coast at regular intervals, varying from a week to a month, with others providing intermittent service. By this point Beirut was receiving more ships than any other port along the Syrian coast.[49]

THE GROWTH OF EUROPEAN COMMERCE

Still more important than the volume of traffic passing through Beirut's harbor during this period was its source and composition. Notwithstanding the port's growing commercial links with its hinterland, following the example of Tripoli and, of course, Aleppo, trans-Mediterranean trade flows made their influence felt in Beirut all the more forcefully as they succeeded in shaping the economic development of the entire region. Beirut was the most active port in trading with Europe, and the least tied to Egypt and Turkey—an orientation that acquired still greater significance in view of the fact that the Egyptian and Turkish shares of Syrian commerce had declined. Whereas between them these two countries accounted for half the commerce with Syria in the 1830s, this proportion had fallen to a third by 1910. The other two thirds were taken up by trade with Europe.

No less decisive for the growth of Beirut was the structure of trans-Mediterranean trade and, in particular, the roles played by its two principal participants, France and Great Britain. France had the greater share of Syrian exports, rising from 25 percent in 1833 to 32 percent in 1910; its share of goods imported by Syria, initially more modest, gradually fell over the same period from 15.9 to 9.3 percent. The pattern of British commerce was more constant but less balanced. Its share of Syria's import trade, initially high at the beginning of the Industrial Revolution, remained stable at around a third for most of the nineteenth century: from 31.9 percent in 1833 it rose only slightly to 35.3 percent in 1910. By contrast, the British were not very active customers for Syrian exports, having little or no interest in silk, which had become Syria's principal export product, whereas the silk factories of Lyon bought it in massive quantities.[50]

Although in the Ottoman Empire as a whole silk exports had increased fourfold in twenty years, rising from 340 tons in 1855 to almost 1,400 tons in 1875,[51] in Beirut imports grew faster than exports. In the space of seventy years, the value of imports passing through its port increased by almost 300 percent, jumping from 19 million francs in 1841 to 54 million francs in 1910, whereas exports grew only by 40 percent during the same period, from 15 million to 21 million francs. Beirut nonetheless held a predominant place in both directions: by 1910, it accounted for a third of Syrian imports and a quarter of exports. What is more, the British share of Beirut's import traffic was greater than its share for Syria as a whole, 43 percent against 35 percent.[52] Beirut was now the principal port of Syria, but it had not eliminated regional competition altogether. Sidon and Tripoli both continued to grow, and Haifa began slowly to assert itself. The rise of Beirut must therefore be seen in the larger context of the renaissance of the littoral stimulated by European commerce, even if its merchants profited from the boom in trade more than others.

And while Beirut's share of Syrian exports was not so large as its share of imports, nonetheless it was an export product that left the most visible impression upon the growth of the city. Dominating the trade in silk from Mount Lebanon, Beirut was subject in turn to its domination from the middle of the nineteenth century onward. Until then, silk had occupied a secondary place among goods shipped from the port of Beirut, behind gold and silver. In 1853 it became the leading export product, and three years later made up a quarter of the total volume. During this period sericulture recorded explosive rates of growth, accounting for as much as 65 percent of the total economic output of Mount Lebanon and, depending on the estimate, between 45 and 62 percent of Syria's entire output. Most of this production, increasingly controlled by Europeans, was meant for export, and Beirut constituted its primary outlet, with between 80 and 90 percent of this trade passing through its port. The largest share went to France, rising from 40 percent in 1873 to 90 percent in 1900.[53]

The impact of sericulture was not limited to the export trade. Mulberry plantations dotted the Syrian countryside. In Mount Lebanon the industry dominated the region's economy and by the middle of the century had filled the landscape with silk-reeling factories and spinning mills.[54] But with the growing influence of foreign capital, modern economic institutions were required that only a city could offer. As both a port city and seat of government, Beirut naturally became the center of the silk industry. Its commercial court provided a forum for settling disputes, and its brokerage houses another for placing and filling orders. Above all, it was in Beirut that the requisite financial instruments could be found. Alongside the Imperial Ottoman Bank (later simply the Ottoman Bank), which had responsibility for managing Istanbul's internal and external debt payments, a number of houses were founded there that provided banking services to the silk trade, among them Veuve Guérin et Fils, a subsidiary of the Lyon silk trading house of the same name that owned a large spinning mill in Qrayyeh; also Bassoul, Pharaon, Habib Sabbagh et Fils, and G. Trad et Compagnie. In association with the major French banks, all of these firms developed increasingly elaborate banking operations.

Nonetheless, the role of intermediary between Lyon-based financiers and local spinning mills was more commonly performed by Lebanese banking institutions operating in Beirut than by Beiruti-owned houses. The distinction is still necessary at this stage, for while the Lebanese economy—which is to say that of the Mountain—fueled the growth of Beirut, by no means did it account for all of the economic activity that took place there. Beiruti-owned firms were part of a larger space, and the city's economic links with Mount Lebanon were less developed than its network of contacts with cities in Syria and Palestine that shared a similar socioeconomic profile, reinforced by ties of kinship and religion and, still more so, by the reforms carried out under the aegis of the Tanzimat. With the reorganization of the Ottoman provinces, this economic network came to be crowned by the emergence of Beirut as the administrative seat of the Syrian coast.

AN ECONOMIC CAPITAL

As both the peripheral economic capital of Mount Lebanon and the main port of Syria, Beirut increasingly tended to serve as something more than a regional transshipment hub. With the development of the city's trading sector, a comparably diversified service economy took shape. European banks opened branch offices, and companies in transportation, insurance, and related industries soon followed in their steps. Owing to the variety of the services offered, in addition to the volume of merchandise passing over the docks of the port, Beirut became transformed into a great commercial city, even if its size hardly seemed to justify the importance it had suddenly acquired.

The population of the Beirut metropolitan area, though it had increased dramatically over the course of the nineteenth century, remained modest in 1914 by comparison with that of other Ottoman cities such as Smyrna (modern Izmir) and Damascus, to say nothing of Istanbul, which had grown from some 400,000 inhabitants in 1840 to 900,000 in 1890. During the same interval Smyrna had almost doubled its population, climbing from 110,000 to 200,000.[55] Damascus experienced a comparable, though probably more gradual, rate of increase: its population in 1920 was estimated at more than 200,000 people, or twice the generally accepted figure before 1840.[56] Beirut, which by the highest estimate did not exceed 140,000 at the end of the Ottoman period,[57] and probably not more than 130,000 (or even 120,000),[58] nonetheless fully merited its place among the great urban centers of the Empire. Apart from the fact that it embodied the new urbanism that was one of the most important results of the Tanzimat,[59] its demographic growth was in line with rates observed elsewhere, despite a certain slowing in relative terms, or perhaps because of it—paradoxically, a sign of its accession to the status of a major city.

But the decline in the rate of growth reflected in the statistics was perceptible only in retrospect. At the time the overall impression was one of relentless increase, and indeed the city's progress seemed dazzling. As we have seen, its population had increased fourfold in only a quarter of a century, beginning in the late 1820s—an already explosive rate of growth that was then accelerated in spectacular fashion by the events of 1860, which disgorged thousands of Christian refugees from the Mountain and Damascus. In the space of three or four years, this influx raised the population to about 60,000.[60] And in the course of the next half-century it doubled again.[61]

Here again, quite obviously, we are dealing with educated guesswork rather than precise figures. Concealed within the discrepancies among the various estimates are staggering margins of error. The crux of the problem is that even the censuses undertaken by the Ottoman authorities cannot be accepted as accurate. Generally speaking, families tried to avoid being counted whenever they could, for fear of increasing the risk that male children would be conscripted for military service. In the case of Beirut, an additional difficulty arises from the fact that censuses did not take into account natives of Mount Lebanon, who were considered residents of the Mutasarrifate. Thus in 1917, for example, 50,000 males were recorded in the register of births, marriages, and deaths for the city of Beirut.[62] Factoring in the estimated share of the resident population born outside Beirut, while making allowance for losses due to emigration and for deaths sustained in the First World War, this figure would appear to corroborate the conjecture of 120,000 inhabitants in 1920.

The apparent incongruence between the size of Beirut's population and the magnitude of its economic role suggests how far this role was a product of external causes, foremost among them international commerce. It would nonetheless be a mistake to suppose that the city was simply a European bridgehead. Foreign businessmen occupied a less important, or in any case less visible, place there than in Alexandria, and moreover they had to contend with the dynamism of local entrepreneurs.[63] The establishment of an indigenous business class occurred in two phases: first, the commercial opening to the West transformed the merchant class into a modern bourgeoisie, enlarged by immigration from Mount Lebanon and other cities of the Levant, especially Damascus; second, to the extent that it profited from this transformation, the new bourgeoisie itself became the vehicle for it.

Local merchants were not without comparative advantages of their own in competing with foreign entrepreneurs. Having no need to buy land or to engage the services of translators and expatriate advisors, and already being familiar with the traditional intermediaries of commerce inside Syria, their costs starting out in business were relatively low. But this was by no means enough to assure success. The ease with which European expansion upset even the best-established social structures of countries in other parts of the world, substituting for formerly dominant classes an imported colonial bourgeoisie, or at least one with direct links to imperial seats of power, is well documented. In Beirut, however, the opposite occurred: trade with industrialized nations favored the dominant indigenous class, transforming local notables into an elite and maximizing their comparative advantages by the device of consular protection.

The reason for this is that the Eastern Question had caught up with the logic of European economic expansion, preventing it from assuming the form of a classic colonial relationship. The consensus of the European powers in favor of keeping the sick man alive meant that no one of them could consider the Ottoman Empire as its private preserve. This had the further consequence of encouraging inter-European rivalries, while at the same time restraining them beyond a certain threshold. Moreover, the continuing survival of an Ottoman state that was determined to recover its former glory, and that, no matter how great its present dependence on the other powers, was still a formidable presence in the life of its provinces, prohibited a cartel of foreign powers from usurping the authority of the local government, as Western nations had been able to do in China during this period, for example. Competition among imperialistic interests came to be diverted instead through the back channels opened up to them by the multidenominational and multiethnic composition of the empire.

In large measure this was made possible by the heritage of the agreements concluded by successive sultans with Christian nations conferring rights and privileges upon foreign subjects resident or trading in Ottoman dominions, known as the Capitulations of the Ottoman Empire. Istanbul's program of modernization ought logically to have abolished these arrangements, but their full application was insisted upon by France and Great Britain, and formalized by the Hatt-i hümayun, the second great series of reforms instituted in 1856. The extension of the concept of protection for non-Muslim communities to economic activity was fully exploited by Christian merchants.[64] Stimulated by competition among foreign consulates, the supply of professional interpreters (or dragomans) increased, although they were occupied with translation only on a very occasional basis, if at all. Thanks to the immunity from imperial taxation granted by consular protection, they could profit from the advantages enjoyed by Europeans, particularly in connection with the settlement of commercial disputes, or from those enjoyed by Ottoman subjects, often by serving as front men in order to obtain concessions for their patrons, or both.

This state of affairs obviously depended on Europe's growing power as the center of the world trading system, notwithstanding its internal rivalries. And yet it was not a question simply of native businessmen playing the role of middleman. Owing to Beirut's rapid economic growth and to the network of intermediaries found in other cities of the Empire, as well as in Egypt (under British control since 1882), an indigenous elite—which was beginning to take on the trappings of aristocracy—suddenly found itself in a position to operate on a European scale itself, setting up offices in Genoa, Marseille, and even Manchester. In addition to their commercial interests in Beirut and the investment of initial accumulations of wealth in real estate, local firms looked overseas in search of opportunities for diversifying their activities. Having started out as quasi-banks financing the silk industry and related trade, they moved very quickly to invest profits abroad and to establish foreign banking and loan operations. The geographical mobility of the new bourgeoisie, in combination with its growing financial sophistication, set it apart from the traditional class of notables from which it descended and brought about a change in the way of life of Beirut that was to be made visible by the lavish architecture of the new homes being constructed on the outskirts of the city.

The experience of the Sursocks, probably the most prominent Greek Orthodox family of the new class, is particularly instructive in this regard. The origins of this family, whose name derives from a contraction of the Byzantine Greek "Kyrié Ishac," are associated with Mersin, a town in southern Turkey, and the region of Tarsus, where it owned land. In the seventeenth century, perhaps even earlier, the Sursocks settled in the village of Barbara, not far from Byblos, where they built up land hold-ings in exchange for services rendered to the Porte as tax collection officials. At the end of the eighteenth century, or perhaps the beginning of the nineteenth, a branch of the family took up residence in Beirut and soon came into contact with foreign consuls. By 1832, one of the family had found employment as dragoman for the American representative. Others were in the service of Greek and Russian patrons, and still another, rather more surprisingly for a non-Latin Christian during this period, had found a French protector. As commercial agents, the Sursocks also made a name for themselves in the grain export trade, later diversifying their holdings through investment in foreign ventures such as the Suez Canal Company and the Damascus Road Company. In Egypt the family associated itself with Muhammad ʿAli's son Saʿid, and later with Saʿid's brother Ismaʿil, who succeeded him as khedive. In gratitude for their support in dealing with British and French creditors, Ismaʿil made a gift to the Sursocks of some of his own shares in the Suez venture. In Beirut, the family had in the meantime taken up residence on Ashrafiyyeh Hill, where it gave its name to the most fashionable suburb of the city, lined with mansions in the Italian style, a taste acquired through travel and association with European high society. These aristocratic pretensions, highlighted during the reception of Grand Duke Nicholas of Russia in 1872, were confirmed when a Neapolitan count later gave his daughter in marriage to Alfred Sursock—not the last of the family's alliances with European royalty. Even so, the Sursocks did not neglect either public life in Beirut or Ottoman politics. Devoted to charitable activities, the most conspicuous emblem of which was the founding of a girls school, Zahrat al-Ihsān, they also par-ticipated, directly or indirectly, in the government of the city. Alfred's brother, Michel, was elected deputy for Beirut to the Ottoman parliament in 1914.[65]

Other dynasties joined the Sursocks in establishing themselves in the front rank of the new business upper class, which was to preserve its influence in some cases until the late twentieth century: Greek Orthodox families, such as the Bustroses and the Fayads; Roman Catholics, such as the Abelas; Greek Catholics, such as the Pharaons; and Maronites, such as the Malhamas. Other families, more recently ar-rived from Damascus, such as the Debbas (Greek Orthodox), who had sought refuge in Beirut in 1860, or indeed from Iraq, such as the Chiha (Roman Catholic), steadily consolidated the Christian character of the city. And yet Muslim merchants were not excluded from Beirut's development. To be sure, competition from European businessmen (and occasionally their native protégés) aroused discontent among them. During the construction of the new port, for example, the dealings of the Compagnie Impériale Ottomane—harshly criticized even by the Europeans—led seventy Muslim merchants to sign a petition denouncing the grant of ownership to a French company, which they described as a danger to the empire.[66] Nonetheless, Muslim notables accommodated themselves to the new state of affairs, in part because the city's economic boom was linked also to the development of commerce with the hinterland, where Muslim entrepreneurs enjoyed a privileged, albeit not controlling, position.

Most of all, the city's business leaders, animated by the spirit of the Tanzimat, now held genuine regional power. With the dismantling of the province of Syria and the establishment of Beirut as a vilayet in its own right, members of this new bourgeoisie found themselves included among the governors of a territory that extended as far north as Lataqiyya and as far south as Nablus—and almost on an equal footing with the leading figures of Damascus.

A Window on Ottoman Modernity

Beneath the sepia tones of the earliest photographs of the city, one has hardly any trouble imagining the reddish orange that now tinted Beirut's skyline. A comparison of the first daguerreotypes from the 1840s with later panoramic views shows that beginning in the 1860s, and more clearly still in the following decade, terracotta roofing tile from Marseille became an integral part of the urban landscape, helping to fashion the image of a modern—which is to say a rather bourgeois—Mediterranean city. The transformation was nevertheless far from being complete, as we know from other tableaus: street scenes, group portraits of college faculty and company staff, and pictures of social events.

In these images one sees a mixture of architectural styles, the novel juxtaposition of traditional and Western dress (Ottomanized by the wearing of the tarbush), and the intrusion of modern public spaces into an ancient and closed environment. The city was passing through a transitional phase, like other Ottoman metropolises in which there was no clear demarcation between the European and the Arab city—the opposite case to Algiers, Tunis, or indeed Cairo. Nonetheless the tendency was clear: a new city was in the process of superimposing itself on an old one and, at the same time, going beyond its borders. Two panoramic views (among a hundred others) taken by the French photographer Adrien Bonfils in 1897 or 1898, with the Mountain in the background to the northeast, reveal new contours.[1] Amid the clutter of the built environment—still perceptible in the city center—a few structures stand out: the great Ottoman barracks, massive public buildings, the pier of the new port, the first straight avenues; what is more, the conquest of new and still verdant expanses gives a sense of spaciousness, while at the same time amplifying the im-

FIGURE 25 A–B. The new contours of the city at the end of the nineteenth century, as seen through the lens of Adrien Bonfils.

pression of movement. Already on the edge of the city, new construction—scattered for the moment—seems to be pulling Beirut outward.

The new city had new needs, and satisfying them helped to reconfigure a landscape that increasingly was punctuated by sprawling and prominent buildings. There were now two universities, boarding and day schools, cathedral churches (one for each of the three principal rites—Greek Orthodox, Greek Catholic, and Maronite—as well as the Roman Catholic cathedral of Saint-Louis des Capuchins), and a few hospitals, the largest of which, the military hospital, adjoined the barracks and dominated the site. Less striking at first sight, but no less indicative of the changes taking place, are novel landscape elements hidden in the furrows of urban topography in panoramic views of the city, but visible in detail in close-up pictures: public squares and gardens, and widened streets, notably Rue de Damas, which led on to the road of the same name that climbed eastward into the mountains. By contrast, the old wall is no longer to be seen. By the 1870s it had been dismantled by the spread of construction and, in some places, the growth of the road network.

BEIRUT IN THE AGE OF REFORM

An important part of this reconfiguration escaped all deliberate planning, and proceeded instead from the influence of demography and the social change that Beirut was experiencing. Another was a consequence of the concurrent and concerted initiatives of the agents of European expansion, and quite particularly of the religious missions that founded school after school there. But the metamorphosis of Beirut remains incomprehensible if one neglects to take into account the resolutely modernist attitude of the Ottoman authorities. Beirut was indeed a proving ground for the "inevitable West."[2] But it was also very much a city of the Tanzimat. The spirit of reform inspired governors, local officials, and notables, all of whom were convinced that modernization was the sole road to salvation, that reform of the tax system and recognition of the equality of subjects before the law favored a city that was prepared to move forward. Moreover, in addition to the general impact on its development of the new laws and the spirit of the age, Beirut also received special attention from reformers in Istanbul, not less than the attention given to Damascus—a sign that in their eyes Beirut had taken its place among the leading Ottoman cities. The wālī Ismail Kemal Bey proclaimed on his arrival there in 1898 that Beirut was a "source of affluence and a center of instruction" and that it was destined to "hasten the progress of civilization."[3] A concrete illustration of this came eight years later, in 1896, when the municipal engineer Amin ʿAbd al-Nur translated and published the text of the new Ottoman law that defined the scope of authority of the various city departments.[4]

With the advent of the Tanzimat, the many facets of a revolution from above that cannot be explained by Western pressures alone stood revealed in the cities of the empire. By reformulating the relations between the sultan and his subjects, now equal before the law, by reforming the justice system to adapt it to the development of capitalism, and by modernizing the state apparatus, and thereby society itself, this revolution amounted to a refounding of an empire that could no longer be reduced either to an immense domain for generating tax revenue or to a machine for making war. Beyond the various administrative measures intended to equip the state with specialized instruments (ministerial departments, civil courts, training in law and public administration, and so on), what the Tanzimat changed was the very mission of the state, which now found itself called upon to meet the needs of its people. The restoration of Ottoman authority—not the least of the Sublime Porte's aims in this connection—therefore depended in large measure on its success in reordering municipal government. This would make it possible, in turn, to devise a new source of legitimacy that would moderate the effects of the affront to the empire's dignity on a symbolic level. Islam having ceased to be the sole basis of imperial power, the view gained currency in official circles that government should cultivate a sense of Ottoman national identity *(osmanlilik)* as the mainspring of popular obedience and support.

Unable to prevent the intensification of ethnic and denominational differences or to hold the West at bay, the state had little choice, then, but to take an active approach to provincial administration and social questions that laid particular emphasis on changing the look of Ottoman cities, which were both the theater and the object of the Tanzimat's most visible changes.[5] Indeed urban policy, even more than the legislative program from which it profited, was the principal expression of the age of reform. This was due, first, to the fact that it translated on a human scale the new relations between the empire and its subjects: in substituting for the old procedures of consultation, which had been the prerogative of the provincial council (*dīwān*), more representative (if not perfectly democratic) local government proceedings, it allied the most dynamic segments of the population with public initiative. The importance of urban policy was due also to the fact that in Beirut modernization produced tangible results, improving the quality of life in ways that could be appreciated by one and all: roads, omnibuses (as horse-drawn carriages were called at the time), water and gas supply, and later electric lighting and streetcars, to say nothing of recreational facilities. And finally it was due to the fact that, in an era of triumphant rationality, the Ottoman style of governing drew upon the advances of a field of study peculiar to the city: urban planning. Distinct from the secular urban tradition of Islam, in its Arab and then its Turkish form, this new discipline sought to put into effect as rapidly as possible the development schemes of European cities while at the same time incorporating elements of a rich indigenous architectural heritage.

Like all the other cities of the empire, Beirut benefited from a desire to restore Ottoman authority in the provinces after the unsatisfactory experiment with self-rule of the eighteenth century, without, however, cutting off local sources of innovation. New mechanisms of popular representation, first on the provincial level, and then on the municipal level, were particularly useful in this regard. They presented the dual advantage of permitting administrative decentralization while simultaneously concentrating political authority in Istanbul; and while allowing the wishes of urban elites to be expressed, they gave the administration of the provinces a formal unity and, by regulating the flow of information in both directions, enlarged the decision-making capabilities of the central government. The first in this series of administrative reforms, which extended over a period of some thirty-five years, was a firman of 1840—a few months after the Gülhane decree issued the previous year—that provided for the establishment in the provinces of councils whose members would speak for the secular and religious leaders of each community.

At the same time as these organs of local government were being created, an expanding web of legislation opened up fresh possibilities of intervention to them. Thus, for example, a law on urban planning defined the new parameters of the road network and regularized the layout of streets and their relative width. By this statute, enacted in 1848 and amended a first time in 1858, then again in 1863, the city's principal thoroughfares were widened to more than eleven meters, while the minor ones were required to be more than seven meters across. Enforcement of the law was later entrusted to the city council, which in Beirut had responsibility for supervising the construction of new roads between the old town and the suburbs, until then connected by rocky paths that were unsuited to travel by the new omnibuses. During the same period, the Land Law of 1858 promoted colonization of the urban periphery throughout the empire; in Beirut, in particular, it encouraged migration outside the old walls of the city.

Municipal policy was formalized by the Provincial Law of 1864, extended and completed in 1877. In its first version, this law stipulated that all provincial capitals were to have an elected and explicitly political administrative council, responsible for approving concessions, assessing taxes and collecting revenues, ratifying land sales and property deeds, authorizing infrastructural projects and other public works throughout the province; and also a municipal council, likewise elected, with responsibility for local affairs, determining and enforcing laws and codes with regard to urban planning, commercial practices, health, and public morality and welfare. But even before the Provincial Law was adopted, Beirut had caught the eye of Fuad Pasha, the Ottoman foreign minister and one of the great figures of the age of reform, who was faced with the task of managing the consequences of the war in Mount Lebanon. Installed in al-Qishla, the great barracks on Qantari Hill, he convened the first provincial assembly, one of whose urgent duties was to organize housing and relief for the victims of the conflict while laying out new directions for urban policy. Fuad kept himself abreast of developments in the city through his brother-in-law, Qabbuli Pasha, the new governor of the province of Sidon, who in 1863, probably on Fuad's recommendation, created a municipal council that anticipated the Provincial Law of the following year and Beirut's subsequent elevation to the status of a municipality. Equipped with its own by-laws, and shortly thereafter its own budget, the council established by Qabbuli Pasha was charged with regulating the increasingly complex provision of public services—this at a time when the territorial expansion of the city and changes in its layout were beginning to alter the course of daily life. In 1868, Beirut was duly constituted as a municipality, almost entirely on the model (as Count de Perthuis observed) of Pera, now known as Beyoglu, which had been established as a separate district of Istanbul in 1856.[6]

A NEW ARCHITECTURAL ERA

If the expansion of Beirut beyond its walls had been accelerated by the Egyptian occupation, planned urban development made its first appearance only in the middle of the century. Public initiative and entrepreneurial drive combined to modify the shape of the city, thanks to two building projects of quite different inspiration that were completed within a few months of each other in 1853: the Qishla and the Antun Bey Inn.

The construction of the military barracks was the first government decision to directly affect the city's development, even if it did not, strictly speaking, arise from a concern with urban planning. Meant to house the seventh regiment of the Ottoman army stationed in Beirut, the Qishla was set atop Qantari Hill, overlooking the old town, almost at the southwest corner of the medieval wall, bordering the paved street built by Mahmud Nāmi Bey. Once the surviving towers had been pulled down the summit of the hill had to be leveled. Although only two stories high, the Qishla dominated the entire city, visible from both the sea and the suburbs. A decade later it was completed by a third story and covered with a roof of reddish orange tiles that accentuated the monumentality of the plan, while its exterior ornamentation reproduced the style of public buildings that had recently appeared in Istanbul and the provincial capitals. Later it became the Grand Sérail (Saraya in Arabic, or Seraglio), briefly the seat of the provincial governor, and after that of the French Mandate; since the declaration of Lebanese independence in 1943 it has been the prime minister's residence. Reconstruction of the building in the 1990s preserved the outer walls, but its general appearance has been altered by the addition of a fourth story.

A smaller version of the famous Selimiyye barracks in Istanbul, the Qishla stood out in the first place by reason of its quadrangular plan and massive volume from the labyrinth of alleys and small buildings at its foot, and announced the advent of the new Ottoman architectural era in Beirut: a seemingly limitless number of outward-opening windows, porches decorated with arcades and surmounted by gables, and a brightly colored roof. Moreover, the transformation in several phases of the adjacent land into an esplanade heralded a new approach to urban planning, especially after the construction in 1861 of a military hospital in the same style as the barracks, though on a more modest scale. By the end of the century the space between the two buildings had been made into a garden, having in the meantime lost its function as a parade ground—a metamorphosis that by itself, before the transformation of the barracks into the Grand Sérail, underscored the implications for city planning of what was originally a military decision.

If the erection of the Qishla immediately came to symbolize the new Ottoman public spirit, the Antun Bey Inn illustrated the new scope available to private initiative in this transitional phase of Beirut's economic development. The owner was himself a man astride two eras. Antun Bey al-Misri—an Egyptian of Armenian descent known as Anton Misrilian in Armenian, or Misrioglu in Turkish (*Misr* being the Arabic word for Egypt)—had made his fortune in Istanbul and become acquainted with the new tastes and fashions that were being introduced in the capital, as in Cairo and Alexandria. His establishment was clearly distinguished from the old caravanserais, shut off from the world in the manner of traditional Arab

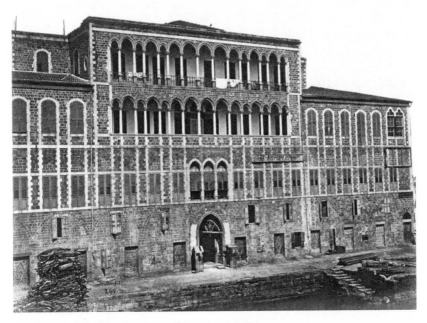

FIGURE 26. The Antun Bey Inn and its private dock.

lodgings, by the delicacy of its architectural details and a façade that gave onto the sea, adorned with two series of arcades on its top floors. A private dock allowed merchandise to be transferred directly from cargo barges to warehouse space inside. And yet despite this last innovation, the Antun Bey Inn was much more than a mere depot. It housed a wide range of modern economic activities (merchant banks, shipping agencies, trading companies, post offices, government departments, and so on), and it was there, as we have seen, that the Imperial Ottoman Bank chose to open its local branch in 1856. This concentration of commercial interests permitted the Antun Bey Inn to exert a significant influence on the development of the Beirut seafront and, beyond that, of the whole lower city.

The beginning of the 1860s represented a turning point, when public works and private enterprise combined to redirect the course of urbanism in Beirut. The initial impetus was given by the start of construction on the Damascus road in January 1859. In itself, the route selected for the first section of this road inaugurated a new way of thinking about the city's future expansion. The original dirt road was located on the eastern side of the old town. Emerging from the labyrinth of narrow streets around the old port, it went out through Porte des Tanneurs (Bāb al-Dabbagha) to the open spaces of Place des Canons beyond the walls. The new road, a bit more than twelve meters (about forty feet) wide, avoided the congestion of the old town while reducing construction costs. Departing from the other end of the port, it followed first the western wall, and then its southern prolongation, as far as Place des Canons, from there branching off toward the suburbs and finally into the foothills of the Lebanon range.[7]

A year and a half after work began, French troops landed in Beirut in August 1860 and took this road to reach the Pine Forest, where they were based for the next year or so. A few weeks later, in October, omnibus service between the encampment and Place des Canons allowed soldiers on leave to come into town easily and also to visit the red-light district, which likewise had moved beyond the walls, reestablishing itself northeast of the old town.[8]

In the meantime, work on the Damascus road had been interrupted. But far from hampering the development of Beirut, this hiatus hastened it. Engineers in the service of Perthuis and their idled teams of workers were put to work extending the network of city streets, in accordance with the plans drawn up by the Ottoman government. This episode turned out to be as revelatory of the spirit of the Tanzimat as the nature of the work itself, since the driving force behind the project was none other than Fuad Pasha,[9] who in a mad panic had rushed to Beirut and Damascus following the massacres. In addition to restoring order in the Mountain, Fuad took charge of provincial administration and concerned himself in particular with the planning of Beirut's expansion, commissioning Perthuis to build three roads between the old urban core and the suburbs.

Work soon resumed on the Damascus road, however. On its completion in 1863, not only was the economy of Beirut profoundly modified, but the plan of the city itself was decisively altered. Use of the new road gave rise to an entire range of activities in the vicinity of the old town, in particular around two open spaces along the enceinte, Place des Canons (El Burj) to the east, and to the southwest Place Assour (from the Arabic phrase meaning "along the wall"). Around the Burj, the first signs of urbanization were now visible. A comparison of maps from 1841 and 1861 reveals the expansion of the built environment;[10] in 1862 the terrain was leveled to create a place for promenades and entertainment. With the opening of the Damascus road, cafés, stores, and hotels sprang up around the square, in addition to a residential neighborhood just to the east. The same thing occurred in the Assour triangle, now brought into contact with the Burj not only by the new road but also by the advance of modern construction. Having formerly served as antechambers to the city, the Burj and Place Assour were suddenly at the heart of the new metropolitan area.

The Damascus road also carried forward the metamorphosis of the lower city around the port. Following the improvements made by the Egyptians, this process had been accelerated by the construction of the Antun Bey Inn, and then further stimulated by the development of a new harbor district. Banks, shipping agencies, and firms providing a wide range of port-related services leased space in buildings that displayed a new style, marked by façades with large bays opening onto the sea beneath a canopy of reddish orange tiles. Introduced first along the wharves, this style gradually moved inland to neighborhoods overlooking the Mediterranean, and thence to farmland to the west, where it was followed almost at once by commercial tenants. Here again the first property lines had been marked out beforehand, and already by 1861 upscale markets and inns were welcoming shoppers and guests. In shifting the port's center of gravity from east to west, albeit only temporarily, the new route of the Damascus road helped to bring about the transformation of the lower city into a business district.

For a time, the old town preserved its residential character, but its growing congestion now began to push newcomers out into the increasingly urbanized outlying areas, with the wealthiest native families settling still further away from the center. A comparison of maps from 1841 and 1876 reveals that the city grew roughly eleven times in size during the intervening thirty-five years.[11] The demand for dressed stone was now so great that it became necessary to dismantle sections of the Roman aqueduct.[12]

By this point, then, the intramural district occupied only a small part of the metropolitan area. This disproportion merely accentuated the contrast between two quite dissimilar urban landscapes: on the one hand, in the old town, a dense mass of winding alleys and cul-de-sacs, overcrowded suqs, and buildings three and four stories high, crammed together; on the other, spacious suburbs where wider streets followed a regular, if not perfectly rectilinear, plan. Often surrounded by private gardens, but in any case set comfortably apart from one another, the modern houses were rarely more than three stories high and increasingly were roofed with Marseille tiles. This break with the city's traditional architecture introduced a new aesthetic. While reproducing the familiar interior arrangement, according to which rooms were laid out around a central court—now covered—that served as the family living room, the new European-inspired style placed great value on openness and letting in natural light through windows (a recent innovation in private homes of the region) and, in the wealthiest neighborhoods, through the triple arcades that, with their ogival (or "pointed") arches, were to become the hallmark of Beirut. No less novel was the cultivation of a visual sensibility that led the most affluent to build their houses on elevated sites, overlooking the sea or on east-facing hillsides, in order to exploit the panoramic views of the sea and the mountains.

Rich merchants from the Greek Orthodox community, for example, began to build lavish residences on the cliffs looking down upon the old town from the east. Together with the small palaces of the Sursock family, they signaled the emergence of a neighborhood with patrician pretensions.[13] From this period date new place names associated with prominent families: Rue Sursock, the Medawar Quarter, the Tuwayni Enceinte, the Debbas Ascent, and so on. An old anecdote about a dispute between the Tuwayni and Debbas families illustrates the new prominence of aesthetic concerns. Dimitri Debbas had come to Beirut from the Mountain in 1860, after the massacres there, and with some difficulty had managed to regain his former status. Disturbed by the prospect of his view of the water being ruined by the house that Debbas was preparing to build, more than fifteen hundred feet from his home, Gerios Tuwayni used his considerable influence to block the project. Finally he was convinced by his wife to sell Debbas another piece of land, a little higher up on the promontory, and the road that led up to the relocated residence was henceforth known as the *montée Debbas*.

The new architectural tendency was further encouraged by a series of public facilities, hospitals, and schools (both public and private) constructed in the nearby suburbs by foreign missions and local religious communities. Thus, for example, l'Hôpital Saint-Georges, the oldest private hospital of Beirut, was built by the Greek Orthodox community in Rmayleh, to the northeast of Saint Dimitri Hill. Even though the original style of the compound was rather traditional, the main building's scale and orientation, looking out over the harbor, signaled the aesthetic transformation underway. On the other side of the city in 'Ayn al-Mrayseh, the hospital dedicated to Saint John, built by German missionaries a little later on a cruciform plan, was more elegant in appearance, with a formal garden and three-story façade, adorned with a gable, that presented a succession of tall windows surmounted by ogival arches. The Prussian deaconess of Kaiserswerth took up residence next door in a U-shaped building whose façade was also divided up into a series of windows, with semicircular arches and *oeils-de-boeuf* (bull's eyes, or oculi). Set within a crenellated wall, with an octagonal corner tower and gardens, the building opened throughout much of its extent onto the sea, its large bays likewise punctuated by ogival arcades. Nearer the old town, across from the enceinte and the southeast gate (Bāb al-Dirkeh), the Sisters of Charity built one of the first structures covered by a roof of reddish orange tiles. It was succeeded in 1950 by the Lazarist Convent, an expansive complex of buildings known as 'Azariyyeh (or Lazariyyeh) that survives today in restored form at the juncture of Place des Canons and the old wall.

The task of uniting the spacious residential area of the suburbs with the densely populated territory of the old town was to fall to Ottoman planners. The origins of city planning in Beirut, as elsewhere in the empire, may be situated in the early 1870s, with the establishment of municipal departments of public works and engineering. The era of the master-builders was over. Private developers now found themselves obliged to hire civil engineers, trained in Istanbul, to draw up plans for new buildings. These plans had then to be officially approved before a construction permit could be issued in the form of a firman. The Law of 1877, which completed the municipal reforms of 1864, improved the functioning of local government by instituting two elected councils, an administrative council and a city council in the true sense, which is to say one concerned specifically with plans for municipal development.

THE DISCOVERY OF URBAN PLANNING

Ottoman municipal reform, though it was applied throughout the Arab provinces, yielded uneven results that largely depended on the interest shown by the provincial governors.[14] After the departure of Fuad Pasha, Beirut profited from the appointment of Midhat Pasha as head of the province of Syria. The last of the great reformist viziers and father of the Constitution of 1876, Midhat Pasha had fallen from favor and now found himself far from the capital (later he was to be banished from it altogether) following the suspension of the Constitution the same year by Abdülhamid II. After the creation of the vilayet of Beirut in 1888, governors had scarcely any chance to leave a lasting mark: sixteen came and went over the next three decades[15]—an average of not quite two years in office through 1918, with rare instances of four years. Nonetheless the city got used to this state of affairs, and despite the resistance to further liberalization during the despotic Hamidian interlude, the central government's abiding concern with urban policy sanctioned municipal initiative. Everything considered, at least in the case of Beirut, the Red Sultan (as Abdülhamid was known for presiding over the massacres of Armenians) did not put an end to the Tanzimat, but continued it by other means. In the matter of urbanism, certainly, it was during the Hamidian period that the spirit of reform received its fullest effect.

Indeed the authoritarianism of the Ottoman regime actually favored bold new departures. Following the contemporary example of Baron Haussmann in Paris, and that of the urban improvements already carried out elsewhere in Europe in the eighteenth century in the name of Enlightenment ideals, deep cuts into the tissue of Beirut had to be made in order to bring about progress, as it was then considered to be, substituting straight lines and right angles for the untidiness of an obsolete network of streets and roads. Freed by advances in military technology from the constraints that had long enclosed cities within walls, planners were now subject to the imperatives of modern transportation. Horse-drawn carriages, railroads, and finally, in the early twentieth century, streetcars all required open space, just as sustained population growth did.

Even before the new reign of orthogonality, a series of improvements had been made in response to the needs of transportation, notably public squares (with room for parking) and, soon, train stations; and also, as an indirect consequence of such development, promenades, cafés, and hotels. The orderly symbols of this progressive urbanism—circular (or, more often, polygonal) public spaces—enlarged the gaps between built-up areas and allowed the city to breathe, giving rise to new forms of behavior in the process.[16] A related sign of the changes that lay ahead was the construction in the center of cities of large public buildings, made necessary by the growth and centralization of Ottoman bureaucracy under Abdülhamid. Housing executive offices and administrative departments, these buildings reproduced from one city of the empire to the next a neoclassical architecture that was among the last manifestations of Ottoman power, now under siege in all other domains.

In Beirut, as elsewhere, the functional purpose of these buildings was combined with variations on traditional Islamic art meant to bring out the distinctive character of the empire in relation to the West, never absent from the minds of its rulers.[17] Throughout the Ottoman lands, and quite particularly the Arab provinces that were the special objects of Abdülhamid's attention, the new imperial concept of osmanlilik made use of these ornamental references to a glorious past in order to proclaim the Porte's continuing and unbroken authority and to demonstrate its perpetual vigor. From Edirna to Beirut, an identical style prevailed.[18] And even though the new look of Ottoman cities borrowed from European ideas about urban planning, it enabled a historically urban empire to give an impression of enduring unity.

Implementing this state-sponsored urban policy was not free of administrative hindrances or local difficulties, however. In Beirut, it was not until the adoption of the Law of 1877 and the transfer of Midhat Pasha to Damascus, following his exile from the Grand Vizierate in Istanbul, that a coherent plan emerged the following year. The city council, now recognized as the competent organ of government in such matters, had the power to substitute regulations for spontaneous arrangements and to plan the large-scale projects that were to define the new public spaces, which included squares, streets bordered by sidewalks, gardens, and promenades lined with administrative buildings, schools, bandstands, theaters, and baths, all built in the currently fashionable neoclassical style.[19]

As emblems of the commitment to progress and civilization, the projects undertaken by the city government after 1878 were aimed chiefly at improving Beirut's appearance and adapting it to contemporary needs. Above and beyond their symbolic usefulness in furthering the purposes of Ottomanism, they answered the necessity of raising standards of public health and making it easier for people to get from one place to another. These aims lent themselves to geometrical solutions that, by means of alignment and perspective, sought to regularize the intramural network of buildings and streets and to link it directly to the old borderlands of the city, which now occupied a central position within a larger metropolitan area. But construction of the three axial roads previously contemplated—two extending southward from the port (the future Rue Allenby and Rue Foch) and one transversal artery, running parallel to the old east-west line of the enceinte—was long delayed by difficulties in acquiring land, and demolition work began only in 1915. By contrast, the Tripoli road, running along an axis parallel to the port, had been substantially widened in 1886. But it was above all the transformation of Place des

FIGURE 27. The garden in Place Hamidiyyeh, with a bandstand behind the fountain and, behind that, the provincial Sérail.

Canons, just outside the old walls, that really marked Beirut's entry into the new era of Ottoman urbanism.

In 1879, the president of the municipal council, Fakhri Bey (son of Mahmud Nāmi Bey), proposed to enlarge the square, which was henceforth to bear the name Hamidiyyeh, in homage to the sultan, by incorporating a public garden inspired by the example of Azbakiyya Park in Cairo. Once approval had been obtained from the wālī of Damascus, Ahmed Hamdi Pasha, Fakhri Bey launched a subscription, to which he was the first to contribute. Designed by the chief engineer of the vilayet, Bishara Effendi, a garden in the Turkish style, planted with Persian lilacs and enlivened by walking paths, a fountain, and a bandstand, was completed two years later, in 1881. On its north side, the square was soon bordered by the new Sérail (also designed by Bishara Effendi, with the assistance of the chief municipal engineer, Yusuf Effendi Khayat), whose cornerstone was laid in a ceremony in June 1882. An interior garden, solemnized at its center by the seal of the sultan *(tughra),* illuminated at night and equipped with its own café, was dedicated with great fanfare in May 1884 in the presence of the city's leading citizens. Eight months later, in December, a still more formal ceremony, presided over by Hamdi Pasha, marked the building's completion.[20] After 1888 the Sérail housed the departments of the governor of the new province of Beirut, as well as the offices of the Mutasarrifate.[21]

The dividing up of land around Place Hamidiyyeh into individual plots and the scale of construction there were likewise meant to call attention to it as an important center of administration. Construction in the old town had been unregulated by municipal codes. The buildings bordering the square, on the other hand, were to be aligned and equal in height, creating a perspective terminated to the north by the Sérail. Together with the square's sultanic name, the Sérail's neoclassical lines and traditional ornamentation, which made it a fine example of Ottoman governmental architecture, conferred an imperial air on the informal space of the old Burj. Indeed, owing to the presence of both provincial and municipal officials in the Sérail itself, and of a police station on its eastern side, Place Hamidiyyeh embodied the revival of the system of direct rule,[22] while improving Istanbul's relations with the governed. In 1910, a wooden building in the Moorish style was erected in the middle of the garden to house the city council. Only seven years later, however, in 1917, the council was moved back to the Sérail, following the transfer of the seat of the vilayet to the barracks overlooking it, henceforth known as the Grand Sérail.

The official character of Place Hamidiyyeh did not prevent it from becoming the city's premier business center as well. In its northern part, along either side of the garden, companies of public and strategic interest established their headquarters: the port and railroad authorities, the municipal gas company, and the state tobacco board on the west side; the Ottoman Bank on the east. The square was livelier in its southern part, on account of the hotels, cafés, and casinos that surrounded it, to say nothing of the brothels lining a side street to the east.[23] A novel type of shop, with windows in front, attracted the curiosity of passersby with displays of merchandise whose appeal was itself recent; booksellers, pharmacists, and watchmakers were all quick to see the advantages of this form of advertising. The new Ra'd and Hani market, built at the southwest corner around a central gallery called the al-Hamidiyyeh Suq and graced with a fountain, further diversified the square's many urban functions by adding a theater and a community center.

Of all these, the bus depot probably did the most to bring new life to the area. Though it was now the heart of the city, the Burj (as the square was still commonly known) remained the gateway to it. Anticipating its future role after the invention of the automobile, it continued to be the final stop made by the caravans before they entered the old town. The omnibus lines that served the new neighborhoods of the city and the villages of the Mountain, and after 1907 the streetcar, departed from sidewalk platforms ranged more or less harmoniously on the south and east sides of the square. The two great intercity routes passed through there as well: the Damascus road—from which another road, to Sidon, branched out at the edge of the

FIGURE 28. An early view of the streetcar line on the south side of the Burj.

city—and the coast road to Tripoli. The construction in 1894 of Rue Nouvelle (the future Rue Weygand), between al-'Umari Mosque and Bāb Idris, improved access to the port, which until then had been provided by the municipal segment of the Damascus road alone, passing through Place Assour. Additionally, the new street eased the congestion of traffic headed toward the rapidly expanding western precincts of the city.

In the aftermath of the revolution of the Young Turks in 1908 and the overthrow of Abdülhamid II the following year, Place Hamidiyyeh was renamed Place de l'Union, and the garden at its center became the Jardin de Liberté. These names were short lived: with the end of the empire the square became Place des Martyrs, in memory of the Arab and Lebanese nationalists executed by the Ottoman government; and this name survives still today, even if the familiar Arabic toponym Sahat al-Burj has continued to be favored by popular use. Even so, despite the disappearance of imperial appellations and, more tangibly, of the garden that once embellished it, the layout and purposes of the square were until 1975 to conform for the most part to the vision of the urban planners of the Hamidian period.

This vision also governed the development of Place Assour (later Place Riad al-Sulh), the other great public space bordering the old enceinte. Mahmud Nāmi Bey's Rue Pavée, the barracks on the adjacent hill, and the Damascus road, which at that time passed through this square, combined to make it an important crossroads of

FIGURE 29. The clocktower designed by Yusuf Aftimos in the forecourt of the Ottoman barracks.

the metropolis, unavoidable for anyone traveling to the new neighborhoods in the west and southwest. In 1882 a suggestion was made to regularize its boundary lines and to create a central garden, but nothing came of the idea. Ten years later, a new plan was proposed by the city council, now presided over by Muhammad Effendi Bayhum, who wished to construct a building there to house the council. Once again nothing came of it, but the streets bordering the square were straightened out, and Rue Émir Bachir on the south side was widened. In the meantime the logic of the city's future development had already pointed to the importance of Place Assour, which soon was occupied on its perimeter by bus stops, businesses, a municipal pharmacy, and the main telegraph office. Despite the failure of two successive city council plans, the square nevertheless came to be recognized in a spectacular way with the erection at the end of the century of a fountain dedicated to Abdülhamid II. Notable for its use of Eastern elements, the monument was the work of Bishara Effendi's son-in-law, Yusuf Aftimos, who had been promoted to chief municipal engineer on his return from studying in the United States, where he discovered a neo-Moorish architecture well suited to the purpose of emphasizing the uniqueness of the Ottoman heritage.[24]

On the hill to the west of Place Assour, alongside the Qishla, an esplanade was laid out in the same spirit in the 1890s. A geometrically proportioned garden set between the barracks and the military hospital looked down upon the port and the old town, and the orientalizing style of the fountain in the square was echoed by a clocktower, due also to Yusuf Aftimos, the first constructed in an Arab city since the Tophane tower in Istanbul, built ten years earlier.[25] In a piece of supreme sophistication, the time was given in both the French and the Turkish manner, as though to acknowledge the city's hesitation between the time of the world, dominated by European expansion, and that of an empire that refused to die.

Completing the regeneration of the lower city, the district nearest the water profited from the joint effects of the expansion of the port and public (especially municipal) investment in infrastructure. To the northwest, the last quarter of the century saw the appearance of commercial streets running perpendicular to the line of the wharves and reserved for pedestrian customers of the modern suqs. Specializing in European luxury articles (silver, passementerie, hosiery, fabrics, and clothes), the shops of this area were distinguished from the old markets by their regular lines as well as their display windows and decorated signs. The first to open was the Suq al-Tawileh (Long Market), which stood where a cactus-lined path used to cut through the mulberry plantation at the northwest corner of the old wall, on the edge of the port. Still more fashionable was the Suq al-Jamil (Splendid Market), built in 1894, which the French orientalist and geographer Vital Cuinet described as "a group of shops, laid out one after the other, that sell only European goods."[26] The shop owners in this district materially benefited from the construction of a new street, Rue Nouvelle, along its east-west axis and, a little later, the improvements to sanitation undertaken by the city. Further to the west along this street the Wadi Abu Jamil neighborhood sprang up, home to the Jewish community following its departure from the intramural town. The northeastern part of the old quarter, by contrast, was slower to change. Expansion of the street network was delayed owing to the municipality's difficulties in acquiring land, and it was not until the First World War that the two great north-south avenues (Weygand and Foch) could finally be constructed. A plan for a monumental line of steps leading from the Sérail on Place Hamidiyyeh down to the port came to naught. Even so, the renovation of the wharves and the area around them exerted a modernizing influence on adjacent neighborhoods.

The harbor itself had managed to escape the city council's authority, but with the construction of the new port facilities, modernization quickly came to the water's edge. Public walkways extended the port's reach along the coast in both directions. The pier became a popular destination for strollers, and the wharves a place for pomp

No. 245. Beirut. Inauguration of Industrial School

FIGURE 30. Dedication of the École des Arts et Métiers in 1907.

and ceremony during military parades or the arrival of an important vessel. The new harbor was completed at the beginning of the new century with the opening of a seaside railroad station. In the meantime, four- and five-story buildings went up in response to the demand for office space from new businesses: banks, hotels, shipping agencies, cafés, restaurants. It was there, on the embankment of the old port, that the Orosdi-Bak department store chain, owned by a Jewish family from Iraq, erected its Beirut branch. Opened for business on 1 September 1900, the store was equipped with elevators, the first ones in the city, and adorned with bas-reliefs and moldings inspired by the European fashion of the period.[27] The Imperial Ottoman Bank constructed new offices in the same style in 1906, at the corner of the wharves, near the Antun Bey Inn, where it had first leased space more than forty years earlier, before moving in 1892 to Place Hamidiyyeh. Older, somber buildings such as the Customs House were given a more contemporary look with the addition of Marseille roof tiles and ogival arches on the façade.

In the majority of the city's neighborhoods the authorities did little more than assist the expansion that had already been set in motion by the economic growth of Beirut and its port. But in at least one case the city council intervened to bring forth from almost nothing a new district, known as Arts et Métiers (al-Sanāyiʿ, or Sanayeh in its French transcription), in the former suburb of Mazraʿat Yammin to the west of Qantari Hill and Wadi Abu-Jamil. The neighborhood took its name from the École des Arts et Métiers and from its adjacent garden, dedicated in 1907 by the provincial governor, which the city council directed to be laid out there along with a hospital, a police station *(karakol),* and a prison.[28] The neighborhood was served by a modern road, Rue Qantari, later extended to form the present-day Rue Hamra; but already in the late nineteenth century it helped to channel the city's westward thrust, spurred on further to the north by the hotels that had gone up along Minet al-Hosn Bay and by the campus of the Syrian Protestant College on the slopes of Ras Beirut.

ASPECTS OF MODERNITY

By the beginning of the twentieth century the center of Beirut had been dramatically reshaped. The very nature of city life had changed with the weakening of the residential component of the inner neighborhoods, new as well as old, and the creation of new public spaces on the edge of the old town. Increasingly modernity was reflected in all aspects of urban life.

This was an official modernity, brought into existence by the Ottoman state in the form of regularly laid out squares, widened streets, and government buildings, and reaffirmed by means of official ceremonies. Military victories, the traditional reason for public celebrations, were no longer available to the empire; but there were more than a few occasions to hold parades and declare holidays, which made it possible in turn, and in spite of all appearances to the contrary, to maintain an image of power and to indicate its extent.[29] Anniversaries of the sultan's reign, visits by European dignitaries, the arrival of high officials, and stopovers by foreign fleets were marked in the new spaces, notably around the port and in Place Hamidiyyeh.

It was an individuated modernity as well. For while the growth of the metropolitan area had not strained family ties, still less sectarian bonds, the city center furnished sites for the open display of a new kind of sociability—one that, far from imposing complete anonymity, lent itself to the assertion of personal identities. Stimulated during the day by commercial activity freed from the physical constraints of the old suqs, by the press of business in administrative offices and the bustle of travelers who filled the cafés and hotels, it was a sociability that also tamed the night through the growing number of recreational venues—restaurants and clubs, of course, but brothels (no less European in influence) as well. While taverns and cafés had to close at sunset, application could nonetheless be made for a special permit allowing the holder to stay open until midnight.[30]

A fresh approach to building further encouraged the free movement of the city's inhabitants. The new suqs that grew up at the periphery of the old urban core to the northwest and the southeast were wide and well ordered. While the lines of the old market were perpetuated through the use of vaults and fountains, and a dense pattern of construction preserved its intimacy, the regular plan and width of the streets accommodated visitors who came in the small horse-drawn carriages known

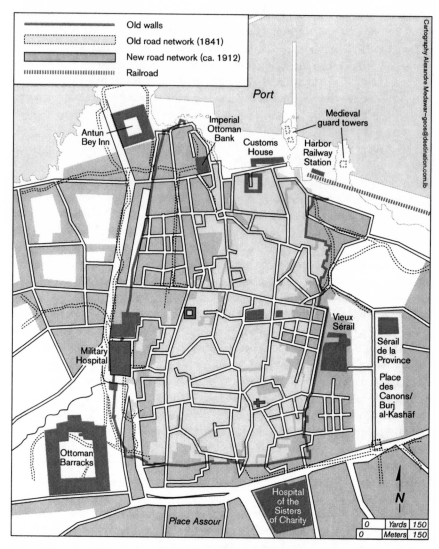

Old walls
Old road network (1841)
New road network (ca. 1912)
Railroad

Port

Imperial Ottoman Bank

Medieval guard towers

Antun Bey Inn

Customs House

Harbor Railway Station

Military Hospital

Vieux Sérail

Sérail de la Province

Place des Canons/ Burj al-Kashāf

Ottoman Barracks

N

Place Assour

Hospital of the Sisters of Charity

0   Yards   150
0   Meters   150

Cartography Alexandre Medawar-geos@destination.com.lb

MAP 6. Extramural Expansion I: Old and New Road Networks

as fiacres. By now, the new architecture had even reached the old town. Although the two north-south thoroughfares meant to relieve its congestion were slow to make their appearance, the development of a series of markets laid out at right angles to one another and dedicated to imported products cut through the labyrinth of narrow paths around the Vieux Sérail, near where the eastern wall once stood, and around the Greek Orthodox Cathedral of Saint George. Thus, for example, the Sursock

Suq, built on the very site of the Vieux Sérail and consisting of two rows of square shops, nonetheless managed to coexist with the old suqs around al-'Umari Mosque that specialized in local manufactures. A decisive feature of the new markets was that they left little or no room for living quarters, formerly an integral part of the commercial space of this district. With the increasingly strict separation of public and private spheres, and the growing emphasis placed on economic activities, the old town slowly but surely ceded its residential function to the old suburbs.

The demarcation between public and private had repercussions for the practice of religion, particularly in the case of the Christian population. The churches lining the old enceinte proved to be ever less capable of ministering to local needs, for want of parishioners, and increasingly came to serve a cathedral function, being enlarged and crowned with tile roofs. In addition to the two existing cathedrals, the Greek Orthodox Cathedral of Saint George, dedicated in 1767, and the Greek Catholic Cathedral of Saint Elijah, erected in 1849, a third was built by the Maronites across from the convent of the French Sisters of Charity. Also dedicated to Saint George, like the old church that it replaced, this monumental Italianate structure by Giuseppe Maggiori was dedicated in 1894 after ten years of construction. The religious monumentality of the city center was further accentuated by the imposing Saint-Louis-des-Capucins, designed by the French architect Édmond Duthoit in the Roman-Byzantine style, overlooking the old wall not far from the barracks. In conjunction with the government offices in Place Hamidiyyeh, the new commercial district around the harbor, and the flight to the suburbs of the old intramural population, this monumentality underscored the center's new status as the focal point of a metropolitan area that expanded beyond it a bit more every day.

What distinguished this new city center more than anything else was precisely the fact that it was a center. Whereas a few decades earlier the old town by itself constituted the entire metropolis (apart from a few embryonic suburbs and a handful of scattered villages), the expanded downtown area, although considerably larger than the intramural settlement, occupied only a limited portion of the land available for development. And here again, outside the center, the density of construction was rising.

By the beginning of the twentieth century, the relocation of residents from the old town was practically complete. Even so, there was constant movement within the limits of the modern city. The first suburbs, having been absorbed by the new business districts or, where they survived, having come to occupy a more central position within the metropolitan area, were now abandoned in their turn by the wealthiest families. The flow of immigrants continued as well, fed not only by the endemic economic difficulties of the Mountain but also by the appeal of urban life and by the opportunities that Beirut's growing prosperity opened up.

The old suburbs now formed a continuous band of settlement, and the villages

FIGURE 31. The Maronite cathedral, a sign of the new religious monumentality, dedicated in 1894.

on the periphery had been swallowed up, together with their farmland, by the expansion of the city. Even the steepest terrain, neglected in the first phase of urbanization, was now claimed by the construction boom. Beirut was still far from filling up the promontory, especially on its western slopes and near the sand dunes to the south. But on its two other sides, bounded by the sea to the north and the river to the east, it was beginning to approach its natural limits. Having outgrown the small square of land on which the city was founded and its initial outer ring of habitation, it now formed an oblong body lying along an east-west axis, and began to push ever further toward the western shore, hugging the coastline—a movement that was to exhaust itself only in the second half of the twentieth century.

To the east of the port, the expansion from the old suburb of Saifi gave rise to the neighborhood of Gemmayzeh, which, reaching almost to Place Hamidiyyeh on

FIGURE 32. The cliffs of Medawar, with new patrician residences in the background, ca. 1895.

one side and touching the cliffs of Medawar on the other, was to stimulate a line of building on the seafront in the direction of the river as far as the Rmayleh area. The spread of urbanization along the water favored in its turn the formation further inland of the Ashrafiyyeh neighborhood, around Saint Dimitri Hill. Profiting from the prestige conferred by the mansions of the new commercial aristocracy, notably on Rue Sursock, Ashrafiyyeh was linked to the center by the great Jesuit institution of higher learning, Université Saint-Joseph (USJ), founded in 1875, which enabled it to incorporate the now-forgotten suburb of Qirat.

To the west, settlement along the coast crept toward Ras Beirut, at the tip of the promontory, above which American missionaries had acquired a huge tract of land for the campus of the Syrian Protestant College (SPC). To the north and east of this, on Saint Andrew Bay, the former suburb of Minet al-Hosn now adjoined the new port; and the hotels that had sprung up around the Antun Bey Inn stretched toward the fishing village of Dar al-Mrayseh (later 'Ayn al-Mrayseh), with a publicly financed promenade leading to the lighthouse there. Under the influence of the neighboring university, 'Ayn al-Mrayseh gradually became urbanized; on the south side of the campus, the future Rue Bliss was to constitute the main axis of a

FIGURE 33. The seafront at Minet al-Hosn.

forward-looking and avowedly intellectual middle-class neighborhood that bore the name of the cape itself, Ras Beirut—an area that as late as the mid-nineteenth century has been poor and insalubrious.[31]

Linked with the city center by the new coastal development extending westward from the port along the corniche, Ras Beirut was connected to it also through Wadi Abu Jamil and the new Qantari neighborhood, the inland route followed by the streetcar line that came into service at the beginning of the century. It nevertheless remained isolated on its southern flank, still a remote outpost despite the steady advance of settlement outward from the center.

On the edge of Place Assour, near the corner of the old wall, Bashura had vigorously expanded toward Basta and, further to the southwest, Musaytbeh, itself linked to Zuqaq al-Blat, the neighborhood surrounding Rue Pavée. Between Basta, a Muslim neighborhood, and Musaytbeh, predominantly Christian, the village of Mazra'at al-'Arab became urbanized in its turn, anchoring the new southern rim of the metropolis under the simplified name of Mazra'a. The old suburb of Ghalghul, adjacent to Bashura and Place Assour, had expanded in the direction of Qirat and the confines of Ashrafiyyeh, and now climbed all the way up to the freshwater springs of Ras al-Nab',[32] an old village along the Damascus road.[33] The construction of a municipal promenade in the direction of the Pine Forest completed this expansion to the south for the time being.

Already, however, a new pocket of settlement was emerging around the Damascus road, before the first foothills leading up into the Mountain, where the village of Furn al-Shubbak (first referred to by that name in 1850)[34] began to assume the form of a suburb. Soon it led on to another such area, an outgrowth of the village of Shiyyah that came to be known as ʿAyn al-Rummaneh.[35]

GREEN AND ORANGE

As the metropolis continued to grow, the distinction between the public space of the city center and the private character of the outlying residential areas was mirrored by the contrast between urban and suburban landscapes. The discrepancy between the density of intramural construction and the spacious geography of the suburbs, still perceptible in the 1850s, had been considerably attenuated by the improvements made to the old town and its immediate environs, where the general use of Marseille tile and the triple-arched window gave an impression of unity. But the distinction between public and private still made itself felt, as a comparison of photographs from the beginning of the twentieth century clearly shows: the central business district, though now abandoned by its former inhabitants, is filled with bustling crowds, especially during the day, whereas the suburban scenes resemble still lifes. Indeed, the new residential neighborhoods were not meant to support a large population.

In all the old suburbs, and especially the three major areas that were to become Ras Beirut, Musaytbeh, and Ashrafiyyeh,[36] buildings were separated from one another by more or less large private gardens. At Jʿitawi, northeast of Ashrafiyyeh, the setting was still bucolic enough in the late nineteenth century to prompt the Jesuits to build a country retreat there (the occasion for the name of the present-day public garden, Jardin des Jésuites). The houses that were erected in these neighborhoods were all the more impressive in the countryside, even if they rarely exceeded three stories (though the ceilings, it is true, were more than fifteen feet high, in some cases almost twenty). The regular layout of the streets as well as the unified treatment of the façades, in addition to their shared ornamental details, nonetheless gave them an urban look.

The characteristic triple arcade, the origin of which is still disputed by architectural historians, was a response chiefly to the requirements of light and ventilation that flowed from the new philosophy of residential design. The concern for hygiene, which to a large extent had led to the abandonment of the intramural city, called for ample exposure to sunlight and adequate circulation of fresh air. But with the conversion of the *īwān* into a great covered hall, light and air could no longer come into the house through an open courtyard and the windows giving on to it; and the

FIGURE 34. Urban expansion in the foothills of Ashrafiyyeh, ca. 1870.

arrangement of the rooms around this central hall meant that additional sources of illumination and ventilation had to be created. The same concern for preventing the spread of disease also dictated that the kitchen and water closets be installed outside, apart from the main building.

Houses with private gardens and outward-facing windows had captured the fancy of the upper class during Beirut's first period of prosperity in the 1840s. As a result of the growing preoccupation with exterior detailing, which drew upon sources as different as the baroque, Moorish, and neo-Gothic, and with new forms of interior decoration that introduced marble columns, wall ornamentation, and painted ceilings to the city,[37] to say nothing of the furnishings themselves, often copied from the homes of the European aristocracy and sometimes purchased directly from its suppliers, the new style of domestic architecture was to give rise to veritable palaces as the century went on. Fine examples still stand today as monuments to the opulent taste of the foreign consuls and the aristocratic pretensions of the wealthiest commercial families, the Greek Orthodox Sursocks, Tuwaynis, and Bustros in Ashrafiyyeh, the Sunni Muslim Da'uqs in Ras Beirut, the Greek Catholic Pharaons in Zuqaq al-Blat, and so on. At the same time, however, the style became more widely affordable. Improved industrial technologies lowered the costs of wood paneling, wrought iron, and glasswork, and middle-class clients could choose from a variety of designs and sizes. But this did not threaten the growing unity of the extramural urban landscape,[38] still less since many public edifices in the city center and elsewhere, particularly police stations, were built in the same style.

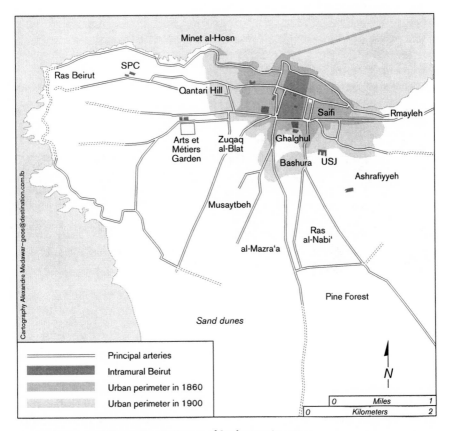

MAP 7. Extramural Expansion II: Extent of Settlement in 1900

The spread of this architecture, in both its domestic and institutional forms, lent an air of distinction to a metropolis that until then had few monumental landmarks apart from its cathedrals and mosques. These structures were themselves converted to the new style, like all the other buildings that came under the authority of the various religious communities. The many sectarian edifices constructed in the new neighborhoods—schools, boarding schools, hospitals, churches—adopted the familiar norms of contemporary Ottoman architecture, abandoning the vault for flat ceilings and making use of new materials such as Marseille tile. In addition to their distinctive roof treatment, the majority of these buildings—one thinks in particular of the Christian Collège de la Sagesse and the secondary school founded by the Islamic philanthropic society al-Maqāsid, the schools of Zahrat al-Ihsān (Flower of Charity), Sacré-Coeur, the Alliance Israélite, and the Hôpital Saint-Georges—bore the mark of the triple arcade on the façade of their central bay. A

51. Beyrouth — L'Université St-Joseph des R. P. Jésuites

FIGURE 35. The Jesuit Seminary, the main building of Université Saint-Joseph.

few great institutions founded by European and American missionaries, among them USJ and the Collège Notre-Dame-de-Nazareth, nonetheless departed from the new fashion.

The building in which the French Catholic Sisters of Nazareth established their school for girls on the hillside of Ashrafiyyeh is visible in most of the panoramic views of eastern Beirut at the beginning of the twentieth century. With its high crenellated walls, the structure seemed to have been imported directly from France. USJ, for its part, was modeled on the plan of European seminaries, creating an atmosphere of contemplative isolation that appeared to contradict Jesuit teaching and the belief that the order's priests must take an active part in the life of the city. The expansion of the university's original foundation was nevertheless to affect the course of development of the entire surrounding neighborhood, which lay at the point of contact between the city center and the rapidly growing residential quarters of Ashrafiyyeh.

A still greater influence on its immediate environment was exerted by the Syrian Protestant College, which transposed the image and ideals of the great American university campuses to the area of Ras Beirut. The very size of the site seemed to come from another world, by comparison with the cramped parcels that were customary in Beirut; indeed the land, acquired by American missionaries from its original Druze owners, was larger than the entire intramural town. In this vast green space, filled with many species of trees, a scattering of buildings reproduced the simplified Gothic of North American academic architecture. With its walking paths opening onto sea and mountain, it was probably the most beautiful site on the promontory, and at all events a place where the recent taste for panoramic views could be memorably satisfied. Just so, its spectacular situation on the northwestern slope of the headland neutralized whatever shock might have been felt on encountering such an unfamiliar style of architecture. Along with the Pine Forest, the other great lung of the metropolis, the American campus at once became a major landmark.

THE GROWTH OF INFRASTRUCTURE

Modern ideas in urban planning and architecture called for corresponding functional adaptations. Government at both the provincial and municipal levels had to manage an increasingly complex set of needs arising from the geographical expansion of the city, which meant that public services—lighting, water, telegraph, streetcar lines, paved roads, and so on—had to be provided on an ever-larger scale. Improving public health, a major issue for the city's nascent press during the age of reform in the mid-nineteenth century, required that measures be taken against the risk of epidemic disease. Here the municipality led the way by its insistence on vaccination programs and regular inspections of hospitals and cemeteries.

The most radical change in this connection was the establishment of a public water system. Until the 1870s, the city was supplied with water from Nahr Beirut by the ancient Roman aqueduct, in addition to a few local springs, and it was not uncommon to see water that had been transported to the city by donkey from the Mountain offered for sale. This arrangement was evidently inadequate to meet the needs of a growing population, and the municipal council in its earliest incarnation had already contemplated bringing water from Nahr al-Kalb (Dog River), some six miles to the north. But finances posed a problem, and as an interim solution two wells were sunk in the 1860s at Ras al-Nabʿ to supplement the principal spring there that had given its name to the area. It was only in 1875 that a scheme for bringing water from Nahr al-Kalb was put into effect, under the management of a British firm, the Beirut Waterworks Company, which three decades later, in 1909, gave way to a French enterprise, the Compagnie des Eaux de Beyrouth. With more than seven thousand subscribers in 1913, the company made a substantial profit for its stockholders.[39] It was nonetheless not until 1922 that the first water tower was built in the city.

A citywide network of public lighting was slow to be put in place as well, but once work began progress was steady. In 1879, a contract for supplying gas was awarded to the Ottoman Gas Company of Beirut, ushering in the general use of street lamps. Ten years later more than six hundred were in service. The advent of electricity soon required large-scale conversion, which the Société des Tramways et de l'Éclairage, founded in 1894 by French investors in alliance with local notables, stepped forward to undertake. Beginning in 1908, a streetcar system operated on four lines in Beirut, two years after Damascus and almost at the same moment as Istanbul; city lighting was fully converted to electricity by 1910. The gas company was less fortunate. Deprived of a public market like the one that existed for lighting, it had little success in attracting private customers. In that same year it counted only 158 subscribers.

Beyond the new needs that these various infrastructure projects sought to satisfy, the government was guided by an idea that was no less novel—quality of life, though it was not yet called that. Hence the importance attached to creating public gardens, which, in addition to reducing the unhealthy congestion of urban neighborhoods, were meant to furnish space for leisure activities. The same was true of the promenades that were laid out during this period, one in the direction of the lighthouse on the corniche, the other toward the Pine Forest.

Beirut, age-old city though it was, appeared at the height of these transformations to be a young city, one that had succeeded in pouring architectural styles from the northern shores of the Mediterranean together with the heritage of Islamic art into the mold of a modernity fashioned by Cairo and Istanbul. On the eve of the Great War, nothing seemed capable of slowing its rise, despite the common opinion that the end was finally drawing near for the Ottoman Empire, now largely drained of its strength by the maneuvering of the European powers as well as by the emergence of a Turkish supremacist nationalism. And if the city suffered in its port and central business district from the bombardment of the Italian fleet in 1912, the ensuing disruption (memorialized by a popular saying that placed all blame on the Italians)[40] was nonetheless overcome, and building resumed during the two years leading up to the war.

Nor did Turkey's entry into the war put an end to the interest shown by the local authorities in city planning. To the contrary, the provincial governor, Bakr Sami Bey, took advantage of the imposition of martial law to put into effect two plans in the old town that had been postponed owing to the opposition of small shopkeepers and the owners of communal property. Armed with the authorization of Jamal Pasha, commander of the Fourth Army and military governor of Syria, the wālī gave three days' notice to the tenants of the suqs who were blocking construction of two roads extending southward from the wharves, the future Rue Allenby and Rue Foch, each some twenty meters wide. On 8 April 1915, a solemn ceremony marked the beginning of demolitions. Three months later there arrived a new provincial governor, 'Azmi Bey, preceded by a flattering reputation acquired in Tripoli—where the main avenue of the city still bears his name. While a committee charged with settling terms of indemnification for the displaced tenants was being appointed, work continued. This led to the loss of a few monuments,[41] but also to the uncovering of the remains of a Byzantine church at the site of the Suq al-Bazirkān.[42]

ʿAzmi Bey went even so far as to study new projects, among them, it would appear, the Place de l'Étoile that was later built by the French. In the meantime the expansion of the war and an economic slump, which was to starve the people of both Beirut and the Mountain, interrupted a part of the work on the road system.[43] Construction of a casino in the Pine Forest was nonetheless completed in 1917. It was in this neo-Moorish building, which housed a movie theater in addition to gambling halls, that two years later the French high commissioner chose first to take up office and then, on 1 September 1920, to roll the dice in proclaiming the state of Greater Lebanon.

PART TWO

The Awakening

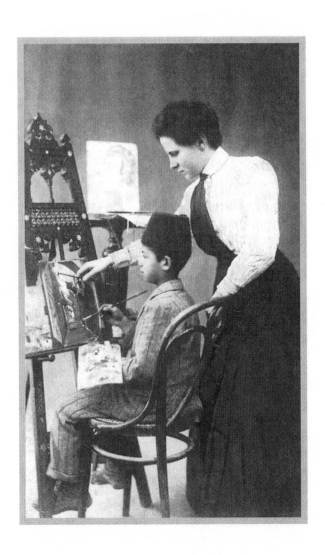

FIGURE 36 *(preceding page)*. Mustafa Farrukh learning to paint.

6

A Cultural Revolution

The evolution of the city during the middle decades of the nineteenth century is not measured solely by its geographic expansion. Lacking schools, newspapers, and any form of organized entertainment when Henri Guys lived there,[1] Beirut changed in atmosphere still more than in size. Forty years after the arrival of Ibrahim Pasha, the premier port of Syria was also a center of learning and intellectual activity. In addition to schools, which were increasingly numerous, and two universities, printing presses multiplied. Two newspapers flourished, and a growing number of books were published. Even theater had made its appearance by mid-century. Marun Naqqash, a merchant who had acquired a passion for the stage in the course of his travels in Italy, adapted and put on a performance of Molière's *The Miser* in his home with the aid of Italian refugees in 1848. Naqqash went on to compose two plays of his own, one of which was devoted to the legendary 'Abbasid caliph Harun al-Rashīd,[2] and in 1853 obtained imperial authorization to establish a proper theater next to his residence in a suburb of the city. Later another theater opened as part of the new Ra'd and Hani Suq. But more than these things it was the intellectual life of the period—marked by debates and controversies that were altogether unimaginable only a few years earlier—that made Beirut, after Cairo, a center of the cultural revolution known as al-Nahda that was sweeping through the Levant.

THE MAN OF AL-NAHDA

Was the leading figure of this "awakening" or "renaissance" a Christian or a Muslim? Even the small cemetery of Hazmiyyeh a few miles from the center of Beirut, where Ahmad Faris al-Shidyaq is buried, gives no clear answer to this question. But the very fact that it can still be posed tells us a great deal about the cultural upheaval that the Mashriq experienced in the period between the Lebanese author's birth in 1805 and his death in 1887.

In the long career of this emblematic figure of the Arab revival, Beirut had not been a major stopping place, and Shidyaq himself had witnessed none of the stages of the transformation that were to make the small town of the early nineteenth century one of the principal urban centers of the region. Yet it was Beirut that conferred posthumous recognition upon him, in the form of an imposing tomb, a privilege not enjoyed by other figures in this revolution who had made great contributions to the rise of the city; and it was in Beirut, the site of Shidyaq's last scandal, that the removal of his remains from Istanbul immediately aroused religious passions and divided one community from another. After sixty years of wandering between Cairo, Malta, Paris, London, Tunis, and Istanbul, Shidyaq regained his native land only in death—intensifying the paradoxes left behind by a passionate, unclassifiable man of letters: lexicographer and author of a monumental dictionary; a lover of Arabic who was eager to make it loved by as many readers as possible and who introduced a great many neologisms into the language; a Christian who translated the Bible for the benefit of Arab Protestants; a pioneering novelist who published an unashamedly erotic autobiography;[3] an advocate of education for women and inventor of an Arab version of socialism (al-Ishtirākiyya); a supporter of Ottomanism; and, above all, a convert to Islam.

Born to a Maronite family in 'Ashqut, in the Mountain, Faris al-Shidyaq converted to Protestantism as a young man after the example of his brother As'ad, whose excommunication from the church of his family and subsequent death in a prison cell in a Maronite monastery caused him to rebel in his turn (an episode that inspired Gibran Khalil Gibran's 1908 novel Spirits Rebellious). At the court of Muhammad 'Ali in Cairo he succeeded the Egyptian scholar Rifa'a al-Tahtawi as the editor of the first newspaper published in Arabic, Al-Waqā'i' al-Misriyya, while teaching Arabic to American missionaries, whom he then followed to Malta. From there he discovered Paris (during the revolution of 1848), London, and socialism, and eventually declared his acceptance of the Muslim faith (taking the first name Ahmad) in Tunis, as the guest of the local reformist government, before finishing out his life in Istanbul, where the sultan had granted him a pension. Successively Christian and Muslim, and perhaps at bottom neither one nor the other, in death he provided both communities in his homeland with a reason to quarrel, each wishing to take possession of his remains and bury them according to its own rites. In the end a compromise brought the two parties together at a funeral ceremony. It had been agreed to respect the wish Shidyaq had expressed in his will, that his body be buried in a small cemetery surmounted at its gate by a crescent, at Hazmiyyeh, between Beirut and Ba'abda, the chief town of the Mountain, where two of the Christian Ottoman governors of the Mutasarrifate had been laid to rest.[4]

The quarrel over Shidyaq's interment, and the final compromise that settled it, gave proof not only of the hegemonic pretensions of the competing religious authorities but also of their limits: the will of the individual had ultimately prevailed, no matter that sectarian protocol was obeyed on each side. The quarrel itself suggested, moreover, that greatness and fame could be attained independently of the community. For want of being able to reform society as a whole, the man who gave birth to the Nahda stamped it with the mark of his own existence instead.

AWAKENING TO THE WORLD

Faris al-Shidyaq received his early education at the Maronite seminary of ʿAyn Waraqa in the Mountain, founded in 1789. His brothers went there as well, Asʿad, a victim of torture at the hands of the patriarchate, and Tannus, a historian who left a valuable chronicle of the disturbances in Mount Lebanon, along with two other prominent figures of the Nahda, Nasif al-Yaziji (1800–1871) and Butrus al-Bustani (1819–83). Although the school's influence is unquestioned, its teaching by no means determined the future course of events. A long and uncertain interval separated the modest cultural revival of the eighteenth century, set in motion by the missionary activity of the Jesuits in the Uniate communities of the Levant, from the complete intellectual and social transformation represented by the Nahda. For ʿAyn Waraqa's most illustrious graduates, the awakening to the life of a wider world occurred after their time at school, in the course of their later professional and intellectual careers, owing to a succession of chance encounters and accidents of fate. Except in the case of Shidyaq, it was in Beirut that these events took place.

Nasif al-Yaziji began his career as personal secretary to Emir Haydar Shihab, and subsequently was taken into the service of Bashir II Shihab, the governor of the Mountain. But the turning point of his life came when he was almost forty. Following Bashir's ouster, he took up residence in Beirut and there came into contact with American missionaries. While teaching in their school he was called upon to make translations, particularly of the Bible, into Arabic; later he taught at the Syrian Protestant College. The author of many essays, among them a commentary on the great tenth-century Arab poet Mutanabbi, Yaziji's principal achievement was to help free Arabic from the formalism of classical models. This contribution was to be extended by his son Ibrahim al-Yaziji (1847–1906), himself a grammarian and teacher, who was also commissioned to translate the Bible, though by the Jesuits— an undertaking that occupied him for eight years, until 1880. But the greater variety of Ibrahim's interests, by comparison with those of his father, revealed how much had changed in the space of a generation. Apart from his linguistic work, particularly his dictionary of synonyms, and his translation of the Bible, Ibrahim al-Yaziji published studies in music, medicine, painting, and astronomy. His innovations included the first modern Gregorian calendar in Arabic and the creation of a sim-

FIGURE 37. Butrus al-Bustani ("the Master"), in a portrait
by Daoud Corm, ca. 1893.

plified font that reduced the number of Arabic characters from three hundred to
sixty, making it possible to reproduce Arabic texts using a recent mechanical invention, the typewriter. And if his poetry was still classical in its form, its patriotic
fervor and scathing exhortations signaled a still more radical change in the ideological atmosphere of the time, illustrated by the well-known verse "Awaken, O
Arabs, the mire has risen up to your knees."

Between the two Yazijis came Butrus al-Bustani, pioneer of Syrian Arab nationalism and encyclopedist of the Nahda. Immortalized by the nickname al-Muʿallim
(the Master), Bustani was himself a grammarian, lexicographer, and educator, but
he also worked as a journalist. As in the case of Nasif al-Yaziji, the turning point of
his life came when he was hired as an instructor in Arabic by the American mis-

sion in Beirut. Although Bustani likewise took part in the translation of the Bible, he cultivated highly secular interests, and despite having converted to Protestantism was able to preserve his freedom of action with regard to the missionaries. During the civil war of 1860 he translated Daniel Defoe's *Robinson Crusoe,* and then published a short-lived newspaper called *Nafīr Sūriyya* (The Clarion of Syria) between September 1860 and April 1861. Nine years later, in 1870, he launched the periodical journal *Al-Jinān* (The Garden), and after that the daily newspaper *Al-Janna* (Paradise), edited by his son Salim, and the weekly *Al-Junayna* (Little Paradise), edited by his nephew Sulayman, who later published a verse translation of the *Iliad* and served as a minister in Istanbul. In the meantime, in 1863, he had opened a secondary school with a comprehensive curriculum that, in addition to offering training in ancient and modern languages (Greek, Latin, Arabic, Turkish, French, and English), was meant to embody the spirit of good will and cooperation that he dedicated his life to advancing. The first secular institution of its kind in the East, it bore the patriotic name al-Madrasat al-Wataniyya (National School). Bustani's great work, after the dictionary *Muhīt al-Muhīt* (The Ocean of Oceans, 1867–70), was the six-volume encyclopedia published under the title *Dā'irat al-Mā'arif* (The Cycle of Knowledge) between 1870 and 1882, to which his heirs and successors, Salim and Sulayman, added five more volumes after his death. Nonetheless he has continued to be remembered for a single aphorism: "Religion belongs to God, the country to everyone"—words that appeared on the masthead of *Nafīr Sūriyya.*

Shidyaq and Bustani were both Maronite by birth. Nasif al-Yaziji belonged to a family divided between two communities, Greek Catholic and Greek Orthodox. The former was born in the 1720s of a schism within the Melkite Church, whose dissidents chose to ally themselves with Rome. Like many families, the Yazijis found themselves torn apart by this quarrel; Nasif himself came from the branch that had transferred its allegiance to the Greek Catholic Church. But the Nahda was not a movement that appealed only to Eastern Christians. Outside Egypt, where it originated, the Nahda managed to avoid particularism, and in Beirut it attracted literate men from all communities, Christian and Muslim alike, notably among them the Druze emir Muhammad Arslan and the Muslim shaykh Yusuf al-Asir. Arslan, appalled by the civil war of 1860, abandoned his post as administrator of the Druze district and settled in Beirut, devoting himself to literature; later he presided over the Syrian Scientific Society. Asir, for his part, had a major influence on the renewal of the Arabic language. Born in Sidon in 1815 and educated at al-Azhar in Cairo, he successively held the offices of judge in Tripoli, mufti in Acre, and public prosecutor of the Mutasarrifate, while devoting a large part of his time to writing. In addition to many poems, he was an author of a commentary on the new Ottoman legal code, and in 1875 assisted 'Abdul-Qadir Qabbani in founding *Thamarāt al-Funūn* (The Fruits of the Arts), a newspaper aimed at the Muslim elite of Beirut. Asir is also remembered, and not least of all, for his revision of the Arabic translation of the Protestant Bible.[5] This labor by a Muslim dignitary on behalf of a sacred Christian work is by itself perhaps the most striking evidence of the humanism of the Nahda.

HUMANISM AND PATRIOTISM

In the Arab perception of history and culture, the Nahda was at once an era and an attitude. In this respect it resembles the model it was meant to copy, the European Renaissance. It was an attitude because, despite the impasses to which Arab modernity were to lead, the Arabic word for a Renaissance man *(nahdawi)* preserves still today a meliorative sense comparable to the one enjoyed by "humanist" in the West. It was an era because the attempt to imitate European historiography was scarcely concealed: following the same tripartite division, rebirth came after an age of decadence that itself had succeeded a golden age.

Strictly speaking, this sequence does not agree with actual history—not only because, outside literature, the presumptive era of decadence coincided at least in part with another golden age, that of the Ottomans, whose glory was especially visible in the realm of architecture, a unifying force for the Arab world until the eve of the First World War; but also because, in both its content and its modes of expression, the Nahda was a product of the European Enlightenment and the ideals of the French Revolution, as well as of technological progress. Its effects were felt above all in their political aspect. This dimension, it must be said, was not wholly free of contradiction, either with regard to the first stirrings of individual identity or to the genesis of a collective awareness that brought about the rise of patriotism, or rather patriotisms: Egyptian patriotism in Cairo, under the influence of Rifaʿa al-Tahtawi, who gave the word *watan* (homeland) its modern sense;[6] Arab-Syrian patriotism in Beirut, with Bustani, who adapted Tahtawi's arguments to the situation in Bilād al-Shām (without, however, rejecting Ottoman citizenship);[7] and shortly thereafter, again in Beirut, Lebanese patriotism.

The Nahda was therefore not only a cultural renaissance but also a protonationalist awakening, comparable in some of its forms to the crystallization of modern Italian identity. And it is precisely because it resembled the *Risorgimento* of the nineteenth century no less than the *Rinascimento* of the fifteenth and sixteenth centuries that a nationalist reading of the history of Islam, in which the Golden Age, Decadence, and Renaissance involve only the Arab peoples, acquires a certain superficial plausibility. But the ferment of ideas represented by the Nahda cannot be confined to the Arab world alone; indeed, without considering the larger movement that in one way or another affected all the ethnic groups of the empire, not least the Turks themselves, it is unimaginable. The Arab nationalism that came later ignored the fact that it was in Istanbul that the desire for renewal and the urge to bring about an Enlightenment in the East manifested itself with the greatest vigor,[8] encouraging reform in the capital and mobilizing social elites in all the cities of the empire, even if here and there some measure of resistance was encountered. Thus Beirut, notwithstanding its enthusiastic embrace of the new thinking, had to deal with the problem of what it meant to be Ottoman, whereas Cairo under the khedives faced no such difficulty.

Historians continue to debate the causes of the Nahda, beginning with the psychological effects of Bonaparte's expedition to Egypt and the subsequent course of development in Arab Muslim lands. But the earliest signs of an awakening can be dated with precision: the founding in 1821, under Tahtawi's direction, of a publishing house in Bulaq, outside Cairo; Muhammad ʿAli's sponsorship of the first Arab scholarship students in France, in 1826, again under Tahtawi's supervision; and the publication by Tahtawi in 1832 of *Takhlīs al-ibriz fī talkhis Bāriz* (The Gold of Paris), an analytical description of Western morality and behavior. The Nahda came a little later to Beirut, in part because it was a consequence not of public initiative, as in Egypt, but of the concerted action of foreign missionaries and local elites. The first innovations in the cultural sphere testified to the primitive state of education and scholarship in what was then still a minor city: the Education Society (Jamʿiyyat al-tahdhīb), founded in 1845 in association with American missionaries; the Syrian Society of Arts and Sciences, created two years later, again with the encouragement of American missionaries, and with the purpose of providing a meeting place for members of all communities; and the Catholic Society, formed in 1849 by the Jesuits. Several years later they were joined by the Literary Authority (al-ʿUmda al-adabiyya), and then in 1857 by the Syrian Scientific Society (al-Jamʿiyya al-ʿilmiyya al-sūriyya), a branch of the Ottoman Scientific Society of Istanbul.

In the absence of institutions of higher learning, slow to develop in Beirut, these associations assisted the diffusion of knowledge in a wide range of fields while also helping to reform traditional ways of thinking. Their members communicated new scientific discoveries and sponsored lectures on historical and contemporary subjects—the advantages of commerce, the necessity of combating superstition, or even the condition of women (the subject of Bustani's talk "On the Education of Women," delivered before the Syrian Society of Arts and Sciences in 1849); in short, on any topic germane to the task of awakening society and helping it to overcome its backwardness. Sometimes frankly expressed in terms of a need to recover a lost faith in reason, the will to escape the hold of decadence was so urgently felt that strictly cultural concerns were seldom dissociated from political issues. The very idea of a renaissance was understood in relation to past greatness, and the notion of patriotism openly discussed; indeed some of these societies saw themselves as providing a forum for those who had begun to call themselves patriots. This was the case with the Literary Authority, initially created to popularize works in Arabic, and still more so with the Syrian Scientific Society, presided over by Muhammad Arslan and including among its members Ibrahim al-Yaziji, whose poems exhorted Arabs to liberate themselves from the control of the "foreigner"—the condition of regaining their past glory.

Even before it gave rise to political action, the interest in renewing Arabic literature and modernizing the language was associated with a frankly nationalist outlook. Thus Bustani made it clear that his *Muhīt al-Muhīt* was meant to be of service to the country, and Shidyaq acknowledged that he had compiled his own dictionary, *Al-Jāsūs 'ala'l-qāmūs* (1881), so that Arabic speakers might learn to love their language more. The selection of Western works for translation, without being based on merely utilitarian principles, was guided more by a passion for new ideas rather than by literary curiosity. The authors of the European Enlightenment were held in particular esteem, as they had been earlier by Turkish readers, and the encyclopedic spirit of Diderot and d'Alembert was carried on by Bustani in his *Dā'irat al-Ma'ārif*.

LINGUISTIC CHALLENGES

For the majority of the men of letters devoted to bringing about this renaissance, perhaps the most immediate challenge was to adapt their language to the new age in which they lived. Not only did the need to describe Western technologies lead to the creation of neologisms, but the confrontation with foreign ways of thinking made it necessary to purge the written language of the dross of outmoded classical forms. Whereas in Cairo—and in Istanbul—the encounter had come about as a result of sending students and diplomats to Europe, in Beirut it was a consequence of Christian missions coming there. Under the influence first of American Protestants, and then of French Jesuits, the translation of Judeo-Christian religious literature was to leave a profound mark on the modernization of Arabic.

Before institutions of higher learning could be established, the need to supply texts illustrating ecclesiastical doctrine led the missionaries at once to enlist the services of the young scholars who were to become prominent figures of the Nahda. At first fragmentary and concerned with popular works, this effort realized its full purpose with the translation of the Bible—or translations, as one should say, since three versions of the holy scriptures were completed within a quarter century. The first, published in 1857, came from abroad, by the hand of Shidyaq (living at the time in London) in collaboration with the Reverend Samuel Lee. Another translation was begun in Beirut in 1847, under the sponsorship of the American Protestants there, by the missionary Eli Smith, Bustani, and Nasif al-Yaziji. Smith was succeeded on his death in 1852 by Cornelius Van Dyck, and the definitive version, corrected by al-Asir, appeared in 1865. Finally, in 1880, Ibrahim al-Yaziji produced a third translation. Commissioned by the Jesuits, this last version represented not only a rejoinder to the work of the Protestants, but also the continuation of a linguistic quarrel that had raged for a number of years already, and whose fiercest protagonists were the translators themselves. The arguments made in the course of this long controversy were often quite technical, whether it was a question of comparing methods of textual analysis or of clarifying semantic relationships between terms in Arabic, Hebrew, Syriac (the liturgical language of a part of Eastern Christianity), and Greek. But something much more basic, and also more general, was at stake: the accessibility of the text. At bottom, this depended on finding a style that was suited both to the spirit of the times and to the genius of Arabic.

The controversy had begun with the appearance of the version by Shidyaq and Lee. Apart from canonical objections raised by Catholic scholars, the closeness of Shidyaq's language to that of the Qur'an aroused reservations; even his collaborator reproached him for it. With the appearance of the second translation, literary disagreements were aggravated by personal rivalries. The liveliest exchanges occurred between Shidyaq and Ibrahim al-Yaziji, who, in advance of bringing out his own version, sought to defend his father's contribution and the classical style that it attempted to reproduce. Shidyaq, for his part, considered the rhymed prose used by Nasif, known as *saj'*, to be a degenerate form of writing. The quarrel was in any case bound to go on once Bustani's magazine *Al-Jinān,* which first appeared five years after the completion of the Beirut Protestant Bible, took an interest in it. Displaying an admirable tolerance, the editor welcomed all opinions, not excluding Shidyaq's harsh criticisms of the translation to which Bustani had himself contributed. Shaykh Asir, though he had assisted in making the same translation, nonetheless sided with Shidyaq. The Maronite archbishop Yusuf al-Dibs likewise supported the London version, calling it the most precise translation of the holy scriptures to date. However this may be, there is no doubt that the new translations of the Bible jointly influenced a whole generation of Arab prose writers, notably among them Gibran Khalil Gibran.

Another linguistic challenge was posed by experimentation with new literary genres in Arabic: drama, introduced by Marun Naqqash; autobiography, which Shidyaq had pioneered while in Europe, and at which Mikhail Mishaqa had tried his hand in a book, published in Beirut in 1873, that retraced his family's history while laying stress on the role of the individual; and above all the novel, first adapted by Salim al-Bustani in *Al-Hiyām fī jinān al-Shām* (Love in the Gardens of Syria, 1870) and *Zenobia* (1871), and later popularized by Jirji Zaydān (1861–1914), a native of Beirut, in a series of historical tales published in Cairo and dedicated to rediscovering the Arab golden age.

But perhaps more than these nascent forms, indeed even more than the translation of sacred and profane texts, the engine of linguistic renewal was the appearance of a modern press that put neologisms, loan-words, and simplified stylistic formulas into general use—a tendency that was strengthened by the fact that news-

FIGURE 38. *Hadīqat
al-Akhbār,* Beirut's first
newspaper, published
in Arabic (shown here)
and French. Reproduced
by permission of
Dār an-Nahār.

papers, inspired by a sense of public service, explicitly espoused an ideology of progress. Here again, unlike in Egypt, where the initiative had come from the government (already under Bonaparte and then, more lastingly, with Muhammad 'Ali's *Moniteur égyptien*), the press in Syria was from the start an undertaking of enlightened entrepreneurs, typically men of letters enamored with progress the way businessmen are obsessed with profitability. Opinion nonetheless usually took precedence over information. The first paper launched in Beirut, by Khalil al-Khuri in 1858, was called *Hadīqat al-Akhbār* (The Garden of News); but other titles saw the mission of journalism as conveying a message, among them *Nafīr Sūriyya* (The Clarion of Syria), launched by Bustani after the events of 1860, and *Lisān al-Hāl* (The Mouthpiece), founded in 1877—to say nothing of the Jesuit weekly *Al-Bashīr*

FIGURE 39. *Lisān al-Hāl*,
a "political, commercial,
and literary newspaper"
(in the description of its
masthead).

(The Herald), which commenced publication in 1870. Still others betrayed a sensual delight in thinking that was itself revelatory of a progressive sensibility: not only the three titles published by Bustani and his son and nephew *(Al-Jīnan, Al-Janna,* and *Al-Junayna),* all deriving from the Arabic word for paradise, but also Qabbani's *Thamarāt al-Funūn.*[9] The preoccupation with transmitting a message was discernible also in the highly ideological treatment of news and information, which explicitly promoted the values of progress and civilization. The encyclopedia articles serialized in Bustani's *Al-Jīnan* and in *Al-Muqtataf,* founded by Ya'qub Sarruf and Faris Nimr in 1876, are perhaps the most notable examples of the new urge to inculcate modern ideas.

These newspapers and magazines depended not only on the dedication of a

FIGURE 40 A–B. Butrus
al-Bustani's magazine,
Al-Jinān, at left; at right
the newspaper edited by
his son Salim, *Al-Janna*.

group of educated men who saw them as the best means of diffusing knowledge, but also on the existence of a literate and growing audience. As the bearer of the spirit of rebirth, the press was also one of the fruits of its popular success. Moreover, in a city that itself was rapidly expanding, reading was no longer the prerogative of an elite. The number of potential subscribers, trained in school not only to read but, above all, to acquire knowledge and to listen to the opinions of others, was expanding as well.

Nothing better explains this enthusiastic and increasingly widespread support for renewal, which gradually became a normative value of social behavior, than the wide-ranging efforts made in the domain of education—the great concern of the Arab Nahda and indeed of the whole Ottoman nineteenth century, one of the most lasting sources for which was to be Beirut itself.

THE SCHOOL OF DIVERSITY

In Ottoman lands the educational system that was established in the nineteenth century was the result of three main directions of activity, more or less sustained, depending on the province, but everywhere mutually reinforcing: the official desire for reform and adaptation to new needs, the work of foreign missionaries, and, as a delayed consequence of these two things, the attempt by provincial elites to supply an alternative to foreign instruction.

Public initiative proceeded in the first instance by the creation of military schools, with the participation of French teachers and later the dispatch of educational missions to Europe after the example of Muhammad 'Ali's program in Egypt. A translation bureau had been set up in Istanbul that was to become one of the chief training grounds for the reformed administration; in the meantime French and Italian were taught in the new schools reserved for children of the military, which very quickly went beyond their primary vocation, training not only officers but also engineers, doctors, diplomats, and civil servants. The experiment was subsequently extended by the creation of a more clearly hierarchical system consisting of colleges (*rushdiyya*) and secondary schools (*sultaniyya*); the system's centerpiece was the prestigious Galatasaray Lisesi in Istanbul, which had trained viziers and court officials since the fifteenth century.[10] Having taken shape first in the imperial capital, this model was then transposed to provincial cities. It was nonetheless slow to reach Beirut, where the first public institution opened its doors during the Hamidian era in the neighborhood of Hawd al-Wilāya.

The need for official intervention was probably less pressing in Beirut, where private initiative had already shown its effectiveness. Under the leadership mainly of religious communities, a fairly extensive and quite diversified network of schools had been put in place by the late nineteenth century. In neighboring Mount Lebanon, the Maronite school of ʿAyn Waraqa had been the first, at the end of the eighteenth century, and another school, coming under the authority of the Greek Catholic Church, had opened at ʿAyn Traz, though without the same success. The Greek Orthodox Church followed, opening its first school in Beirut in 1836 with Russian financial assistance, and then a second in 1852.[11] It was nonetheless not until the economic rise of Beirut was well underway, after 1860, that more comprehensive institutions offering secondary (in addition to primary) instruction appeared. Although the first of these, Bustani's National School, operated independently of sectarian control, the others were associated with religious communities: the patriarchal school of the Greek Catholics, founded in 1865; the Madrasat al-Hikmah (School of Wisdom) of the Maronites, in 1874; the École des Trois-Docteurs (School of the Three Doctors) and the Zahrat al-Ihsān (Flower of Charity), a boarding school for girls, both Orthodox, in 1880. All these schools were meant chiefly for children of the sponsoring faiths. And although they accepted students from other communities, including Muslims, they perfectly reflected the revival during this period of the Eastern churches, perceptible throughout the empire as a consequence of the restored millet system, which favored European expansion and gave protection to missionary works. The Muslims, paradoxically, found themselves disadvantaged by comparison. To the extent that their religious institutions were part of the state apparatus, they tended to trust in official benevolence. After a time, however, the challenge posed by missionary activity, in combination with the efforts of the indigenous Christian communities, brought forth a response from Muslim social elites.

The principal reaction occurred in 1878, with the founding of the Jamʿiyyat al-Maqāsid al-khayriyya al-islamiyya (Society of Islamic Charitable Works), known as Maqāsid for short. The preamble of its first report plainly states the society's educational purpose. Noting the beneficial effect that the "sun of the sciences" had exerted on other communities, it declared its intention to make up for the time lost by failing to reform a primary school system that had been reduced to "a few deserted and foul rooms" under the stewardship of "blind shaykhs" who were unable to see the problems it faced.[12] The governmental network of *rushdiyya* schools and military academies, for all its undoubted virtues, was incapable of remedying them since it was closed to children who had not already received basic instruction.[13] Emphasis therefore had to be placed on elementary teaching that would allow Muslim children to go on to attend public secondary schools. But beyond meeting this immediate and pressing need, the founders of the Maqāsid were committed to a progressive philosophy that, in keeping with the spirit of the age, exalted the place of learning. From the outset great importance was attached to the education of girls, considered to be the "best means of diffusing knowledge" in the community.[14] The first step taken by the society was therefore to open a primary school for girls in the heart of the city, and then a few months later a second school in the nearby district of Bashura. Two other schools for boys followed in the same neighborhoods. In all 430 girls and 218 boys were enrolled in schools in the first year. Eighteen teachers, including eleven women, gave instruction in elementary reading, writing, grammar, and arithmetic in addition to classes in religion and morality.

The value assigned to elementary education was given additional weight with the opening in 1880 of another Muslim primary school called Dar al-Funūn. The Maqāsid's endeavors in this area were guided in the first place by ʿAbdul-Qadir Qabbani, a graduate of Bustani's National School and also a student of Asir,[15] and then by Hassan Muharram. The financial contributions and gifts of property in mortmain to the society, of which its first statement of activity supplied a long list, are proof that the scientific outlook of the founders had met with a warm response from the leading Muslim families of Beirut. The Ottoman provincial authorities took a great interest in this enterprise as well. Midhat Pasha, the governor of Syria (and former grand vizier), had personally encouraged the founding of the society, whose example was to be widely imitated. Soon there were Maqāsids in Sidon, Jerusalem, Aleppo, and Baalbek—all independent of one another.

As a spearhead of the reformist, indeed protonationalist, aspirations that were beginning to emerge in Beirut, the society attested the complex relations between Ottomanism and Arabism. Well before its influence as an incubator for advocates of decentralization came to be felt, the Maqāsid played a leading role in the famous poster affair of 1880–81, a memorable episode in the gathering challenge to Ottoman domination—here again, it would appear, with the implicit support of Midhat Pasha.[16] The Hamidian government seems not to have held this against him, however, and the society was able to devote itself to the development of an impressive educational network in Beirut, going on to establish more schools (including one for girls) early in the twentieth century. The local authorities, for their part, now began to pay greater attention to education. Both there and in Damascus, enrollment in public schools increased more rapidly than elsewhere—and this at a time when the Arab provinces as a whole were deliberately favored by Abdülhamid.[17]

However strong may have been official support for public education, and however great the success of schools founded by private means, these facts did not alter the image of a system dominated by foreign instruction, to the point that the history of Beirut in the nineteenth century seems almost to coincide with that of the Christian missions. In Syria as a whole, the expansion of European commerce had been accompanied from the beginning by the arrival of foreign missionaries. Certain congregations, particularly Franciscans, Dominicans, and Capuchins, had long been represented in the Holy Land, and in Mount Lebanon the Jesuits had established a mission in the seventeenth century that they were forced to abandon after the suppression of the Society of Jesus by Roman decree in 1773, returning almost sixty years later. But it was only with the rising power of the industrialized West that the pedagogical component of missionary activity began to find expression in an immense network of educational institutions, the densest such web in the world outside the European continent.

Stimulated by competition from Orthodox Russia and Protestant America, particularly in Beirut and Jerusalem, and strengthened by the protections historically granted to Eastern Christians, this movement was led mainly by French clerics or ones having links to France, and symbolized by the Jesuits, who returned in 1831 after the reinstatement of their order. Unmistakable evidence of their commitment came in 1843, when the superior general of the Jesuits confided the supervision and recruitment of the Syrian mission to the province of Lyon—a very active chapter, to be sure, but one that was distinguished in particular by the fact that it had its seat in the silk capital of France.[18] The schools founded by these Catholic missions were to play an important role in their turn, cultivating contacts with Europe and firmly laying claim to the allegiance of an increasingly large segment of the Western-educated population.

The later development of Beirut as the cosmopolitan capital of a country that was itself liberal and that imposed hardly any restrictions on freedom of teaching, at a time when the entire surrounding area embraced a strict regime colored with linguistic nationalism, is apt to give a misleading view of the history of education in the Levant in the nineteenth century. Not only did the Ottoman government take an active part in this immense undertaking, but Catholic and Protestant missionaries were allowed to carry on their work throughout Syria, and even the empire. In the last quarter of the century, slightly more than two hundred American missionary institutions were to be found in imperial lands together with several hundred schools run by Catholic missions and some fifty schools of the Universal Israelite Alliance.[19] By 1914, French institutions enrolled roughly ninety thousand students in all, mostly recruited from the Christian population of Syria, of course;

even so, Muslim pupils made up about a tenth of that number.[20] Beirut nonetheless occupied a special position by virtue of its status as a bridgehead of European economic expansion, and therefore a place where everyone wished to be represented. Hence the concentration of missions from all denominations and the appearance of institutions at all levels, among them two rival institutions of higher learning, the Syrian Protestant College, founded by American missionaries in 1866, and the Collège of the Jesuits, established nine years later and rededicated in 1881 as the Université Saint-Joseph. Together they consecrated the city's role as a capital of letters and a center of rebirth.

In the eighty years that separated Ibrahim Pasha's adventure from the First World War, practically every French congregation having an educational purpose in Syria set up an institution in Beirut: Lazarists, Jesuits, De La Salle Brothers, Marist Brothers, Holy Family, Sisters of Nazareth, Sisters of Besançon, Sisters of Saint-Joseph-de-l'Apparition, and so on. The Universal Israelite Alliance, likewise of French origin, opened a school for the city's Jewish community as well. And when the Mission Laïque Française, an overseas outpost of the school founded in 1902 under the Third Republic, established itself three years later in Syria, the Lycée de Beyrouth became its flagship. On the Anglo-American side there was less diversity. Whereas in Jerusalem several Protestant denominations were represented, in Beirut the presence of biblical scholars sponsored by the American Board of Commissioners for Foreign Missions, followed by Presbyterian missionaries, left little room for anyone else.

By a remarkable coincidence, the appearance of American biblicists in the Levant occurred at practically the same moment that the Jesuits were preparing to return following the reinstatement of the order, although in the event nine years separated their arrival in Beirut. The founding of their institutions of higher learning there a few decades later—again with a gap of nine years—suggests that the coincidence is explained chiefly by a spirit of competition. But the passing of more than four decades between the advent of these missions and the emergence of their most tangible and enduring embodiments also suggests that the reasons for such a protracted gestation period were less straightforward. The geopolitical instability associated with the Egyptian interlude, together with the acute social unrest in the Mountain between 1840 and 1860, whose repercussions were vividly felt in Beirut, and the indecision of the Ottoman authorities with regard to the treatment of foreign missions all contributed to the delay, as well as differing assessments of what the situation required on the part of the missionaries in the Levant and their governing bodies abroad, in both America and Rome.

Between Boston and Rome

At the beginning of the twenty-first century, two of the liveliest streets in Beirut still bore the names of Bliss and Monnot, respectively the founders in the second half of the nineteenth century of what became the American University of Beirut and Université Saint-Joseph. The homage these streets pay to them is itself a lesson in history—and in geography.

Other neighborhoods, some of them quite spread out, also take their names from educational institutions that opened their doors during the same period. Along with the Yasuiyyeh (Yasū'iyya, or Jesuit) district, which grew up around USJ, the neighborhood of Nazareth (Nasra) took root on the southwest side of Ashrafiyyeh Hill near the school founded by the Dames de Nazareth. On the other hill, Musaytbeh, the Patriarchal College of the Greek Catholics gave its name to the neighborhood of Batraqiyya. And in the center city, across from the southeast corner of the old enceinte, the residence of the Filles de la Charité left behind the toponym of 'Azariyyeh, or Lazarist, despite its replacement by an immense office building (though this belonged to the same congregation). There is also the medical district (Tibbiyyeh) around the buildings on Rue Damas where the Jesuit School of Medicine moved in 1913, as well as Zahrat al-Ihsān, from the name of the Orthodox girls school founded in 1880 in Ashrafiyyeh, and, in the same part of the city, al-Hikmah, after the Maronite School of Wisdom, founded six years earlier.

The coincidence of official toponymy in these instances with popular usage (not always the case in Beirut) not only reflects the debt owed to customary ways of speaking. It also confirms what photographs from the late nineteenth century reveal, namely, that along with places of worship, before hospitals appeared, educational institutions stood out as the principal monuments of the city—all the more in view of their increasing number. The modern evolution of Beirut, though it was set in motion by explosive economic growth in a political environment that favored it, also marched in step with the cultural revolution of the period.

FROM EVANGELIZATION TO EDUCATION

The American biblicists had set out for the East with proselytization in mind, especially of Jews and nominal but unobservant Christians, but without any precise plan, and certainly not one for a university. The delegation, appointed by a powerful Boston society, the American Board of Commissioners for Foreign Missions, saw itself initially as having an exploratory purpose.[1] The instructions that the two missionaries, Levi Parsons and Pliny Fisk, received before their departure, at a public ceremony in the Old South Church of Boston on 31 October 1819, called only for them to discover what good could be done for the local population and by what means. The geographical scope of the mission was just as vague: if Jerusalem and Palestine were given privileged status, the mandate of the American board also mentioned Egypt, Syria, Armenia, and other unspecified lands. The ministers' first destination was Smyrna, a cosmopolitan city and the only port in the region to be regularly served by the American merchant marine. There they soon learned that settling in Jerusalem was impossible because of informal agreements among the various churches and of the Ottoman prohibition against Westerners ("Franks") taking up permanent residence there.

Parsons nonetheless managed to spend the winter of 1821 in the Holy City, but because of the deteriorating state of his health, and then of his death the following year in Alexandria, this visit had no consequence. Fisk, finding himself alone, chose to abandon Smyrna, considered unsafe following the outbreak of the Greek Revolution, and withdrew to Malta, a British possession where an evangelical mission sent from London had been based since 1815. There he found another minister sent by the American board, Daniel Temple, who was equipped with a small printing press. The two of them were joined at the end of 1822 by Parsons's successor, Jonas King, and then by William Godell and Isaac Bird, who arrived with their wives in January 1823, filling out the American mission to the Holy Land. Malta was plainly incapable of satisfying their purpose, and Fisk set out once again. Finally reaching Jerusalem in the spring of that year, accompanied by King, he noted that in addition to the statutory difficulties facing them there, they had been preceded by a group of British clerics seeking permission to propagate Christianity among the Jews. He therefore resolved to try his luck in Mount Lebanon.

With its substantial Christian population this region may well have appeared as a chosen land, and Fisk moved at once to lease quarters, advancing his own funds, in the village of ʿAntura. As it happened, these premises had belonged to the Jesuits before the suppression of the Society of Jesus. Difficulties quickly arose, despite a rather friendly reception from the Maronite patriarch, who even invited the two Americans to dine with him. In the early fall of 1823, a conference of Protestants in ʿAntura attended by representatives of the two British missions to Malta and Jerusalem, in addition to the Americans, was perceived as a provocation. Emir Bashir Shihab, the governor of the Mountain, having been alerted by the patriarch, disregarded the remonstrations of the British consul and ordered the Protestants to leave. They were not discouraged, however. Resettled in Dayr al-Qamar, the former seat of the wālī, where he set about learning Arabic, King engaged in argument with Maronite priests in the area on points of Christian doctrine. In the meantime it was decided to strengthen the mission's resources. Godell and Bird, held in reserve in Malta since the beginning of the year, reached Beirut in November with instructions to establish a permanent presence there.

Although signs of the city's commercial promise were not yet in evidence, a port such as Beirut presented the advantage of furnishing the Protestants with protection from the resident British consul. In the eyes of the Ottomans, the Americans were subject to the privileges accorded the British under the millet system. This status permitted the biblicists finally to carry out their mission, not very far from the Holy Land, in a place where there were many lapsed Christians. Bird likewise took up the study of Arabic, and Godell of Armenian, and within a short time they had formed the first Protestant church in Syria. Their main evangelical purpose, the dissemination of sacred literature, quickly came to be combined with a commitment to teaching. They began by instructing a few young boys in the rudiments of Italian. In July 1824 these boys formed the first class of seven pupils at their residence in a suburb of Beirut, under the supervision of a native Christian teacher. In the fall the ministers were able to lease a house in the city, which allowed the school to enroll some fifty students, to the dismay of local churches.

Already before the launching of this initiative, the Maronite Church had taken up arms in response to appeals from Rome. In a letter of 31 January 1824, Cardinal della Somaglia, prefect of the Sacred Congregation of the Propagation of the Faith, warned the Apostolic Delegate and the Maronite patriarch against these "bandits of error and corruption."[2] Patriarch Hubaysh proceeded at once to hurl anathemas against the missionaries, whom he denounced as heretics and atheists, and to prohibit use of the Protestant edition of the Bible, on the ground that it excluded certain books held to be canonical since the Council of Trent. Faced with the school's immediate success, it was the turn of the Greek Orthodox patriarch of Alexandria to react. In 1825, Hierotheus I issued an encyclical against Protestant teaching. Not all his flock obeyed, however, for it was from the ranks of this community that Protestantism recruited the majority of its adherents in the Near East. The Maronite Church, on the other hand, succeeded in mounting an effective resistance to the biblicists by supplementing anathema with coercion, as in the case of Asʿad al-Shidyaq. Shidyaq had converted to Protestantism after having taught Arabic to Fisk and King, and then translated the polemical letter of farewell that King had composed before leaving the Levant.[3] Locked up in a prison cell by the patriarchate, in Qannubin, Shidyaq succumbed to privations and mistreatment after a few years.[4]

The American ministers did not give up the fight. In 1826 they received instructions from Boston to continue to seek converts and to enlarge the scope of their educational activity by establishing new schools and subsidizing the operating expenses of existing schools. That same year some three hundred students were enrolled in the mission's own school and the subsidized schools (with a double subvention being paid for girls). The growth of the mission was nonetheless interrupted two years later, in 1828, when the Russo-Ottoman war and rumors of possible intervention by Great Britain caused the Americans to retreat to Malta. Returning to Beirut in May 1830, they had almost to start all over again. Three years later they were running two schools, one for boys and the other for girls, but with a combined enrollment of only a dozen students. The arrival of Ibrahim Pasha strengthened the Americans' resolve, and it was decided to bring the printing press to Beirut from Malta. The press arrived in May 1834, but it took almost two years to be able to republish in Beirut four books that had already appeared in Malta. A new setback came in 1840 with the campaign of the Ottomans and their European allies against Ibrahim Pasha; this time the missionaries withdrew to Cyprus. The following year they came back with new assistants, among them Cornelius Van Dyck, a physician by training who at once took up the study of Arabic with Butrus al-Bustani, another recent convert. Later Van Dyck was to play a decisive role in founding the university. For the time being, however, the missionaries were obliged to moderate their educational ambitions. An envoy of the American board, sent to make an appraisal of progress in Syria, sternly reminded them that they were to give priority to preaching; and that if nonetheless it was necessary to operate schools, this was to be for the sole purpose of training preachers, not of educating the youth of the country. This reprimand seems to have achieved the intended result, for there were enough conversions to justify founding an indigenous Protestant church before the middle of the century.

Similar restrictions weighed upon the mission's growing publishing activity. Boston regularly insisted that Beirut was not to see itself primarily as a publishing center, and in fact secular production remained limited. Apart from work done for local authorities and commercial firms that helped to support the press financially, the small amount of profane literature produced in the two decades between 1834 and 1854 was meant for students: two textbooks of geography and algebra, composed in Arabic by Van Dyck; a book on arithmetic composed by another missionary, Eli Smith; and a manual of Arabic grammar by Nasif al-Yaziji. By contrast, the American mission produced an abundant literature for religious use, and the project of a new Arabic edition of the Bible, undertaken in 1847, occupied its three principal translators—Smith, Bustani, and Yaziji—for more than a decade. It was only in 1860 that Van Dyck, placed in charge of the project following Smith's death, was able to announce the completion of the New Testament. An integral edition, revised in the meantime by Asir, appeared in 1865.

The turning point for the American mission came at the beginning of the 1860s— paradoxically, a moment of crisis, indeed a dual crisis. Not only were the missionaries forced to quit Beirut a third time, following the outbreak of the civil war in Mount Lebanon, but on their return, in 1861, they had to confront the consequences of a still more dramatic conflict that divided the once united states of their homeland. Resources available to the mission became scarce, threatening permanently to interrupt its work, already hampered by Boston's determination to curb the missionaries' educational impulse. At the same time competition was becoming increasingly severe from Catholic missionaries, encouraged by French military intervention and the autonomous status conferred on Mount Lebanon, and from the Orthodox Church, which with Russia's support now found itself able to free up more financial resources for its own schools. Other Protestant associations had begun to operate in Beirut and the surrounding areas as well. Yet it was at this very moment, despite the American board's call to order, that the idea of a great educational institution was formed.

AN AMERICAN UNIVERSITY
FOR A EUROPEAN EDUCATION

As a direct result of the need to face up to competition from Christian missionaries of other denominations, the plan for an American college of higher learning was formulated at the urging of Daniel Bliss, who had been sent to Syria in 1856 by the American Board of Commissioners for Foreign Missions. The board's reaction was circumspect: while refusing to take responsibility for the projected college, and insisting that it be kept separate from the Syrian mission, the commissioners laid down very strict rules for its operation. To obtain their approval, it was necessary first to demonstrate that there existed a demand among the Arab population for European-style education. This was done, and permission was granted in January 1862.

As a practical matter, it meant that the ministers in Beirut were given the latitude to determine the ways and means of going forward with the project, so long as the general instructions of the board were respected. Things moved rather quickly at first. Having for a time contemplated attaching the college to a British institution, the members of the mission initially looked for support in England. In July 1862, however, it was decided to give the institution an American identity, while at the same time making Arabic the language of instruction. This made it necessary to launch a campaign for financing in the United States, despite the obstacles posed by the outbreak of civil war there, in addition to renewing the appeal for funds in Great Britain. Bliss therefore went to New York that fall to attend to the formalities of incorporation and to solicit donations. A board of trustees was appointed, consisting of four members from New York and two from Boston, and a charter was issued by the state of New York the following year. Another council of eighteen members, the board of managers, was set up in Beirut, bringing together all the missionaries in Syria and Egypt, the American consul, the British vice-consuls in Beirut and Damascus, and four local British merchants. Fund-raising proved to be difficult, not only in the United States but also in Great Britain, where Bliss, now officially the president, visited from September 1864 until February 1866, but progress was nonetheless made. In 1865 it was decided to incorporate Bustani's National School in the college as a preparatory section—a short-lived arrangement, though the college continued to be housed in adjacent buildings leased by Bustani. Finally, on 3 December 1866, the Syrian Protestant College opened its doors to sixteen students.

At the beginning there were three teachers, an American named David Dodge and two natives, Nasif al-Yaziji (for Arabic) and Asʿad Shadudi (for mathematics). The SPC rapidly grew in size, however, and after four years its enrollment had reached seventy. Already in the second year of its existence, the curriculum began to be significantly expanded. In addition to the literary department, which itself now offered a variety of subjects, not restricted to languages—Arabic, English, French, Turkish, natural sciences, physics, mathematics, and biblical studies—there was a medical department. Until then only two schools of medicine existed in the entire Near East, one in Istanbul and the other in Cairo. Opening another was therefore a bold undertaking for a city still as poorly equipped as Beirut, not least with regard to hospital facilities. In the meantime, until the SPC could provide itself with its own, a cooperative arrangement was concluded with the Johanniter, the German hospital that had just been opened by the Deaconesses of Kaiserswerth.[5] More problematic was the recognition of equivalences between medical diplomas, which until then could be issued only by the Imperial School of Medicine in Istanbul. In 1871 the Ottoman authorities made a limited concession, allowing Beirut graduates to be examined in the capital, with travel expenses being borne by the government. This arrangement was to last until the end of the century, despite the arguments for its revision brought by the American consul; but it raised another complication, this time of a linguistic nature, since the languages accepted at Istanbul were Turkish and French, whereas the medical students at the SPC took courses in Arabic, to begin with, and then English. It was only in 1903 that Istanbul agreed to send a jury to the American college, as it had been doing in the case of the school of medicine founded in Beirut by the Jesuits in the meantime.[6]

The Syrian Protestant College graduated its first class in 1870. Among its members was Yaʿqub Sarruf, who was immediately recruited to the faculty; later he became one of the great popularizers of the Nahda. That same year the mission to Syria passed from the control of the American board to that of the Board of Foreign Missions of the Presbyterian Church. The college, being independent of the mission from

FIGURE 41. College Hall, the first building on the campus of the Syrian Protestant College, with its clocktower.

the first, was unaffected by this change of authority. Furthermore, although the schools run by the mission continued to experience financial difficulties, the new parent body having proved to be no more generous in educational matters, the SPC could now count on its own fundraising resources. In March 1870 it acquired three immense parcels of land in a place called Tintas, covering almost the entire extent of the north face of the promontory of Ras Beirut, while managing to secure for itself an exemption from tax on the land, which had been granted in mortmain, or perpetuity *(waqf)*, through the intercession of a local notable by the name of Mikhail Gharzuzi. To finance construction, Bliss made another fundraising trip to the United States and England, and three years later the college moved into new buildings.

Now housed on a spacious, verdant campus that served to anchor urban expansion west of the old town, dominated by a tall clocktower and the cupola of the observatory, from which Reverend Van Dyck sent reports twice a day to Istanbul by telegraph,[7] the Syrian Protestant College was poised to become one of the great and enduring landmarks of Beirut. And yet its operations had not yet attained the stability that the grandeur of its facilities seemed to suggest. This was to be achieved only as a consequence of an internal crisis that cost it a bit of its soul—a crisis involving the college's official language of instruction, which led on at once to the question of academic freedom and the relations between Americans and the native population.

DARWIN AND ARABIC

In designing a curriculum, the SPC unambiguously stated that the language of instruction was to be Arabic. This choice was in keeping with the spirit of the missionaries themselves, who as soon as they arrived in Beirut had begun learning the language of the country. But in 1869 a first note of hesitation was sounded by President Bliss, who, while noting the absence of reference works in that language, expressed the concern that local teachers lacked the training to teach advanced courses in the literary department. Not long afterward the college took the unprecedented step of bringing over from the United States two teachers who did not speak Arabic, one a minister and graduate of Harvard Medical School, hired to teach chemistry, the other a graduate of Amherst College, to teach history. The matter of the language of instruction was explicitly discussed at a meeting of the board of trustees in New York in 1875, in the presence of Bliss and David Dodge. On that occasion it was decided to make the learning of English obligatory for all students. Three years later Bliss recommended a "radical" change of approach, and teaching in English was authorized "in a certain measure" for a few subjects.

Arabic ceased to be the recognized language of instruction during the 1879–80 school year. The college then numbered thirty-three students in the literary department and thirty-seven in the medical department. But the transition to English as the sole teaching language met with resistance. Not that the students or native instructors had any say in the matter: with the exception of John Wortabet, son of the mission's first Armenian convert and trained in medicine in England, none of the local teachers—only five in number—held the title of professor. The protest came instead from the heads of the mission itself, who made it clear that they would not have closed their seminary in the village of ʿAbayh if they had known of the board's views in the matter, and that in any case this change was contrary to the intentions of the college's founders. Dissent was also expressed in the professorial ranks, and Arabic managed to survive for a certain time.

Curiously, the liveliest opposition came from the medical department, whereas adoption of English was more readily accepted in the literary department. The reason is that the American Arabic speakers, such as Van Dyck and George Post, in addition to Wortabet, were in the medical faculty and had access to the standard works in Arabic, published in Egypt since the 1820s, as well as to manuals that they themselves had written. In 1881 they managed to delay the introduction of English, but their success was brief. Arabic lost its advantage once and for all in the wake of a new and wholly unrelated dispute that shook the SPC the next year following the death of Charles Darwin.

At the college's graduation ceremony in July 1882 the speaker for the occasion, a professor of chemistry named Edwin Lewis—a physician by training and a minister by profession (though not a member of the mission—and poorly regarded because he served wine at dinner)[8]—shocked the audience by speaking favorably of Darwin's theory of evolution. Controversy was already in the air since the monthly journal *Al-Muqtataf*, edited by two of Lewis's colleagues, Sarruf and Faris Nimr, had announced Darwin's death in its May issue, saluting the memory of "the most learned and illustrious man of his time." The next issue carried an editorial in praise of Darwin, and the July issue another on Darwinism. In August, *Al-Muqtataf* gave new impetus to the controversy by publishing the text of Lewis's speech. In the face of these attempts to promote evolutionism, the board of trustees reacted vigorously, demanding Lewis's resignation, which was submitted and accepted at once. But the crisis had only just begun. In protest against Lewis's dismissal, the students refused to sing hymns and boycotted classes. Forty of them also signed a formal letter of protest, which led to their being suspended for a month. They would be readmitted, the college administration made it clear, only on the condition that they withdrew their signatures—a step that led in its turn to the resignation of Reverend Van Dyke, one of the college's founders, and of all the other professors in the medical department with the exception of Post, the instigator of the campaign against Lewis. The dissident faculty then proceeded to form a short-lived school of their own in order to complete the training of the suspended students, giving lectures in their homes and at the recently founded Greek Orthodox Saint George Hospital.[9] On campus the crisis died down only gradually, and unrest persisted throughout the 1882–83 school year; a few of those who had been accepted back to the college were roughed up by their fellow students. Finally the board in New York decided to entirely rebuild the medical department by recruiting new American instructors. What is more, an oath of theological allegiance was now required of all faculty members. Sarruf and Nimr, though they had received favorable evaluations prior to the outbreak of the affair, and even a promise of promotion, were relieved of their duties at the end of the 1883–84 year. They then left Beirut for Cairo, where *Al-Muqtataf* was henceforth published.[10]

The Darwin controversy bore no relation to the dispute over English as the language of instruction. Edwin Lewis, the lightning rod for the scandal, was not himself an Arabic speaker; indeed, he had been one of the two first non-Arabophone teachers recruited in 1870. Conversely, his chief critic, George Post, had been among those who argued in favor of the linguistic status quo in the school of medicine. None of this prevented Arabic from being one of the victims of the quarrel, however. The medical department having been reconstituted with new American professors, there was no longer anyone capable of teaching in this language, and English prevailed by default.

Calm was eventually restored, and the SPC soon became a center of attraction for elites throughout the region. Nevertheless the period of crisis was not without repercussions, as the articles that Sarruf and Nimr devoted to their alma mater after the transfer of *Al-Muqtataf* to Cairo demonstrated. Bitterness lingered long afterward. Awarded the college's first honorary doctorates in 1890, Sarruf and Nimr refused to come to Beirut to accept them or otherwise to acknowledge its belated gesture of conciliation. A century later passions had not yet entirely cooled, and continued to color even the most balanced accounts of this episode by historians of the American University of Beirut, as it is now known. In combination with the ouster of Sarruf and Nimr, the imposition of English conferred on the missionaries' work a paternalistic character that until then had not been present—all the more since, as a practical matter, the possibility of hiring American and English instructors without regard for linguistic qualifications limited job opportunities for native graduates, denying them the chance of tenured participation in directing the affairs of the college.[11]

Outside the campus the two affairs had significant consequences, however, if not for the development of the Nahda, then at least for the role that Beirut was to play in it. Although linguistic cosmopolitanism—a dominant feature of both Beirut and Lebanon in the twentieth century—won out in the end, the marginalization of Arabic ran contrary to the growing emphasis on linguistic and cultural regeneration in the Arab world. And the assault on academic freedom revealed that Western educational institutions were not in and of themselves synonymous with emancipation. The Egyptian exile of Sarruf and Nimr is instructive in this regard. Notwithstanding that both were linked to the nascent movement of Syrian patriotism, it was because of *imported* religious prejudices that they were forced to leave Beirut, and not as a result of Hamidian absolutism, which at the same moment was driving intellectuals away from Syria into Egypt. Indeed, Ottoman provincial authorities were willing to exempt *Al-Muqtataf* from the general ban that fell upon all printed materials coming from Egypt.

It was a sign of the limits that Beirut had run up against that Cairo was to be chiefly responsible for the diffusion of Darwin's ideas in the Arab world, under the influence of another SPC alumnus, Shibli al-Shumayyil, who had pursued graduate studies in Europe after finishing his medical studies there. Although Shumayyil's articles and translations, published for the most part in *Al-Muqtataf*, aroused hostile reactions in Egypt itself, it was in Beirut that they drew the harshest attacks. This time, however, the most spirited riposte came not from the Protestant missionaries, but from the journal *Al-Bashīr*, published by their Jesuit rivals.

DOING GOOD AND DOING WELL

The experience of the Jesuits following their return to the East presents curious similarities to that of the American biblicists. Both attached the same primacy to preaching, and displayed the same disagreements between missionaries and superiors, the same hesitations in the pursuit of their mission, the same approach to teaching, and, above all, the same assessment of the local demand for education. "These provinces," noted the authors of a proposal for founding a great Jesuit college in Asia, in 1838, "will be at the disposal of whomever is the first to take charge of the education of their young people."[12] Yet in neither case was a plan settled upon far in advance.

The Society of Jesus, suppressed by Rome in 1773, had been reestablished in 1814. But the Levant, where it had been present since the seventeenth century, was not uppermost among its concerns. A petition addressed to the pope in 1816 by the heads of the Uniate churches, asking to be granted the assistance of Jesuit priests, came to nothing. Another fifteen years passed before a return to the region was contemplated. The occasion presented itself in November 1831, when two missionaries, Fathers Riccadonna and Planchet, arrived in Beirut, accompanied by Monsignor Mazlum, a prelate of the Greek Catholic Church who, after a long stay in Rome, volunteered to reopen the school in ʿAyn Traz. Despite the Society's good reputation among the Uniates, the mistrust with which it was regarded by the July Monarchy in France made it impossible to consider establishing a mission on a substantial basis, and the Church of the Gesù seemed resigned to keeping a low profile in the East. The Lazarists, favored by Guizot, therefore found themselves in a position to take over the old properties of the Jesuits in ʿAntura without resistance. At no moment did Fathers Riccadonna and Planchet seek to assert the prior claims of the Society; indeed, in agreement with the superior general, Father Jan Roothaan, they considered withdrawing from ʿAyn Traz, where collaboration with Monsignor Mazlum had proved to be disappointing. In 1836 they argued in favor of relocating to Beirut, which in their view had become the chief port in the Levant, and in any case home to an increasing number of Europeans and native Christians. Rome did not concur. An enlarged Syrian mission was directed instead to establish residences at Maʿallaqa, near the town of Zahleh in the Biqaʿ Valley, and at Bikfaya, in Mount Lebanon. In the meantime an expedition to Chaldea led by Father Planchet suggested the order's growing geographical ambitions.

The mission had therefore just entered into a phase of expansion when the idea arose, in 1836, of founding a great college in Asia. For this task the Congregation of Faith called upon the Jesuits, and the brilliant Polish-born missionary Maximilian Ryllo, who seemed to be promised a fine career, was sent out to the Levant. In 1838, following a tour of inspection that took him as far as Chaldea, Father Ryllo drew up plans for a Gregorian seminary. For a time he considered establishing it in Mosul, but unrest in this region led Rome to prefer a location that benefited from the protection of European consuls. Beirut enjoyed a certain advantage in this regard, and Ryllo, having meanwhile become superior of the Syrian mission, undertook to bring the Séminaire Grégorien d'Asie (also called the Collège Central Asiatique) into existence there. At this point, however, the escalation of the Turkish-Egyptian crisis blocked the way forward.

In the course of these events Ryllo found himself accused of being too close to the Ottomans and of having taken part in the political maneuvering that accompanied the campaign directed by the British against Ibrahim Pasha, thus arousing the displeasure of France and forcing Rome to assign him to other duties outside the Levant. In the interval, however, Ryllo had time to concern himself with the site on which the college and residence of the Jesuits was to be built. The Ottoman authorities, having resumed their control over Syria, even offered a large parcel of land on the edge of the old enceinte that appears to have roughly coincided with the esplanade formed by the Burj. One may well wonder what direction the development of Beirut might have taken if, in what was to become a central public space of the modern city, buildings had been constructed—and, what is more, buildings under foreign protection. Ryllo declined the offer, and instead purchased land nearby, in the vicinity of the Apostolic Delegation. In November 1841, while still under construction, the new residence became home to the first "public schools" in Beirut. This term, used in the plural in the Jesuits' correspondence, is misleading; in fact, it referred to a single primary school, with several grades.[13] The projected college never came to pass.

Exasperated by the partiality for which it rebuked Ryllo, and in any case distrustful of the Jesuits, France intended to leave it to the Lazarists to carry out the Roman scheme for higher education. Furthermore, it agreed to assist in the creation of the Central Asian College only if this were to be established in Aleppo. The Jesuits saw this as nothing more than a maneuver designed to ruin their plans in the Levant. "Aleppo is three days from the sea and in the middle of a desert," Father Planchet (Ryllo's replacement as superior) wrote to Father Roothaan in September 1842, pointing out that the Jesuits could not leave Beirut "without almost destroying" their position in Syria.[14] In another letter, this one to Lamartine, whose help he sought, Planchet emphasized that although Aleppo was a more "considerable" place, Beirut offered better prospects for such an institution, not least because of the greater ease of communication there and the promise of European protection.[15] This protection was not always to be had, however, on account of quarrels among the European powers; and on various occasions the Ottoman authorities intervened to stop construction undertaken by the Jesuits without a firman having first been obtained. In the meantime, the Gesù looked for other solutions. While refusing to abandon the residence in Beirut, as France demanded, it momentarily considered the possibility of establishing the college in Sidon. Consideration was then given to Bikfaya, where the fathers already had a residence and a school.

In Mount Lebanon, local custom made it possible to dispense with the need for a firman. But administrative delays in Istanbul and indecision on the part of Rome combined to hold up the project, and another option began to be investigated, in Ghazir, a village in Kisrawan, where a local notable offered to sell his estate to the fathers. Planchet continued to favor Bikfaya, however. Yet Ghazir, though it was not very far away from the Lazarist institution in 'Antura, suddenly prevailed owing to an accidental hiatus in communications in July 1843 ("the difference of one mail steamer," as the superior later put it). Acting on his own authority, albeit with the encouragement of the apostolic delegate, Planchet effectively created a fait accompli by agreeing to the terms of sale. "Fiat voluntas!" exclaimed the superior general.[16] The opening of the seminary in Ghazir had nonetheless to wait three years, in the first instance because of financial difficulties and the reverberations of international politics in Rome, and then because of the pillage of the new residence during the sectarian fighting that broke out in Mount Lebanon in 1845.

The haste with which Ghazir was decided upon and, more generally, the fevered tone of the epistolary discussions surrounding the plan to found a college suggest the sense of urgency that the fathers must have felt—as if the future of their presence in the Levant depended on the fate of their educational initiative. Yet education was not the first priority in the eyes of the Jesuit hierarchy, as the frequent (and often pointed) criticisms delivered by the superior general make clear. More than once Father Roothaan reprimanded his subjects for having let teaching divert them from their primary task, namely, to do "good" and to conduct communions, as well as "holy exercises," whose regular observance was a recurrent theme in official correspondence. But the Gesù was nonetheless intent on expanding the mission in Syria. If the superior general sent additional missionaries only sparingly, noting that the needs of the Society in the Americas took precedence, he did not hesitate to make funds available as the need arose; and though he found it necessary to curb the enthusiasm of his representatives, by and large he subscribed to the educational orientation that they sought to establish. So great was the local demand for European instruction, impressed upon him by a constant stream of letters and reports, that Father Roothaan came to share their view of education as the lever of every missionary work. What is more, the growing competition from the American biblicists and the success of the school founded in 1836 in Beirut by the Orthodox schismatics argued against procrastinating any longer.

In the face of persistent opposition from the French government,[17] which for a time had succeeded in dissuading Rome from expanding the Jesuits' settlement in the Levant, and particularly in Beirut, the superior general decided in October 1843 to entrust responsibility for the Syrian mission to the province of Lyon, which as a consequence of official favor was one of the most active and wealthiest in France.[18] From that point onward, Catholic teaching in the Levant was to have a French face, even if clerics of other nationalities took part in shaping it. The transformation was still more tangible with the spread of the French language. A letter from the native head of the Société Catholique de Beyrouth to the Société Asiatique de Paris reported in October 1849 that instruction in the language had recently become available thanks to the schools of the Lazarists in 'Antura and of the Jesuits in Beirut: "As a result, our generation is the first, among those who have gone into business, to find itself knowing French."[19]

For the Jesuits, the progressive adoption of French was by no means a foregone conclusion, even after responsibility for the mission had been entrusted to Lyon. In the event it was not a question—not yet—of having to choose between Arabic and French. Faithful to the Society's tradition of enculturation, and in any case resolved to work as effectively as possible, the first fathers had all begun to learn Arabic, like the American missionaries. Such competition as there was came from Italian, already spoken in commercial circles, and which the Jesuits, accustomed to receiving orders from the General Curia in Rome, had naturally enough included in the curriculum of their schools. But the teaching of Italian did not have time to establish itself in the way that French, as the chosen language of the native modernists, both within the entourage of Ibrahim Pasha and in Ottoman governmental circles, had already succeeded in doing. Moreover, it presented the advantage, in the eyes of the Uniate Christians, of being associated with a protective power at precisely the moment when the idea of protection had ceased to be abstract. With the increased speed of communications due to the advent of steamships, the active diplomacy first of the July Monarchy, and then of the Second Empire, had made French influence a daily fact of life. The decision to confide the Syrian mission to the province of Lyon came from that. Yet in a letter written during the fall of 1846, Father Planchet, himself a Frenchman, spoke of the "danger" he found in the French language, "because of its newspapers, its bad books, etc."; the apostolic delegate, for his part, in a report to the Sacred Congregation, denounced the "ill effects" that it had produced in the country.[20] The pragmatic Italian, Riccadonna, argued by contrast in favor of French being taught at the college in Ghazir.[21] A solution had to be found—and French had the "privilege of popular and administrative favor," as a report of December 1855 noted.[22] This was the turning point, which was lastingly to confirm the Francophone image of Beirut and Lebanon (though it was not yet, of course, talked about in these terms) in the twentieth century—and, incidentally, to diminish the appeal of enculturation to the Jesuits, many of whom no longer felt the need to learn Arabic.

THE CALL OF THE CITY

The establishment of the college in Ghazir and the geographic expansion of the Syrian mission did not divert the Jesuits' attention from Beirut. Despite the impossibility of setting up a base of operations there in the near future, the continuing economic boom since the Jesuits' return caused it to become the mission's center of gravity. In 1859, in reply to queries from the hierarchy in Rome as to where the superior's residence should be located, Father Estève (the current incumbent) argued that the answer could not be in doubt: it was "naturally" Beirut.[23] Even though the flagship institution was in Ghazir, the Jesuits' settlement in Beirut had been con-

FIGURE 42. A teacher's
notebook at the Lazarist
college.

siderably expanded, first of all in physical terms. The fathers' residence, built on the
land acquired by Father Ryllo in 1840, occupied a substantial part of the suburban
area that was taking shape outside the city's walls; indeed a whole Jesuit neighborhood sprang up to the east of the Burj, where the church and its outbuildings were
connected to one another by a network of paths and alleyways. The priests' occupations had also been diversified. Communions and spiritual exercises, though regularly reported in letters and diaries, were by no means enough to take up all of
their time. Teaching remained their preferred activity, and in addition to the primary school on the grounds of their new compound another soon opened in Ras
Beirut.

Nor did the Jesuits limit themselves to conducting their own classes. In association with the apostolic delegate, they seem to have played an unofficial role in coordinating Catholic missionary works, calling upon (or urging Rome to call upon)
other congregations to respond to the growing educational needs of the region. In
Beirut, in particular, these needs were thrown into relief by the works of American
and Prussian Protestants and of the Orthodox Church, which opened a second
school in 1852, again funded by Russia. With the exception of the Messieurs de

Saint-Lazare, now firmly established in ʿAntura, and their female counterpart, the Filles de la Charité, who had been operating in Beirut since 1848, the settlement of Catholic congregations resulted from cooperative efforts by Rome in which the Jesuits played a more or less great role. Among these were the Soeurs de Saint-Joseph-de-l'Apparition, who took up residence in Beirut for a short time in 1847, at the request of the apostolic delegate and on the suggestion of the Jesuits, and then permanently twenty-five years later, in 1872, a school in Aleppo having been founded in the meantime;[24] also the Dames de Nazareth, brought to Beirut in 1869 to counterbalance the influence of the Prussian Deaconesses, who operated a flourishing boarding school for girls from the upper class with which the French Sisters of Charity, ministering to less affluent families, could not compete.[25] And if the Brothers of the Christian Schools were soon to oversee a dense network of educational institutions in the Levant, it was in the correspondence of the Jesuit missionaries with the Gesù that the appeal for their assistance was first made.

The Jesuits' influence went beyond the circle of young people whom these various schools enrolled. In addition to the college in Ghazir, which offered advanced courses in theology and philosophy, the fathers sought to attract young graduates interested in furthering their education. Once again in order to keep pace with the Protestants, a Catholic Society was formed in 1849 to sponsor lectures and discussions about the natural sciences, physics, and history. Also referred to in official correspondence by the Jesuits as an academy (or even a congregation), this society nonetheless encountered difficulties, which Father Badour's report four years later attributed to the character of the population,[26] but which seem to have been linked also to the misgivings that the extracurricular occupations of its young members had aroused among the Jesuits themselves. Apart from suggestions of embarrassing political activity, one finds in the Roman archives an echo of the alarms raised by the curiosity of these young people in theater, especially when Niqula Naqqash, who came forward to carry on the work of his brother Marun, following his death in 1855, persuaded some of them to appear in a play.[27] However this may be, the Catholic Society was to go in and out of existence, ceasing to meet for a time and then reappearing under another name.

More lasting in its impact was the publishing activity of the Jesuits, which began toward the middle of the century. Here again denominational rivalries were decisive: from the printing house of the American missionaries, set up in 1833, there issued a regular stream of biblical literature translated into Arabic, and the house of the Greek Orthodox Church, damaged during the bombardment of 1771, had finally come back into operation in 1842. Other presses administered by Uniate orders were established in Mount Lebanon. At first the Jesuits had to make do with autolithography and lithography, using a machine sent from Lyon in the winter of 1847–48, but with the gift of a French patron it was possible to equip a proper printing shop, which commenced activity in 1853. The following year the first book in

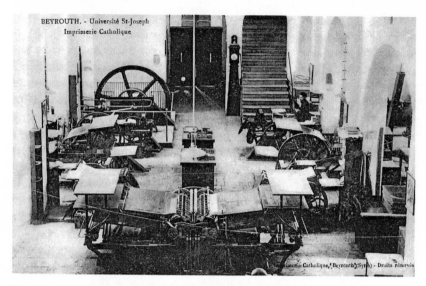

BEYROUTH. - Université St-Joseph
Imprimerie Catholique

FIGURE 43. The Catholic printing house set up by the Jesuit fathers in 1853.

Arabic was issued, and in 1856 the shop's capacity was enlarged by the addition of a second press.[28] As in the case of the American Protestants, priority was given to religious literature, in particular to polemical tracts against this very denomination; but secular works were also produced, such as the Arabic-French dictionary compiled by Father Cuche, following Freytag's Arabic-Latin lexicon, in 1856.[29] The typographical tradition founded by these volumes was to give the Jesuits' printing house a prestige that its American competitor was never to match, and under the name of the Imprimerie Catholique it survived almost until the end of the twentieth century.

Some fifteen years after its inception, the house's business had already become regular enough to support the appearance of the Arabic newspaper of the Syrian mission on a weekly basis. First called *Le Concile du Vatican,* or simply *Le Vatican,* it began publication at the beginning of 1870 in a small format (16.5 × 25.6 cm). In September of the same year the journal changed its title to *Al-Bashīr* (The Herald), and later adopted the royal format (50 × 65 cm) used by other newspapers in order to facilitate postal delivery.[30] As its name suggests, *Al-Bashīr* formed part of the Jesuits' evangelizing activity. This created certain problems with the Ottoman authorities,[31] notwithstanding that the paper was intended mainly as a weapon against American influence, which had recently been further extended by the founding of the Syrian Protestant College.[32]

This year marked another turning point, probably the most decisive one in the

Jesuits' history in the Levant up until then. On 30 July 1870 the Superior of the Syrian mission, Father Ambroise Monnot, was able to announce the acquisition of a piece of land in Beirut large enough to accommodate the Jesuit seminary on its relocation there from Ghazir. Far from being a simple transfer of teachers and students from one place to another, it was in fact the first step toward building Beirut's second university, which was to open its doors in 1875.

Four months earlier, in March 1870, the Americans had bought the parcels in Ras Beirut on which the Syrian Protestant College, which had been operating since 1866, planned to construct its new campus. Although nine years were to separate the creation of the American university from that of the Jesuits, the almost simultaneous purchase of land by the two missions underscores the competition between them. Explicit in the correspondence of the Jesuits, this rivalry was nonetheless equally felt by the Americans; indeed Daniel Bliss, on the founding of the SPC in 1866, is said to have remarked that he had just brought two universities into existence, since the Jesuits would not be slow to reply. The teaching of medicine, in particular, as he might well have known, was reviled by the Gesù as "the most perfidious means that the devil was able to suggest to his sectaries to undermine the faith of a good many of the young and, by their influence, to sow impiety and religious indifference among our good peoples."[33]

A UNIVERSITY FOR FRANCE

The plan to establish a Jesuit college in Beirut had been revived in the wake of the events of 1860. From then on the Society's objectives were to coincide with the interests of France. Competition from the Protestants and the Orthodox notwithstanding, the city's growing importance amply justified such an institution; in the absence of one, there was a genuine risk of alienating the foreign community as well as native Christians from Catholic works.[34] The idea gained ground in the next few years, and soon the relocation to Beirut of the seminary in Ghazir seemed inevitable—so much so that it helped to create a sense of urgency among the fathers, anxious not to miss a vital opportunity and determined to allay the mounting impatience of their community by the announcement of some concrete measure.[35] Practical considerations therefore gained the upper hand, and the task of acquiring land, diligently carried out by Father Monnot, was given precedence over purely academic concerns.[36] The land—held in *waqf* (like that of the SPC) in order to avoid property tax—covered 18,000 square meters (about four and a half acres) in a great quadrilateral southeast of the Burj, a few hundred meters from the Jesuits' original residence. Although this site was large enough to accommodate all the current and contemplated activities of the mission, including the printing house, the share of the construction costs that Rome was not in a position to provide remained to be found. Monnot tackled the problem after the fashion of Daniel Bliss, embarking upon a fund-raising campaign that led him as far abroad as the United States.[37] It is not the least of the paradoxes of the cultural history of Beirut that what was to become a French—and then a Francophone Lebanese—university had been built thanks to American (albeit Catholic) donations.

Dedicated to Saint Joseph, the new institution in Beirut opened its doors in 1875. By virtue of its size it was at once distinguished from the seminary in Ghazir. Whereas the seminary had preserved its ecclesiastical character, most of the students coming from Uniate churches, the urban environment of Beirut lent itself to a larger and more varied enrollment, and from its earliest days the college welcomed the members of all communities, Muslim included. The change in scale was further emphasized by the architecture of the new compound, with its long and imposing outer walls and the monumental façade of its church, consecrated on Christmas eve the same year.

The academic program was different as well, and the *baccalauréat* awarded by the college for secondary studies enjoyed the advantage of equivalence with the French certificate. But the status of the new institution as a university was not asserted at once; to begin with, it accepted students of all age groups, from the primary school pupils of the "petit collège" to seminarians (though advanced instruction was limited at first to theology and philosophy). The foundations of a great institution of higher learning had nonetheless been laid, and in 1881 the college was rebaptized as Université Saint-Joseph, under the auspices—for once conjoined—of the Holy See and the Third Republic: in Rome, Pope Leo XIII granted the university the right to confer academic degrees in theology, while Léon Gambetta and Jules Ferry persuaded the Chamber of Deputies in Paris to approve funding for a medical school,[38] which in 1888 became the Faculté Française de Médecine. The need to supplement classroom instruction with clinical training required a further modification of dogma, however, and the fathers reluctantly entered into a temporary arrangement with the Greek Orthodox Saint George Hospital, recently opened on Ashrafiyyeh Hill, until their students could be placed on the more Catholic path of the Hôpital du Sacré-Coeur, completed in 1885 on the outskirts of the old town.[39] As for recognition of the Jesuit diploma in medicine, there was no obstacle in principle, unlike in the case of the American college, since French was one of the two approved languages of medical instruction in the empire. It was necessary only that final examinations be presided over by professors from the capital, and so beginning in 1895 a jury composed of French and Ottoman authorities came every year to award degrees.[40]

The academic curriculum was further diversified in the 1890s with the introduction of Arab studies, to which the Library of Oriental Letters, newly installed on the university's campus, and the journal *Al-Machreq,* edited by Father Louis Cheikho, gave additional prestige. It was nonetheless not until the eve of the First World War that the study of law—USJ's great contribution to Lebanese political life

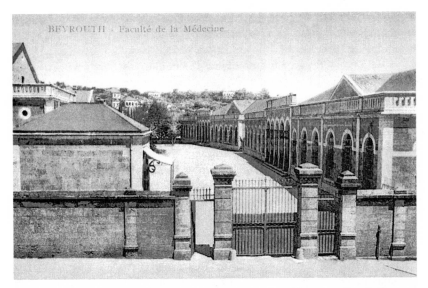

FIGURE 44. The new quarters of the Faculté Française de Médecine on Rue de Damas.

in the decades to come—was inaugurated. Things had greatly changed since 1831. A solemn ceremony on 14 November 1913 marked the opening of the École Française de Droit de Beyrouth, housed in the buildings of the medical faculty, which had just moved to its new location further south on Rue de Damas. Before the assembled dignitaries—the governor of Mount Lebanon, Ohannes Pasha Kuyumjian, accompanied by the representative of the governor of Beirut, as well as Admiral Boué de Lapeyrère, commander of the French navy, the dean of the Académie de Lyon, and the consul general of France—Paul Huvelin, professor of Roman law at Lyon, boldly proclaimed the French identity of the new institution, having first delivered a scholarly dissertation on the heritage bequeathed it by the ancient school of law of Berytus, without omitting to render homage to the "noble Ottoman nation."[41] This nation was yet to have time to disappear before the faculty of law began to function in earnest, in 1919, after the long interruption of the Great War and the upheavals it provoked throughout the Levant.

In 1913, mention of the "two great friendly powers," as Huvelin styled the Ottoman Empire and France, was a piece of conventional courtesy rather than a reflection of political reality. In Istanbul, the Francophilia of the Ottoman elites was beginning to yield to the charms of the Prussian alternative, whereas in Paris the Syrian faction of the colonial party, encouraged by business circles in Lyon and Marseille, was scarcely able to hide its territorial designs.[42] The idea of a protectorate over "French Syria," promoted by a Committee for French Asia under the leadership of the journalist Robert de Caix, an avid imperialist, had succeeded in overcoming a considerable obstacle the previous year when Great Britain let it be known, through the famous correspondence between Edward Grey, secretary of the Foreign Office, and Paul Cambon, the French ambassador to London, that it had neither the ambition nor the intention of acting in Syria.[43] Caix and others recognized that the well-developed network of educational institutions there having ties to France represented a major vehicle of influence, at least as powerful as economic interests, and that the role of the Jesuits in it was far from insignificant. The establishment of the Society of Jesus in Beirut can therefore be seen, if not as a bridgehead of the Quai d'Orsay, in any case as evidence of an expansionist French purpose. And indeed the anticlerical crusade of the Third Republic stopped at the water's edge: French Jesuits, though they were harassed at home by the governments of the Radical Party, benefited from their favors in guiding the Syrian mission, which was to be under the control of the province of Lyon until the 1930s, first as a vice province of the Near East and then as a province in its own right. What is more, as the mission's historian, Father Sami Kuri, was later to emphasize, it profited in particular from an unintended consequence of the campaign against the Catholic Church led by the French prime minister (and former seminarian) Émile Combes and his successor, Maurice Rouvier, in 1904–5, which, by condemning the Jesuits to idleness in France, freed a great many missionaries for reassignment to Beirut. "The Jesuit fathers!" the nationalist writer and politician Maurice Barrès exclaimed. "What a lesson in magnanimity these clerics give us. France hunts them; there will only be more of them to serve it abroad. It disowns them and they no longer have a country? So be it! They will create one [of their own] and set off on the moral conquest of the Levant."[44]

In Syria, certainly, association with France did little harm to the Jesuits' activities. Until the end of the Great War, the plan for a French protectorate was not publicly known. Had it been, this fact probably would not have displeased a large part of the Catholic population, especially in Mount Lebanon, for whom the protection provided by France had become one of the components of its political universe, ever since the intervention of 1860 and the autonomous status subsequently granted the Mutasarrifate. For the others French prestige remained undiminished, and the appeal of French culture, widespread from the time of Muhammad ʿAli and the Tanzimat onward, had seldom been repudiated. The European model of education was valued by the Ottomans no less than by local elites; what is more, as the competition between the missionary orders showed, it was capable of transcending sectarian boundaries. At Université Saint-Joseph, like the Syrian Protestant College before it, the student body was mixed with respect to communal affiliation, and both universities counted Muslim students among their number, even if the Jesuit institution was to remain predominantly Christian. Even more noteworthy than the

FIGURE 45. Scenes commemorating the Jubilee of Université Saint-Joseph in 1900.

educational opportunities they supplied was the vigor of the demand for them, not only in Beirut, where it was sustained by the city's surging socioeconomic development, but also throughout the region (half of the enrollment in the French Faculty of Medicine came from elsewhere than Beirut and the Mountain: Palestine, Damascus, Mesopotamia, and as far away as Persia and Corfu).[45]

Probably the missionaries' greatest virtue, in the absence of any fixed strategy, was to have reacted instinctively to local conditions, often against the advice of their superiors in France, endorsing the dynamic of rebirth that their very presence helped to promote. The attraction of the European model was all the more powerful in view of the contemporary development of higher education elsewhere in the West; many of the colleges and universities in North America had been founded before the Syrian Protestant College, and Georgetown University, the Jesuit university in Washington, D.C., was almost a century older than Université Saint-Joseph. In this sense, the activity of the various missions in the Levant can be seen as an extremely modern application of pedagogical techniques that were themselves still in the process of being worked out. And if Beirut became the privileged vessel of the new learning in the Near East, this is because its economic growth and the way of life that resulted from it encouraged missionaries there to go further in this direction, even if it meant turning away from objectives whose overriding importance they were continually being reminded of by their sponsoring bodies. The cumulative effects of this activity are obvious. In addition to the influence of the French and American universities, the arrival in large numbers of other congregations and the ramification of educational networks, during the second phase of Beirut's expansion after 1860, created a Westernizing wave of modernization that, by scattering the seeds of a foreign culture over the entire metropolitan area, accelerated changes in behavior that were already underway and brought about a transformation of values.

The Horizon of the World

On the eve of the Tanzimat, Shaykh Ahmad al-Agharr was one of the chief notables of Beirut, perhaps even its leading citizen. Holding the office—in this case, to
be sure, more honorific than political—of syndic of the descendants of the Prophet
(naqīb al-ashrāf), he was also the *qādī* of the city and its mufti in 1844. Despite occasional problems with the *wālī* of Sidon, for which he was banished more than
once, he was regarded as the true governor of Beirut, respected by his contemporaries and the authorities alike.[1] During the celebration of the marriage of his
daughter to ʿUmar al-Barbir, scion of another notable family, the gates of the enceinte remained open for four days and four nights. Many years later, in 1887, his
granddaughter Kulthum married Salim ʿAli Salam, son of a wholesaler and a young
man with a future.

Salim Salam's career lived up to its promise, not only in business but also in politics, and when the First World War broke out he became in his turn the most prominent man in the city. Deputy for Beirut in the Majlis al-Mabʿuthān, the Ottoman
parliament, having previously served as a member of the provincial council, president of the municipality, representative of the chamber of commerce to the court
of the same name, president of the Maqāsid Charitable Society and of the Banque
Agricole, this prosperous merchant was involved in every public initiative of the
period. Nothing that happened in Beirut, or indeed the entire province, escaped
his notice.

Although Salim Salam, born in 1868, acquired a preeminence comparable to that
which Ahmad al-Agharr had enjoyed until his death in 1857, the two men had little
in common despite their kinship by marriage. They were divided not only by two
generations, but by an entire world.

THE NEW AGE

Salim Salam's career, as recounted not only by the historian Kamal Salibi but also in the memoirs of his daughter 'Anbara, as well as his own,[2] clearly belonged to a new age. The very offices that he held, successively or simultaneously, testify to a dramatic change in the nature of public life. Still more revelatory of the transformations of the period were the mental horizons that stretched out before a man who played a leading role in both business and politics: while profiting from the change of scale in commercial transactions, Salam also found himself at the confluence of new currents of opinion that divided Arab elites. With the revolution of the Young Turks in 1908 he became one of the principal organizers of the Reform Society of Beirut. In June 1913 he took part in the Arab Congress in Paris as a member of the delegation that met with Stephen Pichon, the French foreign minister, and then as the Ottoman ambassador to France, before transmitting the assembly's grievances to the Liberal Union government in Istanbul. Later Salam objected to the inquisitorial procedures of Jamal Pasha (without, however, casting his lot with the martyrs and exiles who made up the nascent Arab nationalist movement), and under the French Mandate led the protest against the proclamation of Greater Lebanon.

The greatest metamorphosis of all was the one brought about by the emergence of Salim Salam as a public figure—and by his way of life. He did not descend directly from one of the old Muslim families of Beirut. Although the Salam family traced its lineage back to the Maghrib, indeed to Andalusia, it began to acquire a measure of prestige only with 'Ali, Salim's father. While continuing for a time to live in the countryside, among the dunes of Ras Beirut, 'Ali had established himself as a grain merchant in the city. Shortly after Salim's birth the family moved to Musaytbeh Hill, where 'Ali bought a two-story house. He soon added another floor, and Salim later built a fourth, whose unobstructed view looked beyond the city toward both the sea and the mountain, even though in the meantime Musaytbeh had been absorbed into the heart of the metropolitan area. The family's success in business was soon demonstrated, and social advancement followed at once: 'Ali married into the Shatila family, taking as his bride a niece of Ahmad al-Agharr's wife; Salim's wedding to Ahmad's granddaughter allied him to another prominent family, the Barbirs, that like the Agharrs boasted of an ancient line of descent and a long tradition of religious service. Additionally, Salim's commercial skill and his growing political stature enabled the Salams to surpass the Bayhums, an old merchant family that had dominated Muslim society in Beirut since the end of the eighteenth century.

Elegant in manner and possessed of a noble bearing, in public always dressed in the European style while wearing the Ottoman tarbush, Salim Salam embodied a mixture of traditional virtues and new values. Throughout his life he was to maintain a piety attested by his daily observance of religious ritual and his reading of sacred texts, while at the same time displaying an openness of mind that tempered the conservatism of his social class. His father before him had embraced European dress and customs. ʿAli Salam did not hesitate to put his son in a Christian school, the Patriarchal College recently founded by the Greek Catholic community, not very far from the family's home, and he had given his daughter in marriage to one of the first Western-trained physicians in Beirut, Dr. Abdul Rahman Onsi. From this union, in 1901, was born Omar Onsi, a pioneer of modern painting in Lebanon whose interest in profane (and even impious) art, although pursued after the fall of the Ottoman Empire, is in itself one of the most suggestive indications of the transformations undergone by Muslim society after the Tanzimat.

Salim Salam's children had a less unconventional education than their cousin, but one that was no less novel. For the boys of his numerous progeny Salim chose the American college, and from there his eldest son, ʿAli, was sent to study agronomy in Great Britain. The girls were given a modern education as well. His eldest daughter, ʿAnbara, was tutored in French by a Christian cleric, and in Arabic by a man of letters, also Christian. Later she attended the *collège* of Saint-Joseph-de-l'Apparition, until the Maqāsid (under her father's leadership) opened a school for girls run by a young Christian woman, Julia Tohmeh, who was later to marry one of her father's friends, Badr Dimashqiyyeh, also a member of the Maqāsid and an eminent figure in the Muslim community—one of the first freely chosen mixed marriages in Beirut.[3]

Salim Salam's choice of friends was proof of his religious tolerance at a time when communal tensions were intensified by the misfortunes of the Ottoman Empire and the destabilization of the Muslim community by Western penetration. Salam made a point of establishing solid relationships with both the Orthodox archbishop of Beirut, Monsignor Misarra, and Habib Pasha al-Saʿad, the Maronite president of the administrative council of the Mutasarrifate of Mount Lebanon. As a man of his time, Salam regularly took the train to reach his country home in the Mountain on weekends, to go to Damascus, or to tour the ruins in Baalbek with his wife and daughters. In addition to his official visits to Istanbul to take part in the sessions of parliament, and to Paris to participate in the Congress of 1913, he undertook a long trip to Egypt in 1912, once again taking his daughter ʿAnbara with him. To be sure, she had to wear the veil from the age of ten, but this was due more to the wishes of her mother and the pressures of local society than to anything else;[4] in the 1920s she was to be the first Muslim woman in Lebanon to go out in public unveiled. In the meantime she had been sent to study in London, together with her younger sister; a photograph taken during her stay there shows ʿAnbara wearing an elegant cloche hat and a mid-calf skirt in the company of her father, her brother Saeb, and King Faisal of Iraq[5]—proof that Salam readily accepted the idea of women doing away with the veil, in defiance of prevailing social conventions in Beirut.

If the varied public activities of Salim Salam put him in a position to move in step with the new thinking of the age and the changes in political life that accompanied it, his existence was yet much less cosmopolitan than that of his Orthodox Christian contemporary Alfred Sursock—and less affluent as well. The Sursocks had swiftly climbed the social ladder in the decades following the economic boom of the 1830s, owing mainly to consular protection and to business contacts established with the khedival family of Egypt.[6] In the person of Musa Sursock's son Alfred, this success was to translate into intimate familiarity with the highest reaches of the Ottoman government as well as international society. Named secretary of the Ottoman embassy to Paris in 1905, he moved in Europe's wealthiest circles and married Maria Serra di Cassano, the daughter of a Neapolitan count who soon was known in Beirut by the name of Donna Maria. Later his first cousin Nicolas married another daughter of the Cassano family, and Nicolas's sisters married Italian nobles (one of them a scion of the Colonna family in Rome); after the Second World War, Alfred's daughter Yvonne, having married an Irish aristocrat, became Lady Cochrane.

Beirut was far removed from this world, which revolved around an axis linking Rome with Paris, even if in the case of the Sursocks it extended as far east as Istanbul and Alexandria. Just the same, the family did not forget the origins of its fortune. Alfred's brother, Michel, was elected in 1914 to the Ottoman parliament—on the same list as Salim Salam and Kamil al-Asʿad. In religious matters the family established itself as one of the pillars of the Orthodox community, still closely associated with the archbishop of Beirut, and generously contributed to charitable works. Nicolas Sursock's wife, Émilie, founded the girls' school Zahrat al-Ihsān in 1880, entrusting its administration to the nuns of the community.[7]

The experience of Alfred Sursock and Salim Salam was obviously exceptional. But the scope of the changes taking place in the ways of life and thinking in Beirut during this period may be detected in the careers of many of their contemporaries, regardless of background. Three great phenomena had made their effects felt in all segments of society: the expansion and development of educational institutions; adaptation to the needs and opportunities of an increasingly expansive and complex city; and a growing sectarian awareness, complicated by the fact that communal and national identities—Christian and Muslim, on the one hand, Ottoman, Arab, Lebanese, and Syrian on the other—were now juxtaposed or overlapping. Yet none of these three phenomena could resolve the conflict between individual self-assertion and group attachments that had opened up as a result of the encounter with the West.

THE EUROPEAN MODEL

"Having no learned men [of its own] yet, Beirut is trying to create for itself a society in imitation of Europe, as it has many fewer models than some other cities in the East: there not being many Europeans [in Beirut], it does so on the basis of what it imagines Europe to be, rather than what it sees of it."[8] This rather harsh remark by Gilbert Charmes, a French traveler passing through Beirut in the 1890s, was nonetheless probably not inaccurate, at least to judge from the behavior of the city's inhabitants both then and throughout the twentieth century. Despite the element of caricature, it nicely captures the spirit of the Beirut that was being formed under the influence of *al-tafarnuj* (from *Franj,* meaning Franks—a term that denoted not only the French but, since the time of the Crusades, Europeans in general), which is to say, the Westernization that went hand in hand with the city's economic development. The imitation of the West was not always conscious. And if the term "tafarnuj" was applied at first to an indigenous social elite having personal contact with Europeans, its subsequent extension suggests that the urge to imitate foreign models soon became irresistible, affecting all classes and all areas of social activity. From housing to leisure activities, including health and dress, no aspect of urban society was untouched by the changes arising from Western influence.

Probably the most far-reaching of these changes was connected with architecture. We have already noted that the adoption of new forms of construction rapidly transformed the routines of daily life. The home—formerly inward-looking, built around a central courtyard, was now increasingly turned toward the outside, as a result of the new importance attached to windows, and later verandas—also embodied a different conception of personal space, in which rooms were now assigned specific functions, particularly for sleeping and eating.

Until the 1870s bedrooms in the Western style were not common, as we know from the memoirs of the writer and physician Jirji Zaydan, born in 1861, in the neighborhood of the Jesuits' school, to a family that moved twelve times in the space of twenty-two years. Most of the homes in which Zaydan grew up consisted of two rooms, sometimes three, with the same rooms being used for sleeping and receiving guests. Thin mattresses were folded each morning to make room for the day's activities. The absence of raised beds was not a sign of poverty: everyone in Beirut was in the habit of sleeping on a mattress that lay directly on the floor. This practice had struck the traveler Édouard Blondel, who in 1838 noted the lack of bed frames in the homes of the city, while observing that ones made from walnut were to be found in the palace at Beiteddin.[9] Still more revealing is a comparable account by Alphonse de Lamartine of the luxurious house he rented on Ashrafiyyeh Hill six years earlier. Social status depended not on the existence of beds in the Western sense, but on the quality of the mattresses, the sumptuousness of their embroidered sheets, the profusion of cushions, and in some cases the availability of additional living rooms, obviating the need to put away the mattresses in the morning.

Chairs and high tables did not exist either.[10] Furniture consisted for the most part of couches, mattresses, cushions, and curtains, together with small chests and alcoves for removing personal possessions from view, and, most prized of all, carpets for covering the floor (and sometimes the mattresses and walls as well). Meals

FIGURE 46. The interior of a rather well-to-do residence in Beirut in the 1820s, prior to the onset of Westernizing influence.

were served on a low table, or else on a mat placed directly over the floor. Here again, social status varied in relation to the quality of ornamentation, not the quantity of furniture; in addition to finely sculpted chests and low tables, the magnificence of a home was indicated by the display of expensive wall paneling in main rooms and alcoves alike, in accordance with a code of luxury that seemed not to have changed throughout the Arab world since the ʿAbbasid period.

The transformation took shape toward the middle of the century, as a direct consequence of the contact with Europe. In 1858, the English traveler J. Lewis Farley observed that the majority of rich merchants who had visited Europe were furnishing their houses in the style of London and Paris.[11] The fashion appears to have spread beyond the upper classes in only a couple of decades: the newspaper *Lisān al-Hāl,* from the time it began publication in 1878, carried advertisements for furniture in the Western style (chairs, tables, mirrors of "very high quality," and so on), whose tone suggested that these objects had been available for some time.[12] In the years that followed, such notices became ever more numerous—a sign that the market was growing. Adoption of this style had clearly become a mark of social status, or, at the very least, proof of a desire for advancement. Having gotten a foothold by means of the commercial upper class, European furnishings conquered the middle class through force of imitation, especially in Christian communities. Steel-frame beds, armchairs, sofas, dining room tables, sideboards, chests of drawers, chandeliers, candelabras, and "Western carpets" made their entrance into a large number of homes in the late nineteenth century.

There followed from this a concern for interior decoration that found particular expression in the still more recent taste for paintings. European landscapes and images of the Old Testament were especially valued, along with portraits of foreign kings and worldwide celebrities. Here again upper-class Christian families led the way, though initially at least pictorial art was seen simply as another form of ornamentation. Framed pictures and illustrations were much slower to appear in the homes of Muslim families, owing to the Islamic ban on figural representation. Indeed, advertisements for picture sellers were practically nonexistent in the pages of *Thamarāt al-Funūn,* the newspaper of the Muslim modernist elite.[13]

Wall decoration was not limited to painting and reproductions of well-known Western works. Photography was more or less commonly displayed beginning in the last quarter of the century. At a time when this new technology yet remained the prerogative of a select few, pretensions to social status were measured in terms of the number of pictures displayed—especially photographs of the master of the house and his family, whether they were taken by one of the professional photographers then working in Beirut, foreign or native, or by amateurs (advertisements for cameras and equipment indicate the beginnings of photography as a personal hobby, probably among the upper middle class). More widespread was the decorative use of European mirrors, which brought framers a good deal of business, and the arrival of the latest models of gilded frames was regularly announced. But the greatest enthusiasm may have been for music boxes, which made a strong impression on travelers invited into the homes of Beirut. Floral decoration made its appearance as well, giving rise to a hitherto unknown commerce in imported flowers.

Although European-inspired decoration naturally lent itself to the development of differentiated individual tastes, the new approach to interior design, sometimes explicitly identified in the press with the modernization of daily life, was very much a social phenomenon. The magazine *Al-Muqtataf,* which despite its relocation to Cairo continued to be edited by natives of Beirut and had a large audience among educated persons there, made housekeeping the subject of a regular column that encouraged readers, both male and female, to hang paintings on their walls, particularly reproductions of the works of Raphael, and to further enliven rooms with vases of flowers.[14] The results were bound to be uneven. To Dr. Louis Lortet, a French traveler visiting Beirut in the 1870s, the drawing rooms of certain "rich Arabs" appeared as "veritable museums arranged with exquisite taste and would not seem out of place in our more luxurious homes in France."[15] Typically, however, an inauthentic sort of Western luxury prevailed, as Gabriel Charmes was later frankly to point out. It is true that imitation often took precedence over adaptation: one thinks of the installation of purely decorative fireplaces, made of "white marble of the finest effect" but unequipped with chimneys for the evacuation of smoke, observed in 1897 by another French physician, Dr. Benoît Boyer, "in many rich houses."[16] The most common technique of heating remained in any case the brazier, which had the advantage of serving both to make coffee and to provide heat for the hookah (narghile).[17]

The brazier's resistance to Europeanization—it was to survive until the appearance of gas-burning heaters in the twentieth century—was not a unique case. Other traditional household furnishings long remained in use, either for reasons of economy or because they were better suited to local customs, or else owing to sectarian preference. This last factor probably explains why the use of carpets for wall decoration or to cover sofas continued to be widespread, particularly in the homes of Muslim families that had no contact with Europe or Europeans.[18] Even so, the general acceptance of European furniture and related accessories was irresistible, and more or less rapid depending on the item. Demand was so great that factories making European-style furniture were built in Beirut at the turn of the century, advertising their products in local papers.[19] Sellers of passementerie, iron craftsmen, florists, glassmakers, framers, and other artisans specializing in elements of the new interior design set up shops in the city as well.

In addition to modifying the physical surroundings of domestic life, European furniture altered the rhythms of daily existence, introducing new forms of behavior in both the public and the private sphere. The changes in the art of the table brought about by the appearance of the dining room are the most telling example of this. Silverware, no less than high tables and chairs, had been virtually unknown until the middle of the nineteenth century. As early as 1836, in M. Delaroière's account of his travels in the Lebanon, one finds a description of a meal "with silver dinner service, glasses, chairs" given at Zghorta, a fairly rural place at the time, by Shaykh Butrus Karam. But this remained very much an exception, and indeed the traveler noted that his host was "the most European Arab whom I have seen in the whole country."[20] Conversely, the Englishman John Carne reported in 1830 eating a sumptuous meal at the home of a rich "Moorish" merchant in Beirut in which only a spoon was provided, for the soup; the other foods were taken with the fingers directly from a large dish, followed by the ceremonial washing of the hands.[21] It was not until a quarter century later that individual plates, knives, and forks made their appearance in a few wealthy homes of the city, the first documented instance occurring in 1859 with the mention by Farley of a dinner served in the "French style."[22] This practice was nevertheless adopted only by a small minority. The majority of the population long shunned individual place settings, and in particular the fork, which was practically unknown, whereas the spoon was already in common use, along with the knife—inevitably employed for cutting meats, albeit on behalf of a group of diners.

Thus Jirji Zaydan's father, for example, criticized tafarnuj in the 1860s, though he was a restaurateur, challenging the use of individual forks and knives, though not of spoons.[23] The same objection was made by the dragoman accompanying Charmes in 1891, who reproached the nuns not only for teaching girls to "have two or three dresses," but also for "eating off of plates, with knives and forks."[24] And yet European utensils appear to have generally been adopted in the last quarter of the century, to judge from the advertisements appearing in *Lisān al-Hāl* in its early years, where one even finds announcements of Christofle silverware.[25] *Al-Muqtataf* continued to pay attention to the art of the table *(adab al-ma'ida)* in its housekeeping column, which gave advice on entertaining guests and the proper sequence of courses, while disparaging the "Turkish table."[26] The interest shown in this subject by a modern-minded magazine dedicated to promoting discussion of new and often sophisticated ideas shows that the appeal of foreign customs was not only a matter of luxurious display. While it is unlikely that the significance of separate place settings as a recognition of individuality in an environment governed by the communal etiquette of sharing a meal with others (traditionally the members of one's family) was fully appreciated at the time, the metamorphosis of social existence that it represented could hardly have escaped notice. The Western-style dining room, with its high chairs, did not simply introduce novel table manners. It modified the very position of sitting, and in so doing called for windows to be placed at a new height in relation to the floor, while rendering the habit of taking off one's shoes before entering a house obsolete.[27] As a result, the boundary between private and public space was narrowed, and the house became less and less a rampart against the assaults of the outside world.

At the same time as the art of the table was changing, diet was becoming more varied, and the two trends, equally stimulated by the discovery of foreign habits, continued to reinforce each other, accelerating the metamorphosis of daily life. The diversification of diet had first come about in response to the tastes of Europeans who had taken up residence in Beirut. In 1838 Blondel noted that the arrival of a Maltese baker was cheered by the "Franks," who could now eat a bread similar to the one they knew in their homelands. A short time later the menu at Battista's hotel was enlarged to include Italian dishes. Such innovations, though they were meant to please foreign visitors in the first instance, were nonetheless welcomed by the native population. In 1859 Farley reported that European dishes and French wines, in addition to wines from Cyprus and Mount Lebanon, were served at private meals, among them the dinner *à la française* he fondly recollected that year. Here again change came relatively quickly. In the last quarter of the nineteenth century newspapers carried a great many advertisements for imported foods: cheeses from France and Holland, sardines, tuna, macaroni, continental toast, chocolate, sugar-coated nuts, mineral water, and so on.[28] *Lisān al-Hāl* even published notices for charcuterie (ham and salami) and alcoholic beverages (champagne, wine, and beer). Every year there were more and more advertisements around Christmas and New Year, and again with the approach of the Easter season, suggesting that the clientele for such products was to be found mainly among the wealthy Christian population. Among the less affluent, the occasional consumption of imported foods and beverages made it possible to stake out a claim to social status, without abandoning the indigenous cuisine. But little by little a new bourgeois cooking began to emerge that adapted traditional dishes to the dimensions of the individual plate while at the same time incorporating previously unknown ingredients.

THE PASSING OF A WAY OF LIFE

These new social practices did as much, if not more, to transform the appearance of the city than changing styles of architecture. Due in part to the use of signs, the specialization of commerce altered the urban landscape at a moment when the adoption of foreign customs filled the shops and cafés with bustling crowds and the improved flow of information associated with the advent of newspapers produced changes in everyday habits that gave physical reality to the notion of progress. The acceleration of social time brought about everywhere by the Industrial Revolution was sharpened in Beirut by the uneasy coincidence, typical of an era of transition, of what still existed with what was beginning to come into being.

Nothing better illustrated the passing of an age than the revolution in dress that from the middle of the century onward gradually changed the look of the city. No matter that traditional fashions survived for a relatively long time in Beirut, they were incapable of resisting what amounted almost to a change of skin. In the wake of the great political reforms inaugurated in 1839, Istanbul and Cairo were the first places where the effects of contact with the West could be seen. In 1843 the imperial army received new uniforms, inspired by the Prussian style,[29] and the highest officials in the capital, beginning with the sultan himself, adopted European dress,[30] qualified only by a specifically oriental cap, the tarbush, itself a modernizing piece of attire (later, paradoxically, prohibited by Atatürk) meant to supplant the turban. In Istanbul, the turban was abandoned by everyone except religious dignitaries, and provincial officials were quick to follow imperial example. Official taste therefore served to authorize the temptation to imitate foreign models that had already conquered those classes most exposed to European influence. In Beirut, men were visibly the first to give up their customary clothing and dress in the Western style. This was especially the case among wealthy merchants, whose general approval of European costume Farley noticed in 1859,[31] and among dragomans in constant contact with the Europeans—though not among the consular guards (qawwās), who preserved a distinctive style of dress that held great appeal for photographers.

At the same time, the influence of the missionary schools made itself felt among

FIGURE 47. A traveler's guide dressed in the costume of a consular guard.

the young, girls included. In 1855, the French traveler Émile Gentil noted with regret that the girls who attended the school of the Filles de la Charité were "unfor-
tunately" dressed in the European style, but that they changed back into traditional
costume on their return home.[32] It was not until a few years later that this dichotomy
ceased to be observed. Yet for European dress to be widely adopted by women meant
overcoming the problem raised for Christians and Muslims alike by the unveiling
of the head and body.[33] Quite a few upper-class Christian women removed the veil
during the last quarter of the century, but many continued to wear it. In 1917, an
official Ottoman report on the state of the province of Beirut noted that "until recently" Maronite women did not go out to the markets with their heads uncovered.[34]
The habit of covering the hair by some piece of headgear, whether a hat or a scarf,
was nonetheless to survive well into the twentieth century—in keeping, moreover,

with the international style. For Muslim women change came more slowly: the veil, which concealed the face, began to fall into disuse only in the 1920s, having long been worn with clothes tailored in the European manner.

Among both women and men, mixed costume continued to be worn until the end of the nineteenth century. Charmes noticed this in 1891,[35] and one finds local clothes and Western dress juxtaposed in many photographs of the period. Despite resistance, the European (and particularly the French) style made rapid progress in proportion to the rising power of the merchant bourgeoisie, who dealt on a daily basis with European businessmen, and to the emergence of the middle class that had grown up in response to the growth of international commerce and culture. In 1878 a European tailor's shop *(khiyata ifranjiyya)* opened in Beirut. A decade later there were twenty-eight Western-style dressmakers (as against twenty *khayyat 'arabi)*, and advertisements in *Lisān al-Hāl* and *Thamarāt al-Funūn* for English and French fabrics—long dominant in the market—often made a point of noting that they were "perfect for Western dress." Charmes condescendingly spoke of "so-called European outfits," adding that that their "naiveté is sometimes amusing."[36] Yet ready-to-wear clothes could be imported from France, and the great Paris department store Printemps made its illustrated catalogue available by post. It was during this period that the promotional device of "the latest Parisian fashion" first made its appearance, stimulating sales in the manner pioneered by the silkmakers of Lyon.[37]

The propagation of European tastes was all the more rapid as new opportunities for socializing presented themselves in the late nineteenth century. Scenic routes traveled by four-wheeled carriages, public gardens (some of which charged admission), clubs, ballrooms, and theaters—things that were unknown only a few decades earlier—supplied meeting places that modified people's perception of the urban landscape. Public space, formerly confined to a nearby neighborhood, now assumed citywide dimensions; but private space had grown as well, enlarged by new activities and forms of entertainment that encouraged individual expression.

Before the city's expansion, gathering places were limited to cafés, an exclusively male environment, and to baths *(hammam)*. Coffeehouses had long existed in Beirut, but with its opening up to European influence both their decor and their social function began to change. In 1853 the French archeologist Louis Félicien de Saulcy noticed a Café d'Europe that, though it did not seem to markedly differ from other such establishments, managed nonetheless to set itself apart by the sale of cigars and of two French newspapers, *La Voix du peuple* and *Le Charivari*.[38] And though the café was frequented mainly by natives, as Saulcy observed, the name on the sign outside called attention to the high social standing of its clientele. A few years later, the presence of billiard tables in cafés was mentioned by Farley.[39] Old-fashioned establishments featuring the *hakawati,* a storyteller who embroidered episodes from the well-known medieval epics *Sīrat 'Antarah* (The Tale of Antar) and *Sīrat al-Zahir Baybars* (based on the life of the Mamluk sultan Baybars I), survived until the beginning of the twentieth century, and even beyond.[40] Nonetheless, the increase observed in the last quarter of the nineteenth century in the number of European-style cafés, more or less faithful to their models, was striking.

The rise of café culture was particularly favored by the development of the area around the Burj, which was on its way to becoming the central crossroads of the city, and of the seafront at Minet al-Hosn, reinforced in both cases by the presence of foreign visitors and the growing number of hotels that lodged them. According to the guide *Al-Jāmiʿa,* Beirut in 1889 counted seventeen hotels, most of them located in these two neighborhoods, though signs of specialization were already noticeable. Minet al-Hosn catered to the tourist trade with luxury hotels such as the Bassoul and the Bellevue, where rooms were priced between ten and fifteen francs per night, as well as more modest lodgings such as the furnished apartments rented out by Madame Pascall, at two francs per night—the same rate as the Kawkab al-Sharq, on the south side of the Burj—for a less select clientele.[41]

The cosmopolitanism of these places rapidly set the tone for the neighborhood, nowhere better reflected than in the cafés that sprang up around them. Turkish coffee remained the beverage of choice, but imported drinks were also popular. Baedeker's guide for 1893, for example, recommended two cafés in the vicinity of the Hotel Bassoul that served Bavarian beer at eight piasters a bottle and fifty centimes a glass. Four years earlier, *Al-Jāmiʿa* listed two establishments where billiards—the game most commonly associated with European-style cafés—could be played. But the café was more than a place offering new forms of recreation. It had become a source of entertainment in itself that could be enjoyed no less readily by a group than by individuals. Nor was it any longer exceptional to see native customers there, seated alone and reading the newspaper, another recent habit.

Restaurants did not enjoy the same success right away. Not counting a few rather disreputable taverns outside the old town, the first restaurant in the modern sense was opened by the Italian hotelier Battista. Others were opened by natives such as Ilyas Zaydan, the writer's father, whose bakery shop, founded in 1860 not far from Place des Canons, began serving meals the following year. But such establishments had a hard time attracting customers at first, to judge from the account left by Jirji Zaydan, who worked for his father for seven years before taking up the study of medicine. At night the clientele was limited to foreigners, vagrants, and drunks, and during the day to people who worked too far away from home to go back for lunch, though few of these chose to eat in restaurants; typically they brought their lunch with them to work or, in the case of the wealthiest individuals, such as Salim Salam, had it brought to them from home by a servant.[42] The restaurant business became profitable only on account of the growing number of foreigners visiting the city. As a result, the restaurant came to appeal to local merchants as a place to make contact with Europeans. By the end of the century, however, it had begun to become a place to spend one's spare time, and also a place where well-to-do families went to have lunch on holidays. This was especially true of establishments situated outside the city, such as the *guinguettes*—small restaurants with music and dancing—in the Pine Forest described by Abbé Raboisson in the 1880s.[43]

It was not until the French Mandate that the practice of dining away from the home began to spread among the social elite. But the habit of going out at night quickly became popular among the city's most affluent citizens. In 1896, the first nightclub was opened by sons of Musa Sursock. By the beginning of the twentieth century local society already had its own rituals, modeled after those of the Parisian Belle Époque. The most socially prominent ladies received guests at home on a fixed day of the week. Balls and grand dinners were given regularly. Thanks to the immense grounds that surrounded the palatial residences on Rue Sursock in the Ashrafiyyeh district and those of Qantari Hill, the garden party enjoyed a particular vogue. Hundreds of specially invited guests, all turned out in their finest dress, flocked to the homes of the Sursocks, Bustroses, and the Marquis de Freige. The Tuwaynis, in their private park of ten acres, gave "unforgettable receptions."[44]

Clubs for games such as chess also appeared, along with reading societies. The theater gradually became a customary form of entertainment as well. In the wake of the Naqqash brothers' pioneering efforts, foreign Catholic schools managed to overcome the traditional hostility of the Church toward the dramatic arts. Theatrical productions were now part of the year-end celebrations at universities: in 1903 a performance of *Julius Caesar* was staged in the outdoor theater built on the campus of the Syrian Protestant College, followed two years later by a selection of scenes from Shakespeare and the next year by a production of *Hamlet*.[45] Theater began to be appreciated in the city as well. With the appearance of the *Thamarāt al-Funūn*, in 1875, one finds announcements for plays and even critical reviews. Supported by a sizable and devoted audience, though probably it was limited to the wealthiest classes, these early productions were sufficiently successful to justify the construction of theaters such as the one in the new Raʿd and Hani Suq. All of this provides evidence of a transformation of taste that, combined with the changing atmosphere of the cafés, foretold the eclipse of traditional storytellers and the shadow theater known as *karakoz*.

Another form of entertainment inspired by European practices was the promenade. The English-style garden built on the outskirts of the city, in Hazmiyyeh, over the course of a decade beginning in 1873 by the mutasarrif of Mount Lebanon, Rustum Pasha, an Italian aristocrat in the service of the Sublime Porte, at once became the meeting place for the most stylish ladies and gentlemen of Beirut. Charmes described the garden, and the stretch of Rue de Damas leading to it, as "the Champs-Élysées and the Bois de Boulogne of the city."[46] No less popular was the Hamidiyyeh Garden, laid out by the municipality at the center of Place des Canons, whose restricted access (there was a charge for entering) held special appeal for a new urban upper middle class eager to claim for itself a space that satisfied

FIGURE 48. A reading society.

the longing for a Westernized lifestyle.[47] Elsewhere, along the seaside promenade that ended at the lighthouse, elegant young ladies from the best families made regular appearances, decked out in their finest.

Improved means of transport made Dbayeh, five or six miles to the north, another prestigious destination for the city's wealthiest citizens. A 1917 report on the state of the province of Beirut observed that hundreds of motorcars now brought people there to admire the "waterfalls" of Nahr al-Kalb.[48] The four-wheeled carriage had not yet wholly surrendered to the automobile, but the moment was not far off. The first car, a Panhard-et-Levassor, recently imported by Alfred Sursock for his wife, Donna Maria, and driven by an Italian chauffeur, was popularly referred to as the "boat of fire" *(babur al-nar)*. Curiosity soon gave way to emulation. ʿUmar Beyhum was the next to buy one, and the first to drive from Beirut to Damascus, carrying on board gasoline imported from Romania and Russia in 18-liter cans.[49] The growing interest in outdoor excursions was already perceptible with the construction of a track for racing horses to the south of the city in 1893. Though such arenas were a familiar element of Arab tradition, advertising for the new racecourse made a point of noting that it was modeled after European hippodromes. It was not by chance that the developers of this facility belonged to the upper middle class that had grown up with the expansion of Western commerce.

The prior discovery of the pleasures of the seaside proceeded from the same impulse. As in many other Mediterranean cities, only those who resided along the narrow coastal strip, such as the fishermen of ʿAyn al-Mrayseh and Medawar, and

FIGURE 49. A view of the seaside promenade.

FIGURE 50. Doctor Harris Graham of the Syrian Protestant College in one of the first automobiles imported to Beirut.

who made their living from the sea, were in the habit of bathing in it. The rest of the population limited itself to a ritual dip each year on "Job Wednesday," in keeping with the ancestral belief that the waters on that day had the power to cure illness. Ocean bathing had nonetheless begun to be more common by the end of the nineteenth century. In 1888 there were three outdoor bathing establishments (not to be confused with the public bathhouses, of which there were five in the city at this time), beneath the cliffs of Medawar to the east and on the edge of Minet al-Hosn to the west. The sea breezes could also be enjoyed at a few cafés to the west of the port, such as the Hajj Dawud and Amaliyyeh, and at the foot of the cliffs of Rawsheh. These were wooden shacks constructed on stilts, where one could order a snack, washed down with a glass of arak, and smoke a narghile; below them were small cabins, often built into the rock, which served as changing rooms for those who wished to swim—a recreation available only to men, whose costume consisted of baggy linen shorts.[50] It was not until the Mandate that women were welcome to join them.

The introduction of sports in the schools, at a time when the Olympic movement was taking root in Europe, helped to broaden the range of outdoor activities. Scouting was imported practically from the moment of its invention in Europe as well, first in Christian schools and then in those opened by the Maqāsid. A troop of Muslim scouts was formed in 1912, only five years after the founding of the movement by Baden-Powell.

The imitation of all things European, and especially French, extended even to proper names. Many middle-class Christian families simplified the French spelling of their surnames; others, acting out of the same motives, complicated it. Thus Sursuq became Sursock, Fir'awn turned into Pharaon, and the Frayj family, having obtained a title of papal nobility, henceforth styled itself de Freige. But it was above all personal names that changed. Local versions of Christian names were replaced by the French names of patron saints: thus Georges was preferred to Jirjis (or Gerios), Marie to Mariam, Joseph to Yusuf, Jean to Hanna (or Yuhanna), Paul to Bulus, Pierre to Butrus, Antoine to Tanyus (or Tannus), Michel to Mikhail (or Nakhleh), Élie to Ilyas, and so on. Even a secular name such as Kamīl was adapted as Camille. Moreover, names that had been wholly unfamiliar to the region now made their appearance, such as Eugénie (in homage to the empress), Joséphine, Linda, Alice, Albert, Alfred, Émile, and Charles, among others.

THE TRIUMPH OF MEDICINE

These changes affected not only outward appearances. Just as the new architecture had reoriented the traditional perception of spatial relationships and given rise to forms of behavior that broke with social convention, the advance of education modified the very conception of the individual. Even more perhaps than in literary or historical studies, this metamorphosis found expression in the triumph of modern medicine. Apart from the tangible progress made in diagnosis and treatment, the new scientific outlook marshaled popular support for the improvement of public health and personal hygiene, giving medicine an enormous influence over social life and physicians tremendous prestige. By the late twentieth century the medical sector in Beirut was one of the most highly developed in the world.

Until the middle of the nineteenth century, however, medicine was practiced in Beirut and in the rest of Lebanon in a very haphazard manner. Travelers had noted the presence of foreign physicians in Mount Lebanon since the beginning of the century,[51] but for the most part medical care was outmoded and ineffective, having preserved almost nothing of value from the grand Arab tradition of the ʿAbbasid era, and typically delivered by charlatans or by bonesetters with no real training. This situation began to change with the Egyptian reforms and European commercial expansion. The French physician Antoine-Barthélemy Clot, known as Clot Bey, made a visit to Beirut in 1838, and the school that he had founded in Cairo a decade earlier, Qasr al-ʿAyni, began to attract students from the region.[52] The following year Édouard Blondel mentioned a drugstore run by a qualified pharmacist, while noting that other stores did not meet this standard.[53] But it was only in 1847 that a formally trained physician settled in Beirut, a Frenchman named Suguet who stayed for three years.[54] It was also in 1847 that the Great Powers took the unprecedented step of appointing public health authorities in several cities of the Ottoman Empire in response to a cholera epidemic that had spread to Europe from Mecca, beginning in 1831. In addition to foreign physicians who came to Beirut after Suguet, there were missionaries with medical training, among them a Jesuit brother named Henze and the American Cornelius Van Dyck. Soon Arab physicians trained in Istanbul and Cairo, even in Europe, returned home. The first Beiruti graduates of Qasr al-ʿAyni to practice in their native city were Dr. Yusuf Jalkh and Dr. Ibrahim Najjar (the latter went on to become chief physician of the Ottoman army, with special responsibility for the military hospital founded in Beirut in 1846).[55] Other local practitioners included Dr. John Wortabet, son of the first Armenian convert to Protestantism, who had studied in London, and Dr. Shakir al-Khuri, who left Beirut at the age of twenty, in 1867, to study at Qasr al-ʿAyni. But the turning point in medical practice was the founding of the Syrian Protestant College, and then of Université Saint-Joseph. The SPC graduated its first class of medical students in 1871; fifteen years later the school of medicine at USJ, inaugurated in 1881, awarded its first diplomas.

With the growth of these two local institutions, a true native medical corps steadily took shape. Some students who could afford to study abroad chose to do so (during the second half of the twentieth century, by contrast, those of modest means were the ones who would leave their homeland to pursue medical studies, often in Eastern Europe); and many graduates of SPC and USJ went on to acquire specialized training in Europe—a measure of professional success in a society that very quickly showed its preference for Western medicine over traditional forms. To judge from advertisements placed in Beirut newspapers by physicians who had settled there, the demand for modern medical services was both strong and discerning. These notices prominently called attention to the physician's possession of a recognized diploma, even citing its number, and often indicated the place where he had done his postgraduate work—suggesting that the claim to mastery of European medical knowledge and techniques constituted a ground for confidence in the eyes of the public.[56] The results obtained by the practitioners themselves did the rest, whether they were spread by word of mouth or openly publicized through the letters of praise and thanks that patients sent to the newspapers.[57] Even so, medical services were not exclusively reserved for the wealthy; most practitioners set aside hours specifically for seeing indigent patients. In the absence of public institutions for treating the sick, the fact that these consultations were free of charge made it possible to provide all classes of the population with the advantages of modern medicine, while at the same time magnifying the social prestige of the physician, who was now regarded as a demiurge.[58]

At both the Syrian Protestant College and Université Saint-Joseph the teaching of medicine was accompanied by pharmaceutical training, and in 1889 there were fifteen qualified pharmacists in the city. In 1905 a nursing school was opened at the SPC. During this same period there was an expansion of hospital facilities, almost nonexistent as late as the middle of the nineteenth century, and then limited to a single institution with the founding of the military hospital in 1846. Next came the Johanniter, the hospital established by the Deaconesses of Kaiserswerth on land donated in 1862 by Fuad Pasha to the Prussian Knights of St. John. In 1878, a purely local initiative gave birth to the Greek Orthodox Saint George Hospital, which moved twice before finally being established on its present site in 1913. In the meantime other institutions came into existence, among them the Hamidi Hospital in the new Arts et Métiers neighborhood, as well as the Hôpital du Sacré-Coeur, founded in 1885 and run by the Filles de la Charité.[59] At the turn of the century the opening of a psychiatric hospital, the Lebanon School for the Insane (later the Lebanon Hospital for Mental and Nervous Disorders), extended the scope of the health system; built by Theophilus Waldmeier, a Swiss Quaker who had initially come to Mount Lebanon to direct the English high school in Brummana, and financed by both local and foreign donations, it was located outside the city in a place called 'Asfuriyyeh[60] and officially inaugurated in 1902. In a community having no experience of the detention and treatment of the mentally ill (a practice that nonetheless was not without precedent during the Ottoman period, and that was found elsewhere at the time, for instance, at al-Bimaristan in Aleppo), the novelty was such that the name 'Asfuriyyeh, in addition to denoting the hospital itself, came to be synonymous with an insane asylum—including the metaphorical sense of the term (to which the literal meaning of 'asfuriyyeh, a bird shop or aviary, no doubt contributed).

The development of a network of physicians and health-care facilities did not totally eliminate traditional medicine, whose survival may be inferred from the public campaigns conducted with the approval of the city council against archaic and superstitious practices. Newspapers lent their support to the cause, and all the more as they subscribed to the progressive scientism of the day, devoting articles and columns to the improvement of public sanitation as well as to the advances of modern medicine. A medical journal called *Al-Tabib* (The Physician) appeared under the editorship of Ibrahim al-Yaziji, who was succeeded by George Post, still a member of the SPC medical faculty.[61] Unlicensed druggists, another target of these campaigns, gradually disappeared, but traditional healers managed to ply their trade well into the twentieth century, though they were limited now mainly to setting broken bones and treating joint or muscle pain. On the other hand, the recourse to European medical expertise continued to be accompanied by prayer and other prophylactic devices recommended by religious faith. Indeed, the rising trust in the physician-demiurge was not always able to block the intrusion of local prejudice, which under certain circumstances could convert it into reluctance, or even defiance, in the event that the patient was ordered to check into the hospital—an institution that was blamed for dispossessing the family of its traditional role in treating illness, and so for bringing dishonor upon it.[62] The manifest benefits of modern medicine were not yet enough to keep it from coming into conflict with the beliefs and outlook of a world that was only slowly dying out.

INDIVIDUALITY AND COMMUNITY

The transformation of the city was seen most clearly in the new fashions of clothing and the new behaviors, both public and private, that imitation of Western models made popular. Together these things helped to bring about a distinctively malleable modernity that accommodated a multitude of variations, enlarging the range of personal choice in all classes of society. This tendency was further strengthened by the city's geographical expansion and by the practically incessant inflow of immigrants, which led in turn, if not to perfect anonymity, at least to the advent of urban complexity on a scale that allowed a greater measure of individual freedom than ever before. In this respect, too, Beirut took part in a broader pattern of development that could be detected in all the cities of the empire, where the advance of urbanization, the growth of education, and the propagation of the ideals of the French Revolution helped to spread the values of progress and rationality, creating an environment favorable to the assertion of individual identity. The juridical reforms of the Tanzimat, following from the proclamation of the equality of all subjects in the imperial edict of Gülhane in 1839, and the ingenuity of Ottoman officials and civil servants in carrying out the immense task of creating a modern legal system were important, too, for bringing out elements of individualism implicit in the Islamic tradition.[63]

None of this could be perceived at the time in anything but an impressionistic manner, however. Nor can any of its effects be measured with precision now, though the underlying dynamic seems incontestable in view of the many walks of life found in Beirut at the end of the nineteenth century. A few things in particular point to a determination, not always conscious but constantly growing, to achieve greater independence for the individual. There was an attempt, first of all, to reach out beyond and across denominations, sometimes against the will of the religious authorities, as in the extreme case of Orthodox and Maronites converting to Protestantism, or, more pardonably, enrollment by seminarians from the Uniate churches in the Society of Jesus. Such conversions involved only Christians, of course, but the participation of a Muslim cleric such as Yusuf al-Asir in the translation of the Protestant Bible testified to the ecumenical spirit of the Nahda and its ability to transcend divisions among communities. The same spirit led parents to send their children to school in massive numbers; indeed, the excess of demand in relation to supply meant that it was often necessary to overlook denominational affiliation in choosing a school, at least until every community had its own institutions. Even then, a certain intermixing continued to prevail in the foreign schools and, inevitably, in the city's two universities. The range of careers available to students, now broader and more varied than before, likewise set them on paths that were not determined in advance by family background or class. More generally, the new opportunities for social intercourse created by a city open to immigration favored the formation of bonds across social groups, whether in the course of conducting business, practicing a profession, or striking up personal friendships.

A striking illustration of the incipient individuation of society occurred in 1887, as we saw earlier, with the passing of that emblematic figure of the Nahda, Ahmad Faris al-Shidyaq, a Maronite who had converted first to Protestantism and then to Islam. The compromise to which it led—a funeral bringing together the different communities and the choice of a neutral burial ground—showed that a man was now capable of imposing his will on society. Women could do the same as well, as Julia Tohmeh Dimashqiyyeh, a Christian woman who had freely chosen a Muslim husband, demonstrated some years later, and after her 'Anbara Salam al-Khalidi, who marked the end of the Ottoman era by removing her veil. In this case the ideas and achievements of those who had gone before them were of incalculable importance. Although the notion of women's liberation had not been addressed before a general audience prior to the publication of a work by this title (Tahrir al-Mar'a) in Cairo, in 1899, by the Egyptian magistrate Qasim Amin,[64] the problem of female advancement, centered on the education of girls, had been raised in Beirut a half-century earlier in a lecture by Butrus Bustani. Bustani himself had preached by example in marrying Rahil (Rachel) 'Ata, one of the first educated young ladies in the city, who had gone to the American missionaries' school. The same example was set later by Ibrahim al-Yaziji, whose wife Warda presided over a literary salon in the 1870s. This was still a long ways, of course, from the political feminism of the suffragettes, much less professional equality—even in Europe women did not really begin to enter the work force until the First World War. But schooling for girls, introduced by the Christian missionaries and before long very largely accepted by the Muslim population, as the works of the Maqāsid Society attest, was nonetheless a crucial step forward in the integration of women into society—on the one hand, because education gave women access to the teaching profession and, with it, a measure of independence; and, on the other, because a woman's education now came to be seen as one of the criteria of a "good" marriage, at least among the middle and upper classes.

Bourgeois marriage itself underwent a transformation during this period that strengthened the claims to individual autonomy, especially from the prospective husband's point of view. In the past the choice of a bride depended chiefly on the will of the groom's family, and indeed of his extended family, which gave careful consideration to the social rank of the young woman, particularly where an alliance was contemplated with a family from another part of the city or from outside the city. Unions between two moderately educated people suited the perspectives opened up by the nuclear household, itself encouraged by the city's new architecture and the recent appearance of the apartment, which allowed young couples to live apart from the extended family.

If the family was forced to yield ground to the individual in marriage and other matters, it could still assert powerful claims of its own. For many years to come, family ties continued to structure social life. Indeed, rather than a binary opposition between the group and the individual, one should speak instead of an adaptation by the group to the sudden emergence of the individual. The history of Beirut in the nineteenth century, while rich in tales of personal accomplishment, remains in large measure a narrative of families—and not only of the great families that populate the city's most enduring legends. Naturally these families were the most visible, not only because of the ostentation and aristocratic pretensions of their homes, but also, and to a still greater degree, as a result of the commercial dynasties they built up during this period, typically in conjunction with European interests, many of which have served until the present day. Western influence was exerted in a contradictory manner, however, so that while the imitation of foreign models encouraged individual initiative, the agents of European expansion coopted whole families for both business and political purposes. Thus consular protection, granted ever more broadly to a class of obliging dragomans, was extended to include the relatives of these beneficiaries, and then tacitly made a part of the legacy that one generation handed down to the next.

Beyond the power exercised by the new commercial and banking lineages, patterns of family entry and settlement in the various neighborhoods that were incorporated in the metropolitan area during the second half of the nineteenth century

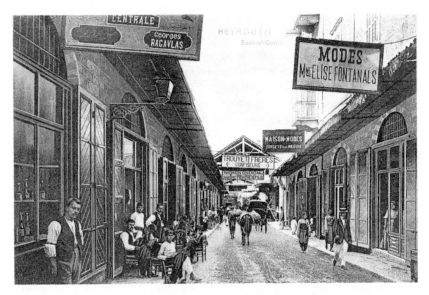

FIGURE 51. The "Beau Souk" with its Parisian-style display windows.

determined the new configuration of Beirut. Immigration, the chief engine of demographic growth, geographically formalized the significance of family ties in all
classes of society. Empty land in the new residential neighborhoods was colonized
by groups of families that had arrived together, or else at very brief intervals, and
that as they grew in size over the years enlarged their holdings. The familial character of urban expansion, attested by customary place names as well as by registers of
land ownership and municipal records of births, marriages, and deaths, was to make
its influence felt well into the twentieth century, and helped to establish a lasting dichotomy between residential neighborhoods—the territory of the group—and districts devoted to business and entertainment—the space of the individual.

Inevitably, this family framework was superimposed on a sectarian geography.
The seat of business and administration in the heart of the city seemed to have no
particular denominational coloring; or, more precisely, it had all of them at once.
Radiating out from the center, residential neighborhoods, urbanized villages, and
former suburbs now formed a continuous band of settlement in which small islands
of well-defined communal groupings lay next to one another. To be sure, this was a
far cry from the abrupt line of segregation that the civil war of the late twentieth century was to institute between an almost exclusively Christian east and a predominantly Muslim west. A hundred years earlier, although Christians found themselves
alone on the slopes of Ashrafiyyeh Hill, other neighborhoods drew them westward,
particularly Musaytbeh and the former village of Mazra'at al-'Arab, soon known sim-

ply as Mazra'a; and enclaves could still be found everywhere, still smaller islands within the small islands—even, in a few cases, individual families professing a different faith from that of their immediate neighbors. This checkerboard configuration, reinforced by the patterns of migration from outside the city, nonetheless did not amount to a battlefield, even if communal territorialization fueled a certain residual level of street violence, especially on the edges of each territory.[65]

Relying on the strength of family authority, religious communities were able for a time to contain the effects of Westernization and curb the assertion of individual identity. Here again, however, one should not speak of a perfect dichotomy, to the extent that communities were obliged to adapt to the new demands for personal autonomy. It would be still less exact to identify the reaction of these communities with an archaic resistance to modernization. If the patrimonial structure of Arab society lent itself to appeals for 'asabiyya, the sense of solidarity exalted by Ibn Khaldun, the sectarian rivalries that now began to develop in Beirut were very much the product of their time.

Through a paradox well known to historians of the late Ottoman period, modernization worked to intensify tensions among communities. Under the contradictory pressures of the European powers, anxious to broaden the basis for trade without forfeiting the advantages they had inherited from the Capitulations, the authors of the Tanzimat, which had originated in the proclamation of the equality of all the sultan's subjects, soon acquiesced in the restoration of the millet system. This enlargement of the jurisdiction of non-Muslim religious authorities, which was to complicate the Eastern Question still further, was more or less pronounced from one province to another depending on the degree of exposure to Western economic, political, and cultural penetration. In Syria, the repercussions of the return to this system were particularly sensitive to both consular behavior and denominational diversity. Western policy encouraged a more assertive posture on the part of Christian minorities there and, in reaction against this, a hardening of attitudes among the Muslim majority.[66]

All the less could a city like Beirut escape the implications of this state of affairs as its rise was directly connected with the development of European commerce—so much so that it had become the main point of entry to the Levant for the West. Against the background of turmoil in Mount Lebanon, and with the redistribution of power and wealth in the city at stake, religious cleavages were aggravated and the sense of communal identity heightened. Just as the opportunities for personal independence had begun to increase, the individual of this new age found it to his advantage to blend into the group.

9

Uncertain Identities

"Then, just before the casket was closed, a young, elegantly dressed Christian who until then had not said a word, wearing a rose in his lapel and a perfumed handkerchief in his breast pocket, . . . walked up to the coffin, leaned over the face of the dead man and kissed it."[1] The scene seems out of a Mafia story, and indeed in a certain sense it is. A few weeks later the man with the rose was to distinguish himself in a much less peaceable manner by assassinating three people, all of them Muslims, in broad daylight. The dead man was avenged—no matter that the new victims were very probably innocent of killing him.

What sort of man was it who deserved such posthumous vindication? He was neither a military leader nor a political official; he was, quite simply, a *qabaday*, a gangster—but one of the most feared in all of Beirut at the turn of the twentieth century. Probably of Greek heritage, Costa Paoli (or Osta Bawli, in the local pronunciation of his name) was regarded as the champion of the Christians. Any member of his community who encountered problems with the government or with rival Muslim gangs could count on being protected—or avenged—by him. As revered by his coreligionists as he was dreaded by his Muslim enemies, Paoli moved about in public with great ceremony, surrounded by a phalanx of bodyguards carrying a slew of revolvers and daggers around their caftans.[2] This did not prevent him from being stabbed to death—in the back, it was said. Inevitably his funeral was the occasion of passionate scenes, in the course of which a frenzied crowd chanted anti-Muslim and anti-Turkish slogans, and the members of his entourage furiously promised a swift revenge, before the elegant young man with the scented handkerchief brought a solemn touch to the theatricality of the moment—and then settled accounts, as the code of honor required.

Typical though it may seem of the violence that is often associated with Beirut and Lebanon in the twentieth century, this episode provides evidence more of change than of continuity. Street violence, at least in this form, was a rather new phenomenon at the turn of the century—no less than the vigor of the sectarian resentments it expressed. Above all, the belligerent confidence displayed by the Christians who had gathered to mourn Paoli's passing revealed a state of mind that had been unthinkable a half-century earlier. Far from being an archaism, sectarian animosity was part of the price that modernity exacted from society. So well adapted was this spirit to the new age, in fact, that it succeeded in swallowing up even nationalism, an impulse of apparently more recent origin.

THE TURNING POINT OF 1860

The intensity of sectarian identification had increased in Beirut as a result of the enduring effects of the events of 1860. If the city proper had been spared the clashes that brought bloodshed to Mount Lebanon and then Damascus, it was not immune either to the tensions that provoked them or to the ones that prolonged them. Throughout Syria, a heightened sense of denominational antagonism was palpable on the eve of the outbreak of hostilities. Noting the mounting sense of exasperation in the city's Muslim community, a Jesuit priest reported in 1859 a "prophecy" announcing the "end of Islamism" that year.[3] When violence erupted in Damascus the following year, the discovery in Beirut of the corpse of a Muslim who had been assassinated prompted the lynching of a Maronite in front of the Sérail. The presence in the outer harbor of European warships, in addition to the Ottoman garrison stationed in the city and reinforced by the timely arrival of two thousand soldiers, prevented the massacres from spreading,[4] however, and Beirut immediately became a haven for Christians fleeing Damascus and the villages of the Mountain. This sudden and lasting influx of population coincided with other developments, notably the construction of the Beirut-Damascus road, that combined to make 1860 one of the major turning points in the history of the city, whose collective memory was henceforth fraught with emotions associated with events that took place elsewhere. Even after the pacification of Mount Lebanon, the incessant flow of immigration continued to strengthen sectarian reflexes in Beirut, sustaining a cold war among its religious communities.

One of the most important consequences of the events of 1860 was to accelerate changes in the denominational composition of the city. Here again, of course, only very rough demographic estimates are available, and the figures given by contemporaries must be regarded with still more caution than estimates of the size of the population as a whole. Nonetheless, a great deal of evidence argues against the popular, but uninformed, view that Beirut remained preponderantly Sunni until the French Mandate. Beginning in the Egyptian era, the number of Christians appears to have substantially increased.[5] Whereas under al-Jazzār, at the end of the eighteenth century, they were so few that (as one visitor put it) it would have been possible for all of them to pray in a single church, the French consul noted in the 1830s that the Christian population in Beirut was the most numerous of the entire coast and that more masses were held there than anywhere else.[6] Henri Guys even went so far as to assert that Christians amounted to more than half of the population, which he put at 15,000: 7,000 Muslims, 4,000 "Greeks" (or Greek Orthodox Christians), 1,500 Maronites, 1,200 "Greek Catholics," 800 Druzes, 400 Armenians and Syrian Catholics, 200 Jews, and 400 Europeans.[7] An Ottoman census cited by the British traveler David Urquhart in 1850 confirmed the tendency, if not the actual estimate itself, in suggesting that Muslims constituted only a slight majority. In addition to immigration for economic reasons, which brought as many Muslims to Beirut as Christians, politically motivated immigration disproportionately added to the Christian population. Its principal cause was the endemic unrest in Mount Lebanon between Druze and Maronites after 1840, though other denominational conflicts also contributed to it, such as the internecine Christian feuds that erupted in Hasbayya in the southern part of the Biqaʿ Plateau following a wave of conversions to Protestantism, and the clashes at Aleppo in 1850 between Christians and Muslims.[8] Then came the civil war of 1860. A steady stream of immigration now became an uninterrupted flood for several months.

Leaving by the unfinished new road from Damascus, thousands of people sought refuge in Beirut during the month of July alone. Their number continued to grow. Eleven thousand were said to have come in the space of one month, three thousand of them arriving together the same day. Despite the efforts of the Ottoman authorities and of the consuls, the exodus went on until autumn, and even beyond. In the years that followed, and as late as 1867, a continuing though reduced flow of Christian emigration could still be observed from Damascus to Beirut.[9]

The influx of refugees radically modified the city's demographic profile. By 1865, compared with the census figures for 1840, the number of Muslims had doubled, but the number of Christians had tripled, with the result that the former now made up one-third of the total population and the latter two-thirds. This new proportion remained stable over the following decades, with the Christian population tripling again between 1861 and the end of the century. In the early twentieth century, mention of a Christian majority could be found in both official and popular sources, the only exception being an Ottoman estimate in the 1908 almanac that spoke of parity between the two groups, although it distinguished between Beiruti and Lebanese, which is to say persons registered in the Mutasarrifate of Mount Lebanon.[10]

Considering only political immigration, motivated by sectarian conflict in the surrounding area, one is apt to see Beirut as a predominantly Muslim city that was suddenly invaded by Christians. It would be more accurate to speak of a new communal balance in which the demographic composition of the Mountain worked to the advantage of the Christian population of Beirut.[11] It was not the only factor, however. The invasion, to the extent there was one, was both Christian and Muslim. The spikes in the city's population, which coincided with massive arrivals of Christians, were roughly balanced by a slow but continuous influx of Muslim immigrants. While the Balkan crises and Slavic pressure on the borders of the Ottoman Empire brought a certain number of Albanian and Caucasian families, Muslim immigration, spread over practically the whole of the nineteenth century, resulted mainly from economic developments that were at work throughout Syria as well as from the administrative reorganization that made them central to the expansion of Beirut. The increase in the Muslim population is attested by the growth in the number of mosques, which rose from six in 1800 to thirty-one at the beginning of the twentieth century. Moreover, according to their own accounts, many Muslim families in Beirut trace their settlement there back to the nineteenth century. And where the absence of a traumatic memory of flight from their homeland, similar to that of the Christian refugees from the Mountain (and those who came from the Balkans), has caused other Muslim families to be uncertain of their origins, it may be assumed in most cases that they came from the Syrian interior or from cities along the coast.

Added to the original Muslim population of Beirut and the villages of the promontory that were gradually absorbed by the city, this steady stream of immigration was to establish, if not perfect parity, then at least a certain equilibrium. Moreover, the Muslims in Beirut almost all belonged to a single community. Although there had long been Druze families, joined by a certain number of their coreligionists after the creation of the Mutasarrifate, as well as a first group of Shi'a that came to the city in the early twentieth century, the overwhelming majority of Muslims were Sunni. The Christians, by contrast, were divided among several rites. No matter that Christians enjoyed a numerical advantage over Muslims in gross terms, a closer denominational analysis brings out the dominant position of the Sunni community, which remained the most numerous of the various sects.

The Greek Orthodox, who were of very ancient settlement in Beirut, had nonetheless reduced the gap that separated them from the Sunnis, thanks mainly to immigration from Damascus; with between 23 and 29 percent of the overall population, they stood in the first rank of the Christian denominations. But the Orthodox now found themselves challenged by the Maronites, who, though they accounted for only a tenth of Beirut's inhabitants in the 1830s, and many fewer than that beforehand, seem to have exceeded a fifth of the total by 1861, and then by the end of the Ottoman period in 1920 amounted to a quarter of it. Next came two other communities of lesser demographic stature, though sizable enough to occupy a discernible place in the political landscape: the Greek Catholics, likewise reinforced by immigration from the Syrian interior, whose prominence in the world of business gave them great visibility; and the Druze, who possessed considerable land-holdings in the western part of the promontory. Further complicating this picture, there were small concentrations of recently converted Protestants and a few other minorities (Armenians, Syriacs, and Latin-rite Catholics), comparable in size to the Jewish community, which accounted for between 1 and 3 percent of the total population. The Jews had preserved their geographic identity in the course of moving from their old intramural neighborhood to Wadi Abu Jamil, which grew up with the expansion of the city and contained, in addition to a synagogue, a school of the Universal Israelite Alliance. Finally, there were the foreigners, who, though their numbers had increased since the opening of Beirut to overseas commerce, did not exceed 3 percent of the total, significantly less than in Alexandria or Cairo.[12]

This uneven distribution was nonetheless heavily weighted in favor of the three principal communities: with Sunnis accounting for more or less a third of the population, a like proportion of Orthodox, and Maronites making up between a fifth and a quarter of the total, there existed a rough balance of power. But this balance itself acted as a source of friction.

A COMMUNAL COLD WAR

In Beirut, as elsewhere, rapid demographic growth combined with ancient prejudices to feed sectarian antagonism. This phenomenon is much more modern than is usually supposed. In the case of Beirut it has often been attributed to the growing frustration of a formerly predominant group, the Muslims, in the face of a newly assertive Christian presence encouraged by the transformation of the Ottoman state under the Tanzimat, the loss of influence that seemed to follow from this transformation, and the interventionism of the European powers. The frustration was quite real and unquestionably played a decisive role in helping to spread the massacres from Mount Lebanon to Damascus in 1860. But beyond these moments of crisis, which were relatively few, sectarian antagonism as a device for mobilizing popular support was also, and primarily, a product of the militancy of minority groups—and all the more so when, intentionally or not, they disrupted the prevailing communal equilibrium. In Beirut this occurred with the arrival of Christian immigrants from the Mountain, whose constantly growing numbers and violent passions upset the delicate balance of civic harmony. These newcomers brought with them the fierce particularism of mountain peoples memorably described by the French historian Fernand Braudel,[13] aggravating and deepening the resentments created by recent events, the memory of which they transmitted to their children. All of this sustained a dynamic of social division despite their gradual integration into urban society, in part because of the persistent rise in population due to continuing immigration. Tensions were already perceptible on the eve of the civil war, then heightened with the arrival of the Christian refugees from Damascus,[14] and exacerbated when those responsible for the massacres were brought to Beirut in order to be taken by ship to Istanbul. Later there were occasional outbursts of violence, although these were limited to more or less localized clashes, notably in 1871, 1881, and 1888.

To a large extent, then, the city was able to absorb the strain of social cleavages. Even at the most critical moment, in 1860, religious loyalties did not translate into an explosive increase in belligerent feeling; indeed, the arrival of refugees even triggered a temporary exodus of upper-class Christians to Alexandria, Smyrna, and Athens.[15] Later, when things calmed down, class identification among the wealthiest citizens came to temper the effect of communal allegiances. The city's growing complexity generated countervailing—and sometimes contradictory—pressures, with the result that interdenominational relations during this period yield a very mixed picture. On balance, however, something like harmony seems to have prevailed under the joint auspices of Ottoman officials, European consuls, and local business leaders. The ongoing economic boom gave rise to new classes that cut across communal lines: bonds were established between merchants and bankers of various religious persuasions, and a spirit of cooperation provided a first glimpse of the sense of decency that was to mark the periods of civil peace in the Lebanon of the twentieth century.[16] Thus one finds the names of Christians in the list of donors to the Maqāsid, among them a member of the Sursock family who, in the first year of the society's existence, donated three hundred Arabic grammars.[17] Similarly, the Orthodox bishop of Beirut, preparing to set off on a trip, instructed the dignitaries of his community to defer to the judgment of Salim Salam during his absence.[18]

But none of this mattered really. An undeclared war had started up among the communities, shaping the daily life of the city. There was a renewed outbreak of violence in the early twentieth century, on a scale that alarmed Maurice Barrès on his visit to Beirut in 1913. Noticeable even in wealthy neighborhoods, sectarian rivalry led to much score-settling among the working classes, and sometimes to assassinations. In 1903 a quarrel between Muslims in the Basta quarter and neighboring Orthodox Christians degenerated into street clashes. Several people were killed, prompting the temporary flight of several thousand Christians; a provisional army of some four thousand Maronites was poised to swoop down from the Mountain and ravage the Muslim neighborhoods of Beirut—in itself a sign of the new confidence that the establishment of the Mutasarrifate had given Christians of all stripes. There grew out of this a rift between the wālī of Beirut, Rashid Bey, and the mutasarrif of Mount Lebanon, Muzaffer Pasha.[19] But the crisis was peacefully resolved before it could spread, thanks to the conciliatory efforts of Muslim and Orthodox notables in the city, and probably also to the imminent arrival of two American warships, dispatched by President Theodore Roosevelt in response to a false report that the vice consul of the United States had been murdered.[20]

THE PRESTIGE OF THE GANGSTER

Even in the absence of such passions, the streets of Beirut were filled with danger. As the privileged theater of a cult of honor, they were regularly the scene of brawls and vendettas that, far from being devalued by the modernization of the city, came to be charged instead with special significance. Perhaps the most striking emblem of this culture of violence, and of its role in determining the balance of power between communities, was the prestige that surrounded the thugs and gang leaders *(qabadayat)* who came to prominence at this stage of the city's expansion.

By promoting the use of force in daily life and making the display of weapons a common sight, the qabadayat made it plain that any individual quarrel was part of a larger conflict between groups. They were colorful characters, to say the least: dressed in the manner of consular guards, an office they sometimes also filled— twirling their moustaches to a point at the ends, sporting the tarbush, caftans, and billowing trousers, with a cartridge belt or two strapped across the chest, brandishing revolvers and daggers, and wielding the wicker cane, a symbol of power—they deployed all the paraphernalia of plebeian charisma. But behind the elaborate apparatus of machismo, which contributed so lastingly to their legend, the qabadayat were nothing less than outlaws, bandits posing as protectors of widows and orphans— so long as they belonged to the same community. These men and their gangs effectively ruled the streets of Beirut.

The qabadayat were descended from the informal urban militias *(ahdāth* and *'ayārūn)* that traditionally maintained order in the working-class neighborhoods of Arab cities.[21] So long as Beirut remained a small town covering only a few hectares, it was neither large enough to warrant this sort of protection nor prosperous enough to afford it. But with the development of the port and increased investment by both business owners and labor—shippers, brokers, dock workers, and so on—as well as expanded opportunities for smuggling across the border with Mount Lebanon, modernization held out the prospect of considerable rewards for criminal initiative. The growth of consular staff offered additional incentives: a number of these specialists in violence were employed as qawwās, among them Sa'id Sununu from the Basta neighborhood (with the French consulate) and Muhammad al-'Anuti from Musaytbeh (with the British consulate).[22] The diplomatic immunity they acquired in this way proved to be very useful in their other occupations. But the differences between their gangs and the old plebeian militias of Damascus and Aleppo were not limited to the economic environment in which they operated. The modern qabadayat of Beirut distinguished themselves as well, and above all, by their involvement in sectarian quarrels. As a consequence of a political reversal having no equivalent elsewhere, Beirut was the only city of the Levant (or at least the first) where Christian neighborhoods had their own bosses. Costa Paoli was but one, albeit the most powerful, among many such gang leaders.

Here again, communal solidarity and class interests overlapped. The development of smuggling and trade in illicit goods by immigrants across the administrative border separating Beirut from the Mountain favored crosscutting alliances. But in marking out their territory, as gangs do in every city in the world, the qabadayat recognized the sectarian dividing lines between neighborhoods.[23] This territorialization of communal rivalry was all the more easily accomplished as the phenomenon of gang conflict, far from being limited to the seedy parts of the city, began to take its place within a clientelist system whose levers were controlled either directly by the Ottoman government or indirectly by local notables.[24] As a neighborhood or street boss, the qabaday was typically the intermediary, or in any case the client, of a za'im, a socially prominent patron who could grant political protection if necessary. And although these notables were capable of maintaining partnerships, sometimes even friendships, across sectarian lines, increasingly they were divided from one another by widening cleavages.

THE WEIGHT OF MOUNT LEBANON

The intensification of sectarian rivalries was due in large part to the growing influence exerted by the semi-autonomous administrative district of Mount Lebanon, where the incessant—and lawful—intervention of foreign consuls and the public role of the Maronite Church had the effect of inverting the traditional balance of power.[25] The new state of affairs appeared so unalterable that voices were raised within the Mutasarrifate demanding nothing less than the annexation of Beirut, notwithstanding that it had become in 1888 the capital of a much larger coastal province that included Tripoli, Sidon, and Tyre and their hinterlands. In disregarding the claims of other denominations in the city, this demand was in itself a provocation, from the point of view both of the Muslim population and of the Porte, even if it is true that the idea of a Greater Lebanon was born, just after the Mutasarrifate had been proclaimed, in the mind of the Ottoman governor, Dawud Pasha.[26] It was reasserted many times, preparing the way for the expansion of Lebanese territory that finally occurred after the First World War.[27] At the same time, however, another attempt was made to get around Beirut by endowing the Mountain with its own outlet to the sea, in the event the little town of Junieh. Despite the importance of the customs house of Beirut for the imperial treasury, and quite particularly for retiring the Ottoman debt, the plan for a Lebanese port won support in the early twentieth century from high officials up to and including the mutasarrif himself, Muzaffer Pasha. In 1903, alleging that travelers from the Mountain were subject to systematic exploitation, and sometimes physical harm, on the waterfront of Beirut, which was controlled by a network of local gangsters and powerful courtiers, Muzaffer authorized a British steamship line to anchor in the roadstead of Junieh, though cargo-handling facilities had yet to be built. A similar arrangement was later concluded with a French line. But faced with opposition from other French interests—dominant in the Compagnie du Port de Beyrouth—and local business circles, the Ottoman government became alarmed and reversed the decision.[28] The matter was brought up once again after the revolution of 1908, and finally, during the crisis of 1912, Istanbul approved the creation of a port at Junieh and of another at Nabi Yunes, on the stretch of coast lying beneath the Shuf Mountains, as the merchants of Dayr al-Qamar had urged.[29] The outbreak of the First World War delayed these plans.

The challenge that certain Mountain elites sought to mount against Beirut encountered resistance on other fronts. The Banque du Liban, created in Paris in 1913 with a capitalization of four million French francs, was greeted with some reluctance by both French investors and merchants in Beirut. Similarly, the Société des Tramways Libanais, which sought to link Sidon and Tripoli, neglected to ask Istanbul for permission to run its line through Beirut—an omission that, because it seemed motivated by political considerations rather than economic expediency, ruined the company's credit and further aroused the mistrust of the city's business class.[30] Moreover, the taxes levied on the revenues of the province of Beirut to help finance the Mutasarrifate did little to mute the hostility arising from the almost simultaneous emergence of two distinct political and administrative entities.

Henceforth the very nature of the relations between the city and its near hinterland was radically changed. The constitution of the Mutasarrifate, with its well-defined administrative and fiscal boundaries, formalized the separation between city and mountain and fed an active trade in contraband, the profits from which were channeled to the dangerous neighborhoods of Beirut and their networks of gangsters. To be sure, this separation did not hinder large population movements, to judge from the continuing flows of immigrants and, in the opposite direction, the seasonal emigration of city dwellers to new holiday resorts. Traditionally a refuge for the inhabitants of Beirut during epidemics on account of its healthier climate, the Mountain now began to be seen as an attractive place to spend the summer. Growing numbers of city residents vacationed there; some even bought second homes in the foothills.

But neighborly relations did not eliminate cultural differences and other sources of animosity. Many immigrants preferred to remain registered as citizens of the Mountain in order to escape the taxation of Ottoman subjects in Beirut. The tax rolls of the Greek Orthodox bishopric, for example, classed the "mountain people" (jabali) with Western foreigners (ajanib).[31] And as the view of the world that the immigrants brought with them suggested, the Mountain cultivated an ideology that was now all the more inward-looking as it could rely on a proto-state structure of government, whereas the city, having one face turned toward the Mediterranean and the other toward the Syrian interior, was subject to the tension between change and resistance to change that soon spread to all the other Arab provinces of the empire. This dichotomy, which was to leave a lasting mark on the constitution of the future Lebanese state, manifested itself in the near term in the form of heightened sectarian tensions in Beirut. But just as the Eastern Question appeared to be nearing its final resolution, the growing attraction of Arab nationalism was forced to yield to an apparent accommodation among Muslim and Christian elites.

BETWEEN CITIZENSHIP AND NATIONALISM

The deepening of communal rivalries helped to accelerate the decline of the Ottoman Empire as well. Ottoman authority itself had not been weakened in the province of Beirut, least of all during the reign of Abdülhamid II. But the echo of the crises that shook the Balkan provinces and the escalation of Great Power competition, thrown into relief by the Congress of Berlin in 1878 and the Fashoda Incident twenty years later, aroused both concerns and expectations. Despite the repressive hand of the imperial police and then, after the revolution of 1908, the hard line adopted by the Young Turk government, the vigor of local demands for self-rule—indeed, for independence—was unmistakable, even if they did not quite amount to a wholesale rejection of Ottomanism.

The first stirrings of an Arab national consciousness in Beirut could be detected at practically the same moment that the idea of osmanlilik, an offshoot of the Tanzimat, was initially formulated. For almost three-quarters of a century, the oscillation between these competing conceptions produced a chronic sort of indecisiveness. Until the outbreak of the First World War, the emerging Arab consciousness went hand in hand with a renewed demand for Ottoman citizenship, the one feeding the other, with the result that it is not easy to identify the various parties contesting the established order, in Beirut as in the other cities of Bilād al-Shām.

The challenge to Ottomanism reached its height with the famous poster affair of 1880–81, when anonymous nationalist appeals were plastered on the walls of Beirut and Damascus. The first declaration, posted in June 1880, was addressed to the "children of Syria" and denounced the "lethargy" that had led to "subjugation to the Turks." It concluded with Ibrahim al-Yaziji's overtly nationalist verse, "Awaken, O Arabs, the mire has risen up to your knees." Six months later a second poster, addressed to the "children of the homeland," hinted at the possibility of taking matters further. A third poster, put up in June 1881, was more explicit. While calling for independence, to be shared with "our Lebanese brothers," it enunciated specific but less radical demands consistent with a revised imperial arrangement: proclamation of Arabic as the official language of Syria, administrative decentralization, and limitation of military service to territories within the borders of the Arab provinces.[32]

Coming in the aftermath of the Balkan crisis and in the context of sultanic absolutism, the affair caused a great stir in the chancelleries, where it was reported in meticulous detail by the consuls to their governments. The mystery surrounding the authors of these documents only increased public curiosity—a mystery that has long intrigued historians of this period, who have advanced a variety of explanations. It is generally believed today that responsibility for the posters resides with the Maqāsid, probably acting with the encouragement of Midhat Pasha, then governor of Syria. The former grand vizier, who had been exiled from the capital after the coup led by Abdülhamid in 1878, was to be exiled once again after his brief tenure in Damascus, this time for good—a sign that the new government would no longer tolerate weakness in the face of a crystallizing Arab political identity. After the ouster of Midhat Pasha the government outlawed the Maqāsid, while nonetheless allowing its educational activities to go forward. It was only in 1907 that the wālī of Beirut permitted the society to be reformed, and not until the next year that its former status was fully recognized with the Young Turks' reinstatement of the Constitution of 1876, suspended by Abdülhamid.[33] Nor was the poster affair unrelated to the decision, taken a few years later, to once again divide up the province of Syria by creating the vilayet of Beirut.

Such an act of defiance was not to be repeated for a long while. Abdülhamid's omnipresent secret police persuaded the majority of intellectuals and militants who advocated change to prefer exile. But repression was not the only reason for their silence. The survival of an empire that had already lost much of its ethnic diversity, along with many of its territories, depended on showing greater attentiveness to the Arab bloc, which now accounted for half of the total population. As part of the new pan-Islamism, whose great symbol was the project of connecting Istanbul with Arabia via the planned Hijaz railroad, the sultan-caliph developed a detailed Arab policy that increased public expenditure in towns between Damascus and Beirut and sought to rally local notables, Muslim and Christian alike, some of whom were even called upon to serve in the government. These included the brothers Salim and Najib Malhama, Maronite businessmen from Beirut with experience in large-scale construction projects; before being made a minister, Najib Malhama was also the head of the dreaded Hamidian secret police in the city.[34] At the same time the foreign menace to the empire strengthened a certain sense of Ottoman solidarity, particularly among Muslim elites, even if the suppression of individual liberties led to abiding dissatisfaction.

For intellectuals in Beirut, especially after 1881, life under the Hamidian regime was stifling. Except in education, the excitement of the early days of the Nahda had been extinguished by the exile of a growing number of men of letters and political thinkers. Cairo and Paris were favored destinations. In Egypt, which was only nominally under Ottoman suzerainty, the new English masters were only too happy after 1882 to welcome "Syrian" journalists and activists opposed to the despotism of Abdülhamid, in the hope that they would act as a counterweight to those, not less numerous, who were attracted to France and supported by her. In any case the time was past when Bustani, Yaziji, and other pioneers were laboring in Beirut to impress on the Arab renaissance its major features. Most intellectual creativity now took place elsewhere—in Paris, where the Muslim reformism of the late nineteenth century was distinguished by the work of the philosopher Jamal al-Din al-Afghani, and in Cairo, by the work of the religious scholar and jurist Muhammad ʿAbduh. So it was, too, with the first works of political Arabism that appeared at the beginning of the twentieth century: *Umm al-Qura* (The Mother of Cities) and *Tabāʾiʿ al-istibdād* (The Nature of Tyranny), published in Cairo by ʿAbd al-Rahman al-Kawakibi of Aleppo shortly before his death in 1902, and *Le réveil de la nation arabe* (The Awakening of the Arab Nation), by the Lebanese Nagib Azoury, published in Paris in 1905. The link that Kawakibi established between Arabism and the reform of Islam nonetheless built upon an idea first formulated in Beirut by a Christian, Ibrahim al-Yaziji, namely, that Islam had been led astray when the Arabs lost control over it. At the same time another independence movement developed in Mount Lebanon, or, more exactly, among the Lebanese elites that were living in exile in Paris. It was given its first expression in 1908, in a book titled *La question du Liban* by Bulus Nujaym (writing under the name Paul Jouplain), who associated the independence of an enlarged (or Greater) Lebanon with that of Syria as a whole.[35] But these ideas, if they reached Beirut, were debated there only insofar as the need for secrecy permitted. Moreover, government repression did not give rise to a radical challenge to Ottoman solidarity, which was nourished and protected by a perception of foreign threats that, particularly among Muslim elites, largely inhibited the development of nationalism.

Ottoman solidarity survived Abdülhamid, at least among the Arabs. With the reinstatement of Midhat Pasha's constitution, the issue of internal reform once again came to the fore, though now the broadening of political horizons favored moderation rather than violent opposition. The annexation of Bosnia-Herzegovina by Austria in October 1908 sparked a mobilization of troops even in Beirut,[36] as well as a demonstration by intellectuals in the Burj. After an interval of almost thirty years the arguments first raised by the posters of 1880–81 were made once more. They were still accompanied, however, by the same hesitation between Ottomanism and Arabism.

Once the news of the sultan's overthrow came to be known, the euphoria of the capital spread to the Arab provinces. The rediscovery of liberty after three decades of absolutism, in addition to the hope of seeing the reform of the state successfully carried out and external threats to its safety dispelled, gave rise to a period of great creativity and excitement. Newspapers were founded, political parties were formed. The first steps taken by the new government pointed in a liberal direction, notably the law regarding the press and another regarding parties and associations (both still in effect in Lebanon today). Between 1908 and 1914, more than sixty new periodicals appeared in Beirut alone.[37] Very quickly, however, the constitutional revolution became a source of a growing misunderstanding between Arabs and Turks, who now with the loss of the last Balkan provinces occupied a binational empire. Where Arab elites saw the end of Hamidian despotism as an opportunity to voice nationalist aspirations and to have a greater say in the conduct of affairs of state, another specifically Turkish—and much more exclusionary—nationalism gained the upper hand with the ascendancy of the Committee of Union and Progress (CUP), the hard-line wing of the Young Turks, dedicated to the defense of Ottomanism.

The reaction of the Syrian Arabs was relatively restrained at first. Some leading figures—Muslims and even a few Christians—belonged to the CUP, such as Sulayman al-Bustani, a deputy for Beirut who was appointed agriculture minister in 1914.[38] The Arab independence movement gained ground among the exiles, of course, but the more or less secret societies that were subsequently formed, from Paris to Cairo and from Istanbul to Damascus, continued to waver between outright independence and autonomy within the framework of empire. The best known, al-'Arabiyya al-Fatat (Young Arabia), formed in Paris in 1911 and then relocated the following year to Damascus, attracted several young activists from Beirut, among them 'Abdul-Ghani al-'Uraysi, the editor of *Al-Mufīd*.[39] In Cairo during this time, Rashid Rida's journal *Al-Manār* made itself the mouthpiece for the challenge to Unionism, and the Administrative Decentralization Party, which enjoyed broad support among the exile community, profited from the convergent ambitions of the khedive, 'Abbas Hilmi, and Great Britain in arguing for the annexation of Syria to Egypt under a British protectorate. Nonetheless the idea of secession by Arab Ottomans was almost never advanced in public, at least not in any collective way. Political debate continued to be dominated by the theme of decentralization, around which the Reform Society of Beirut (Jam'iyyat Bayrut al-islahiyya) was formed in late 1912 by a group including Salim Salam and Ahmad Mukhtar Bayhum. The First Arab Congress, held in Paris in June 1913, did not go any further despite—or indeed perhaps because of—the quickening pace of the Ottoman collapse.

FROM BEIRUT TO PARIS AND BACK AGAIN

What remained of osmanlilik in practical terms now entered into a new and ominous crisis, the last one, as it turned out, before the spoils were divided up. The radicalization of the CUP government poisoned relations between Turks and Arabs while failing to avert the dangers confronting the Porte: the Italian expedition to Libya deprived the Ottoman Empire of its last African possession, and the war that broke out in the Balkans reduced its European territories, already badly eroded by the crisis of 1876–78, to nothing. Despite their geographic remoteness, these threats were directly felt in the Arab provinces. Broadening its field of operations to the eastern Mediterranean, the Italian navy attacked several Ottoman ports, among them Beirut, which on 24 February 1912 was the target of a violent bombardment that was to have lasting repercussions—so many reminders that the end was drawing near. And indeed the conjunction of the Italian bombardment and the war in the Balkans stirred up wild rumors of an imminent French invasion meant to impose a protectorate over Syria.

The plan for a French protectorate, it will be recalled, overcame a substantial hurdle when London made it known, through diplomatic correspondence between Edward Grey and Paul Cambon, that it had neither the ambition nor the intention of acting in Syria, giving France a free hand. Advocated in Paris by the French Asia Committee led by Robert de Caix, the idea won the support of a number of Christian exiles there; in Beirut itself it held appeal for certain notables, also Christian. In the summer of 1912 one of them, Michel Tuwayni, undertook to approach the French consulate—whose protection he enjoyed by virtue of his service as a dragoman—to request a protectorate, even informing Salim Salam, then the most visible member of the Muslim community, of his purpose. But Salam, like the majority of Muslim notables, still was inclined to remain faithful to the empire. Earlier, in February, during a visit to Cairo, he had expressed to the khedive his doubts about the wisdom of annexing Syria to Egypt—doubts that gained force when the CUP was forced to yield power to the Liberal Union in July, just as events in the Balkans were nearing their bloody climax. On learning of Tuwayni's approach to the consul, Joseph-Fernand Couget, Salam became worried. While taking care not to compromise the source of his information, he warned the wālī of Beirut, Adham Bey, of what he had heard, emphasizing the necessity of seizing the initiative.

With the fall of the CUP from power, there was no longer any question of responding to further acts of defiance by empty assertions of authority. In line with the policy of the ruling liberal party that had appointed him, Adham Bey was inclined toward political solutions that would take into account the expectations of the Arab population. What is more, the government had instructed him to obtain the provincial council's approval of its reform program. But even the Liberal Union's closest allies in Beirut preferred a more representative approach, as Salim Salam and Ahmad Mukhtar Bayhum made clear during a conversation with the provincial governor. Thus was born the idea of constituting a Reform Society that would develop a program based on decentralization and reliance on European advisors in each district.[40] Salam had already advocated this approach in an article published in Al-Ittihād al-ʿUthmānī (Ottoman Union) a few months earlier.[41] To achieve the largest possible consensus, each of the various millet councils was asked to appoint representatives of its community. The plan was to bring together forty-two Muslims and forty-two non-Muslims, the latter including sixteen Greek Orthodox, ten Maronites, six Greek Catholics, two Protestants, two Syrian Christians, two Roman Catholics, two Armenian Orthodox, and two Jews.[42]

The inaugural meeting of the Reform Society, attended by sixty-five of the eighty-four representatives, took place on 12 January 1913 in the municipal building. The Society elected two executive officers (Salim Salam, a Muslim, and Petro Trad, a Greek Orthodox) and a secretary (the Maronite Ayub Tabet), and delegated the drafting of its program to a committee composed of twenty-six members (thirteen Muslims, twelve Christians, and one Jew). This parity between the Muslims and the others was to furnish the basis for a campaign launched against the movement by some notables of lesser stature—with the encouragement, it was said, of the CUP.

The Beirut Reform Committee, as it came to be known, rapidly worked up a comprehensive program that defined in great detail the functioning of local governments and specified the role of European advisors and inspectors.[43] Though nothing was said in the program itself, it emerged from previous declarations that these Europeans would be nationals of the smaller countries. At the same time the provincial council, convened by the wālī on the orders of Istanbul, drew up its own program. Revisions negotiated over the following days made it possible to overcome the Reform Society's objections. But just as the positions of the two sides had converged, the coup d'état in the capital that brought the CUP back to power on 23 January blocked progress once more. The liberal provincial governor Adham Bey was recalled, and his predecessor, Abu Bakr Hazim Bey, regained his former post.

Alarmed by these developments, the Reform Society sent a telegram to the new government pointedly affirming its commitment to the rule of law and its continuing determination to push for change. This act of defiance was underscored on the occasion of Hazim Bey's arrival in Beirut on 7 March, when virtually all of the city's leading citizens stayed away from the traditional welcoming ceremonies at the port. The wālī failed to notice this slight, or, if he did, he showed no sign of it. During his first meeting with the leaders of the Society five days later he was conciliatory, but in the days that followed he took a harder line. The reformists dug in their heels: on 17 March Salam refused the governor's nomination to the vilayet council, and off-year elections called to fill the vacancy of two seats on the city council were boycotted. Hazim Bey went ahead and forwarded the vilayet's reform program to Istanbul on 24 March, together with the amendments that had been attached to it at the demand of the reformers, but two weeks later, on 8 April, he ordered the dissolution of the Reform Society and closed the club that the Society had opened the previous month in the Bāb Idris neighborhood. At the same time local agents of the government were directed to take action against the supporters of reform. Among these intermediaries was the qabaday ʿAbduh Inkidar, an arms merchant and smuggler, sentenced in absentia a few months earlier to four years in prison, with loss of civil rights for another five years, for crimes that the CUP chose to ignore.[44]

Despite the closing of its club, the opposition movement did not give up. On 11 April the Reform Society held a meeting on the campus of the Syrian Protestant College and approved a call for a general strike. Hazim Bey reacted by arresting six of the city's leading citizens, among them two members of the Society, and then the next day the editors of three newspapers. Two of these papers, *Al-Ittihād al-ʿUthmānī* and *Al-Mufīd,* the organ of Young Arabia,[45] were shut down. In the meantime the strike had paralyzed the city, despite attempts by the military to force businesses to open. Finally, Istanbul gave its approval to a compromise that freed the prisoners in exchange for a promise to end the strike. The strike was called off on 14 April, but businesses did not reopen until the next day, and leaders of the walkout had to personally appeal to the strikers to go back to work.[46]

These events were closely followed by the foreign chancelleries. The British looked to the Egyptian-based Administrative Decentralization Party in order to win over the reformists in Beirut. ʿAbdul-Karim al-Khalil had come from Cairo, proposing to Salim Salam that they coordinate their efforts with a view to annexing Syria to Egypt under a British protectorate. But even if it is not established that Khalil was knowingly acting as an agent of London, it is clear that the Foreign Office sought to extend its protection to the protesters. After the official dissolution of the Reform Society, the British consul had himself advised its leaders to hold a meeting on the campus of the American college, a protected territory under the terms of diplomatic immunity, as a way of showing their support for the opposition to the CUP. The French were better equipped to play this game, however. They could count on the direct, albeit undeclared, allegiance of a large number of the Society's Christian members, some of whom urged Tuwayni once again to approach the consul, Couget.[47] These advocates nonetheless had to reckon with the hostility of their Muslim partners to French protection in any form, as one may judge from Couget's doubts about the prospects for cooperation with the reformists, Salam in particular.[48] But this did not prevent Salam from accepting an invitation to the First Arab Congress in Paris a few weeks later.

In spite of its name, the representatives brought together by the congress were almost exclusively Syrian. There were two delegates from Mesopotamia. The rest belonged to one of three groups, all of them Syrian: a group of exiles in France, for the most part Christians from Mount Lebanon; a group of exiles in Egypt representing the Administrative Decentralization Party; and the delegation from Beirut, all of them members of the Reform Society. In many respects the latter group was the driving force behind the congress, whose final resolutions by and large recapitulated its program.

The Beirut delegation numbered six representatives: three Muslims (Salam, Bayhum, and Ahmad Tabbara, the publisher of *Al-Ittihād al-ʿUthmānī*) and three Christians (the Greek Orthodox Michel Sursock [Alfred's brother], the Greek Catholic Khalil Zaynieh, and the Maronite Ayub Tabet). The delegation departed on 26 May and arrived in Paris on 3 June, early enough to take part in organizing the conference, which officially opened on 18 June under the gavel of Abd al-Hamid al-Zahrawi, the parliamentary deputy from Hama, who had been appointed by a central committee. The group from Beirut was led by Salam. After five days, on 23 June, the Congress adopted resolutions that, in calling for the link with Istanbul to be maintained, preferred autonomy to total independence. This position was to be communicated on 30 June to the French and Ottoman governments by a predominantly Beiruti delegation.

Led by Zahrawi and comprising four representatives of Beirut (Salam, Bayhum, Tabbara, and Zaynieh) and two exiles from Mount Lebanon (Iskandar ʿAmmun and the writer Shukri Ghanem), the delegation paid a visit to Stephen Pichon, the minister of foreign affairs, to thank him for his country's hospitality and to convey to him their determination to preserve ties with Istanbul. The same delegation next called upon the Ottoman ambassador to Paris, in the presence of his secretary, Alfred Sursock, himself a native of Beirut, in anticipation of a later visit to Istanbul. But before leaving Paris a new delegation was charged with restating the position of the congress at the Quai d'Orsay. This time it was composed exclusively of representatives from Beirut (Salam, Bayhum, Tabbara, Tabet, and Zaynieh)—which did not prevent differences of opinion from emerging in the course of their meeting with Pierre de Margerie, head of the Office of Eastern Affairs. De Margerie reaffirmed the official French position on Ottoman sovereignty, and Bayhum replied that he intended to make this position publicly known. On leaving the Quai d'Orsay, Zaynieh and Tabet rebuked Bayhum for pressing the point, which in their view threatened to annoy the French government, and the members of the delegation began arguing with one another in the street.[49] According to one account that made the rounds in Beirut, Salam actually struck Tabet with his walking stick.[50]

These disagreements did not deter Zahrawi from entrusting the exclusively Beiruti delegation with the task of going to Istanbul. But Zaynieh, citing his fear of being arrested, withdrew from the embassy, which in the end consisted of only three Muslim representatives from Beirut. On 23 August, Salam, Bayhum, and Tabbara were received by Sultan Mehmed Reshad. The sultan, it must be said, had little control over his government. After further meetings with Ottoman officials the delegation came back to Beirut on 2 September to a welcoming crowd. Nothing was settled, of course. But if the government had made no concession, at least it had chosen to stall for time.

The easing of tensions that ensued was confirmed by the elections that took place in the spring of 1914, when Istanbul seemed to look with favor upon the candidacy of Salim Salam for a seat in the Ottoman parliament. And indeed on 9 April Salam was elected a deputy for the province of Beirut, along with the other members of his list, Michel Sursock and Kamel al-Asʿad, running against a list headed by Rida al-Sulh. At the same time, together with other investors from Beirut, Salam obtained a concession for the development of the marshes of Lake Huleh, in Galilee, again prevailing against a group led by Rida al-Sulh. Although the coincidence of these

FIGURE 52. Salim Salam's identification card as a deputy of the Ottoman parliament in 1914.

two things seemed to suggest some sort of under-the-table transaction—as Salam's adversaries repeatedly insinuated—it appears to have been nothing more than a sign of the preference freely granted by the government in Istanbul to a man who had done everything possible to defend the Ottoman bond with Syria. However this may be, the new deputy in his first parliamentary speech abandoned neither his allegiance to the state nor his demands for Arab autonomy.

Nevertheless the CUP was far from having carried the day. The idea of independence, though so far unmentioned in public, had ceased to be abstract. The shadow of French diplomacy gave it a practical dimension, above all once the Grey-Cambon exchange of letters in November 1912 had opened the way to the establishment by France of a protectorate over Syria. The consular reorganization that followed gave still greater importance to the posting in Beirut, soon confided to François Georges-Picot, who from the moment of his arrival initiated contacts with both Arab and Lebanese nationalists. A few months later, the spark of Sarajevo plunged the Old World into war. When it emerged from the conflict, the Ottoman Empire was finished.

FOUR YEARS OF WAR AND
TEN DAYS OF INDEPENDENCE

Beirut had had a foretaste of the misery to come with the Italian bombardment of 1912. The destruction was considerable, bringing with it a degree of social disorder that neither the municipal nor the provincial authorities were able to quickly remedy. But it was nothing by comparison with the desolation that descended upon the city after the outbreak of the world war. As a consequence of the blockade imposed by the British navy, the diversion of food supplies to the sole benefit of the Ottoman Fourth Army under Jamal Pasha, and a catastrophic attack of locusts, a cruel famine struck the Levant. If the Mountain suffered from it particularly, the residents of Beirut were hardly spared its effects, as new waves of refugees increased demand for the bare necessities of life. There were weeks in which dozens of deaths were recorded each day, sometimes as many as two hundred.[51] Additionally, the buildings of the old neighborhood in the historic heart of the city had been pulled down. But owing to the war, the demolition, undertaken finally in the spring of 1915 after a delay of thirty years, was not immediately followed by rebuilding. Next there came in September 1918 the bombing of the city by British airplanes, compounding the destruction. By the end of these terrible years, nothing more was left than a pale reflection of the vitality that had made Beirut the rising metropolis of the region at the beginning of the century.

Political repression deepened the human tragedy. After his failure on the Egyptian front, Jamal Pasha turned against the nationalists, arresting and trying many of them. A court martial convened at ʿAley sentenced several to death; they were hung in Damascus and Beirut. These martyrs, still today commemorated in Lebanon and Syria on 6 May every year, were in part Arab nationalists, in part Lebanese nationalists. Most of the rebels were given prison terms; some were let go. Remarkably, the court martial had in fact respected proper procedure, and it was in the main the official record of the relationships established with these men by the consuls, Couget and Georges-Picot, that formed the basis for the charges brought before the court—Jamal Pasha having managed to extract it from a hiding place inside the French consulate through the treason of a dragoman named Philippe Zalzal.[52] One month after the executions in Damascus and Beirut, in June 1916, Sharif Husayn of Mecca launched the Arab Revolt, proclaiming a *jihad* against the Turks. Kawakibi's prophecy had come true, and several of the freed Syrian militants set off for Mecca and Jidda.

Deliverance did not come until 1918. The Syrian campaign conducted by General Sir Edmund Allenby, with the support of the sharif's troops under the command of Husayn's son, Emir Faysal, came to fruition at almost the same moment as the Allied effort in Europe. On 3 October, Faysal entered Damascus. The Turkish governor having departed a few days earlier, Emir Saʿid al-Jazaʾiri, a descendant of

6. BEYROUTH — Le Grand Sérail

FIGURE 53. Ceremonial raising of the Arab flag over the Ottoman barracks on 6 October 1918.

'Abdel al-Qādir, had formed an Arab government there on 28 September. Emir Saʿid then cabled the president of the city council in Beirut, ʿUmar Daʿuq, to inform him of this development, and asked that Daʿuq in his turn proclaim an Arab government. On receiving this telegram the evening of 30 September, Daʿuq went to consult with Salam at his home. The decision was taken to force the wālī, Ismail Haqqi Bey, to abandon the city. Salam therefore went to see the governor, accompanied by Ahmad Mukhtar Bayhum and the former Ottoman diplomat Alfred Sursock, as well as armed guards who were under orders to fire if anyone blocked their way.[53]

Negotiations lasted all night. The last Ottoman governor of Beirut left the city at six o'clock in the morning on 1 October 1918, escorted to the borders of the city by Salam's son. Haqqi Bey left behind him a city exhausted by emergency military administration, the tension of four years of war, disease and famine—but above all a city that was preparing to divide into two camps. In Beirut, as in Damascus, the end of Turkish domination had been brokered by local elites that had finally come to accept the idea of Arab independence. But between idea and reality, a certain distance remained.

With the wālī's departure the formation of an Arab government in Beirut was announced, following the example of Damascus. Nominally it was headed by ʿUmar Daʿuq, but the real power lay with Salam, who presided over the ceremony at which the Arab colors were raised at the Sérail, on 6 October, before proceeding to the

Shuwayfat Plain south of the city to welcome Shukri Ayubi, whom Faysal had named governor general of Beirut and Mount Lebanon. Receiving Ayubi the next day at his home in Musaytbeh, Salam requested that his friend Habib Pasha al-Sa'ad, president of the dissolved administrative council of the Mutasarrifate, be allowed to serve as the governor of Mount Lebanon. Sa'ad took an oath of allegiance to Faysal during an investiture ceremony that took place later the same day at the seraglio in Ba'abda before the hoisting of the Arab colors there. This, however, was to reckon without either the designs of the French or the calculations of the Christians of Mount Lebanon.[54]

For that same day, 7 October, on the orders of the French Admiralty, its Syrian fleet took possession of the port of Beirut. The next day a first British detachment arrived with Allenby's staff, accompanied by Colonel Philpin de Piépape, representing the French army. On 10 October the Chasseurs d'Afrique, flanked by a "Syrian company" under French command and transported by sea from Haifa, paraded in the streets of Beirut, waving the tricolor flag to the wild acclaim of a throng of Christians. Immediately after their entry into Beirut, the French commanded Faysal's representative to withdraw, took down the Arab flag, and assumed control of the government.[55]

Arab independence would have to wait.

PART THREE

The Capital of the Mandate

FIGURE 54 *(preceding page)*. Poster soliciting subscriptions to a French government bond issue.

France Broadens Its Mission

On 24 July 1921 the Fleur de Syrie, on the south side of the former Place Hami-diyyeh, was devastated by a fire. On the ruins of this theater, which in 1899 had shown the first motion picture in Beirut, a café and nightclub called Parisiana opened a short while later. Imitating Europe was certainly nothing new in Beirut, but this change of name signaled the transition from one world to another. Every-thing had been in the process of changing in the city, at least outwardly, since the autumn of 1918, when French government succeeded Ottoman rule after a brief flirtation with independence.

Outside the city itself everything was changing as well. The geopolitical situa-tion created by the end of the First World War was wholly new. For the first time since the Roman Empire there was no longer a dominant state with roots in the Levant. Turkey, having succeeded in saving what it could, resolutely turned its back on the East, looking to establish a place for itself among the European powers. No other nation was in a position to take over from its defunct predecessor except the two great colonial powers, each then at its height. Now that hopes for a great Arab state had run aground on the shoals of imperialist competition, several smaller states were improvised in its stead in the lands of the old Ottoman Empire under the aegis of France and Great Britain.

The horizons of the world, having been enlarged by the revolution in trans-portation, were just as suddenly compressed in the Near East with the advent of an unfamiliar line of demarcation: the national boundary. In a region that for centuries had been incorporated into one or another of the immense empires that succeeded one another in the eastern Mediterranean, the superimposition of the Westphalian state had the effect of interrupting a territorial, economic, and cultural continuity that had shaped it since ancient times—and all the more ominously since the congruence between state and nation was somewhat less than perfect in the newly formed countries, where the construction of a historical tradition now became a task for the future. Beirut, as the capital of a state that was long to be rejected by a good part of its people, probably better than any other city in the Levant illustrated the ambiguities of this new Eastern Question.

THE IMPERIAL PARTITION

Beirut had been living under Arab government for scarcely a week when General Allenby, bowing to the force of circumstance, consented to the establishment of a French military presence there in the early part of October 1918. French sailors were the first to enter the city, on 7 October. They began at once to prepare the arrival of Colonel Philpin de Piépape the following day. On 11 October the British approved their ally's request to take down the Arab flag. This was done at once.

The new commander of the French troops in the Levant, General Hamelin, disembarked later in the month, followed shortly by François Georges-Picot, who had been named the French High Commissioner of Palestine-Syria in April 1917. Immediately on reaching Beirut, Georges-Picot weighed the balance of forces and cabled Paris: "The only remedy—send 20,000 troops to Syria and ask the English to hand over the administration of the country to us." The British were not really opposed to the idea and in any case did not stand in the way of reinforcements, which arrived in stages over the course of the following year. The French Detachment of Palestine-Syria then took the name French Troops of the Levant, under the command of General Hamelin.[1] In the space of a few months the French military presence, although it was still confined to the coast and in Mount Lebanon, had assumed massive proportions. A French protectorate began to take shape, even before being dressed up as a mandate by the League of Nations and expanded to cover the whole of Syria.

The agreement secretly concluded in May 1916 by Georges-Picot and the British diplomat Sir Mark Sykes called for a substantial part of Bilād al-Shām to be given to France after the Peace of Versailles. This, of course, was far from satisfying French ambitions to assert control over all of Syria—"from the Taurus to the Sinai," as the colonial lobby in Paris led by Eugène Étienne was fond of saying. In the event, even the stipulations of the Sykes-Picot memorandum were not fully respected. Relying on its superior force on the ground, Great Britain had systematically advanced its pawns and forced France to scale back its pretensions in the Levant. With the Balfour Declaration of November 1917, Palestine was first withdrawn from the sphere of partition that had initially been contemplated (the Sykes-Picot agreement had provided for a French zone of influence and an international zone), and then a few months later entirely subjected to British authority in the form of General Allenby's army. Once the war was over, taking advantage of Clemenceau's preoccupation with Germany, London agreed to a thoroughgoing solution to the problem of the Rhineland in exchange for France's willingness to renounce its claims to Mosul, beyond the northeastern border of Syria. This region was to be attached to the new state of Iraq, where the British sought to install a monarchy, finally entrusted to Faysal in 1921 after his ouster from Damascus. The following year the Colonial Office removed the eastern bank of the Jordan River from Palestine to form the Emirate of Transjordan, which it granted to another one of Sharif Husayn's sons, Abdallah. In the meantime France had moved to assert its control over what was left of "French Syria."

Great Britain did not try to push its advantage further than this. Faced with a choice between two alliances, it had evidently preferred the Entente Cordiale to collaboration with the Hashimites of Mecca, to whom it was content to dole out consolation prizes. It had even helped France to realize its ambitions over a certain portion of Syria, first by allowing units of the French army to take possession of Beirut, only a few days after the formation of the Arab government there; then by permitting Georges-Picot to exercise his authority as High Commissioner over the elites of Mount Lebanon in order to present the Arab government with a fait accompli; and finally by abandoning Faysal to a grueling interview with French leaders. The draft agreement concluded between the emir and Clemenceau permitted the colonial lobby in Paris to gain the upper hand and, with the support of Christian advocates of independence in Mount Lebanon, press the case for the protection of minorities.[2] During this time London also worked to neutralize President Wilson's principle of self-determination, joining with Paris to thwart the international Commission of Inquiry that had been set up to resolve claims to disputed places in the Levant, now reduced to an exclusively American delegation and doomed to see its recommendations remain a dead letter.

To get around the problem posed by a right of peoples to self-determination and to take control of the possessions of the conquered countries, Great Britain and France gave their support to the concept of a "mandate," developed by the South African statesman Jan Smuts. This was a kind of protectorate, founded on international law, which itself was to be enforced by a League of Nations—another Wilsonian idea, then in the process of being elaborated. Article 22 of the League's covenant defined the mandate and its function with reference to the stage of development attained by a people, ranked on one of three levels (from A to C), and the corresponding level of intervention required on the part of the supervisory power (or "Mandatory"). Level A provided that the Mandatory have responsibility for leading the country under its tutelage to independence. The peoples of the Levant were grouped in this most favored category—and with good reason, since during the war Sharif Husayn had been treated as an ally, and his son Faysal, who had been awarded the rank of general in Allenby's army, could legitimately con-

FIGURE 55. Emir Faysal, at a reception held in his honor in Beirut in 1919, surrounded by British and French officers and local notables. Photographer: Aziz Zabbal.
Collection: AIF / Roberte Zabbal Sawaya. Copyright © Arab Image Foundation.

sider himself to share responsibility for the victory. What is more, independence
appeared to be an accomplished fact in Damascus and the other Syrian cities that
had been liberated by Faysal's troops, and no one there saw in this state of affairs
justification for imposing a mandate, as the King-Crane Commission acknowledged in 1919. The two Americans to whom it had fallen to conduct the Allies' inquiry into the climate of opinion in parts of the former Ottoman Empire, following the refusal of the French and the British to take part, had obtained an
unambiguous result. Their survey of the various elites in the Levant had shown
that an overwhelming majority, except in Mount Lebanon, rejected any mandate;
if nevertheless one was considered to be indispensable, then an American mandate seemed preferable to any other. But the commission's evidence was to have
value only in the eyes of history. By the time of its return to Paris, Wilson had already withdrawn from the Peace Conference; subsequently it became clear that
the League of Nations he had hoped for would have to go forward without the
United States. The two partners of the Entente Cordiale, who had joined forces to

FIGURE 56. The arrival of General Gouraud in Beirut, in August 1920.

undermine the principle of self-determination, now had the room they needed to impose their partition.

Legalized by the Treaty of San Remo, which officially instituted the mandates in April 1920, France's domination of Syria was not yet fully realized since its troops were present only on the coast and in Mount Lebanon. For the moment the popular legitimacy of Faysal, proclaimed king of Syria on 8 March 1920, precluded any further advance. Even if Faysal had unwillingly assumed his royal office, and even if he himself favored conciliation—going so far as to approve the idea of a French mandate, on the condition that Syria was not to be divided up—he continued to embody the country's aspiration to independence. France chose to employ strong-arm tactics in seeking to rid itself of this obstacle, dismissing Georges-Picot and naming in his place a military high commissioner, General Henri Gouraud. A veteran of Morocco, where he had taken over from General Hubert Lyautey in 1916, and a hero of the Great War, in which he had lost an arm, Gouraud belonged to the most conservative wing of the French officer corps. From the moment of his arrival he was unrelenting in his efforts to drive Faysal out of Syria. On 24 July 1920, at Maisalun, outside Damascus, he sent his forces into battle against the outnumbered and poorly equipped troops of Yusuf al-ʿAzmeh, minister of defense of the Arab Kingdom of Syria, who was killed in the battle. The road to Damascus now lay open. Gouraud's first act on entering the city was to go to Saladin's tomb, to which

FIGURE 57. The Résidence des Pins, shown when it still served as a casino.

he is said to have addressed the taunt, "Saladin, we are back." The time when France was prepared to encourage the idea of an Arab kingdom was decidedly past.

The same crusading spirit animated the reorganization of the territories that France had been entrusted to lead to independence. Five weeks after Maisalun, Gouraud gave practical effect to his government's policy, which was aimed at supporting religious minorities, while at the same time separating them in order to weaken the Arab nationalist movement. On 1 September 1920, on the steps of the old Cercle du Parc—the casino on the grounds of the Beirut hippodrome, now converted into the residence of the High Commissioner and henceforth known as the Résidence des Pins—he solemnly proclaimed the state of Greater Lebanon, which united with the former Mutasarrifate of Mount Lebanon the cities of the coast and four predominantly Muslim provinces on its periphery, against the wishes of a majority of the peoples thus annexed.[3] This measure had been approved by the League of Nations and enjoyed the support of a part of the native population, in particular the clergy and most—but not all—Maronite notables; several leading Christians, among them an ally of Faysal who was also the brother of Ilyas Hoyek, the Maronite patriarch, were deported to forestall the emergence of any opposition. France pushed the logic of backing separate groups of minorities to its extreme by then dividing up the rest of Syrian territory into four entities: a state of Damascus, a state of Aleppo, an Alawite state, and a Druze state. And as if to emphasize that the French mandate, whose stated purpose was to lead these peoples to independence, would not

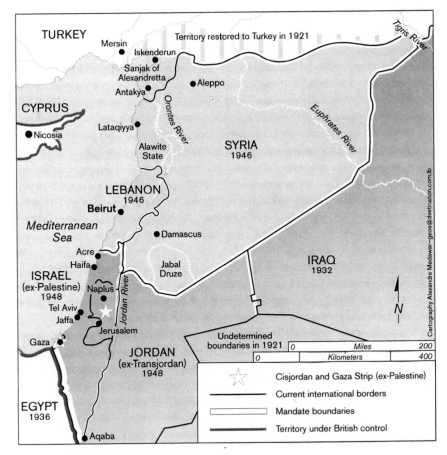

MAP 8. Mandates and Independencies

be needlessly burdened with the weight of sentimentality, it was decided to install the seat of the High Commission in Beirut rather than Damascus—a decision that produced a sense of foreboding in a farsighted young officer who had also trained under Lyautey, the future general Georges Catroux. Catroux warned that exercising the mandate against the peoples of the Syrian interior risked aggravating a feeling of resentment that had already been profound since Maisalun—the source of the Damascene oath that was uttered for many years afterward, "Wli 'ala Ghoro" (Gouraud be damned!)—and prophesied that its repercussions would long make themselves felt. As indeed they were to do.

It still remained to pacify the country, and this was not done without violence. In the Jabal 'Amil, the southern and mostly Shi'i part of Greater Lebanon, the French campaign of 1921 was particularly brutal, unleashing attacks from the air that left lasting traces in the collective memory. In the Biqaʿ Valley, now part of Lebanese territory, and to a still greater degree in the flat eastern borderlands of the Syrian states, the Mandate brought an essentially military solution to the problem of banditry among the Bedouins, whose nomadic way of life had been disrupted by the establishment of boundaries in the heart of a region that had been open since time immemorial. In the cities the situation was relatively tranquil, but a unilateral policy of this sort was bound sooner or later to arouse opposition. Although the French succeeded in buying the cooperation of some Syrian officials by means of sinecures, the political elites remained for the most part orphans of the dream of political independence, and Hashimite appeals from Iraq and Transjordan found a receptive audience. After a quiet period during the two years in which General Maxime Weygand served as High Commissioner, the tactlessness of his successor, General Maurice Sarrail, who in a matter of a few months managed to turn all the religious communities of the land against the Mandate, lit the fuse. Very quickly the revolt launched in 1925 in the Jabal al-Druze by Sultan Basha al-Atrash became transformed into a national uprising that spread beyond the cities of the interior to large parts of the territory incorporated in Greater Lebanon. This time again the response was military, and Damascus was subjected to harsh bombardment.

The alarm went unheard. Despite Sarrail's replacement by a civilian administrator, Henry de Jouvenel, French policy did not change. Jouvenel's only achievement was to endow Greater Lebanon with a constitution, which caused it to be renamed the Lebanese Republic in 1926, and which his successors—Henri Ponsot, Damien de Martel, and Gabriel Puaux—did not fail to suspend whenever native politicians threatened to stray from strict obedience to French wishes. In the meantime the legitimacy of the Lebanese Republic was to remain contested by a large part of its population, as the two Conferences of the Coast, which brought together the principal Muslim figures of the country in support of demands for Syrian unification in 1933 and 1936, were to show. Yet the mandate authority persisted in its determination to play minorities off against one another, refusing to recognize the vigor of sentiments in favor of solidarity and independence that were now expressed through the National Bloc (al-Kutlah al-Wataniyyah), which since its founding in 1928 had organized the nationalist opposition in Syria.

It was only in 1932 that France agreed to the reunion of the states of Damascus and Aleppo. And whereas Great Britain had compromised in 1930 in Iraq, by granting at least formal independence to the Hashimite kingdom, which was at once admitted to the League of Nations, it was not until six years later, in 1936, that France really reconsidered its minorities policy. On the urging of Pierre Viénot, under secretary of state in charge of protectorates and the Levantine mandate under the Popular Front government of Léon Blum, negotiations were entered into with the National Bloc, led by Jamil Mardam Bey and Saʿdallah Jabri. The Franco-Syrian treaty concluded that year recognized Syria's independence, as well as its unity, while remaining silent on the question of Lebanon, which the National Bloc agreed in its turn to drop. In a separate treaty France granted Lebanon nominal independence. In each case, however, the promise turned out to be empty. The French parliament, yielding to colonial pressure groups, refused to ratify the Franco-Syrian treaty;[4] and while the status of "Little Syria" as a distinct political unit was unaffected, and the incorporation of the Alawite and Druze states into the main body of Syria went unchallenged, France at once resumed its repressive policy against the national movement.

As though it had been persuaded from the outset that its own interests were fundamentally at odds with the aspirations of the majority of the population to independence and unity, France never showed any genuine concern for the will of the people, preferring to impose its own will through diplomatic pressure and administrative fiat. The consequence of this attitude was a regime that more closely resembled a protectorate than a mandate, as this latter arrangement was defined by the covenant of the League of Nations, which is to say an interim period of supervision during which interference by the Mandatory Power in internal affairs was prohibited.[5] Although it was manifestly unproductive, interventionism nonetheless found favor in the eyes of successive French governments. While it is true that the cost of occupying the Levant turned out to be much greater than the sums that could be extracted from it through unequal terms of trade, the colonial lobbies were supported by very powerful financial interests. Even so, the requirements of a great power are not reckoned in material terms alone. The immense network of French schools, and the penetration of French as the language of the elites, made Syria a key part of what the Third Republic saw as its universal mission. More than this, France's presence in Syria seemed to many to be a necessary condition of its claim to imperial status: in order to maintain its position as a Mediterranean power and to protect its sea (and later its air) lanes to Indochina, France could not do without the Mandate.[6] The advent of oil as the mainspring of the country's economy only served to confirm this perception. With the installation of a pipeline between Kirkuk and Tripoli, in 1934, France controlled a part of the oil supply from Iraq—this in addition to its interest, duly acknowledged by Great Britain, in protecting the free flow of oil from Mosul and the security of the Compagnie Française des Pétroles there. Ultimately, however, it was the integrity of France's overseas possessions that was at stake. Syria was important in and of itself, but it was even more vital in helping to perpetuate French colonialism in North Africa. Pressing a line of argument that went back to the late nineteenth century, and which the colonial lobby had put forward in the negotiations that preceded the partition of Ottoman lands after the First World War, the occupation of Syria—the heartland of Arabism—was seen as a way of counteracting support for independence in the Maghrib. Hence France's firm insistence on dividing up Syria.

This minorities policy was not without its disadvantages. It permitted neither a regime of wholesale repression, which ran the risk of triggering a backlash in the Maghrib, nor an attitude of conciliation, which, by creating a precedent, might have endangered the architecture of the empire as a whole. France was left, then, with its traditional role as protector of the Eastern Christians. The guarantee of security to a fraction of the population, no matter that it was soon extended to include minor Muslim sects as well, constituted the sole sociological basis of French domination. While assuring the mandate authority of a certain measure of popular support, it also—and for this very reason—blinded Paris to the demands of the majority for independence and unity. That nationalism was at work everywhere, or almost everywhere, transcending communities and weakening the ties that subordinated Levantine minorities to France, was of no consequence. In the view of the High Commission, nationalism was a British creation, introduced in Syria by Iraqi or Transjordanian agents.

In the twenty years of its political presence in the Levant, France never seriously sought, nor did it ever obtain, widespread and voluntary popular support beyond Christian minorities of Roman persuasion and, more crucially, Maronites. This only amplified the nationalist ferment confronting it in Syria, where the refusal of the French parliament to ratify the Franco-Syrian treaty of September 1936 alienated public opinion still further, while in Lebanon at least half the population persisted in its rejection of the separate state proclaimed by General Gouraud. Toward the end of the Mandate, however, the French fait accompli of Greater Lebanon stood poised to become a reality of a different kind. Whereas the second Conference of the Coast in March 1936 had reiterated the demand for reunion with Syria, the treaty signed six months later represented a turning point: the nationalists of the coastal cities were now forced to accept that sooner or later the independent existence of Lebanon would be permanently recognized. There was also a changing of the guard. Salim Salam, who had presided over the Conferences of the Coast, passed away in 1938 at the age of seventy-eight. Practically at the same moment, the son of his old rival from the Ottoman period, Riad al-Sulh, put an end to two decades of wandering. After an already varied career begun under Faysal in Damascus, where he went on to work behind the scenes on behalf of the National Bloc, Sulh now came back to settle in Beirut.[7] The National Pact—the cornerstone of Lebanese independence—was not far off.

THE VISION OF THE MANDATE

Beirut and the Levant occupied an uncertain place in the colonial imagination. The French were not numerous enough to really feel at home there, as they did in Algeria. In the absence of actual colonists, French society in the East was limited to the agents of the Mandate administration and a small circle of expatriate businessmen sent over from France. The civilian staff of the High Commission was rather small, not exceeding five hundred persons for the whole of Syria. And if there were substantially more military personnel, the officers did not stay there long enough (generally two or three years) for a Syrian tradition similar to that of the Moroccan protectorate to be established. Although many of the officials of the Mandate, beginning with Gouraud himself, were veterans of Morocco, there was nothing to encourage the belief that the example that Lyautey had set in North Africa could be imitated, and the particular inconveniences presented by the Levant overcome. In the event, the budgetary restrictions imposed by Raymond Poincaré's government in 1922 very quickly dampened hopes of an Algerization of the Levant.

Volunteers for expatriation were in any case rather rare at the beginning of the Mandate. The climate did not appeal to many, malaria was still rife, the cost of living there was high compared with other parts of the colonial world, and entertainment was in fairly short supply, even in Beirut. Bonuses and other forms of special compensation were approved to alleviate these inconveniences in the hope of attracting qualified candidates. Living conditions soon improved, and Beirut acquired a reputation as a vibrant city with the expansion of modern neighborhoods, progress in supplying water and electricity, the construction of large hotels and cinemas, and so on. A French officer or civil servant was now able to enjoy a standard of living near to that of metropolitan France, with colonial privileges in addition.[8] For men with families, education was available for children up to university age at the various schools set up by the Christian missions. Another advantage was the ease of dealing with the native population, thanks to the existence of a French-speaking elite that was very susceptible to European fashions, above all in Syro-Lebanese Christian communities. Unlike in North Africa, the existence of sizable Christian communities in Syria and Lebanon allowed Frenchmen to socialize in public during the day with young women in a growing number of clubs, restaurants, and cafés, and even on the beaches.[9] Although generally devoid of any real emotional attachment of the sort that often developed in Algeria and Morocco, a posting to Syria under such circumstances was apt to be considered a promising step in an officer's career, so long as one did not linger too long in what after all was nothing more than a "sunny Rhineland."[10]

If the High Commission's staff were denied the familiar comforts of a French colony, which in any case never emerged under the Mandate, they profited from contact with what might be called a creolized environment. The people in Syria were not creoles in the usual sense, of course, on account of their birth and way of speaking, but by virtue of their behavior; indeed one might even go so far as to say that the French presence helped to transform some of them into *petits blancs,* or honorary whites, especially in Lebanon. This will to assimilation dated back to before the Great War, when the death throes of the Ottoman Empire allowed demands for a French protectorate to be openly expressed. Now that France was militarily in control, there was no longer any obstacle to the formation of a distinctive Christian-Lebanese identity that, in seeking to create indigenous points of reference for itself, internalized the ideals of French "civilization." This identity was conceived in opposition to the Arabo-Muslim environment, whether by appealing to the specific historical experience of the Mountain, which constituted the basis of Lebanese nationalism even though it was shared only by a part of the population that came under the jurisdiction of the new state, or by promoting the ideology of Phoenicianism, a doctrine first put forward in 1919 by a group of Christian businessmen and intellectuals led by Charles Corm and Michel Chiha, who sought to legitimize the incorporation of the coastal cities in a future Lebanese Republic by reference to a more ancient heritage. This movement expressed itself in French, rather than Arabic, and developed its own ideology of the Mountain in the form of a privileged relationship between the people and its *doulce mère*—a relationship, it was claimed, that had existed ever since the apocryphal letter of Saint Louis to the Maronites.

The attachment to French ideals continued to manifest itself in everyday life by a sometimes comical urge to imitate foreign models. In addition to christening children with French (or gallicized) names, a practice that was now at least a half-century old, it became common after the First World War to see signs bearing names such as Joffre, Jeanne d'Arc, and França. But it was above all in local high society that the longing for a supposedly French, and more specifically Parisian, style of life was most fully indulged. The social customs of French officials, beginning with the High Commissioners themselves, encouraged this desire, even if in the colonial imagination there was a certain distance between the republic and a land that was likened to a little sister who had been refound—as in the propaganda poster from the mid-1920s that showed Marianne holding the hand of a naked but robust young girl meant to embody the new Lebanon in its march toward civilization.

The suggestion that Lebanon was the object of special favor seemed obvious, but France's purpose extended beyond its borders. The *mission civilisatrice* France claimed for itself was conceived on the scale of the Levant as a whole. French investment, already considerable before the Great War, was to increase appreciably throughout Syria under the Mandate. And there were incontestable achievements in the cultural domain as well. French was now the shared language of elites throughout Syria, not only in Lebanon. In the meantime the expansive network of schools, hospices, and hospitals established by French religious missions in all parts of the region had only grown larger. In addition to the religious orders, there were now the institutions of the Mission Laïque Française, a society founded in 1902 to propagate the secular values of the Third Republic.[11] And following the Moroccan model instituted by Lyautey to give tangible effect to the nation's civilizing mission, the High Commissioners attempted to implant in Syria and Lebanon stable institutions and public facilities under direct French control.[12]

Syria was also integrated into a global strategic vision. Lying between Africa and

FIGURE 58. A Lebanese-Syrian one-pound note.

Asia, it was charged with securing the lines of communication and supply of a colonial empire astride two continents, while contributing to France's stability as a "Muslim power" (yet another element of its self-image). In economic terms, too, Syria was regarded as an avenue for French expansion. Thus Paris contemplated the commercial future of the territories under its control in terms of two great axes or thoroughfares, laid out at the beginning of the Mandate, that were meant to make Syria a crossroads of trade. Departing from Alexandretta (modern Iskenderun), a "trans-Armenian" road connected Aleppo and Mosul with southern Turkey and Armenia, thence passing through northern Iran as far as Azerbaijan. The other "transdesert" route started in Beirut and branched into Syria and Palestine as far as Iraq, southern Iran, and Arabia. Despite the importance of the oil coming from Mosul and the attention paid by the mandate authority to Aleppo, the second road was to enjoy better fortune, especially after the early French disappointments in Cilicia. In part this was because it profited from Beirut's selection as the headquarters of the French High Commission, which effectively made it the capital of Syria and the symbol of the civilizing mission itself.

Beirut experienced its promotion with ambivalence. For many of the city's residents, it was synonymous with Faysal's expulsion from Damascus. Triumph now belonged to the Mountain, to which Beirut suddenly found itself reattached. It was therefore with a paradoxical sentiment of defeat and dispossession that a great many Beiruti saw their city transformed into a capital. Indeed many of them refused to accept the Lebanese identity card delivered by the High Commission. But beyond feelings of resentment, which were especially palpable among the city's Sunni population, the collapse of the old Ottoman order was all the more demoralizing since nothing guaranteed that the historic connection with the Syrian interior would one day be restored, or even that the profits accruing to Beirut's merchants from its

12. BEYROUTH
Siège du Gouvernement Français

Edit. Deychamps, Béziers

2. BEYROUTH
Palais du Gouvernement

Edit. Dey

FIGURE 59. The old Ottoman barracks, now known as the Grand Sérail, seat of the High Commissioner.

FIGURE 60. The former seat of the vilayet, known as the Petit Sérail, now home to the Lebanese government.

position over the past few decades as a transshipment point for goods coming to and from its far hinterland could much longer be sustained. The control exerted by French capital combined with the creation of political borders to produce a generalized sense of alienation. No matter that a small part of the bourgeoisie, especially the Christian middle class, willingly adapted itself to a middleman role, the weight of foreign interests gave rise in time to a certain degree of tension in the labor sector, as the strike against the Compagnie Franco-Belge de l'Électricité et des Tramways, accused of price-gouging, showed in 1931.

Foreign control was perfectly visible in the new administrative topography of Beirut, whose modest dimensions made it seem somehow unsuited to its dual function as the capital of both Greater Lebanon and the Mandate. The mandate authority had made a choice fraught with symbolic significance in installing the offices of the High Commission and its staff in the monumental Ottoman barracks on Qantari Hill. Henceforth this complex was to bear the name of the Grand Sérail, by contrast with what was now called the Petit Sérail on the former Place Hamidiyyeh (now known as Place des Martyrs), reserved for the departments of the Lebanese government. At the same time the French military garrison, composed for the most part of Senegalese riflemen, was lodged in barracks on the outskirts of the city, which thus found itself looked down upon by its occupier on all sides. This state of affairs was not slow to impress its stamp upon Beirut.

THE COURSE OF RECOVERY

On taking office in the autumn of 1918, the French administration first applied itself to the task of erasing the scars of the war, which, to judge from the picture sketched by Count Robert du Mesnil du Buisson, were spectacular still in 1921:

> Today the city of Beirut is a pile of rubble, and soon the modern buildings will make it impossible even for an archeologist to find any traces of it on the ground. Already before the war the ramparts had disappeared, along with the two castles, the oblong donjon to the southeast, and the old port with its picturesque shops, but the city itself still formed a compact core that had endured. During the war the Turkish governor had undertaken to destroy the old neighborhoods, not hesitating to evict without compensation hundreds of unfortunate souls whom disease and famine were soon to decimate.[13]

This description is surely exaggerated, and confuses a number of quite separate things. Thus the disappearance of the ramparts had long preceded the war; they had no longer been visible for some fifty years, and the new port had changed the character of the seafront by the end of the previous century. As for the Turkish governor, his acts of destruction were the consequence of a plan of urban renewal that was thirty years old; and though in the old town he had been able to carry out only the demolition phase, he had nonetheless succeeded in finishing the racecourse and adjacent casino–movie theater, soon to become the residence of the High Commissioner of France in the Levant. No matter. When the Allies arrived in Beirut in October 1918, the demolition begun in April 1915 had been compounded by the effects of bombardment—some of which went back to 1912—to leave an impression of ruin and disintegration, further aggravated by the memory of famine and the ordeals of the war.

The human and material damage prompted the mandate administration to implement a recovery program at once. Food supplies were mobilized to feed a population that had been reduced by about a third from war and famine, and all the more diligently as the British had instituted their own recovery program in Palestine. Health clinics were set up as well. According to the High Commissioner, 10,000 children were hospitalized in Beirut over the first twelve months, and 138,000 adults received emergency care.[14] The French also saw to the reestablishment of public services in Beirut, beginning with the port.

With the lifting of the naval blockade at the end of December 1918, the shore was cleared of mines and facilities were leased to the Suez Canal Company for the purpose of draining the harbor and emptying it of rubble—some of this likewise dating back to the Italian bombardment of 1912. The port was once again fully operational in 1920. In addition to removing wreckage and repairing dockside equipment, steps were taken to reinforce the pier. Thanks to this first round of renovation and repairs, Beirut gradually supplanted Port Said, where the French fleet had anchored during the war, as its major base in the eastern Mediterranean. Civilian traffic also picked up, and whereas Beirut welcomed only 370 ships in 1919, this number had risen to 742 by 1922, restoring the port to its prewar position.

Not less important was the French contribution to restoring confidence in the market for imported goods. An international fair was held in 1921. Opening on 30 April, it welcomed twelve hundred exhibitors from a dozen countries, though the overwhelming majority, of course, were French. The event appears to have been a success; at least all the merchandise on display was sold on the spot. A tourist guide was published for the occasion as well, further helping to burnish the controversial image of the Mandate in local business circles. In the space of a few years Beirut had regained much of its former momentum and begun to take a renewed interest in the fashions of the day. Whereas before the war there had been only a half-dozen automobiles, 376 motor vehicles were registered in 1921. Mechanization also affected leisure activities. Several movie theaters were now in operation, all of them with French names, such as the Chef-d'oeuvre, which opened on Place des Canons in 1919, the Cosmographe, on Rue de Damas, the Pathé, and the Cristal, which presented theatrical productions. "Society life" very quickly resumed. In 1921 we hear of lavish parties given by the city's wealthiest families, inspired by General Gouraud's receptions, which attracted what was now beginning to be called le Tout-Beyrouth to the Résidence des Pins. A tourist guide of the same year mentions a number of restaurants: in addition to L'Astre d'Orient there were five others on Place des

Canons—La Tour Eiffel, La Paix, Les Alliés, the Restaurant d'Europe, and the Restaurant de Paris—and, down along the seafront, Alphonse, where the guide noted that General Gouraud could be seen having lunch[15] (a later account described it as a "Levantino-European" restaurant and cabaret).[16] The guide also recommended Le Chapon Fin for gastronomes, and Al-ʿArab at Bāb Idris for lovers of oriental cuisine. Concerts were also sometimes given at the Saint James Restaurant and the Hotel Bassoul, and the Tabaris Casino (which seems to have been named after the famous establishment in Buenos Aires) welcomed a parade of stars of the period in a magnificent setting that had formerly served as the residence of the British consul.

FROM CITY TO METROPOLIS

The renascent city grew more lively as the years went on. In comparing editions of the *Dalīl Suriyya* (Guide to Syria) for 1923 and 1929, one observes a marked increase in the number of establishments catering to leisure and recreational activities: hotels (jumping from 35 to 62), restaurants (from 21 to 32), cafés (from 22 to 26), and cinemas (from 6 to 10). The hospitality industry was not alone in flourishing. All the other branches of commerce listed by the same guide showed signs of growth, although in highly variable proportions: the number of insurance companies rose (from 26 to 45), along with travel agencies (from 6 to 10), customs clearing houses (from 14 to 24), lawyers (from 86 to 111), physicians (from 164 to 239), and architects and engineers (from 13 to 57).[17]

These figures were in part the result of demographic growth. In the course of the decade dividing the censuses of 1921 and 1932 the city's population doubled. Broken down by communities, Beirut registered an increase of 50 percent each for Sunnis, Orthodox, and Maronites, and a tripling in the number of Shiʿa and Druze. It needs to be kept in mind that this comparison furnishes only very approximate orders of magnitude, since the 1921 census counted only those who wished to be counted. Over the entire territory of Greater Lebanon, and particularly in Beirut, many of the disaffected citizens of the new state made it a point of honor to refuse the Lebanese identity card, which also enabled them to avoid being officially noticed. By the early 1930s this resistance was not so widespread, even if it had not totally disappeared, and a good number of residents who had not been taken into account the first time were now included. This explains virtually all of the 50 percent increase in the number of Sunnis, since there is nothing to suggest a substantial rate of immigration among members of this community during the period. The tripling in the number of Shiʿa is probably a more accurate figure, even if it must also be qualified because of the politicization of the census of 1921, and also because of the novel character of the denomination itself (under the Ottoman Empire, Shiʿa were not counted separately from Sunni Muslims). As for the increase in the Maronite population, it remains debatable on other grounds: apart from the charge often brought later against the mandate authority that it had inflated the rolls of Maronites throughout Lebanon—in both 1921 and 1932—their number in Beirut may have been undervalued for an opposite reason, namely that many of them chose to remain registered in their native village. By contrast, the data are more reliable for the Armenian and Syrian Christian refugees, who seem to have numbered about twenty-eight thousand in the early 1920s. Turkey's recovery under Mustafa Kemal and the failure of the French bid to exercise control over Cilicia had led in 1921 to the displacement into Syria and Lebanon of tens of thousands of Armenians—already forced to flee a first time during the war, after which they were briefly repatriated in 1919. When the treaty of peace with Turkey was signed at Lausanne in July 1923, the territories under French mandate sheltered eight hundred thousand refugees, more than a quarter of them in Beirut, first precariously settled in a makeshift camp at La Quarantaine before gradually, and sometimes very belatedly, being relocated elsewhere.[18]

Whatever the exact figures may be, the demographic growth of Beirut during the first decade of the Mandate is indisputable. Fueled by a flight from the countryside, it could be seen in the expansion of the city with respect to both the area and the density of the built environment. By the end of the decade the number of construction permits issued for all categories of building exceeded a thousand each year: 1,121 in 1929, 1,481 in 1931.[19] This growth helped to revitalize a city whose status as a regional capital at a time of vigorous economic development placed it in the front rank of Levantine commercial centers. The great urban development projects carried out under the Mandate ended up giving it the look of a metropolis, while also determining the main lines of its future development.

In its urban planning dimension the French administration's work began early. Renovation projects undertaken during the proconsulship of General Gouraud initiated an ambitious scheme that in a few years transformed the entire old city within the walls into a modern business center. Even before this scheme was complete the first improvements triggered a real estate boom, as a mandatory official who played a leading role in the modernizing efforts proudly emphasized in the Bulletin de l'Union économique de Syrie.[20] In five years land prices doubled, and in some cases tripled, while the large numbers of construction permits issued substantially added to municipal revenues. During the whole of the first decade of the Mandate, Beirut was an immense building site—all the more since in addition to private construction and projects of urban development proper, other public works of great scope were under way: installation of a sewage system, expansion of street lighting by means of an electrical grid, replacement of the mules used by the city with a fleet of mechanized vehicles. Alongside these elements of infrastructure there were private school and hospital facilities needing to be built, more or less in conformity with the purposes of the mandate administration.

THE CONTINUING COMMITMENT TO EDUCATION

Considering the statistical record alone, one does not find comparably clear evidence of growth among schools and hospitals as in other sectors of activity. And for good reason: the city had already been amply provided for in these two domains since the previous century. Given the rather considerable number of educational and health care institutions, foreign or local in origin, that had been established in almost every neighborhood, the Mandate did not feel a need to take specific action in this area, beyond the introduction of a certificate of primary studies and the opening of normal schools for teachers. Its example was to be followed later by the Lebanese government, which became accustomed to investing relatively little in teaching and health care.[21] Indeed, public secondary and higher education was practically nonexistent in Beirut and the rest of Lebanon for almost the entire period of the Mandate, whereas efforts in this direction were made in the other Syrian states. Beirut nonetheless managed to affirm its commitment to education. The network of French schools, already extensive, grew a bit larger and became more diversified. In 1927, for example, the Collège Protestant Français was founded by Louise Wegman, at the urging of an Alsatian senator, and settled in the premises of the old German hospital. Several years earlier the Mission Laïque Française, present since the beginning of the century, had expanded the enrollment of its secondary school in Beirut, which in 1924 moved to new buildings on Rue de Damas.

It was above all at the university level that the capital of the Mandate asserted its claim as a regional metropolis. The two universities already in existence, although they had been affected by the war, were inestimable assets in this regard. It is true that the American University of Beirut (as the Syrian Protestant College had been renamed in February 1921) could not count on the support of the mandate authority—still less since its president, Howard Bliss, the son of the founder, found himself reproached for having aided and abetted the work of the King-Crane Commission of the League of Nations, whose report had looked so unfavorably upon French colonial ambitions. Nevertheless the unavoidable anglicization of the larger part of the Near East, which now found itself under British rule as a result of the war, combined with the mechanization of transport to assure the university of a massive pool of prospective students beyond the borders of Lebanon. Université Saint-Joseph, on the other hand, as the foremost symbol of France's civilizing mission in the Levant, could not be denied the protection of the High Commission. This privilege failed to be granted only on one occasion: the reopening in Damascus after the war of the university's faculty of medicine and the creation there of a rival school of law. Father Chanteur, the Jesuit superior in Beirut, had appealed the decision at once to the Quai d'Orsay and to General Gouraud, who approved the petition. But General Catroux, Gouraud's representative in Damascus, disregarded

FIGURE 61. The *lycée* of the Mission Laïque Française (left), in its new quarters on Rue de Damas.

his orders and managed to persuade the mandate administration to give its support to the founding by Muhammad Kurd ʿAli of the Syrian University, later merged with the Syrian Academy of Damascus to form Damascus University in 1923. The USJ was nonetheless able to turn matters to its advantage in the post-Ottoman era. It became at once the training ground for the civil service of the future Lebanese Republic and, through its schools of medicine, law, and engineering, the nursery of professional and social elites, while continuing to attract students from Palestine and Syria, as the list of graduates in medicine, pharmacy, and dentistry during the interwar period shows.[22]

The reopening of the Jesuit university after the war amounted almost to a refounding. Whereas the medical school had existed since 1881, the faculties of law and engineering, created in late 1913, had no time to begin operation before the war, and they did not actually open until 1919. Already two years later, when a program in dentistry came to be added to the curriculum, the university was back up and running. In 1920 the faculty of medicine enrolled 250 students, and in 1922 the first class of engineers received its diplomas. But it was incontestably the faculty of law that, because of the implications of its course of instruction for public life, was to become the standard-bearer of French higher education under the Mandate. At a time when the study of law was the indispensable prerequisite to an administrative career, and the practice of law the obligatory condition of a political career, the formation of the state of Greater Lebanon gave USJ an unrivaled opportunity to serve the public interest. The founding of the bar of Beirut in 1919, which coincided with the school's reopening and preceded the creation of the new state by a year, only emphasized its importance. As in the case of the faculty of medicine, whose *diplôme d'État* assured students of the same prerogatives as graduates of schools in France, the law faculty operated in accordance with the same rules that the Jesuit hierarchy had laid down for its counterpart in Lyon. Approval was nonetheless given—this a sign of the special role that the school in Beirut had been called upon to play—for the French syllabus to be supplemented by courses that answered local needs: the three-year cycle leading to the *licence,* instituted in 1920, included a course in Muslim law given in Arabic and, beginning in 1925, a course in Lebanese administrative law. Courses leading to a doctorate were introduced later, with the first thesis defense taking place in 1942.

The French university system in Beirut was crowned by the dedication of a large teaching hospital, the Hôtel-Dieu de France. The project dated from before the war, when the chancellor of the Faculté Française de Médecine (FFM) acquired a piece of land on the south slope of Ashrafiyyeh Hill; architects (among them the famous Yusuf Aftimos) were selected, and a subscription opened under the auspices of the Comité de l'Asie Française.[23] Materials had just been delivered to the construction site when the war broke out. Once it was over, the FFM no longer had enough money to see the project through to completion, and to train its students it was obliged to enter into a cooperative arrangement with the Greek Orthodox Saint George Hospital for three years.[24] A situation so little in agreement with the ambitions of France's *mission civilisatrice* could not long satisfy the mandate authority. Gouraud directed that two million francs be taken from the general administrative budget to relaunch the project, the cornerstone of which he laid himself on 2 May 1922. One year later, on 27 May 1923, his successor, General Weygand, formally opened the hospital, which stood in the middle of seven-and-a-half acres in an undeveloped and quiet area of the city, well suited to the needs of convalescent patients. Largely subsidized by the High Commission, it had a hundred beds and was outfitted with four operating theaters and the most modern surgical equipment. The synergy between the Hôtel-Dieu and the FFM, to which the hospital was now attached (allowing interns to do their training under the supervision of visiting professors from France), further enlarged the Jesuit university's presence in the educational landscape of Beirut. In addition to training doctors, the FFM had to respond to the new staffing requirements of the Hôtel-Dieu. The first class of midwives was graduated in 1924, and some years later construction began on a maternity ward. Finished in 1938, it stood across from the main campus on Rue de Damas, where the direction of a new pediatric unit was entrusted to one of Beirut's two first female physicians, Dr. Hélène Safi.[25]

The educational institutions inherited from the nineteenth century changed little after the early years of the Mandate, and with the advent of an independent Lebanon they survived in much the same form until the 1960s. The only innovations, both attributable to the initiative of the Lebanese state rather than of French authorities, were the creation in 1932 of a national *baccalauréat*, or secondary school certificate, and the opening in the latter part of the same decade of the Lebanese Academy of Fine Arts, a private institution that offered advanced training in architecture and that was to become the womb of the future Lebanese University, a public institution.

THE SHADOW OF HAIFA

The High Commission's record in economic affairs was more mixed. The creation of Greater Lebanon had, in fact, been justified initially on economic grounds. In the transitional period between the end of Ottoman rule and General Gouraud's proclamation, the group of Francophile and Francophone Christian intellectuals associated with the *Revue phénicienne* had urged that the survival of Lebanon depended on a dynamic economy that would permit it to expand and fill up its "natural frontiers." Citing the example of Switzerland, they argued for an economy based on banking and tourism that would also seek to develop the city's advantages as a regional shipping and transport hub. The results were not immediately convincing— though not for want of trying, a charge sometimes brought against France. As the seat of the mandate government and a central component of its universal mission, Beirut was also the anchor of the French colonial economy in the Levant. The High Commission set to work to consolidate its position, instituting emergency recovery programs in the first instance, then undertaking public works and health projects and, not least, improving the city's communications with the rest of the region. But these measures were constantly subject to comparison with those instituted by the British in Iraq, Transjordan, and especially Palestine. Anglo-French competition in the region was particularly sensitive to developments in Beirut, which now had to face up to the challenge that had begun to arise from the cities to the south, most notably from the Galilean port of Haifa.

This commercial threat was an immediate consequence of the invention of national boundaries. It had, moreover, been anticipated, and with some degree of apprehension, by local advocates of imperial partition just after the First World War. At a moment when the *Revue phénicienne* sought to legitimize the new borders by appeal to economic rationality, Amin Mushawar called attention to the emerging rivalry from Haifa: "One wonders if after the conclusion of the peace and the drawing of the Syrian border the port of Beirut will preserve its former predominance or whether, challenged by Haifa, it will no longer be the leading port of Syria, but solely that of Lebanon and of the Biqaʿ. Unpleasant surprises may be in store for us in the future."[26] Another contributor, Ibrahim Tabet, called upon the French authorities to enlarge the port and to improve the rail network, while maintaining the city as a terminus for all the lines of the interior and renouncing plans for the development of the port of Tripoli on the ground that Beirut ought to be the center of French activity in Syria. [27]

In counterpoising its weight to that of Great Britain in the Levant, France was not altogether outmatched. One indisputable success was obtained in the field of communications as a result of timely investments in telephony and wireless telegraphy. Telephone lines were installed in Beirut, and an international communications center was equipped with powerful transmitters in the outer southern suburb of Khaldeh and receivers at Ras Beirut. Broadcasting under the name of Radio Orient, this center linked Beirut with Paris and New York, with the result that the cable laid by the British through Egypt was rendered obsolete and Beirut became the communications node for all the countries of the region, including those that were ruled by London or under its influence. As early as 1930 the *Bulletin de l'Union économique de Syrie,* the organ of the French High Commission, seemed to take a certain mischievous delight in reminding its readers that Radio Orient's broadcast signal reached as far to the east as Persia and that demand for its news service and other programs was increasing, even in Palestine. But despite the High Commission's eagerness to make Beirut a hub for spreading the "influence of French thought throughout this Middle East, so faithful to our language and so attentive to all the manifestations of our culture,"[28] the embryonic world of radio broadcasting came to be dominated instead by Radio Cairo, whose signal reached the entire Levant later in the 1930s, and by Near East Radio, an Arabic-language station established by the British High Commission in Jerusalem. The power of the new medium to modify social habits and popular opinion caused it rapidly to be incorporated as an element in the strategic calculations of both of the rival mandate authorities. But now British influence, radiating outward from Palestine and Egypt, began to reverberate throughout the cultural sphere that the French had grown accustomed to regard as their private domain.

The improvement of transportation infrastructure nonetheless preserved Beirut's advantage over Haifa with regard to shipping, at least during the 1920s. French railway investment was already substantial before the Mandate, and the network of rail lines operated by the Société Damas-Hama et Prolongements served practically all the cities of the interior; the port of Beirut, connected to Damascus by the old cog railway, now found itself linked to the whole of Syria. At first this network served to transport both passengers and merchandise, but over time it was abandoned by travelers and used solely for freight. It took ten hours to reach Damascus by train, whereas by automobile the distance could be covered in only three. The automobile also helped to democratize transportation, since with the appearance of communal taxis, which allowed a group of passengers to share the cost of a trip, travel was now within the reach of every budget. For the old road to Damascus was not the only one to be adapted to motor traffic. Almost all the regions of Lebanon and Syria were gradually connected by a network of asphalt roads and tunnels, whose construction required a high degree of technical skill, sometimes amounting to works of art.

The automobile's growing popularity and the corresponding development of a highway system confirmed the intuition of the French planners who had conceived the transdesert route, the usefulness of which was demonstrated during this time by various private initiatives. In 1925 Francis Kettaneh, a native of Jerusalem who owned an automobile dealership in Beirut, crossed the Syrian desert into Iraq at the head of a convoy that went from Damascus to Baghdad, and from there into Iran—in the process laying the groundwork for a fortune spanning several countries and based in large measure on the sale of cars. In 1931 the French carmaker André Citroën covered a much greater distance during his famous Croisière Jaune (Yellow Cruise), the trans-Asian automobile expedition that set off from Beirut for Beijing: the thirty-some crews accompanying him (one of which included the Jesuit priest and philosopher Teilhard de Chardin) took the Damascus highway, and then the desert road in the direction of Palmyra, thence continuing along one of the ancient silk routes. Less heroically, a regular bus line had been established in the meantime, in 1927, by two Australian brothers whom the war had brought to the Near East, between Beirut and Baghdad via Damascus. Another bus service, inaugurated the previous year between Beirut and Aleppo by the Société Auto-routière Beyrouth-Alep and passing through Tripoli, made it possible to catch the Taurus Express en route to destinations in Europe.

No less than in the stimulus it gave to commercial enterprise, the shrinking of formerly vast distances was perceptible in the life of individuals, whose sense of space and time was radically altered. The trip from Iraq to Syria, which before the Great War took a month, could now be made in a day, and a student from northern Iraq who previously had to go through Bombay in order to reach the American university in Beirut could now get there by an overland route.[29] Furthermore, despite the sudden appearance of political boundaries, the mechanization of ground transportation gave Beirut the chance to exploit its formidable assets in the fields of education and medicine, as well as its image as a dynamic city abundantly supplied with Western consumer goods—yet another advantage over its rising rivals in Palestine.

But the improvement of ground transportation did not benefit Beirut alone. In the late 1920s the plan for a railroad connecting Haifa and Baghdad appeared to threaten the attractiveness of the French transdesert route and, more especially, its access to the Mediterranean. In retrospect it is clear that Anglo-French competition ultimately profited the port of Beirut, the operating concession to which had been granted to the Compagnie du Port, des Quais et des Entrepôts de Beyrouth, a French firm, in 1925. At the time, however, such an outcome seemed less and less likely. In 1929 the *Correspondance d'Orient* expressed anxiety that the fine prospect of seeing Beirut soon become the main port of transit for Mesopotamia, Persia, Afghanistan, and even India was slipping away. It is quite true that emergency repairs had enabled it to quickly regain prewar traffic levels, and that beginning in 1926 a further expansion of facilities was undertaken. But the port could still unload only small steamships at its wharves. Apart from the fact that industrial development was now proceeding at a faster pace in Haifa than in Beirut, the Galilean port posed a dual challenge since, in addition to its own program of expansion, it was the terminus of the pipeline operated by the Iraqi Petroleum Company that carried crude oil from Mosul and Kirkuk to the Mediterranean[30]—deepening the sense of alarm in Beirut.

Beirut's inadequacies were thrown into stark relief by the opening in October 1933 of the new port of Haifa, which, with its enormous docking basins (covering twelve hectares in total, or almost thirty acres) and its more modern facilities, could handle ships of much greater tonnage. Not only was the new Palestinian port twice as large as that of Beirut, its scale of activity stood to expand still further in proportion to the success of the planned rail route to Baghdad, which appeared to constitute a second passage to India.[31] Further aggravating the situation, the *Correspondance d'Orient* alleged, the British were conducting an active campaign in the Iraqi press to undermine the preeminent position of Beirut by suggesting that the transdesert route through Damascus was not secure.[32] "Beirut is dying," one editorialist warned, going so far as to throw the blame for this state of affairs back upon the Sykes-Picot memorandum for having broken up a formerly unified region in which Beirut occupied a privileged position with respect to commerce and trade. One of the consequences of this "disastrous" agreement was that Great Britain had constructed "a modern port at Haifa to combat Beirut while France looked on and did nothing."[33]

Such premonitions were sharpened by the fear that the Turkish port of Mersin might try to capture a share of the lucrative commerce with Iraq and Iran as well. In response both Lebanese and French business interests demanded that Beirut's port facilities be enlarged and modernized. The president of the chamber of commerce, ʿUmar Daʿuq, who had led the campaign against the Iraqi pipeline and for the protection of lines of communication with the interior, wrote to the High Commissioner in early 1933 to request effective action. Faced with the dire threat posed by Haifa, and above all by the adoption of the Baghdad railway plan and Turkish efforts to redirect commercial traffic to and from Persia, the Lebanese economy could not, in his view, be saved from stagnation and decline by half measures such as the construction of a few additional warehouses or the signing of unenforceable trade agreements. Short of making Beirut a free port, Daʿuq recommended the establishment of a free zone within it where goods could be unloaded without payment of customs duties and the construction of a rail line between Tripoli and the Palestinian border.

This approach, which also enjoyed the support of French interests, led by the Compagnie du Port de Beyrouth, was not apt to disconcert the mandate administration—apart perhaps from the prospect of lowered tariff revenue. Despite the unhappiness of native businessmen with what they saw as the inertia of the High Commission, economic questions had gradually come to occupy a sizable place among its concerns. Breaking with the policy of the three military proconsuls and of Henry de Jouvenel, the first civilian high commissioner, Henri Ponsot (who served for seven years, more than all of his predecessors combined) and Damien de Martel (who served for five-and-a-half years) were inclined to look to economic development as a distraction from the political difficulties they had encountered. The local consequences of the worldwide crisis of 1929 only underscored the urgency of such an attitude. Ponsot even went so far that year as to say, in reaction to the crisis, that he saw himself above all else as a high commissioner for economic affairs. But it fell to Martel, who replaced him in 1933, just when the challenge from Haifa had become unmistakably clear, to respond to the expectations of the business community. He did so by energetically committing his government's resources to infrastructure projects, beginning with the expansion of the port.

In early 1934 the free regime demanded by the president of the chamber of commerce came into effect over a rather large part of the harbor complex. In addition to handling cargo in transit, it was designed to accommodate certain forms of industrial production as well. At the same time work began to augment the port's capacity with the construction of a second docking basin to the east of the original one. These measures coincided with another development that, if it did not directly affect Beirut, helped to slow the rise of its chief rival to the south: the opening on 14 July 1934 of an oil terminal in Tripoli, the outlet of a new pipeline from Iraq, whose construction (by an American company from Texas) had begun two years earlier. The implications for Haifa and its own oil pipeline were obvious, since the two conduits followed the same route for roughly 150 miles before splitting at the Haditha pumping station, thence taking different routes of almost the same length: the one about 550 miles to Haifa, passing through five pumping stations; the other about 525 miles to Tripoli, via four stations. Seven years after oil was struck in Kirkuk, the Levantine territories under French control could count on a share of Iraqi crude production, while France saw its own supply increased. What is more, shipping it to Le Havre, which the first tanker from Tripoli reached on 14 August, cost three times less than importing oil from Texas or California.[34]

All these measures helped to restore confidence in Beirut, even if the new port facilities were slow to come into operation. It was not until June 1938 that they were finally opened to commerce, four years after construction began. With a surface area of eight hectares (almost twenty acres), a breakwater of 490 meters, and 800 meters of deepwater docks, the new basin could accept ships of every size, finally relegat-

AIR-FRANCE
Réseau Aérien Mondial

Beyrouth-Marseille en 30 heures
2 FOIS PAR SEMAINE
par hydravion quadrimoteur LIORÉ OLIVIER (départ de Tripoli les Jeudi et dimanche à 6 h.)

Damas-Bagdad en 2 heures 55 minutes
SERVICE HEBDOMADAIRE
par trimoteur DEWOITINE à 10 places (départ de Damas les Mardi à 6 h.)

RENSEIGNEMENTS

BEYROUTH : WAGONS COOK   rue Allenby,   tél. : 66-62
D A M A S : AIR FRANCE,   rue Fouad I", tél. : 12-20
TRIPOLI : AIR FRANCE,   Aéroport d'EL-MINA - tél. : 3-05 - et dans les principales agences de voyages.

FIGURE 62. An Air France advertisement from the 1920s.

ing the old barges to the scrap heap.[35] Beirut's hopes of quickly reaping the rewards of its investment were to be deferred, however, by the outbreak of the Second World War the following year. But if it had not succeeded immediately in turning back the challenge from Haifa, the port had finally placed itself in a position to dispose of it a few years later. In the meantime the expansion of the harbor had welcome consequences for the city's economic activity, the most unexpected of which certainly was the construction of an airport. In the Mediterranean, as everywhere in the world, air traffic had begun to grow in the late 1920s. The first cargo flights between Marseille and Beirut started up at the end of August 1928, and the following year weekly air postal service was initiated between the two cities. The desert was covered by hydroplane. Flying at an average speed of about 85 miles per hour and carrying three to four passengers in addition to a small volume of cargo, the pilots of Air Union-Lignes d'Orient (among them the French writer Antoine de Saint-Exupéry) landed back in Beirut in the old Medawar basin at the port. Visibility was sometimes poor, however, and in 1932 a first fatal accident occurred when a plane strayed off course and crashed on the wharves. The subsequent transfer of the hydroport to Tripoli, in 1935, seemed to foreclose any chance of an airport in Beirut since the geography of the promontory did not readily lend itself to construction of a landing field. But then it became clear that the work just begun to enlarge the port furnished the solution to the problem: the million cubic meters of earth needed to build the embankment for the new basin could be obtained by leveling the dunes at Bir Hasan, southwest of the city, which made it possible to lay out three asphalt runways there in 1936. Three years later, in January 1939, Bir Hasan Airfield welcomed Gabriel Puaux, the first High Commissioner to come to Beirut by air. Regularly served on the eve of the war by Air France, the Egyptian company Misr Air, the Polish airline Lot, and, later, by a Palestinian company, the city was also a stopover for carriers connecting France and Indochina, Warsaw and Teheran, and Berlin and Teheran, with not fewer than thirty take-offs and landings on some days.[36]

The opening of Bir Hasan marked the beginning of Beirut's ascendancy over Haifa, since the aerodrome built by the British in 1936 was located in another city in Palestine, Ludd (later known as Lod under the Israelis, who took over the airport while renaming it Ben Gurion International), near Jaffa; a second facility came into operation at Qalandia, outside Jerusalem. Once again, however, the outbreak of war abruptly dimmed Beirut's prospects as an emerging international center of commercial aviation while at the same time obscuring France's pioneering role in this rapidly growing sector of the economy.

The efforts made under the Mandate to develop infrastructure, particularly with regard to transportation and communications, were more visible in Beirut than in the rest of the French Levant, and substantially strengthened the city's position in relation to its competitors elsewhere in the region. In its turn, this preeminence was both to stimulate and channel a new surge of economic growth within the framework of the Lebanese Republic, even if Beirut remained a part of the larger Syrian economy—in which capacity it had helped to absorb the shocks to the economy of the Mountain arising from the collapse of sericulture, aggravated there by local consequences of the 1929 crisis. In the meantime the flow of emigration to the Americas continued. Much closer to home, Palestine attracted many Lebanese in search of opportunities as well. While the promising environment for industry that was beginning to take shape to the south was perceived by some Beirut businessmen as a threat needing to be met (by higher tariffs, for example, as the mostly French executives of the Société des Ciments Libanais demanded in the face of competition from Palestinian cement producers),[37] the ancient experience of territorial continuity in Bilād al-Shām led others to go try their luck there, as though there were no real border yet. In fact, despite the slowdown in activity occasioned by the Great Revolt of 1936, several Lebanese entrepreneurs began to amass considerable fortunes in Palestine—notably among them the legendary Émile Bustani.

But the most important consequence of the challenge from Haifa, and more generally of competition with the British in Palestine, was a convergence between French and Lebanese economic interests, including those of Muslim merchants in Beirut, at a moment when growing disenchantment in the political sphere was inexorably driving the native population and its foreign governors apart.

The French City

"From the sea, Beirut presents a delightful view, comparable to that of the most famous Mediterranean cities," wrote the author of a tourist guide published in Paris in 1932.

> The city bathes in the caresses of the water, its neighborhoods rising in terraces on the hills, its central mass enlivened by the domes and minarets of mosques, by the steeples of churches, by [so many] imposing monuments—hospitals, convents, and universities—whose austere simplicity is scattered throughout the ensemble of houses and villas, [by] this medley of color, the orange and red of the square roofs with their [Marseille] tiles, the white and pink of the walls, broken by ogival loggias, the green of the gardens and the stands of tapering cypress. Beyond Beirut, the country continues to rise into the first foothills of the mountain. . . . The air is of an ideal purity, the harmony of colors is undisturbed by fog. . . . But it is the sea that enchants, a special, pure, light blue that in places almost imperceptibly acquires an emerald transparency. One understands why it was that Astarte wished to be born from this ocean deep.[1]

Except for a few details, this description—like the famous 1925 poster by Julien Lacaze whose aerial view of Beirut was used to promote French tourism in Syria—recycled the images of the city popularized by travelers during the second half of the nineteenth century. And yet, as the guide assured its readers, Beirut was already highly Europeanized. "One no longer goes there to find the Orient of fifty years ago, but a more colorful copy of Nice." Instead of the famous seaside esplanade in that city, the Promenade des Anglais, here an Avenue des Français ran along the coast. But while the Mediterranean atmosphere of Beirut was apt to call to mind the Côte d'Azur, urban planners during the Mandate incorporated other French references.

As in other cities where the nation's civilizing mission had been undertaken, the colonial model owed something to Baron Haussmann's example, with the result that typically Parisian vistas were re-created in Beirut—though they were soon distorted, and in some cases obscured altogether, by the city's continuing physical and demographic expansion, which before long would conquer the entire promontory.

COLONIAL MODERNITY

Once the emergency measures instituted by the mandate administration after the war had taken effect, modernizing the city's street plan became one of its chief priorities. The chaotic impression left in the heart of the old town by the demolitions of 1915 was clearly incompatible with Beirut's new status as a capital and its role as a showcase for French ideals. And yet by removing physical obstacles that had blocked the renovation of this commercial district for some twenty years, the demolitions marked a great step forward. Henceforth the lower city was organized around three thoroughfares whose construction followed the paths cleared by the Ottoman authorities at the site of three old markets—the Tujjar (Shopkeepers), Khamayir (Winesellers), and Haddadin (Ironmongers) suqs.[2] Two parallel roads now climbed up from the port along a north-south axis and intersected a third road that lay along the east-west axis of Rue Nouvelle, between the Burj (Place des Canons) and the Westernized markets that appeared in the late nineteenth century. If the original plan was hardly new, the Mandate nonetheless impressed its stamp on it, beginning with the street names themselves: the first two streets took their names from General Allenby and Marshal Foch, while Rue Nouvelle, whose improvement had been completed under Weygand's proconsulate, was renamed in his honor.

Bordered by these three roads and by the port on its north side, an elegant neighborhood emerged in the new business district with the appearance of great office buildings constructed out of *ramleh*, a reddish sandstone, and bearing a greater or lesser degree of ornamentation on their ochre façades.[3] The entire southern part of the intramural town was razed, as well as the area that had grown up around the port, and with them vanished a dense network of alleys, markets, and workshops. With the proceeds from a loan granted by a French bank, the city constructed two model office buildings on Rue Foch, the rental income from which was to be used to indemnify dispossessed property owners; in the meantime no repayment of the loan principal was scheduled for twenty years.[4] The main public building of the new neighborhood was the seat of city administration, the Palais Municipal, erected in 1927 on the site of the old al-Fashkha suq. Astride Weygand and Foch streets, across from the al-ʿUmari Mosque, it had no forecourt, nor did its proportions noticeably depart from those of the contemporary office buildings that surrounded it. But despite the lack of monumentality, the neo-Moorish style given it by the architect Yusuf

FIGURE 63. Rue Weygand, with the city hall at the end on the left.

Aftimos, celebrated during the Ottoman period for his designs of the clocktower and fountain for Abdülhamid's jubilee, made it a landmark event in the metamorphosis of the lower city.

The business district was extended across Rue Weygand by still more imposing innovations. What remained of the old fabric of the city—a warren of narrow alleys and rundown houses and clubs inhabited by thugs, ruffians, and drug addicts *(tiryākī)*[5]—gave way to the perfectly precise radial plan of Place de l'Étoile. Although there are some indications that such a scheme had already been envisaged by 'Azmi Bey, one of the last Ottoman governors, the star-shaped design was so intimately associated with Haussmann that it became the signature of the Mandate's urban planning, reproduced on a still larger scale by Place des Omeyyades in Damascus. It was never fully executed, however, since carrying out the original design would have required demolishing the Greek Orthodox and Greek Catholic cathedrals, the

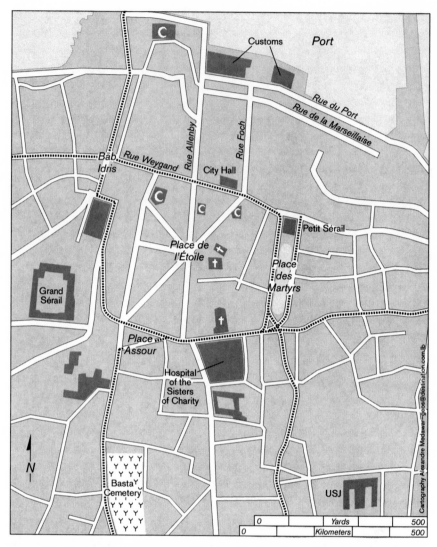

MAP 9. The Center of Beirut under the Mandate: The New Street Plan and Streetcar Lines

old Nuriyyeh chapel, and the Mosque of Mansur ʿAssaf. As a result a connected series of old suqs to the east of the square was saved and others were consolidated. But even stripped of two of its eight radiating branches, the new Place de l'Étoile powerfully indicated the scope of the Mandate's ambitions. And as though to emphasize the modernization of this area, Rue du Maʿrad—the extension of Rue Allenby

FIGURE 64. Rue Foch, looking north toward the water.

FIGURE 65. City Hall, at the corner of Rue Weygand and Rue Foch.

south of Rue Weygand, where it bisected the square—took on the appearance of a Mediterranean Rue de Rivoli with its arcaded sidewalks, while preserving in its name the memory of the Exposition of 1921. The new district was further distinguished by the construction, right on the square itself, of a parliament building in the monumental fashion of the period whose spare geometric lines framed a façade inspired by the ancient architecture of the Islamic East and pierced by massive doors in the Mamluk style. The center of the square was to be occupied in 1932 by a clocktower twenty-five meters high, the gift of a wealthy émigré in Mexico.

With the renovation of the Foch-Allenby district and the emergence of a new neighborhood around Place de l'Étoile, the transformation begun at the beginning of Abdülhamid's reign was at last complete. The entire town within the old walls was now Westernized, or very nearly so; until then, for almost half a century, the heart of the modern city had been confined to a great rectangle formed by Place des Canons and the more modest triangle of Place Assour. Neither of these two areas was in need of major renewal. The Burj, in particular, was more than ever the hub of public transportation and the focus of public life in the city, notwithstanding that it had been demoted as an arena of power: the Petit Sérail on its northern side, where the provincial governor used to sit, now housed only the departments of the Lebanese government and the offices of the president of the Republic, whereas true authority resided in the Grand Sérail, the old Ottoman barracks where the High Commission had been installed. The square nevertheless retained its symbolic importance, henceforth communicated by a new name. Already in 1908 it had been rebaptized Place de la Liberté et de l'Union after the revolution of the Young Turks. Eight years later, in 1916, it became Place des Martyrs (a name preferred to yet another that was briefly considered, Place Pasteur) in homage to the nationalists executed by Jamal Pasha. In 1930 it was finally provided with a monument meant to honor the memory of these martyrs and to celebrate understanding between Christians and Muslims. The sculpture by Yusuf Hoyek, which later was to give rise to controversy, showed two weeping women, one wearing a veil, the other uncovered, face to face and holding hands in commiseration. Whereas the garden inherited from the Hamidian period used to occupy only the northern part of the square, with its bandstand (now vanished) and high gated wrought-iron fence, it was now extended to cover the entire space, almost 5,000 square meters (or about an acre and a quarter)— somewhat less than this, actually, since there was now a series of three gardens in the French style, each bordered by a small balustrade and broad sidewalks that made the square a favorite with strollers. The buildings lining the square on either side remained mostly unchanged, however. The same was true for Place Assour, where the only novelties were the disappearance of the Hamidiyyeh fountain— transplanted to the public garden in the Arts-et-Métiers neighborhood—and the development of Rue Fakhreddine (the future Rue Riad al-Sulh).

The urban renewal projects of the Mandate extended beyond the limits of the

FIGURE 66. A stylized rendering of the National Museum on a bank note from the mid-1980s.

old town, in two directions especially, to the west and the south, and in each case displayed a fine continuity with the works of the late Ottoman period. To the west, Rue Georges-Picot ran through the Jewish quarter of Wadi Abu Jamil, as a prolongation of Rue Weygand; the embankment along the seafront was enlarged with the rubble cleared from the old town, and a retaining wall was built with the remains of the Byzantine basilica, pulled down to make way for Rue Allenby; and the former Rue Minet al-Hosn became Avenue des Français, which, with its wide sidewalks, its palms, and its hotels, became the preferred promenade for the leading families of Beirut. To the south, descending from Place des Martyrs, Rue de Damas left behind the places of entertainment around the square and led onward to a district notable for its educational and cultural institutions. In addition to the Faculté Française de Médecine, which doubled as a maternity ward, the street was home to the *lycée* of the Mission Laïque Française in 1924 (at the intersection with the present-day Sodeco Street) and the Institut Français d'Archéologie du Proche-Orient; in the same vicinity, at the end of the Mandate, the École Supérieure des Lettres was built. In 1931 Rue de Damas was chosen as the site of the National Museum, financed by subscription and finished only ten years later, two hundred meters from the Hôtel-Dieu de France, erected in 1923.

Work was also begun on a ring road with the construction of Boulevard du Fleuve, to the northeast, and Rue Fuad I, to the southeast. They were intended to connect the new Place du Musée with the Résidence des Pins, thence to be continued first by Corniche al-Mazra'a, and then by Avenue de Paris, skirting the cliffs of Rawsheh as far as Avenue des Français. Beyond this proposed beltway, which soon was abandoned, the mandate authority turned its attention further to the southeast, extending Rue de Damas to the suburb of Furn al-Shubbak, and to the southwest, where the airport road now reached its destination in Bir Hassan. To the south of Mazra'a, a stadium covering some ten acres was built by military engineers and inaugurated in 1939.[6]

The growth of automobile traffic during this period called for additional improvements to the road network. The city's success in redrawing property lines and other boundaries as part of its commitment to urban renewal—an initiative unmatched elsewhere in the region and recognized by the League of Nations—made it possible to widen the streets, which then had to be paved with stones, macadamized, or else covered with asphalt. Rue Allenby was asphalted in 1927, followed shortly thereafter by major thoroughfares, especially in the center of the city; but it was a long and drawn-out business, not yet finished by the outbreak of the Second World War. Between 1939 and 1943 some 450,000 square meters (almost 5 million square feet) of roads and sidewalks were asphalted or paved in stone, and public gardens continued to be laid out in various neighborhoods of the city.

By the middle of the 1930s, Beirut could almost have passed for a new city. Even if a broader view going back to the late Ottoman period suggests a process of continual evolution, allowing for the hiatus due to the Great War and its aftermath, the combination of systematic planning and progress in mechanizing transport nonetheless justified talk of a "French" capital. The mandate administration was staffed by veterans of Morocco who drew freely on their experience in North Africa, where a colonial approach to urban renewal relied on the French tradition of grand designs and balanced compositions, mixing the classicism of the seventeenth century with Haussmannian ideas and Beaux-Arts ideals to create a spectacular display of power.[7] Taking into account the exceptional richness of the Levant's history, this striking embodiment of the triumphalist style, with its expansive perspectives and clean lines punctuated by monumental gestures, was calculated to make it unmistakably clear who was now in charge.[8]

The International Exposition sponsored by General Gouraud in 1921 was an opportunity to highlight the first achievements of this colonial urbanism in the Levant. In addition to Place des Martyrs, originally conceived in the Ottoman period, and the Esplanade de la Marine, behind the Petit Sérail, they were to be found on Rue Allenby, whose southern branch, with its arcaded sidewalks, was to keep the Arabic name for a fair or exposition, Ma'rad. Plans for further development under Weygand, drawn up by the French architectural and engineering firm of Deschamps and Destrée, paradoxically confirmed the Mandate's intention to make Beirut a showcase for Western-style development at a time when an arabizing tendency in colonial urbanism was taking shape in the Maghrib. This tendency, which reached its peak with the 1931 Colonial Exposition in Paris, had only a faint resonance in Beirut. More generally, the effort to rescue—and, where necessary, restore—architectural heritage then gathering momentum in North Africa and Indochina, which sought to persuade the peoples of these lands of France's respect for foreign traditions and its commitment to defending indigenous cultures, aroused greater interest elsewhere in the Levant. Unlike Aleppo and Damascus, however, which welcomed this "pose of the protector,"[9] Beirut possessed little that was ancient or otherwise worthy of being protected, and both the mandate authority and local developers felt free to cultivate the spectacle of modernity without unduly encumbering themselves with a concern for preserving the past. Indeed the two plans for building façades chosen by the military governor, Major General Doizelet, to serve as models for private contractors were drawn up by Deschamps and Destrée.[10]

The new private and public architecture that now appeared in the center of the city was not merely a veneer, however. It followed naturally from what already had been constructed à l'occidentale, before the advent of the Mandate, to burnish the image of the bourgeois Mediterranean city that the nineteenth century had begun to fashion for Beirut. The grand designs in the manner of Haussmann were softened by an Italianate vocabulary and Baroque decorative touches, themselves combined with other cosmopolitan influences to form a uniquely Levantine composition. The chronic weakness for pastiche was seen in a hodgepodge of rotundas and elaborate balustrades, bow windows with finely rounded projections, pediments and caryatids, colonnades and corbels—details that seemed unrelated to one another except insofar as they were elements of a novel and distinctive architectural language, no less composite under French rule than it was to be later.[11] And if the tourist brochures and the postcards of the period laid stress on the picturesque quality to which these elements contributed, the predominance of typically ochre (though sometimes pink) sandstone imparted a certain harmony to the overall effect.[12]

A COUNTRY IN A CITY

The growth in public works projects and the boom in private construction that accompanied it gradually gave Beirut the characteristic appearance it was to exhibit until the 1960s. But despite the Mandate's ambitions, the basic shape of the city had not radically changed. The administrative redistricting announced in 1921 had the effect of ratifying the expansion of the second half of the nineteenth century and fixing the configuration of the city limits for the rest of the twentieth century by consolidating the Ottoman mahallāt into a dozen larger neighborhoods (hayy).[13] The oblong footprint constituted by this first phase of expansion, between the coastlines to the north and west, the Beirut River to the east, and the zone of dunes that lay to the south, remained undisturbed. One developer proposed leveling the dunes at Uza'i to construct a new city after the example of Baron Empain's plan for Heliopolis, near Cairo, but nothing came of this idea.[14] Nor was the distinction between a fairly well delimited business district and the sprawling residential areas that occupied the greater part of the municipal territory eroded over time. In these

neighborhoods to the east, west, and south hardly any offices or businesses or retail outlets were to be found, apart from a few small shopkeepers and artisans. Commerce and other forms of economic activity continued to be concentrated in the
center of the city, around its ancient core.

The 1921 redistricting had deprived the intramural town of its Arabic name of
Bayrūt al-qadīma, still common during the late Ottoman era. The terms "medina"
(madīna) and "casbah" (qasaba), formerly sometimes used, were no longer justified
since, unlike in North Africa and Damascus, renewal projects had almost wholly
done away with the old urban fabric. The historic center was now reduced, at least
officially, to a more parochial status, conveyed by the term Hayy al-Marfa'—the
neighborhood of the port.[15] Parts of the Saifi, Bashura, and Minet al-Hosn neighborhoods filled out the rest of the city's business and entertainment district, which
popular toponymy unified under the generic name al-Balad (usually translated as
"country" or "land," but in the restricted sense of "city" also found in Cairo, for example, though not in Damascus)—as if the few acres of land on which it stood could
be made to stand for Beirut as a whole. In the present instance the shorthand had
a certain plausibility to the extent that this area, whose modernization, begun around
the old Place Hamidiyyeh and completed under the Mandate, brought together a
variety of characteristic urban functions: retail and wholesale commerce, entertainment, offices, and residences.

The functional diversity of the Balad was illustrated on the smallest scale by the
mixed-use apartment building, found throughout the renovated part of the lower
city. Given over mainly to commercial space and lawyers' and doctors' offices, such
buildings leased a few apartments on the upper floors; the ground floor and mezzanine levels were reserved exclusively for businesses. Virtually every building had
its own qahwajī, an authorized vendor stationed usually in the mezzanine, near the
stairwell, who delivered coffee and lemonade to office workers.[16] Although not tall
by today's standards (generally six or seven stories, and of varying width), these
buildings broke sharply with what had previously existed in the area, not only as a
consequence of their regular alignment but also because of an impression of verticality that, by comparison with earlier views of the lower city, suggested an abrupt
increase in scale.

Seen from the modern rectilinear street grid on which they were erected, these
towering buildings were unmistakably new. Yet behind them there survived webs of
small streets and alleyways that preserved something of the old atmosphere, most
obviously in the area between Place de l'Étoile and Place des Martyrs, where the jewelers' alley intersected a street lined with markets selling vegetables, fish, and fowl.
But this was not the only such neighborhood. In many areas of the city informal businesses could still be found operating out of workshops, sheds, and warehouses shoe-
horned into small plots of land, or even out of single-room apartments arranged
around a common courtyard (hawsh).[17] Paradoxically, this underground economy

FIGURE 67. Place de l'Étoile, with the 'Abed clocktower in its center and the Parliament Building.

was quick to expand under the French, progressively colonizing the balconies and rooftops of the new buildings with the installation of huts and gambling dens alongside makeshift shelters and dovecotes. Indeed the history of the Balad during the three decades in which the grand designs of the Mandate were carried out was in large part one of the reconquest of the modern by the traditional, and of the legal by the illegal. The most striking example of this was in Place de l'Étoile itself, where the fountain at the base of the 'Abed clocktower—thirty meters from the monumental Parliament Building—soon came to be used by the porters of the old Nuriyyeh suq to wash themselves. Later, when the city council sought to remove this embarrassment by draining the basin, it became an unauthorized garbage dump.[18]

Once construction had gotten underway, however, and in spite of its relatively small scale, the downtown produced an impression in the visitor commensurate with what would normally be expected not only of a great port and commercial city but also of a capital. Beirut was long to be the only city in the Levant adapted to the needs both of international trade and regional consumption, while at the same time offering imported luxury to anyone who desired it, together with entertainment and diversions of every kind—all this under conditions of relative anonymity. Even after Écochard's urban renewal plan was adopted in Damascus in the mid-1930s, Beirut managed to preserve this power of attraction, which brought to it a regular stream of businessmen and tourists in search of European products, from Syria, Palestine, and even Iraq.

No place more fully incarnated this functional diversity than Place des Martyrs. The square remained the center of the city's center, so to speak, even if in strictly geographical terms it constituted the eastern border of the Balad. The enlargement of its central garden and the construction of broad sidewalks on all four sides set off the surrounding Hamidian-era buildings to greater effect. Now a hub for both motorized and horse-drawn carriages as a result of the increase in automobile traffic, it was visited every day by people from both the city and the country on their way to jobs in the buildings around the square or to appointments in the government offices located in the Petit Sérail, on the north side. Nearby hotels, restaurants, and especially cafés helped to carry over the bustling daytime activity into the evening— together with the movie theaters that had recently opened there, a few cabarets, and, above all, the red-light district, located on a back street leading off from the eastern side of the square. There was a double irony of geography and toponymy in this case, for the street ran past the site of the Jesuits' first residence in Beirut and bore the name of the great Arab poet Mutanabbi (who, unlike many of his contemporaries during the ʿAbbasid period, did not compose erotic verse). Popular usage preferred the very frank name "Whore Market" (Suq al-Sharamit)—euphemized as the occasion demanded to "Public Market" (al-Suq al-ʿUmūmi). Regularly inspected by the city health department, the houses on Rue Mutanabbi did not limit themselves to offering love for a price; their drawing rooms, on the ground floor, frequently served as meeting places for notables and politicians. Indeed, the house run by the legendary Greek-born madam Marika Spiridon symbolized a profession that was no longer considered shameful—though this opinion would change later.[19]

Place des Martyrs found an echo nearby to the south in a smaller square, Place Debbas (thus named in 1935, in homage to the first president of the Lebanese Republic), and beyond that along Rue de Damas, where cafés and cinemas had already begun to appear. To the west, however, signs of an earlier age could still be seen: two streets, departing from the middle and the bottom of the square, opened up onto an area of suqs that had managed to avoid the renovations undertaken elsewhere in the Étoile neighborhood, and even found itself enlarged as a result, since the markets that had been forcibly relocated by the Ottoman (and later French) demolitions had come to be added to the ones that were already there.[20] This expanded population of jewelers, cheesemongers, butchers, greengrocers, and other shopkeepers served only to attract more visitors to Place des Martyrs. Though it was to remain dominated by the informal sector of the economy right up until war erupted in 1975, the area was to a large extent hidden, and it did not detract from either the unity of the square itself or its continuity with the rest of the Balad, which depended on two east-west thoroughfares. The first and older one, renamed for Emir Bashir, led out from the bottom of the square past the convent of the Lazarists to Place Assour. The second, Rue Weygand, ran from the Petit Sérail, at the top of the square, toward the area bounded by Foch and Allenby and thence the old Bāb Idris. This neighborhood remained the heart of retail commerce in European merchandise, sold in stores with display windows and in the markets constructed at the end of the nineteenth century—Suq al-Tawileh, Suq al-Jamil, and Suq al-Franj. Next to Bāb Idris stood the European food shops, notable among them Massoud & Cie.[21]

The junction at Bāb Idris could in a sense be considered the fourth pole of the Balad, along with the three squares to the south (Martyrs, Assour, and Étoile). Although it was not laid out for purposes of public assembly, as the others were, it gave the impression of announcing the point of entry to the city's new center, in something like the way the gate from which it took its name had formerly marked off the limits of the old town. Rue Georges-Picot took over at this point from Rue Weygand, heading further west to the Jewish quarter, but it was narrower; similarly, to go southward from Bāb Idris to Place Assour, or northward to the old port, it was necessary to take back streets. At the same time the compactness of the Balad accentuated the impression of energetic activity associated with a modern downtown, all the more since the business district bordered on the port as far to the west as the Antun Bey Inn, the seat of commodity brokers, shipping companies, and law offices. Beyond that the shore road connected the Balad with Minet al-Hosn, a transitional neighborhood, neither residential nor commercial, that catered primarily to tourists—an industry whose origins went back well before the Mandate, and that came to be installed along this stretch of the corniche at the end of the Great War. In addition to the Hôtel Bassoul and other establishments from the Ottoman period, the restaurant-nightclub Alphonse opened in 1921, more than a decade before the city's first luxury hotel, the Hôtel Saint-Georges, went up on Avenue des Français, in 1934, followed a little later by the Hôtel Normandy.

The Balad included a number of religious buildings as well. The four great Christian churches had, of course, been saved from the wrecking ball: the Greek Orthodox and Greek Catholic cathedrals—the one dating from the eighteenth century and the other from the nineteenth—occupied an even more prominent position than before, on Place de l'Étoile, whereas the Maronite cathedral and the Basilica of Saint-Louis-des-Capucins saw their congregations increase as a result of demographic growth and, in the latter case, attendance by the very Catholic representatives of the secular Third Republic. The Mandate's program of urban renewal had likewise left the six mosques of the old town intact. The Mosque of Emir Mundhir, the Majidiyyeh Mosque on Rue Foch, and above all the great al-ʿUmari Mosque, now situated across from the Palais Municipal at the corner of Weygand and Maʿrad, were now shown to greater advantage by the enlargement of the road system. Owing to the small number of permanent residents in the neighborhood, none of these places of worship had any real parish life; the congregants were recruited mainly from the daytime working population and others who came from farther away to celebrate religious holidays. Only the synagogue in the Jewish quarter of Wadi Abu Jamil, now nearer to the city center in the wake of the Balad's westward expansion along Rue Georges-Picot, was an exception to this rule.

THE IRON AND THE JASMINE

Despite its increase in both area and height, and the modern spirit of its architectural innovations, the new downtown did not dominate the physical appearance of Beirut. Panoramic views of the period show that the concentration and verticality of the business district were more than offset by the expanses of a still largely rustic landscape. Although residential areas had doubled in area, beginning with the suburbs of the nineteenth century and the formerly isolated hamlets of the promontory, and while they grew in population from the continuing influx of immigrants, urban development was still far from blotting out the bucolic visage of an earlier era. Taken together, these areas resembled a sort of garden city, rising in terraces over a succession of hillsides and crisscrossed by broad swaths of green against the background of snow-capped mountains. This is the landscape that was to enchant Omar Onsi, Mustafa Farrukh, Georges Cyr, and other pioneers of modern painting in Lebanon, no less than it had dazzled Western travelers of earlier generations. In a sense, the panorama had hardly changed since the appearance of new neighborhoods during the second half of the preceding century. "Considering only its picturesque aspect," a contemporary French visitor remarked, "the principal charm of the landscape of Beirut remains today the still considerable number of fine and large houses from the nineteenth century, sited on the lower slopes of the various neighborhoods, facing the north and the sea, with a central hall opening through three ogival bays."[22]

This hybrid residential design—a Westernized adaptation of the traditional home with its triple-arcaded façade—had resisted the advance of urbanization. Indeed its popularity spread, and with the rise of an urban bourgeoisie eager to assimilate the values of European modernity it was now available in different sizes. On the immediate periphery of the downtown, in Ghalghul and Wadi Abu Jamil, the pace of construction seemed to grow by a process of contagion, at least to judge from photographic surveys of the period; but older patrician neighborhoods such as Zuqaq al-Blat, on Qantari Hill, and Qirat and Rmayleh, on the north face of Ashrafiyyeh Hill, managed to preserve the luxury of large homes set on spacious grounds at a comfortable distance from their neighbors. And despite the increasing density of middle-class neighborhoods near the Balad such as Saifi and Bashura, and the growth of Ras Beirut and Ashrafiyyeh, the new forms of building accommodated themselves to the basic style of the triple-arcaded house.[23] It is true that the gain in height permitted by recent advances in construction technique obscured many existing rooftops, with their reddish orange Marseille tile; but the traditional garden survived, and the structure itself remained unchanged on the whole. Even the dividing up of buildings into large apartments for lease, and with it the loss of the customary correspondence between house and family unit, did not call into question the old domestic arrangements.[24] The life of these houses—or the apartments they contained—continued to be ordered by a central hall that gave access to the other rooms. It alone was partitioned, since in the traditional *dār* the dining room was kept separate from the more informal living room. On the outside walls, still fashioned from *ramleh*, a coating of stucco was applied to conceal defects of workmanship, and probably also to give the house a more modern look, though its distinctive ochre tones were not universally admired; in some cases a yellow or pink—even a plain white—coat of paint was preferred. Concrete made a first appearance during this period, but it did not affect the coherence of the city's built environment, at least until the middle of the twentieth century. Used as a structural material, concrete allowed broad verandas to be substituted for narrow balconies. It was also employed in the decoration of façades, where classical moldings and neo-Baroque festoons could be multiplied more cheaply,[25] accentuating the romantic cachet associated with the architecture of the mandate period.

The recurrence of these ornamental themes, borrowed from older patrician homes that themselves were inspired by a mélange of foreign and native styles, gave most residential areas an air of comfort, if not affluence. And although these buildings were apt to be taller than in the past (some rising to a height of five stories), their large covered verandas and private gardens, giving off scents of jasmine and gardenia, created an atmosphere of tranquility in contrast to the hectic pace of the center city. More than photographs and illustrations, it was perhaps the poetry of Georges Schéhadé, a native of Alexandria, that best captured this atmosphere. His first poems after taking up residence in Beirut gave a glimpse of houses that on summer afternoons "dozed behind their distempered fish-eyed shutters," their verandas "dangling moon linens," their balconies "fluttering in the water," their railings "interlaced in patterns of iron and jasmine," while "behind the garden walls overstepped by the noise of things, jets of water make cats' leaps into the cleavage of the fountains."[26]

Beirut's charms, outside the Balad, caught the fancy not only of poets. To foreign urbanists it suggested comparisons with the garden cities that were being constructed at the time in Europe.[27] Nor were private gardens the exclusive prerogative of the wealthiest neighborhoods. Just as often they were found in more traditional and less affluent districts such as Mazra'a, Musaytbeh, and on the southern and eastern slopes of Ashrafiyyeh. In addition to the small public gardens built throughout the city by the mandate administration and the large orchards that survived here and there, patches of cactus (particularly prickly pears in Ras Beirut) and the wild grasses that took over parcels of uncultivated land seemed to assure that green would continue to enjoy a prominent place in the palette of the urban landscape. The idea of reproducing Cairo's garden city experiment in the Raml district, which was virtually empty at this time, in the hope of attracting middle-class families from the inner city,[28] held no more appeal than constructing a local version of Empain's Heliopolis in Uza'i: demand among this segment of the population did not yet exceed the available supply of land, and gardens were sufficiently numerous in the city itself that they did not have to be created on its outskirts. It may be for the same reason that not enough attention was paid to the master plan drawn up around 1930 by the French urbanist René Danger at the request of the French government, which called for basing the city's future development on the model of the garden city.[29] Once the entire promontory came to be embedded in concrete, after the Second World War, it was too late to regret the neglect of previous decades. For the moment, demographic pressures seemed to be contained on the margins of the city, even if in retrospect the preference for concrete and the emergence of the first peripheral pockets of poverty can be seen to date back to the era of the Mandate.

THE GEOGRAPHY OF COMMUNAL IDENTITY

The city continued to expand, so that gradually the residual empty spaces within and between its various neighborhoods disappeared. And even if the development of the Balad and of the port spilled over into the immediately surrounding area, this expansion for the most part turned its back on the sea—as in many other Mediterranean cities.[30]

To the east, Ashrafiyyeh Hill filled up. The neighborhoods of Ghabeh, Rmayleh, and Medawar now covered its northern face, next to Saifi and Gemmayzeh, which bordered the downtown, and the pace of construction on its eastern and southern flanks increased. Musaytbeh, to the west, gained even more quickly in density, again owing to its proximity to the Balad, from which it was separated only by Bashura and Ghalghul. Between the two hills a more recent pole of settlement, Mazra'a, spread out on one side toward the neighborhood of Ras al-Nabi', which had grown up along Rue de Damas, and on the other toward the old suburb of Basta, which linked it to Bashura, and thence to the center city. In the northwestern part of the promontory, the fashionable district of Qantari stretched toward the new neighborhood of Arts-et-Métiers (Sanayeh) to the south, and toward the former village of 'Ayn al-Mrayseh to the north; west of this stood the American university, and beyond that the neighborhood of Ras Beirut, which grew in prestige with the opening of the consulates of Egypt and Iraq there in the 1930s. But the true extent of the city's expansion was indicated by the emergence of a peripheral zone along a roughly circular arc swinging westward from the Nahr Beirut and passing through an area lying to the south of the city limits that included the former villages of Furn al-Shubbak and Shiyyah (between which the new community of 'Ayn al-Rummaneh

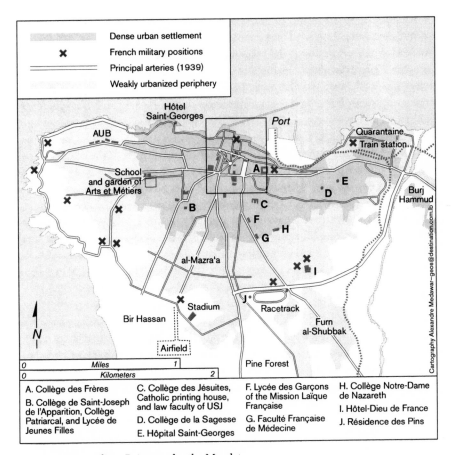

Dense urban settlement

✕ French military positions

Principal arteries (1939)

Weakly urbanized periphery

Hôtel Saint-Georges

Port

AUB

Quarantaine

✕ Train station

School and garden of Arts et Métiers

A

✕

E

D

Burj Hammud

✕ B

C

F

H

G

al-Mazra'a

✕
✕ I

N

Bir Hassan

✕ Stadium

J

Racetrack

Furn al-Shubbak

Airfield

Pine Forest

0   Miles   1
0   Kilometers   2

Cartography Alexandre Medawar—geos@destination.com.lb

A. Collège des Frères

B. Collège de Saint-Joseph de l'Apparition, Collège Patriarcal, and Lycée de Jeunes Filles

C. Collège des Jésuites, Catholic printing house, and law faculty of USJ

D. Collège de la Sagesse

E. Hôpital Saint-Georges

F. Lycée des Garçons of the Mission Laïque Française

G. Faculté Française de Médecine

H. Collège Notre-Dame de Nazareth

I. Hôtel-Dieu de France

J. Résidence des Pins

MAP 10. Metropolitan Beirut under the Mandate

was taking shape), as well as Burj al-Brajneh and Mrayjeh, before being interrupted by an expanse of dunes.

The growth of Beirut continued to be fueled less by its own wealth and industry than by the image of itself that the city propagated abroad and by the haven that it offered to refugees. The urban paradigm of the Tanzimat was extended still further, to the point of anticipating—albeit on a reduced scale—the configuration assumed later in the century by metropolises throughout the Third World. In a city that was pleased to advertise its claims to Haussmannian order and the tranquil nonchalance of bourgeois life, new areas of settlement began to form that were no less modern for being incongruent with the urban core. Whereas Beirut in the nineteenth century had managed to absorb the scattered hamlets on the promontory, even after the shock of the civil war of 1860, its recent promotion to the status of a capital, in combination with the geopolitical changes that followed the First World War and the deterioration of the regional economy in the 1930s, now produced effects that were difficult to control. Not only was the spread of urbanization the result of a lack of systematic planning; it occurred at a pace that outstripped the city's ability to provide basic services,[31] with the result that Beirut could not rapidly assimilate so many newcomers without itself being deformed. It was altered first of all in its physical shape, since the demographic increase could only partially be accommodated by the growth of the old residential areas, which at the same time became more densely populated, and since a part of this increase was therefore diverted to areas outside the municipal grids that furnished water and electricity, disrupting the general impression of prosperity; and next in its social equilibrium, which could not avoid being upset by the arrival in massive numbers of immigrants who brought with them different ways of looking at the world, sharpening the sense of communal identity and aggravating the risk of sectarian antagonism.

Demographic pressures were particularly apparent on the periphery of Beirut, where the new suburbs swallowed up old villages. A few quiet green enclaves survived in Furn al-Shubbak, Shiyyah, and Burj al-Brajneh; elsewhere poorly constructed and nondescript buildings were the rule. Triple-arched windows were rare in these places, and the tall new apartment buildings that recently had begun to appear everywhere else were conspicuous by their absence. Immigrants crowded together instead in old, hastily adapted rural cottages or in new concrete structures, ill-equipped and devoid of elegance, along mostly unpaved roads.[32] Pockets of poverty, and often disease, began to emerge on the outskirts of the metropolitan area, where a growing number of rural migrants came to settle despite the lack of public services. Shantytowns now sprang up, swollen by the influx of Armenian, Syrian, Mesopotamian, and Kurdish refugees.

The Armenian refugees, who had arrived in large numbers and in a very brief period of time, were initially settled by the mandate administration in a transit camp near the old lazaretto. While many of them succeeded in moving out after a few years, spreading into the city and across the banks of the Nahr to the neighborhood of Burj Hammud, where a very densely populated Armenian community took root, the camp in the Quarantaine district still numbered no fewer than three thousand refugees when it was devastated by a fire in 1933.[33] Later this neighborhood was to be occupied by Kurdish refugees. In the meantime other Armenians had settled around the seat of the Armenian Catholic diocese in the Ghabeh neighborhood, on the northeast slope of Ashrafiyyeh; though it offered greater access to municipal services than outlying areas, it was by no means affluent. But however difficult the conditions in which the Armenian refugees lived may have been, their situation was more comfortable than that of the Neo-Aramaic-speaking Christians of Syria and Mesopotamia and of the Syriacs and Assyrians, who received little or no

FIGURE 68. Armenian refugee camp in the Quarantaine district.

assistance from the French authorities. Lacking shelter, they were forced to huddle together in empty lots on Ashrafiyyeh Hill, where the *hawsh* they cobbled together out of discarded materials and debris grew over time into slums, notably at Karm al-Zaytun, on the eastern slope, and in what was later to be known as the Syrian quarter (Hayy al-Siryan), on the southern slope—both of which were to remain without sewers or paved roads until the end of the century.

Within the city limits of Beirut as well as in its suburbs, the poverty of these areas was intensified not only by the absence of urban infrastructure but also by the disregard of governmental agencies. Preoccupied with the ambitious reconstruction projects announced by the Mandate, the municipality of Beirut showed little interest in anything other than the development of the central business district and the port and the improvement of the roads serving them. But lacking any real autonomy, it had no meaningful authority over the new suburbs, which, though they were now contiguous with the limits of the capital itself, had been separately incorporated in 1927 as municipalities in their own right. Even so, their budgetary resources were sadly inadequate. They could scarcely count on making up the difference through taxation, since many of their inhabitants continued to claim domicile in the Mountain, which retained its fiscal privileges from the Ottoman period until the beginning of the 1930s.

If the rural exodus led to overpopulation only in a small number of areas that for the moment were relatively isolated from view, its effects on social and political life were felt practically everywhere in the entire city. No less than in the nine-teenth century, Beirut expanded along sectarian lines of settlement. Still, this was a far cry from the extremely rigid compartmentalization that developed later as a result of civil war in the 1980s. Many neighborhoods continued to exhibit a diver-sity of faiths, as can be seen in the distribution of *mukhtār*—holders of a commu-nal office inherited from the Ottoman system, nominally elected but for the most part appointed, who discharged the duties of civil administration on the local level. The list of such officials drawn up in connection with the administrative redistricting of 1921, for example, indicates that the Christian presence in most Muslim neigh-borhoods was sufficiently large to justify the nomination of both Christian and Mus-lim mukhtār.[34] Yet even if residential districts were seldom perfectly homogeneous, they all displayed a dominant coloring that foreign observers could readily iden-tify with a particular denomination.[35]

The religious character of a neighborhood was still more easily detected when it was associated with a clear geographical demarcation, such as the line passing through Place des Martyrs along Rue de Damas. Very roughly, the Christian neigh-borhoods (or, more exactly, a bloc of almost exclusively Christian neighborhoods) could be said to lie to the east of this line—originally as a result of Greek Orthodox settlement, which over time gave way to a Maronite majority under the influence of the rural exodus. Maronite predominance was further bolstered by another mi-gration from the Mountain, this one repeated on a daily basis, by townspeople from Matn and Kisrawan who came down to the city to buy and sell goods and tend to official business. More generally, the Christian character of this part of Beirut was accentuated by the presence of the Armenians, first in the camp in the Quaran-taine district and then in the surrounding neighborhood, but also by the ongoing flight from the countryside, which increasingly populated the new suburbs to the southeast.

Yet this boundary line was misleading. For if the number of Muslims in the east-ern neighborhoods was small, it did not mean that only Muslims were found west of Place des Martyrs and Rue de Damas. Apart from the Jewish quarter of Wadi Abu Jamil, which now found itself more centrally situated with the growth of the downtown, there were large concentrations of Greek Orthodox in Musaytbeh (where in the late 1920s a young battalion commander named Charles de Gaulle lived for almost two years following his transfer to the general staff of French forces in the Levant)[36] and Mazra'a. This mixed character also obtained to one degree or another in Bashura, Ras al-Nab', Qantari, Sanayeh, Minet al-Hosn, and Ras Beirut; indeed, some of these neighborhoods had a notable Maronite minority. Basta, on the other hand, was almost entirely Muslim—hence the ominous significance of the east-west dividing line.

Very quickly Basta came to represent the Islamic community of Beirut in the popular mind, among both friends and enemies, for its opposition to a Christian

FIGURE 69. The expansion of the urban footprint in the 1920s.

spirit of solidarity *('asabiyya)* that was all the more formidable as it was strength-ened by the twin forces of immigration from the Mountain and the protection of the mandate authorities. Basta was a working-class neighborhood. Preserving the appearance of an old suburb of artisans and craftsmen along the Sidon road, al-though the Sunni bourgeoisie had recently erected some grand residences there,[37] it lent itself to a culture of virility that inevitably assumed the mantle of sectarian rage when the geography of otherness intruded. In local disputes with neighbor-ing gangs from the mixed districts of Mazra'a and Musaytbeh and, still more so, in the neutral territory downtown where they frequently clashed with their counter-parts from Gemmayzeh, the mostly Maronite quarter to the east of Place des Mar-tyrs, the qabadayat of Basta championed Sunni solidarity while proudly embrac-ing their reputation as hoodlums *(zu'rān)*. So fierce and unrelenting was the mutual antagonism between Basta and Gemmayzeh that until the 1960s it continued to shape the public perception of the city's political landscape and to provide jour-nalists with a shorthand way of describing their conflicts.

The logic of sectarian quarrels was not the only force acting to segregate Beirut's various communities. It is a universal law of sociology that rural immigrants tend to stay together and that the relations existing among them in their native villages are transposed to the neighborhoods of their adopted cities. This was especially true in the less affluent neighborhoods on the slopes of Ashrafiyyeh and along the south-eastern periphery where the Maronites chose to settle: those from Kisrawan and the northern part of the Mountain took up residence in large numbers in the neighborhood of Ghabeh, whereas their coreligionists from the Jezzin region, in the south, settled on another flank of Ashrafiyyeh, and still others from the Shuf Mountains in the suburbs of Furn al-Shubbak, Shiyyah, and ʿAyn al-Rummaneh. The Shiʿa of Jabal ʿAmil, for their part, migrated to Ras al-Nabʿ and, outside the city proper, to Nabʿa, Burj al-Brajneh, and Mrayjeh, where these first settlements prepared the way for the massive influx of the 1960s and 1970s. In all these neighborhoods the collective dispositions that the immigrants brought with them from their homelands were found on a smaller scale, through family, clan, and village ties. Sometimes an entire village was reassembled on the same street. As in the nineteenth century, a view of the world and a set of social practices that had been formed in the countryside were transferred almost without modification to the city, with the result that many neighborhoods, especially the less prosperous ones to the east, appeared more like villages, untouched by the anonymity of urban life and remote from the ideal of the melting pot. Without directly contributing to the formation of a belligerent sensibility, any more than the mere existence of different religious denominations did, the importation of rural ways of thinking into an urban environment nonetheless strengthened sectarian attachments.

The latent centrifugal tendencies of greater Lebanon were bound to be strengthened as well in a city whose capacity for assimilating newcomers was challenged by physical growth and the increasing demographic pressures that accompanied it. These tendencies gained momentum in the 1920s and 1930s under the Mandate, with major implications for the long term. In the near term, however, the spreading pockets of poverty and violence were not large enough to mar the splendid panorama, at once bucolic and contemporary, of Beirut. And however much the intrusion of rural values was beginning to alter the city's perception of itself, it was counteracted by the image of modernity arising from the simultaneous emergence of a central commercial district with Haussmannian ambitions and a style of living that, for all its pretensions to Parisian elegance, sought to go beyond the derivative tastes of local elites in order to create a distinctive way of life—a way of life adapted, if only by successive alterations, to a city whose neighborhoods and classes were increasingly separated from one another.

Grand-Liban and Petit Paris

From the opening pages of Pierre Benoît's 1924 novel *La châtelaine du Liban,* the idea is fixed in the reader's mind: whether lounging on the terrace of the Kursaal café or gambling at the Casino Tabaris, French officers stationed in Beirut felt perfectly at ease. Here, only a few years after the end of the Great War, one was worlds away from the ruin it had caused in Europe—far, too, from everything that had troubled the Levant since, far from the uncertain situation in the plains and cities of the Syrian interior, even in the Mountain next door.

However great may have been the tensions aroused by the Mandate's policies, which became still more palpable during the 1930s, the image created by the capital of Greater Lebanon was unavoidably linked with the ineffable lightness of being of a social elite intoxicated by the idea of imitating others—something it succeeded in doing in a way, and to an extent, that impressed visitors. "It is very elegant in Beirut," said the 1932 guide to Lebanon and Syria, foretelling the city's future as the Nice of the Levant. "Everyone speaks French there. 'Society,' the ambiance, the 'salons' (there are even 'literary' ones where writers are given a warm welcome)—in a word, life offers as many possibilities as the visitor may desire."[1] The comparison with Nice may not have met with the approval of *le Tout-Beyrouth,* however, who saw their world as the Switzerland of the East or, better still, as a sort of smaller overseas version of Paris.

The frequent sojourns there by eminent persons from the French capital reinforced a Parisianism that was perceptible especially in women's fashion and the interior decoration of the homes in wealthy neighborhoods. But outward appearances could be deceptive. The very same people who acted at night as though the Belle Époque had not vanished with the war were learning during the day at first hand of the difficulties involved in inventing a country. Immortalized in the society pages of local newspapers for his appearance in the ceremonial dress of a Roman praetor at a costume ball given by Mme Henri Ponsot,[2] Bishara al-Khuri, president of the Council of Ministers and future hero of the struggle for independence, was a more familiar figure in the front pages for his up-and-down relations with his hostess's husband, the French high commissioner.

WESTERNIZATION AND ELECTRIFICATION

As in the majority of the world's cities, the dominant characteristic of the period in Beirut was the advance of technology, which greatly accelerated the movement of people, goods, and information, and above all encouraged the rise of a kind of international citizenship. Originating mainly in Europe, but having roots in North America as well, this mode of existence spread more or less rapidly in the colonial world by means of social elites that found themselves, culturally or economically, or both, in contact with the West—and that often had attained elite status solely as a result of such contact. Beirut was all the less exceptional in this regard as its Westernization had already been well underway since the beginning of the nineteenth century. As a result, it had become acquainted very early on with the latest innovations of technological civilization, from the telegraph to the airplane. With no need of an intervening period of discovery, the interwar years were marked by the increasingly massive adoption of three foreign inventions in particular: the cinema, long a familiar feature of the life of the city; radio, which established itself as a means of communication and a source of entertainment in the 1930s; and the telephone, which, having effectively been reserved at first for government officials, came into private use beginning in the mid-1920s.

Here as elsewhere, the cornerstone and symbol of this new world was electricity, without which none of the other inventions would have been conceivable. To be sure, the Franco-Belgian company that supplied current to the city did not immediately serve every part of it, but the rapid expansion of fraud in this domain suggests that the spirit of private enterprise was not absent. Impressed by the ingenuity of the illegal (and detachable) connections found by the engineers of the Compagnie d'Électricité de Beyrouth, a French observer objected: "And you pretend that you cannot train Lebanese electricians, mechanics, and so on, because the Arabs are unsuited to technology!"[3] The network of streetcars managed by the company was quickly extended beyond the heart of the city as well, once again stimulating widespread, although less sophisticated, forms of corruption: "[R]ather than have a ticket punched, one claims to be a subscriber [and] presents to the conductor, who understands at once, a case of visiting cards with a one-pound note inside."[4] Another and no less paradoxical sign of the success of electrification was the unhappiness aroused by what many felt to be the company's exorbitant rates. Protests soon took on an anti-French tone, culminating in 1931 in a three-month strike during which residents of Beirut refused to pay their electric bills and boycotted the streetcar. A lasting consequence of this boycott was the system of communal taxis (known by the French name *taxis-service,* or simply *services*), already in operation for intercity transportation and now adopted within the city, where a seat could be had for the modest sum of five piasters.[5]

Along with electricity, the other great emblem of technological advance during this period was the automobile. Whereas before the Great War there had been only a half-dozen cars in Beirut, and the government itself owned only five cars in 1920, there were not fewer than 376 motor vehicles the following year. The first drivers' licenses were issued in 1921 as well, and thereafter the number of car registrations rose without interruption. Horse-drawn carriages gradually fell out of use, beginning with the appearance of omnibuses operated by the city. In the space of two years, the number of cars registered in Lebanon tripled; in 1928 there were 5,291, and then almost 10,000 in 1932. Replacement rates were also telling. Of the 18,000 cars imported in 1931 through the port of Beirut, half were destined for the countryside, where they replaced ones that had broken down or that were merely no longer in fashion.[6] Patterns of social behavior in the city had inevitably been changed as well. Every evening, according to the tourist guide of 1932, people drove their cars around Place des Martyrs simply for the pleasure of being seen. Some were even known to sell plots of land in order to find the money to buy the latest model.[7] But it was not necessary to go to such lengths. American cars, in particular, were available at an affordable price. This, together with the option of spreading out payments over twenty-four months, partly explains the preference shown for Detroit products. In 1923, there were 949 American cars in the country, as against only 146 French cars and 112 Italian cars. Fords, both stylish and easy to repair, sold especially well—making a wealthy man of the company's agent, Charles Corm, whose career as a man of letters did not seem to prevent him from popularizing its vehicles and of promoting their manufacturer. So great, in fact, was Ford's popularity that the United States is estimated to have recovered in four years, through sales of Fords in Lebanon and Syria, the equivalent of all the money sent back home by expatriates from these lands in the previous forty years.[8]

The triumph of the automobile and, as a consequence of this, the improvement of the road network had the effect, among others, of encouraging city dwellers to vacation in the mountains. The practice was certainly not new. Natives of the Mountain had always gone back up to their villages to escape the heat and humidity of Beirut in the summer, and wealthy natives of the city (such as Salim Salam) had adopted the habit of seeking relief in higher elevations before the war. Thanks to the railway, villages located on the Damascus road such as 'Aley and Sofar had already acquired a reputation as holiday resorts by the end of the nineteenth century. With the advent of the automobile it now became possible to make day trips be-

FIGURE 70. The Bustros residence, once the site of the British consulate, served as the model for the Tabaris Casino in Pierre Benoît's novel of Beirut.

tween Beirut and the Mountain—a fashion set at the top, since the offices of the high commissioner and the general staff were moved every summer to 'Aley, at the time only a half-hour from Beirut, where the French generals Gouraud, and later Weygand and Sarrail, rented the Bustros residence.[9] Summering in the mountains was not the privilege of local and foreign high society for very long, however. It soon became the norm among much of the middle class as well, regardless of family origins, and helped to spread the city's way of life beyond the Damascus road, bringing restaurants, cafés, and even cinemas to mountain villages north and east of Beirut. In an almost caricatural illustration of this transposition of city to country, and of the Europeanization that accompanied it, the region surrounding the Hôtel du Bois de Boulogne, near Dhur Shuwayr in Matn, came to be known as Bologna. Holidays outside the city were not limited to the summer months, however. The new roads also favored briefer getaways to natural sites such as the gorges of the Nahr al-Kalb, already in vogue at the beginning of the century, and the snow-capped peaks of Mount Lebanon, where skiing soon made its appearance.

TOURISM AND COSMOPOLITANISM

In addition to their impact on people's daily lives, the advances of technological civilization helped to accentuate the cosmopolitan character of Beirut—and of its hinterland. Even before the revolution in air travel, progress in nautical engineering had aroused an interest in tourism, now widespread among affluent urbanites in Europe. If a voyage to the East had lost some of its romanticism, it also gained in comfort because of the new liners put into service on the cruise ship routes. This was still a long way from mass tourism, of course, but the places made famous by the adventurers and literary travelers of previous centuries were now visited by more and more people. Formerly a customary (though by no means obligatory) stopover, Beirut became a regular port of call on bourgeois itineraries, the mid-point of a typical Mediterranean cruise.

Apart from the *Champollion, Lotus,* and *Mariette Pacha,* the three great liners of the Messageries Maritimes favored by French officials, the port was served by a half-dozen other shipping companies: the Fabre Line, Lloyd Triestino, the Byron Line, the Khedivial Mail Line, Sitmar, and the Société Maritime et Coloniale. Leaving from Marseille, ships reached Beirut after seven days via Naples, Messina, Crete, and Alexandria. The return to Marseille took longer, since the northern route was thought to be more scenic, and required twelve days to call at Alexandretta (with a side trip to Antioch) and Smyrna, thence passing through the Dardanelles to Istanbul and from there via the Aegean to Piraeus and Naples.[10]

The boom in tourism had been anticipated in 1919 by the circle of Francophile intellectuals and businessmen who founded the Phoenician Society. In a series of articles published in the *Revue phénicienne* that year, they imagined a country having Beirut for its capital whose political economy would be modeled on that of Switzerland. A little less than a century earlier, as we have seen, Lamartine had been the first to speak of the "Switzerland of the Levant," and in the meantime the analogy had come to occupy a familiar place in the popular imagination, with or without ideological overtones. The expression figured, for example, in a report drafted by two Ottoman officials of Lebanese birth in 1917 on the state of the vilayet of Beirut, where it was employed in a positive way to evoke the natural attractions of vacationing in the mountains.[11] The articles in the *Revue phénicienne,* for their part, laid greater emphasis on local initiative. Without excluding other points of similarity, such as the hydraulic resources of the Mountain, which made it amenable to the development of light industry, or the place of banking and commerce in the economy, they called for investment in holiday resorts as a way of competing for a share of the urban tourist trade from Syria, Palestine, Anatolia, Egypt, and even Europe. "While we do not have money-capital," one writer noted, "we have beauty-capital and climate-capital that are unique in the world. Let us set to work to put them to good use and to make them bear fruit, and we will see Lebanon become before long the Switzerland of the East."[12] Another member of the Phoenicianist movement went on to publish an entire book in Paris devoted to the idea of transforming Lebanon into the "Switzerland of the Levant."[13]

Meanwhile the French authorities were not idle. In 1921, in addition to the *Guide du tourisme* published to coincide with the exposition sponsored by General Gouraud, a national tourism office was opened in Beirut, in coordination with the French railway company PLM (Paris-Lyon-Marseille), as well as an automobile club and an agency of Wagons-Lit Cook. The creation in 1923 of a department within the mandate administration having responsibility for the promotion of tourism confirmed that this sector would be an object of official economic policy. A major publicity campaign was launched through the placement of advertising supplements in Egyptian and Palestinian newspapers, distribution of leaflets in travel agencies, and the publication of small illustrated guides. In parallel with this effort, PLM commissioned large posters in bright colors inspired by the example of the "other France" in North Africa, where tourism had been encouraged by such means since the beginning of the century. Renowned illustrators such as André Frémond, Julien Lacaze, and Geoffroy d'Aboville (who signed his work with the name Dabo) employed the shimmering tones of the reigning Art Deco style to enliven scenes of Beirut against the background of mountain landscapes, as well as Baalbek and other historical sites.[14] On one poster by Dabo, beneath the reddening shadows of a Palmyran temple and the slogan "Syria and Lebanon—Land of Tourism and Vacation," there is the promise: "Clean Air—Beautiful Sites—Beautiful Roads—Good Hotels." No less revealing is a legend in smaller letters that, in giving a pair of addresses for further information, one in Paris, the other in Cairo, identified the two audiences that the promoters sought to reach. The effort to appeal to a European clientele was further supported by promotional posters paid for and distributed by shipping companies and the Orient Express. The mandate administration, for its part, persuaded the Paris publishing house Hachette to publish the first *Guide bleu* to Syria and Palestine in 1927, the old pre-war Baedeker now being hopelessly out of date.

The *Guide bleu* appeared at just the right moment. Interest in the Levant was soon to be stimulated by two events: the Colonial Exposition, staged from May to November 1931 in Vincennes, outside Paris, where the Syro-Lebanese pavilion enjoyed a lively success, and André Citroën's Yellow Cruise that same year. Departing from Beirut on 4 April, the expedition put the Levant on the covers of French magazines and launched a national craze that became still more intense the following year when Éditions Arthaud brought out a new guide on Lebanon and Syria, edited by André Geiger, as part of its "Les Beaux Pays" series. There can be no doubt that Geiger's treatment of his subject, and in particular his prediction concerning Beirut's future as a tourist destination, helped to attract more visitors. The existing hotel stock was neither large enough to accommodate the number of tourists contemplated nor elegant enough to satisfy the type of guest who was now desired, however. The opening in 1934 of a great seaside hotel, the prestigious Hôtel Saint-Georges, testified to a rising demand among wealthy foreigners. Even though the Saint-Georges was the result of private enterprise, it fit in nicely with the Mandate's vision, being managed by the Société des Grands Hôtels du Levant, a subsidiary of

FIGURE 71. The Hôtel
Saint-Georges at night,
as it looked at the time
of its opening in 1934.

the Banque de Syrie et du Grand-Liban, which itself was controlled by French investors. To promote this palace, for the moment the only one of its kind in Beirut, advertisements hastened to assure prospective visitors: "At the hotels run by the Société des Grands Hôtels du Levant you will find a French welcome and French cuisine, and your presence will encourage France's work in the mandated states."[15]

Designed by Antun Tabet, a young architect from Beirut working under the direction of Auguste Perret, the Saint-Georges was to become one of the city's great landmarks, prominently featured in postcards picturing the transformation of the seafront. Six years later, in November 1940, it was joined at the other end of the little bay by a new hotel, the Normandy. The Minet al-Hosn district, and more specifically its Zaytuneh neighborhood along the water, had been identified with tourism since the end of the nineteenth century. In the meantime the construction of Avenue des Français strengthened this initial advantage, and by the 1930s Zaytuneh had firmly established itself as the center of night life in the city. Lucullus—a gastronomic restaurant, as it name suggests—opened there in 1933, followed shortly by the Saint-Georges and the Kit Kat Club, which shared space in a nearby building with the Cercle de l'Union Française and attracted an upscale clientele intent on partying late into the night. The district boasted fashionable beach resorts on

Avenue des Français, famous for their boating displays and entertainments during the summer months. The new facilities built to promote the tourist trade encouraged new forms of behavior as well. The bar at the Saint-Georges, for example, and later at the Normandy, conferred respectability on the consumption of alcohol at any hour of the day by liberating it from the ritual depravity of the old taverns. And in welcoming its guests to the first sidewalk café in Beirut, called the Novelty, the Saint-Georges launched another and no less durable fashion.

More radical still was the introduction of ocean bathing at the Saint-Georges and neighboring establishments. Not only did the newfound fascination with the sea slow the annual summer exodus from the city, but the popularization of bathing costumes accelerated the tendency to adopt more relaxed habits of dress in informal settings. Women increasingly took up swimming as well. Social norms had changed, and with them the design of bathing facilities. The first two establishments to be equipped in a modern way, with restricted entry, changing rooms, showers, diving board, and lifeguard, were the military club at the extreme western tip of the promontory, reserved for officers of the French army, and the club belonging to the American university, next to the beach road bordering the campus. Further to the east, a beach called La Grande Bleue was also adapted for swimming beneath the cliffs of Medawar. But yachting and other boating activities did not really gain impetus until the middle of the 1930s, with the appearance of clubs and marinas in Minet al-Hosn and Uzaʿi.

After the opening in 1934 of the Bain du Saint-Georges—where cases of nudism, probably rare and momentary, were reported—a bath club called the Bain Français sprang up right next to the hotel. Outfitted with a swimming pool, the first in Beirut, where competitions and festivities were held, it was (as the name indicates) patronized almost exclusively by French residents and other foreigners; only a very few Lebanese were admitted. This was also true of its neighbor at the Saint-Georges, but not of two other clubs, ʿAjram and Ondine, whose clientele was recruited from among the young people of the city's middle class.[16] The influence of the Saint-Georges also made itself felt a few miles away. The same year that the hotel opened, a developer named Joseph Semʿan sanctified the French version of his surname by establishing the Saint-Simon in Uzaʿi, on the western shore beyond the administrative limits of the city. The concept was nonetheless different: a broad sandy beach with a restaurant-café and, in addition to showers and two rows of small changing rooms, some sixty wooden bungalows (called "chalets"), all of which gave the place the character of a vacation village ten minutes from the center of the city. Four years later, saintliness descended upon the city again when Semʿan's cousin opened a club called the Saint-Michel on the same stretch of coastline, to the south of Saint-Simon. In the meantime the proprietors of the Grande Bleue in Medawar, who found themselves expropriated as a consequence of the expansion of the port, opened a new beach club further to the east called the Côte d'Azur.[17] Yet another club near the limits of the city, Eden Rock, completed the Lebanese imitation of the French Riviera, whose almost simultaneous boom was not unrelated to the growing enthusiasm for seaside leisure activities, first among Beirut's elites, and then among the middle and lower classes, impressed by the beach scenes they saw in the movies (and also by newsreel reports of the first paid holidays in France under the Popular Front). Popular toponymy retained a special fondness for the heavenly affiliation of the new resorts, much imitated in later years; indeed sainthood was so closely identified with the seashore that soon there came into existence the improbable Saint-Balesh, also known as "Saint-Gratuit"—a free beach with unrestricted access, lacking facilities and not always safe.

LA BELLE ÉPOQUE

Tourism was not alone in making Beirut a cosmopolitan capital. Technological advances helped to spread the values of an international way of life throughout society—beginning, of course, with the wealthiest milieus and then, without great delay, filtering down into the rest of the population. Radio and cinema, in particular, but also newspapers and magazines, which now arrived by sea and air on a regular basis, competed with one another in popularizing new looks and new forms of behavior, adopted so quickly that one forgot they came from somewhere else.

For a growing number of the city's residents there no longer even was an elsewhere: they happened to live in Beirut, but they might as well have been in Paris, Geneva, or Alexandria. And indeed they often were. The progress of maritime transport, and soon of aviation, not only brought tourists to the Levant; these things also made it easier for Levantines who could afford it to travel throughout the Mediterranean. Egypt, nearby and familiar, with its khedivial aristocracy, was still recommended and enjoyed as a stopover; everyone seemed to have a cousin in its affluent Syro-Lebanese community, and eligible bachelors found no shortage of marriageable young women there. But for those who wished to give the impression, or possibly the illusion, of belonging to the modern world, there was no substitute for visiting France. Whether it was to buy new clothes or simply to be *au courant,* one had to go there at least once a year, or else risk being looked down upon at home. The annual—if not semiannual—trip to Paris became a sort of tradition among the rich of Beirut. Some made it part of a longer excursion, dividing their time between the salons of the capital, the nearby casino at Enghien-les-Bains, and the Côte d'Azur.

A few patrician families had long experience in this line, going back to the late nineteenth century, and their offspring could count on being introduced in the right circles. Nicolas de Bustros, one of the privileged few who could postpone marriage for a time in order "to lead the life of a carefree and rich young man in Paris," boasted in his memoirs of having received the "greatest names of Europe" in his furnished apartment at the foot of Avenue de la Grande-Armée.[18] Between gatherings at the

Café de la Paix ("meeting place of all the Lebanese in Paris") and Sarah Bernhardt's drawing room, visits from the Duchesse d'Uzès, outings with Mme Calouste Gulbenkian (wife of Monsieur Cinq-Pour-Cent, as the fabulously wealthy Armenian businessman and philanthropist was known in the international oil industry) and the handsome Count Boni de Castellane, spontaneous infatuations with an Argentine heiress, among others, and larks as an extra at the Opéra and even the film studios in Joinville-le-Pont, Bustros's "marvelous" life[19] may well seem to have been exceptional—and probably it was to some extent, owing to the young man's singularly convivial temperament, which was to win him a shining compliment from André de Fouquières, supreme arbiter of elegance in the Paris of the Belle Époque and later during the Roaring Twenties ("My friend Nicolas de Bustros, who set the tone in Beirut, was a true dandy").[20] But the mention in Bustros's autobiographical reminiscence of so many cousins and uncles and aunts, all of them part-time Parisians, makes it clear that the whole of Beirut high society felt at home in the French capital. Nicolas Sursock, a cousin to Bustros and his neighbor in Beirut, established connections in artistic circles and had his portrait done by no less a painter than Kees van Dongen. Uniquely among the social elites of the French colonial world, the pretensions of this class to membership in international high society were accepted, with perhaps only the barest hint of condescension, by the leading figures of the Paris scene, several of whom came in their turn to be regular visitors to Beirut.

The pillars of Beirut society had no need physically to be in Paris to imagine that they were there. Their clothes and their furniture came from France, along with most of their first names as well. French was the language of everyday life—except for addressing domestic servants below the level of maître d'hôtel; and notwithstanding a tendency to shift the stress within words, an almost universal aversion to rolling the r, and not infrequent barbarisms, all of which betrayed a specifically Levantine style of speaking (also found among the Francophones of Cairo and Aleppo), it was for the most part a quite proper, even affected, French—hardly a creole. The appetite for imitation was whetted all the more by the rituals of daily life and, in particular, the ceremonial devotion to leisure activities. The model for these things, judging from the memoirs of both Nicolas de Bustros and Maud Fargeallah (née Moutran, a native of Baalbek) and from the society columns of the newspapers of the period, was found in the gilded life of the Parisian upper class, even if the Roaring Twenties in Beirut had more in common with the vanished Belle Époque than with the daring energy of the decade as it was experienced by contemporaries in France and elsewhere.

The little Paris that Beirut high society sought to create had always been centered in the Sursock district (usually referred to more simply as "le Quartier"), where since the middle of the nineteenth century the great Orthodox families had constructed huge villas, often inspired by Italian palazzos. It was soon joined by a second patrician enclave on the other side of the city, on Qantari Hill, which attracted Maronite

FIGURE 72. Portrait of Nicolas Sursock by Kees van Dongen. Reproduced by permission of the Nicolas Sursock Museum, Beirut.

and Greek Catholic Christian families whose fortunes came from the port of Beirut and the world of international commerce. In both places, following the example of European aristocracy, hundreds of guests were entertained at dazzling receptions, which in fair weather took the form of garden parties on the spacious grounds of family mansions. Interrupted by the Great War—even though in the first months Jamal Pasha had not declined to honor the *soirées* of the Sursock district with his presence—this sort of merriment quickly resumed, and by the early 1920s the lavish dinners and outdoor parties of the prewar period had regained their former luster. Society hostesses each had a fixed day for receiving guests at home, as in the past, but Sunday was now reserved for the racetrack, where the latest fashions and hairstyles could be paraded in public view. And with the arrival of summer this little Paris was abandoned for the mountains, where the Grand Hôtel de Sofar, popular since the beginning of the century, substituted for the Casino d'Enghien, together with the casino and swimming pool that opened later in ʿAley, in 1930.[21]

To this facsimile of Parisian life, which had preceded the Mandate, native French men and women now added a welcome touch of authenticity. If the French colony in Beirut was not large enough to form a society of its own, the mandate administration could always find enough officers (inevitably "dashing") and high officials (all of them "brilliant") to fill the receptions of le *Tout-Beyrouth*, which were also

FIGURE 73 A–B. The Sursock
mansion: the façade *(left)* and
one of its drawing rooms *(right).*

attended by the executives of local French-owned companies. And increasingly there
were French visitors—among them, familiar figures of *le Tout-Paris* and a number
of noted authors. Apart from Pierre Benoît, who in 1923 resided at the Lazarist college in ʿAntura while writing *La châtelaine du Liban* (though he often "came down"
to Beirut),[22] Linda Sursock welcomed to her villa the likes of Maurice Barrès, who
had known the country before the war, and the academician Henry Bordeaux, who
was to draw from his stay in Beirut a novel called *Yamilé sous les cèdres,* justly forgotten, like the film that it inspired.

But it was perhaps above all Beirut's emergence as a destination on the international theater and music hall circuit that legitimated the aspirations of its high society. Once again the ease of modern transportation played a role, but the improvement of entertainment facilities was no less important in persuading stars of
the Paris stage to come. Two halls in particular vied with each other for headlin-
ers, the Empire and the Grand Théâtre, the latter constructed by Jacques Tabet on
the basis of a design by Yusuf Aftimos. In 1929, for example, the Empire welcomed
a troupe from the Porte Saint-Martin that performed Edmond Rostand's *Cyrano
de Bergerac, L'Aiglon,* and *Chantecler,* while the Compagnie du Mogador and an
Egyptian company were featured at the Grand Théâtre. The following year, Marie
Bell favored both with her presence: having been booked to appear at the Grand

Théâtre with Charles Boyer, she attended the premiere of her film *La nuit est à nous* at the Empire. Such visits became more common during the 1930s, which saw shows by Josephine Baker, Elvire Popesco, Charles Vanel, and Maurice Chevalier, some of whom passed through Beirut more than once.[23]

The strong French presence in the city was nonetheless chiefly responsible for shaping the tastes of a social elite anxious to imitate foreign models, beginning with the example set by the high commissioners themselves (with the notable exception, of course, of the unfortunate General Sarrail). During Gouraud's proconsulate, the Résidence des Pins was the scene of splendid parties attended by members of the great patrician families.[24] Indeed, before moving into the Résidence, the general had been comfortably installed in one of the palaces of the Sursock district[25] and, far from hesitating to take part in social events, he was eager to supervise the arrangements for them personally. It was on Gouraud's suggestion, for example, that sons of the city's leading families joined with members of the French community to put on a play from the classical repertory in the ruins of the temples of Baalbek—an idea that was revived and expanded upon thirty-five years later with the birth of the Baalbek International Festival.[26]

General Weygand was likewise lionized by Beirut society, and after him Henry de Jouvenel, Henri Ponsot, and Damien de Martel. So thorough was the immersion of the Mandate's officials in society life that traditions and precedents came to be established, and it amounted almost to a diplomatic incident if they were not respected, as Mme Ponsot learned to her embarrassment and dismay. Having neglected on her arrival to make the usual calls on the ladies of "the Quarter," neither she nor her husband was invited to the wedding of Nicolas de Bustros. It was not until the new high commissioner awkwardly made it known, through his aide-de-camp, that he wished to be present at the ceremony—a sign of the importance that the mandate authorities attached to social protocol—that an invitation was belatedly issued. In the event Ponsot failed to appear, and this despite the fact that the time of the ceremony had been changed to suit his schedule. A few days later, when Mme Ponsot paid a call on the Bustros residence in order to make her apologies for the unintended breach of courtesy, she was received by the butler.[27] This did not prevent the high commissioner's wife from eventually establishing a prominent place for herself in local society, which developed a great fondness for the masked balls that she frequently gave.[28] Mme de Martel, for her part, also delighted in throwing parties, and indulged a love of riding and visiting the racetrack. In the meantime her husband was able to use the privileges of his office to conceal an affair with the fiendish Raïska de Kherkove, wife of the Belgian consul, until finally evidence of indiscretion fell into the hands of a French official, who hastened to report the matter to Paris, and the high commissioner was promptly relieved of his post.[29]

The fading glow of the Belle Époque served also as a mask for the rivalries playing out under mandate rule. At a party on the eve of the "election" of the first president of the Lebanese Republic, Jouvenel amused himself at the expense of the declared candidates by pretending not to know which one of these three "friends of France"—Émile Eddé, Michel Tuwayni, and Charles Debbas[30]—the mandate administration had chosen (in the end Debbas, the most moderate of the three, succeeded in winning the confidence of the dominant Catroux faction).[31] Martel, for his part, took pleasure at society dinners in openly remarking on the rivalry between Eddé and Bishara al-Khuri.[32] Yet local notables were not without their own cards to play in this game. By involving themselves to such a degree in society life, French officials had helped to make it an opportunity for lobbying by their hosts. Whether it was a question of arranging preferential treatment for a friend or business associate, or of exploiting a certain political advantage, having the ear of the high commissioner, his wife, or his favorite was the quickest and surest way of getting what one wanted. This sort of privileged access to power was not unique to the French mandate, of course. But Beirut nonetheless occupied a special place within the French colonial world: unlike Rabat, Tunis, or Saigon, where similar ballets unfolded before the eyes of the proconsul, here the protagonists were natives, not members of a colonial elite. As a result, issues arising at lower levels of public administration were liable to acquire a political dimension unknown elsewhere to the extent that these socially prominent figures operated at the intersection of two worlds. Linked by bonds of friendship, and often of partnership, with other figures in public life who did not themselves belong to the inner circle of France's friends, the native elite constituted a sort of interface between the Mandate and that part of the political class that continued to reject it. The day was to come when several of its members would dare finally to break ranks with their masters and champion the cause of independence against a France humbled by the defeat of June 1940.

The usefulness of social contacts to the native elite was only to grow with the arrival of the British, who after the Vichy interlude took over the dinners in the city along with control of its territory.[33] Vaudeville, though it had not wholly disappeared, now gave way to geopolitics. Even so, if the tide of great power competition in the Levant turned against France after July 1941, the soirées of le *Tout-Beyrouth* nevertheless preserved their familiar atmosphere. Maneuvers—both on the ground and in the drawing rooms—were in any case admirably conducted by General Edward Spears, a fluent French speaker and a Francophile of long standing, and despite the rejection of French rule there was no break with Parisianism. Once independence had been won, and peace returned to Europe, Maud Fargeallah—muse to Spears after the departure of the Comte de Martel—was very happy to see Paris again.[34]

THE DIFFUSION OF MODERNITY

It scarcely needs to be said that the pleasures of the Belle Époque, in this lingering and suitably affluent overseas variation, were not widely shared. This is not only because membership in Beirut high society was restricted to the families of the commercial and banking upper class, whose relations with foreign interests, dating back in many cases to the late Ottoman period, had grown still closer with the imposition of the Mandate. It is also because class membership was combined with a no less clear-cut communal affiliation—Christian, in the event, whether Greek Orthodox, Greek Catholic, or Maronite. The enthusiasm with which these wealthy Christians embraced their role in the human drama of Beirut had its roots in the conviction, if not that they were now in charge of a country, at least that they were the legatees of a country that France was in the process of forging on their behalf. To be sure, sectarian attachment did not exclude friendly relations, or even partnership, with Muslims of the same social class, particularly in the transitional period between the end of the Great War and the defeat of Faysal, but also after the ouster of Vichy from the Levant. The fact remains, however, that le *Tout-Beyrouth* was a world unto itself.

In the last decades of the Ottoman Empire the Muslim upper class had suffered a first blow with the opening up of Beirut's economy to European influence. French rule weakened its position further, in part because most of the city's Muslim notables were resolved to have the least possible contact with the mandatory agencies. On top of this came the shock associated with the liberalization of morals and the emancipation of women. For the majority of Muslim women, venturing out in public to see a movie or a play—something they did not do very often—required them to respect new constraints that did not fall on their Christian counterparts. Apart from having to wear a veil, or at least a hat with a veil, it was necessary to avoid contact with men by going to screenings reserved for women or by occupying boxes behind the male members of the audience. Since attending society parties remained unthinkable, opportunities for socializing with Christian friends were limited to receiving them at home, and even this was not usually done. The growing prevalence of French styles of dress in Christian high society was certainly one reason for the refusal of Muslim women to take part, even if the veil gradually began to lose some of its coercive authority.

The rejection of the veil was surely one of the most striking features of the interwar period, not least because it was not peculiar to Beirut; indeed, it affected Muslim opinion in the majority of the cities of the Levant. The strongest signal of an imminent cultural revolution came from Egypt in 1922, when the pioneering feminist Huda Sha'rawi, returning from an international women's congress in Rome, removed her veil at the train station in Cairo. Although it was not widely imitated at first in Beirut, this spectacular gesture gave rise to fierce debate, fueled also by the social reforms then being instituted by Mustafa Kemal Atatürk's government in Turkey. The issues at stake were not merely theoretical: women who dared to unveil themselves in the street risked being physically attacked then and there—a not uncommon reaction, captured by the Lebanese painter Mustafa Farrukh in a 1923 painting. The mixed sectarian character of the city exerted a dual influence in this regard. While the freer style of dress worn by Christian women constituted both an incentive and an example for Muslim women, the resentment aroused by the reversal of the communal balance of power, institutionalized by the French Mandate, led men—especially working-class men—to see in the relaxing of vestimentary conventions a betrayal of the Muslim community that had to be punished, where possible in the name of this very community. Conversely, the symbolic celebration of peaceful coexistence between Christians and Muslims licensed the archetypal representation of communal difference in terms of dress, most strikingly in Yusuf Hoyek's 1930 sculpture portraying the shared grief of two women, the one veiled, the other not.

Notwithstanding these obstacles, unveiling was increasingly seen as a step forward and defended on this ground, notably in a book published in 1928 by a young Muslim woman, Nazira Zin al-Din, called *Al-Sufur wa-l-hijab* (Unveiling and the Veil). The book's subtitle ("The Liberation of Women and Social Renewal in the Muslim World") explicitly cast the issue in terms of personal freedom. In the meantime, the majority of Muslim notables in Beirut, educated men who had long been attracted to the related ideas of rebirth and progress, played a supporting role. Thus Salim Salam stood behind his daughter 'Anbara, who on her return home in 1926, after a long stay in London during which she had become accustomed to Western freedoms, chose the occasion of a lecture she had been invited to give on the con-

FIGURE 74. "The Unveiled Young Woman" by Mustafa Farrukh (1923).

dition of women in Europe to present herself without a veil in public—a moment that, though it lacked the theatricality of Huda Shaʿrawi's grand gesture, was no less solemn. The fact that the author of this proclamation was the daughter of the greatest Muslim notable of Beirut, himself a witness to the event, made its exemplary force all the greater. ʿAnbara Salam's younger sister, who had spent her childhood in London, did not even know the veil; as an adolescent in Beirut during the 1930s she rode her bicycle every day to the *lycée* for girls run by the Mission Laïque Française—a liberty that is hard to imagine in an Arab city today, at the beginning of the twenty-first century. It was in any case the daughters of this age, not their mothers, who were to carry out the revolution, just as Egyptian cinema was beginning to popularize among the young the image of the unveiled woman, dressed in Western style, free in her manner of expression and in her way of carrying herself. It was also due more to the determination of young women than of their mothers that the social life of the upper class began to display greater denominational diversity. Another Muslim notable, Abdallah Bayhum, was in the habit of going to official receptions in the company of his daughter Fatmeh, who in 1934 may have been the first Muslim woman to appear "in society,"[35] which is to say to take part openly in the festivities of the Christian elite. Resistance to such behavior came not only from traditionally minded Muslim men, of course, but also from their wives, who had long been accustomed to the reclusive existence common in other Arab societies and disapproved of the idea of accompanying their husbands at social events held outside the home.

And yet however much this *petit Paris* pretended to take the Roaring Twenties as its model, not every kind of diversion was considered acceptable. Beneath the surface attempts to ape the latest fashions, conservatism remained the rule. The first Miss Lebanon contest, which took place in Paris in 1930, aroused hostile reactions in wealthy circles, Muslim and Christian alike—though this did not prevent the competition from being held again, nor its repatriation to Beirut in 1935.[36] If the new conventions could be accommodated by a prudent measure of bourgeois libertinism, a proper education left little room for the assertion of individual freedom, especially in the case of young women. Encounters with men prior to marriage were strictly chaperoned, and great importance was attached to the search for a suitable husband. In the meantime sexual relations were unimaginable—a norm that was to last until the 1970s. Young men had always been able to visit the red-light district, of course; some of them, like Nicolas de Bustros, were able to enjoy themselves in Paris. But sooner or later they had to settle down, and once the time came, exceedingly few managed to escape the dynastic imperative. Marriages were often arranged, with the dowry figuring as one of the major elements of a successful negotiation. The groom's latitude in choosing a professional career was limited to preparing to succeed his father in the family business, bank, or commercial firm, and newlyweds soon found themselves obliged to discharge the ceremonial duties of the Belle Époque following a grand wedding and honeymoon, typically in France, with a side trip to Egypt.

If this *petit Paris* was for all intents and purposes the monopoly of the Christian elite, other classes of society more or less readily followed its example. Parisian life was imitated so successfully by the city's expanding middle class that the adoption of an imported way of life became one of its chief characteristics, indeed one of the main sources of its cohesion. Forged through schooling and shared experience in government and business, this Westernized middle class was among the most powerful agents of modernization—understood as a social phenomenon, and not merely as a fashion—not only in Beirut but in Lebanon as a whole. Its top tier, populated by members of the liberal professions and senior business executives, cultivated links with the patrician upper class of commerce and banking, which was prepared to share its wealth with a select group of outsiders who could be trusted to protect and increase it though marriage. But at the same time, the members of this upper middle class were in close contact with less affluent segments of society, even the working class, not only in the course of their professional lives but also in their capacity as neighbors and parents.

Gradually the mimetic urge began to yield to a desire to think for oneself. Support for female emancipation, in particular, slowly gained ground despite the powerful constraints exerted by social convention over morals and marriage. In 1921, the first year drivers' licenses were issued, a woman was among those authorized to operate a motor vehicle. Together with the relaxation of dress codes and, among

FIGURE 75. A Miss Lebanon contest in the 1930s.

Muslim women, the revolt against the veil, this new freedom made it easier to move about the city. The most decisive impetus may have been the opening of universities to young women—a step that was as important in its day as the admission of girls to secondary school had been in the nineteenth century. In 1924 a new American institution, the Beirut College for Women (later to become coeducational under the name Beirut University College in the 1970s, and then the Lebanese American University in the 1990s), accepted its first class. The American University of Beirut was not slow to follow, welcoming female students to its various departments in 1927 (in addition to the nursing school, where women had been trained since 1905). Université Saint-Joseph, which had created a school for the education of midwives and nurses in 1924, now opened its other faculties to young women as well. In 1931, the first law degrees were awarded to Blanche Ammoun, daughter of a Maronite notable who had been a member of the Mountain's delegation to the conference at Versailles, and Nina Trad, descended from a patrician Orthodox family and future wife of the journalist Charles Hélou, who was to be appointed the first ambassador of independent Lebanon to the Vatican and then, in 1964, elected president of the Republic. Shortly afterward, Dr. Hélène Safi, a graduate of the Faculté Française de Médecine, became the first woman to practice medicine in Beirut.

While access to university departments other than nursing was restricted for the most part to the daughters of the most affluent families, the entry of women into the workforce, though limited to begin with, was more broadly based and did still more to transform urban life. This was not a wholly new phenomenon, of course.

In addition to the many rural tasks that had formed a part of female labor since time immemorial, women had been employed since the middle of the nineteenth century in the silk factories that had been established throughout the Mountain. Suspicions of lax moral conduct were confirmed in many minds when the "charming" women who worked in the spinning mills, reduced to unemployment first by the silk crisis of the early 1860s, and then by the Great War, were forced against their will to convert them into houses of prostitution (with the result that the Turkish word for a silkworm breeding house, *karkhaneh,* now came to signify a brothel, and the Arabic *sharmuta,* or "whore," was substituted for the French *charmante).*[37] With the economic revival of the 1920s the few industrial plants that still operated in the countryside, weaving shops and tobacco factories for the most part, once again took on female workers. But this labor remained largely invisible, at least in the city, and it was above all the hiring of women from the middle class that enlarged the possibilities for social change. Until such time as the legal and medical fields could train young women in large numbers, it fell to the lower middle class to make female labor respectable—in the first place, through teaching. In addition to the many private schools for girls in which instruction was mainly given by women, by the early 1930s there were a dozen female teachers in the public schools, which were likewise segregated by sex. Government also helped to promote the feminization of the workforce in its formative stages. The first female secretaries employed in the various departments of the mandate administration were French, but they were soon to be joined by native stenographers and typists—thirty-five in all by the end of the Mandate. The ABC department stores, opened in 1934, created a new niche by increasing the demand for saleswomen. Along with teaching, nursing, and midwifery, the trade of shop assistant was long to be a common occupation among women of the Christian lower middle class (and indeed of the upper middle class in a few posh establishments), and contributed to a greater mixing of the sexes in the central business district.

Western cultural values, introduced by the city's social elite and now generalized by the middle class, had the effect of making Beirut look more like modern bourgeois cities elsewhere. The resemblance was most plainly apparent in the expansion of the urban footprint, but it could also be seen in the changing routines of daily life. Office work and scheduled hours of operation for businesses gave the life of the Balad—and so the life of the whole city—its characteristic rhythm. Spare time was no longer the exclusive property of persons of independent means. In addition to Saturday afternoons and Sundays, there were lunch breaks on work days (lasting two hours, sometimes three). And when the warm weather came, shorter summer schedules freed most afternoons for trips to the mountains or the beach. But it was above all the conquest of the night, owing to progress in bringing electricity to large parts of the city, that most dramatically changed the perception of social time: now that going out in the evening was no longer regarded as an adventure, except for unaccompanied women, the hours after sunset came to form the favored setting for leisure activities.

At night the theaters and cinemas sustained the liveliness of the commercial downtown, which their new neon signs helped to illuminate. Classical music concerts enriched the variety of entertainments. Chamber music could be heard in one or two hotels, and a symphonic orchestra (and chorus) was founded in 1937, under the baton of Alexis Boutros, an amateur whose success in this endeavor led him to create the Lebanese Academy of Fine Arts.[38] Whereas Western music and French theater required a level of education that unavoidably limited the size of the audience, a much broader public was attracted to performances of Arab popular song, one-man comedy shows (to the detriment of the local storytelling tradition of the hakawati), and of course the movies, the leading form of entertainment for Beiruti, regardless of social class.[39]

But there was no longer any need for shows or concerts in order to have a reason for going out. Nightlife was now its own justification and excuse. More than any other city in the region, Beirut offered entertainment venues for which the night was, if not their very reason for being, then at least the time when they did the most business. The old-fashioned tavern, in becoming a Western-style bar, had gained in respectability, and the cabaret, having rapidly been democratized, saw its clientele expand beyond sophisticated veterans of gai Paris and the carefree French officers described by Pierre Benoît. Even the red-light district just off Place des Martyrs—perhaps the one place where mixing across both class and religious lines occurred—no longer had to conceal itself. Its houses, organized in the European fashion and strictly supervised by the health authorities, were the theater of an undisguised sociability, albeit one reserved for men, and an unofficial headquarters for some of the city's most prominent political figures.

The new value placed on leisure time could also be perceived during the day in the growth of outdoor activities and the adoption, with only a very slight delay, of the vogue for sport that came from across the Mediterranean. In addition to horse racing, which had long been popular, and the recent interest in swimming, disciplines that in their competitive form had only recently appeared in Europe, in the first years of the century or even after the Great War, quickly found enthusiasts in Beirut, notably rugby, skiing, cycling, and soccer.[40] As everywhere else in the world, soccer quickly established itself as the leading sport; from the first it was a popular pastime, like cycling, one that was not only watched but actually played by large numbers of boys and young men from the working classes.

THE ASCENDANCY OF FRENCH

If the modernization of daily life had gotten under way before the Mandate, its pace was now quickened in a city that was permeated by French influence. In this sense

Westernization in Beirut was primarily a form of gallicization, beginning with the language itself. The use of French, already frequent during the late Ottoman period, was further encouraged by the mutually reinforcing effects of the mandate administration and the educational system. In the halls of government French enjoyed the status of a second official language, after Arabic, and even rough fluency in it greatly facilitated dealings with the mandatory authorities. Before the courts, which were composed of French and native magistrates, cases were tried in the language of Montesquieu.[41] The very structure of administration and the judiciary was based on French models, and French norms gradually prevailed in every domain, from the introduction of the metric system[42] to the tax on motor vehicles.

Education was the engine of this gallicization. Schools followed the curriculum then in use in France, including the habitual reference to "our ancestors the Gauls" (though not the anticlericalism of the Third Republic), and when the Lebanese *baccalauréat* was instituted in 1931 it was modeled on the French examination, at the time administered in two parts. In the schools of the Catholic congregations, the primacy of French had a constraining effect: outside a few courses in Arabic language and literature, the poor stepchildren of the parochial program, pupils were forbidden to speak their mother tongue, even during recreation periods, on pain of being issued a *signal*—a warning that carried the force of a reprimand (curiously, this penalty was also applied in the schools run by French orders in Palestine under the British Mandate). But other institutions had to acknowledge the predominant position of French in local life as well. Even AUB's International College felt obliged to create a "French section," which is to say a department in which the language of instruction was French. This pragmatic attitude, devoid of the ideological element that suffused the teaching of the Christian religious schools, met with the approval of well-to-do Muslim families, who were also attracted, for similar reasons, by the separate *lycées* for boys and girls run by the Mission Laïque Française.

The vigor of French as a living language made itself felt outside schools and government ministries. Despite the bilingualism of Beirut's street signs, commercial signs were typically designed in Roman characters and the company names they advertised had a Gallic ring to them. Popular entertainment and culture had a largely French inflection as well. Visiting theater companies and music-hall stars met with a warm welcome from people of all walks of life, not merely the city's social elite; and French films, despite the formidable competition they faced from both Hollywood and Cairo during the 1930s, likewise succeeded in attracting a sizable audience. What is more, everything that appeared on local screens was subtitled in French, even Egyptian productions, and Pathé and Gaumont newsreels were shown before the main attraction *en version originale*—a habit that was long to persist (the regular "Current Events in Lebanon" feature that took their place after independence continued to be narrated in French and accompanied by Arabic subtitles).

FIGURE 76. *L'Orient,*
the newspaper founded
by Georges Naccache,
Francophone and
Francophile.

In the case of the written word, of course, owing to the solid tradition already established by the Arab press in Beirut, there was no comparable linguistic hegemony. Local French-language newspapers—*La Syrie,* published by Georges Samné, together with *L'Orient,* under the ownership of Gabriel Khabbaz and Georges Naccache, and later *Le Jour,* founded by Michel Chiha—nonetheless actively contributed to public debate, and readership of Paris papers and periodicals, which now arrived punctually, extended beyond the small circle of male French expatriates (by 1939, for example, the women's magazine *Marie-Claire* was sold in Beirut). Demand for French newspapers and books was to make wealthy men of the Naufal brothers, whose bookshop La Librairie Antoine (named after the family's eldest son) became a landmark in the city. Young writers were encouraged in their ambitions as a result, and a number of Lebanese authors succeeded in being published in French, among them the poets Charles Corm, Hector Klat, and Fouad Abi-Zeid; a few were published in Paris itself, such as Jacques Tabet and Évelyne Bustros, who tried her hand at fiction with the novel *La main d'Allah* (the first edition of which appeared with Éditions Bossard in Paris, in 1926, with a preface by Jérôme and Jean Tharaud), and above all Georges Schéhadé, whose *Poésies,* published by Guy Lévis Mano's house in 1938, was to arouse the enthusiasm of Saint-John Perse and the envious admiration of Paul Éluard.

The rising tide of *francophonie* did not mean that French had displaced Arabic as the medium of everyday communication for most people—far from it. A knowledge of French amounted instead to a line of demarcation that was at once social and denominational; indeed, to a large extent this continues to be the case today. But even if few people outside the upper classes spoke it fluently, the French language enjoyed a dominant position in the life of the city, nowhere better attested than by the influence that it exerted on the local vernacular. Not only did written Arabic, following a tendency that had been manifest since the time of the great translations made during the Nahda, continue to incorporate French words and turns of phrase, soon so completely assimilated that their foreign origin was forgotten (to choose but one example from among thousands, the expression *dhar al-ramad fi-l-ʿuyun*—meaning to blind someone to the facts, or to impress someone—was borrowed from *jeter de la poudre aux yeux*—literally, to throw dust in the eyes); still more important for purposes of daily communication, the spoken tongue adopted a growing number of French words and phrases, typically altered, as Italian loan words before them had been, though in some cases they retained their original form.

Formulas of greeting and thanks, in addition to a variety of courtesy locutions, were modified in characteristic ways. "Bonjour" and "bonsoir," taken over directly from the French, gave rise to a pair of original responses, *bonjourayn* (two good days [to you]) and *bonsoirayn* (two good evenings); "merci beaucoup" became *merci ktir* (thank you very much); "Monsieur" and "Madame" underwent slight deformations—the latter yielding *al-Madam* (Madam), *Madamti* (my wife), and *Madamtak* (your wife)—as did "Mademoiselle," generally rendered as *Mamouazelle* or *Demoiselle;* "Chérie," employed among women and preceded by the interjection *ya* (oh!) to form *Ya Chiri* (My dear); and "Pardon," sometimes transformed into *Pardon minnak* (I beg your pardon). Such neologisms were inevitably numerous in domains where importation or imitation (or both) were common. In the world of business one signed "contrats" (contracts) and purchased "assurance" (insurance), a term that cohabited with the Italian *suggortà* before replacing it; "banque" (bank) and "chèque" (check) retained their original meanings while bringing forth the plural forms *bnukeh* and *chèquāt.* In the clothing trade one found a great many familiar words, including "boutique" (shop), "vitrine" (display window), "[magasin de] nouveautés" (a store featuring new fashions), "chic" (fashionable), "luxe" (luxury), "tailleur" (tailor), "cravate" (necktie), "papillon" (bowtie), "jacquette" (used instead of the more usual "veste" to refer to a man's jacket), "culotte" (panties), "soutien[-gorge]" (bra), "maillot [de bain]" (bathing suit); and, in the related field of personal grooming, "coiffeur" (hairdresser), "haute coiffure" (stylish hairdressing), "mise en plis" (wash and set), "maquillage" (makeup). In the sphere of entertainment there was "cinéma," with its indispensable "projecteur" (projector), and "piscine" (swimming pool); and in the world of edible delights, "gâteau" (cake), "bonbon" (candy), "chalumeau" (a straw), and "plat du jour" (daily special), which was part of a "menu" prepared by the "chef" and served by a "garçon."

Nor was domestic life immune to this phenomenon. Living rooms were furnished with a "fauteuil" (armchair) and a "canapé" (sofa), which became *canabayeh* in Arabic. Seated in this fashion one could read the *jirnel* (from the French word for newspaper, "journal"), with its "manchettes" (headlines), "portraits" (pictures), and "profils" (sketches of people in the news). But it was perhaps in the mechanical domain that borrowings from the French were most striking: French "tramway" and "autocar" remained almost unaltered *(trènn* and *autobis),* accompanied by their teams of "chauffeurs" (drivers) and "méchaniciens" (mechanics). The same was true of the "automobile" and "camion" (truck), which one might say were driven in French since one had to press down on the "débrayage" (clutch pedal) in order to shift the "vitesse" (gear) and go from "première" (first) into "deuxième" (second), "troisième" (third), and "quatrième" (fourth) or to put the engine in *bamor* ("point mort," or neutral, which gave rise to the verb *bawmara).* If one had difficulty keeping one's car on the road ("tenir la direction," or *dirkission)* there was a risk of smashing up the "carrosserie" (body) in an "accident" and having a brush with the "police" or, worse, of finding oneself in an "ambulance." If need be, one went to a "garage" to repair the "moteur" (engine), "châssis," "amortisseurs" (shock absorbers), "suspension," "pot déchappement" (*ichakman,* or muffler), "joint de culasse" (cylinder head gasket), or "frein" (*freim,* brake). Fortunately, it was still possible to take a "taxi" or, cheaper still, share a *service* with other passengers. Most of these terms are still used today, three-quarters of a century later.

Such semantic enrichments were themselves evidence of the increasing complexity of urban life in a society conquered by Western ideas and inventions. This experience was certainly not unique to Beirut; other cities in the region were undergoing similar transformations, but nowhere else in the Near East, with the exception of Cairo, did the metamorphosis draw an Arab metropolis so closely into the orbit of European culture. The growing importance of new occupations, notably in the liberal professions, and the growing number of trained men and women extended the reach of the imitative impulse, popularizing Western forms of behavior still further. Deepening a tendency already perceptible in the late nineteenth century, the middle class, at least in its Christian branch, turned away from native onomastic tradition in favor of naming children Joseph, Georges, Michel, and Marie— to say nothing of such improbable names as Joffre, Weygand, and Jeanne d'Arc, which now began to make their appearance in provincial families.

But Beirut surpassed even Cairo in the sociological impact of Westernization.

Whereas the public life of the Egyptian capital, especially in Old Cairo, remained to a large degree unchanged, in Beirut the surviving traces of the past (referred to by the adjective *baladi*) were increasingly confined to the outlying neighborhoods, deprived of municipal services, where the country suddenly intruded upon the city and the practitioners of vanishing trades—porters, fruit and vegetable hawkers pushing their wheelbarrows, vendors of heating fuel riding on horse-drawn carts— could still be seen in the streets.

13

A Crucible for Independence

The Greater Lebanon desired by France had come into existence on 1 September 1920, on the steps of a building in the neo-Moorish style that had been intended by the former Ottoman governor to serve as a casino and movie theater, on the outskirts of the city, where a French general and war hero now quietly marked the occasion in the company of a few dignitaries. Then one day in November 1943 another founding image interposed itself. The setting this time was the heart of Beirut, where France had fashioned an urban landscape in its own image. On Place de l'Étoile, itself the emblem of a new age born in the shadow of Paris, voices rang out boldly declaring a determination henceforth to live without France, if not actually against it. The change of scene also signaled a change in the nature of political participation. Instead of the handful of notables and religious leaders who had warmly applauded General Gouraud, now there was a crowd that booed his distant successor, General Jean Helleu, in front of the Parliament Building—perhaps already even a people, not without many differences, but united in optimistic expectation of what world politics had finally made possible. If only for a few days the Lebanese campaign for independence, like the interwar decolonization movements in India and Egypt, managed to imitate the European example of mass mobilization.

Lebanon, that sturdy child of the Third Republic's imperial designs, had visibly succeeded in doing more than the leaders of the colonial faction in Paris had ever imagined it could. The limited form of self-government encouraged by the Mandate—what might be called institutional Lebanonism—had reached a point of maturity; but to reach the point of fruition envisioned by the League of Nations it had to turn away from its tutelary protectors. Gallicized though the country may have been, it was not a part of France, and its exposure to European influence did not prevent it from remaining rooted in the Mashriq. The living culture that was taking shape there, and quite particularly in its capital, showed no interest in ideological quarrels over identity. Beirut had long borne plain witness to a deep-seated and resurgent sense of Arabness, well before the National Pact of 1943 attempted to settle this question by a rather awkward compromise formula that spoke of an "Arab face." Whether the Mountain wished it or not, the course of the city's historical experience led the country to search for a national consensus—a synthesis of its contradictory elements—that could not be achieved without freeing itself from a tutelage that had become unbearable.

THE SECOND RENAISSANCE

No matter how easily the residents of Beirut under the Mandate adapted to the rhythms of life in Paris, or at least the Paris of their imagination, the spread of Western values by no means amounted to a rejection or abandonment of native culture. The penetration of French, as extensive as it was, did not dispense with the need to acquire a mastery of the Arabic language. Even in Christian communities, none of the parochial schools sought to marginalize the teaching of Arabic, which had been an integral part of the missionaries' curriculum; the Maronite Collège de la Sagesse, in particular, came to take pride in the eloquence of its students in Arabic.[1] French-language newspapers, although very much a presence in public debate, were in no position to supplant the Arab press, whose vitality had only been strengthened by the return of journalists forced to leave Beirut for Paris and Cairo during the Hamidian period, and then later under the Young Turks.

In 1921 the interest surrounding the Exposition sponsored by the mandatory authority that year suggested to Michel Zakkur, later a deputy and a minister, the name for a new biweekly paper, *Al-Maʿrad*. In 1924 Gebran Tuwayni, now back from Egypt, launched the daily *Al-Ahrar* (The Free Men), supplemented two years later by an illustrated magazine, *Al-Ahrar al-Mussawwara*; in 1933, following an interval of government service in the office of the Minister of Public Instruction, he founded another daily, *An-Nahar* (The Day), which was to become the paper of record of independent Lebanon. In the meantime new titles—daily and weekly alike—had begun to appear on an almost annual basis: *Al-ʿAhd al-jadid* (The New Times), founded in 1925 by Khayreddin al-Ahdab, a future prime minister; *Al-Sharq* (The Orient), by ʿAbdul-Ghani al-Kaʾki in 1926; *Al-Dustur* (The Constitution), by Khalil Abu-Jawdeh in 1927; *Al-Bayraq* (The Flag), founded before the Great War by Said ʿAkl, one of the martyrs of 1916, and resurrected by his family in 1928; *Al-Nidaʾ* (The Call), by Qadhim al-Sulh in 1930, who sought to promote the nationalist views of his cousin Riad al-Sulh; *Al-Liwaʾ* (The Standard), by Ali Nassereddin, also in 1930; the illustrated magazine *Al-Makshuf* (Exposed), by the writer Fuad Hubaysh in 1935; *Bayrut*, by Muhieddin Nsuli in 1936; *Sawt al-Shaʿb* (The Voice

FIGURE 77. The first issue
of *An-Nahar* in 1933.

of the People), the official organ of the underground Syro-Lebanese Communist Party, founded by Niqula Shawi in 1937; and *Al-'Amal* (Action), the mouthpiece of the Kata'eb faction, in 1939.

The robustness of the Arabic press, often critical of the High Commission and vulnerable on this account to censorship, was to be strikingly demonstrated during the fight for independence, in November 1943, when journalists succeeded in thwarting the ban on publication imposed by the Free France delegate to Lebanon by anonymously producing an impressive series of issues under the banner "?" or "??"[2] But beyond their political content, the roster of Beirut newspapers during this period attested also to the scope of the revival *(al-Tajdid)* of Arab culture, which represented, in effect, a second epoch of the Nahda. At the peak of the renaissance in the mid-nineteenth century, Beirut had been, with Cairo, the principal center of a movement whose influence was particularly perceptible in the domain of the written word. Poets and prose writers joined with journalists in exploring new ways of

enriching Arabic. By the early twentieth century the focus of this effort had shifted
to the Americas, and specifically to New England, where several gifted young writers from Lebanon had emigrated. The best known of these were Amin Rihani, the
first Arab author to publish in English while continuing to write in his native tongue,
and Gibran Khalil Gibran, who likewise worked in both English and Arabic and
took an active role in the New York Pen League *(al-Rabita al-Qalamiyya),* formed
in 1921, where he met his alter ego, the essayist and novelist Mikhail Nuʿaymeh,
and the poet Ilya Abu Madi. Following Gibran's death, in the 1930s, both Nuʿaymeh
and Abu Madi came back to settle in Lebanon. Other expatriate writers, such as the
Maalouf brothers in Brazil, returned to their native land as well.

Of all these authors it was Amin Rihani who most fully embodied the link between the Levantine diaspora and the revival of Arab literature. Before the First
World War he had already lived for long periods of time in America. With the coming of peace he traveled extensively in the lands of the Arab world, beginning with

the Arabian Peninsula, where his avowed agnosticism did not prevent him from forming a friendship with the future king Ibn Saʻud. Having one foot in his native village of Freikeh and the other in the United States, Rihani knew Europe well and alternated globetrotting with a hermitlike existence. By the time of his death in 1940 his fame in the Arab East was immense. Perhaps no one did more to put the new Lebanon into contact not only with its own cultural environment, but also with the wider world. Once repatriated, the "literature of emigration" *(Adab al-mahjar)* resonated powerfully in Beirut, and between the wars reawakened a community of writers who had stayed in the country.

Together with Rihani's accounts of his travels and the realistic vein of the novelist Marun Abbud, the will to renewal revealed itself in poetry. Whereas the neoclassicism of Bishara al-Khuri (no relation to the politician) earned him the nickname Akhtal the Younger—a reference to the great Christian poet of the Umayyad era—and later the epithet "prince of poets," Ilyas Abu Shabakeh cultivated a Baudelairean tone, and the prolific young Said ʻAkl (no relation to the journalist), standing midway between Parnassus and Paul Valéry, reinvigorated Arab prosody. With the stimulus of these innovations, reinforced by the work of an earlier generation of expatriates, Beirut by the 1930s was well on its way to regaining the stature as an Arab cultural metropolis that Bustani and the Yazijis had given it earlier.

This second renaissance may even in a certain way have had greater impact than the first since it was not restricted to writing. Although literature retained its primacy, the scope for artistic expression was now enlarged by the passion for easel painting. Portraiture had already enjoyed a certain popularity in the nineteenth century through the work of Daoud Corm, while the use of reproductions of well-known works of European art as elements of interior design broadened the taste for painted scenes and inspired successive generations of artists whose careers were to flourish in the first two decades of the twentieth century and, to a still greater degree, between the wars. Until the emergence of Habib Srur and Khalil Slaybi, both trained in Paris, painting was almost exclusively an amateur occupation in Beirut. By the 1920s it was recognized as both an art and a profession and attracted a growing number of young talents, Christian and Muslim alike (the Islamic prohibition against figurative representation having lost its force in the interval). It was even possible now to speak of something like a true artistic movement, centered on a dozen or so painters who included Yusuf Hoyek, César Gemayel, Omar Onsi, Mustafa Farrukh, and, a little later, Saliba Duayhi. Still more than in literature, contemporary European styles made their influence felt only with a considerable delay. Although many local artists had spent time in the studios of Paris and Rome, where surrealism was exploding what remained of traditional modes of representation, the realism of the old portrait tradition gave way at first to a belated and very timid impressionism in the treatment of landscapes and still lifes. But then things quickly changed. Duayhi abandoned his classical orientation of the 1930s and went on to make a career as an abstractionist in New York, while Shafiq Abbud, having left for France in the mid-1940s, remained there and become a member of the School of Paris. In Beirut itself the plastic arts now occupied a place in the cultural and social life of the city. It was even possible to find female models who were willing to pose in the nude.

ARABNESS AND LEBANONISM

The effects of this new renaissance were amplified by the progress of technology. Improved transportation made Beirut a frequent stopping point for Syrian and Iraqi painters and Egyptian writers, many of whom contributed to the revival. One thinks, for example, of the poet Ahmad Shawqi, who became a frequent visitor to Lebanon and wrote a famous poem about Zahleh, in the Biqaʿ Valley. And even if authors did not travel, their works did. Egyptian companies often came to Beirut to perform plays directly in Arabic or in translation, such as Edmond Rostand's *L'Aiglon,* staged at the Empire Theater in 1928 with Fatima Rushdi (the "Sarah Bernhardt of the East") in the lead role.[3] But it was also thanks to radio that Beirut fell into step with the world around it. Even though the spread of wireless receivers in the Near East between the wars was concentrated mainly in Egypt and Palestine, programs originating in these places drew a daily audience among Arabic speakers throughout the region. Listeners in Beirut were able to keep up with the work of dramatists and songwriters in Cairo by tuning in to radio broadcasts of plays and, in even larger numbers, of performances by well-known singers. The new style of Arab song, at once a popular and an aristocratic art form owing to the convergence of modern technology and the creativity of Egyptian poets, enjoyed such success, here as in other parts of the Mashriq (as well as the Maghrib), that it worked to counteract the urge to imitate Western models. The same was true for Egyptian cinema, which attracted a massive following throughout the Near East in the late 1920s with the success of Misr Studios, and which all the more rapidly became part of the urban landscape of Beirut as the city was well stocked with movie theaters. The tone of newspaper advertising for the latest "big event," which is to say the premiere of a new film, suggests that even if Beirut was often listening to Paris, above all it had its eyes on Cairo.

But cultural influence did not circulate in only one direction. The emotion aroused in the Arab world by the death of Amin Rihani was merely the most striking indication that ideas and works of art from Beirut now reached across the new political boundaries and shaped elite opinion throughout the Near East. Owing to expanded distribution networks and the broader readership they made possible, Beirut newspapers and publishing houses gained in prestige, attracting new authors as a result. If Egyptian writers naturally tended to remain faithful to publishers in

Cairo, Syrian writers almost instinctively turned to houses in Beirut. It was there that the poet ʿUmar Abu Risha came to be published, along with the historian and political thinker Qustantin Zurayq, perhaps the most prominent advocate of secular Arab nationalism and a graduate of the American University of Beirut, where he taught after completing graduate studies in the United States. And it was in Beirut, in 1946, that another Damascene, Nizar Qabbani, brought out his first collection of poems, launching a fabulous career over the course of which his works sold millions of copies.

Beirut's place in an Arab culture that transcended political borders was still further consolidated by the institutional Lebanonism created as an immediate consequence of French rule. The paradox is only apparent. If the Mandate's great influence gave the French language its hegemonic position and the cult of Paris its normative force, so too did the construction of political institutions in an Arabophone country encourage the flowering of its native culture. It is true that the westward-looking ideology urged by the *Revue phénicienne* just after the war had a lasting influence that was to complicate the formation of a Lebanese national identity. But Phoenicianism assumed no concrete political form of its own, any more than the distinctive character claimed by the Mountain could be made to constitute a separate culture.

Indeed the question of the official language of the new state did not arise. Arabic imposed itself spontaneously, and the Constitution of 1926 only ratified a state of affairs that no one imagined challenging, unless by giving French, for the sake of the Mandate's dignity, a similar status. And although the text of the Constitution, prepared under the aegis of the High Commission, had been composed in French, the formal document was officially promulgated in two versions. When the time came to provide the country with a national hymn, after the adoption of the Constitution, it was in Arabic that the competition for choosing the lyrics was organized; in the end the words of the poet Rashid Nakhleh were selected, set to music by Wadih Sabra.[4] The Chamber of Deputies and of the Council of Ministers deliberated in Arabic, which was likewise the language of governmental decrees, even if the expansive powers of the High Commission and its joint tribunals continued to cast a French shadow over legislative activity. Arabic was also the language of republican ceremony, whether in dedicating a new public building, unveiling Yusuf Hoyek's monument to the Martyrs in 1930,[5] or paying posthumous tribute to Gibran Khalil Gibran the following year—great moments in the life of the new Lebanon. Recognized as a national treasure, notwithstanding his anticlericalism and intemperate outbursts against what he saw as the mercenary mentality of his homeland, Gibran was honored by a solemn funeral over the course of two days. Before being laid to rest in his native village of Bisharreh, in the north, his remains, brought back home from the United States and then conducted by official procession from the port of Beirut, lay in state at the Maronite Cathedral. Next door, at the Grand Théâtre, and for once unaccompanied by its French masters, the Republic commemorated a man who had been above all other things a master of the Arabic language—and only secondarily of English.[6]

AN ARENA OF COEXISTENCE

The construction of an indigenous political society was not limited to celebrations. In spite of the High Commission's insistence on retaining real power at all levels, even suspending the Constitution when it thought it wise to do so, a native elite gradually established itself, sometimes with the consent of the mandate authority, other times against its will. Some of those who believed that they had found a benevolent protector in the French government came to abandon this opinion rather quickly, and it was in opposition to the Mandate that ultimately a majority of Lebanese were to find common ground. In this course of events Beirut played a major role, not only because as the capital of Greater Lebanon—and of the Mandate—the city was the principal theater of political contest, but still more because as a crucible of self-rule, however qualified, it demonstrated the capacity of citizens from different communities to get along with one another.

After the end of Ottoman rule, a small Maronite minority had argued on behalf of a "Small Lebanon" limited almost entirely to the Mountain, whose homogeneous sectarian character would in this way be protected against dilution within a larger population—a plea that was to be reasserted in a different form at the beginning of the civil war in 1975. Another minority, seconded by a majority of Muslims, wished to see their land reattached to Faysal's Syria, but the peace conference and the occupation of the country by French troops following the Battle of Maysalun quickly eliminated this option, though not without coercion (members in every community—among them the Maronite patriarch's own brother—were forced into exile for several years as a result of their support for union with Damascus). In the end the preference of the majority of Maronite notables, led by the church, for a Greater Lebanon under French protection prevailed. Fatefully, the decisions taken by the mandate authority after the fall of Damascus were to determine the future character of Lebanese political society by allowing officials who had begun their careers before the Great War in the formerly autonomous province of Mount Lebanon to establish themselves at its head.

Several of these figures came together at the beginning of the Mandate to form an ephemeral Progress Party (Hizb al-Taraqqi) whose aim was both to legitimize French rule and to strengthen its pro-Christian bias. Armed with the slogan "For Lebanon with France," the party adopted a three-point program: protection of the political independence of Greater Lebanon under French Mandate; defense of "national traditions" and religious liberties; and establishment of a system of electoral representation, according to principles yet to be decided, but based solely on crite-ria of "competence" and "merit"—a thinly veiled attempt to marginalize the Mus-lim population. Exclusively Christian in its membership, the party was led by the papal marquis Jean de Freige; its executive committee included three future presi-dents of the Republic, Émile Eddé, Alfred Naccache, and Bishara al-Khuri.[7] From this common womb, however, two antagonistic groups soon emerged: the National Bloc (not to be confused with the group of the same name in Syria) and the Con-stitutional Bloc. The first was headed by Eddé, whose steadfast allegiance to France was combined with a scarcely concealed mistrust of Muslims, a certain number of whom he urged be relocated to other Arab countries in order to preserve a Chris-tian majority under mandatory administration. The Constitutional Bloc, by con-trast, under the direction of Khuri and his brother-in-law, the banker and author Michel Chiha,[8] positioned itself first as the standard-bearer of those demanding au-tonomy, then as the voice of the opposition, and finally, having joined forces with Muslim nationalists, as the chief proponent of an independent Lebanon.

Whereas the political maneuvering of the Christian notables profited, at least at the beginning, from the benevolent regard of the High Commission, the situation was entirely otherwise for the Muslims, most of whom were hostile to the division of Syria and to the imposition of French rule. They long persisted in their rejection of the new state of Greater Lebanon, and of the institutions with which it was equipped—to the point that many Muslims refused even to be counted in the cen-sus (foremost among them Salim Salam, who later had to go to court in order to obtain Lebanese citizenship for himself and his family). And because of their op-position to the Mandate they were harassed by its administrators, who did not hes-itate to banish enemies. Nonetheless neither the threat of exile, nor of prison, nor of financial ruin succeeded in weakening resistance to French rule, which was syn-onymous with the partition of Syrian territory.[9] The Muslim opposition even suc-ceeded in organizing itself by holding two meetings of the Conference of the Coast and the Four Districts, in November 1933 and March 1936, before the acceptance of a Lebanese state by the Syrian National Bloc, formalized by the Franco-Syrian treaty of November 1936, opened the way to a normalization of its activity.

Muslim antagonism to the Mandate, insofar as it issued from a rejection of the policy of territorial division, cannot be reduced to ideology. It was also fed by dis-satisfaction with the policy that France applied within the new Lebanese borders, which they perceived as fundamentally unbalanced in favor of the Christian pop-ulation. In the terminology of the period, the "people of the Coast" (ahl al-Sahil) were doubly disadvantaged in relation to the "people of the Mountain" (ahl al-Jabal)—a name that in this case was applied both to the Christians who lived in the mountains and to those who were originally from Mount Lebanon and had settled in Beirut. As speakers at the first session of the Conference of the Coast made a point of emphasizing, the dismemberment of Syrian lands had led to an increase in the costs of public administration. Moreover, fiscal outlays were unequally distributed: whereas tax payments by the ahl al-Sahil accounted for more than two-thirds of the Treasury's receipts, a similar fraction of expenditures, in salaries, road construction, contributions to municipal budgets, school and hospital subventions, and tourist promotion, went to Mount Lebanon.[10] Such figures, bandied about for polemical purposes, were surely inaccurate; in particular, the Coast's share of taxation could not have been so high unless the entire remittance of Beirut, from both Christian and Muslim residents, were included. Similarly, the denunciation of exorbitant expenditures on Mount Lebanon underestimated or overlooked the investment in infrastructure undertaken in Beirut, from which once again all of the city's inhabitants benefited, Muslim and Christian, established families and recent immigrants alike. Even allowing for some measure of exaggeration, however, the perception of a lack of evenhandedness was not mistaken. It was aggravated, moreover, by the fact that the principal administrative posts were awarded to Christians. This, the Conference of the Coast rightly pointed out, was contrary to the Constitution, which provided for a proportional distribution of public offices among the various communities.

But in spite of the long-standing refusal of Lebanese Muslims to support the institutions of the Republic, political relations with Christian leaders were not nonexistent. Already, prior to the Franco-Syrian turning point of 1936, bonds between them had been established, or in some cases reestablished, and the reality of everyday life in Beirut as a multidenominational city recommended cooperation for pragmatic reasons, until the unwritten agreement of 1943 gave it a firm basis. As a practical matter, the city's position as an economic and a cultural center, in conjunction with its status as a political capital, meant that the people of the Coast were in permanent contact with the people of the Mountain. This functional multiplicity favored both the Beirutization of Lebanon and the Lebanonization of Beirut—two intertwined processes that were to give the National Pact its social credibility.[11]

By strengthening Beirut's role as a commercial hub and giving tangible effect to the commitment to modernization, the Mandate's economic policies succeeded, if not in winning the approval of the entire population, at least in creating support, declared or not, among a growing multidenominational middle class for the new Lebanese state. But dissatisfaction with other aspects of these policies and with the unwillingness of the mandate authorities to tolerate dissent also marked out an area of common interest among the city's various communities. Christians and Muslims joined together, for example, in opposing the tobacco monopoly, the currency controls imposed after successive devaluations of the franc, and increases in taxes and import tariffs, as well as in denouncing the High Commission's obvious bias in favor of French companies.[12] This was not solely a question of class solidarity among merchants and entrepreneurs. Even among less prosperous segments of the population, opposition to the Mandate's management of the economy transcended communal boundaries, as the streetcar boycott showed in 1931 (inspiring students to demand a reduction of movie ticket prices as well).[13] The abusive behavior of the Franco-Belgian electricity company, now a recurrent grievance, gave rise to a new strike in 1935. All these things signaled a determination to take back control over the public sphere, which, in a heterogeneous city such as Beirut, unavoidably crossed confessional lines.

To some extent this resort to street protest anticipated the Muslim-Christian convergence that was to bring together demonstrators from all communities during the battle for independence. But the reappropriation of the public sphere sometimes went beyond simple agreement among faiths, in response to new forms of political expression that ignored familiar denominational allegiances. Although politics continued to be controlled by a local elite, in part as a consequence of the system imposed by the Mandate, the widespread adoption of modern European values began to weaken traditional divisions. In the most educated circles of society this political modernity assumed the form of a consensus that was independent of any conjunction of confessional interests, whether it involved welcoming Margery Corbett Ashby, president of the International Alliance of Women, for a conference at the Grand-Théâtre in 1935,[14] mobilizing the intelligentsia against Italian intervention in Abyssinia (Ethiopia), or forming a Lebanese Committee for the Support of the Wounded in Armed Palestine.[15] More than anything, however, new forms of political action arose from the emergence of three working-class parties organized along European lines: the Communist Party, the Syrian Social Nationalist Party, and the Lebanese Phalange Party.

POLITICS IN TRANSITION

Socialist thinking had made its first appearance in the Arab world at the beginning of the twentieth century through the efforts of a handful of writers and intellectuals. But it was not until after the October Revolution of 1917, in Russia, that this essentially anticlerical tendency gave voice to a still largely mute working class. Communism attracted a few followers in Egypt in 1919, and Jewish immigrants from Russia propagated Bolshevist ideas in Palestine shortly afterward. In Mount Lebanon, in the summer of 1924, the creation of a tobacco workers union in Bikfaya marked the beginning of a revolutionary syndicalist movement led by Fuad Shimali, a militant worker who had discovered Marxism in Egypt. In October of the same year a People's Party was founded in Antelias, a small coastal town just north of Beirut, not far from Bikfaya, by Shimali and the writer Yusuf Ibrahim Yazbik. A few months later, in the spring of 1925, the celebration of May Day provided the occasion for publicly announcing the existence of this nascent Communist movement at a rally held in the Cristal Cinema in downtown Beirut.[16] Strengthened by the addition of the Spartacus Youth, an Armenian group formed by Artin Madoyan that had broken away from the Hentchag Party, the People's Party renamed itself the Communist Party of Syria and Lebanon (CPSL). Under the direction of a central committee that included Shimali, Yazbik, and Madoyan, as well as Ilyahu Teper, a Jewish revolutionary socialist who had come to Lebanon from Odessa via Palestine, the CPSL was quickly spotted by Moscow. In keeping with the Comintern's usual practice in the colonial world, oversight was delegated to the French Communist Party (PCF), which beginning in the 1930s established privileged relations with the Communists of Lebanon and Syria that were to last until the 1980s. During this time the CPSL broadened its base, at the price of a change of leadership that ousted Shimali and marginalized Yazbik, with three leaders being installed alongside Madoyan who were to guide the destinies of Arab Communism for several decades: Khalid Bekdash, a Syrian of Kurdish origin who became known for his uncompromising enforcement of Muscovite orthodoxy; Niqula Shawi, a subtle tactician who proved capable, when the time came, of accepting the need for change; and Farjallah Hélou, an early advocate of modifying Communist doctrine to admit the possibility that the course of development varies from one nation to another, whose tragic death under torture in 1959 (in the jails of the United Arab Republic in Damascus) was to give him an almost Christlike aura.

Notwithstanding the hostility it encountered from the High Commission, even during the Popular Front government of Léon Blum in France, and despite the fact that it was forced to operate underground, the CPSL managed to combine an active presence in the country's intellectual and cultural life with a growing influence in the workplace. It vigorously denounced clericalism and sectarianism while taking up the campaign against fascism, once the worldwide Communist movement resolved to make it a priority; and gave its support to the Spanish Republic and Abyssinia, notably through efforts of the writer Salim Khayata, even though this meant going against the current of Italian and German sympathies, then very widely shared. In this way, more than any other political movement, it helped to nourish the growth of a democratic culture in Lebanon, however unyielding it may have been in asserting its own authority. In the workplace, too, the Communist Party was a powerful agent for democratization and modernization. Through its control of the printers' union it worked to spread the values of progress and equality beyond communal boundaries. At the same time the CPSL was itself the product of a Christian environment, and its recruitment reflected this fact, though to a greater degree in Lebanon than in Syria. Its preaching met with a sympathetic response in the populous Greek Orthodox neighborhoods of Beirut, whose inhabitants were prone to confuse the Soviet Union and Holy Russia, especially after Stalingrad. Nonetheless it succeeded in establishing a foothold in other communities as well. The leader of the Communist unions, the printer Mustafa 'Aris, came from a Sunni family in Beirut, and through his own union the CPSL acquired enough of a following in the space of two or three years to be able to profit from the repercussions of the Soviet victory over Hitler's armies. With the advent of independence it began to exhibit the characteristic features of a mass party, managing even to achieve the enactment of a progressive labor code, in 1946,[17] before its alignment with Moscow during the civil war in mandatory Palestine in 1947–48 came to undermine most of its accomplishments.

The Syrian Social Nationalist Party (SSNP), though it was diametrically opposed to the Communists, was also an agent of modernization, albeit in an authoritarian mode. Founded in Beirut in 1932 by Antun Sa'adeh, a professor of German at the American university who had spent his youth in Brazil, the SSNP called for the reunification of Syria in its "natural" form—that is, as a nation whose distinctness had been recognized since antiquity and that for this reason deserved to be reconstituted, only now within the framework of a strong state. The idea of a natural Syria was not new (it had been championed by the colonial faction in Paris before the Great War), although in 1947 it was extended by Sa'adeh to include the whole of the Fertile Crescent, conceived as reaching all the way from Cyprus to Iraq. Similarly, the idea that the Syrian nation possessed an ancient and special character—a non-Arab, indeed anti-Arab character—had its roots in the work of a Belgian Jesuit named Henri Lammens, an authority on Islam and author of a concise history depicting Syria as a land that had converted to Christianity in Roman times and was then oppressed by Islam, with the unhappy result that its Christian substrate was now embodied only in Lebanon.[18] This argument, so congenial to the mandate authorities, was to give rise to two antagonistic national myths, one of Lebanon as a historical necessity, the other of an eternal Syria. Sa'adeh's view of Syria was nonetheless distinguished from that of Lammens by its incorporation of a racialist element that drew freely from the philosophy of German nationalism. From Hitlerite Germany Sa'adeh also borrowed the symbolism and rituals of the SSNP, based on the National Socialist model: the party's emblem, a red vortex on a white ground framed in black that recreated the spiral motion of the swastika; the martial salute, arm outstretched; the cult of the leader *(Za'im)*, though "Heil Hitler" gave way to the impersonal exhortation "Tahya Surya" (Long Live Syria); and the paramilitary organization, supplemented by a glorification of violence. Above all, Sa'adeh set himself apart from Father Lammens by his denunciation of sectarian division and his radical secularism.

The SSNP's opposition to imperial partition very quickly brought upon it the wrath of the occupying power, which refused even to recognize its name, calling it instead the Syrian Popular Party (PPS in its French initials)—apparently in the hope of discrediting it by association with the French Popular Party (PPF) of Jacques Doriot. Although forced to operate underground in some places, the SSNP nonetheless managed to attract a large number of followers, more in Lebanon than in the Syrian states. It began by establishing a presence among the Greek Orthodox and Catholics, two communities that had not yet committed themselves to the idea of a Greater Lebanon, and then moved quickly to consolidate support in a few Maronite enclaves in the Mountain, while at the same time winning over Sunni and Shi'i Muslims, as well as Druze, in substantial numbers. Recruiting mainly among the urban and semi-urbanized middle class, the SSNP served as a training ground for a generation of politicians to whom the attempt to create an antidenominational counterculture made a forceful appeal. Many figures who later were to play significant roles in the political and cultural life of independent Lebanon passed through the party for longer or shorter periods of time before finally being alienated by its iron discipline. In this respect the Second World War came at an opportune moment, not only by virtue of the initial success of the German armies and the French collapse, but also because, momentarily deprived of its leader, the SSNP now found itself in the unexpected position of being able to cast its net more widely. When the war broke out Sa'adeh was traveling in Europe. Barred from making his way back to Beirut, he was obliged to spend several years in Brazil and Argentina, and on his return was unable to restrain a renegade faction prepared to make common cause with soldiers for Lebanese freedom. Along with other groups, then, the SSNP materially contributed to the achievement of independence in November 1943; indeed, the only martyr of the struggle came from its ranks.

Whereas the CPSL and SSNP deliberately sought to reach across communal boundaries, the Lebanese Phalange Party (Hizb al-Kata'ib al-Lubnaniyya) had its roots in an exclusively Christian environment populated by recently urbanized Maronites. Here modernity was less a matter of doctrine than of organization. Founded in 1936, the Phalange—like the SSNP—was carried along by the rising tide of European fascism. In this respect its name, an echo of the Spanish Falange *(kata'ib* being the Arabic translation of the Greek *phalanx),* was no less revelatory than the circumstances of its formation by an Egyptian-born pharmacist named Pierre Gemayel, inspired by the Nazis' extraordinary demonstration of force and order at the Olympic Games in Berlin that year. Gemayel himself was one of the pioneers of Lebanese sport (he worked as a soccer referee in his spare time), and at the outset the Phalangists more closely resembled a youth movement, indeed a muscular form of scouting, than a political group equipped with a coherent ideology. The wearing of khaki paramilitary uniforms and short gaiters at their annual parades nonetheless suggested a connection with fascist parties in Europe, which seems to have been partly responsible for the subsequent defection of some of the party's founders, such as Georges Naccache, the publisher of the daily *L'Orient,* and Charles Hélou, editor-in-chief of *Le Jour,* owned by Michel Chiha. Conversely, the sense of order projected by the Phalange Party held a certain appeal in the Christian neighborhoods of eastern Beirut, such as Gemmayzeh and Rmayleh, where recent immigrants from villages in the Mountain now constituted a small lower-middle class.

The absence of ideological sophistication may have been an additional element of attraction to the extent that the Phalangists' uncompromising Lebanese nationalism in no way sought to change the view of the world embraced by their supporters, only to channel it. The doctrine of the party, summarized by the slogan "God, Country, Family," guaranteed it at the very least the blessing of the church and the approval of social conservatives; and it contained nothing that was liable to alarm the mandate authorities, who initially tolerated the Phalangists' uniformed parades. But if the party's nationalism as well as the confessional background and values of its members encouraged them to look with favor upon the French presence, as the guarantor of Greater Lebanon, the same patriotic loyalty could not long suffer the interventionism of the mandatory administration. In the event the Phalange underwent a transformation similar to that of the Constitutional Bloc, despite the differences of class that separated them, and in a manner that was all the more spectacular as its consequences were visible in the street. In 1938, several Phalangist militants, including Pierre Gemayel himself, were wounded during clashes with police and Senegalese infantrymen that in retrospect can be seen to have foreshadowed the demonstrations of November 1943.

And yet neither the rapid growth of its audience in Christian neighborhoods nor its doctrinal conservatism permitted the Phalange to be absorbed by a political society that remained largely dominated by notables—a situation that would not change until the early 1960s. This marginalization was all the more pronounced in the case of the SSNP and CPSL. Notwithstanding their extreme mutual animosity, both parties represented a challenge to the social order; both were forces of subversion that could not hope soon to be allowed parliamentary representation, which was governed after independence, as it had been under the Mandate, by a law that favored both communitarianism and clientelism. Nevertheless, in breaking with traditional forms of political organization, all three parties were to have a profound and lasting influence on the evolution of ways of thinking and the modernization of the public sphere.

More than anywhere else, it was in Beirut that the political reconfiguration of a country that was a mixture of the old and the new made itself felt. Drawing upon almost a century's experience of generating novel institutions and arrangements through the synthesis of opposites, the city that had made itself a capital encouraged the existence of contraries. And nowhere was this talent more strikingly demonstrated than in the battle for independence.

THE END OF THE MANDATE

The First World War had given birth to the modern Mashriq as a collection of states; the Second was, paradoxically, to confirm its results. For although it did away with the imperial hegemony of the two dominant powers of the interwar period, it ratified the national borders they had laid out and, with the advent of decolonialization, gave these boundaries still greater weight. And although the break with the past was much less radical than the one that had put an end to four hundred years of Ottoman rule, a new era was nonetheless about to be entered into.

The first act took place between 1941 and 1946 with the eviction of France from the Levant. France, it must be said, was very poorly prepared for the upheavals brought about by the war. The failure of its treaty with Syria had aggravated the old mistrust in which it was held, and the ceding of Alexandretta to Turkey only made matters worse. The tension was so great, in fact, that the High Commission's first move after the outbreak of hostilities with Germany was to suspend the constitution in Lebanon and Syria. This strategy misfired almost at once. With the rout of June 1940 the mandate authority could no longer lay claim to the prestige of a world power. Its image, undermined by the doubts that affected even France's most faithful friends in Lebanon, was ruined once and for all during the Syrian campaign in May 1941 by the fratricidal fighting between Vichy and Free France and by the domineering attitude of Great Britain. As during the Great War, the British had the advantage of being on familiar ground. The campaign in Syria had been launched on their initiative, for the purpose of bolstering their own position in Iraq following a nationalist and pro-German coup d'état, and the political management of this offensive and its aftermath was largely their responsibility.

Shortly after the campaign began, and at the instigation of London, the French Mandate came to an end. A proclamation by General Catroux, lately the governor general of Indochina and now Free France's representative in the Levant, formally abolished it: Syrians and Lebanese were "henceforth sovereign and independent peoples" who could form "two distinct states or a single state."[19] This turned out to be an empty gesture. Although Great Britain had hastened to give its guarantee, General de Gaulle, anxious to preserve the integrity of the empire, went back on Catroux's proclamation—and on his own word. The official abolition of the Mandate was therefore adjourned. As a practical matter, however, it no longer existed. In its place was a Franco-British condominium that reflected the actual balance of power between the two allies. The British, now in control of the country's supply routes and superior in numbers—having forced the repatriation of the defeated Vichy troops, who were therefore prevented from enrolling in the ranks of the Free French—were free to take advantage of de Gaulle's procrastination in order to turn the demands for independence in their favor.[20] France had no choice but to give in. Curiously, it was obliged to yield first in Lebanon, where it continued to enjoy considerably more support than in Syria—though not so much that the Mandate's backers were in a position to carry the elections that it was obliged to hold in September 1943, under pressure from Great Britain and the United States.

At the urging of the two leaders of the new governing coalition—the Maronite Bishara al-Khuri and the Sunni Riad al-Sulh, named president of the Republic and prime minister, respectively—the new parliament amended the constitution in early November to purge it of all reference to the institutions of the Mandate.[21] The blun-

FIGURE 79. Riad al-Sulh *(left)* and Bishara al-Khuri *(right)*, fathers of the 1943 National Pact and of Lebanon's independence. Reproduced by permission of Dār an-Nahār.

dering of General Helleu, Catroux's replacement as the Free French delegate, did the rest. Instead of slowing the momentum of the independence movement, the arrest of Khuri together with Sulh and the majority of his ministers, as well as the suspension of the constitution and the dissolution of parliament, brought people into the street. Beirut suddenly found itself the scene of massive demonstrations, the most powerful of which in its symbolism was a joint procession of Muslim and Christian women. Under renewed British and American pressure, de Gaulle once more stalled for time, dispatching Catroux to try to salvage the situation. It was too late. Catroux annulled Helleu's edicts and freed the prisoners of 22 November—celebrated ever since as the anniversary of Lebanon's independence.[22]

In committing itself to the cause of independence, Beirut revealed the scope of popular support for open confrontation with the country's overlord, which the shifting balance of power between the mandatory powers themselves had made possible. The protesters who poured into the downtown to defy Senegalese soldiers and demand the release of the president and his government's ministers presented the rare spectacle of a country in transition that had succeeded, if only for a moment, in composing its differences: veiled and unveiled women, Christian Phalangists and members of the Muslim youth movement al-Najjadeh, Communist militants and advocates of a Greater Syria, students and clients of the old notables, flanked by their gangs—side by side, these people, natives and immigrants alike, showed that no matter how much their city had profited from its elevation as the capital of Lebanon under the Mandate, they were ready to throw all this aside. For it was Beirut that gave the new country that was about to be born its substance and its seriousness of purpose.

PART FOUR

The Cosmopolitan Metropolis of the Arabs

FIGURE 80 *(preceding page)*. Place Riad al-Sulh (formerly Place Assour): Rue des Banques (left) and, on the corner of Rue du Parlement, the Esseily Building (with Costa-Gavras's film *Z* showing at the Capitole Cinema).

14

The Switzerland of the East

A country of milk and honey, a city of luxury and delights: twenty years after independence Lebanon seemed to be a success story, and Beirut a rare exception to the tumult of the Near East. In spite of the brief civil war of 1958, Lebanon's capital gave the outward appearance of prosperity, misleading though it may have been, and nowhere more spectacularly than on its seafront with the opening in 1961 of the monumental Phoenicia Hotel.

Looming over the water as an iconic symbol of Lebanese wealth, the Phoenicia excited the wonder of contemporaries—including the vast majority of the city's residents, for whom it was inaccessible. The building itself was splendid to look at, for its white, delicately perforated façade, its unprecedented scale and height (twelve floors), and its oval swimming pool. But it was perhaps the sunken bar that most vividly captured the spirit of the place: incorporating a large glass wall that allowed guests to relax with a cocktail while contemplating the bikini-clad naiads gliding beneath the surface of the pool, it combined a new standard of technological ingenuity with a glamour worthy of the American films that just then were attracting crowds to the brand-new movie theaters of Rue Hamra. Hollywood and its foreign imitators were not slow to take notice of the Phoenicia, whose opulence was memorialized in Technicolor in a succession of romance and adventure films. At long last Beirut had its own internationally recognizable building, henceforth a centerpiece of postcard views of the city. Towering over the beaches, as well as its predecessors, the Saint-Georges and the Normandy, the new palace with its more than three hundred rooms testified to the cosmopolitan vocation of a city where wealth seemed only to beget more wealth.

In the Lebanese narrative of a golden age synonymous with the pleasures of life,

FIGURE 81. The Phoenicia Hotel, iconic symbol of Beirut's postwar prosperity.

entrepreneurial success is the central theme—perfectly illustrated by the Phoenicia, which was the fruit of local private initiative rather than of the will of public authorities in association with foreign business (as in Cairo, for example, where its contemporary, the Hilton, was built by the state and subsequently leased to the American hotel company as managing agent). National prosperity, it is true, depended on the foreign, and particularly Arab, capital that flowed into the Beirut market, especially after the passage of the Banking Secrecy Law of September 1956. The Switzerland of the Levant, first dreamed of by Lamartine and then by the members of the Phoenician Society, had come back down from the holiday resorts of Mount Lebanon to the shores of Beirut. There, downtown, a sparkling street of banks—Riad al-Sulh, which opened on to a square of the same name—came to be united in the popular imagination with the dazzling luxury hotel on the water, giving substance to an analogy that now raised hopes for the future, just as later it would foster nostalgia for the past.

The history of Beirut, though it was henceforth largely bound up with that of the Lebanese Republic, cannot be reduced to it. The capital of Lebanon was also, and perhaps first and foremost, a cosmopolitan regional metropolis, lying at the heart of the convulsions that recently had given birth to a settlement—albeit a very imperfect one—of the Eastern Question. Before being overwhelmed by the political and human tragedies of the Levant, Beirut was able to successfully experiment with a modernity that unfolded in the shadow cast by the gleaming new buildings of its business district. Lebanon's economic success following independence, attested by a great many visible signs of wealth that impressed visitors, sometimes to the point of blinding them, also confirmed by statistics. The most significant figures revealed a pattern of uninterrupted growth for a quarter of a century: between 1950 and 1974 the annual increase in gross domestic product averaged 7 percent, or, taking into account the increase in population, some 3–4 percent per capita.[1] Despite a few dark clouds on the horizon, most obviously the belt of poverty that ringed Beirut, the image of a golden age was by no means unfounded.

THE REIGN OF THE MERCHANT REPUBLIC

The new Lebanon nevertheless got off to a poor start, despite the fair prospects forecast by an American diplomatic report shortly after the declaration of independence.[2] Once the euphoria of November 1943 had worn off, the difficulties of the war economy regained the upper hand. While a few businessmen were able to make enormous profits, the government's inability to remedy widespread shortages aroused harsh criticism, notably against the minister in charge of supplying the capital's needs.[3] Nonetheless the struggle against the former mandate power, which dragged on for another three years, and the diplomatic maneuvering among the Arab states in which Lebanon played an active role served to put matters into perspective. The full extent of the difficulties facing the country was soon revealed after the Anglo-French agreement of December 1945 calling for withdrawal of the last French troops by the end of the following year. Only a few months later, as the new daily newspaper Al-Hayat (Life) observed, the government's failure to address the deteriorating domestic situation was plain to see.[4] A strike by public-sector employees in the summer of 1946 represented the first signal of alarm.[5]

Although the government saw the wisdom of adopting a new labor code, under pressure from the Communist-controlled unions, it showed little concern with establishing an effective system of administration. The question of administrative reform, first raised in 1944 and thereafter insistently demanded by the press and a few politicians, was to recur throughout Bishara al-Khuri's two terms as president of the Republic[6] and well beyond. Within the top leadership the skills needed to undertake reform were in any case absent. Riad al-Sulh, however talented a politician he may have been, and despite his reputation as an able diplomat and a shrewd negotiator, was nonetheless uninterested in the details of public management, and his successors as prime minister—Abdul Hamid Karameh, Saʿdi Munla, and Sami al-Sulh—were no better equipped, either by temperament or training, to deal with them.[7] With a few rare exceptions, their ministers, products of the same milieu of notables, lacked both experience and determination.

As for Khuri, his sense of statesmanship was equal neither to the historical vision that inspired him nor to his commitment, authentic though it was, to the cause of national unity. Preoccupied by petty maneuvering aimed at retaining control over political life, and then in assuring his reelection (this in spite of a constitutional prohibition against seeking a second term), Khuri very quickly moved to place his entourage (beginning with his brother Salim, known as the "Sultan") in charge of official patronage. Far from taking seriously the warning of the British ambassador, who predicted that the course of events would force him to realize that "even a small and unimportant country such as this cannot in these days be run like a petty family business for the benefit of an insignificant minority,"[8] Khuri did nothing to prevent corruption and nepotism from being erected into a system of government.

The distinction between public and private was blurred further by the heritage of the Mandate. The old colonial economy still held sway at the end of the war, and neither France's political and military retreat nor the devolution to Lebanon and Syria of responsibility for managing their "common interests" had affected the position of French investors, who remained closely tied to the commercial and banking upper class of Beirut. Thus the French-owned Banque de Syrie et du Liban (BSL), successor to the Ottoman Bank formerly controlled by Paribas, functioned as the country's central bank; having enjoyed the privilege of issuing money since 1939, and continuing to act in accordance with the terms of the 1943 Constitution as agent of the Treasury until the 1960s, it supervised funds transfers among other banks and siphoned off a large part of the profits from the war for its own use. Under this regime, other French houses could count on benefiting from association with banks owned by prominent Beirut families. Thus, for example, Crédit Lyonnais acquired Banque G. Trad in 1951, and Banque Sabbagh came under the control of the Banque d'Indochine, which was responsible for purchasing the gold used to back the Lebanese currency.[9] The dominant presence of the BSL and other French banks was reinforced by their participation in the affairs of the semi-official trading company SERIAC. As the successor to the French-controlled Office de l'Économie de Guerre, it exercised a de facto monopoly on commercial exchanges between France, on the one hand, and Lebanon and Syria on the other. A similar arrangement obtained with regard to insurance, since covering the risks incurred by French concessionary companies was now the obligation of the Union Nationale d'Assurances, represented by a local company that had taken its name.[10] In spite of the failure to negotiate the preferential treaty terms desired by General

FIGURE 82. One of the first bank notes issued by independent Lebanon.

de Gaulle and blocked by Great Britain, French interests remained safe after the end of the Mandate—for the simple reason that they were guarded by agents of the Lebanese government, who were employed by the large French firms and banks as lawyers and executives.[11]

Wheeling and dealing was not limited to the exchange of services. Ties of kinship and marriage created a situation in which the business and political classes virtually coincided. Even the highest-ranking officials, such as Henri Pharaon, foreign minister in Riad al-Sulh's government in 1944, and Husayn 'Uwayni, who became prime minister in 1949, were known to combine public office with the accumulation of immense personal fortunes. In the latter case the wealth was new, a result of the friendly relations 'Uwayni had established with King 'Abdul-'Aziz of Saudi Arabia, and quickly converted into political capital by virtue of his alliance with the Franco-Lebanese interests that dominated Beirut. 'Uwayni was, among other things, an executive of the Sabbagh bank, whose branch operations in Jidda he oversaw; also a partner of the Union Nationale d'Assurances, and an associate of Air France via its affiliate Air Liban, which owing to the favor of the Saudi monarch enjoyed a long-term monopoly on traffic between Beirut and the kingdom.[12] Most of the fortunes in play already had a few decades behind them, however. Typically they belonged to Beirut families, whether of old stock or more recent adoption, that had been enriched in the second half of the nineteenth century by European commercial expansion, such as the Pharaons, Chihas, and Freiges. Others had only lately entered into the ranks of the city's upper class, such as the Sehnaouis and the Fattals, who transferred a part of their business operations to Beirut from Damascus in the hope of profiting from its central place in the economy of the Mandate, or the Kettanehs, newcomers from Jerusalem who made Beirut the base for an international empire extending as far east as Iran and as far west as the United States.

Born in the late Ottoman period and coming to maturity under French rule, the merchant republic of Beirut now concentrated the nation's wealth in the hands of just a few families, to the point that it could be confused with the new Lebanese Republic itself. The phenomenon went well beyond the protection of French interests after the end of the Mandate; the growing share of imports from the United States was monopolized by the same circle of local magnates. Very few foreign commercial agencies escaped dealing with what was called the "Consortium," whose members controlled banking, insurance, services, and the principal industrial firms.[13] If they were not all directly involved in political life, all of them had gotten their start in business as a result of connections with the governing elite. This intimacy was not new. So long as the French held power, it had remained at least partly hidden from view; but with independence it became flagrant, so much so that the president's entourage no longer made any attempt to disguise its appetite for greater and greater wealth. In the end this naked greed caused a scandal, even in the sight of the class to which Khuri himself belonged, and helped to bring about the White Revolution that led to his resignation in September 1952.

The example set at the highest levels of government hardly encouraged the sound conduct of public affairs. Denouncing the dramatic growth in gambling, smuggling, and drug traffic, a British business magazine in April 1951 exposed corruption on a scale that threatened to jeopardize the country's prosperity.[14] And while the economy did in fact register gains that year, it was the elites of Beirut that almost wholly profited from them.[15] One government after another had thrown up its hands in despair, to the extent that any of them had really tried to eliminate the rot at all. "All the images evoked by the distress that arises from ungoverned things—the abandoned ship, the collapsed building—apply to the current fate of Lebanon," the journalist Georges Naccache lamented in March 1949.[16] It was difficult, under these circumstances, to expect anything resembling a coherent policy for development. Even when the government received the first offer of American aid in March 1947, within the framework of Point Four of the Truman Doctrine, it quickly showed itself to be incapable of drawing up the necessary plans, and it was not until December 1951 that Lebanon qualified for assistance under the terms of this clause.[17] This demonstration of incompetence nonetheless did not prevent the Belgian economist and former prime minister, Paul van Zeeland, engaged as an advisor to the government, from praising its policies. Van Zeeland is said to have concluded that despite Lebanon's disregard for the rules of classical economics, it should continue on the road on which it had set out: "I don't know what makes the economy work, but it's doing very well and I wouldn't advise you to touch it."[18]

THE LEBANESE MIRACLE

Van Zeeland's view, though manifestly incapable of accounting for the extraordinary growth that lay in store, was nevertheless widely shared, nourishing a belief in the country's providential destiny that was to be invoked later. In the absence of natural resources, this "Lebanese miracle"—as it was ritually called—had to be explained by some exceptional circumstance, which, following the helpful suggestion of Michel Chiha, was promptly located in the figure of the eternal merchant descended from the Phoenicians. Though the ingenuity of Lebanese businessmen can scarcely be disputed, essentialist claims about the fundamental character of the Lebanese people that it is customarily thought to support must be qualified in light of the related commercial histories of Aleppo and Damascus. Rather than relying on a tradition of resourcefulness that was, and remains, a constant source of self-satisfaction, one should perhaps speak less grandly of a set of trade practices, common in Beirut since the middle of the nineteenth century, to which families from the Syrian hinterland made significant contributions. Much more important in confirming the wisdom of van Zeeland's advice was the regional economic context of the late 1940s. An unbridled laissez-faire regime brought more reward than it caused damage—at least in the short term—as a result of a unique combination of circumstances that took shape outside the merchant republic and that escaped its control: the disappearance of Arab Palestine in 1948; the breakdown of the Syrian-Lebanese customs union in 1950; and the increase in oil revenues in the Arabian Peninsula from the end of the 1940s onward.

Of all these events it was the rupture with Syria that most profoundly determined the orientation of the Lebanese economy. Indeed one might even argue that the future of Lebanon and, more particularly, of Beirut had until this moment been defined by the relationship with its neighbor, if only involuntarily. A first step was taken in 1947 with Syria's decision to leave the franc zone, formalized by its signing of the Bretton Woods agreement, which meant that the monetary union that in various forms had existed between the coast and the interior for centuries now ceased to exist. The loss of exchange parity that resulted from it suddenly gave the separation of the two countries a tangible significance. Cross-border trade nonetheless continued to be regulated by a customs union, inherited from the Mandate and still in place, despite the temptation to abandon it that was now growing among the merchant bourgeoisie of Beirut.

In view of Lebanon's dependence on its neighbor, not only for its port activity but also for its supply of grain, the government seemed unlikely to run the risks that would follow from a complete break. And in fact the dissolution of the customs union, in the wake of the decoupling of the two countries' currencies, came about at the initiative of the Syrian leaders as a consequence of their decision to place the economy under state control, if not actually a regime of central planning.

But an obstacle lay in the way of adopting a protectionist policy of industrial and agricultural development: so long as Lebanon refused to go along, Syria could not unilaterally raise tariffs. The Syrian government's dissatisfaction with existing arrangements was compounded by what it saw as an inequitable basis for sharing revenues. By the terms of the agreement on the transfer of common interests concluded with France after its departure from the Levant, 56 percent of customs revenue went to Syria and 44 percent to Lebanon—a proportion that reflected the facts neither of geography nor of demography, only the relative size of the two countries' import markets (the Lebanese being reckoned greater consumers in per capita terms). In addition to this fiscal dispute there were complaints from Damascene merchants who felt that the customs union served as a pretext for the monopoly on foreign commercial agencies enjoyed by their competitors in Beirut—some themselves originally from Damascus, such as the Fattals and the Sehnaouis. Relations were poisoned for other reasons as well: the beginning of work to enlarge the port of Lataqiyya, regarded with suspicion by business circles in Beirut;[19] the price demanded by Syria for its grain, higher than that of the wheat imported from the United States; and negotiations over the proposed route of the oil pipeline being built by the Trans-Arabian Pipeline Company (Tapline), an American joint venture formed for the purpose of bringing Saudi oil to the Mediterranean. Whereas Lebanon had hastened to sign the agreement with Tapline in 1946, Syria delayed three years before finally giving its approval; in the meantime, impatient to go forward, the Lebanese advised the American consortium of their willingness to see the route changed, passing through Palestine rather than through Syrian territory.[20]

For a time disagreement was contained by the very close political and personal ties that bound the two governments, beginning with the presidents, Bishara al-Khuri and Shukri al-Quwatli. This brake disappeared with Quwatli's ouster in a military coup engineered by the chief of staff, Husni al-Za'im, in April 1949, succeeded at intervals of a few months by two more putsches. As if to show that an era had passed, Za'im moved to assert his authority by closing the borders with Lebanon, for the first time in May of that year. These reprisals, repeated a few years later, only deepened the cleavage between the two countries, even after Za'im's departure. Partly as a result of the escalation of tensions, the unstable situation in which Syria now found itself led to a continuing deterioration of relations with Beirut, which several times was commanded to choose between full economic union or complete separation. It was with the expiration of a final ultimatum to this effect, no Lebanese response having been received, that the civilian government of Khalid al-'Azm announced the annulment of the customs union and the enforcement of an economic boycott. The decision, announced 15 March 1950, took effect immediately with the installation of customs houses on the border with Lebanon.[21]

The boycott was not without harmful consequences. Not only was Syria the country's principal supplier of agricultural products, it now represented Lebanon's sole means of access to the Arab hinterland with the closing of the Palestinian border in 1948. A whole section of society, traditionally linked to the Syrian economy, stood to suffer from the new constraints on the circulation of goods and merchandise. This was particularly true in Tripoli, the country's second-largest city, where economic hardship combined with political discontent to provoke repeated strikes, even riots against businesses. But apart from a few industrial and agricultural sectors, repercussions from the crisis were relatively mild. In Beirut, in any case, neither the business community nor the political class had grounds for complaint: for supporters of an unregulated free-market economy, maintaining a special relationship with Syria had become too costly; and, in the event, the severing of economic ties more than justified the risk.[22] The state profited no less than its merchants, since a considerable share of Syrian foreign trade continued to pass through the port of Beirut. Not only did customs revenue not decline, but Lebanon saw its competitive position strengthened in many instances. Thus, for example, in response to Damascus's demand that Lebanese imports of Syrian goods be paid for in foreign currency, to offset an unfavorable imbalance in the rate of exchange between the two countries' own currencies, Beirut now began to buy wheat from the United States.[23] Over time the differences between the two capitals became more acute, so that the monetary and customs crises led on finally to a complete rupture of economic relations—with the unanticipated result, at least from the Syrian point of view, that Lebanese autonomy was reinforced.[24]

The divorce with Syria came at a favorable moment. The effects of the cataclysm that swept away Palestine fewer than two years earlier now began to make themselves felt, and for Lebanon they were not all negative—far from it. The country did, of course, have to cope with an influx of impoverished refugees, which at the outset posed the problem of feeding them. The closing of the Palestinian border also disrupted the local economy in the south, whose farmers found themselves cut off from their traditional markets in Galilee.[25] By contrast, Beirut benefited from the transfer of salvaged personal and corporate assets and, above all, by the diversion of transit trade from Palestinian ports. In breaking the link between the Levantine coast and the interior, the creation of the state of Israel not only released Beirut from the threat of domination by Haifa, but also enabled it to claim undisputed supremacy. Long served by the great shipping lines and expanded under the Mandate, the port of Beirut was the natural alternative, and indeed in the space of a few years it managed to take over the bulk of Haifa's traffic. Between 1947 and 1955, the volume of cargo crossing its wharves increased twenty-seven times, not counting merchandise destined for Syria.[26] In other words, the share of Syrian trade that had been lost after 1950 was now more than compensated for by the new commercial relationships established with Jordan, Iraq, and Saudi Arabia.

The consequences for Lebanon of the Palestine War were amplified by the development of the petroleum industry in Iraq and the Arabian Peninsula. Though still small by comparison with later years, oil revenues created a demand for imported goods that, given the inadequate port facilities on both the Red Sea and Persian Gulf coasts of the peninsula, made the transit of cargo through the port of Beirut inevitable. Lebanese industry, suddenly deprived of privileged access to the Syrian market, profited from this situation as well, not least because it now had at its disposal cheap labor drawn from the Palestinian refugee camps, opportunely (if not in fact deliberately) located near centers of production.[27] All the greater, then, was the incentive for local firms to turn away from the domestic market, where they faced stiff competition from foreign products, in order to concentrate on their new export markets.[28] But the decision to link the fortunes of the Lebanese economy to the rising oil wealth of the Gulf States was not only a function of competition or of the interplay of supply and demand. Beyond purely commercial considerations, the closing of the Palestinian frontier forced the Arab oil-exporting countries to incorporate Lebanon in their strategic outlook. The rivalry between the two Iraqi pipelines, and between the refineries of Haifa and Tripoli, had become a thing of the past now that most of Mosul's crude oil production flowed to Tripoli. Similarly, Tapline no longer had a choice in routing its pipeline to bring Saudi production to the Mediterranean: once the agreement with Syria was finally signed in 1949, crude from Qaisumah would end up in Lebanon at the refinery in Zahrani, outside Sidon.

Lebanon's growing attachment to the economy of the oil-producing countries could also be seen, in addition to the role played by its ports in the transshipment of petroleum and other cargos, in the rise of air transport. Beirut had gotten a head start in this domain in the 1930s, and the boycott of Israeli airports gave it a de facto monopoly. For Europeans traveling to Saudi Arabia and the Gulf states a stopover in Beirut was now obligatory and brought prosperity to the two airline companies that were created there in 1945: Middle East Airlines (MEA), founded by Saeb Salim Salam and Fawzi Hoss, whose success led it four years later, in September 1949, to conclude a five-year partnership agreement with Pan American Airlines, which acquired a 36 percent stake (and a management contract); and the Compagnie Générale des Transports, renamed Air Liban in 1951, whose investors included Air France, holding a third of the shares, along with Husayn 'Uwayni and other partners likewise representing French interests. A third company, Transmediterranean Airways, was formed in 1953 to handle freight shipment, joined a little later by a fourth, Lebanese International Airways (LIA). The government had anticipated these developments, and in 1948 dedicated one of the country's first major investments in public infrastructure—not without squandering a great deal of money in the process—to the construction of a new airport to replace the field at Bir Hassan, laid out under the Mandate.

Built among the sand-colored hills of Khaldeh on the coastal plain south of the capital, and formally inaugurated in April 1954 (although it had been partially operational since 1949), Beirut International Airport wore its new and rather impos-

FIGURE 83. Beirut International, the new airport at Khaldeh, officially opened in April 1954.

ing name well. Despite a few Syrian attempts to dissuade foreign companies from serving Beirut,[29] it immediately established itself as the main regional hub for air traffic. The attractiveness of its facilities was further advertised by the warm relations local companies enjoyed with the governments of the Arabian Peninsula. Just as Air Liban benefited from the friendship between Husayn 'Uwayni and the Saudi king, MEA for a time monopolized the Beirut-Kuwait route thanks to ties between Salam and the shaykhs of this emirate, the first of the Gulf states to experience large-scale economic expansion. Beginning with only sixty employees, MEA grew rapidly and by 1956 its staff numbered some nine hundred.[30] In June 1963 it absorbed Air Liban to become Lebanon's national airline and, together with the airport itself, which remained the chief hub of the Near East until 1975, became one of the most visible symbols of Lebanese success.

Still more than through the circulation of goods, people, or even petroleum, Lebanon was connected to the economies of the Arabian Peninsula by enormous capital flows that made Beirut the financial center of the Arab world until just after the first oil shock of 1973. Already in the 1940s, when oil income was limited to the modest royalties remitted by the Western companies, the banks and foreign exchange brokers of Beirut were in an unrivaled position to convert them into secure reserves, typically gold. In 1948, for example, it was estimated that almost a third of world gold shipments passed through Beirut on their way to the monarchs and shaykhs of the Gulf.[31] Financial transactions soon gained in both scope and sophistication as the so-called fifty-fifty profit-sharing rule, first imposed in Venezuela, was adopted by Arab oil-producing countries, whose revenue streams became more

regular and considerably larger during the 1950s. Lebanon was initially well positioned to be one of the beneficiaries of this windfall; its banking sector, active since
the late nineteenth century, had grown in size since independence as a result, first,
of the transfer of Palestinian fortunes to Beirut, and then of the severing of economic ties with Syria, where the implementation of central planning had triggered
another cross-border flight of capital. Lebanon further strengthened its power of
attraction by elevating its laissez-faire policies into dogma with the passage of a law
guaranteeing the secrecy of banking transactions, initially contemplated in 1953
and finally enacted in 1956. From then on Beirut stood to profit from a constant
inflow of capital: in the decade between 1956 and 1966, two-thirds of surplus petroleum revenues found their way from the Gulf to local banks.[32] In the meantime
central planning had reached its peak in several Arab countries, and from 1957 onward a wave of nationalizations made Lebanon the nearest refuge for capital seeking to avoid confiscation.[33] This was particularly true for a large, chiefly Christian
part of the Syrian upper class, and a fewer years later for Syrian-Lebanese families
in Egypt who chose to come back to their homeland, settling in Beirut rather than
in their ancestral towns and villages.

FROM ONE BOOM TO THE NEXT

Looking back, the opening up of the Lebanese economy can be seen to have revealed its structural defects, the most intractable of them linked to the limited size
of the nation's territory and to the poverty of its natural resources, others to the very
nature of the merchant republic itself and the patterns of social organization it generated. And yet for a long while the Lebanese model of economic development managed to evade critical scrutiny. In the eyes of contemporary observers, the miracle
was obviously lucrative for a great many people; and however circumstantial and
extrinsic its origins may have been, its effects were too generally benign to warrant
concern or complaint. The best thing, then, was to try to draw the greatest possible immediate profit from it, trusting to the famous ingenuity that the Lebanese
claimed for themselves to take care of the rest, even if it meant overlooking chronic
sources of weakness.

The dividends of the miracle began to be apparent under the presidency of Camille
Chamoun, one of the leaders of the opposition to Khuri. Elected by Parliament following the White Revolution, Chamoun forced the father of Lebanese independence
to resign in September 1952. In statistical terms, the boom did not reach its peak
until the early 1970s. Yet it was Chamoun's six-year term (1952–58) that was to remain the golden era in the collective memory, at least for the people of Beirut. Far
from undermining the impression of prosperity, the turbulent regional situation of
these years made it stand out all the more clearly. It must be said that the effects on
Lebanon were mixed. If the logic of the cold war, ramified by the military maneu-

vers attending the Pact of Baghdad in the fall of 1955, the Suez Crisis the following year, and the formation by Syria and Egypt of a United Arab Republic in 1958, was not without repercussions for Lebanon, where it helped to fuel the brief civil war of 1958, the quickening pace of events in its vicinity had in the meantime given the country the image of a haven from turmoil. Owing especially to its guarantee of banking secrecy, it commanded a sufficiently large inflow of capital to be able to bring about a certain redistribution of incomes. Corruption had by no means disappeared, any more than economic power had ceased to be concentrated in the hands of a small group of wealthy men. But the excesses of nepotism that had marked Khuri's presidency had come to an end. As a result, the monopolistic control of access to commercial credit was no longer a source of scandal, particularly since redistribution, though it was achieved by market mechanisms, enlarged the circle of those who directly benefited from the nation's economic growth by including an increasingly assertive urban middle class. Beirut profited all the more from the boom since it was there that the rise of this middle class occurred, even if it was hidden from the rest of the country, which came to be reminded of its existence only during the weeks of civil war that engulfed Chamoun's presidency at the end.

The social lessons of the war were drawn by General Fuad Shihab, commander of the army, who succeeded Chamoun in September 1958. In parallel with a redefinition of Lebanese foreign policy to agree with that of Egypt under Nasser and a greater participation of Muslim elites in public life, Shihab sought to address the roots of the domestic crisis. He began by commissioning a study from IRFED, the development research institute run by Father Louis-Joseph Lebret, whose analysis revealed a still tighter concentration of economic power than had been imagined: 4 percent of the population held almost all of the nation's wealth. In response, Shihab moved to create new state institutions designed to promote the redistribution of wealth while at the same time placing economic development in a national perspective. Without inaugurating a comprehensive scheme of central planning, Shihabism (as the president's policy of public sector intervention was called, to distinguish it from the *dirigiste* model favored elsewhere in the Levant) nonetheless brought Lebanon more in step with the economic policy orientation of its neighbors. A planning ministry was created in 1963, along with a central bank—thus putting an end to the anomaly, inherited from the Mandate, by which the privilege of issuing money resided with a private institution, the Banque de Syrie et du Liban, whose capital was supplied mainly by foreign investors. Public expenditures increased in a proportion close to that of Socialist-leaning Syria, and a system of social security was introduced in 1964 to consolidate the gains of the middle class (although it was not until 1971 that a health insurance program had been devised and put into effect). At the same time, the so-called peripheral regions, predominantly Muslim, which had been annexed to the Mountain in order to form Greater Lebanon in 1920, became the object of special attention. The new decentralizing spirit was manifested symbolically by the choice of Tripoli, still the orphan of Syrian unity despite being the country's second-largest city, as the site of an international fair. By way of emphasizing the project's ambition, the design for the main exhibition hall was awarded to the Brazilian architect Oscar Niemeyer, famous for his recent work in Brasilia. In Beirut itself urban improvements were not wholly neglected. But the city's great advantage, overriding all others, was that it profited automatically from the expansion of state agencies housed in government buildings constructed or otherwise converted for this purpose.

The dose of central planning administered by Shihab was not large enough to cause the merchant republic to change its ways, however. Oil money continued to fuel the private banks and the rising volume of transit trade kept the port busier than ever. And since Shihab's reformism was not accompanied by a reorganization of the tax system or by new commercial regulation, the fortunes accumulated by the businessmen and financiers of Beirut remained intact. However resolute may have been the government's will to modernize, and despite the growth of the middle classes, Shihabism did not lead to any radical restructuring of economic power. This was to become clear during the presidency of Charles Hélou (1964–70), who had been chosen by Shihab to continue his policies, and still more so under Suleiman Franjieh (1970–76), whose tenure was marked by a return to unbridled laissez-faire and nepotism, despite a few fresh attempts at reform, quickly aborted. The increasing reliance on the state's police power in carrying out the objectives of regional development during Shihab's regime, uncurbed under Hélou, had made an unfavorable impression on public opinion, dampening popular appreciation of the gains made by the middle classes and their effect in narrowing disparities between the country's religious communities, and so reducing support for pushing reforms further. Ominously, the alarm sounded by the collapse of Intra Bank in October 1966, and by the shock to the banking sector that followed, went unheard.

Intra, founded in 1951 as a currency trading house by the Palestinian financier Yusuf Beidas, had in the space of only a few years become the largest private bank in Beirut, indeed in the entire Arab world. This fact, together with its substantial holdings abroad, including property on the Champs-Élysées in Paris and a stake in the naval shipyards of La Ciotat in Provence, made it one of the most notable embodiments of Lebanese success. But as a result of having grown so quickly, the bank came in for criticism on all sides. Some of it was justified, in view of certain failures of management, though these were hardly unique to Intra; in other cases it grew out of personal vendettas against Beidas himself. The greatest source of disquiet, however, was the central role that Intra now played in the country's economy, thrown into relief by the conjunction of Lebanese, Arab, and Western interests that stood revealed for all to see during the crash and in the months that followed.[34] The Lebanese government did not make the least effort to support Intra, however, even though the bank's deposits and other assets, both in Lebanon and elsewhere, were

FIGURE 84. The port of Beirut in the early 1970s.

more than enough to assure its survival if the liquidity crisis could be brought under control. Moreover, when the government moved to restructure the banking sector, in the hope of absorbing a shock whose effects had immediately been felt by other institutions, its reorganization measures favored Western investors, who were now present in increasing numbers.[35] The consequence of Intra's collapse was a reduced degree of autonomy for Lebanese banks—the price that had to be paid for the regional function that they had fulfilled for some fifteen years now, but also a sign of the fragility of the miracle that had supported their expansion.

It remained possible to ignore such signs, however. In addition to the effectiveness of the reorganization measures from a technical point of view, the unsettling consequences of the banking crisis for Lebanese society were offset by new developments in the region. There was, first of all, the closing of the Suez Canal in the aftermath of the 1967 Arab-Israeli war. The competitive advantage of the port of Beirut, having been firmly established by the 1948 war, was further improved by this second Arab defeat. Over the almost eight years that the Suez Canal was shut down, between June 1967 and April 1975, transit trade through Beirut experienced dramatic growth. Both the port and the airport doubled their volume of traffic during this period.[36] Congestion at the port was so great that cargo ships were often obliged to stand idle in the outer harbor for weeks before being able to unload their merchandise, destined in the main for Iraq and the Arabian Peninsula. Next came the 1973 war and the ensuing oil shock. The banks of Beirut, which had not ceased to attract petrodollars in the interval, were enviably situated to reap the dividends of this price increase. For Lebanon, 1974 was a year of financial euphoria—the last it was to experience in the twentieth century.

The results of these changes in the regional environment were clearly registered in the economic statistics for the period.[37] The tourist sector enjoyed remarkable growth: between 1968 and 1974, its revenues increased fourfold, amounting ultimately to 10 percent of gross domestic product—in large measure due to the influx of Saudi and Kuwaiti vacationers. Another development, whose significance was insufficiently appreciated at the time, was the improved performance of firms that modernized and diversified, despite the lack of encouragement by the government, which remained committed to protecting local producers (though an attempt to enact a slightly protectionist schedule of customs tariffs failed in the fall of 1971 in the face of a strike by the Beirut Traders Association). After holding steady at 12–13 percent during the 1960s, the contribution of industry to gross domestic product rose to between 20 and 25 percent (depending on the estimate) in 1974. Here again the impetus came from the increasing demand for capital goods in the Gulf states, where the accumulation of wealth had stimulated domestic investment. Export-led growth was increasingly oriented toward markets in these countries, which had now become Lebanon's privileged clients.

Still more spectacular, because its effects could be observed in everyday life, was the influence of oil wealth in sustaining the boom in construction and the steep rise in real estate prices, particularly in vacation resort areas and in the most fashionable neighborhoods of Beirut. But already before the advent of large-scale Arabian investment, nearer and older fortunes had spurred the development of certain neighborhoods in the city, particularly Ras Beirut, which was attractive to wealthy Palestinians for its proximity to the American university,[38] and Badaro, to the southeast, where moneyed natives of Aleppo chose to settle.

A PLACE FOR DOING BUSINESS

Notwithstanding the Shihabist policy of guided regional development, Beirut inevitably claimed for itself most of the benefits of an economic miracle that had lasted for twenty-five years; indeed, throughout this period the country's success was usually confused with that of its capital. But Beirut's long experience as an intermediary in international commerce, going back at least a century, gave it additional advantages that could not be found elsewhere in the region. Rising incomes supported demand for a range of goods and services that emphasized the city's modern character and its cosmopolitanism, and in this way amplified its dynamic power of attraction. Beirut now found itself in the avant-garde of the Arab world. It was there that one came to discover novelties from the West—the latest fashions from Paris, the newest models of American and Italian cars, the technological innovations that appeared with increasing frequency over the course of the three decades following the war. In bringing together businessmen, artists, intellectuals, and tourists from near and far, the city impressed visitors as a microcosm of the Arab world that nonetheless fully belonged to a world beyond the Levant.

By the 1950s Beirut's unique position as a liberal and modern city in a region of centrally planned economies had made it a base of operations for businessmen everywhere in the Near East. This transformation could be detected in the rise to prominence of men whose success was all the more exceptional as they belonged neither to the city's financial and commercial oligarchy nor to the political elite of its leading families. After Husayn 'Uwayni, who had been inducted into the society of notables following his early success in Saudi Arabia in the 1930s and 1940s, the two most emblematic figures were Émile Bustani and Yusuf Beidas. Bustani, born into a family from Mount Lebanon and educated at the American University of Beirut, made his first fortune in Palestine; later, in creating a demand for civil engineering projects in the Gulf states, the oil boom converted his Contracting and Trading Co. (CAT) into a veritable empire. But if Bustani's wealth had its origin in other countries, he kept his headquarters in Beirut, where he succeeded in creating a political career for himself. Elected to Parliament as an ally of Camille Chamoun, while at the same time maintaining close ties with Chamoun's adversaries (until Nasser came to power in Egypt),[39] Bustani quickly stood out as one of the rising stars of Lebanese politics, considered by many a serious candidate for the presidency of the Republic. His tragic death in March 1963, when his private jet plunged into the sea, did not fail to arouse a great deal of suspicion. It was nonetheless a sign of the stature he had acquired that his daughter, Myrna Bustani, was called upon by the political leadership to finish out his term. Elected to office without opposition, she became the first woman to enter Parliament, ten years after the right to vote was granted to women. It was to be almost another thirty years before another woman was elected.

Beidas's career, like that of Bustani, had its roots in mandatory Palestine. From there he burst onto the Beirut financial scene in 1948, going on to found Intra Bank three years later. His origins were to be held against him when the moment of his downfall came: a symbol of Lebanese pride so long as his good fortune lasted, he was suddenly demoted in the public mind to the status of a disreputable foreigner following his suicide in November 1968, in Switzerland.[40] In the meantime Beidas had never really been accepted by local elites. In a system still held together by personal ties he remained an intruder—no matter that Intra, in addition to being the leading bank in the Arab world (or perhaps because of that very fact), had become a key actor in the Lebanese economy—and the hostility of his rivals was almost certainly not unrelated to the deliberate inaction of the public authorities at the moment of the collapse.[41]

Beirut was swarming with foreign Arab businessmen during this period. Some were permanent residents, others occasional visitors. There were Palestinians, such as Abdul Hamid Shuman and his brothers, who had transferred to Beirut the head-quarters of the Arab Bank, founded in Jerusalem in 1930 (unlike Intra, its involve-ment with Lebanese firms was relatively limited, though this did not prevent it after Beidas's downfall from dominating the world of Arab finance, thanks in particular to the Palestine Liberation Organization, its principal client from the early 1970s onward); the entrepreneurs Hasib Sabbagh and ʿAbdul-Muhsin Qattan, both par-ticularly active in the Gulf states despite making Beirut their base of operations; and also the Butagys of Haifa, major figures in the furniture trade. There were Christian Syrians, such as the ʿObaji family from Aleppo, proprietors of the bank-ing house Crédit Libanais, and the Sehnaouis, who strengthened their already ven-erable standing in Beirut through association with the Société Générale de Belgique in Brussels; also Muslim Syrians, such as Naʿman Azhari, a former government minister and founder of the Banque du Liban et d'Outre Mer, which began by at-tracting capital exfiltrated from Damascus and Aleppo and later became the pre-ferred bank of the Lebanese Sunni bourgeoisie, establishing itself in the 1980s among the first rank of houses in Beirut. There were Iraqis, such as the Chalabis, promi-nent bankers who had fled Baghdad after the overthrow of the monarchy in 1958 and allied themselves through marriage with important Shiʿi families in southern Lebanon; and Khalid ʿUsaymi, a real estate developer who worked for a time in Da-mascus before coming to Beirut, where he erected its most prestigious office build-ing, the Gefinor, on land for which he had paid a record price. Finally, there were Lebanese from other places than Beirut, such as the ʿAudis, who built up their for-eign exchange business in Sidon into a major bank by attracting Kuwaiti capital, and the Debbanehs, another Christian family from Sidon that went on to dominate the seed import trade. In the end, provincial banking houses that did not succeed in creating a niche for themselves in Beirut fell by the wayside.

In addition to further enriching the most successful newcomers during this aus-picious period, as well as the old but still powerful financial oligarchy, which coopted them more or less quickly, the Lebanese economy was now sufficiently large, owing to the massive inflow of capital from elsewhere in the Arab world, to make the rep-utations of a great many businessmen of lesser stature. Sometimes starting from nothing, talented entrepreneurs were able to achieve a degree of financial reward that lay beyond the reach of the vast majority of the population, assuring the luckiest and most ingenious individuals of rapid social advancement. This freewheeling atmo-sphere added to the list of Beirut's attractions as a place for doing business, where few practices embraced by the euphoric capitalism of the 1960s—respectable or otherwise—were unknown.

It was at this point that Beirut began to emerge as a leading regional center of the world economy. From its banks went out the letters of credit necessary for other Arab countries to pay for their imports, and foreign businessmen gladly accepted having to stay in one or another of its hotels to negotiate contracts for projects in Saudi Arabia, Kuwait, and Iraq. And when the chief executives of American and European companies came to promote their products and services in the Near East, Beirut was inevitably their preferred stopover—often their only one.

A PLACE FOR LIVING

Beirut's allure as a place for work or relaxation for men who made their money elsewhere was due not only to its banks, its port, and its offices. The city's quality of life was not the least of its charms, whether for Arab entrepreneurs who had to work much of the year in the still demanding conditions of the desert countries or for Western businessmen in transit to and from them. No other city in the Near East, not even Cairo, was in a position to provide so many amenities. Public investment in this connection nonetheless remained extremely fragmented. Apart from a few projects—the new airport, halting efforts to expand road and communications infrastructure, construction of the Casino du Liban on the slopes of Ma'ameltein north of the city (leased as a concession but secured by a national monopoly on gaming proceeds), a hotel school intended to supply the tourism industry with trained staff, and, in the cultural domain, support for the Baalbek festival—the state was noticeably absent. The private service sector, already with a long tradition of innovation behind it, succeeded in doing what needed to be done—so efficiently that in addition to the large number of air connections with Europe, on the one hand, and the Gulf states, on the other, and the ease of communication by telephone and telex (which compensated for the continuing deficiencies of postal service), Beirut offered everything that a moderately well-off foreigner could possibly desire, starting with an impressive stock of increasingly well appointed hotels.

In the 1950s and 1960s, a flurry of four-star establishments opened on or near the water: the Palm Beach, the Vendôme, the Martinez, the Cadmos, and, a few hundred yards away, at the tip of the promontory, the Riviera, as well as the Carlton, overlooking the cliffs of Rawsheh. But while the seafront in 'Ayn al-Mrayseh remained the poshest district of the hospitality industry, the west side of the upper city also attracted a certain amount of investment. Before the landmark Phoenicia came to join the Saint-Georges and the Normandy down by the sea, the high-end market had been further enlarged by the Bristol, an elegant establishment in the old neighborhood next to the dunes, not yet highly urbanized. Three-star hotels had also gone up not far from there, in Ras Beirut near the American university, such as the Napoléon, constructed in 1947, and a bit later the Marble Tower and the Mayflower. The development of Rue Hamra in this neighborhood soon heralded

FIGURE 85. The luxury hotel district on the seafront.

the appearance of other three-star hotels, such as the Plaza and the Cavalier, and later the four-star Commodore—which during the civil war was to be the headquarters for the special correspondents of the international press.

The boom in hotel construction remained restricted to the western part of the city. The old hotels around Place des Martyrs were now so many fleabags; a large three-star hotel, the Alexandre, soon outmoded, stood alone on Ashrafiyyeh Hill to the east. Yet things were changing in the mountains nearby, where, independently of the tradition of summer hotels, the descendants of Émile Bustani erected the Bustan (from the Arabic word for orchard), a year-round establishment set beneath the pines of the village of Beit Mery. The increase in the total number of beds in the metropolitan area, substantial though it was, still fell short of meeting the demands of mass tourism, above all in the three-star and (almost nonexistent) two-star range. Nonetheless the luxury end of the hotel trade, which now welcomed a growing number of businessmen and an emerging clientele of convention visitors, had improved enough in scale and quality to help in its own way to justify Lebanon's image as the Switzerland of the East.

In addition to brief business visits, Beirut recommended itself for longer stays, particularly to expatriate families attracted by the educational possibilities it offered. The expansion of the network of private schools in the country enabled foreign children of all backgrounds to continue their studies without interruption. Together with the International College of AUB and the Italian school that had operated in the city for many years, there was a German school and another for the American colony, to say nothing of French schools. These last were so numerous and so well established that they set the standard for the educational system as a whole and constituted one of the most visible proofs of Lebanese uniqueness. Whereas the Suez war sounded the knell for the French cultural presence in Syria and, of course, Egypt, Lebanon chose to maintain friendly relations with its former occupier, and the French secondary school diploma continued to be favorably looked upon by families and schools, even if students had to sit for the Lebanese *baccalauréat* examination as well. The faculties of some institutions, such as the three *lycées* of the Mission Laïque Française and also the Collège Protestant, counted many visiting teachers whose salaries were paid directly by Paris—a source of appeal to French expatriates and French-speaking diplomats. Instruction in the schools run by Catholic missionaries—Lazarists, Jesuits, Marists, and others—was still given for the most part by French friars and nuns, though French men and women of Levantine birth could be found in the teaching ranks more or less everywhere, even in working-class schools. At least until the 1970s coaching in school sports was dominated by the Levantine French, and matches took place at Stade Armand-du-Chayla, built on French-owned land and named after the first ambassador of the Fourth Republic to Lebanon.

Enrollment in schools offering Western curricula was meant chiefly for the benefit of the local population in Beirut, where they did much to strengthen the middle class, while also serving a smaller class of expatriates. But another attraction of the school system, particularly valued in other countries of the region, was Beirut's openness to the outside world and the enhanced prospects for economic advancement that education there seemed to promise. With the development of boarding schools for students from abroad, the analogy with Switzerland now found itself sustained not only in finance and tourism, but in the field of education as well. The greater ease of travel meant that these schools had to depend less and less on enrolling students from Lebanon alone; and even if they permitted families in other parts of the country to preserve a provincial identity (and in many cases to cultivate local political ambitions) while at the same time giving their children a good education in the capital, it was above all the socioeconomic changes taking place in neighboring countries that assured the lasting appeal of private boarding schools. Many parochial schools in Beirut—such as those of the Soeurs de Besançon, Notre-Dame-de-Nazareth, and Saint-Joseph-de-l'Apparition for girls, and, for boys, the Jesuit college, installed in 1960 on the heights of Jamhur, east of the city—maintained boarding departments that regularly received a large contingent of children from the leading families of Damascus and Aleppo, Christian and Muslim alike, all of them restive under the monolingual regime that was taking hold in Syria, and willing, as a result, to pay for tuition abroad. Other institutions, recently founded by private initiative as well but offering a predominantly anglophone course of instruction, welcomed students from the Arabian peninsula.

A similar variety of educational choices was available at the university level. The American University of Beirut and Université Saint-Joseph, whose first decades of existence had accompanied the rise of the city in the nineteenth century, were now mature institutions. Both continued to train local elites, while at the same time fortifying Beirut's regional reputation as a center of education. Owing to the diffusion of the English language since the First World War in the Mashriq and beyond, AUB had managed to establish itself as the leading university in the entire Near East. The availability of student housing on campus or in the adjacent neighborhood of Ras Beirut, together with an unusually expansive curriculum, attracted a diverse student body from as far away as India and Afghanistan. Université Saint-Joseph, by contrast, remained more Lebanese—and Christian—in its enrollment, though both its law school and department of Arab studies accepted a steady stream of Syrian degree candidates. While USJ could not offer housing, the willingness of families in the neighborhood to take in students from the provinces and abroad made it possible to accommodate a regional presence.

In the meantime other institutions made their appearance. The Beirut College for Women, founded in the 1920s, expanded its foreign recruitment as well, and its students now came from the Muslim high society of other Arab cities in addition to Beirut. In the 1970s it approved coeducation, becoming Beirut University College (and later the Lebanese American University), with no apparent harm to its reputation. The course of development of the Lebanese Academy of Fine Arts (ALBA in its French initials), on the other hand, was less straightforward: its branches of law and humanities were effectively nationalized, forming the core of a new state university, while its schools of architecture and fine arts, which remained autonomous and were later joined by a department of graphic arts and advertising, gave it a foremost position in the Lebanese, and even Arab, artistic world.[42] Haigazian College (later University) contributed in its own distinctive way to the regionalization of Lebanese higher education, welcoming young Armenians from Aleppo and other Syrian cities, in addition to the sons and daughters of its sponsoring population in Lebanon. Even the Holy Spirit University of Kaslik, the purest academic expression of local Maronite tradition (established, moreover, in the exclusively Maronite environment of Kisrawan), attracted seminarians from the Christian communities of Syria, Iraq, and Egypt—indeed from as far away as Sudan.

The regional purpose of higher education was to assume still broader scope with the founding in 1959 of Beirut Arab University. Affiliated with the University of Alexandria, it was conceived by Nasserite Egypt as a counterweight to Western institutions in the Levant, appealing exclusively to young Muslims. Attendance was not mandatory, and a great many nonresident students were admitted—Jordanians, even

Egyptians, among them—who needed only to come to Beirut to sit for exams. Foreign enrollment was so massive that non-Lebanese soon accounted for 60 percent of the country's total student population. This proportion had already been skewed by the admissions policy of the Lebanese University, a public institution founded in 1950 that grew in size exponentially despite the indecisiveness of the political class and its reluctance to democratize higher education. The Lebanese University recruited mainly from the rural working class, while also accepting students from other countries on the strength of the official equivalency among the Lebanese, Syrian, and Egyptian *baccalauréats.*

Beirut's ambition to be an educational center for the entire Mashriq is most clearly seen in the medical field. Not only had the number of practitioners trained by its two oldest schools of medicine grown, but the city's openness to Western ideas of progress had permitted them to keep abreast of new developments. Upon graduation the majority of physicians left for Western Europe or America to do their residency; others received all their training abroad. In either case many doctors remained in contact with their teachers and regularly attended international conferences. The relevant technical literature was available in local libraries and bookstores, and constantly updated information about new medicines could be obtained from the moment of their appearance on foreign markets from representatives of the major pharmaceutical manufacturers. Hospitals themselves proved capable of matching the level of care provided in Europe with only a very slight delay. Several institutions had hundreds of beds: the Greek Orthodox Hôpital Saint-Georges, historically the first medical facility in Beirut, was substantially enlarged during the 1960s; the two university hospitals, operated by AUB and the Hôtel-Dieu de France, also equipped with new buildings; the hospital of the Muslim charitable society, al-Maqāsid; the Hôpital du Sacré-Coeur run by the French Sisters of Charity; the Lebanese Hospital operated by Maronite nuns in the J'itawi neighborhood; and so on. In-patient capacity was augmented still further by a series of private clinics, at least three of which—directed by Doctors Rizk, Barbir, and Trad—were as large as hospitals of the period. A suitably dense network of pharmacies supported this extensive medical complex.

Even so, quality care was by no means available to all Lebanese. Public health services were practically nonexistent, perpetuating social divisions in the face of illness. By contrast, the quality of the city's medical and hospital facilities reassured Western residents that, except in the case of rare pathologies, repatriation was seldom necessary. From the point of view of foreigners in nearby Arab countries, medicine in Beirut was clearly superior to anything they could find at home. Many Syrians found it convenient to go there for consultations and sometimes to be hospitalized, not least because of the ease of making the trip—three or four hours by car, with no need to obtain a visa. But the medical reputation of Beirut went well beyond the immediate vicinity. In the still poorly served countries of the Arabian

Peninsula, wealthy patients arranged for Lebanese physicians to come treat them for limited periods of time, while relying on hospitals in Beirut—and particularly that of the American university—as a last resort.

Yet no matter how efficiently its hotels, schools, and hospitals were managed, no matter how irresistible the growth of its banking and commerce, or how justified its reputation as the Switzerland of the East, all this still counted for little next to what constituted Beirut's unique and incomparably seductive quality: an atmosphere that gave visitors, provided they came from far enough away, the impression that the entire city lay at their feet—that here was the one place they could truly feel alive.

Beirut, Male and Female

It was on television that Beirut watched the coronation of its queen. On the evening of 24 July 1971, thousands of miles from the shores of the Mediterranean, in Miami, the Lebanese beauty Georgina Rizk was crowned Miss Universe. An event of this kind would surely have made the front page of the newspapers in other countries as well, but there the reader's attention would have quickly moved on to something else. Here the same thirst for recognition that blew the least achievement of any expatriate Lebanese out of all proportion made this evening more than a momentary reason for celebration, converting it into something like the incarnation of a universalist dream, however frivolous the occasion for it may have been. For her fellow citizens, the crowning of a girl from Beirut represented the culmination of a decades-long effort to adapt their lives to the rhythm of the West in every field of endeavor, from the most serious to the most trifling.

The acceptance of Western modernity appeared now to be almost complete. One had only to compare the performance of the country's economy with that of others in the region, or to look around at the metamorphosis—not altogether edifying, it must be said—of the city's landscape. But nothing illustrated the transformation of Beirut better than the changes taking place in daily life. Westernizing influence had begun to make itself felt among the moneyed classes in the second half of the nineteenth century, but by the middle of the twentieth its effects could be perceived at all levels of society. The assimilation of commercial innovations from abroad now occurred more rapidly than before as well. If consumerism made its appearance in Beirut with an inevitable delay following its initial emergence in America, local merchants scarcely lagged behind their European counterparts in seeking to exploit its advantages. The chief consequence of the boom in retail demand, apart from increasing newspaper revenues thanks to the rapid growth in advertising, was to make Beirut the supermarket of the Near East as well as its luxury department store, attracting visitors from the Arabian Peninsula in addition to those from Damascus and Amman.

The Beirut model of consumption owed its persuasiveness not only to the variety of goods on offer but also, and especially, to the atmosphere created by the city's shoppers, who increasingly conformed to the image that cinema, magazines, and television had manufactured of modern man and, to a still greater degree, modern woman. One of the leading figures in this unfolding drama, as one was constantly reminded, had even been recognized in America as the personification of a universal standard of feminine beauty.

THE ARCHETYPE OF FEMININE MODERNITY

Beyond the exaggerated fit of national pride that seized almost all male Lebanese during the election of "their" Miss Universe, from the president of the Republic down to the lowliest taxi driver, this event had a particular significance for Beirut.[1] Suddenly the most beautiful girl in the world was the girl next door. Not only had every man in the city been able to see her with his own eyes, at the beach, in a fashion show, at a sidewalk café, or otherwise in the society pages of the newspaper and in film advertisements; more than this, and notwithstanding Miss Universe's ideal measurements and the perfection of her features, he found her behind the gaze of any number of other young women in Beirut, who likewise stood as archetypes of the liberated Arab woman—objects of endless masculine fantasies, and yet incapable of being reduced to their appearance alone. Miss Universe herself exchanged fame for tragedy in marrying the head of the Palestinian security services, ʿAli Hasan Salameh (Abu Hasan), assassinated in January 1979 in Beirut by a car bomb planted by the Mossad in retaliation for his role in planning the attack on Israeli athletes at the Munich Olympic games.[2]

The case of Georgina Rizk, who had gone from the world of glamour to the rather less comfortable one of Middle East politics, was not unique. Other women from Beirut high society, whether real or fictionalized, testified to the city's penchant for walking along the razor's edge. One thinks of the picture of Beirut found in the extensively researched and comparably misogynistic *SAS: Mort à Beyrouth,* a detective novel by Gérard de Villiers that was published in Paris in 1974; or of the photos of "Lebanese whores"—obvious code words for corruption—scattered throughout a book savagely attacking the government and morality of the house of Saʿud by an opponent of the regime, himself exiled in Beirut.[3] Notwithstanding the many personal histories that mixed the gay laughter of society life with the rage and fury of the latest chapter in an unending Great Game, and the harsh judgments that they inevitably provoked, the women of Beirut were nonetheless responsible for allowing the city to offer something more precious to its neighbors, the example of a modernity whose burdens were assumed in everyday life, seldom without some measure of pain or misunderstanding.

Many obstacles still stood in the way of sexual equality, in the form of overtly paternalistic legal documents as well as unwritten but no less repressive rules. Apart from a small number of female doctors, lawyers, and journalists,[4] the feminization of the workplace remained limited for the most part to low-ranking positions; and with the exception of Myrna Bustani's inherited parliamentary seat, women had not yet succeeded in gaining entry to the Lebanese political arena. But their growing participation in parties, particularly on the left, suggested that change was in the air.[5] The implications of the revolution taking place in the social condition of women despite these constraints, or perhaps because of them, were profoundly political. For in a region of the world where the second sex was often condemned to relive man's past (the black *izar*-clad silhouettes of women visiting from Saudi Arabia and Kuwait were an insistent reminder of this), the freedom of appearance won by more and more women and girls in Beirut amounted, consciously or not, to a pledge of allegiance.

While Cairo had certainly preceded Beirut on the road to female emancipation, notable advances had also been observed in Damascus and Baghdad. In all three places the veil's authority had been lessened under the influence first of Egyptian cinema, and then of Egyptian nationalism, which was imbued with the rhetoric of socialism and, above all, permeated with Kemalism (although Lebanon did not follow Turkey in recognizing the coercive power of the state to the same degree). Until the early 1970s the veil survived in working-class neighborhoods of Beirut as a way of hiding women's hair, along with the closed cloak that covered the entire body, from the shoulders to the ankles; among older Christian women of the lower middle class, the head scarf was still common. Even so, more women dressed in the Western style in Beirut than in any other city in the Levant. The urban landscape was itself modified as a consequence, since men and women could be seen walking side by side on the street, sometimes together in a single group, and almost as many women drove cars as men. The removal of the veil, especially in the more Westernized neighborhoods, left only the benign form of discrimination that, here as in Europe, preferred women in skirts and dresses to those wearing trousers or suits.

The wearing of pants by women blurred gender distinctions as well. As in more advanced societies, the transgression of symbolic boundaries between the sexes ran up against male resistance, which hid behind the dictates of tradition. Fashion nonetheless ended up prevailing, and in the space of two or three years its hold reached well beyond the upper classes through which it had entered Lebanese society, to the point that by the early 1970s a woman's right to wear pants was scarcely contested any longer. The conquest of most of the world by blue jeans during the same period, which Beirut—unlike other countries of the Near East—did not escape, erased gender distinctions among the young still further, and all the more completely as the vogue of long hair for boys popularized by the Beatles and then by the hippie movement also managed to overcome male chauvinist opposition.

The force of convention was no more successful in stopping skirts from getting shorter. From shorts that ended above the knee to the short hemlines of the French designer André Courrèges—the phrase "coupe Courrèges" came to be commonly used in spoken Arabic—to the miniskirt, and then the micromini, skin came to be increasingly exposed, whether or not it was covered by nylon stockings (and later panty hose). Even the uniforms worn in parochial schools reflected the new interest in economizing on fabric, though many girls managed between getting out of class and arriving home to roll up their skirts still higher. The cult of the naked knee did not fail to give rise to comical situations, especially in social settings, where mothers were ready at all times to warn daughters by means of a reproving glance, or a discreet shake of the head, or a pursing of the lips that a little too much thigh could be seen and that the legs should be uncrossed and straightened. For a few seasons, in fact, skirt length was used by some middle-class parents as a basis for evaluating the moral character of their son's prospective fiancée and for giving or withholding their approval. On the streets, by contrast, and particularly in the business and entertainment districts, no inhibition seemed any longer to restrain the baring of skin, unless it was the countervailing shock of the maxiskirt, also popularized by Western fashion. If the willingness of women to expose themselves may have appeared in certain classes of the population as a subversive form of striptease, the speed with which it came generally to be shared had the paradoxical effect of making it seem normal, and so of lessening its supposed indecency. But for those who came from elsewhere it remained one of the most visible signs of Beirut's distinctiveness—unthinkable in any other city of the region, including Cairo, as one can plainly see from Egyptian films of the period, not known for their concern to defend tradition. Indeed it may have been owing to the rule of the miniskirt in Beirut that Egyptian directors now frequently found an excuse for filming in the Lebanese capital.

It was not only the presence of women on the streets of the city or their style of dress that was novel. Forms of sociability were changing as well. Increasingly the sexes mixed together in public from a young age. Coeducation remained limited to a relatively small number of schools, to be sure, notably those of the Mission Laïque Française. But boys and girls were now brought together in extracurricular activities, particularly sports, where they practiced alongside one another. In the city they were allowed to go out together to the movies or to a café, even if girls from respectable families were sometimes accompanied by a chaperone (typically a brother or a male cousin invested with the authority to command obedience, no matter that he may have been younger than the relative whose virtue he was assigned to protect). The restrictions falling upon young women were relaxed somewhat once they reached college age, and going out to nightclubs, though it often meant having to be home by midnight, was no longer exceptional. These changes seemed in any case irresistible, leading most families, willingly or not, to accept the full range of behavior found in pre-1968 Western society. Soon the sexual revolution made its effects felt in the upper echelons of the city's middle class, almost immediately following its advent in Europe. The devotion to virginity remained vigorous among the majority of the population, however, for another fifteen years.[6]

THE PRIMACY OF THE CONSUMER

This change in outlook, whose most spectacular expression was the new way of life open to women, was largely brought about by the sensitivity of Beirut society to outside influences. But it was not only a consequence of the desire, rational or not, to imitate the West. The urge to do as Paris did was still felt, of course, and not only among those who prided themselves on being *au courant;* only now it was something that seemed to go without saying, so sure was it of its own legitimacy. By this point Western modernity had a tradition behind it in Beirut, together with a set of automatic reflexes that enlarged its impact still further. These reflexes were now supplemented by the internalization of yet another foreign impulse: consumerism.

As in Europe, the consumer society burst onto the scene in Beirut as though it were something waiting to happen. Very quickly it made its mark on the urban landscape, notably in the central business district and the new neighborhood of Hamra, both lined with display windows and festooned with neon signs and billboards. It is true that retail commerce had gotten a head start in Beirut. Following the example of the Orosdi-Bak department store, which at the beginning of the century was the first such establishment in the city to be equipped with an elevator, the Byblos Center overlooking the port introduced escalators six decades later. The ABC department store, opened under the Mandate in the heart of the city, had done well enough in the interval to open a branch on Rue Hamra. Other stores specializing in furniture, household appliances, and lighting likewise invested in large showrooms to attract regular customers.

The new habits of consumption were no less perceptible outside the downtown commercial districts. Refrigerators, gas stoves, and washing machines, and later food processors and dishwashers, soon became basic items of household equipment, while the ubiquity of the television antenna signaled the triumph of a new kind of popular entertainment. Although the first supermarkets did not make their appearance until the second half of the 1960s, neighborhood shops felt the need to update their image. Small grocery stores, now better stocked than before, found themselves next to clothing stores offering the latest fashions (designed and made on the premises) and by de luxe hairdressing salons, whose windows were decorated with posters furnished by the importers of cosmetics and beauty products. Already boutiques featuring ready-to-wear fashions for women had begun to relocate to residential neighborhoods from the downtown without fear of seeing their sales drop.

In Beirut as elsewhere, by liberating women from the most thankless household tasks the consumer society had further strengthened its appeal. The time freed up in this way allowed some women to take jobs, which increased the purchasing power of their families and so made their participation in the workforce less objectionable in the eyes of husbands and male relatives. And for the great majority who still did not work outside the home, and especially those who could afford to hire a live-in maid, the hours when the children were in school was filled by occupations that expanded the range of consumption—whether directly in the form of shopping, or indirectly by multiplying the number of occasions for socializing, which called for constant attention to one's appearance. This made it necessary in turn to visit hairdressers and beauticians more often, to say nothing of the need to buy more clothes. As a result of Beirut's physical expansion, the customary morning visit with neighbors or relatives (sobhiyyeh) was now practiced on a metropolitan scale, which often meant having to make a trip by car. Slovenliness was in any case not an option. The afternoon visit was less firmly rooted in tradition, but it required still more in the way of proper attire, even if it was only for a game of cards. Evening visits to private homes made by husband and wife together, though not necessarily in response to an invitation for dinner (at least not among the middle class), furnished yet another reason to be concerned about making the right impression. And when it came to going out at night, to take in a show or to dine at a restaurant, all the stops had to be pulled out, with both partners dressed to the nines—or the nearest thing to it. For women this involved going to the hairdresser beforehand to have their hair put up in a chignon, or, at a minimum, to get a comb-out.

More than anything, women's fashion showed that consumerism was in the process of being democratized. To be sure, the wealthiest still went to Paris to choose their wardrobe for the season. But they could also find satisfaction without leaving home, and without compromising on quality, by shopping at de luxe houses with a proven reputation or by patronizing a few highly regarded local designers,[7] male and female alike, foremost among them Alfred Mehchi, a native of Aleppo, and Ilyas al-Barizi (Ilyas of Paris, a nickname suggested by his French apprenticeship), whose clientele was willing to overlook his reputation as an active Communist. Other more modest artisans reproduced a variety of styles culled from international women's magazines. The growing availability of ready-to-wear clothing broadened demand, with the result that luxury stores dating back to the Mandate were very quickly joined, and challenged, by a legion of boutiques catering to all classes of society. Men and children were served by an equal number of outlets. Despite the decision by some clothiers to move their businesses to residential neighborhoods, most stores were still concentrated in the suqs built in the late nineteenth century near the old western wall downtown, or else on Rue Hamra, Beirut's gleaming new display window. The congestion of these two main shopping centers amplified everything that seemed chaotic about the city and accentuated the impression of a population governed by an irresistible urge to shop.

The car, of course, was another trademark of the consumer society, in Beirut no less than in Cairo, Damascus, or Baghdad. Although automobile traffic was not noticeably heavier than in these places, the noise level in Beirut—intensified by the excessive and nonetheless chronic honking of horns, and the equally disordered whistling of policemen and the hum of idling engines—made it seem more like the other great Arab cities. If a difference could be perceived it was in the variety of vehicles, greater in Beirut than anywhere else, and probably even than in European cities. In the absence of a national automobile industry, brand preference was influenced by the sales strategies of importers, the cost of spare parts, manufacturers' reputations, and, more than anything else, the social status that attached to each model. The most coveted luxury vehicles were a few extremely rare Rolls and Bentleys. Cadillacs, more numerous, followed close behind, while ordinary comfort and convenience was sought in other large American cars of all makes (although after the war of 1967 the importation of Fords was prohibited because of the company's investments in Israel). Some European cars were nonetheless highly prized. Mercedes, which sold in large numbers in later years, were valued at first only for their durability—apart from the prestigious 600 series, of which only one or two examples could be found in Beirut. The social cachet of Mercedes was also diminished by its association with the tarnished image of the run-down communal taxi fleets. In a similar price range, Volvo succeeded for its part in projecting a dual image of reliability and affluence. French cars—Citroën, Peugeot, and Renault—were also well represented; among Italian models, Fiats were very commonly seen. And here as everywhere, the people's car was the Volkswagen bug, though it was to face competition from the little English Minis before Japanese imports changed the face of the market.

Lovers of fast cars could choose from an even more striking variety. The finest Italian sports cars—Ferraris, Maseratis, and Lamborghinis—were by no means exceptional in Beirut. Young drivers looking for Italian style at a much more affordable price favored Lancias and Alfa-Romeos, as well as Fiat coupes. By the 1980s BMWs had become the privileged vehicle for reckless driving in Lebanon, but in the meantime the handling of the Mini Cooper, which lent itself to wildly acrobatic driving in a city of narrow streets—thanks, not least, to the famous hand-brake U-turn—made it also an exciting sports car within the reach of more modest budgets. American cars were not absent from the lower end of this market, however. Both the Ford Mustang, which became still more mythic after the boycott of 1967, and the Pontiac Trans Am, whose purring engine compensated for the massiveness of its lines in the minds of the most flirtatious show-offs, had their share of admirers. And as for motorcycles, the formidable machines made by Kawasaki and Honda were also to be found at the weekly display of horsepower on Rue Hamra, a great showcase for motor sports held every Saturday afternoon.

THE POPULAR PRESS

The money needed to observe the new social rituals was not spent by the upper class alone. In keeping with the basic rule of the consumer society, supply created demand among all classes. Even if the volume of expenditure was necessarily proportional to income, virtually every household had to allocate a part of its budget to buying new clothes and labor-saving appliances, as well as to entertainment. The relatively large size of the middle class in relation to the total population, in both the country as a whole and its capital, was particularly favorable to the exchange of information and therefore to the rapid development of new fashions. Advertising, direct or indirect, did the rest.

The scope of modern consumerism had been multiplied exponentially by the concomitant transformation of the means of communication. With the expansion of the English- and French-speaking worlds in the first decades of the twentieth century, the international press had become a part of everyday life in the Levant, particularly in the case of magazines, whose circulation took off after the Second World War. The French and American newsweeklies, and to an even greater degree the illustrated periodicals and women's magazines, were attentively read in the upper stratum of the middle class. Doctors and dentists were among the many subscribers to *Paris-Match, Elle,* and *Marie-Claire,* which they made available to patients in their waiting rooms.

Local publishers followed suit. In addition to their daily papers, which devoted considerable space to public figures and celebrities, they sought to compete for readers by producing picture magazines of their own. The old *Revue du Liban et de l'Orient arabe,* founded in Paris in 1928 and later repatriated to Beirut, was enlivened by the prominence now given to fashion and scenes from society life, both international and local. A second French-language weekly, founded in 1960 under the rather obvious name *Magazine,* entered this niche of the market in the expectation of being able to profit from the generous advertising budgets of its owner, a major importer of beauty products and luxury merchandise. The formula seemed so promising that a French monthly devoted to illustrating miscellaneous news items, *Le Beyrouthin,* tried its hand at it in the 1970s. A monthly movie review, *Ciné-Orient,* rounded out the field in French. English-language offerings remained much more limited in Lebanon than elsewhere, but the weekly *Monday Morning,* which took its place alongside the *Daily Star* newspaper in the 1970s, looked to have a bright future by mixing political stories with coverage of society in its turn.

The development of periodical publishing during this period was still more remarkable in Arabic. *Al-Sayyad* (The Fisherman), founded by Said Frayha in imitation of Egyptian models, offered a good dose of entertainment news together with political articles. Its appearance marked the beginning of what advertising professionals were later to call the "pan-Arab press," a term justified not by any firm ideological bias in favor of pan-Arabism but by the magazine's audience, which spanned the region. Two other political weeklies edited by ex-Frayha journalists, *Usbu' al-'Arabi* (The Arab Week)—twin brother of the French-language *Magazine*—and *Hawadith* (Events), also counted on an emphasis on personal news to appeal to Arab readers throughout the Middle East and to attract advertising. Yet the most successful example of this style was another title published by Frayha himself, who, in addition to *Sayyad* and his daily paper *Al-Anwar,* launched an entertainment magazine called *Al-Shabaka* (The Net). Known chiefly for its coverage of the world of cinema and Arab song, *Shabaka* established itself as the leader of the pan-Arab press and became the cash cow of Frayha's stable, later enlarged by other specialized monthly periodicals. An-Nahar, another rapidly growing publishing group of this period, looked to diversify in the same direction, albeit a notch below, by introducing *Al-Hasna'a* (Beautiful Woman), a woman's magazine that prided itself on a certain quality of writing while not neglecting pages on fashion and beauty. Other titles, aimed for the most part at a female audience, appeared in the 1970s.

Continuing growth in magazine readership depended on an increasing demand for advertising space, which until now had guaranteed a rapid return on investment. Profitability was further improved by recent advances in printing technology that had immediately been adopted in Beirut. The most important of these was the appearance of four-color offset printing in the 1960s, which made it possible to use color with greater confidence, at least for the front cover and the three pages of advertising that went with it (on the inside front and both sides of the back cover). Creativity in design was encouraged as a result—all the more since an expanding pan-Arab press now began to attract advertising by large multinational firms.

Beyond the prompt sales response sought by the clients of local advertising firms and the revenue growth their placements assured newspapers and magazines, the message conveyed by advertising had a value of its own. This is true everywhere, but in Beirut it had an additional implication: no matter that the consumerism being promoted was modern Western consumerism, by force of repetition readers gradually forgot that it was imported. The norms of luxury, comfort, and beauty diffused by advertising were naturalized to the extent that they seemed to be authenticated by the magazines in which the advertising appeared; and because they shared the same frame of reference, the articles and pictures in local magazines reinforced the assimilation of foreign values and legitimized still further the daily commitment of their readers to the rituals of consumption. Even when the pan-Arab press aimed at a readership beyond Lebanon's borders, it also worked on behalf of local merchants by suggesting to potential tourists that Beirut was the nearest place where anything worth having could be purchased.

A WINDOW ON THE WORLD

To a large extent the world of magazines overlapped with that of film. Since the 1920s cinema had not ceased to be one of Beirut's principal windows on the outside world. A continually expanding supply of movie theaters, without parallel in the Near East, guaranteed that the city's residents would not miss any major Hollywood production, nor anything from Cinecittà in Rome or the Paris studios, nor, quite obviously, anything from Cairo.[8] In the 1950s a number of new theaters appeared on the edge of the commercial downtown, not far from the old Crystal, Opéra, Empire, and Roxy, with names still drawn from a cosmopolitan repertoire: Métropole, Rivoli, Gaumont-Palace, Pigalle, Radio City, Capitol, and so on (the only concessions to Arab memory were the Dunia and the Schéharazade). But it was not only the number of theaters. The quality of their projection equipment and the comfort of their seats assured the best possible conditions of viewing; what is more, foreign films were shown in the original language (with subtitles in both French and Arabic). The widescreen movie format Cinemascope was immediately adopted and spread almost at once to the neighborhood of Ras Beirut, the site of dazzling growth in the 1960s, and more particularly to Rue Hamra, where in the space of a decade a dozen movie theaters appeared. With the exception of the aptly named al-Hamra, the first to open its doors, their neon signs still alluded to the landmarks of the Western imagination: Eldorado, Colisée, Picadilly, Strand, Pavillon, Commodore, Saroulla (named after the wife of a famous visiting American producer),[9] Edison, Clemenceau (on the street of the same name), Orly, Versailles, Étoile, and so on.

This situation did not escape the attention of international distributors. It was not infrequently the case that American films could be seen in Beirut even before they arrived on screens in Paris. Censorship was less severe than in other Arab countries, and films were banned only rarely, although the cuts regularly insisted upon by the censors continued to arouse protest. Fellini's *Satyricon* and Bertolucci's *Last Tango in Paris* were expurgated of their most daring scenes, but they were at least shown, to considerable popular acclaim. Indeed censorship did not prevent frankly pornographic films from being shown in the 1970s, when a few failing theaters sought to revive their fortunes by riding the European wave of sexual liberation; others specialized in Indian or kung-fu films. No taste was left unattended. Even avant-garde films, from Europe and elsewhere, found an audience thanks to the Ciné-club de Beyrouth, a film society sponsored by a quiet theater that otherwise showed Disney films and other American entertainments for children.

Cinema was at once a reason to go out—and therefore an opportunity for shopping—and indirectly an advertisement for consumerist modernity. Whether it was

FIGURE 86. The al-Hamra Cinema, down the street of the same name and to the right.

a question of inspecting the latest automobile models, clothing fashions, or leisure activities, prospective buyers could scarcely do better than consult the vast catalogue of new products found in films, above all ones from Hollywood, where the archetypal figures of modern man and woman had first taken shape. And if viewers were able to find even a few of these products in local stores, as they could in Beirut, they could also believe that their daily lives shared some of the glamour radiated by the stars they saw on the screen. Instead of being authenticated by reality, the cinema came to validate the world around them—and all the more persuasively when the screen reflected images of the very city in which they lived, as in the case of Egyptian films shot on location in Beirut, even if these films ignored the profound social changes that were taking place.

The world that advertising brought to consumers through magazines was magnified even more by television than by the movies. Television was not a local monopoly, of course, but Beirut was the first Arab city where the new medium became available, in May 1959. The distinctiveness of local television came from its programming, stimulated by competition between two broadcasting companies, both of them created, as one might expect, as a result of private initiative. In Egypt, where it was introduced the following year, television was a state enterprise.

The first to begin operation, the Compagnie Libanaise de Télévision (CLT), was

FIGURE 87. An advertisement for Walt Disney's *Cinderella,* opening at the Capitole on Christmas Day 1950, the same day as in the major cities of Europe.

backed in part by French capital and assisted by the French national broadcasting agency, the Office de Radiodiffusion-Télévision Française (ORTF), which regularly sent *coopérants* (young staff members willing to work abroad in lieu of military service) to Beirut.[10] In exchange the CLT dedicated one of its two channels to a French-language station, Canal 9, which rebroadcast programs shown very recently in Paris. The second company, Télé-Orient, had British partners. The rivalry between the two companies coincided with the advent of color: the CLT made the switchover at once, in 1967, choosing the new French analog system SECAM since it was compatible with the bulk of its material; a little later Télé-Orient chose the German PAL system, then in use in Great Britain. This discrepancy posed technical difficulties in reception for buyers of color television sets, but they were not enough to prevent CLT's Arabic-language channel, Canal 7, from collaborating with Télé-Orient to offer the same kind of programming—American television series and films from Hollywood and Cairo, in addition to locally produced variety shows, dramas, and comedy series.[11] Eventually, in December 1977, CLT and Télé-Orient merged to form Télé-Liban (Lebanese Television Company).

Paradoxically, the local programming seemed utterly incongruent with the modern character of the medium. For the most part it consisted of costume dramas set among the desert tents of Bedouin tribes or in a stereotypical mountain village (the like of which could hardly be found anymore), as well as classical Arab tales. Even when the story was contemporary, it was treated in such an impersonal way that any sense of life as it was actually experienced in urban situations remained foreign to it. One of the longest-running series was set in a small country village and featured a couple, supposed to be the embodiment of Lebanese folk wisdom, who passed their time, week after week and year after year, castigating the morally corrupt. Comedies more readily situated themselves in the city, but it was a city outside of time. Neither the popular comedian Shushu, who played the average Sunni resident of Beirut, nor the Syrian team of Durayd Lahham and Nihad Qala'i succeeded in making any connection with the true, constantly changing life of the capital beyond mere allusions to it. It was not until the 1970s that a series would treat, in a comic vein, the shock of modernity felt by a villager on discovering the big city. During the same period ambitious attempts were made at the CLT, under the direction of Paul Tannous, to adapt literary works for the small screen, including *Les Misérables* (in Arabic) and *Femmes passionnées* (Passionate Women), a collection of risqué episodes whose filming was to be interrupted by the war. Though these experiments were not unsuccessful, it nonetheless must be said that television drama for the most part failed to reflect urban experience.

Variety and game shows, along with the fashion and news magazines, did a better job of capturing the vivacity and complexity of the city. On the eve of the war, however, television news departments began to take their cameras out into the street—the young filmmaker Maroun Bagdadi got his start doing this—with a view to documenting the social transformations then underway. Despite the reluctance of local writers and producers to confront the contradictions of contemporary Lebanon, preferring to substitute in its place an idyllic country that never existed, television nonetheless succeeded in changing its audience's view of the world.

But the principal consequence of television in Beirut was that it popularized a universalist conception of modern life. Not even the cinema did more to make this outlook a part of daily routine than American TV shows. Every evening of the week the immersion in American culture was repeated in homes throughout the city, and on a few Sundays every year a "marathon day" of television (the word "telethon" had not yet been coined) permitted the youngest viewers to watch one series after another. Probably the American dream, in the form given it by television, appealed to people in every society that discovered it, but for a society that at the same moment was internalizing the basic principles of consumer behavior, this dream had additional significance: it invited viewers to accept the legitimacy of the changes taking place around them by placing themselves within the frame of reference constituted by the world they saw on television. Foreign advertising further strengthened viewers in the belief that consumption of this or that product guaranteed their access to this world, while the increasingly successful performance of homegrown products imparted a credible local color to it.

The very technology of television, finally, seemed to confirm the veracity of the message conveyed by advertising. Well before the introduction of video and before images transmitted from satellites had become commonplace, the simple fact of being able to show what was happening on the other side of the world, if only with a delay of a few hours or even a couple of days, assured a television news program of a larger audience than any daily newspaper. And to see the familiar faces of journalists from the two Lebanese companies, some of whom also worked for ORTF, reporting and filming interviews abroad gave viewers the impression that they themselves were eyewitnesses to international events. The advent of satellite broadcasting, shortly after the switch to color, only deepened this impression. In Beirut, as everywhere else, the first worldwide broadcast via satellite was unforgettable—for it was nothing less than the first manned lunar landing by Neil Armstrong and Buzz Aldrin in July 1969. Later broadcasts were less spectacular, but no less popular. Whether it was the incomparable World Cup final between Brazil and Italy in Mexico City in June 1970 or the first heavyweight championship bout between Muhammad Ali and Joe Frazier in New York in March 1971, viewers in Beirut could feel with certainty that they were tuned in to the world. But the high point indisputably came later that year: watching the crowning of their queen, direct from Miami, they could believe at last that the world was tuned in to Beirut.

16

The Pleasures of the World

The triumph of the consumer society, already obvious in the case of clothes and automobiles, was completed by a range of leisure activities whose variety was unmatched in the Near East. In addition to cinemas, there was a boom in restaurants, cafés, and nightclubs not only in the new tourist districts of Beirut, but outside the city as well; and with the leisure industry's conquest of the coast and the mountains around the capital, the Beirut model of urban life came to establish itself in the Lebanese countryside.

Thanks to the new rites of sociability and to the growth of the middle class, the risks of investment in this domain were considerably reduced. In addition to a local customer base having substantial purchasing power, the leisure industry could now count on an expanding foreign clientele. Trilingualism was increasingly common, at least among the middle classes and employees of the service sector, protecting visitors from Europe and the United States against any danger of disorientation; and if this facility with Western languages accentuated the sense of being in a foreign place felt by guests from the Gulf, it also sharpened their fascination with an elsewhere that was so near.

Still, the special delight to which Beirut gave rise—at least among those who had the means to experience it—was nourished by something more than the impression that it had been deliberately created for the pleasure of tourists. Beirut was home to people imbued with the Mediterranean taste for comfort, a characteristically Levantine inclination toward cosmopolitanism, and the Arab tradition of hospitality, from which they fashioned a distinctive art of living. All the more completely, then, did the city's charms captivate guests from abroad, some to the point that they chose Beirut as their permanent residence, where they could be sure not only that nothing they desired would be lacking but also that they would enjoy a mixing of cultures without parallel in the Near East.

EATING AND DRINKING

Nothing better embodied this talent for synthesis, which the city had so inventively claimed for itself, than the restaurant business. As the centerpiece of Beirut's entertainment industry, it succeeded not only in modernizing local cuisine, but also in bringing it into creative contact with the other great culinary traditions, almost all of them present in Beirut. French cuisine had been well established for decades, of course, and practiced with more or less fidelity to its source depending on the audience. The classical repertoire was perpetuated by the restaurants of the great hotels and establishments such as Chez Jean-Pierre, which took its place alongside the older Lucullus, founded between the wars. But even the less select brasseries offered beef Stroganoff and stuffed escalopes of veal as plats du jour. French was the standard, indeed the sole language of restaurant menus, even in the case of other culinary cultures. Italian cooking, popularized in the nineteenth century by Battista, the first restaurateur in Beirut, now made a comeback. At a time when the peninsula's cuisine was only beginning to be rediscovered in Europe, it could be appreciated in Beirut, notably at the Spaghetteria and the Romano, both located in the lively neighborhood around the beachfront hotels, and the Bella Napoli at Rawsheh. The same was true for Asian cuisines, then all but neglected outside their homelands but represented in Beirut by Indian and Chinese restaurants, and soon a Japanese restaurant.

Already, however, harbingers of American standardization had begun to appear. Although the fast-food chains had not yet launched their worldwide offensive (with the exception of Kentucky Fried Chicken, which opened a local franchise in the early 1970s), hot dogs, hamburgers, and fried chicken were quickly adopted—and adapted—by café-restaurants, beginning with the aptly named Uncle Sam, across from the entrance to the American University of Beirut, and then by a multitude of street stalls elsewhere. Irrefutable evidence of the American advance could be found in the fact that, except in prestigious restaurants, fried potatoes increasingly looked like the french fries served in the United States. Here, too, they were eaten with lots of ketchup.

Even so, this cosmopolitanism did not affect local tradition. Beirut made the Westerner feel at home while firmly retaining its regional culinary identity for the delectation of guests from nearer places. Indeed one of the principal elements of value added by Beirut was its interpretation of Turkish-Aleppine cooking. Classics of Syrian bourgeois cuisine that until then required a daunting amount of domestic labor were suddenly and readily accessible in restaurants: stuffed vine leaves and zucchini, fisherman's rice (*siyyadiyyeh*, generally served Fridays), *mughrabiyyeh* (a remote though less sumptuous variation on couscous), *mulukhiyyeh* (which skill-fully combined chopped Jew's mallow leaves, rice, beef, and chicken)—these and other dishes became so many plats du jour, even in establishments featuring an international menu.

Where Beirut's syncretism showed its full vigor was unquestionably in the stylized presentation of the extensive selection of hors d'oeuvres known as *mezze* that accompanies the drinking of arak, the anisette of the Mashriq. A growing number of restaurants specialized in the "glass of arak," a modest name that concealed a long ritual during which the table, already decorated with a great many raw vegetables and condiments, is gradually covered with a flurry of small dishes and salads, sometimes more than twenty in all, before the arrival of brochettes and *kebab*—the whole procession being crowned, three hours or more having gone by, by another and scarcely less rich course of desserts and fruits. There was nothing new about the ritual itself, nor about the dishes that marked its observance: mezze are served from Istanbul to Jaffa, with more or less local variation reflecting the diversity of the region's produce and the willingness of diners to be seen drinking alcohol in public. If Beirut impressed a distinctive mark on the practice (relying in part on the contribution of residents from Zahleh, the center of arak culture in the Biqaʿ Plateau), it was less through the incorporation of dishes specific to Mount Lebanon or the disinhibition of its visitors than through the rationalization of the ritual and its embellishment. The elaborateness of each dish, and sometimes the substitution of low-fat ingredients, if not also the elimination of overly specific flavors, which were replaced by ones that were more widely shared (for both the appetizers and desserts), as well as the interior of the restaurants themselves, indistinguishable from establishments serving European cuisine, with waiters wearing bowties and detailed bilingual menus—all this made the mezze served in Beirut a rather plausible piece of exoticism, and one that defenders of culinary authenticity did not really find offensive.[1] Even if purists turned up their nose at what they considered "Syrian cuisine for tourists," its success was such that the cooking of the Turkish-Aleppine region came to be known, thanks to the popularity of restaurants opened by Lebanese expatriates throughout the world, by the generic name "Lebanese cuisine"—a title sometimes claimed by patrons who were themselves Syrian.

Restaurants were only one aspect of a larger industry purveying food, beverages, and related pleasures. From caterers to bars, cafés, and nightclubs, a whole network of venues existed to satisfy the most diverse tastes,[2] including delicatessens and pastry shops specializing in both Oriental and European styles. Viennese pastries had a harder time carving out a niche for themselves alongside French pastries, probably because of local competition from *manʿusheh* (a sort of pizza flavored with thyme) and *kunefeh* (a sweet cheesecake covered with syrup). The Viennese style began to catch on at last in the early 1970s, having managed to create an indigenous brand with the introduction of the thyme croissant—a fine irony since the Viennese tradition of pastrymaking is popularly believed to have had its origins in the second Ottoman siege of the Hapsburg capital in 1683, when crescent-shaped pastries were found in the camp of the Turkish armies following their retreat, along with coffee beans.[3] The profits from both French and Viennese pastries were put to good use by café proprietors looking to diversify their menus.

The cafés themselves had begun to undergo a transformation that enlarged their clientele. Exclusively male bars still existed in the form of the old *qahwat al-qzaz*, where polite behavior was seldom encountered. Other more recent establishments, in the downtown commercial district, were likewise the preserve of working men who had come to the capital from small provincial towns and villages. New cafés appeared, however, where women were seen in increasing numbers, such as La Ronda, on the edge of the downtown, frequented by artists and intellectuals in the 1950s; the Automatique, on Rue Weygand; and the Cosmos, which formed part of the itinerary of shoppers along the same street, in an atmosphere nearer to that of Vienna than that of Paris.

In the 1960s the Roman fashion of the Via Veneto brought the sidewalk café to Beirut, particularly on the corniche along the cliffs of Rawsheh, a gathering place for intellectual adversaries from throughout the Arab world, and in the emerging neighborhood around Rue Hamra. The Horseshoe, a café for writers and intellectuals that opened in 1959 on the ground floor of a glass building that was home to the street's first cinema, was soon joined by the Café de Paris and a Wimpy Bar, as well as Modca and L'Express. From there the mode spread to the new neighborhood of Badaro, where the Manhattan and the Badaro Inn opened their doors, and above all to the holiday resort of Brummana, one of the city's most popular summertime getaways. In addition to serving beers on tap, most of these places were now equipped with machines for making not only Italian espresso and cappuccino, which attracted long lines of customers, but also ice cream desserts.

THE LURE OF THE NIGHT

Even more than its many Western-style restaurants and cafés, Beirut's nighttime landscape set it apart from the other cities of the Near East. Not only did it make greater and more varied use of neon signs than any other Arab metropolis, but it was the only one to offer itself up so willingly to nocturnal revelry. To be sure, most of the city's neighborhoods cherished their tranquility; the silence of the night in these places was broken only by the distant murmur of conversations and the call of the muezzin, softened here and there by the fragrance of jasmine. Were it not for the smells of the sea that were mixed with it, the atmosphere would scarcely have differed from that of Damascus. But one had only to travel a short distance before coming face to face with the frenzy of a city of pleasures, flooded with light. A growing number of bars and discotheques were clustered around two poles, Hamra and the seafront, while the slightly less bustling area around Place des Martyrs offered cheaper forms of entertainment.

Along the water, the Zaytuneh neighborhood had been an early consequence of the city's westward expansion in the nineteenth century, formally recognized by the laying out of Avenue des Français under the Mandate. Its touristic character, already perceptible by the end of the Ottoman period, was confirmed by the construction of the Hôtel Saint-Georges on the edge of Saint Andrew Bay in 1934, and later by the Normandy and the Cercle Français. Popular with British and Australian officers during the Second World War, the many cabarets in this district sought to re-create the ceremonies of the Parisian night with an admixture of oriental sensuality. The most famous of these was the Kit-Kat Club in the Cercle Français, which remained a beacon of nightlife throughout the 1950s, along with ambitiously named neighbors such as the Lido, Eve, and the Black Elephant. Although cabaret culture soon gave way to the superior allure of the modern nightclub, the seafront did not cease to attract night owls during the 1960s and 1970s. The rooms of Zaytuneh had entered into decline by this point, and now welcomed a less exclusive clientele than before, but the bars in the Saint-Georges and the Normandy preserved intact a prestige associated with their dual reputation as political clubs and nests of spies. The night's center of gravity had in any case shifted only two hundred yards to the west, toward Rue de Phénicie—still near the Saint-Georges and just behind the newly opened Phoenicia Hotel, with its great reception halls, its bar looking out into the bottom of the swimming pool, and its elegant restaurant-nightclub, the Paon Rouge (Red Peacock), offering panoramic views of the city.

Rue de Phénicie began its rise with the opening of an upscale nightclub called Les Caves du Roy (The Cellars of the King), or simply Les Caves, a meeting place for Beirut high society and an obligatory watering hole for foreign film stars (Marlon Brando, Brigitte Bardot, and David Niven among them) and other famous personalities. There were revues at places like the Crazy Horse Saloon and Lucky Luke, and music clubs for a younger crowd eager to perform the latest dances, notably the Stéréo-Club and the Épi-Club. There were new restaurants as well, such as the Grenier des Artistes, which attracted a fashionable clientele intoxicated by its atmosphere of Parisian intellectualism.[4] But Anglomania also flourished at pubs that catered to guests staying at new hotels in the vicinity, including the Vendôme, Palm Beach, Martinez, and Cadmos.

The boom on the seafront in ʿAyn al-Mrayseh, beyond Zaytuneh, extended the city's nightlife to its western residential precincts. A little ways up the promontory on Qantari Hill, five hundred yards away as the crow flies, two dance clubs decorated in the latest style, the Flipper and the Flying Cocotte, were joined by an Austrian restaurant and, a little further on, the Cinéma Clemenceau. Beyond ʿAyn al-Mrayseh lay Ras Beirut, the other great center of nocturnal activity. The atmosphere there was more relaxed than on Rue de Phénicie, but no less cosmopolitan at night, with a predominantly Anglo-American element due to the proximity of AUB. Not far from Rue Hamra, across from the Hôtel Napoléon on Rue Jeanne-d'Arc, stood the Mayflower Hotel with its bar, the Duke of Wellington, and nearby a succession of English pubs and American bars (Your Father's Moustache, Mr. Pickwick, the Rose and Crown, Uncle Sam) and two Anglophone discotheques, the Eleven Twelve (later renamed Nine Clouds) and Jack's Hideaway. It was not only the neon signs in Ras Beirut that testified to the rise of Anglo-American influence. From the moment they entered a pub or discotheque, patrons were engulfed by a wave of English, beginning with the background music, typically American and British pop, more rarely jazz. The drinks served there were no less the product of the Americanization of world entertainment: Bloody Marys, Screwdrivers, B-52s, Long Island Iced Tea, and other new cocktails that had supplanted the native arak (though two national beers, Almaza and Laziza, managed to hold their own with the support of several Dutch brands). There was no official closing time in the pubs and bars of Beirut, and, by way of further contrast with England, though not America, the beer was served cold, a concession to the climate.

The neighborhood that had grown up around the American university evidently cannot be reduced to the den of debauchery that both pious citizens and pan-Arab legend claimed it to be. Bookstores were at least as numerous there as cafés and cinemas. And despite a substantial component of tourist-related businesses, it remained a primarily residential district, notable already under the Mandate for the puritanism of the "Protestants of Ras Beirut" and durably strengthened after 1948 by the settlement there of many families of the Palestinian refugee bourgeoisie.[5] With the construction of the first steel and glass office building on Rue Hamra in 1959, however, it had also become a modern business center. The luxury trade was not slow to take its place alongside the large companies headquartered there, leading to a tremendous rise in real estate values. All of this was nonetheless eclipsed in the popular mind by the flights of fancy given wing by Hamra's industries of the night.

The neighborhood was notable not only for the rapidity of its metamorphosis, unique in the Arab world, but also for the fact that half its population was made up of foreigners, attracted by its modern aura.[6] No less than the orgy of neon that advertised its cafés, cinemas, and pubs, and the Western appearance of the women who frequented these places, the magical air of its name conferred upon Hamra a sort of predestination. Probably few people recalled that the place originally took its name not from the Arabic word for the color red, hamra, but from a community of Hamra, or Persians, who passed through some twelve centuries earlier; and even the rival folk etymology connecting the name with the nearby sand dunes, subsequently planted with prickly pears, carries a connotation of reddishness. The name Hamra has the same resonance in Arab ears as the Alhambra of Granada. Beyond the Andalusian analogy, laden with all the many senses of pleasure, some variations on the name, deliberate or not, made such meanings even more explicit. Thus

"Hamra nights" could be confused with "red nights"—a phrase that conjured up an entire universe of lasciviousness in the Arab imagination. Although its suggestiveness was sometimes decried (notably in the tabloid press, where the epithet was used as a synonym for depravity), its strong sensual charge was more often favorably regarded (as in the film of the early 1970s with the deliberately salacious title *Qitat Shariʿ al-Hamra*—The Pussies of Rue Hamra).

The spirit of individualism in this district, which came to be identified in the popular mind with all of Ras Beirut, including the area around Rawsheh, was further attested by the availability of small but well-furnished, and occasionally luxurious, studio apartments.[7] Generally they consisted of two rooms and were rented mostly by well-heeled students enrolled at AUB, but some were occupied by young men from wealthy families who had left home to live in *garçonnières,* or bachelor pads—contributing still further to Hamra's reputation for libertinism.[8]

If the radiant modernity of Hamra and the glittering affluence of Rue de Phénicie stimulated the libido, not all of the city's residents could afford their pleasures. Men from the lower classes had to settle for Place des Martyrs, which by the 1960s had lost most of its former glamour. The cinemas got by in both good times and bad by specializing mainly in Egyptian films, but the hotels were nearer to flophouses now and sandwich shops selling *shawarma* and *falafel* were more numerous than cafés, whose sparse clientele at night only underscored their decline. Although neon continued to illuminate the buildings around the square, it was more often found in commercial advertisements than in signs for entertainment. No matter that the square remained the nerve center of the city by day, by night it more and more resembled the dockside district of a port of call elsewhere in the Mediterranean.

The red-light district, politely referred to in the press by the euphemistic phrase al-Suq al-ʿUmumi (the Public Market) but more often called Suq al-Sharamit (Whores' Market), and sometimes simply the Suq, without any further qualification, had likewise known better times under the Mandate and during the Second World War. It was nonetheless well preserved until the late 1950s, and the house run by Marika Spiridon, the Greek-born madam who had landed in Beirut on the eve of the Great War, still enjoyed its customary preeminence. Here, as at Bianca, all tastes could be accommodated for a price,[9] by white and black girls alike—Greeks, Sudanese, Egyptians, Syrians, and, of course, Lebanese.[10] No less cordial and polite than in the past, the madams nonetheless knew how to command the respect of both their girls and their clients, and could in any case count on the help of the police in getting rid of troublemakers. Surveillance by the authorities was not oppressive. It mainly took the form, inherited from the Mandate, of an obligatory medical examination administered each Thursday under the supervision of the vice squad. Beyond this the madams were in a position to fend off overly zealous inquiries owing to their connections in the political world. It was an open secret, for example, that a former prime minister was in the habit of holding meetings in

FIGURE 88. Vestiges of the
red-light district, following
the "clean-up" of 1983.

Marika's drawing room because his fundamentalist wife did not wish to receive men
she did not know in her home. He was not alone in doing this.

But the age of easygoing tolerance of prostitution was about to come to an end.
Now that urban development held out the prospect of a dramatic increase in real
estate values, the economy came to the rescue of morality. Most of the land on Rue
Mutanabbi was owned by the Maronite Church and a few prominent families, who
hoped to make more honorable and, above all, more profitable use of it. Toward the
end of Camille Chamoun's term in office, political pressures were brought to bear
to block the approval of permits for new brothels, until then a standard procedure
in a system inspired by the one that had prevailed in France prior to Marthe Richard's
successful campaign to close houses of prostitution there in 1946.[11] The new ordi-
nance had an opposite effect from what its sponsors intended, however, so far as
urban development was concerned, since neither the madams nor their girls were

advanced enough in age for the natural extinction of the existing houses to occur anytime soon. The red-light district therefore remained in operation, ceasing activity only with the outbreak of the war in 1975; and it was not until 1983, during a lull in the fighting, that it was demolished. In the meantime, however, prostitution had increasingly been relocated to bars elsewhere in the city, particularly in Zaytuneh, where its profitability depended less on the traffic in flesh than on the consumption of alcohol that hostesses were responsible for encouraging.

THE WORLD OF SPORT

Beirut was obviously much more than the path to perdition decried by some and praised by others. Other, arguably healthier pleasures enriched the city's quality of life. The temperate climate and the still relatively unspoiled natural environment of the coasts to the north and the south, as well as in the mountains to the east, lent themselves to the pursuit of leisure activities and outdoor life. Although the development of holiday resorts outside the city took away many of its guests during the summer, Beirut's proximity to them made it all the more appealing as a tourist destination. And the growing interest in both land and water sports, some of them unknown in the rest of the Near East, helped to throw the Westernized atmosphere of the capital, and of Lebanon in general, into even greater relief.

Apart from a great sports complex, constructed on the outskirts of the city under Chamoun's presidency—and named after him—to host the Pan-Arab Games in 1957, the city itself was poorly equipped with facilities, and competitive opportunities remained limited on the whole. As a result, young athletes from the working classes tended to prefer sports that required scarcely any investment, such as wrestling and weightlifting—the only two disciplines in which Lebanon won Olympic medals during this era, at Helsinki (in 1952) and Munich (in 1972), respectively. Boxing had less success, though the career of Cassius Clay, later known as Muhammad Ali, aroused enthusiasm in Lebanon, as in other Arab countries. Cycling, deprived of the luster it had enjoyed under the Mandate, had entered a period of stagnation. In the schools and, to a still greater extent, the villages outside the capital, a rather fast-paced form of volleyball predominated, until finally being overtaken by basketball. Here as elsewhere, of course, soccer could boast of an almost universal following, particularly during televised international competitions, though the poor state of local fields and a lack of professional leagues prevented Lebanese teams from advancing beyond regional play. On the edge of sport, horseracing succeeded in maintaining its special position, for Beirut continued to be the only city in the Arab East to have a racetrack. But the track was no longer the stylish meeting place of years gone by, when it attracted rich Damascenes in addition to local worthies. With the exception of the stable owners, members of the upper class tended to stay away to the extent that racing had become a more popular pastime in the interval; gambling at the casino now seemed more attractive than betting on the horses. Professional wrestling enjoyed a brief vogue in the most Westernized circles, but it more nearly resembled the entertainment of the old music hall than true athletic competition.

All these activities clearly benefited from the accelerating pace of modernization in Lebanese society. By a paradox typical of Beirut's fondness for surface appearances, however, it was those sports which lacked a popular base of support that most revealingly emphasized the city's unrivaled status in the Near East. A comparison of the sports pages of the French-language press, which attracted an affluent readership, with those of the Arabic newspapers is especially telling in this regard. While the French papers did not fail to report on the various ball sports, much less the rare international successes of local athletes, they accorded a disproportionate place to sports practiced by a small minority—alpine skiing, golf, riding, tennis, automobile racing, track and field, and various water sports—not because performances in these were any closer to the world level, but because the prestige that attached to them strengthened the social elite in its impression of belonging to the world shown in glossy magazines.

In the winter, skiing provided an incontestable affirmation of class status, as well as a proof of Lebanon's topographical exceptionalism. Together with the Cedars resort in the north of the country, the slopes of Kisrawan and the Matn, nearer to Beirut, were outfitted with trails and chair lifts. The village of Farayya, in particular, reproduced the posh neighborhoods of the capital in microcosm, with its more or less Swiss chalets, its inns and nightclub, and its Francophone exclusivity. A still more elitist recreation was playing golf at the club near the airport in Beirut, where Anglo-Saxon visitors were more numerous on the greens than members, or riding at the Turf Club, whose school, long the only one in the country, admitted only children from wealthy families (in Syria, by comparison, equitation developed a little later through officer clubs).

Tennis, although more widely played, was not more democratic. With the exception of the country's top singles player, a former ball boy, the players who entered amateur competitions all came from privileged backgrounds. Despite growing interest in the sport, due in part to exhibition matches underwritten by large companies that attracted ranked players on the international circuit, courts were few, all of them outdoors, and open only to those who were able to pay prohibitively high fees. The new sport of car racing functioned along similar social lines: in the absence of corporate sponsorship, the hill climbs and rallies that began to gain in popularity in the late 1960s required drivers to pay a substantial entrance fee, part of which went to improving the performance of their cars. Not even track and field escaped the rule of social hierarchy: except in long-distance and cross-country events, the majority of the champions came from the upper middle and upper classes, and the country's two principal clubs were affiliated with local parochial schools, Champville, run by the Marist brothers, and the Jesuit college of Notre-Dame de Jamhour, whose stadium was the first to be equipped with an all-weather synthetic track.

But it was in the rise of water sports that the pronounced Westernization of tastes in Beirut could most clearly be seen, as well as the time-lag that accompanied it. Here the lines of social division were clear: ocean swimming and cliff-diving competitions at Rawsheh were the province of the Beirut working class, and more specifically the Sunni youth of the coastal neighborhoods, whereas waterskiing, yachting, and competitive swimming in twenty-five-meter pools were reserved for the upper classes. For the most part the local champions in swimming and water polo were sons of good Christian families, though in the early 1970s young men from other social and religious backgrounds began to make their mark.

Still more restricted was the circle of enthusiasts for waterskiing and sailing, which could be enjoyed only by members of the Saint-Georges Yacht Motors Club, associated with the hotel of the same name. The international waterskiing competitions that took place there during the 1950s had more to do with society than with sports, at least in the eyes of the public, notwithstanding that at one of them a Lebanese was crowned world champion. The construction of a marina at Kaslik, as part of the government's program for developing Kisrawan, the native region of President Fuad Shihab, enlarged the possibilities for sailing in the late 1960s, but not the number of people who took advantage of them. In a gesture typical of Lebanese inegalitarianism, the entire complex was constructed with public funds, its docks, Olympic swimming pool, tennis courts, and restaurant being leased by the government for ninety-nine years to the Automobile and Touring Club of Lebanon (ATCL), which accepted new members—lifetime members—only a few at a time.

THE BEACH IN THE CITY

The elitism of water sports nonetheless did not curb the growing interest in swimming and the related devotion to sunbathing, which now assumed the dimensions of a social and urban phenomenon. Having first appeared between the wars, it gave rise to a striking expansion in the number of beach resorts—no longer a playground solely for the inhabitants of the coastal neighborhoods and visiting foreigners. Here again Beirut was able to exploit what made it distinctive by comparison with the other cities of the region. The Syrian littoral around Lataqiyya offered a few fine beaches, to be sure, but the absence of facilities prevented it from accommodating a large number of vacationers. Alexandria's star had begun to dim, and 'Aqaba, on the Red Sea, quite far from the centers of Jordanian settlement, attracted only a small fringe of local society. Moreover, in all these countries the residents of the capital had to make plans and reservations well in advance of going on a seaside holiday. In Beirut, by contrast, one had only to travel a few miles to the edge of the city in

FIGURE 89. The Sporting Club near the cliffs of Rawsheh.

order to find safe, sandy beaches, or else to enjoy one of the swimming pools that had been built in the coves on the western coast of the promontory. For most people it took no more than ten minutes to get from the office to somewhere for a swim.

As in the 1930s, the bath club at the Saint-Georges, to which a small marina had been added in the meantime, and the private bungalows at the Saint-Simon continued to be favored by Beirut high society, at least until the opening of the ATCL at Kaslik. The other facilities that opened near the Saint-Georges in 'Ayn al-Mrayseh at about the same time remained popular as well. In addition there was the Sporting Club, established by a Palestinian entrepreneur in the shadow of Rawsheh, which became the preferred haunt for intellectuals and upper-middle-class professionals, and later the Long Beach Club, which, with its three swimming pools and its family atmosphere, helped to inaugurate a trend toward democratization. Owned by a local Sunni family, it opened up the sea to ordinary wage-earners, in spite of its restrictions to entry and membership fees; and although its clientele was mixed from the religious point of view, it was notable especially for providing the Muslim middle class with access to water sports. At the western point of the promontory, the bath club of the Riviera Hotel attracted a more cosmopolitan clientele, like the swimming pool of the Carlton, to the south, which compensated for its greater distance from the sea by a singular panorama overlooking Rawsheh and the reputedly dangerous public beaches of Ramlet al-Bayda.

Still further to the south, beyond the Coral Beach Hotel on the edge of the city, which also featured a bath club and swimming pool, there began a series of private sand beaches. Stretching from the Côte d'Azur to the Beach Club, past the pioneering Saint-Simon and Saint-Michel, as well as the Acapulco and Riviera Beach hotels,

FIGURE 90. The Saint-Simon beach, in the early 1960s.

the southern coastal strip of seaside resorts extended as far as Khaldeh. Things were different to the north, where the beaches running from the city along the littoral of the Matn were interrupted by the planned expansion of the port. Only beyond the cliff that guarded the outlet into the sea of the Nahr al-Kalb did touristic entrepreneurialism again manifest itself, and then only intermittently. The Holiday Beach, at the mouth of the river; the Lagon on the shore at Junieh; Tabarjah Beach, an almost instant sensation in the vicinity of the Casino (soon—thus the price of success—overlooked by the massive construction site of the Aquamarina); further on the King Barjis and the Santa Teresea Playa, just outside Byblos—all of these, a mere half-hour by car from the capital, signaled the terrific explosion of beach resorts that during the war to come was to develop the economy of Kisrawan and destroy its natural surroundings.

Along the coastline in Beirut itself, the ecological damage was for the moment limited, and in any case less severe than the havoc being wrought in the rest of the city. But beyond the deleterious effects of development on the environment, the excessive (and indeed illegal) privatization of the shore blocked poorer citizens' access to the sea while at the same time advertising its charms to them. As a result, the least advantaged had to settle for Saint-Gratuit—the unmonitored stretch of coastline at Ramlet al-Bayda, where drownings were frequent until a short-lived "public beach" was established there in the early 1970s—or the pebbled shore of

Junieh. But the crowds of vacationers who invaded these free beaches and coves every Sunday during the summer, covering them with garishly colored umbrellas, testified at least as forcefully as the elite membership of the closed clubs to the growing popularity of seaside bathing and the central place that the Mediterranean now held in the lives of the city's inhabitants.

The conquest of the coast was accompanied by a transformation in social behavior. During the warm months the beach also served as a café and restaurant, and all the more readily as it was not very far from downtown. A great many people took advantage of their lunch break to go out for a dip before coming back to the office, and still more used the half-workday, in effect from July to September, as an occasion to spend the afternoon in the sun. Sporting a tan was now de rigueur— and was something more than a simple matter of fashion. The aesthetic reversal brought about by the worship of the sun had important social implications: until then a pale complexion was considered one of the conditions of a good marriage. Going to the beach gradually became established as an annual rite of spring, so that lounge chairs began to fill up with the arrival of mild weather, sometimes in late March but otherwise in April. The tanned body also had to be a slender body, of course, in keeping with the canons of beauty propagated by the movies and fashion magazines, and quickly embraced by the city's residents. Among women, as a direct consequence of the worldwide vogue of the bikini, until recently regarded with suspicion in Beirut, dieting was willingly submitted to. This led to a general acceptance of the archetype of the modern mermaid, at once svelte and voluptuous, which in its turn reinforced the capital's glamorous image. Now that the beach was only a few steps away from the office or shopping it became common to see light sundresses worn in town during the week. Combined with the spectacular response to the miniskirt in the late 1960s, and then to shorts, the summertime unveiling of the female body by the sea and on the way there had the effect of making freedom of appearance for the women and girls of Beirut one of the most powerful emblems of the modernism in which, consciously or not, the collective identity of the city was rooted.

CITY IN THE COUNTRY

Under these circumstances, the advantages of Beirut's physical situation were more than ever identified with its location between sea and mountain—the inspiration for a Lebanese tourism slogan that invited visitors to go snow skiing in the morning and water skiing in the afternoon. Strictly speaking, this was possible only for a few days in March and April every year. And yet it was during the summer months that the conjunction of sea and mountain came most fully into play. The expansion of vacation resorts in the near foothills, far from adversely affecting the tourist industry of Beirut, only served to enhance its appeal. The visitor could relax in a benign climate and enjoy superb panoramic views while still being able to regularly come down to the city for its nightlife. For the residents of the capital themselves, the early onset of warm weather made it possible to divide one's time between the sea and the mountains for almost half a year. For many middle-class families it was customary to spend May and June at the beach and the rest of the summer in the mountains. Others preferred to stay a longer time in the city, passing only two or three weeks—generally during the month of August—at an inn in the mountains. Both the school calendar and office hours were still determined by the rhythm of the seasons. Schools opened their doors again only in October, and during the month of June classes followed a half-day schedule, allowing students to go to the beach in the afternoon. In the workplace, civil servants had the right to work half-days throughout the year and private-sector employees from July to September, which left plenty of time to enjoy a late lunch by the sea or in the mountains. Retail businesses did not have the same liberty, of course, but some did not hesitate to close for two weeks in the middle of August. In any case the foothills were not far away, and shopkeepers could always get on the road in the early evening and spend the night in the cool air of the higher elevations. The same ease of moving back and forth between city and country enabled families from Beirut to break up their three-month vacations with a day at the beach from time to time.

The now familiar practice of summering in the mountains, where Lamartine was long ago the first to discover the Switzerland of the Levant, increasingly had an urban feel. If many of the capital's newer residents took advantage of the summer season to go back to their native villages, a greater number of vacationers were now prepared to overlook their provincial origins and congregate in a dozen or more villages so near to Beirut that they were known as "folding suburbs,"[12] opening and closing almost on fixed dates of the year. On the last Sunday of June, or the first of July, the roads leading out of the city were choked by streams of small trucks weighed down with furniture and household appliances—a sight that was repeated in the opposite direction at the end of September, when resorts that had been completely booked up for three months were emptied in the space of one or two days. Apart from the patrician families of Beirut, long accustomed to maintaining a secondary residence in the mountains, and emirs from the Arabian Peninsula who had purchased villas there, most visitors rented more or less large houses for the summer, or else apartments in buildings three or four stories high, seldom more. The tourist industry obeyed a similar schedule. With the exception of a few hotels, the management of inns, cafés, restaurants, and even cinemas was taken over for the season by people who did the same thing for a living in Beirut the rest of the year. The city in the country lacked almost nothing in the way of amenities, other than luxury shops, although even these began to migrate from the capital to the most exclusive holiday resorts in the early 1970s.

This enlarged version of Beirut that came into existence each summer developed

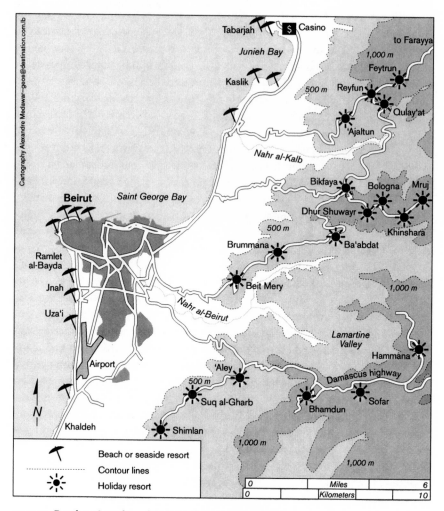

MAP 11. Beaches, Seaside and Holiday Resorts around 1970

along four main axes. The oldest was the Beirut-Damascus road, along which Sofar had welcomed vacationers since the late Ottoman period, later joined by ʿAley, in the foothills, under the Mandate. Between these two, the village of Bhamdun experienced a tremendous boom around its old railway station and, like ʿAley, particularly attracted summer visitors from the Arabian Peninsula. In the same neighborhood, Suq al-Gharb likewise grew in size, while retaining a more rustic atmosphere than ʿAley, and Shimlan, renowned for its "spy school" (where American and British officials learned Arabic), appealed chiefly to the Anglophone intelligentsia that had settled around the American University of Beirut. On the northern side of the highway, Hammana boasted exceptional views looking out onto Wadi Lamartine, the valley popularly associated with the French poet. In addition to the agreeableness of the climate and the ease of getting there, the confessional integration that characterized this entire region, where Druze and Christians lived side by side, was an important element in its success as a tourist destination—though, in attracting the Sunni middle class of Beirut as well, the area around ʿAley set itself apart from the other three centers in the Matn and Kisrawan, where Christian vacationers were clearly predominant.

The cluster of resorts adjoining the Beirut-Damascus road was followed during the time of the Mandate by a second one that developed first around Bikfaya and Dhur Shuwayr in the Matn mountains, and then extended eastward to Bologna (the "Bois de Boulogne," as it was locally known), Mruj, and Khinshara. An abundance of parasol pines was the principal attraction in this area, though Bikfaya and Dhur Shuwayr relied also on cafés, restaurants, and cinemas to bolster their appeal. The transplantation of the city to the country came to be most fully achieved by a third pole, also in the Matn, consisting of the villages of Beit Mery, Brummana, and Baʿabdat. A quarter of an hour from Beirut (no further away than ʿAley), Beit Mery had the advantage of being served by a road that, because it carried fewer trucks, was thought to be less dangerous. Its proximity to the capital caused it eventually to become a permanent suburb, whose cachet was significantly added to by the settlement there in the late 1950s and the early 1960s of some of the leading names of Beirut society. Kamil Muruwwah, the owner of the newspaper *Al-Hayat* and a man famous throughout the Arab world, was the first to build a home in Beit Mery. He was followed by the no less illustrious Ghassan Tuwayni, the proprietor of *An-Nahar*, who, with his wife, the poet Nadia Tuwayni, formed one of the most socially prominent couples in Beirut, and by a small group of Kuwaiti notables who preferred to keep their distance from their compatriots in Bhamdun. The construction of the al-Bustan Hotel, which unlike the other hotels in the mountains was to operate year round, announced Beit Mery's impending transformation into a wealthy suburb of the capital, though its primary function as a holiday resort was never to be abandoned. Yet once summer arrived it was the neighboring commune of Brummana that most resembled an urban neighborhood in a rural setting. Brummana was the first place in the mountains to offer restaurants serving French food that were open twelve months a year, and its sidewalk cafés lining the main street, together with a nightclub, made it a sort of Hamra beneath the pines, whose joyful noise was swallowed up a few miles further on by the rustic quiet of Baʿabdat.

The creation of an urban environment in the mountains, especially at Brummana, was imitated a short time later in Kisrawan. There, as a consequence of the regional development policy promoted under Fuad Shihab, a fourth hub of holiday resorts came into existence in the second half of the 1960s. On the road leading to the ski resort of Farayya, the villages of ʿAjaltun and Feytrun offered a tranquil residential atmosphere; between them, the communes of Reyfun and Qulayʿat sought to follow the example of Brummana by arranging sidewalk cafés and restaurants along a broad ring road. Here, however, there were obstacles to reproducing the denominational richness of the city. Unlike the area around ʿAley, marked by a mix of Druze and Christians, and even in the Matn, breeding ground of the two great Lebanese secular parties, where several Christian sects—Maronites, Greek Orthodox, and Greek Catholics—cohabited with a small Protestant community affiliated with the English Quaker boarding school in Brummana and the Druze minority of Beit Mery, Kisrawan was exclusively Maronite. It attracted mainly middle-class Maronite families, whose roots in Beirut were recent for the most part; consciously or not, the experience of passing the summer among one's own people tended to strengthen a sense of communal identity that was apt to be frayed by the strains of urban coexistence. Other less traditional norms of behavior nonetheless somehow succeeded in establishing themselves, notably with regard to relations between old and young and between the sexes.

Far from amounting to a simple return to nature that glorified the virtues of rural life, the modernization of the summer resort industry amplified the Beirutization of Lebanon. This was true literally to the extent that these great bands of folding suburbs enlarged the capital beyond the promontory on which it had been perched until now, intensifying the overconcentration of population in a single metropolitan area that was the distinguishing feature of the country's human geography. And just as the other cities of the country were eclipsed by Beirut, more distant resorts such as Ehden in the north and Jazzin in the south saw their business contract in the face of the preference for summering in the suburbs of the capital. But this Beirutization also had a symbolic dimension, to the extent that imported fashions, once domesticated in Beirut, were now able to be elaborated and varied on an increasingly large scale.

Beirutization in both these senses was further emphasized by the urbanization of the northern coast, largely under the influence of the tourism industry. The Casino du Liban, opened in 1959 on a hillside overlooking Junieh Bay to the north, in Maʿameltein, seemed to be an outcrop of Beirut. Granted a monopoly over gambling throughout Lebanon, and equipped with an "Ambassadors' Room" where Las Vegas–style revues were presented, as well as a theater having the largest stage in the country, it very quickly became a popular nighttime destination as work on the northern highway progressed. Restaurants and bars soon sprang up in the vicinity, notably Tziganes, a club with a French name (meaning "Gypsies") and a reputation for lewd behavior that attracted a young, wealthy, music-loving crowd.[13] The gradual appearance of several seaside resorts stimulated the city's centrifugal impulse to a still greater degree. Increasingly Beirut lay beyond its own borders.

A DESTINATION FOR THE INTERNATIONAL JET-SET

Beirut's extrovert style of life was best appreciated by visitors. The cosmopolitanism that was visible in every domain, from cars to clothing, to say nothing of the rapid adoption of European and American musical fashions, was not only ramified by its exportation beyond the city's limits; it was validated by the presence of foreigners who had come to live permanently in Beirut. Foreigners had never been absent since the beginning of its rise in the nineteenth century, of course, and both the Mandate and the Second World War had a multiplying effect in this regard. But the city's charms were never more seductive than during the three decades of rapid economic growth following the war. The extinguishing of Alexandria's flame only revealed Beirut's cosmopolitanism to greater advantage, and this at a moment when the anti-Westernism encouraged by the Soviet Union in Egypt, Syria, and Iraq assumed the form of a sort of moral Jacobinism unsuited to the display of hospitality.

And yet the foreign community in Beirut had deep roots. The principal element was the Levantine French, some of whom had settled there even before the Mandate period, alongside more or less arabized families of Italian and Greek origin. With the nationalization of businesses and industries in neighboring countries after the Second World War, another wave of French and Italians came from Syria and Egypt, just as French-speaking White Russians had come to Beirut after the first. From an even earlier date the two great universities had contributed to the formation of an international community by hiring professors from abroad, French in the one case, British and American in the other, who often chose to stay, causing English to be widely spoken in Ras Beirut. With the economic boom of the postwar period, the world of commerce attracted more newcomers. In addition to the French dynasties that had long been active in the city, there was an influx of Western businessmen and other professionals, particularly bankers but also hotel managers, oil engineers, and, in later years, broadcasting technicians.

Around this core of permanent residents, a second and larger circle was constituted by the regular visitors for whom the city was an obligatory, or simply a convenient, stopover on the way to other places—beginning with airline flight crews. The importance of Beirut as a regional hub, served by almost every international airline, guaranteed the daily presence in its hotels and bars of a foreign population that was all the more emblematic of a change in popular attitudes as the pilot and airline hostess embodied the quintessence of glamour during this period; indeed many families made Sunday outings to the airport to take in the spectacle of planes landing and taking off. Less frequent but no less closely associated with this image of openness were the visits of the foreign correspondents of the international press, who felt almost obliged to pass through Beirut between assignments. While enjoying the pleasures of a capital whose way of life was freer than elsewhere in the region, notably around the bar at the Saint-Georges, they could nonetheless justify over-drawing their entertainment accounts on the ground that Beirut provided an un-matched vantage point for surveying regional politics, and that in fact they were likelier to make a scoop there than on the front lines of a battle zone. Similarly, many businessmen traveling in the Near East looked to combine business and pleasure there, hoping in this way to spare themselves the risk of a doubly dry stretch in neigh-boring countries. Western expatriates living in the Arabian Peninsula, on the other hand, needed scarcely any professional excuse for passing a few days in Beirut. Like Peter O'Toole, who came to unwind there during the filming of *Lawrence of Arabia* in Jordan, many less famous people took short vacations there as well, break-ing up long periods of asceticism in a socially conservative desert environment by drunken weekends in the Lebanese capital whenever possible.

And yet mass tourism remained unknown. With the exception of regular visits by Mediterranean cruise ships and a few brief organized tours to the ruins of Baal-bek and other archeological sites, Lebanon drew only a scattering of middle-class European tourists. There were few three-star hotels, and the two-star establishments around Place des Martyrs were badly run down. Another obstacle was the absence of great expanses of sand beach, outside the private seaside clubs. Lebanon was far-ther from Western Europe than either Spain and Greece, too, which meant that get-ting there was more expensive as well. In any case it was not in a position to profit from the vogue for beach vacations that in the 1960s attracted the European mid-dle class to the Costa del Sol and the islands of the Aegean Sea, and it was not until the 1980s that the Near East was to gain a substantial share of cultural tourism. Though Beirut was a stopping point for hippies on their way to Katmandu (helping to spread the reputation of Lebanese hashish around the world), its image as a mod-ern capital of glittering exoticism depended on luxury tourism, which was sustained in large measure by wealthy and longer-term visitors from the Arabian Peninsula.

In bringing more or less well-known figures of European high society to Beirut, along with stars of international stage and screen, this form of tourism built upon a habit acquired during the Mandate when the city emerged as a Levantine pole of the "Other France," more remote than the metropolises of North Africa. Eminences of the Paris social scene were assured of finding respectable companions there, many of whom were already known to them. The intimate acquaintance of Beirut's patri-cian families with European social life, forged in the early part of the century and expanded during the interwar period, was an effective form of publicity. In the af-termath of the Second World War, *le Tout-Beyrouth* scored a great success when one of its young lions, Georges 'Arida, managed to buy Adolf Hitler's yacht, put up for auction by the British, and brought it to its new home port with the intention of rent-ing it out as a cruise ship to a select list of wealthy clients.[14] Ultimately the enterprise foundered on the yacht's high maintenance costs, but it had been widely advertised in the meantime, helping to create an image of great riches that gave Lebanese ty-

FIGURE 91. President Chamoun and his wife flank the king of Saudi Arabia; to the right, a future president, Charles Hélou.

coons a peripheral place among cosmopolitan celebrities. This image was further enhanced in the 1950s by the prestigious state visits made during Chamoun's presidency by crowned heads enjoying an exalted status in international society, notably Mohammed Reza Shah Pahlavi of Iran and Paul, King of the Hellenes.[15] Owing, too, to the brilliant figure cut by the country's very Anglophile president and his wife, Zalfa Chamoun, herself partly of English descent, the impression was reinforced not only that Lebanon was a friend of the West during the cold war, but that it constituted a rare Western outpost in the Near East.[16]

With the development of air travel, and especially after the advent of jet service, the ease of going to and from Beirut helped to deepen friendships established with people throughout the Mediterranean. In the 1960s the trip from Paris took only four hours aboard a comfortable Caravelle, scarcely an hour more than it took to reach Athens. Royally received by their hosts in lavish residences and entertained in elegant restaurants and fashionable clubs, inevitably with a detour to view the Roman ruins at Baalbek—all this against the background of conversations of the greatest courtesy in French or, as it sometimes happened, English—visitors to Beirut might well have imagined they were guests at a posh vacation resort somewhere in Europe. There was nothing in the least odd about this—had not Europe been born, they were asked between glasses of champagne, on the ancient shore of Phoenicia? By a fitting reversal, it was now on this same shore that Europe each year crowned the young woman who was supposed to embody her: for a decade, from 1959 to 1969, Miss Europe was chosen at the Casino du Liban, at the end of a competition that did much to advance the cause of national tourism.[17] And in 1964 the thirtieth anniversary of the Bal des Petits Lits Blancs, sponsored by a French charity for hospitalized children, was held in the courtyard of the palace at Beiteddin.[18] Strictly speaking, these great moments in the life of Lebanese high society did not have the capital for their backdrop, but Beirut profited from them nonetheless, if only because it fell to its hotels to take care of the many foreign visitors.

The same was true, in a more sophisticated vein, with regard to the Baalbek Festival, which between 1956 and 1974 stood out as the main cultural event of the year in Lebanon, and whose reputation very quickly spread beyond the country's borders. The popularity of such festivals, propagated by the success of the first ones at Avignon and Aix in France, had not yet reached the Provençal, Italian, and Tunisian coasts of the western Mediterranean, and it was not uncommon for European visitors to make a special trip to Baalbek, where the temples of Jupiter and Bacchus formed an imposing setting for a program of memorable performances. Subsidized by the state since Chamoun's term in office, with additional support from the private sector, the festival presented year after year an impressive roster of artists of the first rank—among them Mstislav Rostropovich, Sviatoslav Richter, Ella Fitzgerald, Rudolf Nureyev and Margot Fonteyn, Herbert von Karajan, Merce Cunningham, the New York experimental theater company La MaMa, Joan Baez, and Umm Kulthum. The 1974 edition of the festival, which no one at the time knew would be the last before the fires of war were put out, featured the world premiere of a production inspired by Louis Aragon's book of poems *Le fou d'Elsa,* staged in the presence of the author with scenery by André Masson.[19] But Baalbek was only a momentary diversion. However stirring the shadows cast by the Roman vestiges may have been, the festival goers—drawn mainly from Beirut society, with the addition of a certain number of affluent foreigners—hastened to return to the capital or a nearby mountain resort for supper after the end of the show. The surrounding region was hardly equipped to handle the influx of visitors, much less to benefit from the money they were prepared to spend on meals and accommodations: the old Palmyra Hotel, built at the beginning of the century, could put up the artists themselves only for the night of their performance (and then only if they were not too many), and the number of rooms at the Kadri Hotel in Zahleh and the Park Hotel in the mountain town of Shtaura, on the Baalbek road, remained limited. Yet again Beirut profited from an event that took place elsewhere: although more than three hours distant from Baalbek, its hotels provided lodging for the performers and foreign visitors for most of their stay. It was also in the capital, or in one of its summer encampments in the mountains, that the guests who came to Baalbek were honored by Beirut high society in a succession of brilliant evenings and suitably sumptuous lunches.

FIGURE 92. A poster for the 1966 Debutantes' Ball.

In addition to the briefly remembered young women who held the title of Miss Europe and the lastingly famous artists who performed at Baalbek, many other figures of international renown passed through the hotel lobbies of the capital, which had now become a regular stop on the jet-set circuit. The frequent visits of film stars and musical performers, in particular, gave local audiences the impression that Beirut occupied a privileged place among the theaters of the world. Carrying on a tradition that dated back to the time of the Mandate, almost all the great names of French *chanson* came to town, often staying longer than their contractual obligations required. With the exception of Johnny Hallyday, whose engagement was cancelled by the minister of the interior as part of a campaign to ban popular Western dances such as the Twist, all these stars—among them Jacques Brel, Juliette Greco, Charles Aznavour, Gilbert Bécaud, Mireille Mathieu, Tino Rossi, Georges Moustaki, Serge Reggiani, Catherine Sauvage, and Dalida—seem to have enjoyed their visit, at least to judge from the many photos scattered about the city's restaurants and nightclubs. Movie actors included David Niven and Françoise Dorléac, who came to film *Where the Spies Are* (1965); Mireille Darc, starring in Georges Lautner's *La grande sauterelle* (1967); and Richard Roundtree, Max von Sydow, and Marie-José Nat, in *Embassy* (1972), a premonitory film in view of the difficulties that American diplomacy was to experience in Lebanon in the near future. Two years later Roger Moore was scheduled to shoot the James Bond film *The Man with the Golden Gun* there, but already the political situation was judged to be dangerously unstable by the producers, and a substitute location was found. Other stars came simply to promote a film, unless they had been invited to vacation there by a well-connected Lebanese acquaintance. Marlon Brando was one; another was Brigitte Bardot, accompanied on her first visit to Beirut by her husband at the time, Gunter Sachs, and subsequently by her new companion, Omar Sharif, whose family came from Zahleh, less than two hours away. There were many others.

Beirut was also, and especially, a destination for the Arab jet set. Saudi emirs were frequent visitors, both during and after the tourist season. The same was true for Egyptian movie stars, whether they came to shoot a film or for a short vacation. At a time when Gamal Abdel Nasser was engaged in a test of strength with the petromonarchies of the Gulf, Beirut was the only place, outside of meetings of the League of Arab States, where Arabs could talk to Arabs.

Whether they were Arab, European, or American, these visitors obviously could not see everything. It comes as no surprise that they should have left with a misleadingly idyllic picture of the city, deaf to the antagonisms that now rumbled beneath the surface and blind to the dangers that were beginning to gather on the horizon. For Beirut managed to pull the wool over everyone's eyes. It is an extraordinary paradox, but one altogether revelatory of a country where the well-being of a few was so dearly paid for, that its capital—a city that was hedonistic to the point of making an art of living out of material comforts, and of making beauty the singular obsession of its inhabitants—had lost its own beauty, so celebrated only a few decades earlier. But not its charm.

17

Écochard's Lost Wagers

"Beirut," lamented the French architect and urban planner Michel Écochard in 1955, "has one of the most beautiful sites in the world. It could have been made into one of the most beautiful cities in the world—if the master plan had been followed."[1] Écochard's use of the past conditional mood testified to the scale of the disappointment that already was felt a decade after the Second World War. He spoke from experience: having won praise for his work in Damascus and Casablanca, he was assigned the task at the end of the Mandate of drawing up a plan for the city's future development. Nothing came of it. Neither Écochard's plan nor any other was acted upon. Instead of trying to think ahead, this second age of Beirut's modernity contented itself with muddling through.

For a century Beirut had succeeded in combining modernization and urban harmony. This balance was suddenly disrupted in the middle of the twentieth century, prompting a few warnings that went almost completely unnoticed. "What is Beirut today?" L'Orient had asked in 1954, indignantly answering its own question: "A monstrous pile of miscellaneous architecture."[2] And yet worse—far worse—was still to come. A decade later Écochard himself abandoned any pretense at understatement. Approached by the Lebanese government, which had finally become aware of the gravity of the situation, his attitude was frankly alarmist: "Beirut can still be saved, but action must be taken immediately. In a few years this will no longer be possible, even by spending hundreds of millions." His pessimism had hardened by the time he delivered a new master plan, which he likened to "a life preserver [thrown] to a drowned man."[3]

In the interval, the architecture of the 1960s had begun to take its toll. There were, of course, a few fine achievements, which, taken individually, illustrated the ability of local architects to incorporate new uses of metal, concrete, and glass in their designs. Here as elsewhere, however, the Western curtain-wall office building was on the whole dismally imitated, quite apart from the fact that the results tended to age very badly. In these cases, at least, the unfortunate consequences were limited to the central business district. The malign legacy of residential building was even more devastating. Almost everywhere apartment towers shot up, eight or ten stories high, and before long between thirteen and eighteen, in a jumble of styles and clashing exterior ornamentation. The absence of alignment along the street accentuated the impression of disorder, and the growth of neighborhoods unserved by municipal utilities on the periphery of an expanding metropolitan area aggravated the sense of dislocation still further.

Just as the Switzerland of the East now existed only by virtue of its banks and boarding school students, so too the Nice of the Levant had vanished except for its seaside promenade and the leisure opportunities it afforded its richest residents. Urban planning, or the lack of it, had caused Beirut to let its mask drop. At bottom, the Lebanese capital was a third-world city that had ventured into the no-man's-land of uncontrolled urbanization, beyond which loomed the specter of environmental and social catastrophe—a far cry from the noble dream of creating a functional and harmonious whole that had led modern Beirut from its humble nineteenth-century origins to the glorious vision of Écochard's initial plan. As the country looked forward to independence, the capital's prospects still seemed endlessly promising.[4]

THE BEIRUT OF THE POSSIBLE

When Michel Écochard was commissioned in 1943 to draw up a plan for Beirut's future development, he had already known the country for more than a decade. He had arrived in the Levant in 1932, immediately upon graduating from the École des Beaux-Arts in Paris. Assigned to the Department of Antiquities in Damascus, he threw himself into the study of the Arab architecture of Syria and began his career with the restoration of Palmyran and Umayyad monuments, dismantling and rebuilding minarets stone by stone. Fascinated by the simplicity of the region's medieval architecture, which he compared to that of the Bauhaus, he tirelessly traveled throughout Syria and Lebanon on foot and by motorcycle, even at the controls of an airplane. It was this passion that led him to urban planning. Charged with responsibility for creating a department of urban planning within the Syrian government, he received his training on the job, not without success as it turned out.[5] Before being conscripted and sent back to France upon the outbreak of war in the fall of 1939, he was able to work out a plan for the expansion of Damascus that called for the construction of new neighborhoods and the creation of a formal entrance to the city along the Beirut road.[6] The part of Écochard's plan that was carried out following Syria's declaration of independence in April 1946 embodied one of his leading ideas: the new neighborhoods in the capital, and particularly that of Abu Rummaneh, were laid out along tree-lined avenues and populated by small, modestly scaled buildings of five or six stories whose balconies and terraces gave onto small gardens. Although there was nothing remarkable about the architecture of these buildings, which Écochard had no hand in designing, the layout of the neighborhood and its integration with the physical environment revealed a sense of urban life and a relationship to nature that had been missing in the modernization of the cities of the Near East. A similar intuition was to guide him when he came back to Lebanon on the eve of its independence to devise a plan for Beirut.

The point of departure for this first plan was an analysis of the city's expansion in terms of its relation to its natural site, considered for the first time as a whole, disregarding administrative and municipal boundaries. The project covered the entire area between Nahr al-Mawt (Death River), to the north, and Uzaʿi to the south. Committed at this juncture of his career to the principles of the modernist movement in architecture, having rejected the Beaux-Arts classicism of his formative years, Écochard turned away from the monumentality of the "grand compositions" that had been built under the Mandate and the underlying assumptions of its approach to urban planning. Speaking of Casablanca, he was later to write: "The general planning of a city, taking into account the economic, social, and demographic problems of the country as a whole, means having to provide for areas of expansion and laying out neighborhoods within a network of main thoroughfares linked to ports and air fields. The study of neighborhoods, for its part, is based on a certain conception of the city, applied to the social unit. This conception of life must be the same for all its inhabitants, for they all have the same need for light, space, hygiene, education, and work."[7] In the case of Beirut this environmental perspective called for the planted spaces and the gardens of the metropolitan area to be methodically surveyed, and measures proposed for safeguarding the shoreline and wooded spaces. On a smaller scale, this perspective informed the design of several buildings Écochard went on to construct in the city, including the Collège Protestant in 1955 and the new lycée of the Mission Laïque Française in the early 1960s.

The concern for Beirut's physical context went far beyond any interest in pleasing visual effects. As part of a detailed zoning scheme by which the city was divided into twelve areas, it helped to determine the siting of industries, residential neighborhoods, and civic centers. This scheme was regulated in turn by an overall conception of urban functions that structured the city's development around a network of main arteries leading to and from the downtown business district, on the one hand, and, on the other, a network of highways connecting the capital to the hinterland. With respect to commerce, the plan recommended that the port be expanded through the construction of an additional and larger docking basin and that the field at Bir Hasan be replaced by a new airport.

The airport was in fact built on the site Écochard had suggested, but very few of his other proposals were to be accepted. And the ones that were acted on inspired no more than half-hearted measures, yielding only bits and pieces of the original conception, as though a deliberate attempt had been made to empty it of its meaning and purpose. Despite being largely ignored, Écochard's work was nonetheless decisive in the history of urban planning in Beirut, if only because it tacitly fixed the rules of a game that was never to be played, set forth a vision of the landscape that was to be systematically violated, and sketched the contours of Beirut as it might have been—a vision of the city's possibilities that was constantly to be disregarded, like his heroic but no less doomed attempt to rescue it twenty years later.

Although Écochard's ideas have not been immune to criticism, something very like a cult continues to surround this "third-world architect"[8] in Lebanon, more so, paradoxically, than in Syria, where his plans for Damascus and for Aleppo were actually put into effect (twice in the case of Damascus).[9] Part of the reason for this has to do with the professional—and cultural—environment in which Écochard operated in Beirut. Here he was not a foreign expert working on his own, but the leader of a school surrounded by colleagues and disciples, some of whom went on to hold important positions in government, whereas in Syria architects tended to emigrate. The high regard in which Écochard is held still today is due also to the general opinion that his recommendations, beginning with those of 1943, can now be seen as so many missed opportunities.

However this may be, it was not on account of its defects, real or imagined, that this first plan for managing Beirut's growth failed to be implemented, but because of its rigor and coherence. In assigning a preeminent role to the state in deciding questions of future land use, Écochard's approach to urban planning entailed the depreciation in value of many parcels of real estate that would no longer be available for private development. The threat to entrenched interests was plain.

THE UNBRIDLED CITY

The laissez-faire attitude that dominated the merchant republic under the presidencies of Bishara al-Khuri and Camille Chamoun had no patience for such restrictions on profitability. The first dividends of the Lebanese miracle, tangible shortly after the Écochard plan was submitted, held out the prospect of being able to obviate the need for formal planning policy. So closely were business interests interlocked with those of the public sphere that the question of the proper relationship between the private sector and city planning did not even arise. Growth was the order of the day, and the construction industry was accustomed to getting its way. Whereas 390 building permits were approved in 1945, 1,261 were issued in 1955; the built area of the city rose during the same period from 626 hectares (2.4 square miles) to 2,730 hectares (10.5 square miles), and total commercial floor space from 100,000 square meters (1,075,000 square feet) to more than 600,000 (6,460,000 square feet).[10] Moreover, the municipality itself had no real authority to curb the natural tendency to speculation. By virtue of its status as the country's capital—and in keeping with the Parisian model of the era—the city came directly under the supervision of the central government, represented by the prefect *(muhafiz)*. Even had the city been in a position to intervene, it would in any case have lacked the power to legislate effective limitations. It therefore remained dependent on governmental initiatives, which in this case were scant.

In the absence of a concerted plan, new urban construction was bound to follow existing patterns of development under the impetus and guidance of speculation. The configuration that gradually emerged around the central business district in the 1940s and 1950s traced two congruent half-circles on either side of a semi-commercial ring where the bulk of the city's public institutions were grouped, including schools and hospitals. Within this outer circle new and increasingly dense residential neighborhoods spread over the empty spaces of the hills of Ashrafiyyeh and Musaytbeh, leveled the sand dunes of Raml al-Zarif and Saqiyat al-Janzir, and overran the truck farms of Furn al-Shubbak—outside the city limits—and Ras Beirut, where the proximity of the American university attracted the Palestinian bourgeoisie. Extending outward from its periphery was a belt of unincorporated settlements, already becoming overpopulated.[11]

At this juncture the state was chiefly concerned to strengthen the city's commercial and tourist appeal by improving access to the downtown. The new airport at Khaldeh, under construction in the late 1940s, had to be connected to the city by its own road. At the same time the Department of Municipalities and Urban Planning, headed by the Swiss architect and city planner Ernst Egli between 1946 and 1951, undertook several related projects, inspired by Écochard's proposals, linking the center to highways leading out to Damascus, Tripoli, and Sidon; completing the corniche, begun under the Mandate, that ringed the western precincts of the city; and laying out two main thoroughfares in the downtown. Egli nonetheless had greater ambitions, as the International Urbanism exhibition he organized in 1950 made clear. Real estate speculators, powerfully connected in political circles and within the city council, easily gained the upper hand,[12] however, with the result that the Master Plan for Beirut approved four years later limited itself to adopting only a part of the road network sketched out in Écochard's plan. An additional but already belated step was taken in 1956 with the enactment of a zoning law that divided metropolitan Beirut into ten zones defined by the ratio of surface area to building height. If adoption of a zoning principle seemed finally to signal acceptance of the idea of integrated planning, it was deprived of all force by the language of the law, which officially recognized only the state of the constructed site and sanctioned a building footprint in the city center equal to between 70 and 100 percent of the area of the site, with a maximum height of eight floors. Still, developers were not satisfied. A few months later Parliament went even so far as to amend the General Construction Code, in effect since 1940, by authorizing the addition of two floors beyond the heights permitted until then.[13]

The merchant republic was nonetheless capable of accommodating itself to a regime of planned development when it found it convenient to do so. The renovation of Rue Riad al-Sulh (also known as Rue des Banques, since the international banking houses had their headquarters here), carried out beginning in 1952 by means of the government's expropriation power, presented the opportunity to build the only coherent group of buildings in the downtown since the Mandate, apart, of course, from the great reconstruction project of the late twentieth century. Deploying a tempered neoclassical language while at the same time borrowing rather successfully from New York façades—though without reproducing their elevation— the architecture of Rue des Banques achieved a level of distinction comparable to the competitive performance of the companies that occupied its buildings. The street's clean new lines came fully into view in 1955 with the completion of the Pan American Building (built according to the designs of Georges Rayes and Theo Kanaan, both of Palestinian origin and trained in London), whose massing and relation to the ground closely echoed the imposing perpendicularity of the Grand Sérail, at the corner of the old city wall,[14] thus announcing itself as one of the main entrances to the city center.

The same concern with rationalizing street plans was found elsewhere, although only sporadically. In several places near the downtown the government did not hesitate to step in, demolishing old buildings (among them a house where Lamartine had stayed)[15] along with more modern additions. But without a master plan having the force of law, such interventions ran up against the opposition of real estate interests. The state no longer sought to deflect the course of architectural practice by means of edicts that might have set a different tone and preserved the visibility of historical landmarks in the city. Beyond the new airport, Khuri's administration called attention to itself only through the construction of the monumental UNESCO Headquarters, expressly built (from the plans of Farid Trad) to serve as the site for the organization's general conference in November 1948.[16] The great project of Chamoun's presidency, an eponymous Sports City Stadium, was also undertaken in response to an imperative of external prestige, namely, the invitation to host the Pan-Arab Games in October 1957. A new northern highway was planned as well, but construction began in 1955 only on the stretch leading to Maʿameltein, site of the future Casino du Liban. With regard to patronage of the arts, the state limited itself to commissioning an Italian sculptor to create a new statue of the Martyrs to replace the original by Yusuf Hoyek, which, having been partially disfigured by a crazed man, and for many years unjustly disparaged, was declared ineligible for restoration. The new monument, a pompous piece of classicism thought to be more in keeping with the demands of national pride, succeeded in regaining some-

FIGURE 93. Buildings along Rue des Banques, seen from the rear, overlooking the Roman baths, excavated during the 1990s.

thing of its former relevance only once it had been post-modernized, as it were, by the wounds of the civil war.

It fell to private firms, then, much more than to the state or to the city, to search for an architectural language capable of allying the innovations of modernism with the distinctive character of a Mediterranean Arab city. Already under the Mandate, Antun Tabet had applied himself to this task in an imaginative series of office buildings, churches, and schools. Architects who came after him were to place greater emphasis on volumetric simplicity, articulated through the interplay of solid masses and space, without any ornamentation other than the curved façades and painted surfaces, typically yellow, displayed by many new buildings in the expanding residential neighborhoods of the 1950s.[17]

In more than one of these buildings a hint of the Bauhaus could be detected. Still today it is impossible to say whether this influence came directly from Europe or whether it had passed through other places along the way, possibly Turkey, where one of Walter Gropius's associates had worked. Another path of transmission may have been through Palestine. The troubled state of relations between Lebanese and Palestinians since the war of 1975 and, to a still greater degree, the apprehension that existed prior to 1948 regarding the possible consequences of Zionist statehood have combined to cast doubt on this possibility. A concert—the only concert, it must be said—given in Beirut by a Jewish symphony orchestra from Palestine has, for example, disappeared from memory. Is a similar phenomenon at work in architecture? We do know that a Bauhaus-style neighborhood was constructed in Tel Aviv in the 1930s, at a time when this quite recent settlement (dating only from 1911) ceased to be simply a suburb of Jaffa; and that several buildings in this quarter bear a resemblance to what was constructed in Beirut in the 1950s. Obviously no direct link between the two can be asserted without further evidence. Yet one has only to recall that before 1948 the border was hardly impenetrable, in either direction. What is more, the majority of the German architects who worked on this neighborhood in Tel Aviv were not Zionists; to the contrary, they were anti-Zionists, and some even joined the Palestinian Communist Party, which was itself associated with the Syrian-Lebanese Communist Party. One may well imagine that those architects who were party members, as well as ones who were fellow travelers, talked to one another.[18] We know, too, that the exodus of 1948 brought Palestinian architects to Beirut, such as Rayes and Kanaan, as well as the structural engineer Bahij Makdissi. Makdissi's Polish associate, Karol Shayer, himself came to Beirut via Palestine. Shayer, moreover, had also been a colleague of the German architect Fritz Gotthelf, whose designs owed something to Gropius.[19] Whatever its geographic origin may have been, the minor legacy of Bauhaus influence in Beirut testifies to the possibility of harmoniously employing a modern language even in the absence of a master plan. This was to be increasingly difficult in the years that followed, however.

In the city center itself, a few private projects in the vicinity of Rue des Banques also showed that real estate development could be compatible with the tradition of urban planning created first by the Ottomans and then by the French. One thinks of the Lazariyyeh complex, designed by the French architect André Leconte in 1953 to fill the site of the convent of the Sisters of Charity, at the intersection of Rue Émir Bachir and Place des Martyrs. The first example of a large-scale commercial center uniting office buildings with a shopping gallery around a vast central court, its massiveness was moderated by a spacious and varied plan, the fluidity of its horizontal lines, and yellow stone cladding. At the other end of the street, sitting athwart and across from the Pan American Building, Georges Araman and Giorgio Ricci gave the Esseily Building—home to the Capitol cinema—the appearance of a great ocean liner surmounted by a rotunda. On Place des Martyrs a new office tower erected by the Maqāsid society, which owned the land, and designed by Said Hjeil filled out the north face of the square on its completion in 1954. Standing on the site of the old Petit Sérail, demolished four years earlier on the pretext that renovation would be too costly, its construction had been strenuously opposed by advocates of opening the square up to the sea. Though this vista was closed off, the building's neorealism and American-style façade, which displayed the marquee of the Rivoli cinema and monumental posters advertising Egyptian films, made it one of the most engaging landmarks of the downtown business district.[20] In all three cases, construction had been made possible by the availability of a large undivided parcel of land. Elsewhere in this district the fragmentation of ownership favored incoherence and improvisation, with the notable exception of the Fattal Building, at the foot of Rue Allenby, which likewise benefited from unrestricted access to an ample site.

The shortcomings of municipal planning were to be highlighted by the development of Rue Hamra, beginning in the late 1950s, though they were not enough to prevent it from mounting a challenge to the commercial heart of the city during the decade that followed.[21] Already in the nineteenth century, of course, the city had begun to expand toward the empty spaces in the western part of the promontory, and the growing power of attraction exerted by the campus of the American university only strengthened this tendency in the interval. But Hamra was born and grew up almost without warning. The point of departure was the construction in 1958 of a modern office building, soon to be famous for the opening on its ground floor the following year of a storied sidewalk café, the Horseshoe. Designed by Makdissi, Shayer, and Wathek Adib, it was the first in Beirut with a glass and steel façade. A similar inspiration guided Georges Rayes's work on the building that went up next door, housing the street's first movie theater as well as a second sidewalk cafe, the Café de Paris. Here was a rare example of architects—and developers—choosing, in the absence of any municipal plan for development, to do the work of urban planners themselves by regularizing the height of the floors and coordinating the horizontal lines of the façades.[22] This happy initiative failed to set an example, however. Hamra's growth in the years that followed was haphazard, and the state did little more than tag along, content simply to pave the old country lanes of the neighborhood.

Notwithstanding their undoubted talents, the architects of this period (and of the one following) could not by themselves compensate either for the absence of the state or for the short-term calculations of developers, many of whom regarded the architect as a mere executor hired to do their bidding. In fact, hiring an architect was not actually necessary, since a loophole in the law allowed applications for construction permits to be signed by a civil engineer. Assured of obliging treatment from the city and the national government, developers could also, once a permit had been obtained, make changes to the plans drawn up by an architect. This loosely regulated approach to urban planning led to overbuilding in the downtown and adjacent districts, despite intermittent attempts at harmonizing designs, and to rampant expansion along the coastline and around the main arteries, radiating from the center like the fingers of a hand, at the extremities of which unincorporated areas grew more crowded, sinking tens of thousands of inhabitants ever more deeply in poverty. Toward the end of Chamoun's term, American development aid financed an IRFED study of housing conditions in Lebanon, conducted by an Athens-based

FIGURE 94. By the 1970s the empty spaces of the western part of the city had been filled in, here between the sea and the campus of the American university; at right, toward the water, the new Holiday Inn can be seen under construction.

firm of consulting engineers, Doxiadis Associates, which devoted a large part of its inquiry to Beirut.[23] But the outbreak of civil war in 1958 quickly put an end to the project.

The garden city ideal of the Mandate period was now a distant memory, having given way to an increasingly compact and, at the same time, expansive urban imprint. In the center, the unchecked search for profits superimposed additional floors on older buildings, covered over their courtyards, and filled in all remaining empty lots. Outside the center, the absence of a land policy prevented both the state and the city from building up property reserves that might have been drawn on afterwards to spread out the metropolitan area and reduce population density. The few surviving fragments of rural landscape that punctuated the vast expanse of new construction were hardly a substitute; indeed they had the contrary effect of accentuating its discontinuity. Not even the road network was adequate to guide the development of residential neighborhoods, where large avenues were apt to abruptly turn into narrow streets.[24] The problems of expropriation, chronic since the late nineteenth century, were aggravated by the lack of any effective distinction between public and private in state administration, and public works, almost all of them carried out piecemeal, inevitably had an unfinished air about them.

ÉCOCHARD'S RETURN

The harmful consequences of uncontrolled development were already quite pronounced when the government finally resolved to intervene in a more radical manner during the presidency of Fuad Shihab (1958–64). Shihab's policy of stimulating regional economic growth undertook to bring about administrative reform by
a variety of measures, including the creation of new organs (among them a planning ministry) to consolidate the state's power and to circumvent the bureaucracy,
the establishment of a central bank and a system of social security, grand projects
aimed at stimulating commerce in the provinces (such as the Tripoli International
Fair, laid out according to Niemeyer's designs), and an increase in public expenditures to a level equal to one-third of gross national product, or almost the same proportion as in the command economy of Syria at the time.[25] Although it was meant
chiefly to correct the imbalance between the capital and outlying areas, the government's policy nonetheless did not neglect Beirut. Alongside an executive council that took over responsibility for regional development projects from the ministry of public works, a similarly autonomous body was charged with oversight of
projects in the capital. Beirut stood to benefit from a new spirit in parliamentary
legislation as well. A law adopted in 1963 considered a variety of issues that until
then had gone unaddressed, particularly in connection with the environmental impact of development, and it entrusted the tasks of urban planning throughout the
country to a unified authority.

This centralizing policy had the defects of its virtues. An overreliance on purely
technical analysis made it hard to grasp the particular difficulties facing Beirut. The
city center was more than a hundred years old in its oldest areas, including Place
des Martyrs and some of the surrounding suqs. Although it had been renovated
under the Mandate, the terrible mess that had been made since then, in the space
of only a few years, was enough to make the downtown seem like the "old" Beirut—
a hopelessly congested and disordered place where it was now too late to do anything.[26] Even the new business district of Hamra, where country lanes had been
hurriedly transformed into asphalt streets, gave rise to the same sense of fatalism.
Planning therefore tended to ignore the heart of the city, and tried only to limit the
damage by building new roads and highways that drew a kind of cordon sanitaire
around the center, as though the disarray of the inner precincts could in this way
be prevented from contaminating newly urbanized areas on the periphery of the
metropolitan area.

The perception of a city center that had become unmanageable led the government to attempt to physically extricate itself from Beirut. While the Parliament
remained where it was, on Place de l'Étoile, and the offices of the prime minister
continued to be located in the old Ottoman barracks, now the Grand Sérail, the
president of the Republic abandoned Khuri's former residence on Qantari Hill,

where Chamoun had lived, for his native region of Junieh. Soon the idea of creating a government city outside Beirut was proposed for consideration. The local office of Doxiadis Associates, already familiar with the country, was called upon to advise with regard to the site and scope of the project. Four sites, all them outside the administrative limits of the city, were then suggested as candidates for this giant administrative complex, which was meant to group together all the ministries.[27] At this point Écochard, who had continued to follow developments in Lebanon from abroad, was brought in as a consultant. The government city was then split in two, and in 1962 two sites were selected, one in Hadath, to the southwest, and the other at Bir Hasan, on the land of the old airfield. But then the project came to a sudden halt. In the event only a single building was constructed, the postal and telecommunications ministry in Bir Hasan. The objective of relocating public agencies nonetheless continued to be pursued elsewhere, and a new presidential palace was built on the eastern outskirts of Beirut in the foothills of Ba'abda. Alongside the palace, finished in the late 1960s and used by Charles Hélou in the final months of his term, the ministry of defense was soon installed. Other ministries were also exiled to the suburbs, where they were quickly overtaken by the growth of the city, however. Even the ministry of foreign affairs, housed in one of Bustros's sumptuous mansions on Rue Sursock in the Ashrafiyyeh district, considered moving.

In the meantime options for the development of the metropolitan area continued to be examined in the wake of the IRFED mission's study on social development, which coined the expression "Greater Beirut." A master development plan was to bring the new entity into being—a vast metropolis stretching from the edge of Junieh in the north to Na'meh in the south that would bring together almost half of the country's population. To give effect to this great ambition, Écochard was once again called upon. Since the end of his years in Morocco, in 1953, and in parallel with his work in Africa, Écochard had made frequent visits to Lebanon, often extended ones, to supervise various design projects in cooperation with local associates: the Collège Protestant (with Claude Le Coeur) and the *lycée* of the Mission Laïque Française (with Fayez Ahdab), both in Beirut; the Sacred Heart Hospital (with Henri Eddé, a future minister) and the Antonine Fathers College (with Gabriel Tabet) outside the city, in the vicinity of Hazmiyyeh-Ba'abda; and the Marist Brothers' school in Sidon (with Amin Bizri, another future minister) and that of the Sisters of Charity in Tripoli. He also concerned himself with urban planning, working on development schemes for Sidon, and later for Junieh and Byblos,[28] before being asked in 1961 to take part in the government city project in 1961. During these stays he could not fail to look back upon the unfinished work of 1943, nor to cast his gaze upon the runaway growth that in the interval had rendered it partially obsolete. "Twenty years ago I thought about the problem of Beirut, and I believe that on a certain number of points time has not shown me to have been mistaken," he wrote to a high-ranking government official, adding that he would be pleased if

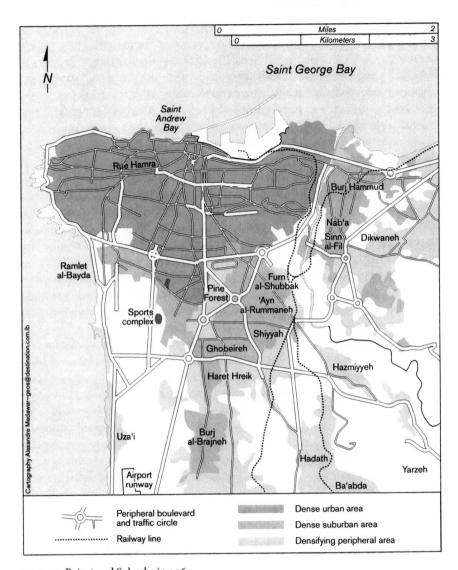

MAP 12. Beirut and Suburbs in 1964

the patience he had "placed in the service of this city" were to yield some result.[29] We can be sure, then, that the Greater Beirut project was dear to his heart. And yet Écochard could not bring himself to endorse the government's approach and ended up dissociating himself from the final plan, issued in 1964.

Taking into account the expansion of the city and its future possibilities for growth, Écochard had marked out a perimeter that extended from the al-Kalb River in the north to Na'meh in the south and encompassed the foothills of the mountains up to a height of 450 meters (almost 1,500 feet). The bursting of Beirut's old boundaries under the force of demographic pressures did not mean that some larger agglomeration could not have the shape and function of a city. The solution, he argued, was "to prevent the uncontrolled proliferation of suburbs by grouping the inhabited areas together so that they do not stretch out indefinitely along the highways."[30] But in order to incorporate these areas into a new municipality it would be necessary to substitute for the mononuclear structure inherited from the city's first era of explosive growth, which no longer suited contemporary conditions of development, a polynuclear structure organized around green spaces and green belts that would constitute the lungs of a Greater Beirut. Beyond this, and not less importantly to Écochard's way of thinking, it would be necessary to radically transform the existing state of housing if Beirut were to cease being what he saw as a "seat of social injustice." A survey of the suburbs that he commissioned found some 60,000 inhabitants crowded into 300 hectares (750 acres) of hovels, and almost 200,000 others living in substandard conditions. Drawing on his experience in Morocco, he set himself the task of providing adequate housing for the entire metropolitan area, without neglecting the need to protect the environment.[31]

Écochard translated this comprehensive vision into a series of specific recommendations: decentralization of activities that until then had been concentrated in the center; creation of a new city that would absorb the bulk of future population growth on the sands of Burj al-Brajneh and Hayy al-Sillum, to the south and east; replacement of the hard-core shanty towns in the suburb of Burj Hammud, considered to be unfit for habitation, by areas of high-density housing for workers at the industrial plants in Jdeideh, Jisr al-Basha, and along the Beirut River; protection of the wooded hills overlooking Beirut and the olive groves of Shuwayfat by classifying them as areas of low-density housing where new construction would be subject to severe restrictions; and classification of beaches and woods as prohibited areas for building.[32]

Once again, only bits and pieces of Écochard's proposals were adopted. The master plan issued by the government codified a functional scheme that did no more than define the extent of industrial zones and certain major facilities, and instituted a freeze on construction along the beaches and certain protected areas. Residential building regulations were amended to permit the construction of an additional "roof story" enclosing service rooms and roof-top elevator equipment.[33] More fundamentally, however, the plan altogether disregarded Écochard's analysis of how the city actually worked and how best to manage its growth in the years to come. Far from recasting the contours of the capital, this timid and unimaginative exercise in planning served only to intensify the effects of uncontrolled development. The existing concentric structure of the metropolitan area continued to expand, further stifling the center city. As for the new city that Écochard had envisioned to the south and east of Beirut, it never saw the light of day. In its place, free from administrative regulation and largely unserved by public utilities, there grew up an outer suburb where apartment buildings and individual houses stood next to vacant lots and desperately poor shantytowns—the core of the belt of squalor that was soon to emerge, forming the future bastion of Hezbollah in the 1980s and beyond.

AN UNFINISHED CITY

Among the various planning initiatives sponsored by Shihab's administration and sustained under his successor Charles Hélou, albeit with many interruptions, a series of great road projects in Beirut stand out. The first of these, begun in the early 1960s although decided upon long before, created a new thoroughfare, named after Bishara al-Khuri, that connected the Pine Forest with Place des Martyrs, running next to Rue de Damas on arriving in the vicinity of Université Saint-Joseph, where it encountered the congestion of the existing downtown street grid. Extending both the improvements made under the Mandate and those implemented by Ernst Egli, the cliffs of Rawsheh were linked to the Beirut River by means of the Mazra'a corniche (later Boulevard Saeb Salam) and Avenue Fuad I, which passed by the national museum and the new Palais de Justice, forming an inner beltway. In the northwestern corner of the promontory, the connection between Avenue des Français and the Manara coast road remained unfinished, though there was time enough to disfigure the coastline at 'Ayn al-Mrayseh, where the old fishing port was preserved by building a bridge over it. For the moment a short stretch known as the Corniche de la Télévision continued the coast road in the vicinity of Hamra. Between the two great residential districts in the east and the west, a pair of transversal roads made it possible to avoid the commercial downtown. The first began as Avenue de l'Indépendance and connected Ashrafiyyeh Hill with Musaytbeh Hill, passing through Basta and extending as far as the Télévision road and the outskirts of the new luxury residential neighborhood along Rue de Verdun. The second, a highway later named after Fuad Shihab that made Ashrafiyyeh only a three-minute ride from Hamra (not allowing for the traffic jams at either end), was the belated reply to a suggestion made by Écochard in 1943 to relieve congestion in the central business district. In the event, this idea was placed in the service of the integrationist policy adopted by Shihab's government in the wake of the short civil war of 1958, which by constructing new thoroughfares sought to weaken the internal cohesiveness of neighborhoods marked by a strong sense of confessional identity while at the same time putting them in closer contact with one another.

The government's resolve was nonetheless undermined in more than one instance by recurrent problems of expropriation and later, after Shihab, by a reversion to the habit of administrative delay. Not only were the intended effects of public intervention often cancelled by the unchecked expansion of the city, but some projects never even got underway. Thus, for example, construction of the northern segment of the road meant to connect the Damascus highway to the port, near the Collège de la Sagesse, was blocked for years by the opposition of the Maronite Church, a major landowner in the neighborhood. The segment between the Collège and the Palais de Justice, begun under the presidency of Suleiman Franjieh, remained unfinished at the time of the outbreak of civil war in 1975, and the southeastern segment was not finished until the 1990s. Another road, meant to link the Sidon highway with the city center, was completed only after the end of the war as well.

None of these projects aimed at reorganizing traffic patterns inside the downtown itself, where the city's commercial activity was concentrated. The sole exception was the new bus station, on the edge of the port, which was designed to allow freer circulation around Place des Martyrs. Though it was completed just before the start of the war and named after Charles Hélou, entrance and exit ramps had not yet been constructed. Once the war was over, the station had to be repaired before it could finally be put into operation. But by then Place des Martyrs had ceased to exist. Even less successful were two projects undertaken in the Ghalghul and Saifi neighborhoods of the old intramural town, which had been bypassed by the new roads built under the Mandate and ignored by the speculative fever that accompanied Lebanon's independence. Neither of these projects—the one awarded to Nabil Tabbarah and Raymond Dawud, the other to Assem Salam and Pierre Khoury, with Écochard himself acting as coordinator (several sketches in his own hand have survived)—got beyond the preliminary study phase.[34]

The mark left by the Shihab and Hélou presidencies in architecture is less perceptible, at least in Beirut. The priority given to regional development produced some fine results here and there, among them government buildings in provincial cities, such as Assem Salam's administrative complex in Sidon and the neighboring complexes in the outer Beirut suburbs housing the ministry of defense (designed by André Wogenscky, one of Le Corbusier's last associates,[35] and Maurice Hindieh) and the offices of the president of the Republic (designed by the Swiss firm Addor & Julliard), to say nothing of Niemeyer's imprint on the international fair in Tripoli. In Beirut itself a few ambitious buildings nonetheless deserve to be mentioned: the Palais de Justice, built according to the designs of Farid Trad in a monumental style that sought to reflect the commanding status now accorded, at least rhetorically, to the law; the Banque du Liban, due also to Addor & Julliard[36] and completed in 1964, whose massing and lines identified it as an innermost sanctuary of the republic, and which was reproduced on a smaller scale in other cities of the country; the ministry of tourism, where Salam introduced references to the Arab past in a modern idiom, the like of which could also be seen at this time in Baghdad; the offices of the municipal electric utility overlooking the port, designed by Pierre Neema, Joseph Nassar, and Jacques Aractingi and influenced by Niemeyer; and finally, the Maison de l'Artisan, an airy masterpiece designed in 1965 by Neema, notable for its ogival arcades set between sky and sea.

A series of privately sponsored construction projects also helped to make this a prosperous period for architects. Coming after the Horseshoe Café and the Hamra cinema, the headquarters of the Lebanese television company, designed by Willie Sednawi in 1959, confirmed the new willingness to work with glass and steel. The Swiss-designed Starco Center on Rue Georges-Picot, on the edge of the Jewish quarter, came to symbolize this style of architecture, and provided local developers with a model for future complexes consisting of two or three buildings,[37] such as the Gefinor. On the cliffs of Rawsheh, still a formidable site from the technical point of view, Makdissi, Shayer, and Adib—the three architects who had collaborated on the Horseshoe—enjoyed equal success with the Shell Building (1959), a mixed complex of offices and apartments with large balconies that, despite its height, managed to achieve an effect of lightness, emphasized by a roof cast in the shape of an airplane wing. The Carlton Hotel, built four years earlier on the same stretch of shoreline, was another triumph for this trio, admired for its gardens overhanging the coast road. Despite being more massive, the Phoenicia Hotel (designed by the American architect Edward Durrell Stone, in collaboration with Ferdinand Dagher and Rodolphe Elias) also succeeded in attenuating an impression of monumentality through the orientalizing ornamentation of its balconies, to say nothing of the tour de force of its bar, looking into the swimming pool. On its completion in 1967, the building designed for the American Life Insurance Company by the English architect Anthony Irving, on the road to the airport, demonstrated yet another way of adapting the vocabulary of local architecture to contemporary purposes (it was later to be the setting for the film *Embassy*), as did the new School of Arts and Sciences on the campus of the American university, conceived at about the same time by Samir Khairallah, and the mosque in the Pine Forest, where Assem Salam substituted a floating hull for the traditional dome and gave the minaret the shape of a campanile. The modernizing impulse made itself felt in the heart of the city as well. Near the Lazariyyeh Center, at the foot of Avenue Béchara al-Khoury, a new group of buildings enclosed the Radio City cinema in a doubtful egg shell; at the northeast corner of Place des Martyrs, Henri Eddé designed the Byblos Center (1960), a commercial complex that was home to a cinema of the same name.

Many other architects—Pierre Khoury, Khalil Khoury, Grégoire Sérof, Raoul Verney, and Jacques Liger-Belair among them—distinguished themselves during the 1960s and 1970s, both in Beirut and in its environs, by a range of projects, including apartment buildings, schools, and private homes.[38] Even the great Finnish architect Alvar Aalto impressed his stamp—albeit from a distance—on Rue Hamra in the form of the Banque Sabbagh building (later the Fransabank Center), designed with the Swiss architect Alfred Roth, director of Das Neue Schulhaus in Zurich. The level of professional talent that was available to the city is therefore not in question. But the achievements of architects, like the plans of Écochard himself, in the end amounted to little more than a tantalizing suggestion of what Beirut might have been. Apart from the inferior, and indeed sometimes catastrophic, copies they inspired, good buildings were still more apt to find themselves next to shapeless structures of no appeal, lost in the endless concrete expanses of an urban forest whose growth nothing seemed capable of restraining, least of all the return to laissez-faire policies under Franjieh's presidency.

The end of Shihab's term had already seen a slackening of planning efforts, and with the departure of his successor and ally, Charles Hélou, the days of the interventionist state were over. Despite the presence of Henri Eddé, an innovative architect and a former associate of Écochard, as a minister in the first government of Franjieh's mandate, support for urban planning waned. Although it was intended to give architects greater freedom, the abrogation of the height limit of 26 meters (85 feet) in residential neighborhoods, originally enacted under the Mandate, turned out to be a godsend for developers. Gradually a de facto limit of 40 meters (130 feet) came to be observed, although without any corresponding obligation to respect the constraints that applied in the case of other buildings classified simply as "very tall." The oil boom only made the situation worse by giving fresh impetus to land speculation, after three lean years of stagnant prices. If the road projects somehow or other managed to avoid being cancelled, the white paper published by the Directorate General of Urban Planning in 1973 with the purpose of demonstrating the continuity of planning efforts was above all an admission of their failure.

What little continuity there was resided instead in the popular resistance to any coherent attempt at urban planning. Beyond the speculation and the influence peddling, the wheeling and dealing of the developers, and the docile acquiescence of the engineers and architects, due notice must be taken of the reluctance of the people themselves to accept the constraints either of law or the environment—when it was, after all, their own way of life that was at stake. The most obvious symptom of this selfish rejection of civility was—and remains —the readiness to scrounge out additional space in residential buildings by closing off balconies and loggias with glass and aluminum, in contempt of the façade and disregard for construction permits. Against all the ruses and subterfuges to which developers and residents alike resorted for the sake of cobbling together an extra floor or converting an underground parking garage (obligatory in new buildings) into a warehouse, no collective interest weighed very heavily.[39] To the contrary, it was the private domain in all of its many parts that invaded the public sphere and everywhere hacked away at its flailing carcass, from the richest neighborhoods of the center to the poorest shantytowns of the periphery. As a consequence of this, and urged on by the ongoing population explosion, the metropolitan area was henceforth to be little more than a mass of infringements and trespasses against the ability to breathe that is no less essential to a city than to a person.

A MACROCEPHALIC COUNTRY

As in the majority of the world's developing countries, the social history of Lebanon in the second half of the twentieth century was inseparable from the growth of its urban population. In 1950, two-thirds of the country's people still lived in the countryside. Twenty years later the proportions were reversed: 62 percent of its inhabitants lived in cities, a level that was to rise to 70 percent by 1975.[40] And most of this urban majority lived in Beirut.

Under the Mandate, Beirut already had a sizable population, with 180,000 inhabitants, or almost a quarter of the total population of Lebanon in 1930.[41] This number grew considerably in the years that followed—by two-thirds between 1930 and 1950 alone, when it reached 300,000. But it was above all after 1960 that demographic growth accelerated. By 1970 the population had more than tripled by comparison with 1950, and the Beirut metropolitan area, having now passed a million, accounted for 42 percent of the country's inhabitants. Finally, in 1975 it reached 1.2 million, or half of the national population.[42] In a century and a half, the population had therefore grown by a factor of 200. If one accepts the figure of 15,000 inhabitants for the end of the Ibrahim Pasha interlude, this amounts on average to a doubling every twenty years. The actual rate of increase was greater than this after independence, since it took only ten years to double the 1959 population of 450,000, and sixteen years almost to triple this figure.[43]

Demographic increase on this order obviously could not have been due solely to natural causes. It is true, of course, that the improvement of living conditions in the city favored growth, since the lowering of infant mortality compensated for the drop in the birth rate. But modernization in another and more decisive respect contributed to the rise in population: the city attracted newcomers, as it had not ceased to do since the late Ottoman period. Stimulated in the nineteenth century by the political and economic situation in the Mountain, the inflow peaked in 1860 and was renewed under the Mandate, when the transformation of Beirut into the capital of Greater Lebanon brought a wave of Maronite immigrants from the highlands. This reaction continued until the late 1950s and even beyond. While the adoption of a regional development policy under Shihab succeeded in opening up the last Maronite villages to have remained immune to the city's charms, it had unanticipated consequences, above all in the Shiʿi communities of the Biqaʿ and southern Lebanon. The rural exodus from these regions that had begun in the 1940s now assumed massive proportions[44] in the two decades before hostilities in the south were to channel the waves of refugees fleeing Israeli bombardment toward the outskirts of Beirut. Inexorably, the emptying of the countryside, under the influence of large-scale investment in the country's cities, the elimination of sharecropping, the collapse of small peasant landownership, and the aftermath of the Arab-Israeli conflict transformed Lebanon into an urban society concentrated around a macrocephalic capital.[45]

Not all the new residents of Beirut came from the countryside. Migration originated no less in the various provincial towns and cities, including Tripoli and Sidon, in part because Lebanon's limited geographic area multiplied the power of attraction that the centralization of government services and cultural life conferred on the capital.[46] A comparison of estimates for 1970 and 1975 suggests moreover that other cities did not record a rise in population during the interval; indeed, something closer to the opposite occurred. Excepting Tripoli, which now counted more than 100,000 inhabitants, and to a lesser degree Sidon and Zahleh, the country's largest towns were little more than overgrown villages: in 1970 the majority of them numbered barely 10,000 inhabitants each, often less in the south and in the Biqa'— evidence of an abrupt discontinuity between the countryside and the capital.[47] With regard to the gap between the country's first and second cities, Lebanon ranked among the leaders in the Middle East, behind Iran, Sudan, and Iraq. And if one considers the four-city index, which measures the gap between the size of the principal city and the next three largest in a country, Beirut came well ahead of all the other capitals in the region.[48]

The effects of earlier migrations to Lebanon following each of the world wars continued to be keenly felt. Between these two waves, and afterwards, there were several surges of lesser magnitude spread out over larger intervals, chief among them the Kurds, who began to arrive from Turkey during the interwar period, often in desperate circumstances, and the Christian Syrians and Assyrians, who came from Iraq at about the same time. Although these inflows were episodic, apart from the Kurdish case, the settlements that resulted from them were characterized by very high birth rates, which, like those of rural migrants within Lebanon, contributed to the natural growth of the population. Economic refugees from Egypt and Syria in the 1950s, though they were both far less numerous and a great deal wealthier, nonetheless encouraged population increase by promoting the concentration of economic activity in Beirut.

This tendency toward concentration was to continue unabated: whereas the city center monopolized the service sector—to the point of atrophy, in fact, and at the price of constricting the city's circulation—factories sprang up in the inner suburbs of Beirut, where the associated increase in population created an irresistible impulse to expand, soon as far as the first foothills to the east. By the late 1960s, Beirut's municipal limits could scarcely any longer be detected; and although the urbanized area was rather small by comparison with the expansion that was to take place after 1975, population density had increased. Within the metropolitan area a high-rise architecture now came into general use, with the result that most of the buildings constructed from the late 1960s onward were eight or nine stories high, often more. Outlying neighborhoods attained some of the highest densities in the world during this period, making social inequalities all the more glaring. And in accordance with a rule obtaining in most cities of the third world, the growth in unem-

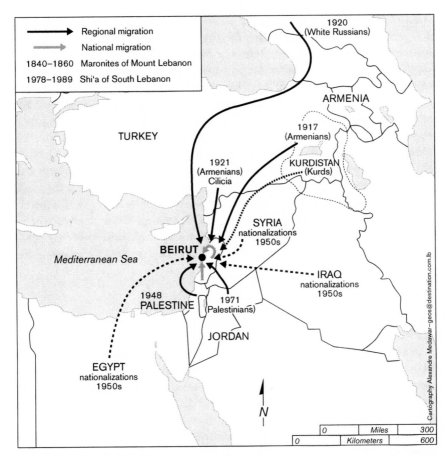

MAP 13. Beirut, City of Refuge

ployment, disguised though it may have been in official statistics, now combined with the relentless centrifugal diffusion of neighborhoods lacking access to basic municipal services to call into question Beirut's ability to survive as a cohesive unit.[49]

The most striking illustration of the city's dysfunction was the widening belt of poverty constituted by these unincorporated suburbs, punctuated by a series of wretched shantytowns. More and more wealthy residents began to flee the old peripheries, themselves on the verge of overpopulation and now threatened by rising rates of crime, to take refuge in small residential enclaves overlooking the city in the first foothills leading up into the mountains. By the early 1960s it was in any case clear that Beirut had now fully occupied its natural site,[50] except perhaps for the area of dunes around the airport. The city's distention beyond the promontory was sufficiently obvious to attract the attention of the IRFED mission of 1958–59, and gave rise to the notion of Greater Beirut that the master development plan subsequently sought to clarify. This term was meant to take in the whole of the metropolitan area, composed of the city proper and outlying unincorporated suburbs, as well as a few villages accessible by coastal highways. It remained vague, however, at least to the extent that a still greater Greater Beirut could be imagined that would encompass the Mountain; indeed, Lebanon itself, as the victim of this extreme case of macrocephaly, might not unreasonably be thought of as a Very Great Beirut. Still today the proper definition of Greater Beirut remains a subject of dispute. In 1984 the French-Lebanese Mission for the Development of the Metropolitan Region of Beirut proposed situating it between al-Kalb River in the north, Damur in the south, and Baʿabda in the east. Other studies argued in favor of including Byblos further to the north, and ʿAley, in the first foothills to the southeast. But these shifts of focus did not amount to a redefinition either of the city's administrative scope or of the limits of municipal jurisdiction,[51] and still less to a consistent, comprehensive, and robust vision of the future.

THE ATROPHY OF THE CITY CENTER

Just as the Beirut metropolitan area had come to bear a macrocephalic relation to Lebanon as a whole, so too was it connected on an urban scale with another form of hypertrophy, one that had immeasurably enlarged the heart of the city. The increase was neither geographic nor, in the strict sense of the term, demographic. The area comprised by the downtown commercial district—roughly speaking, the old intramural town, bordered to the north by the sea and the port—and the first half-ring of inner suburbs from the late Ottoman period covered only 130 hectares (320 acres), or a bit more counting the area adjacent to the port, whereas the city within its municipal limits covered some 1,700 hectares (6.5 square miles), and the metropolitan area as a whole some 8,000 (31.25 square miles).[52] In this smaller area, now typically known as the Balad, the population density was between 176 and 192 per hectare (71 and 78 per acre)—considerably lower than that of the city proper, which exceeded 250 per hectare (100 per acre). Still less did the increase involve the size of the resident population, which represented only a very small part (about 2.3 percent) of the municipal population. This picture changes completely, however, when one considers the daytime population: whereas only one in forty-three people actually lived in the center, one out of every three members of the metropolitan labor force worked there.[53]

The concentration of jobs in the Balad could also be measured in terms of the functional uses of the built environment. Only 3 percent of the space in the downtown was used for residential purposes, with the other 97 percent being occupied by businesses and other commercial entities. Despite recent competition from the

FIGURE 95. Aerial view of the city center in the 1960s.

area around Rue Hamra in the 1960s, the downtown remained the principal site of economic life, absorbing the bulk of service sector activities.[54] These activities were of many different kinds, framed by a subtle and complicated geography that wedged dead-end streets and alleys in among larger thoroughfares, themselves scarcely less congested, and set tall buildings, the majority of which dated from the 1920s and 1930s (though some went back to the late nineteenth century, and others appeared only in the 1950s), cheek by jowl with the more modest structures of the markets, most of them only two or three stories high. Almost everywhere there were signs of overcrowding, a courtyard closed off here, an extra floor added on there—reinforcing the impression that a point of saturation had at last been reached.

The sights and sounds of congestion were immediately apparent on entering the Balad. For most people the way in was through Place des Martyrs, still popularly known as the Burj—the center of the center, as it might be said, although it was no more centrally located with respect to the downtown than the downtown was with respect to the city as a whole. As the terminus of the city's main roads and highways, the square had become a vast outdoor bus station. Including its southern extension toward Place Debbas and Avenue Béchara al-Khoury, there were some fifty parking areas for communal taxis and private bus lines ("garages," as they used to be called), from which passengers departed for some neighborhood of the city, or region of the country, or city in Syria, Jordan, or Iraq. Until the opening of the Fuad

FIGURE 96. The bus depot at the Burj.

Shihab ring road, the square had also been the hub of automobile traffic in the city, almost impossible to avoid in passing from one neighborhood to another. This was also true for those who did not have a car of their own, since it was both the origo
inating point and destination for the majority of taxis, and connecting bus service could be had in no other place. Traffic was so backed up during the day that speeds of more than five miles per hour were seldom possible, condemning drivers to asphyxiation. Consideration was therefore given to building a proper station, four stories high overlooking the port. In the meantime various attempts were made, without great conviction, to unclog the roads—campaigns to prohibit parking on the square,[55] never actually carried out, and, in the 1970s, to restrict driving by allowing only cars with even-numbered license plates one day and odd-numbered plates the next. At night the rhythm of activity was slower, but it never ceased altogether, being sustained by the cinemas and seedy hotels nearby as well as establishments on Rue Mutanabbi.

The Burj itself had changed little since the improvements made by the Ottomans and then under the Mandate, despite the replacement of Place Hamidiyyeh, in the center, by French-style gardens that could scarcely be seen any longer behind the rows of cars. Instead of the Petit Sérail, the Rivoli cinema now blocked the northerly view from the square to the sea. To the east, the police headquarters stood between the square and the red-light district. The western side opened on to pedestrian mar-

FIGURE 97. Rue Weygand, with suqs on either side.

kets, the old suqs. To the south, beyond Place Debbas along Rue de Damas, the eastern suburbs stretched as far as the eye could see. Rue Weygand, at the northwestern corner of the Burj, led to the more modern suqs and, beyond the intersection with Rue des Banques, on to Ras Beirut; alternatively, one could travel along Rue Émir Bachir, departing from Place al-Sulh at the southwestern corner of the square, across from the Lazariyyeh Center.

On the western side of the Balad, Rue des Banques (more formally, Rue Riad al-Sulh) was another and obviously more symbolic connecting point. The money that circulated there resembled the automobile traffic of Place des Martyrs, at once intra-urban, inter-urban, and transnational. But though the look of the street was more modern, the congestion was scarcely less great. The office buildings in the area bounded by Rue de Banques, Rue Foch and Rue Allenby, and the Lazariyyeh Center were laid out in an orderly fashion, yet the offices themselves were often small and overcrowded. Some companies were forced to lease space in a number of different buildings haphazardly situated in relation to one another, and occasionally separated by warehouses. The total population of white collar workers in the downtown business district was estimated at 35,000. But this was only a small part of the daytime population. In 1973, for example, between 180,000 and 270,000 people entered the downtown every day,[56] for the most part through Place des Martyrs. The rest of this population was made up of shopkeepers and staff (as many as 39,000, or 48 percent of those employed in the Balad); artisans and civil servants; and, in still greater numbers, all those who regularly came to the downtown, some almost every day, to conduct business in government offices or banks, or else to buy or sell goods in one or another of the many retail outlets in the district—more than seven thousand by one count, of varying sizes. Most of these businesses were very small, occupying on average thirty-five square meters (375 square feet), though sometimes scarcely more than fifteen square meters (160 square feet)—or even less in the suqs off the main streets.[57]

The memory of these pedestrian markets is the chief reason for the nostalgia that has filled their old customers since the destruction of the city center in 1975. It should not be supposed that they were more picturesque than the ones in other Arab cities, however, or that their historical character was any more remarkable; indeed the suqs of Beirut were not very old. Few of them dated back more than a few decades, which is to say to the late nineteenth century at the earliest. More than the particular atmosphere of these markets, it was the variety of architectural styles and customers that gave them their distinctive quality, scattered throughout a maze of streets that was nonetheless modern, unlike the much older suqs of Tripoli, Damascus, and elsewhere, which were set apart in a quarter of their own. Here one could pass almost without noticing from the hawkers' cries and vivid colors of a narrow alleyway to the relatively serene ambiance of the Café l'Automatique. Here men and women in European dress went straight from a retail fabric market to the ABC department store and the Antoine bookshop without the least impression of having crossed a boundary.

The suqs themselves were very different from one another.[58] Leaving the Burj one came to al-Sagha (Jewelers' Market), the only suq to have metal gates that were closed at night—all except the one gate that opened onto the square (right across from the police station). Nearby were the decidedly less opulent Abu-l-Nasr, specializing in tools and supplies for odd jobs as well as canned food products; the vegetable and fish market al-Nuriyyeh, named after an adjacent chapel dedicated to the Virgin of Light, which led on by a muddy path to Place de l'Étoile; suq Sursock, which (contrary to what its patrician name seemed to suggest) sold cheap clothes off the rack and fabrics by the meter; and al-Lahhamin (Butchers' Market), which, as one would expect, sold meat, not far from the flower and perfume markets. On reaching Place de l'Étoile one found oneself in an apparently more orderly environment, though the arcades along Rue Maʿrad—lined with stalls trading in sweets and pastries, sandwich shops, and more or less specialized grocery stores, all of them filled with fragrant odors—hardly lived up to its ambition of being the Rue de Rivoli of Beirut. A short distance south and east from the square stood the Lazariyyeh Center, which, although recently built, had seen its vast interior courtyard turned into a booksellers' market, whereas to the north of Étoile the Parliament Building barely concealed al-Bazirkān, a suq selling woven goods, as well as al-Munajjidin

(Carders' Market) and al-Haddadin, where tinplate was worked, next to another space for locksmiths. Further on was al-Ayyas, a vendor of fabrics and cheap ready-to-wear clothing, and then, near Rues Weygand and Foch, al-Wqiyyeh, which priced its fabrics by the ounce and also offered toys and various low-end manufactured items; al-Hisbeh and Māl-Qabbān, occupied respectively by wholesale greengrocers and grain dealers; and finally al-Jukh, which sold tweed. To the west, between Rue Allenby and the old wall of the city, there were fancier establishments: suq al-Franj (the Franks' Market), which dealt in select fruits and vegetables for a cosmopolitan clientele; al-Jamil, long ago recommended by the French geographer Vital Cuinet; and al-Tawileh, whose windows featured stylish off-the-rack fashions.[59]

This list is far from exhaustive. One might also mention suq al-Najjarīn (Woodworkers' Market) to the southeast of Place des Martyrs; the millers' market, housed right in the middle of the red-light district; the lumberyard down by the port; another market selling eggs; and the minuscule suq al-Fashkha (or what remained of it). Nor should one omit the many artisans, notably bootmakers and typesetters, concentrated on the eastern edge of the Balad in Rue du Liban, or the many moneychangers who helped tide over travelers while also assisting the city's banks in handling all kinds of financial transactions.

Another view of the downtown, seen through the prism of sectarian identity, reveals a harmonious mosaic, if not quite a melting pot. There were Sunni and Greek Orthodox, of course, who claimed—and still today claim—to be "authentic" Beiruti. They came from all social classes: among the Sunni, greengrocers, fishmongers, and grain wholesalers in the Sursock and Abu-l-Nasr markets, shopkeepers on Rue Maʿrad, butchers, warehousemen from the port, sellers of tweed (who plied their trade next to Palestinians in suq al-Jukh, themselves Sunni), tin plate craftsmen; among the Orthodox, some were also tenants of the Sursock and Abu-l-Nasr markets, while others—wealthier and the majority—were to be found at suq al-Tawileh and in banking. There were many Armenians as well: jewelers, stall vendors in the Sursock market, cobblers, moneychangers, typesetters, zincographers, and lockmakers, to say nothing of the market that by tradition was reserved for them, suq al-Arman. Shiʿa, whose exodus from their homeland in southern Lebanon was more recent, were inevitably less well represented; some worked as wholesale fabric merchants, but many men shined shoes for a living. The Druze had still less commercial visibility, even if they had long been settled in Beirut and owned a good deal of land in the western part of the city. Maronites, by contrast, were numerous, without any particular specialization apart from woodworking and dealing in wood; they were also present in substantial numbers in the state administration. Greek Catholics, for their part, were found in the upper levels of banking and import-export businesses, like families of other Christian denominations professing allegiance to Rome. Jews, though very much a minority in national terms, did not participate any less actively in the life of the Balad, being concentrated in and around the Wadi

Abu Jamil neighborhood, where the majority of them lived near the synagogue and the school of the Alliance Israélite. Merchants of varying stature, they worked notably in the Sursock and al-Tawileh markets, as carders, toy sellers, and money changers. Kurds—porters and laborers for the most part, who had begun to settle in the Jewish quarter—completed this mosaic of Lebanese diversity.

The confessional geography of the Balad was further enriched by the number of different places of worship, although none had been constructed in the recent past. A plan for a new grand mosque for the Sunni, on Place des Martyrs, was contested even within the community, and finally took shape only in the twenty-first century. Owing to the low residency rate of the city center, all these places—except the synagogue—were as a practical matter deprived of any parish function. This was already true during the time of the Mandate. But even their cathedral function was not unduly emphasized. Without being quite invisible, they now occupied a less prominent place in the life of their neighborhoods, living side by side in some cases, peaceably and without quarrel (the competition among muezzins and church bells that no visitor to the downtown of Beirut can fail to hear today is a postwar phenomenon). Indeed the Balad seemed for the most part to avoid denominational polarization: apart from two or three incidents, it was spared by the civil war of 1958, and by the unrest of the late 1960s as well; the great student demonstrations of the 1970s, which traditionally wended their way to the Parliament Building, only added to the Balad's reputation in the public mind as a place where the city's powers of synthesis could still be brought to bear. The merchants' strike in protest against protectionist legislation concerning customs duties in the fall of 1971 had much the same effect.

No one in any case could have foreseen that the Balad, which by virtue of its very name claimed to sum up and stand for an entire country, would soon be one of the first parts of the metropolitan area to go up in flames and, more than that, become the place where this conflagration would take on the meaning of a suicide. Having finally reached the limits of its capacity to absorb differences, as though exhausted by the weight of the city, which now more than ever stood revealed as the seat of social injustice that Écochard had futilely taken up arms against, and having exhausted the city in its turn, the Balad could henceforth perpetuate its centrality only by transforming itself into a field of battle, there to be consumed by its own violence.

PART FIVE

The City of Every Danger

FIGURE 98 *(preceding page).* The City Center clock, at the head of Rue Béchara al-Khoury, south of Place des Martyrs, damaged in the violence of 17 September 1975.

18

On the Knife's Edge

War did not take Beirut by surprise. Even if its central districts were to be spared on the whole by the recurrent manifestations of the state of discord that was the lot of independent Lebanon,[1] neither the prosperity of its economy nor the sparkle of its way of life could always mask a premonition that the city—and with it the entire country—was walking along a knife edge. Well before the turning point of the 1967 Arab-Israeli war, which slowly but surely gave rise to the habits of extremism, Beirut had become acquainted with all of the many shadows of polarization that the abrupt, yet inconclusive, settlement of the Eastern Question by the Second World War continued to cast over the Levant.

The cosmopolitan metropolis of the Arabs did not live in isolation from their passions and their quarrels. Nor did the capital of the Lebanese Republic manage to sidestep the difficulties of building a nation. And all the less could Beirut hope to escape the realities of the world around it as the life of the city was, if not intrinsically belligerent, in any case well suited to the expression of political violence. Beirut's shifting demographic composition, constantly reshaped since the nineteenth century by streams of migration from abroad, near and far, superimposed, layer by layer, the divisions and antagonisms of the new settlers on older sectarian allegiances that had never wholly been abandoned by those who had come before them. More ominously, these layers were laid down in an urban landscape riven by social fractures and dislocations, some of them visible to the naked eye. The most recent of these ran along the broken line of corrugated metal roofs and bare cinder-block walls of the ring of squalor that had grown up on the outskirts of the city, crowded to overflowing with the newest wave of immigrants, Shi'i peasants from southern Lebanon and Palestinian refugees who had come since 1948, as well as a smaller number of Kurds. Within the city itself the fault lines were better disguised, but they were nonetheless there, and many neighborhoods that were already old had the appearance of isolated territories, even of villages, as if they had been transplanted from somewhere else.

Yet the original city—if this expression has any meaning—was not a victim, as accounts that lay emphasis on the city's origins seek to suggest. The picturesque but ruthless tradition of its qabadayat had long sustained a culture of violence; before they disappeared, the "patriotism of the communities"[2] embodied by these gangsters had succeeded in adapting itself to the dynamics of an apparently more modern form of political mobilization, and in transposing the convulsive upheavals of regional geopolitics to the urban level. Above all, Beirut showed it was incapable of functioning in any durable way as a melting pot. Notwithstanding the exceptional circumstances of the country's independence, and despite Beirut's success in creating a common way of life, its talent for blending disparate elements was overcome at last by ideology and politics. Its meeting places, no longer forums of gregarious civility where the corrosive effects of narrow self-interest were resolutely combated, turned into desolate crossroads from which each person could pridefully depart without having had to cede the least part of his dignity. Henceforth the synthesis of the city's contradictions was to be achieved in the perpetuation of war.

A COMPOST FOR POLARIZATION

The most visible of these contradictions, and also the most lasting, if not the most constant, grew out of the soil of communal pluralism. In combination with each other, the turbulent history of Eastern Christianity and the no less volatile consequences of schisms within Islam[3] had created a patchwork of incongruous parts whose stability had long been known to be fragile. Such pluralism was peculiar neither to Beirut nor to Lebanon. But though it was found in other countries of the Mashriq—Syria, Iraq, and Palestine, as well as Egypt—its effects in these places were counterbalanced by the existence of a clear majority of Sunni Muslims, except in Iraq, where Shi'is were more numerous. In Lebanon, no community constituted a majority. Even considering only the most general division, between Christians and Muslims, neither of the two blocs before the war could stake a claim to preeminence; after the war the relative size of the country's Christian population was reduced, with the most widely accepted estimates placing the Muslim majority somewhere between 60 and 65 percent of the total. The prewar situation was reproduced in Beirut, at least with regard to the resident population (and not only to the registered electorate, formed mainly of Sunni, Greek Orthodox, and Armenian Christians). Moreover, the diversity of the communities in the capital was amplified by their cohabitation within a restricted area, where peoples of different faiths unavoidably found themselves in close contact with one another. And while their interaction weakened particularisms, it also strengthened the narcissism of small differences.

These differences were, of course, striking—no less so, in fact, than the similarities between the various groups. In no part of the country, either today or in the past, did communal affiliation overlap with ethnic identity,[4] apart from a few very unusual cases, notably the Armenians, who had come to Lebanon at the beginning of the century, and who by now were remarkably integrated, if not into Lebanese culture, then into certain sectors of the economy. The White Russians and the Levantine French, on the other hand, very few in number on the eve of the war, did not represent distinct sociological groups, many of them having been culturally Lebanized and linguistically Arabized, at least to the extent of having acquired the local dialect; the Kurds, for their part, had been largely assimilated by the Sunni working class. All the religious communities, whether they were native or had come from elsewhere at some point, were Arab by language and culture; and many Christians, including Maronites, had contributed to the revival of one or the other at the time of the Nahda, and then in the next century during the interwar period. The variety of accents was therefore a result not of denominational attachment, but of geographical location or origin.[5] Throughout Syria and Lebanon—the old Bilād al-Shām—Muslims and Christians shared the same structures of kinship,[6] the same class divisions, and, to a very large extent, the same social values. The routines of daily existence revealed no major distinction between them either, prior to urbanization: domestic arrangements, culinary traditions, and the kinds of work they did[7] were largely common to both, and the life of the modern city only accentuated these similarities.

The theological dimension is no more enlightening. If the nominal line of demarcation between religious communities coincided, inevitably, with the forms of worship that they claimed to follow,[8] the controversies between Islam and Christianity belonged to the distant past. No one had seriously disputed either the nature of Christ or the legitimacy of 'Ali for centuries—a situation that did not change even after the Iranian revolution. In each community, the dogmas that historically were at the root of religious belief were often little known; in the extreme case of the Druze, they could be taught only once students had reached a certain age. Knowledge of these tenets was unnecessary, in fact, to the extent that membership in the community, acquired at birth, did not require a reasoned commitment. Adherence to dogma was something almost incidental. Indeed, with the exception of Protestants who sought to convert those whom they considered Christians in name only, proselytizing was virtually unknown. The tolerance shown in normal times—and even in times of war—toward the religious practices of others was therefore not so paradoxical as it seemed. Popular tradition sometimes went still further, promoting syncretism. There is the cult of Saint George/al-Khodr, for example, venerated in Beirut—and in Palestine—by both Christians and Muslims, as well as the devotions performed by Muslim fishermen to the Virgin of Nuriyyeh in the little chapel next to the vegetable and fish market of the same name, between the Burj and Place de l'Étoile.[9]

Divisions between communities in Beirut were independent of forms of worship or any specific anthropological substrate. At bottom they had to do—and still have to do today—with the fact that an individual cannot help but belong to a group. Imprisoned by the system of relationships to which he owes his ancestry, he finds himself by virtue of this very fact set apart from those who belong to another group. In this sense, religious communities can be considered as so many tribes,[10] whose exclusive sense of solidarity is akin to the *'asabiyya* detected by Ibn Khaldun in his sociology of Arab dynasties and clans.[11] Neither "religious community" nor "confessional community" denotes a very useful category. Although such terms may help to explain why certain groups can be mobilized for certain political purposes, they do not explain how these groups come into peaceful contact or into conflict with one another. One must keep in mind that the Arabic word *tā'ifa* (pl. *tawā'if*) does not specifically refer to religious groups; it denotes simply a "grouping" or "group." What is more, its meaning has changed over the course of Arab history, having been used at different times to designate different kinds of collectivities: corporations, political factions (thus, for example, the *mulūk al-tawā'if* and the *reyes de taifas* in eleventh-century Andalusia), and religious sects.[12] In this last sense, it is instructive to recall that *tā'ifa* was translated by European travelers and consuls until the early nineteenth century as "nation"—a rendering that would be very doubtful in modern French or English, but which has the virtue of pointing out the similarity between religious communities and other social structures and, in this way, of emphasizing the need to subsume this category under a broader one, as the French Arabist Maxime Rodinson proposed to do by endorsing the term "suprafunctional groups," coined by his compatriot, the sociologist Georges Gurvitch.[13] This suprafunctionality is embodied within each community by religious, educational, charitable, and even political institutions that allow more or less cohesive groups to navigate the challenges of modernity mostly intact, by providing a permanent framework for the activities of their members while at the same time insulating them against outside influences.

And yet communities are not monolithic; nor is their cohesiveness exempt from the tensions of internal dispute. This was already true in Lebanon under the Ottomans. After independence, political competition within a national state frequently caused a "community's sense of decency"[14] to take precedence over narrow factional interests, with the result that cooperation across groups was encouraged—a situation that was most visible in electoral alliances. Urban experience, particularly in the Beirut metropolitan area, also favored the dissolution of traditional points of reference. Both the secularizing tendencies of social life and the new interest in artistic creativity lent themselves to a freer expression of individual identity.[15] Increasingly children were given names having no explicit religious or historical connotation. Boys born between 1943 and 1975 were likelier to bear names such as Amin, Kamal, Karim, Ziad, Sami, Samir, and Walid, and girls' names such as Mona, Nada, Samia, Randa, and Rima, than in the past.

One consequence of the growing complexity of urban life and of the permeability of native society to Western influences was a decline in religious observance, apparent in Beirut and especially among young people, which weakened the intermediary role that parish churches and neighborhood mosques had traditionally played in their communities. The same was not true of schools, which were to remain a powerful source of support for confessional identity. Secular or nondenominational private institutions, few in number, educated a minority of children by comparison with the network of Christian religious schools—both foreign and local—and, to a lesser degree, with those of the Maqāsid society, deeply rooted in Sunni communities since the late nineteenth century and imitated by Shiʿa through the ʿAmiliyya society (named after Jabal ʿAmil, an area of southern Lebanon known for the tradition of its Shiʿi ʿulamas). Public schools were secular, but unassertively so, and they did little to promote communal integration since their students came from the neighborhoods in which they were located, the majority of which in Beirut had remained relatively homogeneous from the confessional point of view.

At all events, the secularization of daily life stopped on reaching the threshold of the law. The maintenance of a distinct legal system for religious communities preserved their separation from one another while reinforcing their integrity as sociological entities. By virtue of this regime, the various communal courts continued to be endowed with full jurisdiction over questions of personal status (involving marriage, divorce, and inheritance) that arose from civil legislation, the communities themselves being considered as moral persons in public law.[16] Inherited from the Ottoman millet system governing non-Muslim communities,[17] which itself codified the Qur'anic prescriptions concerning the "peoples of the Book," the communal regime was formally instituted as part of the Organic Law of Mount Lebanon that the Great Powers had ratified in 1861 (and again, with modifications, in 1864). It was subsequently brought over into the new Lebanese state with one major difference, namely, that for the first time the regime was extended to cover Muslims (whose religious institutions under Ottoman rule had come under the direct authority of the state). Moreover, apart from the recognition of civil marriages performed abroad, citizens seeking to escape the constraints of this system found no other recourse available to them.

THE DEAD ENDS OF COMMUNALISM

Not content with laying down sectarian boundaries in law, the communal regime made its influence on the institutional life of the country felt through what it is con-

venient to call "political confessionalism," which is to say the rule of communal proportion that governed the assignment of governmental posts and public positions,
as well as the composition of the National Assembly. This principle likewise had its
origin in the prehistory of the Lebanese state, in both Beirut and the Mountain: in
the city it was embodied by the advisory council (Majlis al-Shūra) that had been
created by the Egyptian administration under Ibrahim Pasha; in the mountains, by
the protocol of Shakib Effendi instituting a dual system of administration over
separate regions (one presided over by Maronites, the other by Druze), and then
by the Organic Law of Mount Lebanon, which established the Mutasarrifate and
equipped it with an administrative council whose seats were apportioned according to a rule of denominational representation.[18] The principle was subsequently
adopted by the Mandate and formally enshrined in Article 95 of the Constitution
of 1926.[19] Although this proposition was stipulated to be temporary, as a practical
matter, in the absence of any challenge to the communal regime as an "indivisible
whole,"[20] it remained in force.

In Beirut, political confessionalism manifested itself in the composition of the
city council, made up mainly of Sunni and Greek Orthodox, as well as in the tradition of naming a Christian—typically Greek Orthodox, but occasionally Greek
Catholic—as prefect (muhafiz), who constituted a counterpart to the Sunni mayor.
In the event this balancing arrangement was illusory since the city of Beirut (like
Paris before 1977) had no independent power of its own. Whichever person of old
patrician stock nominally held local power as muhafiz was for the most part an instrument of the central government, which is to say he represented, in the view of
the communities, the "Maronite government"—whose symbolic legitimacy came
from elsewhere, no matter that this elsewhere was very near. In a sense, then, the political confessionalism that characterized Beirut by virtue of its being the country's
capital overdetermined the political confessionalism that was peculiar to Beirut as
a city. Inevitably this was a source of frustration, aggravated by the chronic exacer-
bation of intercommunal tensions in the nation as a whole. As the primary vessel
of these tensions, Beirut remained the bellwether of the Republic, even when the
seat of the president moved to the outer suburbs.

The confessional mosaic that presented itself to view in the city's economy, in
its cultural life, and, physically, in its business centers takes on another aspect when
looked at through the prism of national politics. Whereas the city mixed people of
different denominations horizontally, as it were, or at least juxtaposed them (not
always harmoniously, of course, but without necessarily favoring certain individuals as a consequence of the relative weight of their communities), the capital
stacked them on top of one another in a vertical structure—in the event, a pyramid, in which the mosaic of the fifteen communities then officially recognized
(eleven of them Christian, three Muslim, and the last Jewish) shrank in both size
and complexity as one drew nearer to the summit. At the middle of the pyramid,

seven communities—Druze, Greek Orthodox, Greek Catholic, and Armenian Orthodox among them—were each represented in the governments of a dozen or more prime ministers; each had its share of other public posts as well. The upper level, however, was occupied only by the three largest communities—Maronites, Sunnis, and Druze. Since 1943 these communities had shared the three highest offices of the state.

In practice, however, power was concentrated in a still higher echelon, occupied by representatives of the Maronite community alone. The presidencies of the Assembly and the Council of Ministers were of minor importance. For although the regime created by the Constitution of 1926 was theoretically parliamentary in nature, having largely been modeled on the Third Republic in France, the institution of the presidency of the Republic was fortified by elements borrowed from both the Belgian constitution and that of monarchical Egypt,[21] giving it almost regal authority. More than this, the preeminence of the Maronites recurred in every domain of public life, since the main levers of power—notably the command of the army, military intelligence services (the Deuxième Bureau), police, and the general secretariat of the ministry of foreign affairs, as well as the rectorate of the Lebanese University and the governorship of the central bank following the creation of these two institutions in the 1960s—were in their hands. This vertical political power exercised a controlling influence over the horizontal urban mosaic by structuring the class relations that underlay it, in the same top-down manner. Although popular perceptions of this state of affairs inevitably blurred fine distinctions—to those who lived in the belt of poverty around Beirut, mainly Shi'i Muslims, their subjugation seemed to be due to the Maronite government, when in fact it was the result of a much more complex set of interlocking factors—they were no less consequential for that.

In a country in which institutional inertia had not yet managed to arrest social mobility, consociationalism—the term used by sociologists to describe the form of power-sharing by means of guaranteed group representation practiced in Lebanon and elsewhere—naturally tended to promote the growth of polarization. The communal regime, exposed to public view by the composition of governments and by the pattern of parliamentary representation, in which Christians (all denominations included) outnumbered Muslims and Jews by a factor of five or six, did not amount to a system of deliberate democratic choice—whatever the advocates of consociationalism as a way of managing conflict in deeply divided societies may say. While political confessionalism was sometimes described by architects of the National Pact such as Michel Chiha as a means of ensuring equilibrium among the religious "minorities" that composed Lebanon,[22] it was more often disparaged, at least rhetorically. Riad al-Sulh had already emphasized its defects in the governmental declaration of 7 October 1943—the only written trace of the National Pact—while conceding the "temporary" necessity of bringing about an equitable representation of the different communities. It was not a question only of furnishing a guarantee to the Maronites, by granting them a monopoly on the presidency of the Republic, but also of assuring the participation of the Sunnis in the government of the country, notably through the post of prime minister.

Confessionalism weighed all the more heavily on the nation as it was connected with a tradition of clientelism that had long weakened Lebanese political society to the advantage of a small number of prominent families. Clientelism is neither a specifically Lebanese phenomenon nor the inevitable corollary of a communal form of social organization. It is present in many societies, particularly along the Mediterranean rim, and even in neighboring countries one finds the two principal forms it has assumed in Lebanon, where patrons *(zuʿamaʾ)* are either large landowners or clan chieftains who, in the countryside, impose feudal-style relationships, or else urban notables who control networks of qabadayat.[23] Nonetheless the amplifying effects of confessionalism, through the institutional and political immobility to which it gives rise, on a clientelist system that already exerted its own power of resistance to democratic reforms cannot be ignored.

The influence of notables within each community was strengthened by a peculiar electoral regime, adopted by the Mandate authorities and subsequently retained by the Lebanese Republic, which led to the representation of both communities and electoral districts. The practice of choosing from representatives of more than one party under either a list system or a single-candidate system[24] naturally presented the advantage, given the condition of universal suffrage within constituencies, of obliging candidates to seek at least some minimum of intercommunal cooperation. But at the same time it increased the local power of notables, or of coalitions of notables, without whom the lists could not be drawn up in the first place.[25] And because voting was based on a person's theoretical place of residence, which was generally only his place of birth, even in the case of municipal elections, the influence of notables was reinforced still further. Although candidates in general elections could run anywhere they liked, voters wishing to change electoral district had to declare their intent well in advance, without any assurance that their petition would be approved. Indeed very few such transfers were authorized. As a result of this fossilized state of parliamentary representation, political life was incapable of keeping pace with economic and social developments.

No better example can be found of the system's inability to allow the popular will to express itself than the redistricting of Beirut for the 1960 parliamentary elections, which combined two weaknesses that together amounted to a refusal to acknowledge exactly these developments. The city was divided by the electoral law of the same year into three districts: Beirut 1 (three Armenian Orthodox seats, one Armenian Catholic, one Greek Orthodox, one Maronite, one Greek Catholic, and one Protestant), Beirut 2 (one Sunni seat, one Shiʿi, and one for "minorities," which is to say the smaller communities—those pledging allegiance to Rome, as well as Jews and

Neo-Aramaic-speaking Christians), and Beirut 3 (four Sunni seats, one Greek Orthodox). This method of partition had the effect of creating in each of the two large districts, 1 and 3, a communal bloc that was all the more likely to prevail as it was freed from the necessity of competing against the other: a Sunni bloc insulated against a Christian bloc (even if the latter was weighted by the Armenian vote—wholly controlled by the Tashnag party, and so generally to the advantage of moderate and loyalist candidates). At the same time, the size of the districts made them vulnerable to manipulation by local power brokers. This was especially the case in the third municipal district, where the za'im could hope that the other candidates on his list would be elected on his coattails. Moreover, the allocation of seats bore only an approximate relationship to the actual composition of the city's population. As part of a more general arithmetic used to determine electoral districting in the country as a whole, this allocation reflected a voting population composed of citizens registered in Beirut, which is to say that it recognized only long-established residents or, in any case, a demographic profile that no longer existed. The most recent immigrants had to leave to vote elsewhere. As for the inhabitants of the suburbs, even if some of them were registered to vote there, their voices were muffled by being mixed in with those of people in distant villages, whose concerns were wholly removed from theirs. A neighborhood such as Furn al-Shubbak, which had been part of the metropolitan area for decades, was—and still is today—part of a district that extended as far as the Biqaʿ, on the other side of the mountains. The only exception to this rule was Burj Hammud: most of its Armenian population had been registered in Beirut since the Mandate, but the Armenians also had a deputy in the Matn district, where Burj Hammud was located.

This electoral regime had the effect, among others, of effectively prohibiting modern parties from winning parliamentary representation, unless they were able to appeal to voters along strictly communal lines. Among the Christian population, the Phalange Party was in a position to do just this; indeed it was founded for the express purpose of defending Christian interests. Among the Sunni population, however, the old Najjadeh youth movement proved to be incapable of imitating its example and thereby supplanting notabiliary influence. The Independent Nasserite Movement, for its part, despite the extraordinary popularity of the Egyptian president among the Sunni working class, likewise failed to wrest control from the notables, and in 1972 managed to elect only a single deputy—a Christian, as it happened.

No matter that the notables, Muslim and Christian alike, profited from the parliamentary fragmentation produced by this electoral regime,[26] the proliferation of communal factions mainly benefited the holder of executive power, which resided with the president of the Republic rather than the head of the government. However important a figure the prime minister may have been, whether he came from Beirut or Tripoli, the government he directed answered to the president; and however fierce the debates in Parliament may have been, the national assembly, from the moment it gave the government a vote of confidence, ceased to matter—not once did it succeed in bringing down a government. Yet factionalism did little to strengthen political stability. To the contrary, it gave the country merely the appearance of a republic, and one that was all the more precarious since the preeminence of the Maronites, symbolized by their unchallengeable and permanent claim to the presidency, confirmed Muslim politicians in the impression that they had been left nothing more than the crumbs of political power. More generally, and more disturbingly, the confessional disequilibrium that had existed at the highest institutional levels from the beginning, and that then deteriorated further in the early 1970s, made it plain to Muslim citizens that still, a half century after the founding of Greater Lebanon, the state was not really theirs.

At bottom, the difficulty was that the negotiations surrounding the National Pact and the attainment of independence in 1943 did not succeed in doing away with the original dissymmetry of a multicommunal state constructed by France around, and on behalf of, the Maronite population. The desire of the people to live together, forcefully expressed at that time by great anti-French demonstrations, could not be doubted; even at the height of the crises that came later, it was no less clear. But it was not enough to guarantee communal integration. Whereas the National Pact sought to lay the groundwork for lasting understanding between Muslims and Christians, in practice it worked against the construction of a common identity. The internal cleavages created by institutionalized confessionalism were reinforced by outside influences—or, more precisely, by the inclination of domestic political factions to internalize these influences—with the result that Lebanon was, to an even greater degree than neighboring countries, structurally sensitive to changes in the world around it.

A DIVIDED IDENTITY

In the meantime, the reverberations of European power politics, formerly symbolized by the Eastern Question, had not ceased to make themselves felt throughout the Arab world. The Palestinian problem, which was one of its consequences, had first aroused popular feeling during the 1930s and subsequently concentrated the attention of all the more or less independent states in the region. Two decades later, in the 1950s, all the countries of the Mashriq were shaken at one moment or another by the collision between Arab nationalism and Western imperialism. Lebanon did not by any means escape the effects of either controversy. What set it apart from neighboring states, however, was the fact that the internal resonances of regional politics affected not only governmental policies, but the very possibility of holding the country together. For want of a genuine consensus about national identity, the various elements of the Lebanese polity regarded the regional and international environment in very different ways. The principal line of cleavage among them was to emerge with growing disagreement over Lebanon's proper place in the Arab world and its position in relation to the West.

Again, these differences in perception are explained by the peculiar circumstances surrounding the genesis of a state constructed by France in the interest of the Maronites. In spite of the eminent contribution of Maronite men of letters to the Nahda, and of the spirit of Arab-Syrian patriotism that in Beirut had motivated the Bustani and Yaziji families, the ideological world of the new state was characterized by a strict particularism that insisted on Lebanon's ancient history, uniquely rooted in the Mountain, independently of the rest of Bilād al-Shām. This view depended in turn on two mythical sources of legitimacy: the continuity of a quasi-sovereign Lebanese entity since the Maʿnid emirate,[27] and, going further back, the unbroken tradition of a "national" church dating to the eighth century.[28] In order to justify the enlargement of the Mountain to include Beirut, resort was had to this still more fanciful claim of direct descent from the merchant cities of Phoenicia.[29] At the same time, the landmarks of Arab history that guided the Muslims of Greater Lebanon—to say nothing of the cultural Arabness of the Maronites themselves—were ignored, and the modern outlook propagated by everyday life in Beirut was dismissed as a matter of little or no consequence.

The Lebanese Republic's relationship to the West was no less problematic.[30] Despite the renunciation of French protection, formalized by the National Pact, a sentimental regard for France as the nation's *doulce mère* (in Arabic, *al-umm al-hanūna*) survived in the Maronite imagination. This enduring attachment was symbolized by the celebration twice a year of a "mass for France": on Easter Monday, at the cathedral of the Maronite patriarch in the presence of the ambassador of the secular Fourth (and, after 1958, the Fifth) Republic; and on 15 August, the feast of the Assumption, at the summer residence of the archbishop of Beirut, to which the French chargé d'affaires was traditionally invited. Outmoded though it may have seemed, this Francophilia did not spring from simple nostalgia. Beyond its obvious religious echoes, the foundational link with the West had lost none of its force in relation to political power. Commemoration of the legacy of French imperial rule, which is to say the creation of Greater Lebanon itself, remained for Maronites the badge of Lebanese distinctiveness as well as the solemn expression of their own dominant position.[31] Associated with this was a tendency to play the role of honorary Westerners as well as a certain cultural provincialism, despite the fact that both impulses stood wholly in contradiction to the Maronite claim to a venerable history. The situation was altogether different, of course, in the case of the Muslims, of whom it is not an exaggeration to say that they continued to suffer from the dual trauma of the ruin of the Ottoman Empire and the defeat of Maysalun, both inevitably called to mind by renewed confrontation with the West. But here again Beirut's singular talent for synthesis was of no help whatever.

From now on these two questions, of Lebanon's Arabnesss and its relationship with the West, were destined to become the crux of the disagreement over national identity as well as the stake of the internal power struggles between Muslims and Christians, or, more exactly, between Muslims and Maronites. In the other Christian communities, the notion of Arabnesss encountered less resistance, and sometimes none at all. The National Pact, of course, had plainly acknowledged that Lebanon was "a country with an Arab face," and it was considered altogether natural that Lebanon should have been one of the five founders of the League of Arab States; indeed the Alexandria Protocol, which in October 1944 had prepared the way for the creation of this alliance, devoted a whole paragraph specifically to the recognition of Lebanese independence. The National Pact also tried to resolve the ambiguity inherent in the country's relationship to the West by stipulating—in the words of Riad al-Sulh, speaking on the floor of Parliament—that an independent Lebanon should be "neither a sanctuary nor a throughway for colonialism" (whose destination, Syria, scarcely needed to be mentioned). The inadequacy of these fine expressions of purpose was not slow to become apparent after Sulh's death, undermining still further the perilous state of the country's institutions.

AN INCOMPLETE NATION

The structural problems of Lebanese political society were plain even during the presidency of Bishara al-Khuri, although the good will given expression by the National Pact managed to preserve enough of its impetus to curb confessional polarization for a time. France's delay in disengaging the last of its troops, not finally withdrawn until the end of 1946, promoted unity among members of the political class. The warm relations that Khuri and Sulh made a point of maintaining with both Syrian and Egyptian leaders also helped to keep a damper on the latent controversy over the country's identity. Moreover, the most ardent Francophiles, such as Émile Eddé, were still discredited. The government's support for Great Britain, still the dominant power in the Near East, and the official friendship with the United States, now gradually moving to assert its influence there, aroused no misgivings. And in spite of the sense of solidarity felt in Lebanon, as elsewhere, in response to the escalation of the war in Palestine and the bitterness created by the defeat of the Arab armies in 1948, popularly perceived as a disaster (al-Nakba), the unsettling effects of the establishment of the state of Israel were to resound throughout the region only later. For the moment, while it had to cope with the influx of refugees from Palestine, Lebanon profited from the loss of Haifa to Arab commerce and the contributions made by Palestinian capital and ingenuity to the prosperity of Beirut. The war in Palestine had the additional advantage, for the ruling classes, of removing the threat posed by the Communist Party, whose support for the United Nations partition plan of November 1947, in accordance with Moscow's instructions, alienated many sympathizers and resulted in its being banned. The other main source of dissent, the

Syrian Social Nationalist Party (more worrisome perhaps on the national level, although it had been kept on a tight leash by the British), was also neutralized as a consequence of the alarm triggered by defeat in Palestine. Its chief, Antun Sa'adeh, was delivered to the authorities in Beirut by the short-lived Syrian dictator Husni al-Za'im, and executed for armed rebellion at the end of a hasty trial in July 1949.

The opportunities presented by the international and regional situation—on the whole favorable, despite the Palestinian disaster, to building institutions in the young state—were nonetheless neglected. The influence of the notables extended to every level of public life and encouraged the machinations of President Khuri, who even before the departure of French troops had begun to look for ways to prolong his mandate, due to expire in 1949. Rather than mend the alliance with Sulh, with whom he had broken a year after independence, Khuri went through several prime ministers before finally appealing (not once, but twice) to his former partner to form a new government. But the primacy of the presidency of the Republic was not yet seen in terms of the intercommunal balance of power, in large part because Khuri and his circle had stirred up still greater discontent among the Christian notables, who were treated as adversaries for opposing the chief of state's unconstitutional ambition of remaining in power for a second term and complaining about nepotistic excesses whose spread he had done nothing to check. Nor did the vote-rigging orchestrated by the government during the legislative elections of 1947 distinguish between Christians and Muslims; it aimed at destroying the whole of the opposition, without regard for sectarian attachment. Nevertheless the president's discretionary power with regard to the selection of the prime minister permitted him to retain some useful Sunni interlocutors (among them Sulh himself, much against his will), and with his control over a compliant Chamber assured, Khuri seized upon the occasion of the war in Palestine, where the Lebanese army was engaged, to amend the Constitution and renew his mandate, a year in advance.

The enforced stability of the presidency in no way meant that the government could count on its authority being respected. Apart from the scheming of Khuri's circle and the financial appetites of the Consortium, against whom the law raised little or no obstacle, a diffuse violence was now beginning to manifest itself—ordinary, almost unremarkable violence, even if the newspapers became worked up about a few particularly bloody incidents. There was, on the one hand, clan violence in traditionally anti-statist regions of the country, where the police were welcomed with gunfire. There was also political violence of the sort witnessed in August 1951, when supporters of the president's brother bombed the offices of the newspaper *Al-Bayraq* in Beirut, thus provoking a retaliatory assault on the home of the man who was believed to have ordered the attempt. Finally, there was intercommunal violence. In addition to the riots that shook Tripoli after the dissolution of the economic union with Syria, thereafter rapidly assuming the form of confessional conflict, and recurrent brawls between gangs in the neighborhoods of Beirut, the death of Riad al-Sulh—assassinated in Amman in July 1951 by a member of the SSNP (a Christian, in the event) to avenge Sa'adeh's death—ended in an atavistic settling of old scores. A fresh wave of violence was then unleashed in the center of Beirut, where, on hearing the news, rioters decreed a strike. A few Christian shopkeepers who did not close quickly enough were beaten, and one death was recorded. Four other victims were added to the list the next day, along with acts of vandalism that, it must be said, were partly motivated by anger arising from the economic distress of the Sunni working class.[32] This flare-up was nonetheless exceptional. Of greater and more troubling consequence was the dissatisfaction excited by Khuri's policies in political and media circles generally, which for the time being pushed communal polarization into the background while inviting violent reprisals unmarked by denominational prejudice, such as the attack against *Al-Bayraq*—all of this against the changing landscape of regional geopolitics.

The Near East had irrevocably entered the cold war era in May 1950 with the Tripartite Declaration, by which the United States, Great Britain, and France announced their intention to control the sale of arms to countries in the region and to freeze the armistice demarcation lines between Syria and Israel, with the purpose of containing the expansion of Soviet influence. Despite the protests that greeted this declaration in Damascus and in other Arab cities, Beirut among them, and that ushered in a brief period of neutralism, the dynamics of superpower conflict superseded regional opinion. Great Britain, having persuaded the United States to agree to its coordinating the defense of the Near East against Soviet aggression, sought first of all to shore up the remnants of its empire. Supported by the two branches of the Hashimite family, in Amman and Baghdad, it now turned its attention to Egypt, where Mustafa an-Nahas, the elderly head of the Wafd party, had been returned to power as prime minister in January 1950. British pressure soon produced an unintended result. Rejecting the idea of integrating the structure of regional defense, which would only have served to give new life to the British protectorate, Nahas repudiated the Anglo-Egyptian treaty of 1936, which he himself had signed. Beirut was among the cities that followed Cairo in passionately demanding an end to the monarchy and complete independence. In addition to demonstrations by the Sunni working class, Arab nationalist students at the American university took to the streets and then, after the expulsion of the leaders of the protest, successfully went on strike to gain their readmission.

President Khuri himself, though not an enemy of Great Britain, was friendly with Nahas and hostile to the Hashimites. He therefore refused to subscribe to the defense pact, without, however, reaping any benefit from the build-up of British forces in the region, as he had hoped to do. To the contrary, London skillfully maneuvered to exploit the discontent aroused by his domestic policies. In the ensuing course of events the absence of Riad al-Sulh, in whom the pro-British capitals as well as Cairo had placed their trust as an interlocutor, was keenly felt.[33] A few weeks after the coup d'état carried out in Egypt on 23 July 1952 by the "Free Officers" under the leadership of General Muhammad Naguib and Colonel Gamal Abdel Nasser—not yet favorably disposed to the Soviet Union, and indeed reputed to be pro-American—the death blow was struck. The withdrawal of the British security umbrella left the field open to the Lebanese opposition, now joined by the shopkeepers of Beirut,[34] who on 15–16 September called a strike that partially paralyzed the downtown. The government's attempts to suppress the strike succeeded only in widening it. Khuri once again sought a new Sunni ally to form a government—and for a moment thought that he had found one in the person of Saeb Salam, son and political heir of Salim. The general strike obliged Salam to refuse, however, leaving Khuri no choice but to resign, having first appointed the army commander, General Fuad Shihab, to preside over a transitional government until elections could be held to name a successor. This turned out to be the impeccably Anglophile Camille Chamoun.

In the collective memory of Beirut's middle class, above all that of its Christian element, Chamoun's presidency was to be cherished as an era of carefree prosperity. Yet it was during this period that the communal problem came to be fatally conjoined with the country's growing sensitivity to external shocks. Notwithstanding a few halting efforts to improve housing and basic services, the predominantly Muslim regions on the periphery of the city were abandoned in favor of ensuring the primacy of the market, which in Lebanon now constituted a pure and unrestrained form of capitalism, albeit a highly profitable one in the short term. The successes of economic liberalism could not long mask the cleavages within Lebanese society, however, which became all the more acute as the regional conflict between Arab nationalism and Western foreign policy now began to infiltrate local politics.

With the sudden appearance of a neutral Egypt under Nasser's direction, Arab nationalists had escaped British domination at last. But by a curious shift in cold war strategy, containment of the Soviet Union soon gave way to containment of Arab nationalism and Nasserite Egypt, and Lebanese foreign policy, like that of the other states in the region, gradually came to be preoccupied by the problem of the "defense" of the Near East.[35] As a friend of the Hashimite kings, before becoming an ally of the United States, Chamoun hastened to make his influence felt, without worrying unduly about the consequences for Lebanese society.

In Syria, Jordan, and Iraq the controversy over Arab nationalism had the effect of pitting governments against the main driving forces of the society, if not actually of society as a whole. In Lebanon, support for Nasser was concentrated in the heart of urban society: although the Egyptian leader's rhetoric aroused a fervor in Beirut similar to the excitement observed in Damascus, it was restricted to the Arab street. Christians, choosing to align themselves for the most part with the "free world," to which they felt attached by the dual bond of Westernization and free-market economics,[36] remained unreceptive to Nasser's advocacy of national liberation, no matter that it formed a part of the intellectual heritage of the modern Western world. Between these two opposing positions there were many intermediate shades of opinion among politicians and intellectuals, the most unexpected of which was articulated by Georges Naccache, who, despite having raised Francophilia to an art form, now considered Nasser's ideas more favorably. The communal divide was nonetheless less clear outside elite circles, where Arabism was perceived by some as a threat to sectarian equilibrium and by others as an instrument of mobilization against Maronite preeminence. As a result, the advance or containment of Arab nationalism became a domestic political issue, and civil war for the first time a possible outcome.

Even so, nothing was fated to happen automatically. Saeb Salam had not yet reconstituted the political organization he had inherited from his father. In the meantime Riad al-Sulh's cousin, Sami al-Sulh—prime minister several times under Chamoun and, on the whole, an accommodating one—presided over the Sunni machine in Beirut with the easygoing manner of a neighborhood boss (hence his affectionate nickname, Baba [Papa] Sami). The shock wave unleashed by the Suez crisis in the summer and fall of 1956 overwhelmed this delicate balance, however. Whereas Chamoun aligned himself still more closely with the pro-Western Hashimite camp, the adulation of the majority of Muslims for Nasser was boundless, and the uneasy equilibrium of local and regional antagonisms quickly degenerated. Chamoun's reckless embrace of the Eisenhower Doctrine, in disregard of the constraints of the National Pact, was reinforced (according to the subsequent testimony of a local CIA official) by daily American interference in local politics.[37] At the same time the Syrian-Egyptian alliance, concluded in February 1958, revived the unificationist sentiments of the majority of Lebanese Muslims—although now, by an irony of history, Arab unity was to be constructed in opposition to the Hashimites.

The situation had been made still more explosive by the deadlock that increasingly gripped the political process. In the spring of 1957 the government moved to take matters in hand, once again rigging legislative elections to achieve a massive victory. This was all that was needed for Chamoun himself to be accused of seeking to extend his term in office, and indeed he did nothing to deny the allegation. It remained only to wait for the spark: the assassination of Nasib Matni, an opposition journalist (and, as it happened, a Maronite), on 7 May 1958. The uprising that then broke out against Chamoun quickly turned into civil war—a foreshadowing on a small scale of the grand suicide of 1975, minus the Palestinians. In Gemmayzeh, the barricades were erected by Christian loyalists belonging to the Phalange Party, curiously supported in this instance by their traditional adversaries, the anti-Nasserite and pro-Hashimite SSNP. In Musaytbeh, Saeb Salam and his brothers directed the revolt on the Muslim side.

Given that Matni's assassination was attributed to people around the president, himself a Christian, the crisis plainly cannot be reduced to a purely Islamic-

Christian confrontation.[38] Not all of the country took up arms, and many places where Muslims and Christians lived together remained untouched by the war. In Beirut, the hostilities were almost entirely limited to the perimeter of the city center, along an arc stretching from Qantari to Gemmayzeh and including Musaytbeh, Basta, and Bashura, but not the downtown itself. In fact, the violence was largely restricted to the highest seats of the government, notably the presidential palace on Qantari Hill where Chamoun had dug in, personally firing on rebel forces; to the redoubts of the opposition, such as Salam's headquarters on Musaytbeh and that of the Karameh family in Tripoli; and to Chamoun's native region, the Shuf Mountains, dominated by the Druze Kamal Jumblatt. The commercial district of Beirut was largely spared, with the exception of one or two bloody episodes. It is true that there was little reliance on artillery, mainly small-caliber mortars and bazookas—unlike the situation in 1975. Although the fighting claimed a few hundred victims over the course of two months, it had more the quality of a murderous family quarrel than of a battle to the last bullet. Nonetheless it revealed the extent of the unresolved problems of independent Lebanon. Confessionalism was the most obvious of these, of course, together with the absence of agreement over national identity that flowed from it, and the dysfunction of the political system that it brought about. The institution of the presidency, in particular, stood exposed as the focal point of communal conflict, although the personalization of power worked to attenuate the degree of confessional polarization,[39] in this case by setting Christian politicians against Chamoun.

Hostilities were brought under control in a few weeks, following the landing of American marines in Beirut, which itself came in response to the overthrow of the monarchy in Iraq on 14 July 1958. An agreement between Nasser and Eisenhower's envoy, Robert Murphy, then brought to power Fuad Shihab, descendant of the emirs of the same name and commander of the army, which he had succeeded in holding together. In charting a path of recovery from the crisis, Shihab sought not only to renew the purposes of the National Pact, seriously damaged under Chamoun, but also to give it the largest possible scope by defusing the principal sources of tension.

On the regional scale, Shihab adopted a policy of entente with Egypt that acknowledged the support of a large part of the population for Nasserism. Alignment with the dominant Arab power, however hedged with qualifications, served to guarantee the integrity of Lebanon's territory—symbolized by the meeting in March 1959, at a military outpost on the Syrian border, between Shihab and Nasser, now president of the United Arab Republic (UAR)—and therefore of Syria as well. Even after the break-up of the Syrian-Egyptian union in June 1961, Shihab held to his course and continued to prefer the UAR (as Egypt continued to be called after Nasser's death, until 1971) to neighboring Syria as a strategic partner. A call for the establishment of diplomatic relations between Lebanon and Syria, issued in Damascus by Khalid al-'Azm, met with a flat refusal in Beirut. In return, Nasser made a show of respect for Lebanon's special position in the "Arab civil war" that soon opposed Egypt to Syria, Iraq, and Saudi Arabia.[40] Policy coordination between Egypt and Lebanon, described by one commentator as a process of "endosmosis,"[41] was to go on growing, above all after the end of the Algerian War, when France, still looked upon with sympathy by Lebanese Christians, and no longer standing in an antagonistic relation to Nasser, adopted a new attitude to the Arab world under the influence of General de Gaulle.[42]

Lebanese diplomacy, for its part, was placed in the service of a domestic policy that sought to rally Muslim support for the state and to increase the Muslim presence in the upper levels of the administration, this with a view to remedying once and for all the imbalance formalized by the creation of Greater Lebanon in 1920. On assuming office, Shihab brought the leaders of the 1958 uprising into the government, naming Rashid Karameh prime minister, with special responsibility for Tripoli, and putting Saeb Salam in charge of Beirut. He mandated the equal distribution of civil service jobs,[43] while working to integrate the predominantly Muslim peripheral regions into the economic life of the country—an ambition that went well beyond simply cleaning up the aftermath of the civil war.[44] Ultimately this belated attempt at nation-building failed, but the political gamble paid off in the short term: Shihabism enjoyed a degree of support in outlying areas proportional to the resistance that was shown a few decades earlier to the prospect of their annexation to Greater Lebanon.[45] Shihab himself enjoyed genuine popularity outside the capital, a sign that he had in fact succeeded in establishing among Muslims a new relationship to the state. In Beirut the situation was more ambiguous to the extent that Salam, having restored his family's claim to leadership as a result of the insurrection of 1958, soon broke with both Shihab and Nasser in the hope of winning the support of the pro-Saudi camp in the Arab contest for power.

For Shihab, as he was to state in a rare public explanation of his aims, what mattered was constructing a new society, one in which inherited privileges would disappear and the state would be transformed into an arbiter of social relations by acquiring a margin of autonomy in relation to the short-term calculations of the entrenched business class. Yet the prevailing doctrines of economic liberalism were never seriously challenged, and the interests of the Beirut merchant republic suffered no lasting injury during Shihab's presidency. The leaders of this republic were equally adept at playing the game, without directly taking issue with official policy. One of the few moments of public opposition was the lawyers' year-long strike of 1961–62 in protest of the authorization granted to the Arab University of Beirut, founded by Nasserite Egypt, to teach law. But this complaint, despite its class and confessional aspects, did not rise to the level of confrontation with the government.

If Shihab sought to address the structural problems of Lebanese society by promoting regional economic development—not altogether unsuccessfully, it must be said—his administration's inability to forge a new vision of politics created other problems. The program of electoral reform adopted in 1960 only preserved the power of the very notables whom Shihab was fond of calling *fromagistes* (French slang for the passengers on a gravy train). In the event, the strengthening of the state was scarcely perceptible apart from an enlargement of the security apparatus. After the failed attempt by the SSNP to overthrow the government at the end of December 1961, the army's intelligence branch expanded its control over public life, though without any express authorization to do so, imposing serious restrictions on the freedom of speech and association. Nonetheless the hegemony of the military did not encourage modernization, as it had done in other countries in the region, albeit in authoritarian form.

Far from neutralizing clientelism, the system of control instituted by the Deuxième Bureau served as a means of manipulating it to its own advantage. The government moved to exert its authority over urban gangs, especially in Beirut, and the clans that held sway on the country's borders. Otherwise it sought to supplant traditional patrons only to the extent that they were opposed to its policies, and granted obliging notables the support of its administrative and police apparatus. This had the effect of marginalizing political newcomers committed to Shihab's program, who, having no client networks of their own, found themselves excluded from the 1964 legislative elections because they threatened to hurt the chances of the government's local allies.[46] And in the event that zu'ama' rallied opposition forces in the countryside, as Saeb Salam had done in Muslim Beirut, the regime used its own patronage resources and, if necessary, the police power of the state to ensure the victory of more congenial candidates.[47] Obviously these measures were not enough to bring about the reform of the political class that Shihab sought. A more decisive step in this direction came from the Phalange Party, which, with the encouragement of the government, anxious to mitigate the hostility of the traditional Maronite elites, began to transform itself into a mass political movement. Whereas in the villages of the Mountain it asserted itself as a counterweight to the leading families, in Christian Beirut it recruited members of the lower middle class who had moved to the city. In both cases, the aspirations of its supporters dovetailed with the regime's program of regional development.[48] By the nature of its appeal, however, the Phalange was also a vehicle of ideological expansionism and communal polarization— tendencies that became clear in 1968, as it began to win over Maronite opponents of Shihabism, and still more so with the mounting extremism of the 1970s.

Secular parties were unlikely to be more reliable partners. The only two existing ones, the SSNP and the Communist Party, were fatally handicapped by their ideological rigidity. The SSNP was fiercely hostile to Nasserism, as it had shown in both Syria and Lebanon, where it did not hesitate to take part in the civil war of 1958 alongside its old Phalangist adversaries in support of Chamoun's government. The lingering resentment produced by its exclusion from Shihab's government of national reconciliation led it to attempt a coup d'état three years later, unsuccessfully, erasing whatever room for maneuver was left to it. As for the Communist Party

(LCP), it had been outlawed ever since endorsing the Soviet position in favor of the partition of Palestine in 1947. Nevertheless it had managed to preserve its apparatus. Already in June 1948 a report by the American intelligence services emphasized that the Lebanese Communists were the best organized among all those in the Near East, and accused them of disseminating propaganda from Moscow in neighboring countries.[49] Although forced to operate underground, the LCP succeeded that year in instigating a violent protest against the decision to hold the UNESCO conference in Beirut; and despite the ensuing crackdown, it was able to collect signatures for a Soviet-inspired manifesto denouncing nuclear weapons.[50] Al-Tarīq, the review founded by the architect Antun Tabet, was allowed to continue publication, enabling it to keep an audience among the intelligentsia. The LCP also maintained its influence in a few labor unions, notably among the typesetters and, more surprisingly, workers in the hospitality industry. Paradoxically, however, like the other Communist parties of the Mashriq, its difficulties were liable to increase to the extent that the Soviet Union managed to make its presence felt in the region. Although the LCP supported Nasser following the first Asian-African conference, held in Bandung, Indonesia, in 1955, and during the Suez crisis the next year, it joined the Syrian Communist Party, to which it was organically linked, in opposing the Syrian-Egyptian union. For this association it paid a heavy price, through the loss of many members and by the martyrdom of its secretary general, Farjallah Hélou, tortured to death in the prisons of the Syrian province of the United Arab Republic. Furthermore, under Shihab the LCP was unable to profit either from its participation in the uprising against Chamoun or from its traditional rivalry with the SSNP, abominated though this party was by the regime. In addition to the repressive effects of police control, which now extended over the whole of Lebanese political life, the country's alignment with Egypt, where Communists were still persecuted, deprived it of any hope of regaining lawful existence, still less a position of official favor.

The political and structural impasse that condemned Shihab's reformist vision, predicated on economic development, to remain unrealized was reason enough for the president to resist the temptation of trying to prolong his term in office. His chosen successor, Charles Hélou, preserved the basic orientation of his foreign policy, in particular the warm relationship with Nasser. In May 1965 Hélou made the first official visit by a Lebanese head of state to Cairo, the first leg of a tour that took him to Paris, and then the Vatican, as though he meant in this way to illustrate the order of priorities for Lebanese diplomacy.[51] The result in any case was that stability was protected in Lebanon while its neighbors exhausted themselves in internecine quarrels. And even if the gradual intensification of the Arab-Israeli conflict aroused apprehensions in Beirut, Nasser refrained from pressuring Lebanon to join with Jordan and Syria in order to thwart Israel's plan of diverting the headwaters of the Jordan River from their natural storage basin, the Sea of Galilee.[52] The Egyptian president could still count on enthusiastic support among the Sunni population of Beirut. Large crowds turned out to protest a visit there by the Tunisian president Habib Bourguiba shortly after his speech in March 1965 at Jericho—then under Jordanian sovereignty—calling for the peaceful settlement of the conflict with Israel, which was interpreted as an attack on Nasser's policy. Reassuringly, or so it must have seemed, the demonstrators who booed Bourguiba chanted Hélou's name in addition to that of his more famous ally.

Continuity prevailed also in domestic policy, at least at the beginning. As a protégé of Shihab, Hélou was supported by the same parliamentary majority and supervised by his predecessor's confederates, in particular the military leaders who, thanks to the omnipresent Deuxième Bureau, held real power. Very quickly, however, Shihabism lost its impetus. The modernization effort was slowed by the failure of a reform bill being pushed by the administration and the judicial branch, and then seriously harmed by the collapse of Intra Bank in October 1966 and the banking crisis that shook the Beirut market in its wake. The following year, the immense upheaval in the geopolitics of the Near East caused by the Six-Day War in June upset the fragile equilibrium of Lebanese politics, which ultimately Shihabism had not succeeded in bracing to the point that it was capable of withstanding severe external shocks. The project of building a nation was therefore doomed to remain incomplete, and the identity of the country to remain undecided in the eyes of its citizens. Those who supported the cause of Arab nationalism had nonetheless begun to become accustomed to the idea of Lebanon's exceptional status among Arab nations. But the persistent hostility toward Arab nationalism on the part of those who insisted upon a thorough-going Lebanonism threatened to ruin everything that had so far been accomplished.

THE REPUBLIC OF ARAB LETTERS

Arab geopolitics found expression in Beirut not only by means of diplomacy or through demonstrations in the street. The city's intellectual life exerted an equal or even greater authority. In this regard, however, perceptions of identity were still more blurred. As the capital of a political republic that was not prepared to unambiguously affirm its Arabnesss, the city was also the seat of a republic of letters that recognized the cultural reality of Arabism while at the same time displaying the full range of its many variations.

Since the Nahda, the cultural and intellectual purpose of Beirut had not gone unfulfilled. Over time literature had come to occupy a place of honor, and the world of men (and women) of letters went well beyond the few writers who could make a living from their books, including a good many lawyers and teachers, to say nothing of journalists. Although the Lebanese Republic in the years after independence had shown scant interest in endowing the country with cultural institutions (apart from welcoming UNESCO, whose new exhibition hall was well suited to hosting various types of events), private initiative sometimes succeeded in making up for the shortcomings of the state. In the late 1940s, for example, Michel Asmar established the Cénacle Libanais, a nonpartisan academic circle that served as a laboratory for new mainstream thinking, disseminated by its own publishing arm. A quite different, but hardly less influential, institution was the musical theater founded a bit later by the brothers 'Asi and Mansur Rahbani. Unmistakably identified with the voice of the great Lebanese diva Fairuz (née Nuhud Haddad), it was to do more than any textbook in constructing a statist-nationalist mythology—though this did not prevent the company from celebrating Palestine or, in the 1950s, from recording dozens of songs in praise of Damascus on Arab radio. Curiously, although they were working at the crossroads of a great many diverse, and indeed cosmopolitan, tendencies in Beirut, the Rahbanis set their productions in an archetypal country village, paying no regard to the experience of city dwellers. It was not until the 1970s that Fairuz's and 'Asi Rahbani's son, the *enfant terrible* Ziad Rahbani, attempted to express Beirut's unique synthesis in song and musical comedy.

Lebanese authors and artists were not the only players on this stage. The openness of Beirut's economy had its cultural counterpart, with one slight difference, namely that the emergence of the cultural sphere had preceded economic prosperity in the modern history of the city. The Nahda had left its mark on Arab societies well beyond Bilād al-Shām when Beirut was only the port of Damascus; the Revival of the 1930s likewise occurred before the postwar boom. The city's promotion to the rank of a major financial market and commercial hub of the Near East nonetheless favored the production and transmission of cultural goods. The appeal of its way of life attracted writers in particular, who were no longer content merely to send their manuscripts there and who now, in increasing numbers, preferred to take up permanent residence near their publishers and one or another of the many places of recreation and inspiration that filled the city. By virtue of their presence, the republic of Arab letters ceased to be something diffuse and delocalized. Indeed, its physical boundaries could now be described. They extended from the Lazariyyeh Center in the commercial downtown, where the majority of publishing houses were located among a clustering of book shops near the Dolce Vita café, to the cliffs of Rawsheh, passing along the way by the Horseshoe Café on Rue Hamra and the offices of *An-Nahar*, the newspaper founded on the same street in 1933, which gladly opened its columns to poets and writers—not to mention the campus of the American university and the two unavoidable brasseries across from it, on the other side of Rue Bliss, Faysal and Uncle Sam (whose name did not prevent it from serving as the favorite meeting place of supercilious anti-imperialists).

Between the two world wars the success of Beirut publishing, supported by what was already a deeply rooted tradition of typography and bookmaking, began to attract manuscripts from other parts of the Arab world. This trend was considerably amplified after 1945. The first foreign author to settle in the city was probably Nizar Qabbani, from Damascus, who became a part-time resident and whose love poems—no less (and possibly more) than his patriotic works—were intended as a statement of emancipation. Beirut houses were also to publish the leading Iraqi poets, notably Badr Shakir al-Sayyab, whose masterpiece, *Unshudat al-Matar* (Song of the Rain), appeared in 1960. One house, with the frankly revanchist name of Dār al-'Awda (Return Publishers), specialized from the mid-1960s onward in Palestinian poetry. Mahmud Darwish, then living in Haifa, brought out his first collection to appear outside Palestine with Dār al-'Awda in 1966. Seven years earlier, in 1959, Beirut had welcomed an iconoclastic novel by Naguib Mahfouz called *Awlad haratina* (Children of the Alley), for which the author could not find a publisher in Cairo. But the nerve center of the Arab republic of letters was situated among a group of less well known poets associated with *Shi'r* (Poetry), a review edited by Yusuf al-Khal. The sensibilities that found expression in it were as diverse as the paths that had led its authors to Beirut. In addition to Khal himself, a native of Wādī al-Nassara (Valley of Christians) in northern Syria, *Shi'r* was dominated by the towering figure of Adonis (the pseudonym used by Ali Ahmad Said Asbar), who came from the Alawite region near Lataqiyya and espoused the ideology of Greater Syria. *Shi'r* also introduced a third Syrian poet, Muhammad al-Maghut, while nurturing the careers of several Lebanese authors, among them Shawqi Abi-Shaqra and, above all, the young Unsi al-Hajj, who with his collection of prose poems *Lan* (Never), published before he was twenty years old, in 1960, exploded what remained of Arabic metrics. Although poetic invention mattered first and foremost for these writers, their work was at the same time invested with the mission of changing the world, or, failing that, the Arab world. In this sense the *Shi'r* group was not unrelated to the circle of more overtly politicized writers who were published in Beirut. All of them shared the ambition of bringing about a cultural revolution, which, ultimately, meant encouraging political protest.

The republic of letters was also an academy, and in this role the American University of Beirut worked miracles. There is no question that AUB was the premier center of cultural and ideological extraterritoriality in Beirut in the twentieth century. Already under the Mandate, when Université Saint-Joseph still specialized in training the administrative and professional elites of the Lebanese Republic, students came to AUB from throughout the Near East. It was there that an obscure professor of German named Antun Sa'adeh founded the Greater Syria Party (forerunner of the SSNP) in the early 1930s, and there that the student group al-'Urwa al-wuthqā (The Firmest Bond—an echo of the famous phrase from the Qur'an [2.256]) later argued the case for Arab nationalism. In 1948 another faculty member, the Damascene historian Qustantin Zurayq, published *Ma'nā al-Nakba* (The Meaning of the Disaster), a work whose influence among the generation that grew up with the loss of Palestine was unrivaled. The exodus of that year brought with it a number of Palestinian teachers, most of whom had studied in Beirut, and still more students. One of these, a student in the school of medicine who indefatigably put his learning to humane use by helping to care for his countrymen in the refugee camps around Beirut, was named George Habash. Harakat al-Qawmiyyin al-ʿArab, the campus organization Habash founded in the early 1950s with friends from Palestine, Lebanon, and elsewhere—known after 1958 as the Arab Nationalist Movement (ANM)—soon established itself as a mainspring of Nasserite advocacy in several countries; in 1967 it joined with other revolutionary groups to form the Popular Front for the Liberation of Palestine (PFLP), which later became, after Fatah, the largest element of the Palestine Liberation Organization (PLO). Throughout the 1950s AUB served as a rallying point for Arab nationalists who opposed the Algerian war, the trilateral expedition to Suez, and, above all, American foreign policy. Protest became a habit. It was at AUB that students formed the Arab Cultural Club as a counterweight to both the Cénacle Libanais and Francophone influence. Until 1975, and well beyond, the American campus was to remain perhaps the safest haven for the spirit of rebellion in Beirut, as well as a place where cosmopolitan ideas and ways of living came into contact with a radical commitment to nationalism.

On the margins of literature, and free of academic attachments, political exiles further enriched and complicated Beirut's intellectual life. Even if not all of them were published authors, they were forever scribbling away. What is more, they lived in permanent contact with journalists and editors, whether they drank with them in the cafés or deliberately sought them out in their offices, prevailing upon them to circulate this or that item of news or to soften or harden an editorial line on this or that subject of controversy. A babel of Arab accents, Beirut was the impromptu capital of various political groups forced to relocate by police repression in their native countries, beginning with the Syrian Baʿth Party, whose founders, Michel ʿAflaq and Salah al-Din al-Bitar, endured several periods of exile in Beirut. Only two hours from Damascus, they remained well informed about the situation there and ready to return home at once in case circumstances changed, even though it meant having to head right back to Beirut at a moment's notice if events took an unforeseen turn. Other Baʿthists joined them in the Lebanese capital, from both Syria and Iraq. Saddam Hussein, a young party member on the road to exile in Egypt following the failed attempt to assassinate Iraqi general Abdul Karim al-Qasim in October 1959, stayed for several weeks in an apartment on Rue Hamra. Hafez al-Assad, a young Syrian army commander, was also seen paying a visit to Salah Bitar before the schism within the Baʿth Party of May 1963.

Even when repression in their homelands did not make exile unavoidable, Baʿthist leaders found it agreeable to be in Beirut, where communication was unhampered and information readily collected. And then there was the force of habit:

in going day after day to the Dolce Vita, which had become their headquarters, they found themselves among friends—but also enemies. For the Ba'thists were not alone in the city. Quite apart from the agents of the various intelligence services whom their presence attracted, they could hardly escape contact with their rivals in the ANM (who, in addition to Palestinians and Lebanese, included Syrians, Iraqis, Yemenis, and Kuwaitis), to say nothing of the socialist and communist militants who came from almost every country, Iraqis and Yemenis among them again, as well as a handful of Saudis (who generally rejected this name, derived from the name of the ruling family, preferring to say that they were natives of the Arabian Peninsula); even distant Morocco had representatives in Beirut, at least intermittently, in the persons of Muhammad al-Basri, ally of the nationalist leader and politician Mehdi Ben Barka, and the journalist Bahi Muhammad. Not all the exiles could be found together at the same time; indeed, they often sought to avoid one another. But even if each group had its own preferred meeting place, the promontory of Beirut was by no means a place of vast distances and from time to time their paths were bound to cross—particularly when they made the rounds of the newspapers, especially *An-Nahar,* where on some days the office of the brilliant columnist Michel Abu Jawdeh looked like the Arab League. How many alliances were concluded or undone there, how many reconciliations proposed, how many schemes hatched? Naturally there is no way of knowing. What is certain, however, is that the concentration in the space of a square mile or two of so many conflicting allegiances promoted the free discussion of ideas, which had become impossible elsewhere, and helped to form points of convergence between rival—and often antagonistic—doctrines, as the virtually symmetric movements of the Lebanese left toward Arab nationalism, and then from Arab nationalism toward socialism, were to show in the late 1960s. The same phenomenon of increasing radicalization was to be observed among the Palestinians in Beirut.

Of all the exiles, the Palestinians and the Syrians felt the least out of place there. In both cases their links to Beirut were of long standing, and were it not for the dramatic political circumstances that had sent them into exile, visiting the city would have seemed an altogether normal thing to do. Neither the intellectuals nor militants who came in the aftermath of the Ba'th coup of February 1966 in Damascus had really been uprooted, least of all since they could hear the accents of their own countrymen all around them. A good part of the Syrian middle classes, and especially the Christian bourgeoisie, had already moved with weapons and suitcases to Beirut. And if these older immigrants were more or less allergic to the rhetoric of armed struggle, in which they could not help but recall one of the sources of their own exile, family ties and bonds among former neighbors tempered whatever uneasiness they may have felt. For Palestinians who arrived in the wake of the June 1967 war, paradoxically, things were easier: bourgeois families, both Christian and

Muslim, that settled in Ras Beirut after 1948 had no reason to be wary of the younger generation of partisans, who after all were fighting for land whose loss was lamented by all Palestinians, rich and poor alike, even if the doctrine that guided this struggle was part of a broader pan-Arab ideology. Unlike their Syrian counterparts, the Palestinian combatants could be sure of finding not only moral support, but also financial assistance from their prosperous compatriots. Significantly, the weakness that many educated middle-class Palestinians were to feel for the radicalism of George Habash dates from this period.

The Palestinian militants had yet another advantage, by comparison with the other exiles of the Arab world, in that they had access nearby to a pool of popular and readily mobilized support. Although the refugee camps in the south—unlike the Beirut cafés frequented by intellectuals—were under the strict police control of the Lebanese state, they constituted a sort of political compost in which ideas could be translated into action. Thanks to the many medical services that the Doctor (al-Hakīm, as Habash was familiarly called) had rendered there, the ANM had long been favorably regarded in the camps before the radical Palestinianism of Fatah, a product of the impasse in which Arab nationalism came to find itself as a result of Nasser's wrangling for control with his neighbors, began to attract a following in the mid-1960s. Founded in Kuwait in 1959 by young Palestinians who for the most part had been educated in Cairo, though some in Damascus, Fatah came from a world far removed from the Beirut of the intellectuals. It was not slow in making its appearance there, however. While militants in the camps tried to break free of police surveillance long enough to enlist new recruits, others went around to editorial offices in the capital with copies of a newspaper called simply *Filastinuna* (Our Palestine), which, without claiming officially to follow Fatah, stood the slogan of Arab nationalism on its head by asserting that the liberation of Palestine was the road to Arab unity, and not the other way around. Soon these partisans were distributing communiqués in addition to newspapers. Among them was a message from al-ʿĀsifa (The Storm), the clandestine military wing of Fatah, which announced in early January 1965 the first guerrilla operation on Israeli territory and the launching of the armed struggle.

THE WAR OF THE NEWSPAPERS

Beirut was the only place in the Arab world where such a communiqué could be issued—and, more than that, published. In spite of the constant preoccupation of the Lebanese government to avoid provoking Nasser, whose intelligence services reacted violently to al-ʿĀsifa's initiative, which they characterized as a maneuver by the CIA, the pluralism of the press in Beirut guaranteed that no Arab voice would be stifled, even when it explicitly conveyed a challenge to Egyptian authority. An even broader degree of freedom was allowed in the treatment of Arab politics than in the coverage of Lebanese news, which the Deuxième Bureau sought either to control by intimidating journalists or to manipulate by planting false or misleading information—the source of its rhyming nickname "Dactylo" (Typist).

As governments in other parts of the region took steps to shackle public opinion, and many times physically to lock up its spokesmen, the newspapers of Beirut had come to represent the free Arab press. In spite of its far larger circulation, *Al-Ahram* in Cairo was only an Egyptian newspaper, and a semi-official one at that. In Damascus the press had slowly been strangled, and many newspaper owners and journalists, such as Riad al-Rayes, whose father Najib had founded the nationalist newspaper *Al-Qabas* during the Mandate period, and Rafiq Khuri, a longtime member of the Syrian Communist Party, took refuge in Beirut along with Palestinian émigrés such as Nabil Khuri and the short-story writer Ghassan Kanafani. Other temporary exiles worked as journalists during the course of their stays in Beirut as well.

Thanks to the diversity of its contributors as well as the availability, right next door in the corner café, of all the human resources of the exile community, the Beirut press transformed the Arab republic of letters into an actor in Arab politics—only an actor playing multiple roles with discordant voices. In all of the Arab world there was not a single sensibility that did not find expression there, not one capital that did not seek to exploit the possibilities that existed there. Very quickly pluralism became a weapon of combat in the hands of governments engaged on every front of their cold war. Although *An-Nahar, Al-Hayat, Al-Jarida, Al-Anwar,* and *Lisān al-Hāl,* among the daily papers, and *Al-Sayad, Al-Usbuʿ al-ʿArabi,* and *Al-Hawadith,* among the weeklies, were able to turn a profit, the advertising market, despite its rapid growth, was still not large enough to support all of the city's papers. Nor could they all count on surviving from their sales in the rest of the country outside Beirut. As for distribution in other Arab countries, foreign exchange controls—now instituted practically everywhere—no longer permitted the repatriation of profits, except in the form of officially authorized and disguised subventions. There was hardly any need to disguise subventions, however, since banking secrecy laws in Lebanon made it possible for many publications to be silently financed by Arab governments for the purpose of broadcasting the accusations and insults that they tirelessly hurled at one another.

Punctilious in its monitoring of domestic politics, but tempted to relax its vigilance by the prospect of so many unsolicited contributions to the country's economic well-being, the Lebanese government was willing to put up with the cacophony to which they gave rise. Charles Hélou, himself a former journalist, openly made light of the situation. Receiving the leaders of the local press, which is to say the nominal Lebanese proprietors of the city's newspapers, he greeted them with the words, "I bid you welcome to Lebanon, your second country." And when one of the assembled chiefs of state at the first Arab summit in Cairo, held in January 1964, raised the issue of the war of information that was being conducted from

Beirut, Hélou good-naturedly replied that he had himself been meaning to bring up the subject himself but that, since his fellow dignitaries seemed interested in concluding a truce, he recommended that they consider shutting down the papers they were so busy financing.

Not every betrayal in this war could be forgiven, however. Real passions drove its protagonists: not all the Nasserites were hired guns, and not all their adversaries, liberal or conservative, were paid off in oil or kept on the payroll of the CIA. The United States, of course, was widely suspected of interference. In the 1950s it had launched a publication called *Hiwār* (Dialogue) in Beirut, which nonetheless failed in its apparent purpose of forestalling the rise of Arab nationalism. Later the Bureau of Studies and Research, a think tank serving the Gulf states that assembled a team of pro-American scholars, earned for itself in the eyes of nationalists the reputation of being a branch office of the CIA. But in the small and feverish world of intellectual Beirut, antagonisms scarcely needed an American sponsor in order to flourish.

Both *An-Nahar* and *Al-Hayat,* although resolutely opposed to Nasser (whom they had a special talent for annoying, to the point of causing him to lash out against them in his public speeches), were nonetheless able to retain their credibility. Ghassan Tuwayni, the Greek Orthodox publisher of *An-Nahar,* was careful to qualify his American sympathies (he had studied at Harvard) in more or less subtle ways; in addition to giving Michel Abu Jawdeh free rein in his daily column to relay the latest gossip and anecdotes pertaining to Arabist controversies, he invited a number of Arab nationalists to join his editorial staff, among them the Damascene Riad al-Rayes, a native of Damascus, and Clovis Maqsud, a future ambassador of the Arab League, and opened up his opinion pages to a variety of points of view.

Tuwayni's friend and neighbor Kamil Muruwwah, a Lebanese Shi'i Muslim who had started *Al-Hayat* in 1946 (in a back room of the *An-Nahar* offices kindly made available by Tuwayni's father, Gibran), was able for his part to boast of an old commitment to Arab nationalism going back to the days of the Mandate. Formerly a close aide to Hajj Amin al-Husayni, the British-appointed Mufti of Jerusalem, he had spent the Second World War in Germany (his future wife was half-German), without, however, embracing Nazism, at least to judge from the series of articles he wrote about his time there and from the willingness of the British and their Hashimite friends to grant him favorable treatment in the 1950s. During this period *Al-Hayat* sold thousands of copies in Iraq, and Muruwwah suddenly found himself at the forefront of the Hashimite reaction to the rise of Nasserism. Following the Iraqi revolution and the ensuing reconciliation between the Jordanian Hashimites and the house of Sa'ud, he managed to win the confidence of the conservative camp, led by Saudi Arabia, which had itself broken with Nasser and opposed him in Yemen. A few bridges to Cairo were nonetheless left unburned, and Ahmed Sa'id, a high official of the Nasserite radio station Sawt al-'Arab (Voice of the Arabs), let it be known that plans had tentatively been made for Muruwwah to visit the Egyptian capital.[53]

But this announcement may have been motivated by a desire to absolve Nasser's regime of responsibility for the tragic end to this story. One evening in the spring of 1966 a Sunni gangster—notorious for his Nasserite sympathies—entered Kamil Muruwwah's office and shot him down in cold blood. Thus it was that the Beirut street finally got even with the republic of letters.

19

The End of Innocence

It was to be a New Year's Eve like any other in Beirut. Despite the gloom provoked by the Arab-Israeli war of the previous year and the tensions of domestic politics, the capital looked forward to celebrating the arrival of 1969. The newspapers were filled with advertisements for the various menus being offered by local restaurants. Then thunder struck. Three days before the new year, during the night of 28–29 December 1968, Israeli commandos launched a raid against Beirut International Airport, destroying sixteen aircraft owned by Middle East Airlines and two other Lebanese carriers. Even if it did not spoil the upcoming festivities for all of the city's residents, the attack did mark the end of Beirut's age of innocence.

During the seven years that followed, Beirut looked to be rapidly recovering from the shock of the event. Its economy was operating at full capacity, the airport remained the hub of regional air transport, and the city's skyline shone as brilliantly as ever. Consumerism created ever more varied demands among the middle classes, and even those with only mild cultural curiosity no longer knew where to turn, so great was the competition for their attention from exhibitions, plays, lectures, and an endless stream of movies. In the drawing rooms of the city's high society, in its grand restaurants and its chic nightclubs, *le Tout-Beyrouth* imperturbably went on making the rounds of what was now known as the Paris of the Middle East.

Nonetheless alarms were being sounded on all sides—by artists, the press, street protests, the worsening Arab-Israeli conflict, and above all by the widening arc of hovels that lay between the well-off, if not uniformly wealthy, neighborhoods of the city and their increasingly affluent extensions in the foothills beyond. Even if statistics showed a narrowing of social inequalities, overcrowding in the ring of poverty that surrounded the city disturbed the consciences of people already troubled by the contradictory and lasting effects of the second defeat of the Arab states by Israel in June 1967. With the loss of influence by Nasserite Egypt, a new actor in Arab politics—the Palestinian Resistance—made its appearance in Lebanon, but with one crucial difference: it was no longer a question of foreign influence but of an actual physical presence, both in the southern part of the country and in the suburbs of Beirut, and eventually in the streets of the city itself.

This geopolitical realignment led in turn to a new and more intense phase of communal polarization. Undermined by its own unresolvable disagreements, the political system found itself challenged also by the emergence of another force on the left, whose transformation during the years of the Lebanese miracle was sharpened by the trauma of 1967 and invigorated by the mobilizing energies of the Palestinian resistance. After two decades of obscurity the Communist Party was now on its way to becoming once again a mass party, stimulated by the expansion of Marxist thought throughout the world and by rivalry at home from new and more radical groups. Beyond the sphere of ideology, this suddenly plural left began to merge on the ground with revolutionary elements of the Palestinian resistance that had now infiltrated the poorest neighborhoods encircling the capital, among which the refugee camps were so many outposts of the struggle being carried out in the south.

THE TURNING POINT OF 1967

Although it was the only one of the four neighboring states of Israel not to take part in the war, Lebanon fully partook of its atmosphere. Even in those places that were furthest from the frontier, windows in buildings and the headlights of cars were tinted blue. Schools remained open, but all economic activity ceased on the morning of 5 June 1967. Beirut felt the same calm anticipation, the same sense of imminent euphoria as the cities of Syria—though not the nervous anguish of their soldiers' parents. With the news of imaginary victories broadcast by the Voice of the Arabs from Cairo the streets resounded with exultant cries of triumph. Reality would be a harder thing. On the evening of 9 June, Nasser announced Egypt's defeat and his own resignation. Beirut mourned that night no less bitterly than Cairo. And as in Cairo, thousands and thousands of people descended into the streets to proclaim their refusal to accept defeat and their loyalty to the vanquished leader—and to execrate the United States, which no one doubted for a moment had been the true instigator of this lightning war. At the southern entrance to the city the most visible symbol of American domination, the Coca-Cola bottling plant, was burned, and later the parent company, along with Ford Motor Company, was placed on the list of firms to be boycotted by Arab nations in retaliation for their investments in Israel. During this time Israel completed its conquest by occupying East Jerusalem, the West Bank of Jordan, and the Golan Heights in Syria.

Lebanese territory, by contrast, remained virtually intact. Perhaps a dozen border villages were partially occupied, not more. Yet because of its extreme structural sensitivity to external shocks, Lebanon had little chance of escaping the consequences of so total a defeat. Two decades after the Nakba of 1948, a new trauma had been inflicted upon all of Arab society, not merely those countries in which the fighting had actually taken place. The geopolitical situation, familiar if not in fact stable since 1956, now tottered. Israel, which had withdrawn into itself after Suez and set aside Ben-Gurion's strategic ambitions, now found itself a conqueror, its territory enlarged and henceforth assured of American support. Moreover, it was now in a position to exploit the consequences of a victory that had left its enemies routed and demoralized. Not the least of these was the shift in the balance of Arab power, which passed from Nasserite Egypt to the advantage of the conservative states, headed by Saudi Arabia. And yet neither the scope of the defeat nor the upheavals that resulted from it caused the Arab peoples to abandon hope. Coming in the wake of massive demonstrations in Cairo and elsewhere by crowds of people who declined to accept Nasser's resignation, declaring instead their determination to fight on, the triple refusal of the Khartoum summit in November 1967—either to negotiate with Israel, recognize it, or make peace with it—translated the spontaneous defiance of the street into official policy. Given Israel's military supremacy, however, this renewal of Arab hostility could not be given practical effect on the battlefield before Egypt's shelling of the Bar-Lev line launched the War of Attrition along the Suez Canal in March 1969.

In the meantime, popular frustration served to promote both ideological mobilization and a radicalization of purpose. For if the deep and abiding consequence of the 1967 war can be seen in retrospect to have been the rise of the most conservative Arab regimes, the three or four years immediately following the defeat of Egypt and its allies were marked by a maximalist, quasi-Marxist rhetoric devoted chiefly to attacking "petit bourgeois" regimes. In Egypt itself, domestic politics were characterized by a hardening of the Nasserite stance. In Syria, the leftist neo-Ba'th movement was unperturbed by the loss of the Golan Heights; the Ba'th Party in Iraq, returned to power in July 1968, began its long reign by steadily exacerbating the tone of anti-Western invective, a habit it was later to abandon. The Libyan Arab Republic, a newcomer to the camp of self-styled progressive states, contributed its oil revenues and Colonel Muammar Qadhafi's global populism. More than through the action of governments, however, radicalization was fueled by the revolutionary aspirations of the Palestinian Resistance, whose guerrilla fighters filled the void created by the collapse of the Arab armies, providing concrete political and indeed military support for the refusal to accept defeat and, by its mystique as the avantgarde of a people's war of liberation, encouraging hopes for revenge. Nasser, long wary of a movement that initially had seemed to represent a challenge to his leadership, eventually came around and agreed to give control of the Palestine Liberation Organization (PLO), created by the initiative of the League of Arab States in May 1964, to Fatah and its allies. In February 1969, Yasser Arafat, one of Fatah's founders, became chairman of the PLO's executive committee.

From the point of view of the Lebanese political establishment there was nothing good in these developments, apart from the closing of the Suez Canal, which allowed Beirut to capture a part of its traffic. Neither the populist ideology of a war of liberation nor Israeli strategic supremacy, much less Nasser's reduced stature, was favorable to maintaining the delicate balance of domestic politics. Such stability as had been achieved by Shihab's foreign policy and program of economic development, sustained in the face of growing pressures under Hélou, was not yet sufficiently robust to survive profound changes of this sort.

With the end of the old regional order, the alignment of Lebanese diplomacy with Egypt—a source of internal equilibrium as well as a means of keeping Syria at bay—no longer served its purpose. The forces opposed to Nasserism perceived this and saw an opportunity to press their advantage. In June 1967, the mood changed in Beirut. On the day following the outbreak of war, Camille Chamoun emerged from almost a decade of ostracism,[1] immediately resuming his place as one of the central figures of Lebanese politics. At the same time the Phalange Party, until then, as one of the chief supporters of Shihabism, a defender of the policy of entente with Nasser, was no longer able to suppress its growing doubts about the Arabist movement, which it saw as a mixture of communal atavism and ideological extremism.[2] Even before the Palestinian struggle had become a domestic issue in Lebanon, the formation of a Maronite bloc under the name of al-Hilf al-Thulāthī (Tripartite Alliance) signaled a resurgence of confessional polarization. By itself the Hilf—which brought together Chamoun, Raymond Eddé (another implacable foe of Shihabism), and the Phalangist leader Pierre Gemayel, who thereby withdrew his allegiance to the regime—demonstrated that the Deuxième Bureau's attempts to intimidate the opposition had lost their effectiveness. Chamoun's political resurrection was consecrated during the 1968 legislative elections by the Hilf's success in the Christian regions of the country, and particularly in the first district of Beirut.[3] President Hélou, only too happy to be able finally to distance himself from Shihab, ratified the new state of affairs by bringing a few of the general's adversaries into his government.

Nor was it possible any longer to sum up Lebanese politics in terms either of parliamentary maneuvering or the distribution of ministerial portfolios. The Arab-Israeli conflict, which had ceased to concern policymakers since the armistice of 1949, first made a timid reappearance in the early 1960s with Israeli plans for diverting the upper tributaries of the Jordan River. In the wake of the 1967 war, however, the reality of the relationship between Arabs and Jews—namely, that it was first and foremost a conflict—could not continue to be ignored. Indeed, Israel no longer felt itself bound by the armistice, which in fact did not apply to the territory it had just conquered on the Golan Heights.[4] The occupation of these highlands had the consequence of extending the front with Israel by some twelve miles and giving the Lebanese border region of 'Arqub, at the foot of what were now Israel's northern mountains, greater strategic importance.[5] It was here, already before the war, that the Palestinian resistance began to make its presence felt as a new force in Arab politics.

THE TIME OF THE FEDAYEEN

The first mention of the Palestinian resistance in Beirut newspapers occurred in 1965. The Israeli occupation two years later of what remained of mandatory Palestine renewed its original intent, and the discredit brought upon the established Arab regimes and their armies redoubled its resolve. Having come into existence in several countries at once as a result of the Palestinian diaspora, the resistance was able immediately to exert an influence over regional politics, in part, too, because by the primacy it attached to armed struggle it incarnated the entire mystique of the Arab "rejection"—in the sense that Maxime Rodinson gave this term[6]—as well as the struggle of the peoples of the Third World against the imperialist West. In Lebanon, as in Jordan, this struggle benefited additionally from the presence of a large number of refugees and powerful support from the local population.

Since 1948 many Palestinians had been assimilated into Lebanese society, and more than a few of these had, like Yusuf Beidas, amply contributed to its economic prosperity. A few thousand, most of them Christians, had even been naturalized as citizens under Chamoun's presidency. Several of the leading cultural figures in Lebanon were of Palestinian origin, such as Sabri Sharif, who played a decisive role in the theatrical success of the Rahbani brothers and the career of the singer Fairuz, and Wadi'a al-Jarrar, who helped to shape the Lebanese folk tradition in dance. The painters Paul Guiragossian and Julian Sarufim, like the composer Halim Rumi, came from Palestine. Radio Lebanon profited from the professionalism of both Palestinians and Lebanese who had been trained at the Voice of the Orient (Sawt al-Sharq) under the British Mandate. Palestinians, notably Ihsan Abbas and Walid Khalidi, were also among the most prominent members of the faculty at the American University of Beirut. At Khalidi's urging, the Institute of Palestinian Studies was established in Beirut in 1963, with the backing of Qustantin Zurayq (a native of Damascus) and Edmond Rabbath (from Aleppo), as well as eminent Lebanese figures of various intellectual and religious persuasions.

Refugees in the strict sense of the term, which is to say those whose welfare was the responsibility of the United Nations Relief and Works Agency for Palestine Refugees in the Near East (UNRWA), had also been integrated into the Lebanese economy, though only in the capacity of cheap labor. Over time the tents that had temporarily sheltered them in improvised camps had been replaced by permanent housing. But these camps, into which the majority of the refugees had been herded together, remained just that—miserable shanty towns staggered along the periphery of the inner suburbs and closely monitored by the police.[7] Around Beirut there were six of them: Shatila, Burj al-Brajneh, Tall al-Za'tar, Jisr al-Basha, Mar Elias, and Dbayeh; the last two, populated by Christian refugees, were smaller than the others. It was in camps such as these, not only in Lebanon but also in Gaza, Jordan, and Syria, that Fatah grew beyond its initial core of Kuwaiti militants. It was also in these camps that the Palestinian resistance was truly born. After the inception of the armed struggle, announced by a communiqué that had been issued in Beirut, the refugees in the camps began to organize themselves in defiance of police surveillance; some received clandestine training in the use of weapons. Fatah's growing support among refugees was to lead the Palestinian component of the Arab Nationalist Movement, under the direction of George Habash, to stray from Nasserite orthodoxy by endorsing the armed struggle. The urge to join was especially keen in the camps of Lebanon, because it was owing to the existence of the republic of letters in Beirut that the various Palestinian sensibilities, and those of Arabs in general, could be freely expressed. Lebanon also had a frontier with Israel. Although the first armed operation was launched from the West Bank, not yet occupied, in January 1965, Lebanese territory was used to mount a few further attacks later that year. The fedayeen's freedom of action was nonetheless restricted in southern Lebanon, where it had been placed under the jurisdiction of the army. On several occasions permission to carry out commando missions, including ones led by Arafat himself, was denied.[8]

This situation changed dramatically after 1967. Although the Israeli occupation of the West Bank upset the strategic balance, causing priority to be given to the Jordanian front, the fedayeen became emboldened in Lebanon. And while the leaders of the resistance were based in Jordan, it was always from Beirut that they issued their communiqués. In the camps the prestige of the fedayeen had grown in proportion to the disrepute in which Arab governments were held after the defeat, inciting more and more refugees to join resistance organizations and, to that extent, weakening police control. As in Jordan, Fatah quickly attained the status of a movement of national liberation. Guerrilla operations were attempted with increasing frequency from the south of Lebanon since the landscape there presented no natural obstacles.[9] Whereas only two operations were launched across the Lebanese-Israeli border in 1967, there were twenty-nine such missions in 1968 and one hundred fifty in 1969.[10] By the autumn of 1968, occasional fedayeen raids had given way to the establishment of actual bases in the 'Arqub, whose rugged terrain was all the better suited to guerrilla warfare as the proximity of the Syrian border made it possible to directly supply the fedayeen along what Western journalists nicknamed the "Arafat trail" (by analogy with the Ho Chi Minh trail in Vietnam).[11] The villages of the region—mostly Muslim—made up for the absence of a Palestinian population such as the one found in Jordan by providing the fedayeen networks with indispensable assistance. A general readiness to identify with the new agents of Arabism, noticeable throughout the Arab world, was reinforced in southern Lebanon by neighborly feelings arising from the memory of the historical bonds that had existed before the creation of a border, which had the effect of dividing Galilee.[12] Additionally, the fedayeen were often greeted as liberators by peasants in the south who until then had been subjected to both the rule of the Lebanese army and the feudal domination of the great landed families. In the border village of Khiyam, the first to receive them, the fedayeen made their entrance in 1968 at the head of a demonstration by residents who had occupied the local office of the Deuxième Bureau and then expelled its agents.[13]

The same sense of solidarity could be observed elsewhere in the country, and particularly in the capital. Beyond the border region, broad segments of Lebanese society openly expressed their commitment to the guerrilla movement and, like many other Arabs, sizable numbers of young Lebanese joined fedayeen units in Jordan. When the remains of Khalil al-Jamal, the first Lebanese martyr of the Palestinian Resistance, were repatriated from Amman in April 1968, nearly 150,000 people lined the route from Damascus to Beirut. Some belonged to left-wing parties and Arab nationalist groups, but the majority had no partisan affiliation. The range of public figures who attended the funeral supplied further evidence that support for the objectives of armed struggle had no predominant political coloring, even if in confessional terms it was almost exclusively Muslim. The Mufti of the Republic led the prayer, and even the prime minister, Abdallah al-Yafi, took part. The gesture in this case was not only a matter of personal feeling: approval of the resistance signified above all recognition of its right to organize the Palestinians in the camps and to conduct the struggle from Lebanon.

Such support naturally could not be total in a society as deeply polarized as Lebanon. Indeed, the opposing positions were still more starkly contrasted than on the eve of the civil war ten years earlier. Faced with the sudden emergence of an external force that was nonetheless intimately associated with Lebanese society, communal atavism and class fears combined to arouse a hostile reaction among the Christian middle and lower middle classes. In the aftermath of the defeat of 1967, however, it was no easier in Lebanon than elsewhere in the Arab world to oppose the Palestinian resistance in principle. Its presence on Lebanese territory provoked a few public challenges, and opposition was expressed initially in roundabout ways for the most part—ways that nonetheless were pregnant with consequence. There was the frequent use, for example, of the word *gharīb* (plural *ghurabā'*), which in its strict sense means "foreigner" but in this case carried the pejorative connotation of an intruder, and only in connection with an Arab foreigner; a European or an American was called *ajnabi* (plural *ajanib*). Originally employed by certain Beirut newspapers in the context of real estate deals involving wealthy citizens of the countries of the Arabian Peninsula, *gharīb* suddenly underwent a change of meaning with the intensification of xenophobic feeling in the press in early 1968 and came to be used against Palestinians as well as Syrian workers.[14] This mentality, typical of a class of people who did not mind enriching themselves by taking advantage of the very external sources of labor and capital they demonized, was later to be responsible for some of the most appalling atrocities of the war. Opposition to the Palestinian resistance was also obliquely expressed by the appearance of the Hilf, which nominally had been formed to combat the increased reliance on police power under Shihabist rule, but whose election campaign was marked by the aggressive assertion of Maronite identity. Even the Virgin Mary's help was enlisted: Our Lady of Harissa, her great statue overlooking Junieh, was said to have changed position on its pedestal in order to protect Camille Chamoun.

The electoral success of the Maronite Tripartite Alliance nonetheless indirectly aided the activities of the Palestinian resistance. The Deuxième Bureau had lost a decisive battle on the national level, and now found itself substantially weakened in trying to contain the spread of guerrilla bases in the south and the growing support for the fighters in the camps, or to curb the effort made by many political figures, among them old Shihabist allies, to loosen the constraints imposed on the Palestinians. The prime minister, Yafi, was himself won over to their cause, which in turn drew personal attacks from Christian politicians and helped to make the armed Palestinian presence a domestic Lebanese issue. At this stage, the Palestinian leadership continued to direct the main part of its attention to the front bordering on Israel and Jordan, where Arab volunteers poured in following the battle of Karameh in March 1968. In Lebanon, the fedayeen and their Lebanese sympathizers were able to operate practically free of any restraint, excited, too, by the prospect of leading a people's war of national liberation, and now with the encouragement of Damascus as well. But if Amman figured more and more as the Hanoi of the Arab-Israeli conflict, Beirut remained abreast of what was happening there. The guerrilla movements, which in the meantime had multiplied, continued to publish their bulletins in Beirut, and it was there that the Popular Front for the Liberation of Palestine, the splinter organization directed by George Habash, issued calls for Western airliners to be hijacked. It was in response to one of these communiqués that Israel dispatched its own commandos to attack the Lebanese civil aviation fleet in Beirut at the end of the year.

The airport raid dealt a severe blow to the authority of the state and, especially, to the prestige of the army, which had failed to react. Two weeks later Yafi's government was forced to resign. Very quickly it became clear that the debate over the Palestinian presence was inextricably bound up with the problem of communal division. Yafi's successor, Rashid Karameh, a key figure of the Shihabist era who was often praised for his sense of statesmanship, immediately invited Parliament to recognize the right of the Palestinians to fight for the liberation of their homeland. On the ground the government found itself overwhelmed on all sides, and no longer only in the south; indeed it was in Beirut, and then Tripoli, that the most decisive episodes played out later that year. The crisis erupted in the capital in broad daylight on 23 April 1969, when the army moved to break up a demonstration that united left-wing militants and the Sunni working class in support of the resistance. The ensuing furor plainly showed that, despite the decree of a state of emergency and a curfew, the army could not hope to impose its will on the fedayeen without running the risk of a civil war that would tear its own ranks apart. Yet clashes between the military and guerrilla forces, many of whose fighters were Lebanese, grew more numerous. During this time the Palestinian camps rose up, providing the resistance with dramatic proof of their wholehearted commitment. Filled with the revolutionary fervor that the cause of the fedayeen aroused everywhere, and impatient to reclaim their long-suppressed political liberty, the refugees broke free of the control of the commando organizations, whose leaders managed to establish their authority over the camps only once the uprising had been quelled.[15] In October the fever of insurrection spread to the old city in Tripoli, where Nasserite militants stormed the army's entrenched positions inside the Crusaders' citadel. Additionally there was economic pressure from Syria, which, by closing its frontier, had frozen transit trade from Lebanon. But, above all, there was the paralysis of the Lebanese government—or, more exactly, the effective absence of a government for more than nine months. Refusing to approve a massive military operation against the resistance, Rashid Karameh, called upon by Hélou to form a new cabinet following Yafi's resignation on 15 January 1969, required as a precondition of serving as prime minister that a national accord be reached with regard to the Palestinian question.[16]

Faced with the danger of an irremediable rupture, Hélou and the army agreed to negotiate with the PLO, now presided over by Arafat, within the framework of talks sponsored by Nasser. This led to the Cairo Agreement, signed on 3 November by Arafat and Émile Bustani, the Lebanese army commander. Subsequently ratified by Parliament, the agreement unquestionably amounted to formal recognition of the fedayeen—Lebanon having explicitly acknowledged the PLO's right to wage the armed struggle from bases on its territory. While forbidding the presence of commando groups along the coast of southern Lebanon and specifying authorized crossover points in the central zone of the border with Israel, the accord granted them great freedom of maneuver in the ʿArqub, the principal area of guerrilla activity. More than this, it provided a basis for the extraterritorial status of the refugee camps, spelled out in detail three months later by protocols that prohibited the Lebanese government from exerting its authority there, reserving complete jurisdiction to the PLO.[17]

In this way the crisis seemed to have been resolved. The newly appointed interior minister, Kamal Jumblatt, leader of both the Druze community and the

Lebanese left, sought to avoid a recurrence of domestic unrest by using his standing within the resistance to see to it that the agreement was respected and that there would be no encroachment beyond the zones stipulated by the Cairo Agreement; additionally, he imposed restrictions on funeral processions, prohibited the wearing of uniforms as well as gunplay in urban areas, and ordered that military positions be relocated to at least one kilometer outside towns and villages. The PLO cooperated, and in the spring of 1969 created the Palestinian Armed Struggle Command (PASC), an organization that effectively became its military police. But despite attempts at centralization and coordination between the Lebanese army and PASC, the dispersion of guerrilla units reduced the chance that they could be completely kept under control. At the same time the Cairo Agreement, seen as the symbol of a loss of national sovereignty, provoked vigorous resentment among those within the army who, like much of the Christian population, had accepted it only as the lesser of several evils. Shortly afterward, in March 1970, Phalangist militants staged an assault on a Palestinian convoy in Kahaleh, a small town just outside the capital on the Damascus highway. During the course of the fighting that then broke out in the Beirut suburbs, Bashir Gemayel, the youngest son of the Phalangist leader and one of the party's most daring junior commanders, was taken captive at a Palestinian roadblock and detained for a few hours.[18]

Concerted efforts by the Lebanese army and the PLO succeeded in containing the violence. The Cairo Agreement seemed to be working. Indeed there were no new clashes in the three years that followed, and the first World Conference of Christians for Palestine, held in Beirut in May 1970, showed that mutual understanding was still, in fact, possible. Yet the adversaries of the Palestinian presence, far from disarming, prepared to form their own militias well out of the view of television cameras.

THE IMPOSSIBLE CAPITAL OF THE PLO

An easing of tensions between Lebanon and the Palestinian resistance seemed at first to be favored by the conjunction of three events that occurred in the space of a few weeks, in August and September 1970: a change of Lebanese political leadership, the ouster of the Palestinian resistance from Amman, in the wake of violent clashes with the Jordanian army, and Nasser's death. In a longer perspective, however, these same three events could be seen to have had devastating consequences for the balance of political power in Lebanon.

Suleiman Franjieh, elected president of the Republic by a majority of the votes cast in an epic session of Parliament (the first to be broadcast on television) on 17 August 1970, made a clean break with Shihabism. The prototype of a traditional provincial za'im, Franjieh had scarcely distinguished himself in 1957 by authorizing a retaliatory attack against political rivals that had left some thirty people dead inside a church. Although he came from a family known for its openness to Arabist ideas and support for close relations with Syria, and although he himself had been a minister under Hélou, Franjieh's apparently centrist candidacy had been endorsed by Chamoun and the Hilf—as well as by Saeb Salam and, discreetly, by Kamal Jumblatt. Joyous gunfire had greeted his election in the Mountain and in the Christian neighborhoods of Beirut, where it was interpreted as marking the end of the dictatorship of the state intelligence services, but also as heralding a strong presidency that would restore Maronite preeminence after the demotion of the previous year. Following his inauguration in the new presidential palace at Baʿabda, Franjieh did in fact move at once to dismantle the apparatus of the Deuxième Bureau, though it had already lost much of its ability to control popular protest.[19] By contrast, he took no immediate steps against the Palestinian resistance. As an ally of Salam, whom he named prime minister, he was manifestly eager to begin his term, as all his predecessors had done, by appearing to adopt a consensual approach. The leadership of the PLO, for its part, was not unfavorably disposed to the new president; it even claimed that of the two candidates on the list, he was the one it preferred. What is more, the PLO was busy coping with the aftermath of its disastrous expulsion from Jordan—Black September, as it was thereafter known. The disarray in which Arab politics now found itself following Nasser's death on 28 September, five days after Franjieh took office, hardly encouraged precipitous action in any case.

It rapidly became clear that Nasser's death had the effect of confirming the geopolitical implications of the defeat of 1967, notably by delaying the rebuilding of the Egyptian army, now engaged in the War of Attrition along the Suez Canal. An offensive meant to reconquer the Sinai Peninsula, planned for the spring of 1971,[20] was postponed by the reorientation of Egyptian policy, both domestic and foreign, under Nasser's successor, Anwar al-Sadat, who broke off relations with the Soviet Union and threw out its military advisors. General Hafez al-Assad, who had been promoted from the ministry of defense to the presidency of Syria in the wake of a coup d'état in October 1970, introduced a spirit of moderation there as well that grew out of the perceived need to improve relations with the West and to foster economic liberalization. The new regime of Ahmad Hasan al-Bakr and Saddam Hussein did the same in Iraq, without, however, renouncing its penchant for inflammatory rhetoric. King Hussein of Jordan, once more an actor in Arab politics now that the country had succeeded in ridding itself of the PLO, now hoped to be able to recover the West Bank in the event that the United States could devise a peaceful resolution of the conflict with Israel. In the face of these changes, especially the last, the PLO's first concern was to make sure that the progress that had been made so far would not be erased. With its ouster from Jordan, complete by July 1971, and the closing of the Syrian front to commando operations, ordered by Assad, the possibility of conducting such operations was now restricted to Lebanon, henceforth the only option for independent maneuver available to the Palestinian resistance.

Driven out of Jordan, the fedayeen made their way to the Lebanese camps, above all around Beirut, through the still porous Syrian border. Accompanied in some cases by their families, the Palestinian fighters swelled the number of unofficial refugees—unofficial in the sense that they were not counted by the UNRWA—even if subsequent calculations showed that this inflow was not as massive as often supposed. Whereas the total number of refugees prior to the Cairo Agreement was some 223,000 according to official Lebanese figures (the UNRWA figure was only 166,000), it rose to 260,000 in 1972 and to 289,000 in 1975, an increase that can largely be explained by a sharp rise in population growth in the camps, estimated to be 3.6 percent annually.[21] It is true that the actual figures mattered less than what people reckoned them to be, and that the concentration of Palestinians in and around the camps reinforced popular perceptions, magnifying the refugee presence in the eyes of adversaries and allies alike, and perhaps even in the eyes of the Palestinian leaders themselves. This was especially the case in Beirut, where refugees represented 16 percent of the resident population at the beginning of the 1970s, as against 10 percent on a national scale.[22] The demographic shift was accompanied by a still more striking transfer of political power, since the command structures of the resistance and of the various fedayeen units were all based in Lebanon. Even if the official seat of the PLO was in Damascus and Yasser Arafat himself spent a great deal of time in Cairo, Beirut was for all intents and purposes the capital of Palestinian political life. The inadequacy of the framework created by the Cairo Agreement was obvious, with the result that resentments among the Lebanese military hierarchy and anti-Arabist segments of Lebanese society grew increasingly bitter. Israeli policy did the rest.

Jerusalem had inaugurated its policy of retaliation following the first guerrilla operations in 1965: after interventions against Jordan and Syria, Israeli units launched a raid against two Lebanese border villages. In the aftermath of the 1967 war Israeli attacks increased in number and frequency, in both Lebanon and Jordan. To call these attacks "reprisals" would be misleading, however. They were so common, and so disproportionate to the original provocation, as to become a horrific element of daily life. Israel committed more than three thousand territorial violations between 1968 and 1974, according to statistics compiled by the Lebanese army, or an average of 1.4 incidents per day,[23] killing or wounding more than eight hundred Lebanese and Palestinians.[24] Such violations often took the form of aerial bombardment. Lacking any means of anti-aircraft defense, Lebanon saw its skies become the preserve of the Israeli air force, which, when it was not bombing ground objectives, made its presence felt by unleashing sonic booms. The scale of assault was soon to be enlarged, with an average of seven territorial violations per day recorded for the period 1974–75. This campaign was not limited to border areas, as the raid against the Beirut airport had shown in late December of 1968. International reaction—including the second French arms embargo against Israel, ordered by General de Gaulle in response to the airport attack[25]—had a deterrent effect only for a time. The Israeli intelligence services also resorted to underground warfare against Palestinian figures, more often intellectuals than politicians. The first episode was the assassination carried out by the Mossad in July 1972 of the author and journalist Ghasan Kanafani, spokesman for the PFLP, by means of a car bomb detonated in front of his house in a Beirut suburb. This was followed by a letter-bombing campaign that severely injured several people, among them Anis Sayegh, director of the Palestine Research Center, and Bassam Abu Sharif, Kanafani's successor as chief press officer of the PFLP. Finally, on 10 April 1973, the Israeli army repeated its bold stroke of December 1968 by aiming a blow again at Beirut, this time in the heart of the city: seaborne commandos linked up with infiltrated agents to kill two former leaders of Fatah, Abu Yusuf al-Najjar and Kamal 'Adwan, as well as the PLO's spokesman, the poet Kamal Nasir, in the residential neighborhood of Rue de Verdun. Their funeral was the occasion of the largest political demonstration in the history of Lebanon: a crowd estimated at two hundred and fifty thousand, or a little less than a tenth of the country's total population, poured into the streets of Beirut to convey the remains of the victims (including those of Kamal Nasir, a Christian) to the Muslim Martyrs' Cemetery in the Pine Forest.

The Israeli stratagem had nonetheless succeeded. The old antagonism between the Lebanese state and the resistance reappeared, dividing the country's population almost equally. Three weeks later, at the beginning of May, Beirut once again found itself in the grip of violence. The army had done nothing to defend against the recent Israeli incursion in the capital, recalling its failure to intervene during the raid on the airport. In the ensuing controversy, having been disappointed in his attempt to have the commander-in-chief of the army removed, Saeb Salam quarreled furiously with President Franjieh, a longtime ally, and submitted his government's resignation. Franjieh could not bring himself to call upon Rashid Karameh, the other leading figure of the Sunni community, to serve as Salam's successor, and instead appointed a politician of considerably lesser stature named Amin al-Hafiz on 25 April. The uproar in the Sunni community that followed forced Hafiz to name a cabinet that was unrepresentative of the political class as a whole. This served only to inflame passions further—and all the more dangerously since during the interval Palestinian groups had gone back on the offensive after the attack on Rue de Verdun, provoking renewed friction with the army. The arrest of two armed Palestinians within the airport compound and the retaliatory kidnapping of two Lebanese soldiers brought matters to a head. The army responded by harnessing firepower on a scale that had not been seen in 1969. Its resort to air attacks on the camps around Beirut, in particular, seemed to indicate a determination to eliminate the armed

FIGURE 99. One of the demonstrations held in April 1973 in support of Palestine and against the United States and the Arab governments.

Palestinian presence, as in Jordan—hence the talk that began to be heard of a "Black May." Franjieh nonetheless was obliged to stop short of this point on account of the opposition he met with from the Arab states, chiefly Egypt and Syria, who were preparing to launch the October war (Cairo urging the general secretary of the Arab league, Mahmud Riad, to put pressure on Beirut, and Damascus once again closing its border with Lebanon, as it had done in 1969). A still greater source of opposition, however, came from inside Lebanon itself, as a consequence of domestic political discord.

Hafiz's government, weak and under attack since the moment it was formed, had not yet been formally presented to the Chamber of Deputies. Far from being able to manage the crisis, the government became one of its elements. In the eyes of the Sunni establishment, this unrepresentative body, led by an unrecognized figure, was

evidence of a worsening imbalance of power in favor of the Maronites. Hafiz's departure therefore became the condition of resolving an impasse in which the
Lebanese-Palestinian conflict had become entangled with Lebanese communal
conflicts. Franjieh ended up giving in after less than two months—an outcome that
had been made all the more unavoidable by the fact that by mid-June the army's
offensive, despite its initial successes, had stalled. Hoping to avoid a loss of face,
which would have been the result of naming either Salam or Karameh, Franjieh
turned to a Sunni figure of unchallenged stature, Taqieddin al-Sulh, Riad's nephew
and one of the architects of the National Pact; moreover, in order to avoid offend-
ing anyone, he saw to it that the new government counted the largest number of
ministers ever seen in the history of Lebanon. In the meantime, far from having
eliminated the PLO or even reduced its freedom of maneuver, the crisis had led to
the opposite result. The Melkart Accord, signed in the Beirut hotel of the same name
on 17 May, substantially broadened the terms of the Cairo Agreement, ceding still
greater autonomy to the PLO.

Just as the 1969 crisis had been a national crisis, so the turning point of 1973
once again exposed the acute structural divisions of Lebanese society. Not only was
one part of the nation strongly supportive of the Palestinian resistance, while the
other was prepared to enter into confrontation with it; developments on the ground
now seemed to point to an imminent collapse of state authority. While the fighting was taking place, Phalangist militias had been seen in some streets of Christian
neighborhoods and on rooftops. During periods of cease-fire, such deployments
required the authorization of the army, and it seems clear that the army had un-
officially charged the Phalangist militia with responsibility for conducting the defense of the eastern precincts of Beirut.[26] On the other side of the city, barricades
had been erected by the new Nasserite gangs to protect Muslim neighborhoods close
to the camps against attack by the army.[27] Left-wing militants had also taken part
in clashes alongside Palestinian fighters. Even more seriously, perhaps, during the
course of the crisis itself, the disagreement among the country's elected officials over
the status of the armed Palestinian resistance had laid bare a contradiction directly
connected with the question of governmental power: whereas the PLO had regained
much of its independence and taken full advantage of the resources of Beirut's media to broadcast its message, the animosity catalyzed by its very presence in the country continued to grow more intense.

These antagonisms cannot be reduced to the traditional opposition between Muslims and Christians. It is quite true, of course, that the struggle for power continued
to set notables on both sides against one another. But a new force of radical protest,
fed by all tendencies on the left, now challenged the system in its entirety. The growing strength of this force derived in part from its success in conjoining the causes of
socialism and Arab nationalism, but also from its embrace of a revolutionary ideology whose mobilizing potential had been demonstrated by the Palestinian resistance.

A CRUCIBLE OF RADICALISM

The birth of a new left-wing alliance, in March 1965, united patriotic and reformist elements in a Front for Progressive Parties and National Forces. The significance of the event was not fully appreciated at the time. Ten years later this coalition was to be one of the declared belligerents in the civil war, now under the name of the Lebanese National Movement (al-Haraka al-wataniyya). At its head in 1975—as in 1965—was Kamal Jumblatt, a complex figure whose career symbolized better than any other the transformation of the left in Lebanon, and perhaps of Lebanon itself.

Long a well-known figure of the political establishment, Jumblatt came from an old Druze family of Kurdish origin whose roots in the Mountain are attested since at least the seventeenth century. Although it had not played a prominent role in the government of the Mountain under the Ottomans, the family had embodied the Druze community's resistance to demographic and political changes that favored the Maronites. One of its leaders, Bashir Jumblatt, clashed with Bashir II Shihab in the early nineteenth century, meeting a violent death at the emir's hands. Turkish reprisals in the wake of the massacres of 1860 directly touched his heirs, further deepening a bitter resentment of Maronite influence that was powerfully to affect Kamal Jumblatt many years later, to judge from his posthumously published memoirs.[28] In 1921, when Kamal was not yet four years old, his father was assassinated. At the age of eight he was sent away for schooling with the Lazarist fathers in ʿAntura and a sort of regency was instituted, with a cousin holding the family's hereditary seat in Parliament under the political guidance of his mother, Nazira, a moderate advisor as it turned out. *Sitt* Nazira, who never appeared in public unveiled, refrained from joining the opposition to the French Mandate, despite the revolt in the Jabal Druze range in southwestern Syria (later renamed Jabal al-ʿArab), favoring instead alliance with Émile Eddé against Bishara al-Khuri's Constitutional Bloc. When the time finally came for Kamal Jumblatt to stand for Parliament himself, in 1943, he did so as a candidate on Eddé's anti-independence list. In the event, it was the leader of the other great Druze family, Majid Arslan, who distinguished himself in the battle for independence.

Unlike Eddé and his fellow Maronite partisans, Jumblatt's status as one of the two traditional leaders of the Druze community assured him of participating more or less quickly in government. He was not yet thirty years old on receiving his first ministerial portfolio (Economy, Agriculture, and Social Affairs) in 1946. At this point began Jumblatt's double life as a notable and an anti-establishment figure. In keeping with the role he had inherited as his birthright, he converted to socialism following a brief flirtation with Antun Saʿadeh's Syrian Social Nationalist Party, and in March 1949 founded the Progressive Socialist Party (PSP) with a number of Christian and Muslim figures, among them the modernist shaykh Abdallah al-ʿAlayli, while at the same time persisting in his anti-Communism. Two years later the PSP joined the gathering opposition to Khuri (collectively known as the Patriotic Socialist Front), even if it was more as a Druze notable than as a party leader that Jumblatt helped to bring about the fall of the regime. He soon broke with Chamoun, now president, initially for electoral reasons—the two men were from the same region, the Shuf—and later on political grounds. Attracted to Hindu culture and influenced by Jawaharlal Nehru's advocacy of neutralism between the superpowers, Jumblatt gradually came to adopt the cause of Arab nationalism in the form given it by Nasser. In 1958 he constituted one of the main centers of opposition to Chamoun, and his supporters took an active part in the civil war, with the result that the PSP became one of the two principal guarantors and beneficiaries, together with the Phalange Party, of the new regime's policy of regional economic development. And so it was that in early 1965, a few months after Shihab's departure, this atypical and occasionally perplexing figure, who combined asceticism with a feudal-style clientelism, and who until then had not shown any interest in enlarging his party's appeal, agreed to head up a new movement on the left: the Front for Progressive Parties and National Forces, which later became the Lebanese National Movement (LNM).

In addition to the PSP, the new coalition brought together the Lebanese branch of the Arab Nationalist Movement, the Lebanese Communist Party (still semi-clandestine), the Ba'th Party (likewise without legal existence), and a few unaffiliated political figures. Apart from Jumblatt, all of them were obliged to operate at the margins of the system, and no immediate impact could be expected from their alliance. Combining forces in this way nonetheless had the advantage of permitting not only fringe parties, but also other segments of public opinion that had no institutional voice, to profit from Jumblatt's credibility. At the same time, the conjunction of Arab nationalism and socialist ideals gave substance to a movement whose appeal extended well beyond the militant base of the various elements of the new Front,[29] including Jumblatt's own PSP.

The heart of the coalition was the Lebanese Communist Party, the oldest party in Lebanon. Throughout its history the LCP's attention had never been entirely distracted from the national question. Its links with the Syrian Communist Party, with which it had long formed a single entity, the CPSL, naturally inclined it to look beyond its own borders; and the memory of the many members it had lost as a result of its position on the partition of Palestine furnished ample reason to recall the salience of Arab nationalism in public opinion. Nonetheless the LCP continued to attach priority to class-based objectives, out of a desire not least to avoid the confessional entanglements of Arabist movements. Although the party did not prohibit occasional collaboration with such movements,[30] its decision to join a coalition in which Arab nationalists played a major role appeared to represent a change of direction, the implications of which went beyond Lebanon itself. Like the Egyptian Communist Party, which that same year merged with the Arab Socialist Union (originally founded by Nasser as the country's sole political party), the LCP demonstrated the possibility of forming an alliance with nationalist parties that allowed Communists to preserve their ideological identity while giving them greater leverage over both domestic and foreign policy.

The 1967 war broadened the movement further. To be sure, the Front for Progressive Parties and National Forces was forced to suspend its activity owing to disagreements among its members in the wake of the defeat. But the convergence of socialism and Arabism was not challenged. For if the defeat discredited Nasserism and the other nationalist regimes, the internal party dispute to which it gave rise sprang from a similar Arabist impulse, while at the same time sharpening the anti-imperialist tone of leftist rhetoric. Moreover, the LCP confirmed the change of direction to which it had committed itself in 1965—albeit at the price of an internal schism—by officially agreeing at its Second Congress, held in quasi-secrecy in Beirut in July 1968, to address the issues raised by the growing power of the movement for Arab national liberation. The new line was formally ratified in January 1972 by the Third Congress, the first to be openly convened; meanwhile one of the party's most brilliant intellectuals, Mahdi 'Amil, attempted to give it a theoretical foundation with reference to the writings of the French philosopher Louis Althusser.[31]

In parallel with this transformation, though from the opposite direction, the advocates of Arab nationalism were increasingly inclined to adopt aspects of Marxist—indeed, Leninist—doctrine. This was particularly true of the ANM, whose Palestinian wing became the Popular Front for the Liberation of Palestine (PFLP) in December 1967; the Lebanese wing, led by Muhsin Ibrahim, reconstituted itself the following year as the Organization of Lebanese Socialists.[32] In their turn, former Ba'thists who had converted to Marxism created the Socialist Lebanon movement, which, under the guidance of Waddah Sharara and Fawaz Traboulsi, rallied a small circle of intellectuals around a radical critique of the Communist Party.[33] The leftist reorientation of these two nationalist movements was crowned in May 1971, when the Organization of Lebanese Socialists and Socialist Lebanon united to form the Communist Action Organization in Lebanon (CAOL). This convergence affected not only those groups that from their inception had embraced either Marxism or Arab nationalism, but many smaller and more radical groups as well, especially in student circles, where the events of May 1968 in France and the anti-imperialist tendencies of the European extreme left exerted a reinforcing influence.

Nothing more clearly attested the transformation of the political landscape than the ideological reversal of the Syrian Social Nationalist Party (SSNP). Although its authoritarianism and quasi-fascist structure firmly situated it on the right, the SSNP had always constituted a challenge to the system. Over the years its secularism had attracted many intellectuals alienated by organized religion, many of whom, after a more or less short-lived membership in the party, went on to become enlightened establishment figures, such as Jumblatt himself and Ghasan Tuwayni. The SSNP's unrelenting animosity toward Zionism, attractive to young Palestinians (most of them Christian) after the creation of the Jewish state in 1948, was another point of contact with Arab nationalists. It had long clashed with this latter movement, however, to which it was opposed for fundamental ideological reasons (Saʿadeh held, among other things, that Syrians were not ethnically Arab), though this did not prevent it from winning the support of the Hashimites in the 1950s. Moreover, the party's visceral hostility to Nasserism deprived it of any possible sympathy for the new ideological synthesis that took shape in Beirut in the mid-1960s. And yet not only did the SSNP ally itself with Arab nationalism after the 1967 defeat, it also showed a willingness to entertain Marxist ideas. In 1973 a change of party leadership, subsequently consolidated by a split within the ranks, formalized this remarkable reversal, which in the meantime had been encouraged by the emergence of the Palestinian resistance. The large proportion of Palestinians in the militant ranks of the party as well as its anti-Zionist heritage enabled it to appreciate the radical promise of this rising force sooner than other parties on the right.

In time the appearance of the resistance in Lebanese territory came to influence these other parties, but the readjustment of leftist thinking had begun earlier. As everywhere else in the Arab world, progressive elements of public opinion spontaneously pledged their support for the only force that seemed to be in a position to take over from Nasserism. In Lebanon, where the PLO and its cohorts were physically present, this solidarity could manifest itself in tangible ways. To the impoverished peasantry in the southern part of the country, the resistance seemed to be both the new incarnation of Arabism and a harbinger of the revolution to come. There was nothing abstract about the synthesis of Marxist and nationalist discourses in this case. It was capable of finding immediate expression—as indeed it was to do, particularly in student circles—in the growing appeal of a socialist ideology that was both secular and Arabist, and whose accompanying revolutionary dimension assumed the form of popular support for the resistance.[34] Beyond ideology, the effectiveness of this alliance could be seen in the institutional repercussions of the crisis of 1969, following which the LCP and the two Baʿth parties (pro-Syrian and pro-Iraqi, respectively), as well as the SSNP, were legalized by Jumblatt, then serving as interior minister in the government formed after the signing of the Cairo Agreement. Several years later, in 1973, the left's determination to defend the resistance revived the fortunes of the Front for Progressive Parties and National Forces, to which the SSNP now belonged.

Rather than an alliance between two autonomous entities, the Lebanese left and the Palestinian resistance, it would be more accurate to speak of a process of osmosis. Lebanese militants, like other Arabs, hastened to join the various groups that composed the resistance, Fatah foremost among them. But the specifically Palestinian orientation of the PLO's principal faction was tempered by the avant-garde

image of the broader Arab national liberation movement that attached to the resistance as a whole and that the majority of its cadres had internalized. Membership in a radical faction such as Fatah had in any case more of an Arab than a strictly
Palestinian character: its student brigade (al-Katība al-tullābiyya) was made up
mostly of young Lebanese; other Lebanese militants worked to mobilize the rural
population in regions where there was no Palestinian presence, such as ʿAkkar, in
the extreme northern part of the country. In Beirut, as well as in Tripoli and Sidon,
Fatah also took over supervision of a number of Nasserite groups that had been or-
phaned by the new course of Egyptian politics.[35]

The Lebanese-Palestinian osmosis could be seen most clearly perhaps in the
Communist Action Organization in Lebanon. Without losing sight of the distinctive features of Lebanese society, on which it had drawn in seeking to revitalize Marxist thought, the CAOL aimed to provide a forum where Lebanonism and Arabism
could find common ground. Its leader, Muhsin Ibrahim, had been valued by Nasser
for his advice as one of the heads of the ANM; now Ibrahim found his opinion sought
after by all the Palestinian leaders, and by Jumblatt himself. The product of a rupture within the ANM, the CAOL was to share its weekly newspaper, *Al-Hurriyya,*
with a Palestinian group of similar origins, Nayef Hawatmeh's Democratic Front
for the Liberation of Palestine (DFLP)—itself issued from a schism within the PFLP.
Militants from the SSNP likewise became involved with the most radical factions
of the Palestinian resistance, without abandoning their ideological (though not always their party) affiliation. At the head of the left, Jumblatt found his own stature
enhanced: while continuing to function as the Druze leader, and in this capacity
unavoidably a figure of consequence within the Lebanese establishment, he now
enjoyed a growing Arab, and even international, reputation. Unsurprisingly, when
parties from throughout the Arab world gathered in Beirut in November 1972 to
create the Arab Front Participating in the Palestinian Revolution, he was elected its
general secretary.[36] Later the same year he received the Lenin Prize, a rare distinction for a non-Communist.

At this juncture the left was stronger than it had ever been. Once again it could
hold demonstrations free of legal restrictions, and in October 1974 the Communist Party was able to celebrate its fiftieth anniversary with great fanfare. Increasingly the left took part in public debate as well. Every other year a leftist was elected
head of the Student Union of the Lebanese University and the Writers Union. More
significant still, support for the left was growing among workers and farmers, and
also among those who found themselves in the no man's land between city and country. Here, in the ring of squalor that surrounded Beirut, home to the many who had
been left out of the Lebanese miracle, the rhetoric of anger and alienation that accompanied the deteriorating state of relations between Palestinians and their hosts
was a familiar feature of everyday life.

ON THE MARGINS OF THE MIRACLE

Even if the political events that succeeded one another with accelerating speed had redressed the domestic balance of power, the merchant republic did not show undue concern. And for good reason: if there was one domain in which the 1967 war did not seem to represent a dramatic turning point, it was the economy. In bringing about the closing of the Suez Canal, the war had been highly profitable for the Lebanese transit trade. The beginnings of the petroleum age had already been very rewarding as well. With the nationalization of Iraqi reserves in 1972, and the rise in the price of crude oil the following year during the October war, purchasing power rose in tandem with demand in parts of the Arab world that remained largely undeveloped. Lebanese financiers, forwarding agents, and industrialists were ready and willing as always to satisfy needs. The business class profited even at the expense of the PLO: first, because in carrying on the war and looking after the families of its many soldiers, the PLO had mouths to feed and salaries to pay; second, because the money that came to it from Palestinians in the Gulf states as well as from Arab governments could not help but pass through one or another of the many banks in Beirut.

In spite of the country's political turmoil, then, the Lebanese miracle remained essentially intact. The port, whose activity increasingly derived from trade with Iraq and Saudi Arabia, was experiencing unprecedented growth. In the meantime the banking sector, now largely controlled by foreign capital, had shaken off the effects of the Intra crisis. Industry seemed ready at last to take off, accounting now for a quarter of gross domestic product, and joint ventures, stimulated by the new markets of the Gulf, brought Lebanese businessmen into collaboration with foreign companies. In almost all the city's neighborhoods, but especially in the new business district around Rue Hamra, an unparalleled real estate boom gave rise to rampant speculation. Construction sites multiplied, especially for luxury residential buildings and business complexes. The tourist trade was sufficiently promising to attract the notice of American hotel chains, in partnership with Arab investors. Overlooking the prestigious Saint-Georges and the Phoenicia on the beachfront, the Holiday Inn opened in 1974. Both its rooftop revolving restaurant and its movie theater, the most luxurious in the city, were topics of conversation. Meanwhile, a few hundred yards away, the massive frame of the Hilton was being erected above the Normandy.

Yet the economy's prosperity did not benefit all Lebanese. Indeed, both inflation and property speculation worked to widen existing inequalities. Even so, an initial round of wealth redistribution measures instituted under Shihab began to produce their intended effect,[37] and after 1960 growth was recorded in middle- and upper-income brackets. The gap between the level of economic development in different regions of the country also began to shrink, thanks to public expenditures on in-

FIGURE 100. The Holiday Inn (at left) in 1974: not yet open for business but already available for war.

frastructure and expatriate remittances. Outlying rural areas saw a sharp rise in their standard of living during the 1960s: 44 percent in southern Lebanon, 40 percent in northern Lebanon, and 15.6 percent in the Biqaʿ.

Even when interpreted in communal terms, the figures showed progress. It is true that control over every sector of the economy remained in the hands of Christian businessmen—a state of affairs that had not changed for a century.[38] But the improvement of living standards in the predominantly Muslim rural areas nonetheless seemed to suggest that Shihab had been right in counting on regional development to strengthen national unity. The confessional profile of occupations requiring higher education (lawyers, doctors, engineers, high-ranking civil servants) also indicated a narrowing of the gap between communities. This trend appeared likely to continue, at least to judge from the composition of the university-level student population, which now approached parity between Muslims and Christians. If Muslims remained a minority at Université Saint-Joseph (20 percent), they accounted for a little less than half of the students at the American University of Beirut, and overall enrollment at the Lebanese University, which had grown steadily since its founding in 1952, was 60 percent Muslim,[39] although largely in disciplines that offered few prospects of professional advancement.

The fact remains that the extent of the progress made in reducing inequalities was not perceived at the time. Social mobility, though obvious as a matter of casual observation, was harder to measure than before since the changing composition of economic growth had upset traditional demographic categories.[40] Moreover, the reversion to laissez-faire principles at the beginning of Franjieh's term interfered with the corrective mechanisms of fiscal policy, which was now less efficient than emigration as a means for narrowing income discrepancies across communities.[41] But it was above all the contrasts visible in daily life, and especially in Beirut, that had become more glaring. Between the ostentatious luxury of the upper classes and the no less palpable misery of its most impoverished residents, the capital remained the seat of social injustice denounced by Michel Écochard more than a generation earlier. Immense Muslim fortunes did exist, of course, but they were not enough to offset the image of a communal cleavage that coincided with the social divisions of the country. Indeed Lebanon's human geography accentuated these divisions, wealth being concentrated in the Mountain, overwhelmingly Christian and historically the first region to be developed, and in a few neighborhoods of the Beirut metropolitan area, which every day extended its reach a bit further. It was here, in and around Beirut, that both the most brilliant successes of the Lebanese miracle and its most abject failures were to be found.

By the early 1970s the metropolitan area had surpassed the million mark in population, which is to say that one in three Lebanese resided there. Certainly a good part of the appeal of urban life was associated with this hypertrophy. But most of the newcomers, stranded on the margins of the capital, to which they had been driven by the rural exodus and, increasingly, the Israeli strikes against southern Lebanon, had no access to its charms. The suburbs of Beirut, home to some four hundred thousand people,[42] were hardly uniform. Along the outer edge of the great arc of settlement, wealthy communities had recently sprung up to the southeast around Yarzeh, overlooking Baʿabda, and to the northeast around Rabieh, above Antelias, that coexisted with long-urbanized villages having a lower-middle-class, mainly Christian population. A similar pattern could be observed in the already venerable suburbs of the southwest such as Furn al-Shubbak, Shiyyah (known locally as ʿAyn al-Rummaneh), and Sinn al-Fil, where the original homes had mostly been replaced with comparatively tall buildings having several apartments on each floor and occupied by the families of public employees and factory workers. These neighborhoods could not be considered impoverished, but neither were they in any sense affluent. Even there the population density was relatively high: 142 persons per hectare in Furn al-Shubbak and 84 in Sinn al-Fil (57 and 34 persons per acre, respectively).[43] Alongside these established suburbs, however, two other forms of habitation accommodated the larger part of the extramural population: unincorporated neighborhoods and shantytowns, most of them wretchedly poor, among which were scattered the Palestinian camps. It was this haphazard concentration of

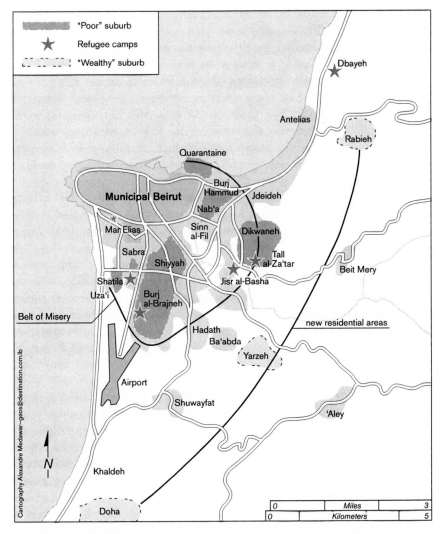

MAP 14. Greater Beirut on the Eve of the War, 1975

unemployed workers and destitute refugees that constituted what was now known simply as the belt of misery.

This ring of appalling slums, the dark side of Lebanese prosperity, had abruptly grown in the second half of the 1960s. It stretched from the Quarantaine district, at the mouth of the Beirut River (site of the first settlement of Armenian refugees, which later gave way to Kurds and to Bedouins from the Biqaʿ), to the dunes on the edge of the airport. In the shantytowns and camps, Lebanese represented only a little more than a tenth of the total; the rest (87.3 percent) were foreigners, of whom the Palestinians accounted for the largest share in addition to smaller numbers of Syrians and Turkish Kurds.[44] In some of the older neighborhoods, such as Nabʿa and Burj al-Brajneh, the majority were Lebanese, for the most part Shiʿa from the south. If the housing in these places was more sophisticated and some buildings a few stories high, the quality of life there was scarcely better than in the shantytowns and camps: the sewer system was fragmentary, water supply intermittent; and while the large number of television antennas showed that difficulties in hooking up to the electrical grid (due generally to a failure to obtain building permits) could be overcome, telephones were practically nonexistent.

There were many other squalid areas within municipal Beirut itself, such as Hayy al-Siryan (the Syrian Quarter) and Karm al-Zaytun in Ashrafiyyeh, and Wata in Musaytbeh. Inner-city slums were prevented from expanding by the development of middle-class housing on all sides, and in any case their population was not swollen by the massive inflows that bloated the periphery. The belt of misery, by contrast, only grew wider, until its advance was finally halted by the first foothills of the Mountain or by insurmountable obstacles, such as the banks of the Beirut River (which blocked the westward expansion of the Armenian suburb of Burj Hammud and the adjacent community of Nabʿa) and the new airport. Above all, this ring became more and more densely populated, reaching levels unknown in the city itself. In the area formed by Burj Hammud and Nabʿa, the density rose to 518 persons per hectare (210 per acre).[45]

Beyond the primitiveness of its buildings and the sordidness of its living conditions, what distinguished the belt of misery from the sociological point of view was the fact that it was almost exclusively Muslim, apart from the Armenian Christians of Burj Hammud. And because a growing proportion of this population came from southern Lebanon, whose residents were now regularly confronted with the brutal reality of the Arab-Israeli conflict, Beirut soon became a fertile breeding ground for left-wing parties urging the cause of social justice in conjunction with the paramilitary campaign for Arab national liberation. At the same time the extension of the protected area of the Palestinian camps made it easier to recruit refugees, who on taking up the armed struggle made revolutionary rhetoric a part of the daily life of the most impoverished inhabitants of the metropolitan area.

Suddenly able to exploit the human resources furnished to it by the belt of misery as well as the autonomy that the Palestinian guerrilla movements had managed to acquire, thanks at least in part to its efforts at mobilization, the left could now look forward to the day, not far off, when it would at last be recognized as a major actor in Lebanese, and even Arab, political life. The Palestinian presence had done nothing more than accelerate this course of events—it was not its cause. For the parties of protest perfectly distilled the various and mutually reinforcing influences of modernity that were most vividly registered in Beirut, the site one day of a student demonstration, the next of a teachers' strike, the day after that of a new play—and witness every day to the power of the press. Yet neither social upheaval nor unorthodox ideas could hope to be acknowledged and given their due weight by a political system that was spent. Under these circumstances it is hardly surprising that far more vigorous forces were soon to gain the upper hand.

Beirut, O Beirut!

Beirut was accustomed to being a film set. Yet something had changed, so that now the city was called upon to play the hero—and the antihero. These were the roles that Maroun Bagdadi assigned it for the film he submitted as a thesis in satisfaction of the degree requirements of the Institut des Hautes Études Cinématographiques (IDHEC). Made in 1974 on a small budget, but even so with the great Egyptian actor ʿIzzat al-ʿAlayli, *Beyrouth ya Beyrouth* (Beirut, O Beirut!) was the complaint that a young man, twenty-five years old, unable any longer to repress the political, intellectual, artistic, existential, and sexual anxieties of his generation, felt obliged to address to the city of his birth. It was to be a letter of farewell.

Unflinchingly honest in the witness it bore to the present, just before the fall from grace, though not without hope for the future, *Beyrouth ya Beyrouth* showed another city than the one that formed the background for Egyptian films of romance and intrigue and the detective movies made by European and American directors of the period. Already one sensed in it the mixture of tension and gaiety that the German filmmaker Volker Schlöndorff, in *Die Fälschung* (Circle of Deceit, 1981), and the Algerian Farouk Beloufa, in *Nahla* (1979), were later to detect during the war, before Bagdadi himself created a still more absurdist picture of the city in *Petites Guerres* (Little Wars, 1982), his second film. But the violence that lay ahead, when *Beyrouth ya Beyrouth* was being filmed, was not yet inevitable. If the young artist unquestionably had a premonition that the end was drawing near, he was more concerned with capturing the spirit of a generation that, like him, sought to bring about change by embracing all the causes of the left.

Bagdadi did not exaggerate. Beirut, long a shrine to conspicuous consumption and economic liberalism, had suddenly taken on the appearance of a left-wing city, at least on the surface. The demonstrations and the theatrical productions, the strikes, the painting exhibitions—all these things gave the impression of a place where the air itself was red. Even at the École Supérieure des Lettres, the children of the Lebanese miracle and of the Francophone Christian middle class were soon to crack open the champagne to celebrate General Giap's final victory with the fall of Saigon in April 1975.

In the meantime the class struggle had faded away, or else been obscured by events. The like of this had already happened in the nineteenth century: Tanyus Shahin's revolt, though it attracted the notice of Karl Marx, only prefigured the civil war between the Druze and Maronites of the Mountain. A century later the communal landscape of Lebanon, a larger country than before, was more crowded, and the paths of divergence more numerous. The Palestinian resistance, by its very presence, nourished a radically anti-imperialist view of the world, dedicated to bringing forth "one, two, several Vietnams," while at the same time sharpening other, more ancient antagonisms between Christians and Muslims. The prospect of a divorce, if not actually civil war, acquired its plausibility from just this fact. Even if its implication was never explicitly formulated, the neologism "Cypriotization" (al-Qabrasa)— suggested by the example of the neighboring island of Cyprus, where the Turkish invasion in the summer of 1974 ended in a de facto partition of the country, and frequently heard in the months leading up to the outbreak of the war—spoke volumes.

The experience of living beneath the volcano restrained neither the passions of those who challenged the status quo nor the behavior of those who were determined to preserve it at any cost, and still less the insouciant verve with which Beirut pursued its quest for riches and pleasures. As a reading of the newspapers of the period shows over and over again, the country and the city could not help but tear themselves apart in their desire to go in every direction at the same time. After three decades of independence, racked by all the economic, social, and ideological changes that Beirut's explosive growth had produced in the interval, Lebanon found itself subjected to a profound transformation that constitutionally it was poorly equipped to withstand. Since the mid-1960s, many signs—not all of them immediately legible—testified to a longing for new modes of expression and, ultimately, a way to reconceive the basis of political life. This broader ambition was to remain unfulfilled. Nevertheless, the almost ineffable impulse that gave rise to a sense of perpetual motion—the relentless and continually growing appetite for political confrontation limned by *Beyrouth ya Beyrouth*—increasingly animated every aspect of social life, beginning with the cultural sphere.

A CULTURE IN FERMENT

Emblematic in this regard, among a thousand others one could name, is the career of Roger Assaf, one of the great figures of Lebanese theater. The son of a French mother and, like his younger contemporary, Maroun Bagdadi, raised in a West-ernized middle-class Christian family, Assaf scarcely spoke Arabic at all in his youth. He started out as an actor in Francophone productions in the mid-1960s, appear-ing initially in plays sponsored by the Catholic Student Youth theater, and then on television. In almost no time he was the talk of the town for his staging of *Majdaloun*, a play written by a member of the SSNP, Henri Hamati, and starring Nidal Ashqar, daughter of one of the elders of the same party, which denounced the government's inaction in southern Lebanon in the face of Israeli provocation and called upon the audience to support the Palestinian resistance. It was shut down by military order on the evening of its premiere in 1968. The cast and audience decamped at once to the Horseshoe Café, where the play was then performed—an event that remains one of the most powerful moments in the recent memory of Beirut intellectuals. Assaf's insistence on authenticity led him subsequently to engage the famous co-median Hasan 'Alaeddin, known as Shushu, to act under his direction in *Akh ya baladna!* (O, Our Country!), a play with populist overtones, in 1974. Assaf later converted to Islam and, under the spell cast by the Iranian Revolution, made him-self the herald of the Shi'i peasantry of southern Lebanon, finding inspiration in the inventiveness of Ariane Mnouchkine's Théâtre du Soleil. After the war he re-turned to urban themes, while continuing to call attention to the plight of the poor and helpless.

For Roger Assaf, as for other artists of his generation, the turning point came in 1967. Suddenly, in a manner recalling Freud's notion of a return of repressed ele-ments from the subconscious, the Arab-Israeli conflict invaded the cultural scene. Until then the republic of Arab letters had figured prominently in the Beirut intel-lectual landscape; but from now on its influence was paramount. Politics had never been wholly absent from the city's cultural life, of course, and in the wake of the de-feat a skeptical opinion of authority took root and spread among artists and intel-lectuals. Dār al-Fann (House of Art), founded by Janine Rubeiz (known, despite her bourgeois origins, as Janine the Red), hosted passionate debates in addition to important exhibitions of painting, in which the ascendancy of leftist ideas could plainly be seen. But the intelligentsia was not the only audience. The public showed considerable interest as well, and particularly in the development of a highly polit-ical form of theater in which eminent actors were eager to take part.[1] Jalal Khoury (son of the well-known Communist couturier to Beirut high society, and himself a fellow traveler) attracted large crowds for his adaptation of Bertolt Brecht's *The Re-sistible Rise of Arturo Ui*, recast in the light of the Arab-Israeli conflict. Later Khoury enjoyed remarkable success with a series of plays featuring the comic character Geha, whose naive acceptance of official explanations for government policy in southern Lebanon was used to denounce the situation there. The theater of the absurd pio-neered in Lebanon by Raymond Gebara, though less overtly political, also took its place among the great challenges to orthodoxy of the moment.

Literary life was nevertheless not wholly immune to official harassment. The publication in Beirut in 1969 of *Naqd al-fikr al-dini* (Critique of Religious Thought) by the Syrian philosopher Sadiq Jalal al-ʿAzm, a penetrating examination of traditional Arab culture, prompted Muslim religious authorities to demand that all copies of the book be confiscated. While the ensuing protest failed in its purpose of having the ban lifted, it did at least manage to deter new instances of political censorship, with the result that increasingly bold productions were mounted in the theater and accompanied by greater daring among publishers. Indeed, despite the precedent set by ʿAzm, the bulk of intellectual debate in the Arab world continued to take place in Beirut, where it was marked by a frankly leftist tone that established the reputation of new houses such as Dār al-Talīʿa, set up by the Baʿthist Bashir Daʿuq, and Dār Ibn Khaldun, directed by Muhammad Kishli, a former member of the Arab Nationalist Movement who had briefly been affiliated with the Communist Action Organization in Lebanon. Marxist analysis of current events also continued to reach an audience well beyond the borders of Lebanon through Dār al-Farabi, the publishing organ of the Lebanese Communists. These houses were joined by the Arab Institute for Studies and Publication, headed by the Palestinian historian Abdul Wahid al-Kayali, as well as the Palestine Research Center, founded in 1965 by the PLO under the direction of Anis Sayegh, and the independent Institute of Palestinian Studies, both of which fueled debate during this period by means of translations from Hebrew and works examining the historical development of Israel and the Arab-Israeli conflict. Lebanese and Palestinian researchers mixed with one another to such an extent that these last two centers were scarcely distinguishable. Other Lebanese scholars—notably Waddah Sharara and Ahmad Beydun, two future eminences of the intellectual scene in Beirut—were later recruited by an ambitious Arab Development Institute, financed by Libya, which barely had time to commence its publishing activities before the war broke out. A series of theoretically minded journals also sought to respond to the major questions of the post-1967 period, notably the LCP's review *Al-Tarīq, Dirāsāt* (Arab Studies), *Al-Fikr al-ʿarabi al-muʿāsir* (Contemporary Arab Thought), and *Mawāqif* (Positions), the last of which, under the editorship of the pseudonymous poet Adonis following his departure from *Shiʿr,* combined a reverence for literary invention with philosophical inquiry.

Now more than ever, as the center of Arab publishing, Beirut attracted authors and artists. The Dolce Vita café had, of course, lost its former luster. With the Baʿth Party now in power in both Damascus and Iraq, Beirut was no longer the magnet for political exiles it had been when Michel ʿAflaq lived there almost permanently. Some Baʿthists who had broken with the party still sought refuge in Lebanon, but the ferocious vindictiveness of the two ruling regimes and the capacity of their secret police to intervene there (notably in the case of the kidnapping in July 1974 of the columnist Michel Abu Jawdeh, often critical of the Syrian regime) made it advisable for dissidents to keep a low profile. Nevertheless the appeal of the Palestinian resistance largely filled the Ba'thist void by bringing together in Beirut, often in institutions controlled by the PLO, intellectuals and militants from Tunisia, Morocco, Sudan, Iraq, and even Egypt, to say nothing, of course, of the Palestinians themselves. Mahmud Darwish, who had come from Haifa via Moscow (having until then been a member of the Israeli Communist Party), made only a brief stopover of a few months in Cairo before settling in Beirut in 1972. Over the next ten years he succeeded in transforming himself from a bard of combat into one of the great poetic voices of the later twentieth century, a voice long marked, as his work shows in innumerable ways, by the syncretism in which he had immersed himself in Beirut—before moving to Paris.

The city's press, as a microcosm of a microcosm, was bound to reflect the mood of these years. The end of the Arab cold war had not interrupted the funneling of money to local newspapers by foreign governments; indeed, oil wealth had only increased such transfers. But the incessant quarreling of the recent past had given way to a sort of communion in doubt and radicalization, and even if differences had not yet wholly been erased, all papers had shifted at least some ways to the left. In 1974, Libyan financing enabled Talal Salman to launch *Al-Safir*, which billed itself as "the newspaper of Lebanon in the Arab nation and the newspaper of the Arab nation in Lebanon," and which was to train some of the best writers of the Arab press. It succeeded in competing with *Al-Muharrir* (The Liberator) and *Al-Bayrūt*, both pro-Iraqi, which, along with *Al-Nida'*, now the official organ of the LCP, rounded out the list of the left-wing dailies. The same sensibility was found elsewhere as well, even in *An-Nahar*, the city's leading paper, which regularly topped its own sales records. All of Lebanon's contradictions were concentrated in its building on Rue Hamra. Michel Abu Jawdeh's office, where Ba'thist officials often came to visit, followed at once by Palestinian leaders, remained the capital of radical Arab politics; Ghassan Tuwayni's office three floors above continued to be the meeting place for the Arab establishment, which used it to make and unmake governments, and the intelligentsia. On the third and fourth floors, the editorial offices of this liberal newspaper were a nursery for left-wing militants, among them the young Amin Maalouf, who served as a foreign correspondent. The paper's cultural supplement, *Al-Mulhaq*, launched in 1967 under the direction of Unsi al-Hajj and housed in a nearby annex, quickly made itself the main outlet for new poetry as well as for fresh departures from political and intellectual orthodoxy.

Even the Francophone press participated in the ferment. Under the direction of Georges Naccache, who had started out under the Mandate as a supporter of the nationalist French writer and politician Maurice Barrès and then moved further and further to the left, *L'Orient* carried on the venerable Lebanese tradition of Francophilia, particularly in its literary section (edited for a time by Georges Schéhadé), while enriching it with a spirit of dissent embodied by men such as Samir Franjieh, nephew of the future president, whose activity in the Communist Party (and later on its margins) was to win him the nickname "Bey Rouge." *Le Jour,* relaunched in 1965 by a group of anti-Shihabists led by Ghassan Tuwayni and backed by the leading figures of the merchant republic, did not lag behind. Under the direction of Jean Choueiri and Édouard Saab, who was also a foreign correspondent for *Le Monde* in Paris, the liberal (if not actually libertarian) bent of its young editorial staff put the paper on a different course than the one set by its original founders. One rising journalist who particularly distinguished himself was Marwan Hamadeh, brother of the poet Nadia Tuwayni and a future minister with close ties to Kamal Jumblatt's Progressive Socialist Party. Later a new section of the paper, *Le Jour des Jeunes,* spoke to young people captivated by the excitement of May 1968 in France as well as by the allure of post-1967 Arab radicalism. The merger of the two papers in 1971 under the name *L'Orient–Le Jour* served to pool the relatively small but nonetheless impressive supply of journalistic talent and anti-establishment thinking in mainstream Beirut circles.

STUDENTS IN THE STREET

The experience of *L'Orient* and *Le Jour,* like the career of Roger Assaf, testifies to the change of direction that Lebanon underwent during this period, when the aftermath of the Arab-Israeli War converged with the student revolutions of the following year to persuade some observers that by adding together 67 and 68 Beirut got 69, which is to say the Cairo Agreement. This convergence was felt particularly in the universities and more than a few schools. As a side-effect of Westernization, the events of May 1968 in Paris immediately influenced the Francophone intellectual elites and a large number of the sons of good families in Beirut. At the beginning of the 1968–69 school year an action committee was formed at the *lycée* of the Mission Laïque Française, where a number of young teachers working abroad in lieu of military service acted as intermediaries for the transmission of radical ideas. But the radicalization of the city's affluent youth occurred chiefly at the École Supérieure des Lettres, founded in 1945 by Gabriel Bounoure and headed at this time by Michel Corvin, a professor of literature specializing in theater studies. In combination with the dissenting tradition of the American University of Beirut and, even more important, the large enrollments of the Lebanese University, a state school founded in 1952, this radicalization was to give rise to a broad-based student movement between 1968 and 1975.[2]

In spite of the disproportionate use of force by the police, the number of strikes and demonstrations rose—from day to day during certain periods. The processions that made their way to the UNESCO headquarters, where the Ministry of Education had its offices, or to the Parliament Building on Place de l'Étoile, sometimes involved tens of thousands of young people, among them the children of several ministers and deputies. More than once the nephews of the president of the Republic and of the prime minister were seen neglecting their studies. But the spirit of protest exhilarated students from all backgrounds, at all universities and a great many schools—not only the private institutions esteemed by the middle class (such as the French *lycée*) and the upper class (such as the International College of AUB), but also the public high schools. In part this was due to the fact that, in addition to the urgency of political and ideological issues, there were increasingly pressing social motivations.

The social dimension of protest was particularly perceptible at the Lebanese University, whose students came from the working and lower middle classes, and where the doubtful prospects of finding employment after the completion of their studies helped to create an atmosphere of discontent.[3] The curriculum offered no professional outlets other than teaching and government service. The only field that permitted access to a "satisfying" profession was law, but the bar was already overcrowded and a judicial career no longer promised the social advancement it once did. The establishment of faculties of engineering and medicine at the state university was a recurring demand of the student movement there, repeatedly rejected by the administration. At the time, Lebanese physicians trained in the Soviet Union whose education had been financed through scholarships handed out by the Communist Party were not automatically admitted to practice on their return, unlike those who came back from France and the United States, and were required first to pass a special examination known as the Colloquium.

The political system was plainly incapable of adapting to the situation. Ghassan Tuwayni, appointed minister of education in the first government of Franjieh's presidency, sought to defuse protest by going into the street and talking with the demonstrators—a futile gesture since he did not have the president's support. When Tuwayni resigned a few months later, it was the students' turn to make common cause with him by means of new demonstrations. The job was to take its toll on a succession of other ministers, among them the architect Henri Eddé, relieved of his duties by Franjieh in 1972 after fewer than two months in office—the only instance of a minister being dismissed in the entire history of the Lebanese Republic.

The perceived failings of the educational system, and of the Lebanese University in particular, did not exhaust the sources of student dissatisfaction.[4] Occupying an intermediate position between intellectual debate and social struggle, the student movement also contributed to the increasingly political character of union mobilization among the working and lower middle classes. The government's bloody crackdown on a demonstration by small farmers in the south brought the students out into the streets in Beirut, as did a strike by workers at the Ghandur chocolate plant in November 1972. A protest singer popular among the Francophone youth of the École des Lettres named Paul Matar drew inspiration from this last episode, in which strikers died, for a song that advised his listeners—in French—to be wary of eating chocolate because there was blood inside. The mood of the time was also, and especially, influenced by the proximity of the Palestinian resistance. Already in 1968 the first strikes had anticipated debate in Parliament and the newspapers by raising the question of the place of Lebanon in the Arab-Israeli conflict and its support for the Palestinian armed struggle.[5] In the months and years that followed, students regularly assembled to demand that southern Lebanon be defended against Israeli attacks and to proclaim their anti-Americanism, nowhere more stridently than at the American university.

Left-wing student organizations were not without rivals during this period of course, though their rhetoric rubbed off on all the groups that were active in university circles, the Phalange Party included. Notwithstanding the epic brawls in which Bashir Gemayel traded punches with adversaries from the École des Lettres, the Phalangists' student section, led first by Karim Pakraduni and later by Michel Samaha—both future ministers during the postwar era—was much less to the right than the rest of the party. Open to dialogue and Arabist ideas, it managed to achieve consensus with parties on the left on a number of questions, particularly with regard to demands concerning the Lebanese University. And it was on that campus, in the middle ground between the Phalangists and the left, that a movement known as the Awakening (Sahwa) first emerged, whose secular perspective and concern for social justice attracted a growing number of young Christians, generally from the provinces.

To all of this the government seemed to remain oblivious. Under Hélou, Shihabism had manifestly reached an impasse. Yet opposition to change only grew under Franjieh, who rapidly showed himself to be incapable of grasping the new dynamics that were reshaping Lebanese society. To be sure, he appointed a "youth cabinet" composed of men in their forties and headed by Saeb Salam, while continuing to support social programs that had been established under Shihab and Hélou[6] and in some cases built upon them (thus a program of health insurance, for example, introduced in 1971, extended the provisions of the social security scheme that had been instituted in 1964). Once the euphoria of the first months had worn off, however, it became clear that the state was no longer fully committed to modernization. To the contrary, Franjieh refused to support his most innovative ministers—Ghassan Tuwayni in the first instance, and later Dr. Émile Bitar, the minister of health, who sought to challenge the pharmaceutical monopoly that had long kept prices of prescription medicines artificially high; Elias Saba, the finance minister, who attempted to favor industrial expansion through higher tariffs on imports that would be used to finance a six-year development program for infrastructure; and Henri Eddé, minister of public works, summarily removed from office.[7] With the fall of this government, after only a year of existence, Franjieh restored clientelism and nepotism to their former places of honor (going so far as to appoint his own son as a minister) and freed laissez-faire policies from all impediment, without feeling the least need to try to address the fundamental questions that had continued to face Lebanon since independence, and whose urgency was now further emphasized by events in the street.

Apart from Franjieh's first cabinet, quickly jettisoned, governments made little or no attempt to make room for representatives of the new social forces. Indeed, nothing better symbolized the official resistance to change than the very presence of Franjieh as head of state. While Beirut—culturally the most creative, if not also the most sophisticated, metropolis in the Arab world—was alive with the clamor of experimentation and argument, Lebanon found itself saddled with the dullest and most uncouth president in its history. Routinely drawn by cartoonists in peasant costume, with a hunting rifle slung over his shoulder, Franjieh personified to the point of caricature the contrast between the Mountain and the City famously described by Albert Hourani.[8]

It was not only the president himself. The whole system seemed incapable of evolution, much less imagination. The legislative elections in the spring of 1972 brought to Parliament only the usual run of zuʿamā' and notables. Nonetheless there were a few promising indications that a page was about to be turned. In Tripoli, the Baʿthist candidate received more votes even than Rashid Karameh. Still more suggestive was the outcome in the third district of Beirut. Although Saeb Salam was able to get two of the three Sunni candidates on his list elected, his Greek Orthodox ally was defeated by a twenty-five-year-old Nasserite named Najah Wakim. Closer analysis of the results showed that the district's Sunni electorate had combined the support of notables for Salam—who after all was one of their own—as prime minister with a sectarian refusal to vote for the Christian candidate—despite Salam's personal endorsement—in the case of the parliamentary seat. But apart from the two Sunnis elected from the prime minister's list, along with a few other figures of the moderate left, elevated for the most part owing to Jumblatt's established network of alliances, and, at the other end of the political spectrum, a few deputies from the lists of the Phalange Party—altogether scarcely more than 15 percent of the total number of parliamentary seats—the new Chamber, like the old one, reflected only to a very small degree the changes taking place in Lebanese society. The obsolescence of the system was plain, if only by virtue of the startling contradiction between the growing urbanization of the population over the past two decades and the obligation of urban voters to cast their ballots in the district where they were born, and not where they lived, which is to say the place where they actually worked, where they made their homes, and, most importantly of all, where they created their identity as individuals.[9]

From obsolescence to paralysis turned out to be but a short step, as yet another crisis the following year was to make clear.

THE QUARREL OF THE COMMUNITIES

The crisis of 1973 had its origins in the long-standing question of power-sharing among the notables of the various religious communities.[10] In spite of a certain improvement in Lebanese-Palestinian relations, the issue remained unresolved. The solidarity shown by Lebanese Muslims had assured the Palestinian resistance of a certain margin of security in its dealings with the state—a significant development, in the event, since it gave the Muslims an awareness of their strength and exposed the depth of the frustration (*ghubn*) of which their leaders complained. Anything was liable to fray nerves, so that minor procedural delays, or even insistence on simple points of protocol, came to be considered assaults on the "dignity" of the Muslim community. Yet the same leaders took no more than a token interest in the social inequalities from which a large part of their electorate suffered.[11] Their platform—a strictly political one—called only for a renegotiation of the power-sharing arrangements by which the preeminence of the Maronites was incarnated in the all-powerful presidency of the Republic.

In the eyes of Muslim notables, the president behaved as though he were operating in a genuinely presidential regime, while at the same time being constitutionally unaccountable and therefore immune from any attempt to remove him from office. By contrast, the kind of participation (*mushāraka*) they called for assumed the existence of a true parliamentary regime in which the prime minister, chosen by the deputies rather than by the chief of state, served as head of the executive branch. Reform would also mean strict parity between Christians and Muslims in Parliament, instead of the prevailing ratio of six Christian representatives to five Muslims. Finally, there was a military implication: the army ought to be reorganized for the purpose of defending the country against Israel and its command entrusted to a multiconfessional body of officers rather than a single Maronite general. Far from challenging the National Pact, this rather modest set of proposals claimed to honor it. Nonetheless it ran up against the categorical opposition of Franjieh and the majority of the nation's Christian politicians. The Ta'if Accord of September 1989 that ended the civil war finally adopted all of these points, except for the one abolishing the position of commander-in-chief of the army, and the following year they were enshrined in the revised Constitution.

The resettlement of the Palestinian resistance in southern Lebanon also affected the Shi'a, among whom the perception of an unbalanced political system was still more keenly felt. The presidency of the Chamber of Deputies, which had now devolved to them, was even more liable to be drained of its nominal authority by the growing power of the president of the Republic than the post of prime minister. More than this, the community objected to what it considered to be its severe under-representation in the state administration, and particularly in high public offices, on the ground that it had become the most numerous denomination in the

country—a claim that, though it was repeatedly made and not entirely without foundation, was nonetheless greatly exaggerated. The fundamental issue in any case
involved more than the sharing of power among communities. Within the Shiʻi community, the notables were themselves regarded as allies of "the Maronite government," and under the influence of Imam Musa al-Sadr, an Iranian cleric who had
emigrated to Lebanon in 1959, becoming head of the Higher Shiʻa Council a decade
later, a demand for social justice arose in tandem with a protest against the traditional leaders of the community, accused of hampering its advancement, by what
Sadr called the "disinherited" masses *(mahrūmīn)*.

Imam Sadr's interest in organizing the Shiʻi community had initially been encouraged in the 1960s by the Deuxième Bureau, which looked to him to do two
things: thwart the anti-Shihabist obstructionism of the community's zuʻamāʼ while,
at the same time, channeling its rapidly expanding subproletariat in the suburbs of
Beirut onto the path of moderation.[12] Sadr's rhetoric, if not his behavior, quickly
hardened as a result of a series of developments in the early 1970s that included the
intensification of social protest, confessional polarization, the crumbling of the state's
authority in southern Lebanon and the devastation of this region by the Israeli army,
and the rise of the Marxist left. In 1973 and 1974 the imam held vast rallies that attracted tens of thousands of people, most of them armed; at one of them he called
upon his listeners to carry weapons, celebrating them as "the ornament of men" *(zī-
nat al-rijāl)* and the bearing of arms as a "sacred duty." But if repeated use of the
term *mahrūmīn* conferred upon the imam a revolutionary aura, symbolic gestures
such as his participation in public debates held at a Beirut church during Lent gave
him the reputation of a reasonable man who was open to opposing points of view,
and the general opinion of his community continued to favor the reformulation of
communal power-sharing arrangements through the introduction of new Shiʻi elites
into the system.

Nevertheless popular support for the Palestinian cause gave impetus to another,
more radical strategy. Beyond the rebalancing of the institutional status quo that
the leaders of the Muslim communities now felt themselves in a position to insist
upon, parties on the left found in this support the means they lacked for competing with both the traditional notables and the broad-based appeal of Imam Sadr.
But if the left stood to gain by challenging political confessionalism and the whole
existing structure of power, this strategy had the unintended consequence of deepening the quarrel among the communities. By virtue of the very mobilization that
had been set in motion by the concern to defend Palestinian claims, and under the
cover of a struggle for national liberation, an equivalence was established between
Muslim aspirations and the rejection of the status quo. What is more, an increasingly widespread confusion over who actually constituted the "masses" often caused
it to be forgotten that there were many Christians among them as well.

Imam Sadr had himself been influenced by the social agenda of the left, despite his resolute anti-Communism, several times publicly declared,[13] and his development of the theme of the disinherited unmistakably borrowed from its rhetoric. Clumsy formulations lent credence to the idea that the Shiʿa formed a disinherited community—even a community-class *(al-tabaqa al-taʾifa)*, a hybrid notion over which much ink was spilled. Although often attributed to the CAOL, this expression did not figure in any official document, and, despite its use by journalists, it was never erected into a concept or endowed with any theoretical status.[14] It nonetheless had a devastating effect. By a series of gradual and almost imperceptible shifts, the left ended up embracing a doctrine of communal division. Indeed the confessional composition of the militant base of both the LCP and the SSNP underwent a change, substantially reducing old pockets of support in Christian circles. The presence of Jumblatt at the head of the alliance on the left—a figure who, notwithstanding his reformism, increasingly presented himself as the spokesman of all the Muslim communities, and not only of the Druze—further strengthened this identification of class and community.

Support for the transformation of politics, manifest in the student movement and in the cultural sphere, led in practice to a regeneration of denominational loyalties. Except for the most committed militants, communal attachment continued to dictate the definition of identity, Arabist or Lebanonist, even among the young.[15] A few on the left were aware of this, notably the playwright Jalal Khoury. His play *Rafiq Sijʾan* (Comrade Sijʾan), produced in 1974, portrayed a village—in the event, a Christian village—where political allegiance, whether to Moscow or Washington, was a function of parochial quarrels. On a national scale, ideological preference pitted the bell towers against the minarets, and vice versa.

The polarization of political life was now a fact of daily life,[16] even if in Beirut the economy, culture, and the entertainment industry continued to thrive. Not all Christians or Muslims found themselves in a state of permanent confrontation, of course. Notwithstanding the tensions between Franjieh and the Sunni notables, public administration continued to embody the inertial force of coexistence. Taqieddin al-Sulh's expanded government having outlived its usefulness by October 1974, the new cabinet—directed by one of his cousins, the deputy Rashid al-Sulh, who was reputed to be close to Jumblatt—managed once again to bring together representatives of various parliamentary blocs, including the Phalange Party. And yet the fundamental questions of the day, to the extent that they were considered at all, were considered against a background of controversy and crisis. The chronic dispute over "Lebanese Arabness" once more flared up, and it was forgotten that the same government that had found a way to wind down the civil war in 1958, to which the Phalange leader Pierre Gemayel himself belonged, had solemnly affirmed this Arab identity. Assertions of communal patriotism, whether explicit or disguised, dominated debate and brought forth frenzied calls for change while at the same time reinforcing ideological and political rigidity. Having become entangled in domestic political antagonisms, the question of the Palestinian presence was now posed only in polemical terms, and this at a moment when progress in improving the regional situation might yet have made it possible to ease tensions within Lebanon.

THE RISE OF EXTREMISM

The test of strength of May 1973 had shown that the divided state of Lebanese society and of its political class ruled out any chance that the Palestinian presence could be reduced, still less eliminated, without exposing the country to grave risks. There seemed to be some reason to believe that the lessons of the past had been learned, however. A dialogue was officially initiated between the Phalange Party and the PLO, and the government's support for Syria during the war of October 1973 permitted a rapprochement with General Assad's regime. Franjieh was even deputized at the October 1974 Rabat summit conference of Arab leaders to represent them at the United Nations in New York during the special session of the General Assembly to be held the following month, at which Arafat was to make his first appearance before the world community. The delegation that accompanied Franjieh included Camille Chamoun and Charles Hélou, in their capacity as former presidents, along with former prime ministers and presidents of the Chamber of Deputies, to illustrate Lebanon's confessional diversity and to emphasize its unity in defense of the Arab cause. Developments on the regional level, following the October War, appeared to provide grounds for cautious optimism. For the moment at least a spirit of moderation prevailed in all the Arab capitals, as the Rabat summit showed. Saudi Arabia, an American ally, saw its influence amplified as a result of the oil embargo and the new financial leverage it enjoyed with the increase in the price of crude oil. The United States, despite having sided with Israel during the war, was once again welcome in both Cairo and Damascus; indeed Richard Nixon had made a triumphal eight-day tour of Near Eastern capitals in June 1974, only a few weeks before his resignation. Prospects for a peaceful settlement of the Arab-Israeli conflict looked brighter than before. Even the PLO seemed to accept the idea, suggesting that the objective of the total liberation of Palestine might be renounced in favor of a two-state solution granting Palestinians the West Bank and the Gaza Strip.

The apparent willingness to contemplate diplomacy as a substitute for preparing for war was nonetheless misleading. Whereas the Arabs announced their desire for a peaceful settlement, the United States, now in the position of referee, sought only to contain the conflict, in keeping with its own priorities, which placed crisis management ahead of conflict resolution.[17] Events on the ground threatened to upset these calculations, however. In spite of the sudden conversion to pragmatism by the Palestinian resistance, its behavior in Lebanon seemed to point to a different purpose, not only in view of its continuing cross-border commando raids but also, and especially, of the international audience whose sympathetic attention the

PLO was now accustomed to command via the media in Beirut. Israel, for its part, did not mistake the implications of Palestinian activity, and far from diminishing its interventions in Lebanese territory, it began to step up attacks. Air strikes were even directed against PLO camps in Beirut and Tripoli in November 1974—at practically the same moment that Arafat and Franjieh went before the United Nations to declare the Arab interest in pursuing a moderate course. A few weeks later, the village of Kfarshuba, in the ʿArqub, was entirely leveled.

Not only did circumstances in Lebanon, the weak link of the Mashriq, stand in the way of any attempt to resolve the Arab-Israeli conflict; now Lebanon saw focused on its own territory the whole potential for instability that the American policy of crisis management was intended to suppress in the rest of the Near East. It was there, and only there, that Arab-Israeli animosity and popular discontent with American influence in the region could find expression so long as the Palestinian resistance remained the vessel of both impulses. No matter that the PLO had publicly endorsed the search for a negotiated solution, the survival of its original motivation encouraged it to continue on the path marked out by revolutionary rhetoric, and indeed by revolutionary action—all the more since large segments of the Lebanese population spontaneously demanded that it do just this.

The question of the Palestinian presence therefore lost none of its pertinence in domestic politics. On the contrary, the campaign conducted by Christian leaders against what they saw as the PLO's abuses and assaults on the sovereignty of the Lebanese state only gained in intensity. In early 1975, it took on a still graver tone when Pierre Gemayel presented Franjieh with a memorandum formally denouncing the state's relinquishment of sovereignty, and then, in concert with Chamoun, demanded a referendum on the question. By this point, however, political controversy had exceeded its usual limits and quickly reached the stage of popular mobilization. Militias associated with the Christian parties were being trained in the use of arms, thanks to the support lavished on them by influential elements of the army, up to and including the highest levels of both the general staff and the intelligence services. By now it was plain for all to see that the adversaries of the Palestinian presence had taken a hard line regarding the political paralysis that arose from the 1973 crisis: if it was impossible for the army to impose its will on the PLO, for both internal and external reasons, other means could be found.

Weapons had long been available in Lebanon, as the celebratory gunfire that for several hours greeted Franjieh's election in the Mountain and in almost all the streets of the Christian neighborhoods in Beirut demonstrated more than four years earlier. Militias were not a totally new phenomenon in Christian circles either. The Phalange Party had had a paramilitary arm since its founding in 1936, and the party's anniversary every year was the occasion of a uniformed procession through the streets of the capital. Regularly involved in the brawls between the Communists and Syrian nationalists, the Phalangists had vigorously taken part in the clashes of 1958.

The Armenian Tachnag Party also had a paramilitary wing. But beginning in the late 1960s this phenomenon assumed an increasingly broad scope. After the emergence of the Palestinian resistance, the Phalange's paramilitary units gave way to larger and more sophisticated formations.[18] Already by 1973 its armed force was robust enough to take up positions in the streets of Beirut, and indeed to take responsibility for the defense of its Christian neighborhoods. Chamoun's National Liberal Party (NLP) was also equipped with a militia, the Tigers (Numur—plural of *nimr*, Chamoun's middle name and his father's given name), and the current president of the Republic kept a unit under his personal command in his hometown of Zghorta, in northern Lebanon, where the cult of weapons had long been widespread. This devotion was now noticeable in Beirut itself, where there was a growing tendency in the Christian population to acquire military weapons, particularly the Kalashnikov AK-47 rifle. Typically the *Klashin* (as it was known locally) was purchased in a Palestinian camp.

After 1973, such expedients were no longer felt to be sufficient. The army command, with Franjieh's encouragement, adopted an unofficial policy of substitution that permitted Christian militias to receive regular supplies of arms and furnished them with training facilities. The top generals also turned a blind eye toward the behavior of mid-ranking officers, among them the future general Michel Aoun, who set about establishing a new militia, called simply the Organization (al-Tanzim), that recruited mainly from the urban professional classes. Enrollment in a militia came to precede membership in its sponsoring party—when there was a sponsoring party. Established political organizations were no longer the sole source of military training. The existence of a militia became in itself an instrument of mobilization, as if appeals to ideology no longer mattered. Political allegiance did in fact continue to play an important role, as the war was to demonstrate, but membership in militias nonetheless transcended traditional partisan divisions, amounting to normal behavior in communities obsessed with the need to defend the sovereignty of the state. Some parts of the Christian population resisted the temptation, of course. Among politicians, several figures took care to distance themselves from Chamoun and Gemayel, notably Raymond Eddé, one of the pillars of the Hilf, the old tripartite alliance. Eddé was nonetheless very troubled by the Palestinian campaign in the south: he had not approved the Cairo Agreement, and for years had called for the neutralization of the border with Israel with the assistance of a U.N. peacekeeping force—yet he could not prevent the formation by some of his own supporters of a local militia, in the suburb of Dikwaneh, near the Palestinian refugee camp at Tall al-Za'tar.

The word "sovereignty" was now constantly on the lips of those who lived next to the refugee camps and who no longer felt at home in their own homes. But for the most part sovereignty was the cherished symbol of national and confessional identity, as this was embodied in the structure of power[19]—whence the central role of the Phalange Party, which for decades had seen itself as a sort of surrogate state, a strategic reserve.[20] The tendency to regard minor disagreements arising from the expansion of the security perimeter of the camps into settled areas nearby as so many offenses against sovereignty deserving to be punished was forcefully illustrated in July 1974 by a quarrel among petty criminals that degenerated into armed clashes between Phalangist militiamen and Palestinians in Dikwaneh.

The Christian parties were not alone in protecting themselves. Militants on the left took up arms as well, albeit belatedly, as their unpreparedness in the spring of 1975 was to show. Although many Lebanese had been trained in the use of weapons, as a direct consequence of joining the various Palestinian groups, the established left-wing parties did not enter upon this path until after the crisis of May 1973. At that point the osmosis that had developed between the left and the Palestinian resistance led the PLO to provide military training to the members of friendly parties and to furnish them with weapons, however sparingly. Whereas the growth of militias among the Christians had proceeded from a perceived need to protect national sovereignty, among the Muslims it was justified in terms of the "defense of the Palestinian Revolution and of the Arabness of Lebanon." Behind this slogan the left was certainly searching for something else, although the idea of forcibly taking power had not been put forward and probably was not being contemplated. As a member of the establishment and at the same time committed to bringing about its transformation, Jumblatt regarded the Palestinian presence less as a lever that could catapult him to power than as a card to be played with his fellow politicians, who were both partners and adversaries; in exchange for a minimum of socioeconomic reform and a modification of the power structure through greater Muslim participation, the natural allies of the PLO would be in a position to make it accept a strict interpretation of the Cairo Agreement, as Jumblatt himself had done with some success on becoming interior minister in 1970.[21]

This fundamentally evenhanded strategy was also shared by other parties, notably the LCP and the CAOL, both now closely associated with Jumblatt. Nonetheless it did not permit him or anyone else to control the course of events. The proliferation of weapons and the revolutionary rhetoric that accompanied it combined to overwhelm all such calculations. In the extreme case, small groups having their roots in the subproletariat undertook direct action. A raid on the Bank of America branch in the heart of Beirut by the Lebanese Socialist Revolutionary Organization, in which hostages were taken and a $10 million ransom demanded in support of the armed struggle against Israel, gave a startling example of this in October 1973. The Arab Communist Organization, a radical group made up of both Lebanese and Syrians, appeared in Beirut and Damascus in the spring of 1975 after the outbreak of the war. In the meantime the interventionism of Arab states also helped to promote violence. In the poor Sunni neighborhoods of Beirut, the Nasserite political machine was now highly fragmented, and the system of clientelist control that had still functioned in the 1960s broke down following Gamal Abdel Nasser's death and the dismantling of the Shihabist Deuxième Bureau.[22] The new qabadayat were now linked to foreign patrons—Syria, Iraq, Libya, and, above all, the various Palestinian groups.[23] The left's identification with Muslim partisans also favored the neglect of older forms of local mobilization, which increasingly became the province of gang leaders.[24] Far from weakening the forces of communal activism, however, foreign interference failed to prevent the Sunni establishment from encouraging action at the neighborhood level, even when it could no longer control street violence.

The dangers that flowed from confessional polarization and the proliferation of political factions were to be dramatically highlighted in late February 1975, in the course of what may be considered the prologue to the war.[25] It unfolded first in Sidon, then in Beirut. While marching at the head of a small demonstration of independent fishermen protesting the award of a concession to a large mechanized fishing company, Ma'ruf Sa'd, a former Nasserite deputy from Sidon who had led the uprising against Chamoun in this city in 1958, was mortally wounded by a soldier's bullet. Aggravating suspicions was a rumor that linked Chamoun personally to the new enterprise, which it was feared would quickly monopolize the local fishing economy. The ensuing riots quickly gave way to clashes between left-wing Nasserite militants, supported by Palestinian elements, and the army, which finally withdrew from the city. In Beirut, where Sa'd lay dying in an American hospital, opposing forces began to mobilize as well. Although Jumblatt, hoping to save the government, did his best to avoid an escalation of tensions, the parties of the left mounted large demonstrations, both in the capital and in other cities. The Christian parties, for their part, responded to the army's ouster from Sidon with a massive show of strength. The call for their loyalists to gather in Beirut brought together the whole of provincial Christian Lebanon: preceded by a police motorcycle escort, the procession that passed through the Christian neighborhoods of the city supplemented the traditionally active student wings of the Phalange Party and the LCP with teenage boys and young girls in their school uniforms who had been bussed in from their villages in the mountains under the approving eye of nuns and staff.

All the ingredients of catastrophe had finally been assembled. Each of them was discernible in the Lebanese capital, where the chain reaction that would result from their combination could be foreseen as well. It had been anticipated the year before by the eighteen-year-old Ziad Rahbani, child prodigy and prodigal son of Fairuz and 'Asi Rahbani, in *Nazl al-Surur* (Inn of Happiness), a musical comedy about the sudden appearance of a tramp bitten by the bug of revolution at a boardinghouse filled with the most dissimilar people imaginable. Beirut, this miscellaneous city where people from all places were thrown together, had long attracted contraries, but it was no longer capable of making a synthesis from them, from the contradiction between the idea of urbanization and the actual experience of urban life, the hesitation between the temptations of individualism and the reassuring comfort of the communal cocoon, the tension between economic and cultural openness and the dynamics of political mobilization, which aroused the most deeply seated impulses. In short, it could not find any way out from the impasse into which the withdrawal into sectarian identity had led Beirut, now the capital of the Arab cause.

A HOME FOR SUFFERING

After the prologue of Sidon, the fatal spark was struck on Sunday 13 April 1975 in 'Ayn al-Rummaneh, a populous Christian suburb where Pierre Gemayel was attending the dedication of a new church. Shots rang out, killing one of Gemayel's bodyguards. Later the same day, a bus bringing Palestinians back from a commemorative ceremony at Tall al-Za'tar to their own camp in Shatila was caught in an ambush by Phalangist gunmen, killing twenty-seven. Clashes broke out at once between residents of 'Ayn al-Rummaneh and the adjacent Shi'i suburb of Shiyyah, one of the most densely populated neighborhoods in the belt of misery. Armed squads appeared in almost all districts of the city.

On the evening of this day, 13 April, Lebanon descended into civil war. The descent occurred in stages. With the second of these, in early May, the conflict reached Rue de Damas, henceforth the line of demarcation between east and west. In the beginning the Lebanese wished only to speak of the "events" (*hawādith* or *ahdāth*) of the spring, and it was only in the fall that the word "war" came to be used. But behind the veil of euphemism, war had indeed been taking place since the spring, and Beirut seemed to embrace it with morbid delight. If combat in the strict sense developed only gradually, the militarization of daily life immediately foretold the intensification of violence. The fronts of this war did not form in the countryside, outside of the cities, nor was the urban population a simple spectator or victim of a clash between military units that was forcibly imposed on it. The war began as a battle of neighborhood against neighborhood, then of city against city, and then spread throughout the country under the influence of a viral dynamic of proximity. Confessional polarization gave way to face-to-face combat. The adjacent neighborhood abruptly became a terra incognita, into which no one could venture without exposing himself to the risk of kidnapping and murder. Nor were its residents any longer the only threat: major military operations in an urban environment, exchanges of artillery fire between residential districts, and isolated rifle fire from the *qannās*—the "sniper" who lay in wait on high ground, determined to bring death at close range—now laid down a clear, if not yet completely drawn, line of separation between "them" and "us." The communal geography of the city, where many neighborhoods had remained homogeneous, helped to deepen the sense of distance that increasingly divided what was to become East Beirut from West Beirut.

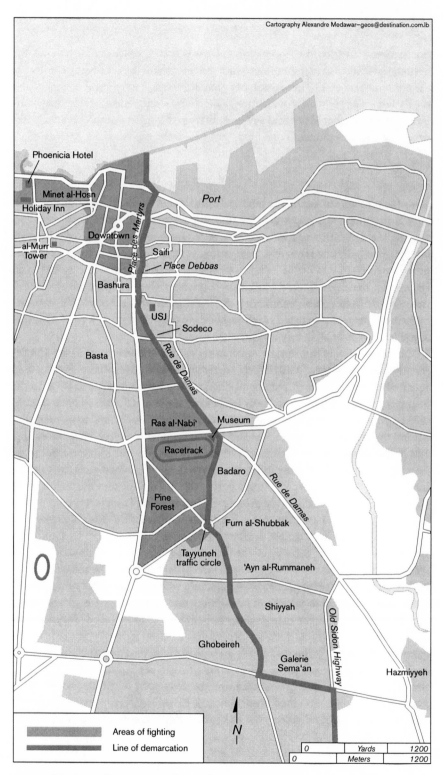

Phoenicia Hotel

Minet al-Hosn

Holiday Inn

Port

al-Murr
Tower

Downtown

Place des Martyrs

Saifi

Place Debbas

Bashura

USJ

Sodeco

Basta

Rue de Damas

Ras al-Nabi'

Museum

Racetrack

Badaro

Pine
Forest

Furn al-Shubbak

Rue de Damas

Tayyuneh
traffic circle

'Ayn al-Rummaneh

Shiyyah

Old Sidon Highway

Ghobeireh

Galerie
Sema'an

Hazmiyyeh

Areas of fighting

Line of demarcation

N

| 0 | Yards | 1200 |
| 0 | Meters | 1200 |

MAP 15. The Line of Demarcation during the War

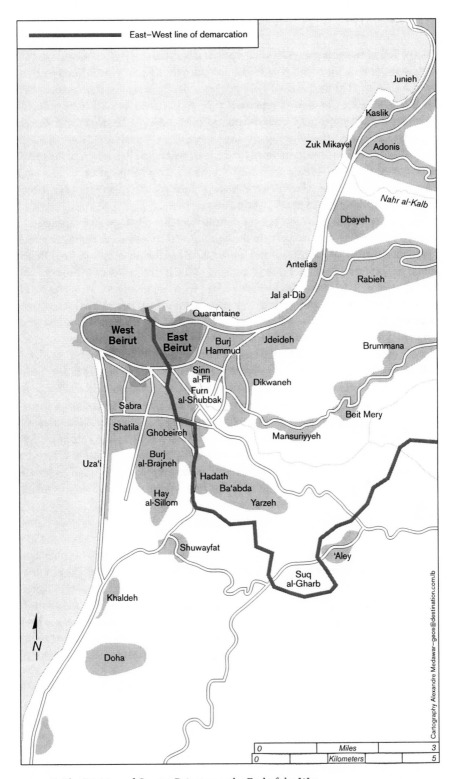

| 0 | | Miles | | 3 |
| 0 | | Kilometers | | 5 |

MAP 16. The Division of Greater Beirut near the End of the War

The lull of the summer, following upon a third round of violence, served only to give more time for mobilizing forces on each side, and the streamlined government of national unity installed on 1 July, presided over by Rashid Karameh and including Camille Chamoun as minister without portfolio, proved to be quite incapable of achieving unity even within its own ranks. After making a detour through Zahleh, and then through the front that suddenly established itself between Zghorta and Tripoli—the hometowns of the president of the Republic and the prime minister, respectively—the war settled into Beirut. On 17 September, the old suqs to the west of Place des Martyrs were burned to the ground. A month later the violence reached the grand hotels overlooking the sea.

At the beginning of December, the commercial downtown, which struggled to come back to life with each pause in the fighting, was sentenced to death: an attack that killed dozens of Muslims—and a few Christians by mistake—showed that it could no longer hope to be a public meeting place. Even the lull of February 1976 failed to revive it. In March the war reappeared there once again, this time for good. In the wake of combat came looting; indeed sometimes combatants and looters were one and the same. The British Bank of the Middle East and the Banco di Roma were cleaned out, and the port methodically plundered.[26] Just as the conflict was beginning to take on the aspect of a total war, matters became still more complicated. On 1 June, the Syrian army entered Lebanon to do battle with its former allies on the left and the Palestinian resistance. The offensive against positions held by the Christian militias having stalled earlier, these forces were now able to count on the simultaneous support of Syria and Israel in laying siege to the Tall al-Za'tar camp, which was to fall after two months and thousands of deaths. In the autumn, a reconciliation between Damascus and Cairo gave the Syrian intervention a broader mandate and, by the authority of the Arab League, established an Arab Deterrent Force with the purpose of strengthening the hand of the new Lebanese president, Elias Sarkis, who succeeded Franjieh on 23 September 1976.

The war was not over, however. The assassination on 16 March 1977 of Kamal Jumblatt, probably on the orders of Assad, made orphans of the parties of the left, despite the efforts of his son Walid as the new head of the PSP to hold the old coalition together, and communal antagonisms became still more deadly. The elimination of the left as a political force gave Syria greater opportunity to assert its control over the country, while also enhancing the prominence of the PLO in Lebanese affairs. Although Beirut was pacified for a brief time, making it possible to think about reconstructing the destroyed downtown, the war immediately shifted to the south, where Israel had gotten a foothold in the form of three enclaves controlled by Christian militia. After Anwar al-Sadat's visit to Jerusalem in September 1977, Israel was to have still more freedom of action. An initial invasion in March 1978 led to the enlargement of the security zone patrolled by its local allies, now a twelve-mile-wide buffer meant to protect Israeli territory from cross-border attacks, as well as the establishment of a United Nations Interim Force in Lebanon (UNIFL), which rapidly found itself condemned to stand on the sidelines, however, sometimes coming under fire. In the meantime shifting geopolitical alignments in the region ruptured the alliance between Syria and the Christian parties. The tensions that had been building in East Beirut since the winter of 1978 led on to more than three months of violent clashes during the summer, an episode known as the Battle of Ashrafiyyeh or the Hundred Days' War. Despite a new compromise, the downtown areas affected by this battle remained a front in the wider conflict until 1982; and despite a return to something like normalcy, the widening of communal cleavages continued. The increasingly close cooperation between Christian parties, under the leadership of Pierre Gemayel's son Bashir, and the right-wing government in Israel led by Menachem Begin culminated in three moments of crisis: first, in the spring of 1981, the battle of Zahleh and the deployment of Syrian missiles in the Biqa' Valley, which provoked diplomatic intervention by the United States; then, in July of that year, Israeli air raids on the PLO headquarters in West Beirut, killing three hundred; and finally, in June 1982, the launching of the main Israeli invasion of Lebanon.

The invasion, begun on 6 June and directed by the minister of defense, Ariel Sharon, turned a few days later into a full-scale siege of West Beirut. For three months this part of the city, where Palestinian fighters and their left-wing Lebanese allies had dug in, was to be bombed almost without interruption from air, land, and sea. The Israeli air force, assured of total mastery of the skies, might as well have been putting on a show for civilians except for the fact that it left thousands of them dead. One day a building in the Sanayeh neighborhood in which Arafat had been spotted was reduced to rubble by a vacuum bomb—moments after he had left, as it happened. But apart from the bombardment of Beirut and an attempt at breaking through to the city via the airport, the Israeli army ran up against fierce resistance. Finally, a political solution was imposed by the United States, which dispatched its marines, together with a force of French Foreign Legion paratroopers and Italian Bersaglieri, to protect the orderly evacuation of the Palestinian leadership and most of its fighters. During this time the presence of an occupying army had made it possible to constitute a quorum of initially recalcitrant deputies in the Chamber to elect Bashir Gemayel to the presidency of the Lebanese Republic. It was 23 August 1982.

The Christian war leader did not have time even to take office, though he had tried to tone down his rhetoric. On 14 September—three weeks after his election, and ten days before the date set for his inauguration—an assault against the Phalange party headquarters in Ashrafiyyeh put an end to his life and killed several of his men. The Israeli army immediately used this as a pretext to occupy West Beirut, from which enemy artillery had been withdrawn and the multinational force had departed. At once a new resistance began to take shape. While George Hawi, the general secretary of the Communist Party, and Muhsin Ibrahim, his counterpart in the CAOL, jointly called for the formation of a Lebanese National Resistance Front (LNRF), a small band of militants loyal to them, together with others from the SSNP and a few Palestinian fedayeen who had stayed behind, began to harass Israeli army patrols. Shortly afterward three Israeli soldiers who made the mistake of thinking they could safely sit in a sidewalk café on Rue Hamra were cut down by fire from an SSNP rifleman.

By this symbolic gesture, as the first Arab capital to be subjected to Israeli occupation, Beirut launched a wave of defiance that three years later was to lead to the withdrawal of Israeli forces from most of the territory it held in Lebanon, and in particular from the cities of Sidon, Tyre, and Nabatiyyeh. Alas, it was for something else that the month of September 1982 was to be remembered: the massacre of more than a thousand Palestinian and Lebanese civilians in the Sabra and Shatila refugee camps by Phalangist members of the Lebanese Forces militia, let into the camps by the Israeli army.

The massacre aroused universal condemnation and brought the U.N. multinational force back to Beirut. There, in addition to protecting the civilian Palestinian population, it was to assist the new president, Amin Gemayel, Bashir's older brother, who had been elected almost unanimously in the emotion of the moment. Despite being more moderate than Bashir, though ultimately perhaps for that very reason, Amin Gemayel was able neither to make the Lebanese Forces see reason nor to obtain an Israeli commitment to withdraw without ceding a portion of Lebanese sovereignty. The old communal antagonism between the Maronite Phalangists and the Druze (now led by Walid Jumblatt) resurfaced with the return of the civil war through the Shuf Mountains. Syria, which had been rearmed by the Soviet Union, was once again in a position to exert pressure. In the meantime the quarrels between Iran and the West were prolonged by a suicide attack against the American Embassy in West Beirut in April 1983, followed by two related assaults in October against the U.S. Marine barracks and the Drakkar post of the French forces. By the autumn of 1983 the war had come back to Beirut, and by February of the following year East Beirut was once more separated from West Beirut, with the same line of demarcation running between the two, and the center of the city still lying in ruins as before. Thus the "war of liberation" confidently proclaimed by General Aoun against the Syrian army came to an end.

The geography of the war had hardly changed in Beirut, nor would it change in the years ahead. West Beirut, the largest part of the city proper, shrank by comparison with East Beirut, which during the 1980s sprawled northward along the coast and climbed up into the mountains. Every neighborhood in both parts of the city had been damaged by the fighting, simultaneously or in alternation, or would be by the time the fighting was over six years later. More than anywhere else, however, it was in the battle zone of downtown that the sense of war without end made

FIGURE 101. The statue of the Martyrs, riddled with bullets and pieces of shrapnel.

FIGURE 102 A–C. Scenes of the
destruction downtown, 1990.

FIGURE 103. The Barakat Building, designed by Yusuf Aftimos, on the old line of demarcation running along Rue de Damas (not yet restored in 2003).

itself felt most deeply. After each lull in the violence, it was here that the refusal to seek peace first manifested itself, even if after 1976 no one died there, unless by taking his own life. When from time to time life showed signs of reviving elsewhere, it was here that the familiar front lines of combat came to be reestablished, as if by some automatic reflex. Only the deserted Rue des Banques managed to escape destruction, thanks to the deterrent effect of money. Here, on its edges, squatters relocated fragments of the belt of misery, itself demolished by the war. In the heart of the old downtown—between Place des Martyrs, Place de l'Étoile, Rue Foch, Rue Allenby, and the Tawileh suq—the only pedestrians were stray dogs. Weeds ran rampant, taking over the streets and sidewalks, as though to proclaim the death of civility. Watched over by mute sentinels, the burned-out shells of the Phoenicia and the Saint-Georges, the heart of the cosmopolitan capital of the Levant was now only a home for suffering.

Epilogue

FIGURE 104 *(preceding page)*. Aerial view of the city and the northern coastline, ca. 1995.

To Be or to Have Been

One fine day people suddenly stopped talking about Beirut and Lebanon. It was in the fall of 1990. After fifteen years of almost constant violence, television viewers throughout the world and readers of the international press might not have realized, at least not right away, that the war was over. Then, beginning in the mid-1990s, Beirut and Lebanon began to be talked about again, this time in the pages of travel magazines. Since then many articles have been written in the hope of attracting tourists. Guides have appeared, promoting the image of a country that could safely be visited again and of a capital where life had returned to something like normal.

Tourists coming to Beirut at the beginning of the twenty-first century do in fact have the impression that that city has been put back on its feet. At the airport they are welcomed by modern facilities of the sort found in all the great cities of the world. An embankment was built along the shore of the Mediterranean to accommodate longer runways, the old terminal was pulled down, and a new one went up in its place that can handle up to six million passengers a year. On leaving the airport perimeter, visitors find themselves on an expressway that brings them into the city in seven minutes while sparing them the sight of the hovels on its outskirts. If they knew Beirut before the war, it takes them a little time to get their bearings, but very quickly they feel at home again. If they did not know it at all, they are apt to be favorably impressed, especially after everything that they have heard and read.

TROMPE-L'OEIL

Visitors have an embarrassment of choice in the way of hotel accommodations, but this has been true only since the late 1990s. The Phoenicia has reopened its doors, with its indented façade meticulously restored and new annexes added, but without the famous bar looking into the swimming pool. The Vendôme and the Riviera preceded it, and the Martinez became a Holiday Inn. Another, entirely new Holiday Inn was built as the anchor of a luxury shopping complex on Rue de Verdun. The Bristol, above Hamra, though it was not damaged during the war, has been remodeled. The Commodore is once again open to welcome journalists, now as part of the Méridien group. The Alexander, in Ashrafiyyeh, to which reporters had retreated in the 1980s, has been modernized. Three hundred yards away, on the highest point in Beirut, the French-based Sofitel chain constructed Le Gabriel. The Mövenpick, built into the cliffs of Rawsheh, opened in 2002 as part of the hotel empire created by the Saudi billionaire Walid bin Talal, grandson of both King ʿAbdul ʿAziz and Riad al-Sulh. On the other side of the city, in Sinn al-Fil, an Emirati entrepreneur constructed the imposing Metropolitan Hotel, and a wealthy Iraqi opened the Royal Hotel in Dbayeh, north of the city on the Junieh highway. The Hilton, whose unfinished frame, having survived the entire war, was then demolished, is scheduled to reopen soon in a part of the beachfront that seems destined to become the most expensive neighborhood in Beirut. The original Holiday Inn, where the first fighting of 1975–76 took place, remains just as the war left it, a devastated shell, though hidden from the view of the Phoenicia's guests by a gigantic trompe-l'oeil screen, hastily installed before the opening of the Arab Summit in Beirut in March 2002. Those who have fond memories of the bar at the Saint-Georges or the panoramic view from the Carlton must resign themselves to a different reality: the one has not been restored (a consequence of unresolved litigation between the hotel's owner and the prime minister), and only its swimming pool is open; the other went out of business, after having stubbornly clung to life through the darkest years. Nostalgic visitors may nonetheless console themselves at the Albergo, a boutique hotel designed by the French Relais & Châteaux group, whose themed rooms (offering a selection of orientalist, European, colonial, and Mediterranean styles) has won it the praise of well-traveled journalists. Other places outside the metropolitan area also attract a prosperous clientele: the Bustan Hotel in Beit Mery, the Printania Palace in Brummana, the Palais du Mir Amin in Beiteddin, and the Century Park and the Regency in Junieh. Less affluent visitors can choose from a number of wholly or partially renovated three-star hotels in the Hamra district.

Assured of comfortable accommodations (during the high season it is still advisable to reserve a room in advance), tourists will be pleased to discover that they can get around without any major problems. The streets are relatively clean, much more so in any case than before 1975, thanks to the privatization of garbage collection (though this initiative has recently been challenged in the courts). Traffic flows smoothly, slowed only by a lack of organization and the aggressive style of driving that years of anarchy made common throughout the city. The same is true of intercity travel. The roads leading out from Beirut have been widened, except for

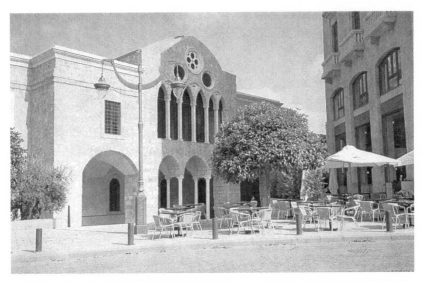

FIGURE 105. The newly restored Greek Orthodox Cathedral of Saint George, looking out upon Place de l'Étoile and its outdoor cafés.

the Northern Highway, and the entire network of expressways has been improved, even if the road surface is often cracked or, because of the low-grade asphalt used, undulating. Tourists nonetheless will have no trouble reaching major tourist centers such as Baalbek, Byblos, and Beiteddin, the vacation resorts in the Matn Mountains and the ones that have been rebuilt along the Damascus highway, or the new coastal developments to the north and south of the capital. In addition to hotel swimming pools in Beirut and the seaside resorts that have disfigured the shoreline in Junieh, a recent and more welcome fashion has revived the tradition of sand beaches—modernized and upscale versions of the old Saint-Simon and Saint-Michel bath clubs, themselves still occupied by refugees and by now an integral part of the southern suburb.

Natives are scarcely better able than tourists to recognize the new landscape of entertainment and leisure activities. The old movie theaters, demolished in the downtown and run down in Hamra, have been superseded by multiplexes on Rue de Verdun, along Rue de Damas (the wartime line of demarcation) and beyond in Furn al-Shubbak, and elsewhere throughout the metropolitan area. For lunch and dinner, the restaurant industry—which had relocated to Junieh and the mountains—has begun once again to offer a full range of international cuisines in Beirut, where now, as everywhere in the world, sushi is the rage. Nightlife offers even more choices. Beirut is once again a city of bars and nightclubs. During the last years of the war,

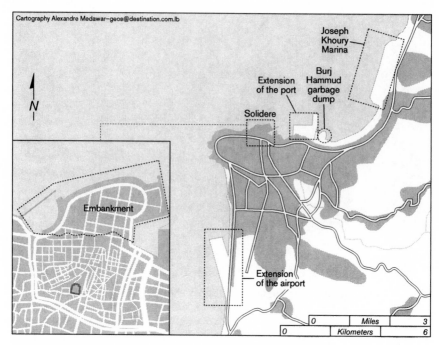

Cartography Alexandre Medawar–geos@destination.com.lb

Joseph
Khoury
Marina

Burj
Extension Hammud
of the port garbage
dump

Solidere

N

Embankment

Extension
of the airport

| 0 | | Miles | 3 |
| 0 | | Kilometers | 6 |

MAP 17. The Solidere Plan (inset) and Coastal Embankment Projects

and the first years of the postwar period, only the Blue Note in West Beirut and the Beirut Cellar and La Closerie in East Beirut had managed to hold on. Then suddenly there appeared two or three top-end restaurants, the Rabelais, Al Dente, and Mijana, and two all-night clubs that were to become legendary destinations for postwar youth: Bo18 (named after a bunker where the club's owner hid out during the war), in an industrial district on the northern edge of the city, and Babylon, in a still devastated and almost deserted neighborhood fifty yards from the line of demarcation. Whereas Bo18 is sunk into the ground in a corner of the Quarantaine District like a communal grave (Bernard Khoury's design, which incorporates coffins as seats, was meant to evoke repressed memories of the war's violence), Babylon is located on Rue Monot (named after the Jesuit father who founded the nearby Université Saint-Joseph) along with several dozen bars and a few restaurants that have sprung up in the immediate vicinity. Frequented for the most part by college (and some high school) students, Rue Monot has already gained a reputation in the Arab world equal almost to that of Hamra before the war, and no article about Beirut in the international travel magazines omits to mention this quarter-mile stretch of pulsating nightlife. Tourists can also spend their money in the casino, still in its original location at the end of the Bay of Junieh and now renovated, or in the bars of

FIGURE 106. The new seafront district built on land reclaimed from the sea.

Ma'ameltein, attended by Ukrainian and Romanian hostesses. In any case they will not have failed beforehand to stroll down Rue Monot as far as the downtown, where in the last several years an enclave has grown up that seems to be entirely dedicated to the pursuit of luxury and leisure.

Both during the day and at night it is this part of the city, the Beirut Central District (BCD), at once new and old, that draws the attention of visitors; or, more exactly, the periphery that was developed during the Mandate—Place de l'Étoile and Rue Ma'rad, and Rues Allenby and Foch together with the back streets that run between them. Transformed into a permanent pedestrian zone, except for parliamentary deputies' cars (the legislature having now come back to its original seat, deserted for fifteen years, and imposed a prohibition on other vehicular traffic), Place de l'Étoile and the great colonnaded avenue that bisects it have become the favorite place of many residents to go out for a stroll. On holidays the area around the 'Abed clocktower, restored to its original place at the center of the square, is even a playground for children, where rollerbladers and kids on scooters weave their way

FIGURE 107. The façade of the
restored Parliament Building.

among the baby carriages. The adjacent streets are filled with cafés and restaurants.
When Casper and Gambini's, an American-style restaurant and coffeehouse, first
opened on Rue Ma'rad in 1999, across from a sidewalk café overlooking the Roman ruins, just breaking even looked to be a rather daunting challenge. It was followed by a Café Place de l'Étoile, across from the Parliament Building—and that
was all for a year or so. Then fashion caught up. In the space of two years a host of
restaurants and bars have appeared in this area, which once was the very heart of
the city, and which seems to be in the process of regaining this role. Now that
Lebanese tourism has been reunited with its former clientele from Saudi Arabia and
the other Gulf states since 11 September 2001, the pedestrian streets of the downtown, along with Rue Monot, are the liveliest in the city on summer evenings.

Both tourists and natives will therefore join in acclaiming Beirut's rebirth. Indeed, the reconstruction of the downtown (or what has been completed of it) has
met with universal approval. From the architectural point of view, at least, its suc-

FIGURE 108. A peaceful gathering on Place de l'Étoile. Reproduced by permission of the Beirut Ministry of Tourism.

cess is beyond dispute—and all the more welcome because this very success represents a fitting piece of revenge by buildings that for a time were doomed to disappear, and because their restored façades, for the most part condemned by the original postwar master plan, are wonderfully picturesque. Solidere, the development company in charge of the reconstruction of the city's central district (its name is a popular abbreviation of Société Libanaise pour le Développement et la Reconstruction de Beyrouth), nonetheless deserves some measure of credit for this outcome. Its standards are far higher than any that had previously been enforced in Lebanon, and not least with regard to the coherence of its planning: before being granted a construction permit by the city, projects must first obtain Solidere's approval, which ensures conformity with both the purposes and technical requirements of the revised master plan as well as their suitability to the proposed site. And even if in the case of a few new complexes the result seems to border on pastiche, the overall effect is nonetheless impressive.

On closer inspection, however, the matter assumes a different aspect. Beirut is already losing its momentum, like the country as a whole. Its recovery, tangible though it is, has left too many questions unanswered and given too many unsatisfactory replies to others. The affluence of its wealthier citizens falls short in any case of the prosperity (itself only relative) of the prewar period. Above all, Beirut only superficially resembles its public image: the renascent city has not succeeded in making itself the Renaissance city it once was. However incontestable the success of the downtown may seem to be, it is but an illusion—and what is more, an illusion that is not finished, and that will not be finished even on the most optimistic assumptions before 2015, a quarter century after the end of the war.

To be sure, the spirit of adventure and daring that presided over the reconstruction of the central district is not the only reason for the dead end in which Beirut as a whole now finds itself. But it was nonetheless decisive in ensuring that the opportunities of postwar Lebanon would be squandered.

TABULA RASA

The general appearance of the BCD today bears practically no resemblance to the original scale model unveiled in 1991 by Rafiq al-Hariri, the future prime minister. This model represented a clear departure not only from the morphology of the prewar Balad, but also from the two plans that had been previously adopted during the long lulls of 1977–78 and 1983. The first of these plans, commissioned by Amin Bizri—formerly an associate of Michel Écochard who now served as minister of public works in Elias Sarkis's cabinet—and drawn up by the Paris Urbanism Workshop (APUR in its French initials), already contemplated the creation of a private joint-venture company to overcome the difficulties posed by the existence of so many persons and corporate entities bearing legal claims to property. With the resumption of the war during the summer of 1978, nothing came of this idea. The second plan was part of a larger master plan for the metropolitan region of Beirut, prepared by a Franco-Lebanese team associated with the Development and Urbanism Institute of the Île-de-France region (which includes metropolitan Paris). Begun in 1983, at the beginning of Amin Gemayel's presidency, it was completed only three years later, when the war was back in full swing.

Hariri, an exceedingly wealthy entrepreneur who had made his fortune in Saudi Arabia in the 1970s (and who, having won the confidence of King Fahd, was granted the rare privilege of naturalization as a Saudi citizen), had been thinking several steps ahead. Although a native of Sidon, he gave a first indication of his concern for Beirut's future following the Israeli siege of the summer of 1982 by offering to finance the clearing of the rubble from the streets downtown and then the refacing of building façades on Rue Maʿrad. In this connection he made a point of acquainting himself with the plan being prepared by the Franco-Lebanese team, already complete when the war ended in October 1990. But Hariri had anticipated events once again. As a close advisor to the Saudi sovereign, he played an active role in helping to negotiate the Taʾif Accord, which took its name from the holiday resort in Hijaz where Lebanese deputies approved a draft agreement for ending the war. With the cessation of hostilities, Hariri privately commissioned a master plan from Dar al-

Handasah, the global firm of engineering consultants that had been founded in Beirut in 1956. Although it would fall to Henri Eddé, briefly a minister under Franjieh and himself a former associate of Écochard, to carry out the plan, it was nonetheless Hariri's vision that directly prevailed on a number of key points.

In the form in which it was presented to the public in 1991, Hariri's plan suffered from a severe case of gigantism: skyscrapers, a world trade center on an artificial island in Saint Andrew Bay, underground tunnels for expressways. Still more disturbingly, it contemplated destroying the Burj, once the vibrant symbol of the city's unity and later the morbid emblem of its division, to make way for a boulevard that Hariri specifically ordered to be wider than the Champs-Élysées, leading on to a seaside esplanade—in short, a sort of Dallas-on-the-Mediterranean, without any relation to the city that had once existed or even to the city that remained. For this pharaonic project required not only that the rubble be cleared in order for a new downtown to rise in its place, but also the demolition of several neighborhoods that had survived the war.

As a self-made man, and as a newcomer to Beirut who was therefore supposed, perhaps unjustly, to be without memory of it (having served his apprenticeship in construction and civil engineering, urbanism, and public life in the new cities of the Saudi desert, where he equipped himself with ambitions commensurate with his wealth), and who was in any case already obsessed with a desire to make his mark in the world, Hariri had everything it took to arouse opposition to his schemes—all the more as he seemed to take a malicious pleasure in advertising his arrogance and his contempt for dissenting views. For Hariri, everything was an object to be bought, whether the silence of some or the conscience of others. He therefore managed to deepen still further the controversy that inevitably surrounded Solidere—especially once he had forfeited his status as a private citizen, doubtful in the first place, by placing himself in charge of a public project and imposing his personal wishes on the government, and then, finally, in the autumn of 1992, on assuming the office of prime minister, by making himself the beneficiary of the privatization of Beirut.

In the meantime two conferences, one held in the United States at the Massachusetts Institute of Technology, the other in France at the Institut du Monde Arabe in Paris, facilitated a preliminary exchange of views between supporters and critics of the project. In Beirut, expressing criticism was more difficult, since the favorable opinion of local newspaper owners toward Hariri had left little room for the public to state its case. And yet a small circle of detractors managed to make itself heard. Among its distinguished members were the architects Assem Salam, who since the 1960s had designed a number of fine projects, and Jade Tabet, who had extensive experience in the renovation of run-down neighborhoods in Paris and who, moreover, was the son of Antun Tabet, whose Hôtel Saint-Georges, among other buildings, had been a prominent symbol of Beirut before the fall. Two of their younger colleagues who had recently finished their studies in the United States, Hashim Sarkis and Usama Qabbani, were also active at this stage. In addition there were the economist Georges Corm, the sociologist Nabil Beyhum, and the novelist Elias Khoury, the new editor-in-chief of *Al-Mulhaq*, the cultural supplement of *An-Nahar*, which became the chief outlet for dissent at a time when its mother publication preferred to maintain a charitable neutrality.

Criticism of the project reached a first crescendo with the demolition of the area around Place des Martyrs in 1992. What remained of the old red-light district, which had already been "cleaned up" in 1983 during the second long lull of the war, was simply razed, along with adjacent buildings along the whole east side of the square, including the old police station, a perfectly salvageable jewel of Ottoman architecture. On the west side only two buildings remained. The south side vanished entirely: not only were the buildings pulled down, but the square itself was opened up to the streets converging upon the Burj, as a first step to consolidating them into a grand Parisian-style boulevard. On the north side, finally, the Rivoli movie theater—which, despite its unfortunate position blocking the view of the sea, had become the square's most distinctive landmark and the focal point of every postcard—was destroyed in order to permit an unobstructed vista, looking down upon the planned waterfront promenade and completing the new "Champs-Élysées," as Hariri's critics called it.

As if to add a small touch of romantic defiance to the destruction of old Beirut, the Rivoli resisted implosion three times before finally being brought down. By contrast with this symbolic recalcitrance, long to be emphasized by the plan's opponents, the demolition of the suqs and of the Bashura neighborhood, which likewise presented no obstacle to restoration, aroused much less of an outcry. Nonetheless the campaign was to reach another peak of intensity when work began to tear down Wadi Abu Jamil, the old Jewish quarter. In spite of the damage it had sustained and its occupation by an overwhelming number of squatters driven out from southern Lebanon by the war, Wadi Abu Jamil remained the site of many architectural treasures and had managed in spite of everything to retain its coherence as an urban neighborhood. In this instance, however, the urge to discard the past seems to have had less to do with a desire to benefit developers than with considerations of political expediency arising from the illegal refugee settlements, which had become a major source of corruption and fiscal waste; indeed, indemnities paid to the squatters, many of whom were fictitious—though nonetheless well represented by Amal and by Hizbullah, the two principal Shi'i political groups—had reached such heights that the neighborhood was known as Wādī al-Dhahab (Valley of Gold). Landowners in the downtown as a whole, by contrast, were much less generously compensated for their losses, and the level of anger and recrimination was rising.

The very idea of a joint venture was publicly justified by the complex structure of land ownership in the city center, where the tangle of titles to ecclesiastical and public property, as well as private holdings fragmented by successive inheritance, was further complicated by the large number of leaseholders. There is no doubt that this situation required legislative intervention. But a more imaginative approach, possibly providing for the establishment of a series of private companies in those cases where the fragmentation of property ownership made it necessary, might have resolved the outstanding difficulties without going so far as to place the entire central district of the city in a state of quasi-extraterritoriality, beyond the reach of municipal jurisdiction. In the event, the creation of a single joint-stock company came to be seen as a de facto form of expropriation, all the more as the lack of adequate financial mechanisms in support of private reconstruction efforts effectively prohibited the majority of landowners from exercising the rights of repossession to which they were entitled by law. Unsurprisingly, perhaps, the evaluation of ownership and leaseholder claims prior to indemnization (through the distribution of shares in Solidere) was to give rise to a great many disputes, spilling over from the field of intellectual debate into the political arena.

The scope of this reconstruction project, in its first version, signaled its sponsor's ambition to make the commercial district of Beirut a business hub for the entire Middle East. To skeptical observers it seemed obvious, however, that Lebanon by itself was incapable of generating a demand proportionate to the supply of office space that the plan contemplated, and that it would therefore be necessary to count on being able to persuade a great many foreign companies to make Lebanon their regional headquarters—a hazardous wager to say the least, in the absence of even a faintly reliable market survey. Apart from the study commissioned from Dar al-Handasah by Hariri himself and subcontracted to Bechtel, the giant American civil engineering firm, the result of which was an unhelpfully vague document titled "Beirut 2000," no firm estimate of corporate interest had been developed. Without any careful assessment of probable demand, the project seemed condemned to place its trust in a policy of maximizing supply, in the hope—and nothing more—that once the new office space was built companies would hurry to occupy it.

Even in the event that this expectation were to be rewarded, the economic logic of the project remained doubtful. The abnormal growth it promised in the city center was bound to reproduce the excessive centralization that Beirut's macrocephaly had created before the war, especially since the Hariri plan, unlike the one drawn up in 1986, was not part of any larger scheme for the regional development in Lebanon as a whole, or even for the repair and renovation of the metropolitan area. Taken together, the demolition of the old central precincts, the dismantling of the structure of land ownership, and the imposition of a regime of urban and economic planning aimed at attracting large foreign corporations amounted to a potentially lethal assault on the city itself.

As the ensuing debate made clear, the reconstruction of old Beirut along these lines could only come at the expense of modern Beirut. A connected series of arguments demonstrated, first, that the narrowness of the east-west axes downtown, by comparison with the north-south axes, would make it difficult to restore the area's old purpose as a place where people from different confessional backgrounds could freely mix together. In particular, the transformation of Place des Martyrs, one of the foremost such places in the city, into a segment of a massive north-south thoroughfare threatened to install a durable boundary between Muslim and Christian residential neighborhoods. In the second place, the new central district was destined to turn its back on the people who used to live there, now uprooted by the war and deprived of a voice. The loss of a traditional residential function would spell the end for a web of small urban trades while at the same time substituting a class of wealthy native professionals and expatriate businessmen for the socially richer and more varied population that had managed to hang on just until the eve of the war, and even during its first years: the scions of old moneyed families fallen on hard times who still lived in decayed ancestral homes they could no longer afford to keep up; middle- and lower-middle-class families that had lived in the Balad for generations; small shopkeepers and artisans who lived in the apartments above where they worked; and the sort of cosmopolitan migrants that a port city attracts and that boardinghouses and inns had long housed—in short, everything that made the old center a microcosm of the country, and even of the Arab Mediterranean, whose disappearance would make the new downtown a sterile island of commercial rationality cut off from the rest of the capital.

By proposing to start over with a blank slate, making a clean break with the city's familiar morphology in the service of a poorly specified economic purpose, Hariri's reconstruction scheme had the appearance of a plan for a new city, but one without any continuity with what had gone before—in other words, without memory. This memory was of several kinds. First, there was architectural memory, the heritage of Ottoman and French Beirut, dominated by the reddish sandstone and pastel colors of these periods, now totally faded or darkened by years of neglect and pollution. But there was also social memory, lost with the emptying of the neighborhood's composite imagination—largely a working-class, even populist impulse that joined the imagination of the republic of letters that Beirut had nurtured since the 1950s with a nascent national imagination that held out the prospect of finally transcending the old communal ways of thinking. And, finally, there was the memory of the fall, which is to say the civil war. As an enduring reminder of violence and conflict, the city center called for a memorialization, if only in stylized form, of the sense people had during the war of standing outside of time; for a kind of anamnesis, a ritual of collective spiritual cleansing.

ARCHITECTURAL OVERREACH

Fortunately, despite the adoption of a master plan by Parliament in 1991 and approval of the proposed public-private partnership, the logic of the blank slate was not pushed to its inevitable conclusion. Debate was fierce. In the absence of any clear economic purpose, Hariri's motivations in supervising the project lent themselves to a variety of interpretations. In the view of some it was purely a vehicle for financial speculation; for others it was evidence of a determination to "Islamize" the capital, or even part of a calculated political strategy aimed at laying the groundwork for the normalization of relations between Israel and the Arab nations. Denunciations quickly migrated from technical journals into the newspapers and onto the floor of Parliament. The press, while happy to report the attacks launched by politicians, remained quiet about the objections brought by architects, even when the plan's detractors received the unexpected support of its principal designer, Henri Eddé, exasperated by Hariri's arrogance and interference. A sign of the discontent within the profession was the election of Assem Salam, the leader of the protest against Solidere's proposals, as president of the Order of Engineers and Architects in 1996 over the candidate supported by Hariri.

This show of opposition helped to bring about a change of course. Financial considerations were still more decisive, however, in leading Solidere after its official founding in May 1994, and the appointment of Nasser Chammaa as chief executive officer, to scale back Hariri's initial ambitions. A closer examination of the constructible area persuaded the company that it had nothing to gain from the demolition of buildings dating back to the 1920s and 1930s in the Foch-Allenby sector, and that it would make more sense to restore them. Unforeseen delays also caused other assumptions to be reconsidered. In particular, the emergency archeological excavations that the promoters of the Solidere plan had been forced to accept, following a campaign to sway public opinion supported by UNESCO, postponed the beginning of infrastructural work by at least three years.

In the interval Solidere was able to gauge the impact of enlightened opinion on its corporate image. Not only did the results of the restoration already undertaken in the Foch-Allenby sector sharpen its appreciation of the cost savings that could be realized by preserving traditional examples of stone architecture elsewhere, while at the same time renovating building interiors; the excavations were yielding artifacts that could be exposed to public view on a permanent basis, either by leaving them in place or by loaning them for museum exhibition. Support grew for the idea of preserving everything that was discovered, notably the Phoenician rampart uncovered by digs in the area of the suqs, and for sponsoring a competition for the design of a "Garden of Tolerance" to be built among the vestiges of the old Roman road, set between three more recent religious monuments. Even Hariri's Champs-Élysées stood to be affected by these discoveries, since the ruins of the ancient tell and the Hellenistic vestiges unearthed nearby on the southern flank of the Burj were now to be protected, no matter that they lay in the path of the grand boulevard. Solidere resolved therefore to construct a new image for itself on the basis of the idea of historical continuity, rather than the rupture with the past proclaimed by the original master plan. Already on the occasion of its founding in 1994 the company had adopted the slogan "Madina ʿariqa li-l-mustaqbal" (An Ancient City for the Future), devised by the Beirut office of the London-based communications conglomerate Saatchi & Saatchi. To advertise Solidere's change of perspective more directly, a flea market was set up in the initially restored area in the hope of getting people to come downtown and take a look. In the same spirit, the company now made a point of welcoming criticism. One of the young opponents of the initial project, Usama Qabbani, was recruited. Among other duties, Qabbani was to act informally as liaison with Assem Salam, recently elevated to the presidency of the Order of Engineers and Architects, and with Jade Tabet, who himself was later invited to consult on the master plan for the suqs. Tabet's suggestions, despite having been granted official approval, were never acted upon.

The pharaonic projects of the early days were now forgotten. The artificial island (whose theoretical stability was found to be compromised by the existence of a trench in the seabed) was replaced by a coastal embankment—a simpler undertaking from the engineering point of view, but nonetheless expensive, in part because of the excessively large scale on which it was built. The idea for a world trade center was abandoned, and the high-rise office buildings banished from the edge of the old downtown on account of rising cost projections. Apart from the famous al-Murr Tower—one of the most symbolic places of the war, unfinished in 1975 and now, following its sale to Solidere, assured of reconstruction—skyscrapers were to be confined to the embankment on Saint Andrew Bay, and for that very reason consigned to a very late phase of the construction schedule. Although building expressways (and therefore underground tunnels) within the Solidere perimeter was no longer contemplated, it was still envisioned that Place des Martyrs would form part of a broad avenue opening on to the sea.

These revisions to the original plan did a great deal to dampen controversy. But the construction schedule was still more important. Infrastructural work was finished in 1998 and the downtown then reopened to pedestrian traffic. The high quality of the renovations completed by this point provided the incentive for a form of internal tourism, partly spontaneous, partly orchestrated by Solidere, which had begun organizing seasonal events to get people in the habit of going to the downtown again on a regular basis. The importance of timing was to be further emphasized the following year, though in an opposite fashion, when the new government of General Émile Lahoud, having embarked on an anti-Hariri crusade, sought to throw spanners in Solidere's works. One of the first moves made by the new minister of finance, who turned out to be none other than Georges Corm, was to suspend construction of the new headquarters for his ministry on the Solidere perimeter while also canceling several other projects under state contract. The downtown now faced the danger of embodying the so-called jack o'lantern effect dreaded by urban planners, with new buildings standing next to empty lots—so much so, in fact, that Solidere increasingly appeared as a necessary evil, consecrated by the passage of time.

The slowdown in construction produced an abrupt fall in the value of Solidere's shares, and then to cuts in its staff, while at the same time accelerating the metamorphosis of the downtown into a place for sightseeing and recreation. With office buildings still empty for the most part, and work on the new markets stalled, small retailers were much slower in coming back than forecast. By the beginning of the new century business had picked up, however, at least for shops and restaurants, though many of them chose to establish themselves elsewhere than the planners had intended. Office occupancy rates nonetheless remained very low.

AN ENCLAVE OF LUXURY

The bustling streets and sidewalks did not mean that Solidere could consider its work finished. There still remained several contracts from the initial plan to be fulfilled, one for demolishing the old nineteenth-century suqs, though they were salvageable, and replacing them with new markets, on which construction has yet to start despite the adoption of a specific master plan (revised most recently by the Spanish architect Rafael Moneo). Other contracts concern the Bashura neighborhood, leveled and now used for parking lots while waiting for work to begin on a shopping complex (in which the French architect Jean Nouvel's participation is rumored), and Wadi Abu Jamil, where, by a cruel irony, it is now proposed to meticulously reconstruct the very houses that had been torn down. But the most serious predicament, considering the city as a whole, remains that of Place des Martyrs, deprived of its statue still, though it was long ago restored, and still an empty space apart from three buildings on its perimeter. One is occupied by an insurance company, another by a Virgin Megastore, whose brisk business only throws the surrounding void into starker relief. On the north side, on the site of the old Rivoli theater, the An-Nahar group has constructed new offices. So far no one has followed its example.

Far from once more becoming the crossroads that it used to be, the vacant Burj stands apart from the rest of the city, making the Balad as a whole look even more like a suburb, albeit a very luxurious one. The impression of ghettoized opulence was reinforced with the completion of a large gated community called Saifi Village that occupies the site of the old carpenters' quarter—an exclusive enclave, with its own private security detail and waiting areas for chauffeurs, whose homes and villas attempt to reproduce the style of what was destroyed to make room for them. The Foch-Allenby district, the center of prestige shopping, accentuates the discontinuity still further. It is true that the opening of United Nations House on the edge of Place Riad al-Sulh has given demonstrators a regular reason to come downtown to protest the Iraq war or the Israeli attacks against the autonomous Palestinian ter-

FIGURE 109. A rebuilt street
off Place de l'Étoile.

ritories, and that the pedestrian space around Place de l'Étoile, which at first appeared to repel the less well off, has now begun to attract working-class visitors. Nevertheless the concentration of the entertainment and hospitality industry in this neighborhood, the well-heeled crowds that fill the square on summer evenings, and the proximity of high-end shops combine to give it more the appearance of a resort for wealthy tourists from the Arabian Peninsula.

The scope of the projects undertaken in reconstructing the downtown had the unintended consequence also of highlighting the neglect suffered by the other neighborhoods of Beirut and its suburbs, including ones that had been devastated by the war, such as Rue de Damas and the area straddled by Shiyyah and 'Ayn al-Rummaneh. Public assistance has been sparing and slow in coming, and the repercussions of the war in these places lasting. A no less serious matter from the point of view of architectural preservation is the demolition of several of the city's most romantic homes, memorably described by Georges Schéhadé and other poets. Despite the growing sophistication of urban planners and the development of an architectural sensibility among the city's residents, Lebanon's Second Republic has

proved to be as pusillanimous as the first. Old houses are placed on the historic register, then suddenly declassified and immediately torn down. Some buildings are
eligible for protected status only insofar as they are used for purposes of tourism
(restaurants, for example), while others remain under suspended sentence and so
fall into neglect. Nor has the state shown any greater interest in arresting the deterioration of less prestigious properties. A number of building owners immediately
after the war went ahead and cleaned the façades of their buildings themselves, and
in many cases painted them white, as if they hoped in this way to exorcise the curse
of the dark years; the original ochre and pink tones were later rediscovered, thanks
to the efforts of a private society that helped to defray the cost of restoring the historical appearance of the city's older neighborhoods. New construction exacted a
terrible toll—with official encouragement, and despite resistance from the most talented and innovative younger architects—through the widespread application of a
pompous and convoluted "national style." Bernard Khoury is one of the few to have
given form to a true meditation upon the war, including both its symbolism and its
geography, with his homage to the anonymous dead, the B018 club, as well as a
restaurant set inside a guard tower on the line of demarcation.

Beyond the mess that has been made from the architectural point of view, the
primacy given to the downtown portends a new phase of atrophy for Beirut as a
consequence of the lack of any corresponding plan for regional economic development. The folding suburbs of the prewar period have pulled back into themselves.
Junieh, prosperous before the war, has increasingly become a dormitory town. The
plans for a new city to be built on the slopes of Dbayeh, drawn up by the Spanish
architect Ricardo Bofill, remain a great question mark. An immense embankment
has been completed, but apart from a luxurious marina the area is still deserted.
The Linord project, meant to improve road access to Beirut from the north by building a vast seaside embankment around the garbage dump in Burj-Hammud, is at
a standstill. The belt of misery, concentrated in the southern suburbs and now the
bastion of Hizbullah, constitutes another source of atrophy on the edge of the capital, and one that is all the less easily dealt with since, in addition to the crisis of
public finances, all proposals for development there, such as the Elyssar project, are
likely to run into political obstacles.

THE LOST POSTWAR

Beginning in 1996, about four years after Hariri was first elected prime minister,
both the public treasury and private citizens felt the relentless and paralyzing effects
of economic crisis, aggravated by unavoidably massive expenditures on infrastructure. The earliest signs of crisis became apparent a decade before, in 1985–86
(until then the economy had seemed to resist the effects of the war), in the form of
a vertiginous depreciation of the currency. Somehow people managed to adapt to

a new world in which goods and services were denominated in dollars. The end of hostilities did not succeed in curbing either depreciation or inflation, however, and in May 1992 the first postwar government, headed by 'Umar Karameh, fell in the aftermath of riots in Beirut. After a transitional government presided over by Rashid al-Sulh, which had responsibility for organizing something resembling legislative elections, Rafiq Hariri was called to power in the autumn of 1992. Hariri immediately set to work renovating his new offices, even before forming a government. This suggests that he counted on being able to stay there for a certain time. Although the "springtime" he promised came to pass neither at the predicted time nor afterward, the mere fact of his election had the effect of momentarily restoring confidence and blocking the collapse of the Lebanese pound. Linking the defense of the currency to his own prestige, he succeeded in engineering a rise in its value, with the result that the pound's exchange rate against the dollar fell from 2,000 to 1,500. This rate was to be defended at any cost, even if it meant exhausting the reserves of the Banque du Liban and increasing the state's indebtedness to private banks through the issuance of a great many treasury bonds bearing exceedingly attractive yields. The assistance frequently promised by the rich Arab states came only in dribs and drabs, making it impossible to finance the reconstruction of the nation's infrastructure—itself a rich source of opportunities for graft and embezzlement by both Lebanese and Syrian politicians—except by further borrowing. From 1996 onward the Treasury was able to survive only by resort to ad hoc measures and by raising taxes, especially indirect taxes, with the result that the gathering storm now made itself felt in the daily lives of the people, and spending by both businesses and consumers began to decline.

Arab-Israeli tensions, which had continued to project themselves into Lebanon in the interval, only added to the uncertainty of the situation. In July 1993, Yitzhak Rabin's government launched a massive aerial assault on southern Lebanon that devastated whatever infrastructure was still intact. After Rabin's assassination a new campaign of intensive bombing in April 1996 provoked an exodus in the direction of Beirut. A month later the return of the right to power in Israel dashed all hopes of a negotiated settlement in the Near East—this at a moment when resistance to the Israeli occupation of a part of the south, now directed by Hizbullah, in collaboration with Syria, was beginning to show signs of success. The Israeli air force was later to intervene twice in the suburbs of Beirut, attacking electrical stations in June 1999 and February 2000. The Israeli retreat in May 2000 was not enough to put an end to the uncertainty, however. Three years later, in August 2003, Israeli fighters broke the sound barrier at very low altitudes above Beirut, causing tourists to flee the city the next day.

Meanwhile the politicians holding real power in Lebanon, whose claim to legitimacy was undermined in most cases by the support they received from Syria, did their utmost to ignore the necessity of national reconciliation and a collective labor of memory. As a result, confessional allegiance weighed more heavily than ever before in peacetime. After the rigged elections of the summer of 1992, managed down to the smallest detail by the Syrian proconsul stationed in 'Anjar, in the Biqa', a sense of despondency *(ihbat)* set in among the Christian population, which already considered itself the loser of the war. Coming in the wake of General Aoun's exile, the arrest in April 1994 of Samir Geagea—the head of the Lebanese Forces and the only war leader to be imprisoned, whereas the others went on to occupy ministerial posts and the presidency of the National Assembly—and his subsequent conviction for war crimes deepened feelings of bitterness and mistrust. From this point onward the bulk of Lebanese savings abroad, held by Christians, ceased to be repatriated.

In addition to its economic consequences, the deteriorating political situation now began to cast a pall over everyday life. Although the postwar period proved to be much more peaceful than anyone would have dared to predict, and despite the fact that there were very few episodes of street violence, police and soldiers continued to patrol with rifles at the ready, even at rock concerts. Police abuses and human rights offenses multiplied, both in the investigation of common-law crimes and the prosecution of cases against political enemies. Graver still, perhaps, the feeling of being above the law—shared by civilian and military members of the political class and made visible by their convoys of official limousines and teams of personal bodyguards—created an atmosphere in which influence peddling, misappropriation of public funds, and clientelism (which had been transformed by the habits acquired during the war into a Mafia-style system of enforced corruption) all flourished.

This novel and often brutal style of politics did not always find Hariri's readiness to pay off anyone who threatened him with blackmail to its taste, much less the growing intrusiveness of the intelligence services *(mukhabarat),* larger than before and no less addicted to intrigue. For the businessmen, war traffickers, and militia leaders who together formed a new sort of imperial nobility (in Dominique Chevallier's phrase), money was in any case easily come by, and where that was not enough to settle disagreements, these could be submitted to the Syrian proconsul in 'Anjar—and, if necessary, to Damascus—for arbitration. With armed forces of thirty thousand men in Lebanon and legions of its own *mukhabarat* well established there, even in Beirut, which it did not really need to support since they lived off the land, Ba'thist Syria's presence resembled less an occupation than a sort of Mafioso protectorate.

Elias Hrawi's succession by General Émile Lahoud as president in November 1998 modified the internal equilibrium of this system of control only to a small extent. Lahoud presented himself in his inauguration speech as a Savonarola, but neither corruption nor nepotism ceased. His campaign to reform the administration was converted into a purge exclusively directed against Hariri, who was forced to step down as prime minister. Two years later, having gained the upper hand as a result of the first round of parliamentary elections in Beirut, in May 2000, Hariri resumed his office in the fall. In these same elections the president managed to get his son elected as a deputy from Beirut, and then proceeded to name his son-in-law, Elias Murr, as interior minister (in succession to Murr's own father, Michel, owner of the eponymous office tower) and his brother, Nasri, as president of the court of cassation. During this time the intelligence services hounded unfriendly journalists and manipulated others, interfered with the private lives of citizens, managed clientelist networks, and monitored relations among government officials.

In the face of the disastrous postwar situation—an even greater moral disaster than it was an economic one—what was left of civil society nonetheless showed impressive resilience. Associative life blossomed once more, the bar rallied in defense of the rule of law, new talk shows sprang up on radio and television. Cultural institutions struggled to overcome the provincialism that had conquered the city in the last years of the war. The Théâtre de Beyrouth, which reopened its doors under new management in 1992, managed to survive for six years. During this time it provided the people of the city with a number of memorable moments, including performances by the Tunisian companies of Fadel Djaibi and Tewfiq Gibali, a production of Jean Genet's *Les Bonnes* by the Iraqi director Jawad As'adi, and the return of Roger Assaf to a classical though nonetheless inventive form of drama, as well as the stormy commemoration of the fiftieth anniversary of the Palestinian Nakba of 1948 (stormy owing to the participation of several Arab Jews) and the launching of a campaign to organize municipal elections. Al-Madina Theater, for its part, began from nothing on the stage of the old Cinéma Clemenceau: guided by the shrewd instincts of the great actress Nidal Ashqar, it won praise for its production of the two last plays of the Syrian dramatist Sa'dallah Wannus and also for many fine concerts. Both halls nonetheless faced financial difficulties, and although the Madina had initially been supported by one of Hariri's banks, it now found itself forced to cut back its schedule. During this time the city's schools had been working furiously to train a new generation of stage actors, but they were obliged to content themselves with roles in television series on the various Arab stations. Writers were luckier in this respect. A number of younger authors have been able to draw upon the experience of the war to create a place for themselves among the elite of contemporary Arab novelists, and while some of them reside in Paris or London, others have stayed in Lebanon. Jabbur Duayhi, for example, still lives in his native province; Elias Khoury, Hassan Dawud, Rashid Daif, Muhammad Abi Samra, and Rabih Jaber all make their home in Beirut.

Writers from other Arab countries also continue to publish in Beirut, which managed to maintain its reputation as a regional center for publishing throughout the war, despite growing competition from new houses in London, Tunis, Rabat, and later in the Persian Gulf. With the return of peace, paradoxically, freedom of speech suffered. Censorship—unknown since the 'Azm affair of 1969—was reinstated more than once at the demand of the Sunni religious hierarchy for the purpose of block-

FIGURE 110. Le Grand Théâtre, to be restored and remodeled to accommodate several restaurants.

ing publication of both the erotic poetry of ʿAbduh Wazen and the allegedly icon-oclastic works of the Libyan thinker Sadiq al-Nayhum. The need for editors to work with many of their authors at long distance posed another obstacle to restoring Beirut houses to their former position of eminence. Many Arab intellectuals who had stayed in the city until the departure of the PLO in 1982 were slow to come back. Moreover, they were not always welcome: whereas nationals of the wealthy Arab countries were automatically let in, like visitors from Western Europe and North America, intellectuals from poorer Arab countries had to apply for a visa—apart from the Syrians, although few of them who had something to say would have dreamt for a moment of doing it in Beirut, where they were still within the reach of the mukhabarat. Things were yet more difficult for the Palestinians, however. The literary scholar Edward Said, an American citizen, was allowed to visit in 1996, the occasion of a triumphant lecture at the American university, which many saw as a step toward reconciliation between Ras Beirut and Palestine. Said was to come back there several times. But true reconciliation had to await the return of Mahmud Darwish, who was able to come back for the first time only in November 1999, when he was met by an overflowing crowd at the Palais UNESCO. Later he made a second visit to Lebanon, before finally returning to the capital once more, this time during Yasser Arafat's siege of Ramallah, when he filled the stands of the reconstructed Sports City Stadium.

Lebanon's return to the diplomatic scene, if only nominally, as host of the Arab summit in March 2002 officially marked the reunion of the intellectual world of the Mashriq and Beirut. Even so, the link with the republic of letters was not restored, for want of local sponsorship: the Lebanese press had now been superseded. No matter that *Al-Hayat,* having become an organ of Saudi interests since its reappearance in London in 1988, ended up moving a large part of its editorial staff back to Beirut, it deliberately refrained from setting up its political desk there. In Beirut the newspapers were, if not muzzled, in any case emptied of all substance, and therefore left vulnerable to every kind of manipulation. There were indeed some attempts at renovation within the An-Nahar group, which brought out once again its weekly supplement *Al-Mulhaq,* now edited by the left-wing Lebanese author Elias Khoury and the poet 'Aql Awit, with a new group of reviewers; and also at the daily paper *Al-Safir,* where Joseph Samaha, one of the most inventive Arab journalists, was intermittently in charge. The results were disappointing. A prolix and increasingly bland style of writing alienated potential readers by making it difficult to decode the abstruse verbiage, teeming with unidentified sources and undefined terms, in which the news was couched. The total circulation of Beirut's Arabic-language newspapers after the war did not exceed that of *An-Nahar* alone in 1975. The Francophone press fared no better. Just when the return of recent expatriates from France, Canada, and French-speaking Africa gave journalism in this language a new chance, provincialism continued to prevail. The young staff of the monthly magazine *L'Orient-Express* had shown that a team consisting in the main of beginners could reinvent journalism in French—very good French, by the way—by putting it in touch once more with both Lebanese society and Arab culture, but it was put out of business after two years by advertising and publishing executives who preferred a superficial and unthreatening *francophonie.* They gave their support instead to magazines that amounted to little more than a catalogue of society evenings, unscrupulously combining a tiny bit of editorial content with intrusive and unapologetically upscale advertising. In an apolitical environment, the formula was bound to succeed. Indeed it was subsequently adopted by the city's Arabophone press and, then, not long thereafter, exported to Jordan and Kuwait.

Television had not waited to export appearance rather than substance, despite the competitive advantages Lebanon enjoyed as a result of the proliferation of channels at the end of the war and the transition made by two of these, LBC and Future TV, to pan-Arab broadcasting by satellite. Lebanese television made its presence felt very quickly in the homes of Yemen and Kuwait, but solely through its variety-show programming and the scantily clad female stars it featured. When a cultural or political program of real quality, expected to last no more than a couple of months in the Beirut market, went on to become the leading talk show in the Arab world for several years, foreign interests saw to it that the show was cancelled. Instead the Saudi station MBC (broadcasting from London) and Orbit 2 (likewise Saudi but originating in Cairo), followed shortly by Al-Jazeera (from Qatar) and soon there-after Abu Dhabi TV and Al-ʿArabiyya (from Dubai), were allowed to dominate the Arab audiovisual landscape in the field of politics and commentary—very often thanks to journalists, producers, and technicians who had received their training at stations in Beirut. By the time LBC realized what was happening the scale of in-vestment required to compete in regional markets had become prohibitively great, and it found itself forced in its turn to look to a Saudi prince for assistance, though without any guarantee of success.

Despite the lack of resources, a few writers and other voices stubbornly persisted. When intellectuals mobilized in Cairo to defend the French Marxist philosopher and Muslim convert Roger Garaudy against charges of denying the Holocaust, it was in the columns of *An-Nahar* as well as those of *Al-Mulhaq, Al-Safir,* and *Al-Hayat* in Beirut that readers were warned against the unworthiness of their cause. Journalists also spoke out against the country's drift toward a Syrian-style police state and against the protectorate imposed by Damascus. To the surprise of some this protest touched a nerve, provoking a police response and then, in reaction to this, a campaign by intellectuals (rather than journalists, who for the most part had been tamed by this point). But the strongest signal in this regard was to come from Syria—the other Syria, where during the "Damascus Spring" of 2001 intellectuals signed a petition of support for a persecuted Lebanese journalist. In the modern memory of Beirut and Damascus, no one had ever seen such a thing.

WHICH CITY FOR WHICH ROLE?

Between the pressure of the economic crisis and the complacency of the forces of opposition, intellectuals in Beirut were too exhausted to argue with anyone who believed that their traditional function as a tribune of the people had subsided into insignificance. Their influence in the academic sphere was no more vigorous. If pri-vate universities had regained their prewar level of operation while at the same time negotiating partnership agreements with foreign institutions, the Lebanese Uni-versity had been allowed to fall apart—as if deliberately sacrificed in favor of the reinvigorated forces of confessionalism and mercantilism that had united to form more than three dozen institutions throughout the country, hastily dignified with the name of a university.

What purpose remains, then, for Beirut to fulfill, beyond serving simply as a place for recreation and entertainment? In Sidon, only half an hour away by the new high-way, the resurgent tide of puritanism now prevents popular singers from appear-ing in concert. In Tripoli, a Sunni Islamist movement publicly condemned Future TV, owned by the head of the municipal government, himself Sunni, because of the hugely successful Arab version of "Pop Idol." In view of the official indulgence from which both Arab and Islamic nationalism, fossilized in a fundamentalist hatred of the West, benefit in Lebanon and Syria alike, one may well wonder whether this puritanism will not reach Beirut in its turn.

So long as Beirut's downtown continues to be a getaway destination for tourists from the Gulf, it seems more likely that a suitably rebranded merchant republic will find a way to triumph over the enemies of pleasure. Nevertheless Beirut is troubled by a lack of confidence, unsure whether even this role will be left to it. Companies from the Gulf increasingly operate in the local tourist industry without Lebanese intermediaries, taking direct control of hotels, car rental agencies, and shops selling perfume and other luxury goods. The sting of doubt has been particularly felt with the emergence of the Emirate of Dubai as the communications capital of the region, as well as an air hub and a relaxed (not to say freewheeling) center of tourism, at least in the bars and hotels. Playing the extrovert is a role with which the merchant republic has long been familiar, of course, and indeed Shaykh Muhammad bin Rashid al-Maktum, the crown prince of the Emirate, makes no secret of the fact that he has taken Beirut as his model. More disturbing still, the rise of Dubai—where tens of thousands of Lebanese now work—did not come about while Beirut had fallen into eclipse during the war, but only in the second half of the 1990s, when Lebanon and its capital were doing their utmost to throw away the opportunities presented by reconstruction.

On maps of the world, and apart from the historical accident of Ibrahim Pasha's entry into the old walled town, Beirut first reappeared as a consequence of the projection of the European economy into the eastern Mediterranean, via a colonial axis that was to link its port to Damascus in a system of unequal trade with the West. This axis was to endure under the Mandate, despite the creation of borders within the Bilād al-Shām and the Franco-British competition that accompanied it. It next required the misfortune of some—of Haifa and the Palestinians, and of the Syrian bourgeoisie—and the neediness of others—the new oil states of the Gulf—for Beirut to become the cosmopolitan metropolis of the Arabs and the Switzerland of the Near East. Whoever wished to fly from Europe to the Arabian Peninsula in those days had to make a stopover, and he gladly made it in Beirut. Now there are direct connections between Europe and the Gulf, and if one wishes to make a stopover on the way to the Far East, it will be in Dubai. For the banks, things were easier still: once the oil fortunes found ways to dispense with the services of Lebanese banks during the war, there was no longer any need for either a hotel reservation or a local intermediary.

Since 11 September 2001, the merchant republic has no doubt smiled upon the new misfortune of some, and smiled no doubt again to see tourists from the Gulf flocking to the downtown of Beirut and the resorts that lie beyond it. And yet, having already experienced such misfortune itself, and very painfully indeed, Beirut is no longer unaware that it enjoys no special protection against it. And so perhaps Beirut must patiently await the return of prosperity in order to discover happiness, which is to say democracy for everyone—and not only in a few of its neighborhoods—and peace for the Palestinians. Thus the two essential conditions for creating a new regional market, which alone can give it new life. And permit it at last to be, after having so well and truly been.

Beirut
August 2003

NOTES

PROLOGUE

1. Élisée Reclus, *L'homme et la terre . . .* , 6 vols. (Paris: Librairie universelle, 1905–8), 2:43.

2. See Miles Copeland, *The Game of Nations: The Amorality of Power Politics* (New York: Simon and Schuster, 1970).

3. See Jonathan C. Randal, *Going All the Way: Christian Warlords, Israeli Adventurers, and the War in Lebanon* (New York: Viking, 1983).

4. Reclus, *L'homme et la terre . . .* , 2:44.

5. See Ahmad Beydoun, *Identité confessionnelle et temps social chez les historiens contemporains* (Beirut: Publications de l'Université Libanaise, 1984); also Kamal S. Salibi, *A House of Many Mansions: The History of Lebanon Reconsidered* (Berkeley and Los Angeles: University of California Press; London: I. B. Tauris, 1988).

CHAPTER ONE

1. Nina Jidejian, *Beirut through the Ages* (Beirut: Dār el-Mashriq, 1973), 11–12.

2. Louis Dubertret, *Géologie du site de Beyrouth* (Beirut: Délégation Générale de France au Levant, 1945), 50.

3. Roger Saydah, "The Prehistory of Beirut," in *Beirut—Crossroads of Cultures* (Beirut: Salwa Nassar Foundation for Lebanese Studies/Librairie du Liban, 1970), 10.

4. Jidejian, *Beirut through the Ages,* 13.

5. Ibid., 14–15.

6. Ibid., 15.

7. Herodotus, *The Histories,* 5.58–61.

8. May ʿAbbud Abi-ʿAql, *Wasat Bayrūt bayn al-iktishāfāt wa-l-jarrāfāt* (Beirut: Milaffāt an-Nahār, 1999), 64–68.

9. Reclus, *L'homme et la terre* . . . , 2:21.

10. Ibid., 2:43–44.

11. René Mouterde, S.J., *Regards sur Beyrouth phénicienne, hellenistique et romaine* (Beirut: Imprimerie Catholique, 1966), 9.

12. Ibid.

13. Maurice Sartre, *L'Orient romain: Provinces et sociétés en Méditerranée orientale d'Auguste aux Sévères (31 avant J.-C.–235 après J.-C.)* (Paris: Éditions du Seuil, 1991), 310.

14. Sanchuniathon is described in ancient sources as a pre–Trojan War author; modern scholarship places him between 700 and 500 B.C.E., though it cannot be excluded that he may have lived sometime during the Seleucid period (312–60 B.C.E.).—Trans.

15. Maurice Sartre, *D'Alexandre à Zénobie: Histoire de Levant antique, IVe siècle av. J.-C.–IIIe siècle ap. J.-C.* (Paris: Fayard, 2001), 288. [An abridged edition of this work, containing all the sections on Roman administration together with a new introductory chapter on the Hellenistic legacy, is available in English as *The Middle East under Rome*, translated by Catherine Porter and Elizabeth Rawlings with Jeannine Routier-Pucci (Cambridge, Mass.: Belknap Press of Harvard University Press, 2005).—Trans.]

16. Herodotus, *The Histories*, 3.37; cited in Jidejian, *Beirut through the Ages*, 6, 53.

17. Mouterde, *Regards sur Beyrouth*, 10–11.

18. Nonnos, *Dionysiaca*, 41.13–19, 41.143–49, quoted in Mouterde, *Regards sur Beyrouth*, 11, and in Jidejian, *Beirut through the Ages*, 54–55. [W. D. Rouse's 1940 translation, slightly modified.—Trans.]

19. See Louis Cheikho, S.J., *Bayrūt tārikhuhā wa āthāruha*, 3rd ed. (Beirut: Dār el-Mashriq, 1993).

20. Mouterde, *Regards sur Beyrouth*, 13.

21. Ibid.

22. Ibid., 14.

23. Jidejian, *Beirut through the Ages*, 26–27.

24. Ibid, 27–29.

25. 'Abbud Abi-'Aql, *Wasat Bayrūt bayn al-iktishāfāt wa-l-jarrāfāt*, 65–69, 99–100.

26. Ibid., 65, 99–100.

27. Helen Sader, "Ancient Beirut: Urban Growth in the Light of Recent Excavations," in Peter G. Rowe and Hashim Sarkis, eds., *Projecting Beirut: Episodes in the Construction and Reconstruction of a Modern City* (Munich and New York: Prestel Verlag, 1998), 30.

28. 'Abbud Abi-'Aql, *Wasat Bayrūt bayn al-iktishāfāt wa-l-jarrāfāt*, 70.

29. Herodotus, *The Histories*, 2.44, 8.67.

30. Sartre, *D'Alexandre à Zénobie*, 43n.

31. Ibid., 40.

32. Ludvig Müller, *Numismatique d'Alexandre le Grand* (Copenhagen: B. Luno, 1855), 310, quoted in Cheikho, *Bayrūt tārikhuhā wa āthāruha*, 31.

33. Cheikho, *Bayrūt tārikhuhā wa āthāruha*, 32.

34. Mouterde, *Regards sur Beyrouth*, 24–25.

35. Sartre, *D'Alexandre à Zénobie*, 147.

36. Sartre, *L'orient romain*, 338n.

37. Jules Rouvier, "Une métropole phénicienne oubliée, Laodicée métropole de Canaan,"

Al-Mashriq 1 (1898): 17–20; P. Roussel, "Laodicée de Phénicie," *Bulletin de correspondance hellénique* 35 (1911): 433–40; see also Cheikho, *Bayrūt tārikhuhā wa āthāruha,* 33.

38. Sartre, *D'Alexandre à Zénobie,* 147.

39. Quoted in Mouterde, *Regards sur Beyrouth,* 16–21.

40. Sartre, *D'Alexandre à Zénobie,* 432.

41. Strabo 16.2.18; see *The Geography of Strabo,* 8 vols., trans. Horace Leonard Jones (Cambridge, Mass.: Harvard University Press, 1960–70), 7:263.

42. Mouterde, *Regards sur Beyrouth,* 22.

43. Sartre, *L'orient romain,* 332.

44. Strabo 16.2.19; see *The Geography,* 7:265.

45. Sartre, *L'orient romain,* 338.

46. Strabo 16.2.19; see *The Geography,* 7:263–65.

47. Pliny, *Natural History,* 5.17, quoted in Mouterde, *Regards sur Beyrouth,* 23.

48. Sartre, *L'orient romain,* 71n, 316, 338.

49. Sartre, *D'Alexandre à Zénobie,* 646.

50. Sartre, *L'orient romain,* 337.

51. Mouterde, *Regards sur Beyrouth,* 25.

52. Ibid.

53. Sartre, *The Middle East under Rome,* 170; see also Sader, "Ancient Beirut," 33.

54. 'Abbud Abi-'Aql, *Wasat Bayrūt bayn al-iktishāfāt wa-l-jarrāfāt,* 117.

55. Jidejian, *Beirut through the Ages,* 48–49.

56. See *An-Nahār,* 17 and 29 January 2001.

57. Mouterde, *Regards sur Beyrouth,* 26–27.

58. Sader, "Ancient Beirut," 34.

59. Ibid.

60. Sartre, *L'orient romain,* 322.

61. Ibid., 323.

62. Flavius Josephus, *The Jewish War,* 1.422; see the nine-volume Loeb edition, trans. H. St. J. Thackeray (Cambridge, Mass.: Harvard University Press, 1976), 2:199.

63. Ibid.

64. Sartre, *L'orient romain,* 158.

65. Flavius Josephus, quoted in Mouterde, *Regards sur Beyrouth,* 27.

66. Sartre, *L'orient romain,* 351.

67. Sartre, *D'Alexandre à Zénobie,* 548.

68. Cheikho, *Bayrūt tārikhuhā wa āthāruha,* 38.

69. Sartre, *L'orient romain,* 346.

70. Sartre, *D'Alexandre à Zénobie,* 686.

71. Sartre, *L'orient romain,* 344n.

72. Cheikho, *Bayrūt tārikhuhā wa āthāruha,* 37.

73. Ibid., 52–53; see also Mouterde, *Regards sur Beyrouth,* 33–34.

74. Sartre, *L'orient romain,* 78.

75. Ibid., 122.

76. Sartre, *The Middle East under Rome,* 185–86.

77. Sartre, *L'orient romain,* 350.

78. Sartre, *D'Alexandre à Zénobie*, 894.

79. Sartre, *L'orient romain*, 490.

80. Ibid., 491, 494; see also Sartre, *D'Alexandre à Zénobie*, 898.

81. *Al-Mashriq* 11 (1908): 31, 81–98; see also Jidejian, *Beirut through the Ages*, 25.

82. Sālih bin Yahya, *Tārikh Bayrūt*, edited by Francis Hours, S.J., and Kamal Salibi (Beirut: Dār el-Mashriq, 1969), 17; also, Francesco Suriano, *Il Trattato di Terra Santa* (1485), quoted in Cheikho, *Bayrūt tārikhuhā wa āthāruha*, 43n, 117.

83. See Houda Kassatly, *Si proche, si extrême: Rituels de sursis du Liban et de Syrie* (Beirut: Layali, 1998).

84. Cheikho, *Bayrūt tārikhuhā wa āthāruha*, 43.

85. Sartre, *The Middle East under Rome*, 338.

86. Paul Collinet, *Histoire de l'École de droit de Beyrouth* (Paris: Sirey, 1925), 28–29.

87. Mouterde, *Regards sur Beyrouth*, 34.

88. Cheikho, *Bayrūt tārikhuhā wa āthāruha*, 57.

89. Ibid., 41.

90. Ibid., 42.

91. Sālih bin Yahya, *Tārikh Bayrūt*, 17.

92. Collinet, *Histoire de l'École de droit de Beyrouth*, 17.

93. Sartre, *The Middle East under Rome*, 289–90.

94. Ibid.; see also Collinet, *Histoire de l'École de droit de Beyrouth*, 20–21.

95. Paul Huvelin, "Leçon inaugurale (14 novembre 1913)," reprinted in *Mélanges à la Mémoire de Paul Huvelin* (Paris: Sirey, 1938), on the occasion of the twenty-fifth anniversary of the École Française de Droit de Beyrouth.

96. Collinet, *Histoire de l'École de droit de Beyrouth*, 16–18.

97. Ibid., 45.

98. Quoted in ibid., 31.

99. Ibid., 36.

100. See *Life of Severus*, quoted in Mouterde, *Regards sur Beyrouth*, 39. [The biography of Severus (465–538), Patriarch of Antioch, is attributed to Zacharias of Mytilene and survives only in Syriac.—Trans.]

101. Collinet, *Histoire de l'École de droit de Beyrouth*, 126–29, 139.

102. Ibid., 149.

103. The Latin phrase ("in Berytiensium pulcherrima civitate quam et legum nutricem bene quis appelet") is from *Constitutio Omnem* § 7, quoted in Collinet, *Histoire de l'École de droit de Beyrouth*, 53.

104. Jidejian, *Beirut through the Ages*, 68.

105. Collinet, *Histoire de l'École de droit de Beyrouth*, 5.

106. Cheikho, *Bayrūt tārikhuhā wa āthāruha*, 46.

107. See René Mouterde, S.J., "Le temple de Vénus dans la Beyrouth romaine," *Al-Mashriq* 22 (1924): 195–200.

108. Sartre, *The Middle East under Rome*, 323–25.

109. Quoted in Collinet, *Histoire de l'École de droit de Beyrouth*, 36.

110. Quoted in ibid., 53.

111. A lyrical description of the city is found in Nonnos of Panopolis, *Dionysiaca*, 41.13–

50; see the 3-volume Loeb edition, trans. W. H. D. Rouse (Cambridge, Mass.: Harvard University Press, 1963), 3:197–201.

112. Sālih bin Yahya, *Tārikh Bayrūt*, 11–12; see also Cheikho, *Bayrūt tārikhuhā wa āthāruha*, 50.

113. Sartre, *The Middle East under Rome*, 242–244; see also Cheikho, *Bayrūt tārikhuhā wa āthāruha*, 51.

114. Jidejian, *Beirut through the Ages*, 71.

115. Quoted in Collinet, *Histoire de l'École de droit de Beyrouth*, 56–57.

116. Joannes Barbucallus, *Anthologia Graeca*, 9.425–27; quoted in Jidejian, *Beirut through the Ages*, 8.

117. Ibid., 150.

118. Sader, "Ancient Beirut," 34.

119. Sālih bin Yahya, *Tārikh Bayrūt*, 23.

120. Cheikho, *Bayrūt tārikhuhā wa āthāruha*, 69.

121. See the article "Al-Awzāʿī," in *Encyclopédie de l'Islam*, 2nd edition (Leiden: E. J. Brill and Paris: Maisonneuve and Larose, 1960–89).

122. Sālih bin Yahya, *Tārikh Bayrūt*, 23–24.

123. "Al-Awzāʿī," in *Encyclopédie de l'Islam*.

124. Jidejian, *Beirut through the Ages*, 81.

125. Cheikho, *Bayrūt tārikhuhā wa āthāruha*, 72.

126. Quoted in Jidejian, *Beirut through the Ages*, 84.

127. Cheikho, *Bayrūt tārikhuhā wa āthāruha*, 76.

128. Jidejian, *Beirut through the Ages*, 85.

129. Sālih bin Yahya, *Tārikh Bayrūt*, 43–44.

130. Ibid., 61.

131. Jidejian, *Beirut through the Ages*, 89–90.

132. Sālih bin Yahya, *Tārikh Bayrūt*, 52–53.

133. Ibid., 58.

134. The Bahri, whose name derived from their garrisoning in Egypt on the Nile *(Bahr)*, were former slaves—Slavs, Greeks, Cherkesses, and above all Turks. The Burgi, so called because they were settled in the citadel *(Burg)* constructed by Saladin, were Cherkess. The latter were distinguished chiefly by their system for electing the sultan, which, by doing away with the hereditary transmission of power, favored conspiracy and assassination.

135. "Bahriyya," in *Encyclopédie de l'Islam*.

136. Sālih bin Yahya, *Tārikh Bayrūt*, 59.

137. Ibid.

138. Cheikho, *Bayrūt tārikhuhā wa āthāruha*, 105; see also Kamal S. Salibi, *A House of Many Mansions: The History of Lebanon Reconsidered* (London: I. B. Tauris, 1988), 121.

139. André Raymond, "Les provinces arabes (XVIe siècle–XVIIIe siècle)," in Robert Mantran, ed., *Histoire de l'Empire Ottoman* (Paris: Fayard, 1989), 341–420.

140. Antoine Abdel-Nour, *Introduction à l'histoire urbaine de la Syrie ottomane (XVIe siècle–XVIIIe siècle)* (Beirut: Publications de l'Université Libanaise, 1982).

141. Raymond, "Les provinces arabes," 370–72.

142. Two other regimes were commonly administered in Ottoman lands: *timar,* the al-

most feudal practice of granting land (typically to soldiers) in exchange for services to be rendered, particularly in Anatolia; and *emaneh,* which confided responsibility for tax collection to a government official.

143. Dominique Chevallier, *La société du mont Liban à l'époque de la Révolution industrielle en Europe* (Paris: Geuthner, 1971), 3–15.

144. Ibid., 82–85.

145. Cheikho, *Bayrūt tārikhuhā wa āthāruha,* 111.

146. Abdul-Karim Rafeq, *The Province of Damascus, 1723–1783* (Beirut: Khayats, 1970), 76, 179.

147. Ibid., 116–17.

148. Rafeq, *The Province of Damascus,* 179.

149. Cheikho, *Bayrūt tārikhuhā wa āthāruha,* 112.

150. Laurent d'Arvieux, *Mémoires du chevalier d'Arvieux . . . contenant ses voyages à Constantinople, dans l'Asie, la Syrie, la Palestine, l'Égypte, et la Barbarie. . . .* (Paris: C. J. B. Delespine, 1735).

151. Antoine Abdel-Nour, *Tijārat Saydā maᶜ al-Gharb* (Beirut: Publications de l'Université Libanaise, 1973).

152. Robert Mantran, "Les débuts de la question d'Orient (1774–1839)," in Mantran, ed., *Histoire de l'Empire Ottoman,* 421–25.

153. Following the dismantling of their state in 1517, the Mamluks retained the title of *bey* and the right to govern Egyptian provinces annexed to the Ottoman Empire. Gradually they managed to reduce the power of the pashas appointed by the Porte, and in the eighteenth century effectively reestablished themselves as the masters of the country, though they remained subject to Ottoman sovereignty.

154. The holding of the office of *wālī* in two provinces at the same time was not without precedent, but this was the only occasion when such an expansion of power involved both Sidon and Damascus.

155. Rafeq, *The Province of Damascus,,* 293–94.

156. Ibid., 299.

157. Ibid., 300–302.

158. François Charles-Roux, *Les Échelles de Syrie et de Palestine au XVIIIᵉ siècle* (Paris: P. Geuthner, 1928), 106n.

159. Ibid., 106, 212.

160. Rafeq, *The Province of Damascus,* 3, 312.

161. Ibid., 315.

162. Houda Kassatly, *De pierres et de couleurs: Vie et mort des maisons du vieux Beyrouth* (Beirut: Layali, 1998).

CHAPTER TWO

1. C.-F. Volney, *Voyage en Égypte et en Syrie,* edited by Jean Gaulmier (Paris: Mouton, 1959), 290.

2. Albert Hourani, *A History of the Arab Peoples* (Cambridge, Mass.: Belknap Press of Harvard University Press, 1991), 261.

3. Dominique Chevallier, "Signes de Beyrouth en 1834," *Bulletin d'études orientales* 25 (1972): 211–29; reprinted in Chevallier, *Villes et travail en Syrie: Du XIXe au XXe siècle* (Paris: Maisonneuve et Larose, 1982), 9–28.

4. Hourani, *A History of the Arab Peoples*, 267.

5. Henri Guys, *Beyrout et le Liban: Relation d'un séjour de plusieurs années dans ce pays*, 2 vols. (Paris: Comon, 1850), 1:13n.

6. Henry Laurens, *Le royaume impossible: La France et la genèse du monde arabe* (Paris: Armand Colin, 1990), 37–42.

7. Paul Dumont, "La période des Tanzimât (1839–1878)," in Mantran, ed., *Histoire de l'Empire Ottoman*, 501.

8. Chevallier, *La société du mont Liban*, 243–72.

9. See Leila Tarazi Fawaz, *An Occasion for War: Civil Conflict in Lebanon and Damascus in 1860* (Berkeley: University of California Press, 1994).

10. Pierre Marthelot, "Une ville remplit son site: Beyrouth," *Méditerranée* 4, no. 3 (1963): 37–39.

11. Alexander Schölch, "Le développement économique de la Palestine, 1856–1882," *Revue d'études palestiniennes*, no. 10 (Winter 1984): 93–113.

12. Ibid.

13. Chevallier, "Signes de Beyrouth en 1834."

14. Latīfa Muhammad Sālim, *Al-Hukm al-masrī fī-l-Shām, 1831–1841*, 2nd ed. (Cairo: Madbuli, 1990), 17–22.

15. Cheikho, *Bayrūt tārikhuhā wā āthāruha*, 133.

16. Chevallier, *La société du mont Liban*, 90–105.

17. Sālim, *Al-Hukm al-masrī fī-l-Shām*, 41.

18. Ibid., 83.

19. Chevallier, *La société du mont Liban*, 49–62.

20. Laurens, *Le royaume impossible*, 122–23.

21. Fawaz Traboulsi, "Le pas de deux de l'émir Abdel-Kader et de Youssef bey Karam," *L'Orient-Express*, no. 11 (October 1996).

22. Laurens, *Le royaume impossible*, 148–49.

23. Engin Deniz Akarli, *The Long Peace: Ottoman Lebanon, 1861–1920* (Berkeley: University of California Press, 1993), 39, 60–61, 184.

24. Albert Hourani, "Ideologies of the Mountain and the City," in Roger Owen, ed., *Essays on the Crisis in Lebanon* (London: Ithaca Press, 1976), 33–41.

CHAPTER THREE

1. This quotation and the ones preceding are from Gérard de Nerval, *Voyage en Orient*, 8th edition, 2 vols. (Paris: Charpentier, 1875), 1:327–30.

2. Dominique Chevallier, "Signes de Beyrouth en 1834," *Bulletin d'études orientales* 25 (1972): 211–29; also "Les villes arabes depuis le XIXe siècle: Structures, visions, transformations," *Revue des travaux de l'Académie des sciences morales et politiques*, 4e série, 1er trimestre, 125 (1972): 116–28; both reprinted in Chevallier, *Villes et travail en Syrie*, 9–28 and 29–30, respectively.

3. Nerval, *Voyage en Orient*, 1:329.

4. Édouard Blondel, *Deux ans en Syrie et en Palestine (1838–1839)* (Paris: P. Dufart, 1840), 11.

5. Alphonse de Lamartine, *Souvenirs, impressions, pensées et paysages, pendant un voyage en Orient (1832–1833)*, 4 vols. (Paris: C. Gosselin, 1835), 1:127.

6. Leila Tarazi Fawaz, *Merchants and Migrants in Nineteenth-Century Beirut* (Cambridge, Mass.: Harvard University Press, 1983), 12.

7. See the photographs taken around 1875 by Jean-Baptiste Carlier and reproduced in Fouad Debbas, *Des photographes à Beyrouth, 1840–1918* (Paris: Marval, 2001), 60.

8. Blondel, *Deux ans en Syrie et en Palestine*, 13–14.

9. Joseph-François Michaud and Jean-Joseph-François Poujoulat, *Correspondance d'Orient, 1830–1831*, 7 vols. (Paris: Ducollet, 1833–35), 6:124.

10. Blondel, *Deux ans en Syrie et en Palestine*, 11–12.

11. Fawaz, *Merchants and Migrants in Nineteenth-Century Beirut*, 12.

12. Debbas, *Des photographes à Beyrouth*, 5.

13. May Davie, *Beyrouth et ses faubourgs (1840–1940): Une intégration inachevée* (Beirut: Centre d'Études et de Recherches sur le Moyen-Orient Contemporain, 1996), 23–29.

14. Chevallier, *La société du mont Liban*, 41.

15. Fawaz, *Merchants and Migrants in Nineteenth-Century Beirut*, 28–32.

16. Léon de Laborde, *Voyage de la Syrie* (Paris: Didot Frères, 1837), 37.

17. Michaud and Poujoulat, *Correspondance d'Orient*, 6:123.

18. John Lewis Burkhardt, *Travels in Syria and the Holy Land* (London: John Murray, 1822), 182.

19. Chevallier, "Signes de Beyrouth en 1834," 9.

20. Davie, *Beyrouth et ses faubourgs*.

21. Sālim, *Al-Hukm al-masrī fī-l-Shām*, 71–74.

22. Ibid., 225.

23. Ibid., 73.

24. Ibid., 40.

25. Ibid., 80.

26. Moshe Ma'oz, *Ottoman Reform in Syria and Palestine, 1840–1861: The Impact of the Tanzimat on Politics and Society* (Oxford: Clarendon Press, 1968), 90–91.

27. Sālim, *Al-Hukm al-masrī fī-l-Shām*, 82.

28. Ibid., 82.

29. Ibid., 67.

30. Muhammad Sabry, *L'Empire égyptien sous Mohamed-Ali et la question d'Orient, 1811–1849: Égypte, Arabie, Soudan, Morée, Crète, Syrie, Palestine* (Paris: Paul Geuthner, 1930), 346; see also Chevallier, "Signes de Beyrouth en 1834," 19n.

31. Assad Rustom, "Idārat al-Shām, rūhuha wa haykaluha wa atharuha," in al-Jam'iyyah al-Misriyah lil-Dirāsāt al-Tārīkhīyah, ed., *Dhikrā al-batal al-fātih Ibrahim Pasha, 1848–1948*, reprint (Cairo: Madbuli, 1990), 121.

32. Sālim, *Al-Hukm al-masrī fī-l-Shām*, 83.

33. Ibid.

34. Blondel, *Deux ans en Syrie et en Palestine*, 14.

35. Debbas, *Des photographes à Beyrouth*, 13.

36. Davie, *Beyrouth et ses faubourgs*, 32.

37. Fawaz, *Merchants and Migrants in Nineteenth-Century Beirut*, 34.

38. Blondel, *Deux ans en Syrie et en Palestine*, 14.

39. Frédéric Goupil-Fesquet, in N.-P. Lerebours, *Excursions daguerriennes* (Paris: Béthune et Plon, 1841–42), quoted in Debbas, *Des photographes à Beyrouth*, 6.

40. Rustom, "Idārat al-Shām," 112.

41. Guys, *Beyrout et le Liban*, 1:32–33.

42. Baron d'Armagnac, *Nézib et Beyrout: Souvenirs d'Orient de 1833 à 1841* (Paris: J. Laisné, 1844), 126–27, quoted in Debbas, *Des photographes à Beyrouth*, 7.

43. Sālim, *Al-Hukm al-masrī fī-l-Shām*, 212.

44. Fawaz, *Merchants and Migrants in Nineteenth-Century Beirut*, 33–34.

45. Debbas, *Des photographes à Beyrouth*, 7.

46. Guys, *Beyrout et le Liban*, 1:11.

47. Ibid., 1:143.

48. Davie, *Beyrouth et ses faubourgs*, 34.

49. Letter from Father Paul Riccadonna, S.J., to Father Jan Roothaan, Superior General, 22 June 1836, quoted in Sami Kuri, S.J., *Une histoire du Liban à travers les archives Jésuites (1816–1973)*, 3 vols. (Beirut: Dār al-Mashriq, 1985–96), 1:200.

50. Letter from Father Roothaan to Father Benoît Planchet, S.J., 19 March 1838, quoted in Kuri, *Une histoire du Liban*, 1:243.

51. Chevallier, "Signes de Beyrouth en 1834," 15, 18n.

52. Fawaz, *Merchants and Migrants in Nineteenth-Century Beirut*, 26.

53. Sālim, *Al-Hukm al-masrī fī-l-Shām*, 223.

54. Ibid., 213.

55. Fawaz, *Merchants and Migrants in Nineteenth-Century Beirut*, 34.

56. Sālim, *Al-Hukm al-masrī fī-l-Shām*, 215.

57. Rustom, "Idārat al-Shām," 123–24.

58. Guys, *Beyrout et le Liban*, 1:8.

59. Fawaz, *Merchants and Migrants in Nineteenth-Century Beirut*, 33.

60. Ibid., 32–33.

61. Quoted in Debbas, *Des photographes à Beyrouth*, 7.

62. Fawaz, *Merchants and Migrants in Nineteenth-Century Beirut*, 32.

CHAPTER FOUR

1. Guys, *Beyrout et le Liban*, 1:11, 21.

2. Quoted in Debbas, *Des photographes à Beyrouth*, 27.

3. Quoted in Fouad Debbas, *Beyrouth, notre mémoire: Promenade guidée à travers la collection de cartes postales*, 3rd ed. (Paris: Éditions Henri Berger, 1994), 19.

4. Quoted in Kuri, *Une histoire du Liban*, 1:335.

5. Letter from Father Jean-François Badour to Father Pieter Beckx, 3 September 1853, quoted in ibid., 2:117.

6. Chevallier, *La société du mont Liban*, 268n, 185–86.

7. Fawaz, *Merchants and Migrants in Nineteenth-Century Beirut*, 26.

8. Ibid., 61.

9. Debbas, *Des photographes à Beyrouth*, 8.

10. Fawaz, *Merchants and Migrants in Nineteenth-Century Beirut*, 61.

11. Letter from Father Raymond Estève to Father Jan Roothaan, June 1850, quoted in Kuri, *Une histoire du Liban*, 2:60.

12. Quoted in Dominique Chevallier, "Lyon et la Syrie en 1919: Les bases d'une intervention," *Revue Historique* 224 (1960): 275-320; see Chevallier, *Villes et travail en Syrie*, 43.

13. Fawaz, *Merchants and Migrants in Nineteenth-Century Beirut*, 61.

14. Ibid., 26.

15. Letter from Father Jean-François Badour to Father Pieter Beckx, 3 September 1853, in Kuri, *Une histoire du Liban*, 2:117.

16. Ibid., 2:113.

17. Fawaz, *Merchants and Migrants in Nineteenth-Century Beirut*, 34.

18. Ibid., 36-37.

19. Ibid., 34.

20. Quoted in Debbas, *Des photographes à Beyrouth*, 47.

21. Ibid., 21.

22. Ibid., 31.

23. Cheikho, *Bayrūt tārikhuhā wā āthāruha*, 136-37.

24. Debbas, *Des photographes à Beyrouth*, 9.

25. Fawaz, *Merchants and Migrants in Nineteenth-Century Beirut*, 33.

26. Debbas, *Des photographes à Beyrouth*, 31.

27. Fawaz, *Merchants and Migrants in Nineteenth-Century Beirut*, 68.

28. Ibid.; see also Chevallier, "Lyon et la Syrie en 1919."

29. Fawaz, *Merchants and Migrants in Nineteenth-Century Beirut*, 68; see also Dumont, "La période des Tanzimât," in Mantran, ed., *Histoire de l'Empire Ottoman*, 496.

30. Fawaz, *Merchants and Migrants in Nineteenth-Century Beirut*, 69.

31. Ibid.

32. Butrus Abu-Manneh, "The Establishment and Dismantling of the Province of Syria, 1865-1888," in John P. Spagnolo, ed., *Problems of the Middle East in Historical Perspective: Essays in Honour of Albert Hourani* (Reading, England: Ithaca Press, 1992), 7-26.

33. May Davie, *Beyrouth, 1825-1975: Un siècle et demi d'urbanisme* (Beirut: Ordre des Ingénieurs et des Architectes, 2001), 43.

34. Cheikho, *Bayrūt tārikhuhā wā āthāruha*, 160.

35. Davie, *Beyrouth, 1825-1975*, 42.

36. Fawaz, *Merchants and Migrants in Nineteenth-Century Beirut*, 61.

37. Davie, *Beyrouth, 1825-1975*, 61.

38. Fawaz, *Merchants and Migrants in Nineteenth-Century Beirut*, 71-72.

39. Debbas, *Des photographes à Beyrouth*, 34.

40. Fawaz, *Merchants and Migrants in Nineteenth-Century Beirut*, 72; see also Debbas, *Des photographes à Beyrouth*, 28.

41. Fawaz, *Merchants and Migrants in Nineteenth-Century Beirut*, 72.

42. Debbas, *Des photographes à Beyrouth,* 36.

43. Fawaz, *Merchants and Migrants in Nineteenth-Century Beirut,* 69–70.

44. See Jacques Thobie, *Intérêts et impérialisme français dans l'Empire ottoman, 1895–1914* (Paris: Imprimerie Nationale, 1977).

45. Fawaz, *Merchants and Migrants in Nineteenth-Century Beirut,* 70.

46. Cheikho, *Bayrūt tārikhuhā wā āthāruha,* 159.

47. Fawaz, *Merchants and Migrants in Nineteenth-Century Beirut,* 71.

48. Ibid., 72.

49. Ibid., 61–62.

50. Ibid., 62.

51. Dumont, "La période des Tanzimât," in Mantran, ed., *Histoire de l'Empire Ottoman,* 494.

52. Fawaz, *Merchants and Migrants in Nineteenth-Century Beirut,* 62–63.

53. Ibid., 63.

54. Ibid., 63–64.

55. Dumont, "La période des Tanzimât," in Mantran, ed., *Histoire de l'Empire Ottoman,* 487.

56. See Badr al-Hājj, *Des photographes à Damas* (Paris: Marval, 2001).

57. François Georgeon, "Le dernier sursaut (1878–1908)," in Mantran, ed., *Histoire de l'Empire Ottoman,* 551.

58. Chevallier, *La société du mont Liban,* 292.

59. Dumont, "La période des Tanzimât," in Mantran, ed., *Histoire de l'Empire Ottoman,* 487, 490.

60. Chevallier, *La société du mont Liban,* 292.

61. Fawaz, *Merchants and Migrants in Nineteenth-Century Beirut,* 32.

62. Rafīq al-Tamīmī and Muhammad Bahjat, *Wilāyat Bayrūt,* 2 vols. (Beirut: Matbaʿat al-Iqbāl, 1917), 2:19 [erratum at 1:8].

63. Fawaz, *Merchants and Migrants in Nineteenth-Century Beirut,* 85.

64. Ibid., 86.

65. Ibid., 91–94.

66. Ibid., 96.

CHAPTER FIVE

1. Debbas, *Des photographes à Beyrouth,* 112–13 and 124–25, respectively.

2. Chevallier, *La société du mont Liban,* 291–92.

3. Jens Hanssen, "Your Beirut Is on My Desk: Ottomanizing Beirut under Sultan Abdül-Hamid II (1876–1909)," in Rowe and Sarkis, eds., *Projecting Beirut,* 53.

4. Ibid., 51.

5. Dumont, "La période des Tanzimât," in Mantran, ed., *Histoire de l'Empire Ottoman,* 490–93.

6. Hanssen, "Your Beirut Is on My Desk," in Rowe and Sarkis, eds., *Projecting Beirut,* 53. [On the respective responsibilities of provincial and municipal councils, see Jens Hanssen,

Fin de Siècle Beirut: The Making of an Ottoman Provincial Capital (Oxford: Oxford University Press, 2005), 70–73, 139–40.—Trans.]

7. Davie, *Beyrouth, 1825–1975*, 41.

8. Debbas, *Des photographes à Beyrouth*, 13.

9. Dumont, "La période des Tanzimât," in Mantran, ed., *Histoire de l'Empire Ottoman*, 463.

10. Davie, *Beyrouth, 1825–1975*, 42.

11. Davie, *Beyrouth et ses faubourgs (1840–1940)*, 45.

12. Ibid.

13. Fawaz, *Merchants and Migrants in Nineteenth-Century Beirut*, 102.

14. "Baladiyya," in *Encyclopédie de l'Islam*.

15. Cheikho, *Bayrūt tārikhuhā wā āthāruha*, 142–43.

16. Davie, *Beyrouth, 1825–1975*, 51.

17. Ibid., 52.

18. Georgeon, "Le dernier sursaut," in Mantran, ed., *Histoire de l'Empire Ottoman*, 553.

19. Davie, *Beyrouth, 1825–1975*, 53.

20. Ibid., 54.

21. Hanssen, "Your Beirut Is on My Desk," in Rowe and Sarkis, eds., *Projecting Beirut*, 60.

22. Davie, *Beyrouth, 1825–1975*, 53–55.

23. Debbas, *Des photographes à Beyrouth*, 13.

24. Davie, *Beyrouth, 1825–1975*, 58–59; see also Hanssen, "Your Beirut Is on My Desk," in Rowe and Sarkis, eds. *Projecting Beirut*, 59–60.

25. Hanssen, "Your Beirut Is on My Desk," in Rowe and Sarkis, eds., *Projecting Beirut*, 57–58.

26. Quoted in Debbas, *Des photographes à Beyrouth*, 46.

27. Ibid., 34.

28. Davie, *Beyrouth, 1825–1975*, 60.

29. Hanssen, "Your Beirut Is on My Desk," in Rowe and Sarkis, eds., *Projecting Beirut*, 45.

30. Ibid., 54.

31. Kuri, *Une histoire du Liban*, 2:113.

32. Davie, *Beyrouth, 1825–1975*, 61.

33. Kuri, *Une histoire du Liban*, 2:75n.

34. Ibid.

35. Davie, *Beyrouth et ses faubourgs (1840–1940)*, 62.

36. Ibid., 61.

37. See Claire Paget, *Murs et plafonds peints: Liban, XIXᵉ siècle* (Beirut: Éditions Terre du Liban, 1998).

38. See Kassatly, *De pierres et de couleurs*.

39. Cheikho, *Bayrūt tārikhuhā wā āthāruha*, 160.

40. "Al-haqq ʿala-l-tiliyān" ("It's the Italians' fault"). This expression is still used today to mock government officials who try to avoid taking responsibility for their mistakes.

41. Debbas, *Des photographes à Beyrouth*, 66.

42. Tamīmī and Bahjat, *Wilāyat Bayrūt*, 1:81.

43. Ibid., 1:64.

CHAPTER SIX

1. Guys, *Beyrout et le Liban*, 1:14.

2. David Urquhart, *The Lebanon (Mount Souria): A History and Diary*, 2 vols. (London: T. C. Newby, 1860), 2:178–81.

3. Ahmad Faris al-Shidyaq, *La jambe sur la jambe*, trans. René Khawam (Paris: Phébus, 1991).

4. Fawaz Traboulsi, "Ahmad Farès al-Chidyaq, de la modernité en tant que femme," *L'Orient-Express*, no. 5 (April 1996).

5. Taha al-Wāli, *Bayrūt fī-l-tārīkh wa-l-hadāra wa-l-ʿumrān* (Beirut: Dār al-ʿIlm li-l-Malāyīn, 1993), 293–94.

6. Bernard Lewis, *The Political Language of Islam* (Chicago: University of Chicago Press, 1988), 40–41; see also Albert Hourani, *Arabic Thought in the Liberal Age, 1798–1939* (London: Oxford University Press, 1962), 79–81, 194; and Henry Laurens, *L'Orient arabe: Arabisme et islamisme de 1798 à 1945* (Paris: Armand Colin, 1993), 75–77.

7. Hourani, *Arabic Thought in the Liberal Age*, 99–102.

8. Louis Bazin, "La vie intellectuelle et culturelle de l'Empire ottoman," in Mantran, ed., *Histoire de l'Empire Ottoman*, 716–24.

9. Taha al-Wāli, *Bayrūt fī-l-tārīkh*, 295–96.

10. Dumont, "La période des Tanzimât," in Mantran, ed., *Histoire de l'Empire Ottoman*, 480.

11. Kuri, *Une histoire du Liban*, 1:525, 2:202.

12. *Al-Fajr al-sādiq li-jamʿiyyat al-maqāsid al-khayriyya al-islāmiyya fī Bayrūt: Aʿmāl al-sana al-ʿūlā* (Beirut: Thamarāt al-Funūn, 1879), 4.

13. Ibid., 5.

14. Ibid., 7.

15. Hisham Nashabi, "Shaykh ʿAbd al-Qadir al-Qabbani and *Thamarāt al-funūn*," in Marwan R. Buheiry, ed., *Intellectual Life in the Arab East, 1890–1939* (Beirut: Center for Arab and Middle East Studies, American University of Beirut, 1981), 84–91.

16. Laurens, *L'Orient arabe*, 98–99.

17. Georgeon, "Le dernier sursaut," in Mantran, ed., *Histoire de l'Empire Ottoman*, 535.

18. Chevallier, "Lyon et Syrie," in *Villes et travail en Syrie*, 47.

19. Dumont, "La période des Tanzimât," in Mantran, ed., *Histoire de l'Empire Ottoman*, 480–81.

20. Georgeon, "Le dernier sursaut," in Mantran, ed., *Histoire de l'Empire Ottoman*, 541.

CHAPTER SEVEN

1. On the American evangelists in Beirut see A. L. Tibawi, "The Genesis and Early History of the Syrian Protestant College," *Middle East Journal* 21, nos. 1 and 2 (1967): 1–15 and 199–212.

2. Quoted in Abdul-Latif Tibawi, *American Interests in Syria, 1800–1901: A Study of Educational, Literary and Religious Work* (Oxford: Clarendon Press, 1966), 27.

3. Jonas King, "Wadāʿ Yūnus Kīn ilā ahbābihi fī Filastīn wa Sūriyya" (5 April 1825); cited in Tibawi, *American Interests in Syria*, 27.

4. Toufic Touma, *Paysans et institutions féodales chez les druzes et les maronites du Liban du XVIIe siècle à 1914*, 2 vols. (Beirut: Publications de l'Université Libanaise, 1972), 2:550.

5. Robert M. Khouri, *La médecine au Liban: De la Phénicie à nos jours* (Beirut: Éditions ABCD [ca. 1990]), 169.

6. Ibid., 110.

7. Ibid., 100.

8. Ibid., 114.

9. Ibid., 116.

10. Ibid. See also Shafiq Jeha, *Darwin and the Crisis of 1882 in the Medical Department; and the First Student Protest in the Arab World in the Syrian Protestant College (Now the American University of Beirut)*, edited by Helen Khal and translated by Sally Kaya (Beirut: American University of Beirut Press, 2004).

11. *Al-Muqtataf* 9 (1884–85): 468–72, 633.

12. Quoted in Kuri, *Une histoire du Liban*, 1:221.

13. Ibid., 1:335, 525, 528.

14. Letter from Father Benoît Planchet, Superior, to Father Jan Roothaan, Superior General, 8 September 1842, quoted in Kuri, *Une histoire du Liban*, 1:357.

15. Quoted in ibid., 1:335.

16. "[God's] will be done!" Reply of Father Jan Roothaan to Father Benoît Planchet, 3 August 1843, quoted in Kuri, *Une histoire du Liban*, 1:397.

17. Letter from Father Benoît Planchet to Father Jan Roothaan, 8 September 1842, quoted in Kuri, *Une histoire du Liban*, 1:357–59, 369.

18. Letter from Father Jan Roothaan to Father Louis Maillard, Provincial of Lyon, 31 October 1843, quoted in Kuri, *Une histoire du Liban*, 1:409.

19. Quoted in Kuri, *Une histoire du Liban*, 2:409.

20. Letter from Father Benoît Planchet to Father Jan Roothaan, 26 November 1846; and Report of the Apostolic Delegate to the Sacred Congregation, 26 September 1847, quoted in Kuri, *Une histoire du Liban*, 2:25, 36, respectively.

21. Ibid., 2:83n.

22. Report from Father François Badour to Father Joseph de Jocas on the state of the mission to Syria for the previous three years, 12 December 1855, quoted in Kuri, *Une histoire du Liban*, 2:139.

23. Letter from Father Raymond Estève to Father Pieter Beckx, 17 February 1859, quoted in Kuri, *Une histoire du Liban*, 2:219.

24. Kuri, *Une histoire du Liban*, 2:525n–526n.

25. Letter from Father François-Xavier Gautrelet to Father Pieter Beckx, 17 February 1859, quoted in Kuri, *Une histoire du Liban*, 3:292.

26. Letter from Father François Badour to Father Pieter Beckx, 3 September 1853, quoted in Kuri, *Une histoire du Liban*, 2:118. See also Report of Father Édouard Billotet to Father Jan Roothaan, 4 January 1851, quoted in Kuri, *Une histoire du Liban*, 2:73; letters from Father Raymond Estève to Father Jan Roothaan, 9 February and 4 March 1851, quoted in Kuri, *Une histoire du Liban*, 2:77–78; and Report of R. Louis-Xavier Abougit to the President of the Central Council of the Society for the Propagation of the Faith in Lyon, 8 September 1851, quoted in Kuri, *Une histoire du Liban*, 2:91–92.

27. Kuri, *Une histoire du Liban,* 2:410, 423.

28. Letter from Father Édouard Billotet to Father Jan Roothaan, 1 March 1853, quoted in Kuri, *Une histoire du Liban,* 2:110; and letter from Father Jean-François Badour to Father Pieter Beckx, 3 September 1853, quoted in Kuri, *Une histoire du Liban,* 2:119.

29. Letter from Father Philippe Cuche to Father Pieter Beckx, 19 June 1856, quoted in Kuri, *Une histoire du Liban,* 2:154–56; and letter from Father Louis-Xavier Abougit to Father Pieter Beckx, 22 March 1860, quoted in Kuri, *Une histoire du Liban,* 2:247–48. See also Antoine Talon, "Renseignements sur la fondation de tout ce qui regarde l'imprimerie S.J. à Beyrouth," quoted in Kuri, *Une histoire du Liban,* 3:425–29; and Talon, "Développements de l'Imprimerie catholique," quoted in Kuri, *Une histoire du Liban,* 3:429–32.

30. Reply of Father Pieter Beckx to Father Ambroise Monnot, 18 January 1870, quoted in Kuri, *Une histoire du Liban,* 3:355.

31. Letter from Father Ambroise Monnot to the Consul General of France, 2 January 1871; and letter from Father Ambroise Monnot to Father Sébastien Gaillard, 20 January 1871, quoted in Kuri, *Une histoire du Liban,* 3:389, 391.

32. Letter from Father Ambroise Monnot to Father Pieter Beckx, 29 June 1870, quoted in Kuri, *Une histoire du Liban,* 3:377.

33. Quoted in M. Julien, *La Nouvelle Mission de la Compagnie de Jésus en Syrie, 1831–1895* (Paris, 1899); also in Kuri, *Une histoire du Liban,* 3:133.

34. Undated letter from Father Louis Canuti to Father Pieter Beckx, quoted in Kuri, *Une histoire du Liban,* 3:108.

35. Letter from Father Ambroise Monnot to Father Pieter Beckx, 29 May 1870, quoted in Kuri, *Une histoire du Liban,* 3:374.

36. See the observations of Father Ambroise Rubillon on the plan for a college in Beirut, 1873, quoted in Kuri, *Une histoire du Liban,* 3:408–11.

37. Kuri, *Une histoire du Liban,* 3:409.

38. Chevallier, "Lyon et Syrie," in *Villes et travail en Syrie,* 47.

39. Khouri, *La médecine au Liban,* 186–87.

40. Ibid., 146.

41. Huvelin, "Leçon inaugurale (14 novembre 1913)," reprinted in *Mélanges à la Mémoire de Paul Huvelin.*

42. Chevallier, "Lyon et Syrie," in *Villes et travail en Syrie,* 47.

43. Ibid., 71n.

44. Maurice Barrès, *Une enquête aux pays du Levant,* 2 vols. (Paris: Plon-Nourrit, 1923), 1:32.

45. Khouri, *La médecine au Liban,* 163–74.

CHAPTER EIGHT

1. Hassān Hallāq, *Bayrūt al-mahrūsa fī-l-ʿahd al-ʿuthmāni* (Beirut: Al-Dār al-Jāmiʿiyya, 1987), 252–53; see also al-Wāli, *Bayrūt fī-l-tārīkh,* 282.

2. Kamal Salibi, "Beirut under the Young Turks as Depicted in the Political Memoirs of Salīm ʿAlī Salām," in Jacques Berque and Dominique Chevallier, eds., *Les Arabes par leurs archives: XVIᵉ–XXᵉ siècles* (Paris: Éditions du CNRS, 1976), 193–215; see also ʿAnbara Salām al-Khālidī, *Jawla fī al-Dhikrayāt bayn Lubnān wa Filastīn* (Beirut: Dār an-Nahār, 1978).

3. See the account of their son, Nadīm Dimashqiyyeh, in *Mahattāt fī hayātī al-diblūmāsiyya* (Beirut: Dār an-Nahār, 1995), 17–20; also Salām al-Khālidī, *Jawla fī al-Dhikrayāt bayn Lubnān wa Filastīn*, 66–72, and Jacques Berque, *Les Arabes d'hier à demain* (Paris: Seuil, 1960), 163.

4. Salām al-Khālidī, *Jawla fī al-Dhikrayāt bayn Lubnān wa Filastīn*, 37–38.

5. See inset plate in Hassān Hallāq, ed., *Mudhakkirāt Salīm ʿAlī Salām* (Beirut: Al-Dār al-Jāmʿiyya, 1981).

6. Fawaz, *Merchants and Migrants in Nineteenth-Century Beirut*, 91–92.

7. Ibid., 93.

8. Gabriel Charmes, *Voyages en Syrie, impressions et souvenirs* (Paris: Calmann-Lévy, 1891), 153.

9. Blondel, *Deux ans en Syrie et en Palestine*, 91.

10. Ibid., 17–18.

11. J. Lewis Farley, *Two Years in Syria* (London: Saunders and Otley, 1858), 29–30.

12. Nada Sehnaoui, *L'occidentalisation de la vie quotidienne à Beyrouth, 1860–1914* (Beirut: Dār an-Nahār , 2002), 119.

13. Ibid., 120.

14. Ibid., 121.

15. Louis Lortet, *La Syrie d'aujourd'hui, voyage dans la Phénicie, le Liban et la Judée, 1867–1880* (Paris: Hachette, 1884), 73.

16. Benoît Boyer, *Conditions hygiéniques actuelles de Beyrouth et de ses environs immédiats* (Lyon: Alexandre Rey, 1897), 26.

17. Sehnaoui, *L'occidentalisation de la vie quotidienne à Beyrouth*, 126.

18. Ibid., 127.

19. Ibid., 121.

20. M. Delaroière, *Voyage en Orient* (Paris, 1836), quoted in Sehnaoui, *L'occidentalisation de la vie quotidienne à Beyrouth*, 130.

21. John Carne, *Syria, the Holy Land, Asia Minor &c. Illustrated*, 3 vols. (London: Fisher, 1936), quoted in Sehnaoui, *L'occidentalisation de la vie quotidienne à Beyrouth*, 128.

22. Farley, *Two Years in Syria*, 200–202.

23. Sehnaoui, *L'occidentalisation de la vie quotidienne à Beyrouth*, 129.

24. Charmes, *Voyages en Syrie*, 203.

25. Sehnaoui, *L'occidentalisation de la vie quotidienne à Beyrouth*, 131.

26. Ibid., 133.

27. Ibid., 136.

28. Ibid., 135.

29. Mantran, "Les débuts de la question d'Orient," in Mantran, ed., *Histoire de l'Empire Ottoman*, 454.

30. Dumont, "La période des Tanzimât," in Mantran, ed., *Histoire de l'Empire Ottoman*, 460.

31. Farley, *Two Years in Syria*, 29–30.

32. Quoted in Sehnaoui, *L'occidentalisation de la vie quotidienne à Beyrouth*, 153.

33. Guys, *Beyrout et le Liban*, 1:83–84.

34. Tamīmī and Bahjat, *Wilāyat Bayrūt*, 1:21.

35. Charmes, *Voyages en Syrie*, 240.

36. Ibid.

37. Sehnaoui, *L'occidentalisation de la vie quotidienne à Beyrouth*, 154, 158n.

38. Ibid., 164.

39. Farley, *Two Years in Syria*, 28.

40. Salām al-Khālidī, *Jawla fī al-Dhikrayāt bayn Lubnān wa Filastīn*, 25.

41. Marwan R. Buheiry, "The Rise of the City of Beirut," in Marwan R. Buheiry, *The Formation and Perception of the Modern Arab World*, ed. Lawrence I. Conrad (Princeton, N.J.: Darwin Press, 1989), 483–87.

42. Salām al-Khālidī, *Jawla fī al-Dhikrayāt bayn Lubnān wa Filastīn*, 24.

43. Abbé Antoine Raboisson, *Récit et notes d'un voyage en Palestine et en Syrie, par l'Égypte et le Sinaï* (Paris: Librairie Catholique de l'Oeuvre de Saint-Paul, 1886), 312.

44. Nicolas de Boustros, *Je me souviens* (Beirut: Librairie Antoine, 1983), 16.

45. Marwan R. Buheiry, "Notes on the Beginnings of the English Open-Air Theater at the SPC and Its Social Context," in Buheiry, *The Formation and Perception of the Modern Arab World*, ed. Conrad, 569–74.

46. Charmes, *Voyages en Syrie*, 137–38.

47. Sehnaoui, *L'occidentalisation de la vie quotidienne à Beyrouth*, 174.

48. Tamīmī and Bahjat, *Wilāyat Bayrūt*, 2:141–42.

49. Joseph G. Chami, *Le Mémorial du Liban*, 6 vols. (Beirut: Joseph G. Chami, 2002), 1:32.

50. Bassem El-Jisr, "Les plages de Beyrouth: Privatisation et communautarisation d'espaces publics," in Nabil Beyhum, ed., *Reconstruire Beyrouth: Les paris sur le possible* (Lyon: Maison de l'Orient, 1991), 76.

51. Khouri, *La médecine au Liban*, 79.

52. Ibid., 81–83.

53. Blondel, *Deux ans en Syrie et en Palestine*, 47.

54. Sehnaoui, *L'occidentalisation de la vie quotidienne à Beyrouth*, 61.

55. Khouri, *La médecine au Liban*, 84–85, 219.

56. Sehnaoui, *L'occidentalisation de la vie quotidienne à Beyrouth*, 68.

57. Ibid., 74.

58. Ibid., 69–70.

59. Khouri, *La médecine au Liban*, 106, 186–87, 193.

60. Ibid., 62.

61. Buheiry, "The Rise of the City of Beirut."

62. Sehnaoui, *L'occidentalisation de la vie quotidienne à Beyrouth*, 74.

63. Nawaf Salām, "L'émergence de la notion de citoyenneté en pays d'Islam," in *La condition libanaise: Des communautés, du citoyen et de l'état* (Beirut: Dār an-Nahār, 1998), 124ff.

64. Qāsim Amīn, *Tahrīr al-Mar'a* (Cairo: Maktabat al-Taraqqi, 1899).

65. Michael Johnson, *Class and Client in Beirut: The Sunni Muslim Community and the Lebanese State, 1840–1985* (London: Ithaca Press, 1986), 19.

66. Chevallier, *La société du mont Liban*, 272, 294–96.

CHAPTER NINE

1. Edward Atiyah, *An Arab Tells His Story: A Study in Loyalties* (London: John Murray, 1946), 11–12.

2. Ibid.

3. Letter from Father Édouard Billotet to his brother, Abbé Billotet, curate at Rozey (Franche-Comté), Beirut, 27 June 1859, quoted in Kuri, *Une histoire du Liban,* 2:225.

4. Henry Harris Jessup, *Fifty-Three Years in Syria,* 2 vols. (New York: Fleming H. Revell, 1910), 1:184–90; see also Johnson, *Class and Client in Beirut,* 19.

5. Fawaz, *Merchants and Migrants in Nineteenth-Century Beirut,* 47.

6. Guys, *Beyrout et le Liban,* 1:8–9.

7. See Henri Guys, *Esquisse de l'état politique et commercial de la Syrie* (Paris: Chez France, 1862).

8. Fawaz, *Merchants and Migrants in Nineteenth-Century Beirut,* 48, 55–56.

9. Ibid., 56, 60.

10. Ibid., 48–50.

11. Chevallier, *La société du mont Liban,* 291.

12. Fawaz, *Merchants and Migrants in Nineteenth-Century Beirut,* 51.

13. See Fernand Braudel, *The Mediterranean and the Mediterranean World in the Age of Philip II,* trans. Siân Reynolds, 2 vols. (New York: Harper & Row, 1972), 1:34–41.

14. Fawaz, *Merchants and Migrants in Nineteenth-Century Beirut,* 113.

15. Ibid., 60.

16. See Beydoun, *Identité confessionnelle et temps social.*

17. *Al-Fajr al-sādiq,* 34.

18. Salām al-Khālidī, *Jawla fī al-Dhikrayāt bayn Lubnān wa Filastīn,* 15.

19. Hanssen, "Your Beirut Is on My Desk," in Rowe and Sarkis, eds., *Projecting Beirut,* 55.

20. Johnson, *Class and Client in Beirut,* 19.

21. C. Cahen, "*Ahdāth*," in *Encyclopédie de l'Islam.*

22. Johnson, *Class and Client in Beirut,* 20.

23. Fawaz, *Merchants and Migrants in Nineteenth-Century Beirut,* 113–16.

24. Johnson, *Class and Client in Beirut,* 22.

25. Akarli, *The Long Peace,* 163–83.

26. Ibid., 40.

27. Marwan Buheiry, "Bulus Nujaym and the Grand Liban Ideal, 1908–1919," in Buheiry, ed., *Intellectual Life in the Arab East,* 62.

28. Ibid., 65–66.

29. Ibid., 79; see also Thobie, *Intérêts et impérialisme français dans l'Empire ottoman, 1895–1914,* 379–84.

30. Thobie, *Intérêts et impérialisme français dans l'Empire ottoman, 1895–1914,* 330.

31. See May Davie, *Atlas historique des orthodoxes de Beyrouth et du Mont-Liban, 1800–1940* (Tripoli, Lebanon: Publications de l'Université de Balamand, 1999).

32. Laurens, *Le royaume impossible,* 98–99.

33. Salibi, "Beirut under the Young Turks," in Berque and Chevallier, eds., *Les Arabes par leurs archives,* 202.

34. Hanssen, "Your Beirut Is on My Desk," in Rowe and Sarkis, eds., *Projecting Beirut,* 47–48.

35. See Paul Jouplain [Bulus Nujaym], *La question du Liban: Étude d'histoire diplomatique & de droit international* (Paris: A. Rousseau, 1908).

36. Hanssen, "Your Beirut Is on My Desk," in Rowe and Sarkis, eds., *Projecting Beirut,* 63.

37. Rashid Khalidi, "'Abd al-Ghanī al-ʿUraisi and *al-Mufīd:* The Press and Arab Nationalism before 1914," in Buheiry, ed., *Intellectual Life in the Arab East,* 39.

38. Hasan Kayali, *Arabs and Young Turks: Ottomanism, Arabism, and Islamism in the Ottoman Empire, 1908–1918* (Berkeley: University of California Press, 1997), 40–44, 74, 176.

39. Khalidi, "'Abd al-Ghanī al-ʿUraisi and *al-Mufīd,*" 44.

40. Fawwāz Saʿdūn, *Al-Haraka al-islāhiyya fī Bayrūt fī awākhir al-ʿasr al-ʿuthmānī* (Beirut: Dār an-Nahār, 1994), 26–27.

41. *Al-Ittihād al-ʿUthmānī,* 22 January 1912, quoted in Saʿdūn, *Al-Haraka al-islāhiyya fī Bayrūt,* 28–29.

42. Saʿdūn, *Al-Haraka al-islāhiyya fī Bayrūt,* 30–31, 34–35.

43. Ibid., 39–46.

44. Johnson, *Class and Client in Beirut,* 21.

45. Khalidi, "'Abd al-Ghanī al-ʿUraisi and *al-Mufīd,*" in Buheiry, ed., *Intellectual Life in the Arab East,* 44.

46. Saʿdūn, *Al-Haraka al-islāhiyya fī Bayrūt,* 106.

47. See the appendix in Hallāq, *Mudhakkirāt Salīm ʿAlī Salām,* 244–45.

48. Adel Ismaïl, ed., *Documents diplomatiques et consulaires relatifs à l'histoire du Liban et des pays du Proche-Orient du XVIIᵉ siècle à nos jours. Première partie: Les sources françaises* (Beirut: Éditions des Oeuvres Politiques et Historiques, 1975–), 20:106–7.

49. Saʿdūn, *Al-Haraka al-islāhiyya fī Bayrūt,* 116–17.

50. Johnson, *Class and Client in Beirut,* 64.

51. Khouri, *La médecine au Liban,* 237–50.

52. Gérard D. Khoury, *La France et l'Orient arabe: Naissance du Liban moderne, 1914–1920* (Paris: Armand Colin, 1993), 67.

53. Hallāq, *Mudhakkirat Salīm ʿAlī Salām,* 48–49.

54. Ibid., 49.

55. Khoury, *La France et l'Orient arabe,* 132–34.

CHAPTER TEN

1. Pierre Fournié and Jean-Louis Riccioli, *La France et le Proche-Orient, 1916–1946: Une chronique photographique de la présence française en Syrie et au Liban, en Palestine, au Hedjaz et en Cilicie* (Paris: Casterman, 1996), 58–59.

2. See Khoury, *La France et l'Orient arabe,* passim.

3. Ibid., 397; see also Meir Zamir, *The Formation of Modern Lebanon* (Ithaca, N.Y.: Cornell University Press, 1988), 2–11.

4. Charles-André Julien, "Léon Blum et les pays d'Outre-mer," in *Léon Blum, chef du gouvernement, 1936–1937* [Proceedings of a colloquium held in March 1965 at the Fondation Nationale des Sciences Politiques] (Paris: A. Colin, 1967), 337–90.

5. André Raymond, "La Syrie du royaume arabe à l'indépendance," in *La Syrie, d'aujourd'hui,* ed. André Raymond (Paris: Éditions du CNRS, 1980), 55–85.

6. Chevallier, "Lyon et la Syrie," in *Villes et travail en Syrie,* 73.

7. Khaled Ziyadé, "Riad al-Solh, l'enfant des villes, l'homme des mutations," *L'Orient-Express,* no. 1 (November 1995).

8. Fournié and Riccioli, *La France et le Proche-Orient,* 97.

9. Ibid.

10. Ibid., 192.

11. See Élisabeth Jacquet, "La Mission laïque française en Syrie, 1925–1929" (Master's thesis in history, Université de Paris-IV [Sorbonne], 1987).

12. Howard M. Sachar, *Europe Leaves the Middle East, 1936–1954* (New York: Alfred A. Knopf, 1972), 5–11.

13. Robert du Mesnil du Buisson, "Beyrout el-Quadimé," *Bulletin de la Société historique et archéologique de l'Orne* 40 (July–October 1921).

14. Fournié and Riccioli, *La France et le Proche-Orient,* 97.

15. Chami, *Le Mémorial du Liban,* 1:81.

16. Rondot, "Beyrouth 1930," in Beyhum, ed., *Reconstruire Beyrouth,* 71.

17. Ilyās and Jirji Jad'un, *Dalīl Suriyya* (Beirut [no publisher indicated], 1923 and 1929).

18. Davie, *Beyrouth et ses faubourgs,* 86.

19. Marwan R. Buheiry, *Beirut's Role in the Political Economy of the French Mandate, 1919–39* (Oxford: Centre for Lebanese Studies, 1986), 11.

20. M. Poupon, "La modernisation de Beyrouth," *Bulletin de l'Union économique de Syrie* 7 (1928): 23–29, and 8 (1929): 18–22, quoted in Buheiry, *Beirut's Role in the Political Economy of the French Mandate,* 11.

21. Rondot, "Beyrouth 1930," in Beyhum, ed., *Reconstruire Beyrouth,* 73.

22. See Khoury, *La France et l'Orient arabe.*

23. Ibid., 194.

24. Ibid., 193.

25. Ibid., 195.

26. Amin Mushawar, in *Revue phénicienne,* July 1919.

27. Ibrahim Tabet, in *Revue phénicienne,* December 1919.

28. [No author indicated], "Le centre de T.S.F. de Beyrouth," *Bulletin de l'Union économique de Syrie* 9 (1930): 10–11.

29. Hourani, *A History of the Arab Peoples,* 338.

30. May Seikaly, *Haifa: Transformation of an Arab Society, 1918–1939* (London: I. B. Tauris, 2002), 62–63, 68–69, 74.

31. See article in *al-Ma'rad* (6 February 1935), quoted in Buheiry, *Beirut's Role in the Political Economy of the French Mandate,* 14.

32. Quoted in ibid., 13.

33. See editorial in *Al-'Āsifa,* 15 April 1934, quoted in ibid.

34. Chami, *Le Mémorial du Liban,* 1:154–55.

35. Fournié and Riccioli, *La France et le Proche-Orient,* 172.

36. Chami, *Le Mémorial du Liban,* 1:209–10.

37. Fournié and Riccioli, *La France et le Proche-Orient,* 155.

CHAPTER ELEVEN

1. André Geiger, *Le Liban et la Syrie* (Paris: Arthaud, 1932); quoted in Chami, *Le Mémorial du Liban*, 1:129–36.

2. Jade Tabet, "La ville imparfaite: Le concept de centralité urbaine dans les projets d'aménagement et de reconstruction de Beyrouth," in Beyhum, ed., *Reconstruire Beyrouth*, 88; this article is largely reproduced in Tabet, *Beyrouth* (Paris: Institut Français d'Architecture, 2001). See also Davie, *Beyrouth*, 73, and *Beyrouth et ses faubourgs*, 88n.

3. Tabet, "La ville imparfaite," 92.

4. Davie, *Beyrouth et ses faubourgs*, 87n.

5. Rondot, "Beyrouth 1930," in Beyhum, ed., *Reconstruire Beyrouth*, 71.

6. Fournié and Riccioli, *La France et le Proche-Orient*, 169.

7. François Béguin, *Arabisances: Décor architectural et tracé urbain en Afrique du Nord, 1830–1950* (Paris: Dunod, 1983); quoted in Tabet, "La ville imparfaite," 88.

8. Tabet, "La ville imparfaite," in Beyhum, ed., *Reconstruire Beyrouth*, 88.

9. Ibid., 89.

10. Davie, *Beyrouth, 1825–1975*, 76.

11. Tabet, "La ville imparfaite," in Beyhum, ed., *Reconstruire Beyrouth*, 89.

12. See the album of photographs compiled by Houda Kassatly, *De pierres et de couleurs*.

13. *Lisān al-Ḥāl*, 26 February 1921, quoted in Davie, *Beyrouth et ses faubourgs*, 89n.

14. Davie, *Beyrouth, 1825–1975*, 89.

15. Davie, *Beyrouth et ses faubourgs*, 89.

16. Tabet, "La ville imparfaite," in Beyhum, ed., *Reconstruire Beyrouth*, 90.

17. Ibid., 91.

18. Chami, *Le Mémorial du Liban*, 1:123.

19. Farès Sassine and Ghassan Tuéni, *El Bourj, place de la liberté et porte du Levant* (Beirut: Dār an-Nahār, 2000), 116–22.

20. Davie, *Beyrouth et ses faubourgs*, 88.

21. Rondot, "Beyrouth 1930," in Beyhum, ed., *Reconstruire Beyrouth*, 71.

22. Quoted in ibid., 74.

23. Davie, *Beyrouth et ses faubourgs*, 90.

24. Ibid., 91.

25. Tabet, "La ville imparfaite," in Beyhum, ed., *Reconstruire Beyrouth*, 92; see also the photographs in Kassatly, *De pierres et de couleurs*.

26. Georges Shéhadé, *Poésies* (Paris: GLM, 1938).

27. Tabet, "La ville imparfaite," in Beyhum, ed., *Reconstruire Beyrouth*, 91–92.

28. Davie, *Beyrouth et ses faubourgs*, 91n.

29. Tabet, "La ville imparfaite," in Beyhum, ed., *Reconstruire Beyrouth*, 91.

30. Ibid.

31. Davie, *Beyrouth et ses faubourgs*, 90.

32. Ibid., 91.

33. Fournié and Riccioli, *La France et le Proche-Orient*, 185.

34. *Lisān al-Ḥāl*, 23 February 1921, quoted in Davie, *Beyrouth et ses faubourgs*, 90.

35. Rondot, "Beyrouth 1930," in Beyhum, ed., *Reconstruire Beyrouth*, 73.

36. Ibid.

37. Ibid.

CHAPTER TWELVE

1. Geiger, *Le Liban et la Syrie;* quoted in Chami, *Le Mémorial du Liban,* 1:129.

2. Ibid., 1:127.

3. Rondot, "Beyrouth 1930," in Beyhum, ed., *Reconstruire Beyrouth,* 74.

4. Ibid.

5. Ibid.

6. Chami, *Le Mémorial du Liban,* 1:207.

7. Geiger, *Le Liban et la Syrie;* quoted in Chami, *Le Mémorial du Liban,* 1:131.

8. Chami, *Le Mémorial du Liban,* 1:207.

9. Boustros, *Je me souviens,* 37; see also Fournié and Riccioli, *La France et le Proche-Orient,* 145.

10. Ibid.

11. Tamīmī and Bahjat, *Wilāyat Bayrūt,* 2:10.

12. Fouad al-Khoury, "L'industrie hôtelière au Liban," *Revue phénicienne,* August 1919; see also Albert Naccache, "L'industrie de la villégiature au Liban," *Revue phénicienne,* December 1919.

13. Jacques Tabet, *Pour faire du Liban la Suisse du Levant* (Paris, 1924); quoted in Buheiry, *Beirut's Role in the Political Economy of the French Mandate,* 6.

14. Abderrahman Slaoui, *L'Affiche orientaliste* (Casablanca: Malika Éditions, 1997); see also the portfolio by Badr al-Hājj, *Excursions en Orient: 24 reproductions d'affiches de tourisme et de voyage* (Beirut: Layali, 2002).

15. Quoted in Fournié and Riccioli, *La France et le Proche-Orient,* 149.

16. Jisr, "Les plages de Beyrouth," in Beyhum, ed., *Reconstruire Beyrouth,* 76.

17. Ibid., 77; see also Chami, *Le Mémorial du Liban,* 1:219.

18. Boustros, *Je me souviens,* 26–27.

19. Ibid., 27–34.

20. André de Fouquières, *Cinquante ans de panache* (Paris: Horay, 1951), 405, quoted in the preface to Boustros, *Je me souviens,* 9.

21. Chami, *Le Mémorial du Liban,* 1:128.

22. Boustros, *Je me souviens,* 26.

23. Chami, *Le Mémorial du Liban,* 1:128.

24. Ibid., 1:126.

25. Boustros, *Je me souviens,* 122.

26. See *Baalbeck: Les riches heures du Festival* (Beirut: Dār an-Nahār, 1994).

27. Boustros, *Je me souviens,* 49–50.

28. Chami, *Le Mémorial du Liban,* 1:127.

29. Boustros, *Je me souviens,* 65–66, 81–82.

30. Ibid., 43.

31. Fournié and Riccioli, *La France et le Proche-Orient,* 122.

32. Boustros, *Je me souviens,* 65.
33. Maud Fargeallah, *Visages d'une époque* (Paris: Cariscript, 1989), 91–104.
34. Ibid., 178–79.
35. Chami, *Le Mémorial du Liban,* 1:128.
36. Ibid., 1:126.
37. Fawaz Traboulsi, "Un amour de soie," *L'Orient-Express,* no. 6 (May 1996).
38. See Denise Ammoun, *Alexis Boutros: ALBA, le défi culturel* (Beirut: Éditions Alba, 2002).
39. On the new tradition of Arab song that was being invented in Beirut at this time by young performers who later attained great fame, such as ʿAbdel-Wahab and Umm Kulthum, see Nawaf Salam and Farès Sassine, eds., *Liban, le siècle en images* (Beirut: Dār an-Nahār, 2000), 93.
40. On the growth of sporting clubs and the organization of a league of soccer teams, see Chami, *Le Mémorial du Liban,* 1:97, 217–20.
41. Pharès Zoghbi, *À livres ouverts, une vie de souvenirs* (Beirut: Dār an-Nahār,1998), 80–81.
42. Chami, *Le Mémorial du Liban,* 1:149.

CHAPTER THIRTEEN

1. Zoghbi, *À livres ouverts,* 41–49.
2. Reproduced in Ghassan Tuéni, *Le livre de l'indépendance* (Beirut: Dār an-Nahār, 2002).
3. Salam and Sassine, *Liban, le siècle en images,* 87.
4. Chami, *Le Mémorial du Liban,* 1:106–8.
5. Ibid., 1:124.
6. Ibid., 1:124–25.
7. Buheiry, *Beirut's Role in the Political Economy of the French Mandate,* 15.
8. See Michel Chiha, *Politique intérieure* (Beirut: Éditions du Trident, 1964).
9. Johnson, *Class and Client in Beirut,* 22–26.
10. Buheiry, *Beirut's Role in the Political Economy of the French Mandate,* 15–19.
11. Ibid., 20.
12. Ibid., 21.
13. Chami, *Le Mémorial du Liban,* 1:138–39.
14. Salam and Sassine, *Liban, le siècle en images,* 109.
15. Ibid., 113.
16. Ibid., 77.
17. See Jacques Couland, *Le mouvement syndical en Liban, 1919–1946* (Paris: Éditions Sociales, 1970).
18. See Henri Lammens, *Syrie, précis historique* (Beirut: Imprimerie Catholique, 1921).
19. Quoted in Sachar, *Europe Leaves the Middle East, 1936–1954,* 202.
20. See ibid., 194–217, 282–334.
21. Eyal Zisser, *Lebanon: The Challenge of Independence* (London: I. B. Tauris, 2000), 68–82.

22. Kamal S. Salibi, *The Modern History of Lebanon* (New York: Praeger, 1965), 151–91; see also Edmond Rabbath, *La formation historique du Liban constitutionnel et politique,* 2nd ed. (Beirut: Publications de l'Université Libanaise, 1986), 455–93.

CHAPTER FOURTEEN

1. See André Chaib, "The Export Performance of a Small, Open, Developing Economy: The Lebanese Experience, 1951–74" (Ph.D. thesis, University of Michigan, 1979), quoted by Roger Owen, "The Economic History of Lebanon, 1943–1974: Its Salient Features," in Halim Barakat, ed., *Toward a Viable Lebanon* (London: Croom Helm; Washington, D.C.: Center for Contemporary Arab Studies, Georgetown University, 1988), 33.

2. Zisser, *Lebanon,* 209.

3. Ibid., 113.

4. See editorial in the 25 March 1946 issue of *Al-Hayat.*

5. Zisser, *Lebanon,* 121.

6. Ibid., 116, 121, 123.

7. Ibid., 112, 119.

8. Cable from Sir William Evelyn Houstoun-Boswall to the Foreign Office, 5 October 1949, quoted in ibid., 144.

9. Fawaz Traboulsi, "Identités et solidarités croisées dans les conflits du Liban contemporaine" (Doctoral thesis in history, Université de Paris-VIII, 1993), 267.

10. Ibid., 267–68.

11. Ibid.

12. Ibid.

13. Ibid., 278–97.

14. *The Economist,* 28 April 1951, quoted in Zisser, *Lebanon,* 199.

15. Ibid., 229.

16. *L'Orient,* 10 March 1949.

17. Zisser, *Lebanon,* 199.

18. A possibly apocryphal remark, quoted by Carolyn Gates, *The Merchant Republic of Lebanon: Rise of an Open Economy* (London: Centre for Lebanese Studies/I. B. Tauris, 1998), xv.

19. Zisser, *Lebanon,* 171.

20. Ibid., 172.

21. Ibid., 173.

22. See Gates, *The Merchant Republic of Lebanon,* 91–93.

23. Traboulsi, "Identités et solidarités croisées," 269–70.

24. Zisser, *Lebanon,* 174.

25. Ibid., 159.

26. Traboulsi, "Identités et solidarités croisées," 271.

27. Ibid., 273.

28. Ibid.

29. Chami, *Le Mémorial du Liban,* 2:429.

30. Traboulsi, "Identités et solidarités croisées," 271.

31. Ibid., 270.

32. Ibid.

33. Claude Dubar and Salim Nasr, *Les classes sociales au Liban* (Paris: Presses de la Fondation Nationale des Sciences Politiques, 1976), 71.

34. Kamal S. Salibi, *Cross Roads to Civil War: Lebanon, 1958–1976* (Delmar, N.Y.: Caravan Books, 1976), 29–30; see also Rabbath, *La formation historique du Liban constitutionnel et politique*, 573, and Traboulsi, "Identités et solidarités croisées," 401.

35. Clement Henry Moore, "Le système bancaire libanais: Les substituts financiers d'un ordre politique," *Maghreb-Machrek* 99 (1983): 30–46; see also Dubar and Nasr, *Les classes sociales au Liban*, 70.

36. See Boutros Labaki, "L'évolution du rôle économique de l'agglomeration de Beyrouth, 1960–1977," in Dominique Chevallier, ed., *L'espace social de la ville arabe* (Paris: Maisonneuve et Larose, 1979), 215–44.

37. Owen, "The Economic History of Lebanon, 1943–1974," in Barakat, ed., *Toward a Viable Lebanon*, 35–37.

38. Samir Khalaf and Per Kongstad, *Hamra of Beirut: A Case of Rapid Urbanization* (Leiden: Brill, 1973), 31–33, 111–13.

39. This according to Ahmad Said, one of the producers of "The Voice of the Arabs" [a half-hour radio program first broadcast 4 July 1953] for Cairo Radio, in an interview with the author.

40. Salibi, *Cross Roads to Civil War*, 29–30.

41. Ibid.

42. See Ammoun, *Alexis Boutros.*

CHAPTER FIFTEEN

1. Asma Freiha and Viviane Ghanem, *Les Libanais et la vie au Liban de l'Indépendance à la guerre, 1943–1975* (Beirut: Dār Assayad, 1992), 523.

2. See Michael Bar-Zohar and Eitan Haber, *The Quest for the Red Prince* (New York: Morrow, 1983).

3. See the illustrated plates in Nāsir al-Saʿīd, *Tārikh āl Saʿūd* (Beirut: [no publisher indicated], 1978).

4. Freiha and Ghanem, *Les Libanais et la vie au Liban*, 497–515.

5. See "Quand la politique faisait rêver," special report of *L'Orient-Express*, no. 1 (November 1995).

6. Claude Eddé, "Fragments expurgés des carnets d'une jeune fille pas très rangée," in "Ah! qu'il était joli le Liban de papa," special report of *L'Orient-Express*, no. 14 (January 1997).

7. Freiha and Ghanem, *Les Libanais et la vie au Liban*, 518.

8. Ibid., 416–17.

9. See Muhammad Suwayd, *Yā fuʾādī* (Beirut: Dār an-Nahar, 1994).

10. See Jean-Claude Boulos, *La Télé, quelle histoire!* (Beirut: Éditions FMA, 1996).

11. Freiha and Ghanem, *Les Libanais et la vie au Liban*, 233.

CHAPTER SIXTEEN

1. See Farouk Mardam-Bey, *La cuisine de Zyriab* (Arles: Actes Sud, 1999).

2. Freiha and Ghanem, *Les Libanais et la vie au Liban de l'Indépendance à la guerre*, 414.

3. I am indebted to Melhem Shaul's unpublished contribution to the conference "The Lebanese System: A Critical Reassessment," held in Beirut on 18–19 May 2001 under the sponsorship of the Fondation Michel Chiha and the Center for Behavioral Studies.

4. Omar Boustany, "Berytian Graffitis," in "Ah! qu'il était joli le Liban de papa," Special report of *L'Orient-Express*, no. 14 (January 1997).

5. Khalaf and Kongstad, *Hamra of Beirut*, 31, 33, 110–11.

6. Ibid., 4, 78.

7. Ibid., 48, 97–98, 103, 134.

8. Ibid., 127.

9. Omar Boustany, "Les dames du temps jadis," in "Ah! qu'il était joli le Liban de papa," Special report of *L'Orient-Express*, no. 14 (January 1997).

10. See Max-Pol Fouchet's account, quoted in Sassine and Tuéni, *El Bourj*, 125.

11. Boustany, "Les dames du temps jadis," in "Ah! qu'il était joli le Liban de papa."

12. André Bourgey, "La guerre et ses conséquences géographiques au Liban," *Annales de géographie* 94 (1985): 1–37.

13. Boustany, "Berytian Graffitis," in "Ah! qu'il était joli le Liban de papa."

14. Freiha and Ghanem, *Les Libanais et la vie au Liban de l'Indépendance à la guerre*, 408–9.

15. Chami, *Le Mémorial du Liban*, 3:276–77, 301.

16. Ibid., 3:258–59.

17. Freiha and Ghanem, *Les Libanais et la vie au Liban de l'Indépendance à la guerre*, 523.

18. Ibid., 531.

19. See *Baalbeck: Les riches heures du Festival.*

CHAPTER SEVENTEEN

1. Quoted in Chami, *Le Mémorial du Liban*, 3:160–61.

2. *L'Orient*, 24 October 1954.

3. Chami, *Le Mémorial du Liban*, 3:161.

4. Tabet, "La ville imparfaite," in Beyhum, ed., *Reconstruire Beyrouth*, 93–95; see also Michel Terrasse's article on Écochard in *Dictionnaire des architectes* (Paris: Encyclopaedia Universalis/Albin Michel, 1999).

5. Tabet, "La ville imparfaite," in Beyhum, ed., *Reconstruire Beyrouth*, 93; see also Marlène Ghorayeb, "The Work and Influence of Michel Écochard in Lebanon," in Rowe and Sarkis, eds., *Projecting Beirut*, 107.

6. Samir Abdulac, "Damas: Les années Écochard (1932–1982)," *Les Cahiers de la Recherche architecturale*, nos. 10–11 (April 1982).

7. See Michel Écochard, *Casablanca: Le roman d'une ville* (Paris: Éditions de Paris, 1955).

8. Abdulac, "Damas: Les années Écochard," 42.

9. Ghorayeb, "The Work and Influence of Michel Écochard in Lebanon," in Rowe and Sarkis, eds., *Projecting Beirut*, 119.

10. Khalaf and Kongstad, *Hamra of Beirut*, 17.

11. Tabet, "La ville imparfaite," in Beyhum, ed., *Reconstruire Beyrouth*, 97.

12. Tabet, *Beyrouth*, 22.

13. Ibid., 23.

14. Ibid., 25.

15. See volume 3 of Chami, *Le Mémorial du Liban*, passim.

16. Jade Tabet, "From Colonial Style to Regional Revivalism: Modern Architecture in Lebanon and the Problem of Cultural Identity," in Rowe and Sarkis, eds., *Projecting Beirut*, 88.

17. Tabet, *Beyrouth*, 24–25.

18. Interview with Jade Tabet.

19. Tabet, "From Colonial Style to Regional Revivalism," in Rowe and Sarkis, eds., *Projecting Beirut*, 90–91.

20. Tabet, *Beyrouth*, 24–25.

21. Khalaf and Kongstad, *Hamra of Beirut*, 21–22.

22. Ibid., 26–27.

23. See Hashim Sarkis, *Circa 1958: Le Liban à travers les photos et les plans de Constantinos Doxiadis* (Beirut: Dār an-Nahār, 2003).

24. Tabet, "La ville imparfaite," in Beyhum, ed., *Reconstruire Beyrouth*, 97.

25. Michael C. Hudson, *The Precarious Republic: Political Modernization in Lebanon* (New York: Random House, 1968), 312.

26. See Georges Riachi, "The City of Beirut, Its Origin and Evolution," in Berger, ed., *The New Metropolis in the Arab World*, 103–14.

27. Tabet, "La ville imparfaite," in Beyhum, ed., *Reconstruire Beyrouth*, 101.

28. See Terrasse, "Écochard," in *Dictionnaire des architectes*.

29. Quoted in Tabet, *Beyrouth*, 30.

30. Presentation of the Master Plan for the Development of Beirut and Its Suburb by M. Écochard (1963), quoted in Tabet, "La ville imparfaite," in Beyhum, ed., *Reconstruire Beyrouth*, 102.

31. Tabet, *Beyrouth*, 31.

32. Tabet, "La ville imparfaite," in Beyhum, ed., *Reconstruire Beyrouth*, 102.

33. Tabet, *Beyrouth*, 23.

34. Ibid., 32.

35. Tabet, "From Colonial Style to Regional Revivalism," in Rowe and Sarkis, eds., *Projecting Beirut*, 97.

36. Ibid.

37. Helmut Ruppert, "Beyrouth, une ville d'Orient marquée par l'Occident," translated and edited by Éric Verdeil and Laurent Combes, *Les Cahiers du Cermoc* 21 (1999): 92–93.

38. Tabet, "From Colonial Style to Regional Revivalism," in Rowe and Sarkis, eds., *Projecting Beirut*, 100.

39. Tabet, "La ville imparfaite," in Beyhum, ed., *Reconstruire Beyrouth*, 104.

40. See Bourgey, "La guerre et ses conséquences géographiques au Liban."

41. Albert Hourani, "Visions of Lebanon," in Barakat, ed., *Toward a Viable Lebanon*, 5.

42. Bourgey, "La guerre et ses conséquences géographiques au Liban."

43. Ibid.

44. Nabil Beyhum, "Espaces éclatés, espaces dominés: Étude de la recomposition des espaces publics centraux de Beyrouth de 1975 à 1990" (Doctoral thesis, Université de Lyon-II, 1995), 114.

45. Tabet, "La ville imparfaite," in Beyhum, ed., *Reconstruire Beyrouth*, 105.

46. Hourani, "Visions of Lebanon," in Barakat, ed., *Toward a Viable Lebanon*, 5.

47. See Youssef Courbage and Philippe Fargues, *La situation démographique au Liban* (Beirut: Publications de l'Université Libanaise, 1974).

48. Beyhum, "Espaces éclatés, espaces dominés," 116.

49. Tabet, "La ville imparfaite," in Beyhum, ed., *Reconstruire Beyrouth*, ed., 105.

50. See Marthelot, "Une ville remplit son site: Beyrouth."

51. "Grand Beyrouth, trop grand Beyrouth," Special Report of *L'Orient-Express*, no. 4 (April 1996).

52. Beyhum, "Espaces éclatés, espaces dominés," 120.

53. Ibid., 121.

54. See Catherine Paix, "La portée spatiale des activités tertiaires de commandement économique au Liban," *Revue Tiers-Monde* 16, no. 61 (1975); also André Bourgey, "L'évolution du centre de Beyrouth de 1960 à 1977," in Chevallier, *L'espace social de la ville arabe*, 244–78; and Chadia Sinno, "Évolution des structures urbaines du centre-ville de Beyrouth" (Master's thesis in urban studies, Université de Paris-VIII, 1986).

55. Chami, *Le Mémorial du Liban*, 3:135.

56. Beyhum, "Espaces éclatés, espaces dominés," 121.

57. Ibid., 113.

58. Ruppert, "Beyrouth, une ville d'Orient marquée par l'Occident," 67–80.

59. Ibid., 111–12.

CHAPTER EIGHTEEN

1. See Elizabeth Picard, *Liban, État de discorde: Des fondations aux guerres fratricides* (Paris: Flammarion, 1988).

2. See Maxime Rodinson, "La dimension religieuse du conflit libanais, ou qu'est-ce qu'une communauté religieuse libanaise?" in Bassma Kodmani-Darwish, ed., *Le Liban—Espoirs et Réalités* (Paris: Institut Français des Relations Internationales, 1987), 73, reprinted in Rodinson, *L'Islam: Politique et croyance* (Paris: Fayard, 1993).

3. See Salibi, *A House of Many Mansions*, passim.

4. See Nawaf Salam, "Les communautés religieuses au Liban," *Social Compass* 35 (1988): 455–64; reprinted in Salam, *La condition libanaise*.

5. H. Fleisch, "The Eastern Dialects," in *Encyclopedia of Islam*, new edition, 11 vols. and supplement (Leiden: Brill, 1960–2004), 1:574–78; also Samia Naïm-Sanbar, *Le parler arabe de Rās-Beyrouth, 'Ayn al Muraysa: La diversité phonologique, étude socio-linguistique* (Paris: Geuthner, 1985).

6. Chevallier, *La société du mont Liban*, 66–79; see also Robert Cresswell, "Parenté et pro-

priété foncière dans la montagne libanaise," *Études rurales*, no. 40 (October–December 1970): 7–79.

7. Chevallier, *La société du mont Liban*, 150–56.

8. Traboulsi, "Identités et solidarités croisées," 7–8.

9. Beyhum, "Espaces éclatés, espaces dominés," 11.

10. Salibi, *A House of Many Mansions*, 55.

11. Salam, "Les communautés religieuses au Liban."

12. Rodinson, "La dimension religieuse du conflit libanais"; see also Chevallier, *La société du mont Liban*, xi.

13. Rodinson, "La dimension religieuse du conflit libanais."

14. See Beydoun, *Identité confessionnelle et temps social*.

15. Salam, "Les communautés religieuses au Liban."

16. Rabbath, *La formation historique du Liban constitutionnel et politique*, 65, 138.

17. See the essays on the millet system during the nineteenth century in Benjamin Braude and Bernard Lewis, eds., *Christians and Jews in the Ottoman Empire: The Functioning of a Plural Society*, 2 vols. (New York: Holmes & Meier, 1982), 1:261–400; also, in the same collection, Samir Khalaf, "Communal Conflict in Nineteenth-Century Lebanon," 2:107–34.

18. Akarli, *The Long Peace*, 148–49.

19. Edmond Rabbath, *La Constitution libanaise: Origines, textes et commentaires* (Beirut: Université Libanaise, 1982), 517–18.

20. Rabbath, *La formation historique du Liban constitutionnel et politique*, 616.

21. Nawaf Salām, "The Institution of the Presidency in Elections in Lebanon," in Nadim Shehadi and Bridget Harney, eds., *Politics and the Economy in Lebanon* (Oxford: Centre for Lebanese Studies, 1989), 69.

22. Michel Chiha, "Philosophie du confessionalisme au Liban," in Chiha, *Politique intérieure*, 303–6.

23. Hourani, "Ideologies of the Mountain and the City," in Owen, ed., *Essays on the Crisis in Lebanon*, 35.

24. Rabbath, *La Constitution libanaise*, 179, 181.

25. Hudson, *The Precarious Republic*, 214.

26. Ibid., 232.

27. Beydoun, *Identité confessionnelle et temps social*, 520; see also Salibi, *A House of Many Mansions*, 126–27.

28. Salibi, *A House of Many Mansions*, 87–107.

29. Hourani, "Ideologies of the Mountain and the City," in Owen, ed., *Essays on the Crisis in Lebanon*, 39; see also Salibi, *A House of Many Mansions*, 167–81.

30. Chevallier, *La société du mont Liban*, 291.

31. Waddāh Sharāra, *Al-Silm al-ahlī al-bārid, Lubnān, al-mujtamaʿ wa-l-dawla, 1964–1967* (Beirut: Dār an-Nahār, 1980), 390.

32. Zisser, *Lebanon*, 202.

33. *Al-Hayat*, 15 July 1952.

34. Rabbath, *La formation historique du Liban constitutionnel et politique*, 560; see also Hudson, *The Precarious Republic*, 96.

35. Irene Gendzier, "The Declassified Lebanon, 1948–1958: Elements of Continuity and Contrast in US Policy toward Lebanon," in Barakat, ed., *Toward a Viable Lebanon*, 178–79.

36. Chevallier, *La société du mont Liban*, 24.

37. See Wilbur Eveland, *Ropes of Sand: America's Failure in the Middle East* (New York: W. W. Norton, 1980), especially 252, 266.

38. See Nawaf Salam, "L'insurrection de 1958 au Liban" (Doctoral thesis in history, Université de Paris-IV [Sorbonne], 1979).

39. See Hudson, *The Precarious Republic*, 290; also Traboulsi, "Identités et solidarités croisées," 374.

40. See Malcolm H. Kerr, *The Arab Cold War: Gamal 'Abd al-Nasir and His Rivals, 1958–1970*, 3rd ed. (New York: Oxford University Press, 1971).

41. Rabbath, *La formation historique du Liban constitutionnel et politique*, 581.

42. Samir Kassir and Farouk Mardam-Bey, *Intinéraires de Paris à Jérusalem: La France et le conflit israélo-arabe*, 2 vols. (Paris: Revue des Études Palestiniennes, 1992–93), 2:35–43.

43. Rabbath, *La formation historique du Liban constitutionnel et politique*, 570.

44. Sharāra, *Al-Silm al-ahlī*, 60–61.

45. Ibid., 443.

46. Ibid., 87.

47. Johnson, *Class and Client in Beirut*, 142–43.

48. See Sharāra, *Al-Silm al-ahlī*, 49n.; also Frank Stoakes, "The Supervigilantes: The Lebanese Kataeb Party as a Builder, Surrogate, and Defender of the State," *Middle Eastern Studies* 11, no. 3 (October 1975): 215–36; and Traboulsi, "Identités et solidarités croisées," 390.

49. Zisser, *Lebanon*, 215.

50. Ibid., 216.

51. Charles Hélou, *Mémoires, 1964–1965* (Araya, Lebanon: Imprimerie Catholique al-Araya, 1984), 105–30.

52. See Kerr, *The Arab Cold War*, 98–100.

53. Interview with the author.

CHAPTER NINETEEN

1. Bishara Menassa, a senior civil servant on the staff of the Chamber of Deputies who wrote under the pseudonym Benassar, recalls Chamoun's return that day to the corridors of power, making the rounds of lawmakers' offices; see his memoir *Anatomie d'une guerre et d'une occupation* (Paris: Galilée, 1978), 45.

2. Sharāra, *Al-Silm al-ahlī al-bārid*, 457.

3. Wade R. Goria, *Sovereignty and Leadership in Lebanon, 1943–1976* (London: Ithaca Press, 1985), 89–90.

4. Frederic C. Hof, *Galilee Divided: The Israel-Lebanon Frontier, 1916–1984* (Boulder, Colo.: Westview Press, 1985), 66–67.

5. Ibid., 68.

6. Maxime Rodinson, *Israël et le refus arabe: 75 ans d'histoire* (Paris: Éditions du Seuil, 1968), 218.

7. Rosemary Sayigh, *Palestinians: From Peasants to Revolutionaries* (London: Zed Press, 1979), 130–36.

8. Alan Hart, *Arafat: Terrorist or Peacemaker?* (London: Sidgwick and Jackson, 1984), 214–15.

9. Hof, *Galilee Divided*, 46–47, 74.

10. Bard E. O'Neill, *Armed Struggle in Palestine: A Political-Military Analysis* (Boulder, Colo.: Westview Press, 1978), 242.

11. Xavier Baron, *Les Palestiniens, un peuple,* 2nd ed. (Paris: Le Sycomore, 1984), 189; see also Hof, *Galilee Divided*, 72.

12. Hof, *Galilee Divided*, 17–21; see also Rashid Khalidi, *Under Siege: PLO Decisionmaking during the 1982 War* (New York: Columbia University Press, 1986), 21.

13. Traboulsi, "Identités et solidarités croisées," 410.

14. Sharāra, *Al-Silm al-ahlī al-bārid,* 742n.; see also Traboulsi, "Identités et solidarités croisées," 398.

15. Sayigh, *Palestinians,* 156–171; see also Rex Brynen, *Sanctuary and Survival: The PLO in Lebanon* (Boulder, Colo.: Westview Press, 1990), 52.

16. Baron, *Les Palestiniens,* 193ff.

17. Ibid., 198, 201–2.

18. Ibid., 202; see also Brynen, *Sanctuary and Survival,* 58–59.

19. Goria, *Sovereignty and Leadership in Lebanon,* 126–27.

20. Mahmoud Riad, "Au coeur du conflit," interview in *Revue d'études palestiniennes* 19 (Spring 1986): 7–16.

21. See Georges Kossaifi, "Contribution à l'étude démographique de la population palestinienne," 2 vols. (Doctoral thesis, Université de Paris-I, 1976); also Salma Husseini, "Redistribution de la population du Liban pendant la guerre civile (1975–1988)" (Doctoral thesis, École des Hautes Études en Sciences Sociales, Paris, 1992), and her article "Les mouvements de population palestinienne durant la guerre civile libanaise," *Revue des études palestiniennes* 11, no. 50 (1994): 11–124.

22. See Bourgey, "L'évolution du centre de Beyrouth de 1960 à 1977," in Chevallier, ed., *L'espace social de la ville arabe,* 244–78.

23. See *Fiches du monde arabe (Beyrouth),* no. 933 (19 April 1978).

24. Michael C. Hudson, "The Palestinian Factor in the Lebanese Civil War," *Middle East Journal* 32 (1978): 263.

25. Kassir and Mardam-Bey, *Intinéraires de Paris à Jérusalem,* 2:68–69.

26. See Stoakes, "The Supervigilantes."

27. Johnson, *Class and Client in Beirut,* 83.

28. See Kamal Joumblatt [with the assistance of Philippe Lapousterle], *Pour le Liban* (Paris: Stock: 1977); also Nawaf Salam, "Lecture dans le miroir des Mémoires," in *Mythe et politique au Liban: Trois essais* (Beirut: Éditions FMA, 1987).

29. Hudson, *The Precarious Republic,* 178–200.

30. Sharāra, *Al-Silm al-ahlī al-bārid,* 634.

31. See Mahdī ʿĀmil [pseud. Hassan Hamdan], *Muqaddimāt nadhariyya li-dirāsat athar al-fikr al-ishtirākī fī harakat al-taharrur al-watanī al-ʿarabiyya* [Theoretical Prolegomena to

the Study of the Influence of Socialist Thought on the Arab National Liberation Movement], 2 vols. (Beirut: Dār al-Farābī, 1972).

32. See Muhsin Ibrahīm, *Limādhā Munadhammat al-ishitirākiyyīn al-lubnāniyyīn?* [Why the Organization of Lebanese Socialists?] (Beirut: [no publisher indicated], 1970).

33. See [Anon.], *Al-ʿAmal al-ishitirākī wa tanāqudāt al-wadʿ al-lubnānī* [Socialist Action and the Contradictions of the Lebanese Situation] (Beirut: [no publisher indicated], 1969). The authors, identified only as "Ishitirākiyyūn lubnāniyyūn" [Lebanese Socialists], were in fact Waddah Sharāra and Fawaz Traboulsi.

34. Halim Barakat, "Social Factors Influencing Attitudes of University Students in Lebanon towards the Palestinian Resistance Movement," *Journal of Palestine Studies* 1 (1971): 87–112.

35. Brynen, *Sanctuary and Survival*, 66.

36. Baron, *Les Palestiniens*, 303.

37. Boutros Labaki, "Rapports de force intercommunautaires et genèse des conflits internes au Liban" (unpublished paper, annual meeting of Violence and Conflict in Divided Societies section of the European Consortium for Political Research, Fribourg, March 1983).

38. Johnson, *Class and Client in Beirut*, 33.

39. Labaki, "Rapports de force intercommunautaires et genèse des conflits internes au Liban."

40. Dubar and Nasr, *Les classes sociales au Liban*, 276.

41. Traboulsi, "Identités et solidarités croisées," 425.

42. Beyhum, "Espaces éclatés, espaces dominés," 124; see also Fuad I. Khuri, *From Village to Suburb: Order and Change in Greater Beirut* (Chicago: University of Chicago Press, 1975).

43. Beyhum, "Espaces éclatés, espaces dominés," 125.

44. See Bourgey, "La guerre et ses conséquences géographiques au Liban."

45. "Beyhum, Espaces éclatés, espaces dominés," 125.

CHAPTER TWENTY

1. See Ghassan Salamé, *Le théâtre politique au Liban (1968–1973): Approche idéologique et esthétique* (Beirut: Dār al-Mashriq, 1974).

2. See Agnès Favier, "Logiques de l'engagement et modes de contestation au Liban: Genèse et éclatement d'une génération de militants intellectuels (1958–1975)" (Doctoral thesis, Institut d'Études Politiques d'Aix-en-Provence, 2004).

3. Dubar and Nasr, *Les classes sociales au Liban*, 328.

4. See Barakat, "Social Factors Influencing Attitudes of University Students in Lebanon"; also J. Jabra and N. Jabbara, "Political Culture and the Rural-Urban Dichotomy in Lebanon," *Political Science Review* (Jaipur, India) 19, no. 3 (July–September 1980), containing the results of a poll of secondary school students conducted in 1969.

5. Sharāra, *Al-Silm al-ahli al-bārid*, 767.

6. Traboulsi, "Identités et solidarités croisées," 413.

7. See Charles Winslow, *Lebanon: War and Politics in a Fragmented Society* (New York: Routledge, 1996), 164–65.—Trans.

8. Hourani, "Ideologies of the Mountain and the City," in Owen, ed., *Essays on the Crisis in Lebanon,* 40.

9. Traboulsi, "Identités et solidarités croisées," 444.

10. Goria, *Sovereignty and Leadership in Lebanon,* 142–46.

11. Walid Khalidi, *Conflict and Violence in Lebanon: Confrontation in the Middle East* (Cambridge, Mass.: Center for International Affairs, Harvard University, 1979), 73.

12. Johnson, *Class and Client in Beirut,* 149.

13. Fouad Ajami, *The Vanished Imam: Musa al-Sadr and the Shia of Lebanon* (Ithaca, N.Y.: Cornell University Press, 1986), 48–49; on the sacred obligation of Shi'is to bear arms, see 171–72.

14. Traboulsi, "Identités et solidarités croisées," 17–18, 28–30.

15. See Jabra and Jabbara, "Political Culture and the Rural-Urban Dichotomy in Lebanon."

16. Goria, *Sovereignty and Leadership in Lebanon,* 157–172.

17. Philippe Rondot, *Le Proche-Orient à la recherche de la paix, 1973–1982* (Paris: Presses Universitaires de France, 1982), 68.

18. Juzīf Abu Khalīl, *Qissat al-mawārina fī al-harb: Sīra dhātīyyah* (Beirut: Sharikat al-Matbūʿāt lil-Tawzīʿ wa-al-Nashr, 1990), 17–18, 27.

19. Samir Kassir, *La Guerre du Liban: De la dissension nationale au conflit régional (1975–1982),* 2nd ed. (Paris and Beirut: Karthala/Centre d'Études et de Recherches sur le Moyen-Orient Contemporain, 2000), 76–79.

20. See Stoakes, "The Supervigilantes"; also Karim Pakradouni, *La paix manquée: Le mandat d'Elias Sarkis, 1976–1982* (Beirut: Éditions FMA, 1983), 100; and Abu Khalil, *Qissat al-mawārina fī al-harb,* 18.

21. Traboulsi, "Identités et solidarités croisées," 454.

22. Johnson, *Class and Client in Beirut,* 180.

23. Ibid., 178; see also Khalidi, *Conflict and Violence in Lebanon,* 99.

24. Johnson, *Class and Client in Beirut,* 182.

25. Kassir, *La Guerre du Liban,* 95–102.

26. On all of the events of the war between 1975 and 1982, see ibid.

GLOSSARY OF ARABIC AND TURKISH TERMS

Arabic words are given here with long vowels, together with words transcribed from the spoken language that regularly figure in local toponyms and patronymics. The origin of Turkish and gallicized terms, and also of abbreviated Arabic forms, is indicated in parentheses by a complete transcription.

Abdul or *Abdül* (*'Abd al-*)	slave of (epithet attached to names of gods)
abu (abū)	father of
ajānib	Western foreigners
'asabiyya	esprit de corps, solidarity
'ayn	source, spring
bāb	gate
balad	country or land; in Beirut used also to refer to the central business and entertainment district
bey	title accorded to notables and high officials
Bilād al-Shām	the country of Syria
bin or *ibn*	son of
burj	tower
dār	house, abode
dhimma	pact of protection
dhimmī	a member of a protected Christian or Jewish community under the Ottoman Empire

dīn	religion
dīwān	counsel, advice; by extension, a municipal or provincial council
drogman or *dragoman*	a consular official (from *turjumān,* "interpreter" or "translator"); also a fictive office accorded to clients of foreign powers
effendi	title of nobility accorded particularly to ʿulamas and men of letters
emaneh (amāna)	Ottoman system of tax collection administered by government officials
emir (amīr)	chief, or prince; title borne by the members of noble families of the highest rank
franj (sing. *franji*)	Franks; and, by extension, Europeans in general
furn	oven, bakery
hakawati	traditional storyteller
hammam	Arab baths
harakat	period of unrest in the Mountain between 1845 and 1860
haret (hārāt)	neighborhood
Hatt-i sherif	the Gülhane imperial edict of 1839
hawsh (pl.)	the courtyard of a house (and specifically the small apartments arranged around it); or any vacant lot and the makeshift lodgings that have been illegally built on it
hayy	neighborhoods
iltizām	tax farm
ishitirākiyya	a version of socialism devised by Ahmad Faris al-Shidyaq
īwān	central courtyard in traditional nineteenth-century homes
izar	black material used to make the veil worn by women in traditional Islamic societies
jabal	mountain, massif
jabali	mountain people
jamʿiyya	association, company
Jamʿiyyat al-Maqāsid al-khayriyya al-islamiyya	
	Society of Islamic Charitable Works
jisr	bridge
jizya	head or poll tax
jund (pl. *ajnād*)	military district
karakol	police station
karm	vine
khan	commercial inn or hotel comprising rooms and shops ranged around an interior courtyard

madīna	city
Maghrib	the Arabic-speaking countries lying to the west of Egypt and to the north of the Sahara
mahalla (mahallāt)	neighborhood
Majlis al-Shūra	advisory council
Maqāsid	*See* Jam'iyatt al-Maqasid
mār	saint (from the Syriac, used always with the saint's name)
marfa'	port
marj	meadow, plain
Mashriq	the Arabic-speaking countries lying to the east of Egypt and north of the Arabian Peninsula (the Levant)
millet (milla)	non-Islamic religious community enjoying official recognition in the Ottoman Empire
minet (mīnā')	port
mu'allim	master
mufti	interpreter of the canon law, often serving as the religious leader in a particular city
mukhabarat	intelligence services, secret police
mukhtār	communal officials under the Ottoman regime whose authority survived into the Mandate period
muqāti'ji	farmer general, i.e. official of a *muqāta'a* (tax farm)
muqātila (pl.)	soldiers, troops
murābit	holy warrior
mutasallim	governor of a city or an administrative district
mutasarrif	governor of a provincial district *(sanjak);* title of the governor of Mount Lebanon after 1861
mutasarrifiyya	administrative district endowed with some measure of autonomy; name of the district of Mount Lebanon after 1861
nahda	rebirth, revival; used particularly in connection with the Arab cultural renaissance of the nineteenth century
nahr	stream, river
naqīb al-ashrāf	syndic of the descendants of the Prophet
osmanlilik	the notion of a national Ottoman identity shared by the peoples of the Empire in the nineteenth century
pasha	title given to Turkish ministers, provincial governors, generals, and admirals
qabaday (pl. *qabadayat*)	thug, gangster, strongman

qāḍī	judge
qahwajī	café proprietor
qāʾimaqāmat	Arabic name for Ottoman system of sectarian power-sharing (from the Franco-Turkish term *caimacamat*)
qannās	sniper
qasaba	citadel (anglicized as "casbah," referring to the native Arab quarter of a North African city)
qawwās	consular guard (literally "marksman")
al-Qishla	military barracks on Qantari Hill, originally housing the seventh regiment of the Ottoman army; later the Grand Sérail and the Prime Minister's residence
raml	sand
ramleh	reddish, loosely cemented sandstone
rās	cape, promontory
ribāt	settlement on the borders of the territory of Islam
sajʿ (sajaʿ)	a style of rhymed and cadenced speech or writing (literally, the cooing of a dove), associated mainly with prose compositions
sanjak	district of a province (*vilayet*)
shariʿa	Islamic holy law
sharīf (pl. *ashrāf*)	from *sharaf* (honor), a term used to refer to notables claiming descent from the Prophet
shaykh (sheikh)	title borne by ʿulamas and by members of certain important families
suq (sūq)	market
tafarnuj	Westernization (literally, acting like Europeans)
tāʾifa (pl. *tawāʾif*)	a group or grouping
Tanzimat	the reorganization of economic and legal affairs in the aftermath of the Gülhane decree, issued in 1839, shortly after the death of Mahmud II; literally, a reordering
tell (tall)	hill, slope
timar	assignment of land in exchange for services rendered, particularly service in the cavalry
tiryākī	drug addict
vilayet (wilāya)	province
wadi (wādī)	vale, valley
wālī (sing. and pl.)	provincial governor
waqf	property whose income is assigned in perpetuity to charitable purposes

watan	homeland or country (equivalent to the French *patrie)*
zaʿīm (pl. *zuʿamāʾ)*	socially or politically prominent patron
zāwiya	shrine, mausoleum
zuqaq (zuqāq)	alley, back street
zuʿrān (sing. *azʿar)*	hoodlums

BIBLIOGRAPHY

DIPLOMATIC RECORDS, TRAVEL NARRATIVES, AND MEMOIRS

Armagnac, Alfred, Baron d'. *Nézib et Beyrout: Souvenirs d'Orient de 1833 à 1841*. Paris: J. Laisné, 1844.

Arvieux, Laurent d'. *Mémoires du chevalier d'Arvieux ... contenant ses voyages à Constantinople, dans l'Asie, la Syrie, la Palestine, l'Égypte, et la Barbarie....* Paris: C. J. B. Delespine, 1735.

Atiyah, Edward. *An Arab Tells His Story: A Study in Loyalties*. London: John Murray, 1946.

Barrès, Maurice. *Une enquête aux pays du Levant*. 2 vols. Paris: Plon-Nourrit, 1923.

Benassar [pseud. Bishara Menassa]. *Anatomie d'une guerre et d'une occupation*. Paris: Galilée, 1978.

Blondel, Édouard. *Deux ans en Syrie et en Palestine (1838–1839)*. Paris: P. Dufart, 1840.

Boulos, Jean-Claude. *La Télé, quelle histoire!* Beirut: Éditions FMA, 1996.

Boustros, Nicolas de. *Je me souviens*. Beirut: Librairie Antoine, 1983.

Boyer, Benoît. *Conditions hygiéniques actuelles de Beyrouth et de ses environs immédiats*. Lyon: Alexandre Rey, 1897.

Burkhardt, John Lewis. *Travels in Syria and the Holy Land*. London: John Murray, 1822.

Carne, John. *Syria, the Holy Land, Asia Minor &c. Illustrated*. 3 vols. London: Fisher, 1936.

Catroux, Georges. *Dans la bataille de la Méditerranée: Égypte, Levant, Afrique du Nord, 1940–1944*. Paris: R. Juilliard, 1947.

Charmes, Gabriel. *Voyages en Syrie, impressions et souvenirs*. Paris: Calmann-Lévy, 1891.

Delaroière, M. *Voyage en Orient*. Paris, 1836.

Dimashqiyyeh, Nadīm. *Mahattāt fī hayātī al-diblūmāsiyya*. Beirut: Dār an-Nahār, 1995.

Al-Fajr al-sādiq li-jamʿiyyat al-maqāsid al-khayriyya al-islāmiyya fī Bayrūt: Aʿmāl al-sana al-ʿūlā. Beirut: Thamarāt al-Funūn, 1879.

Fargeallah, Maud. *Visages d'une époque*. Paris: Cariscript, 1989.

Farley, J. Lewis. *Two Years in Syria.* London: Saunders and Otley, 1858.

Geiger, André. *Le Liban et la Syrie.* Paris: Arthaud, 1932.

Guys, Henri. *Beyrout et le Liban: Relation d'un séjour de plusieurs années dans ce pays.* 2 vols. Paris: Comon, 1850; reprinted by Dār Lahd Khater, Beirut, 1985.

———. *Esquisse de l'état politique et commercial de la Syrie.* Paris: Chez France, 1862.

Hallāq, Hassān, ed. *Mudhakkirāt Salīm ʿAlī Salām.* Beirut: Al-Dār al-Jāmʿiyya, 1981.

Hélou, Charles. *Mémoires, 1964–1965.* Araya, Lebanon: Imprimerie Catholique sal Araya, 1984.

Ismaïl, Adel, ed. *Documents diplomatiques et consulaires relatifs à l'histoire du Liban et des pays du proche-Orient du XVIIᵉ siècle à nos jours. Première partie: Les sources françaises.* Beirut: Éditions des Oeuvres Politiques et Historiques, 1975–.

Jadʿūn, Ilyās, and Jirjī Jadʿūn. *Dalīl Sūriyya.* Beirut, 1923 and 1929.

Jessup, Henry Harris. *Fifty-Three Years in Syria.* 2 vols. New York: Fleming H. Revell, 1910.

Kuri, Sami, S.J. *Une histoire du Liban à travers les archives Jésuites, 1816–1973.* 3 vols. Beirut: Dār el-Mashriq, 1985–96.

Laborde, Léon de. *Voyage de la Syrie.* Paris: Didot Frères, 1837.

Lamartine, Alphonse de. *Souvenirs, impressions, pensées et paysages, pendant un voyage en orient (1832–1833).* 4 vols. Paris: C. Gosselin, 1835.

Lortet, Louis. *La Syrie d'aujourd'hui, voyage dans la Phénicie, le Liban et la Judée, 1867–1880.* Paris: Hachette, 1884.

Michaud, Joseph-François, and Jean-Joseph-François Poujoulat. *Correspondance d'Orient, 1830–1831.* 7 vols. Paris: Ducollet, 1833–35.

Nerval, Gérard de. *Voyage en Orient.* 8th edition, 2 vols. Paris: Charpentier, 1875.

Raboisson, Antoine, l'abbé. *Récit et notes d'un voyage en Palestine et en Syrie, par l'Égypte et le Sinaï.* Paris: Librairie Catholique de l'Oeuvre de Saint-Paul, 1886.

Randal, Jonathan C. *Going All the Way: Christian Warlords, Israeli Adventurers, and the War in Lebanon.* New York: Viking, 1983.

Salām al-Khālidī, ʿAnbara. *Jawla fī al-Dhikrayāt bayn Lubnān wa Filastīn.* Preface by Kamal Salibi. Beirut: Dār an-Nahār, 1978.

Sālih bin Yahya. *Tārikh Bayrūt.* Edited by Francis Hours, S.J., and Kamal Salibi. Beirut: Dār el-Mashriq, 1969.

al-Shidyaq, Ahmad Faris. *La jambe sur la jambe.* Translated by René Khawam. Paris: Phébus, 1991.

Tabet, Jacques. *Pour faire du Liban la Suisse du Levant.* Paris, 1924.

al-Tamīmī, Rafīq, and Muhammad Bahjat. *Wilāyat Bayrūt.* 2 vols. Beirut: Matbaʿat al-Iqbāl, 1917; reprinted by Dār Lahd Khater, Beirut, 1979.

Urquhart, David. *The Lebanon (Mount Souria): A History and Diary.* 2 vols. London: T. C. Newby, 1860.

Volney, C.-F. *Voyage en Égypte et en Syrie.* Edited by Jean Gaulmier. Paris: Mouton, 1959.

Zaydān, Jirjī. *Mudhakkirāt.* Beirut: Dār al-Kitāb al-Jadīd, 1968.

Zoghbi, Pharès. *À livres ouverts, une vie de souvenirs.* Beirut: Dār an-Nahār, 1998.

ALBUMS AND ILLUSTRATED VOLUMES

Baalbeck: Les riches heures du Festival. Beirut: Dār an-Nahār, 1994.

Chami, Joseph G. *Le Mémorial du Liban.* 6 vols. Beirut: Joseph G. Chami, 2002.

Debbas, Fouad. *Beyrouth, notre mémoire: Promenade guidée à travers la collection de cartes postales.* 3rd ed. Paris: Éditions Henri Berger, 1994.

———. *Des photographes à Beyrouth, 1840–1918.* Paris: Marval, 2001.

Fani, Michel. *L'atelier de Beyrouth: Liban 1848–1918.* Paris: Éditions de l'Escalier, 1996.

Fournié, Pierre, and Jean-Louis Riccioli. *La France et le Proche-Orient, 1916–1946: Une chronique photographique de la présence française en Syrie et au Liban, en Palestine, au Hedjaz et en Cilicie.* Paris: Casterman, 1996.

Freiha, Asma, and Viviane Ghanem. *Les Libanais et la vie au Liban de l'Indépendance à la guerre, 1943–1975.* Beirut: Dār Assayad, 1992.

al-Hājj, Badr. *Des photographes à Damas.* Paris: Marval, 2001.

———. *Excursions en Orient: 24 reproductions d'affiches de tourisme et de voyage.* Beirut: Layali, 2002.

Jidejian, Nina. *Beirut through the Ages.* Beirut: Dār el-Mashriq, 1973.

Kassatly, Houda. *De pierres et de couleurs: Vie et mort des maisons du vieux Beyrouth.* Beirut: Layali, 1998.

———. *Si proche, si extrême: Rituels de sursis du Liban et de Syrie.* Beirut: Layali, 1998.

———. *Beiteddine, silences et lumières.* Beirut: Layali, 2001.

Paget, Claire. *Murs et plafonds peints: Liban, XIXe siècle.* Beirut: Éditions Terre du Liban, 1998.

Salam, Nawaf, and Farès Sassine, eds. *Liban, le siècle en images.* Beirut: Dār an-Nahār, 2000.

Sarkis, Hashim. *Circa 1958: Le Liban à travers les photos et les plans de Constantinos Doxiadis.* Beirut: Dār an-Nahār, 2003.

Sassine, Farès, and Ghassan Tuéni. *El Bourj, place de la liberté et porte du Levant.* Beirut: Dār an-Nahār, 2000.

Slaoui, Abderrahman. *L'affiche orientaliste.* Casablanca: Malika Éditions, 1997.

Tuéni, Ghassan. *Le livre de l'indépendance.* Beirut: Dār an-Nahār, 2002.

al-Wali, Taha. *Bayrūt fī-l-tārih wa-l-hadāra wa-l-ʿumrān.* Beirut: Dār al-ʿilm li-l-malāyin, 1993.

STUDIES AND MONOGRAPHS

ʿAbbud Abi-ʿAql, May. *Wasat Bayrūt bayn al-iktishāfāt wa-l-jarrāfāt.* Beirut: Milaffāt an-Nahār, 1999.

Abdel-Nour, Antoine. *Tijārat Saydā maʿ al-Gharb.* Beirut: Publications de l'Université Libanaise, 1973.

———. *Introduction à l'histoire urbaine de la Syrie ottomane (XVIe siècle–XVIIIe siècle).* Beirut: Publications de l'Université Libanaise, 1982.

Abdulac, Samir. "Damas: Les années Écochard (1932–1982)." *Les Cahiers de la Recherche architecturale,* nos. 10–11 (April 1982).

Abu Khalīl, Juzīf. *Qissat al-mawārina fī al-harb: Sīra dhātīyya.* Beirut: Sharikat al-Matbūʿāt lil-Tawzīʿ wa-al-Nashr, 1990.

Abu Manneh, Butrus. "The Establishment and Dismantling of the Province of Syria, 1865–1888." In John P. Spagnolo, ed., *Problems of the Middle East in Historical Perspective: Essays in Honour of Albert Hourani*, 7–26. Reading, England: Ithaca Press, 1992.

Ajami, Fouad. *The Vanished Imam: Musa al-Sadr and the Shia of Lebanon*. Ithaca, N.Y.: Cornell University Press, 1986.

Akarli, Engin Deniz. *The Long Peace: Ottoman Lebanon, 1861–1920*. Berkeley: University of California Press, 1993.

ʿĀmil, Mahdī [pseud. Hassan Hamdan]. *Muqaddimāt nadhariyya li-dirāsat athar al-fikr al-ishtirākī fī harakat al-taharrur al-watanī al-ʿarabiyya*. 2 vols. Beirut: Dār al-Farābi, 1972.

Amīn, Qāsim. *Tahrīr al-Marʾa*. Cairo: Maktabat al-Taraqqi, 1899.

Ammoun, Denise. *Alexis Boutros: ALBA, le défi culturel*. Beirut: Éditions Alba, 2002.

[Anon.]. *Al-ʿAmal al-ishitirākī wa tanāqudāt al-wadʿ al-lubnānī*. Beirut: [no publisher indicated], 1969.

Ayalon, David. *Gunpowder and Firearms in the Mamluk Kingdom: A Challenge to a Mediaeval Society*. London: Valentine, Mitchell, 1956.

Barakat, Halim. "Social Factors Influencing Attitudes of University Students in Lebanon towards the Palestinian Resistance Movement." *Journal of Palestine Studies* 1 (1971): 87–112.

Barakat, Halim, ed. *Toward a Viable Lebanon*. London: Croom Helm; Washington, D.C.: Center for Contemporary Arab Studies, Georgetown University, 1988.

Baron, Xavier. *Les Palestiniens, un peuple*. 2nd ed. Paris: Le Sycomore, 1984.

Bar-Zohar, Michael, and Eitan Haber. *The Quest for the Red Prince*. New York: Morrow, 1983.

Bazin, Louis. "La vie intellectuelle et culturelle de l'Empire ottoman." In Mantran, ed., *Histoire de l'Empire Ottoman*, 716–24.

Béguin, François. *Arabisances: Décor architectural et tracé urbain en Afrique du Nord, 1830–1950*. Paris: Dunod, 1983.

Berger, Morroe, ed. *The New Metropolis in the Arab World*. New York: Allied Publishers, 1963.

Berque, Jacques. *Les Arabes d'hier à demain*. Paris: Seuil, 1960.

Beydoun, Ahmad. *Identité confessionnelle et temps social chez les historiens libanais contemporains*. Beirut: Publications de l'Université Libanaise, 1984.

Beyhum, Nabil. "Espaces éclatés, espaces dominés: Étude de la recomposition des espaces publics centraux de Beyrouth de 1975 à 1990." Doctoral thesis, Université de Lyon-II, 1995.

———, ed. *Reconstruire Beyrouth: Les paris sur le possible*. Lyon: Maison de l'Orient, 1991.

Bourgey, André. "L'évolution du centre de Beyrouth de 1960 à 1977." In Chevallier, ed., *L'espace social de la ville arabe*, 244–278.

———. "La guerre et ses conséquences géographiques au Liban." *Annales de géographie* 94 (1985): 1–37.

Boustany, Omar. "Berytian Graffitis" and "Les dames du temps jadis." In "Ah! qu'il était joli le Liban de papa," Special report of *L'Orient-Express*, no. 14 (January 1997).

Braude, Benjamin, and Bernard Lewis, eds. *Christians and Jews in the Ottoman Empire: The Functioning of a Plural Society*. 2 vols. New York: Holmes & Meier, 1982.

Brynen, Rex. *Sanctuary and Survival: The PLO in Lebanon*. Boulder, Colo.: Westview Press, 1990.

Buheiry, Marwan R. *Beirut's Role in the Political Economy of the French Mandate, 1919–39.* Oxford: Centre for Lebanese Studies, 1986.

———. *The Formation and Perception of the Modern Arab World: Studies.* Edited by Lawrence I. Conrad. Princeton, N.J.: Darwin Press, 1989.

———. "The Rise of the City of Beirut." In *The Formation and Perception of the Modern Arab World,* 483–87.

———. "Notes on the Beginnings of the English Open-Air Theater at the SPC and Its Social Context." In *The Formation and Perception of the Modern Arab World,* 569–74.

Buheiry, Marwan R., ed. *Intellectual Life in the Arab East, 1890–1939.* Beirut: Center for Arab and Middle East Studies, American University of Beirut, 1981.

Chaib, André. "The Export Performance of a Small, Open, Developing Economy: The Lebanese Experience, 1951–74." Ph.D. thesis, University of Michigan, 1979.

Charles-Roux, François. *Les Échelles de Syrie et de Palestine au XVIIIᵉ siècle.* Paris: P. Geuthner, 1928.

Cheikho, Louis, S.J. *Bayrūt tārīkhuhā wa āthāruha.* 3rd ed. Beirut: Dār el-Mashriq, 1993. [First edition 1926.]

Chevallier, Dominique. "Lyon et Syrie en 1919: Les bases d'une intervention." *Revue Historique* 224 (1960): 275–320.

———. *La société du mont Liban à l'époque de la Révolution industrielle en Europe.* Paris: Geuthner, 1971.

———. "Signes de Beyrouth en 1834." *Bulletin d'études orientales* 25 (1972): 211–29.

———. "Les villes arabes depuis le XIXᵉ siècle: Structures, visions, transformations." *Revue des travaux de l'Académie des sciences morales et politiques* 125 (1972): 86–98.

———. *Villes et travail en Syrie: Du XIXᵉ au XXᵉ siècle.* Paris: Maisonneuve et Larose, 1982.

Chevallier, Dominique, ed. *L'espace social de la ville arabe.* Paris: Maisonneuve et Larose, 1979.

Chiha, Michel. *Politique intérieure.* Beirut: Éditions du Trident, 1964.

Collinet, Paul. *Histoire de l'École de droit de Beyrouth.* Paris: Sirey, 1925.

Copeland, Miles. *The Game of Nations: The Amorality of Power Politics.* New York: Simon and Schuster, 1970.

Couland, Jacques. *Le mouvement syndical en Liban, 1919–1946.* Paris: Éditions Sociales, 1970.

Courbage, Youssef, and Philippe Fargues. *La situation démographique au Liban.* Beirut: Publications de l'Université Libanaise, 1974.

Cresswell, Robert. "Parenté et propriété foncière dans la montagne libanaise." *Études rurales,* no. 40 (October–December 1970): 7–79.

Davie, May. *Beyrouth et ses faubourgs (1840–1940): Une intégration inachevée.* Beirut: Centre d'Études et de Recherches sur le Moyen-Orient Contemporain, 1996.

———. *Atlas historique des orthodoxes de Beyrouth et du Mont-Liban, 1800–1940.* Tripoli, Lebanon: Publications de l'Université de Balamand, 1999.

———. *Beyrouth, 1825–1975: Un siècle et demi d'urbanisme.* Beirut: Ordre des Ingénieurs et des Architectes, 2001.

Dubar, Claude, and Salim Nasr. *Les classes sociales au Liban.* Paris: Presses de la Fondation Nationale des Sciences Politiques, 1976.

Dubertret, Louis. *Géologie du site de Beyrouth.* Beirut: Délégation Générale de France au Levant, 1945.

Du Mesnil du Buisson, Robert. "Beyrout el-Quadimé." *Bulletin de la Société historique et archéologique de l'Orne* 40 (July–October 1921).

Dumont, Paul. "La période des Tanzimât (1839–1878)." In Mantran, ed., *Histoire de l'Empire Ottoman*, 459–522.

Écochard, Michel. *Casablanca: Le roman d'une ville.* Paris: Éditions de Paris, 1955.

Eddé, Claude. "Fragments expurgés des carnets d'une jeune fille pas très rangée." In "Ah! qu'il était joli le Liban de papa," Special Report of *L'Orient-Express*, no. 14 (January 1997).

Encyclopedia of Islam. New edition. 11 vols. and supplement. Leiden: Brill, 1960–2004.

Eveland, Wilbur. *Ropes of Sand: America's Failure in the Middle East.* New York: W. W. Norton, 1980.

Fani, Michel. *Dictionnaire de la peinture au Liban.* Paris: Éditions de l'Escalier, 1998.

Favier, Agnès. "Logiques de l'engagement et modes de contestation au Liban: Genèse et éclatement d'une génération de militants intellectuels (1958–1975)." Doctoral thesis, Institut d'Études Politiques d'Aix-en-Provence, 2004.

Fawaz, Leila Tarazi. *Merchants and Migrants in Nineteenth-Century Beirut.* Cambridge, Mass.: Harvard University Press, 1983.

———. *An Occasion for War: Civil Conflict in Lebanon and Damascus in 1860.* Berkeley: University of California Press, 1994.

Gates, Carolyn. *The Merchant Republic of Lebanon: Rise of an Open Economy.* London: Centre for Lebanese Studies/I. B. Tauris, 1998.

Gendzier, Irene. "The Declassified Lebanon, 1948–1958: Elements of Continuity and Contrast in US Policy toward Lebanon." In Barakat, ed., *Toward a Viable Lebanon*, 187–209.

Georgeon, François. "Le dernier sursaut (1878–1908)." In Mantran, ed., *Histoire de l'Empire Ottoman*, 523–76.

Ghorayeb, Marlène. "The Work and Influence of Michel Écochard in Lebanon." In Rowe and Sarkis, eds., *Projecting Beirut*, 106–21.

Goria, Wade R. *Sovereignty and Leadership in Lebanon, 1943–1976.* London: Ithaca Press, 1985.

"Grand Beyrouth, trop grand Beyrouth." Special Report of *L'Orient-Express*, no. 4 (April 1996).

Hallāq, Hassān. *Bayrūt al-mahrūsa fī-l-ʿahd al-ʿuthmāni.* Beirut: Al-Dār al-Jāmiʿiyya, 1987.

Hanssen, Jens. "Your Beirut Is on My Desk: Ottomanizing Beirut under Sultan Abdül-Hamid II (1876–1909)." In Rowe and Sarkis, eds., *Projecting Beirut*, 41–67.

———. *Fin de Siècle Beirut: The Making of an Ottoman Provincial Capital.* Oxford: Oxford University Press, 2005.

Hart, Alan. *Arafat: Terrorist or Peacemaker?* London: Sidgwick and Jackson, 1984.

Hof, Frederic C. *Galilee Divided: The Israel-Lebanon Frontier, 1916–1984.* Boulder, Colo.: Westview Press, 1985.

Hourani, Albert. *Arabic Thought in the Liberal Age, 1798–1939.* London: Oxford University Press, 1962.

———. "Ideologies of the Mountain and the City." In Owen, ed., *Essays on the Crisis in Lebanon*, 33–41.

———. "Visions of Lebanon." In Barakat, ed., *Toward a Viable Lebanon*, 3–11.

———. *A History of the Arab Peoples.* Cambridge, Mass.: Belknap Press of Harvard University Press, 1991.

Hudson, Michael C. *The Precarious Republic: Political Modernization in Lebanon.* New York: Random House, 1968.

———. "The Palestinian Factor in the Lebanese Civil War." *Middle East Journal* 32 (1978): 261–78.

Husseini, Salma. "Redistribution de la population du Liban pendant la guerre civile (1975–1988)." Doctoral thesis, École des Hautes Études en Sciences Sociales, Paris, 1992.

———. "Les mouvements de population palestinienne durant la guerre civile libanaise." *Revue des études palestiniennes* 11, no. 50 (1994): 11–124.

Huvelin, Paul. "Leçon inaugurale (14 novembre 1913)." Reprinted in *Mélanges à la Mémoire de Paul Huvelin.* Paris: Sirey, 1938.

Ibrahīm, Muhsin. *Limādhā Munadhammat al-ishitirākiyyīn al-lubnāniyyīn.* [No publisher indicated], 1970.

Jabra, J., and N. Jabbara. "Political Culture and the Rural-Urban Dichotomy in Lebanon." *Political Science Review* (Jaipur, India) 19, no. 3 (July–September 1980).

Jacquet, Élisabeth. "La Mission laïque française en Syrie, 1925–1929." Master's thesis in history, Université de Paris-IV (Sorbonne), 1987.

Jeha, Shafiq. *Darwin and the Crisis of 1882 in the Medical Department; and the First Student Protest in the Arab World in the Syrian Protestant College (Now the American University of Beirut).* Edited by Helen Khal and translated by Sally Kaya. Beirut: American University of Beirut Press, 2004.

el-Jisr, Bassem. "Les plages de Beyrouth: Privatisation et communautarisation d'espaces publics." In Beyhum, ed., *Reconstruire Beyrouth,* 75–82.

Johnson, Michael. *Class and Client in Beirut: The Sunni Muslim Community and the Lebanese State, 1840–1985.* London: Ithaca Press, 1986.

Joumblatt, Kamal, with the assistance of Philippe Lapousterle. *Pour le Liban.* Paris: Stock: 1977.

Jouplain, Paul [Bulos Nujaym]. *La question du Liban: Étude d'histoire diplomatique & de droit international.* Paris: A. Rousseau, 1908.

Julien, Charles-André. "Léon Blum et les pays d'Outre-mer." In *Léon Blum, chef du gouvernement, 1936–1937* [Proceedings of a colloquium held in March 1965 at the Fondation Nationale des Sciences Politiques], 337–90. Paris: A. Colin, 1967.

Kassir, Samir. *La Guerre du Liban: De la dissension nationale au conflit régional (1975–1982).* 2nd ed. Paris and Beirut: Karthala/Centre d'Études et de Recherches sur le Moyen-Orient Contemporain, 2000.

Kassir, Samir, and Farouk Mardam-Bey. *Intinéraires de Paris à Jérusalem: La France et le conflit israélo-arabe* (vol. 1: 1917–1958; vol. 2: 1958–1991). Paris: Revue des Études Palestiniennes, 1992–93.

Kayali, Hasan. *Arabs and Young Turks: Ottomanism, Arabism, and Islamism in the Ottoman Empire, 1908–1918.* Berkeley: University of California Press, 1997.

Kerr, Malcolm H. *The Arab Cold War: Gamal 'Abd al-Nasir and His Rivals, 1958–1970.* 3rd ed. New York: Oxford University Press, 1971.

Khalaf, Samir. "Communal Conflict in Nineteenth-Century Lebanon." In Braude and Lewis, eds., *Christians and Jews in the Ottoman Empire,* 2:107–34.

Khalaf, Samir, and Per Kongstad. *Hamra of Beirut: A Case of Rapid Urbanization.* Leiden: Brill, 1973.

Khalidi, Rashid. *Under Siege: PLO Decisionmaking during the 1982 War.* New York: Columbia University Press, 1986.

———. "'Abd al-Ghanī al-'Uraisi and *Al-Mufīd:* The Press and Arab Nationalism before 1914." In Buheiry, ed., *Intellectual Life in the Arab East,* 38–61.

Khalidi, Walid. *Conflict and Violence in Lebanon: Confrontation in the Middle East.* Cambridge, Mass.: Center for International Affairs, Harvard University, 1979.

Khouri, Robert M. *La médecine au Liban: De la Phénicie à nos jours.* Beirut: Éditions ABCD [ca. 1990].

al-Khoury, Fouad. "L'industrie hôtelière au Liban." *Revue phénicienne,* August 1919.

Khoury, Gérard D. *La France et l'Orient arabe: Naissance du Liban moderne, 1914–1920.* Paris: Armand Colin, 1993.

Khuri, Fuad I. *From Village to Suburb: Order and Change in Greater Beirut.* Chicago: University of Chicago Press, 1975.

Kossaifi, Georges. "Contribution à l'étude démographique de la population palestinienne." 2 vols. Doctoral thesis, Université de Paris-I, 1976.

Labaki, Boutros. "L'évolution du rôle économique de l'agglomeration de Beyrouth, 1960–1977." In Chevallier, ed., *L'espace social de la ville arabe,* 215–244.

———. "Rapports de force intercommunautaires et genèse des conflits internes au Liban." Unpublished paper, annual meeting of Violence and Conflict in Divided Societies section of the European Consortium for Political Research, Fribourg, March 1983.

Lammens, Henri. *Syrie, précis historique.* Beirut: Imprimerie Catholique, 1921.

Laurens, Henry. *Le royaume impossible: La France et la genèse du monde arabe.* Paris: Armand Colin, 1990.

———. *L'Orient arabe: Arabisme et islamisme de 1798 à 1945.* Paris: Armand Colin, 1993.

Lewis, Bernard. *The Political Language of Islam.* Chicago: University of Chicago Press, 1988.

Makdisi, Ussama. *The Culture of Sectarianism: Community, History, and Violence in Nineteenth-Century Ottoman Lebanon.* Berkeley: University of California Press, 2000.

Mantran, Robert, ed. *Histoire de l'Empire Ottoman.* Paris: Fayard, 1989.

Ma'oz, Moshe. *Ottoman Reform in Syria and Palestine, 1840–1861: The Impact of the Tanzimat on Politics and Society.* Oxford: Clarendon Press, 1968.

Mardam-Bey, Farouk. *La cuisine de Zyriab.* Arles: Actes Sud, 1999.

Marthelot, Pierre. "Une ville remplit son site: Beyrouth." *Méditerranée* 4, no. 3 (1963): 37–55.

Moore, Clement Henry. "Le système bancaire libanais: Les substituts financiers d'un ordre politique." *Maghreb-Machrek* 99 (1983): 30–46.

Mouterde, René, S.J. "Le temple de Vénus dans la Beyrouth romaine." *Al-Mashriq* 22 (1924): 195–200.

———. *Regards sur Beyrouth phénicienne, hellenistique et romaine.* Beirut: Imprimerie Catholique, 1966.

Müller, Ludvig. *Numismatique d'Alexandre le Grand.* Copenhagen: B. Luno, 1855.

Naccache, Albert. "L'industrie de la villégiature au Liban." *Revue phénicienne,* December 1919.

Naïm-Sanbar, Samia. *Le parler arabe de Rās-Beyrouth, 'Ayn al Muraysa: La diversité phonologique, étude socio-linguistique.* Paris: Geuthner, 1985.

Nashabi, Hisham. "Shaykh 'Abd al-Qadir al-Qabbani and *Thamarāt al-Funūn.*" In Buheiry, ed., *Intellectual Life in the Arab East,* 84–91.

O'Neill, Bard E. *Armed Struggle in Palestine: A Political-Military Analysis.* Boulder, Colo.: Westview Press, 1978.

Owen, Roger. "The Economic History of Lebanon, 1943–1974: Its Salient Features." In Barakat, ed., *Toward a Viable Lebanon,* 27–41.

Owen, Roger, ed. *Essays on the Crisis in Lebanon.* London: Ithaca Press, 1976.

Paix, Catherine. "La portée spatiale des activités tertiaires de commandement économique au Liban." *Revue Tiers-Monde* 16, no. 61 (1975).

Pakradouni, Karim. *La paix manquée: Le mandat d'Elias Sarkis, 1976–1982.* Beirut: Éditions FMA, 1983.

Picard, Elizabeth. *Liban, État de discorde: Des fondations aux guerres fratricides.* Paris: Flammarion, 1988.

Poupon. M. "La modernisation de Beyrouth." *Bulletin de l'Union économique de Syrie* 7 (1928): 23–29, and 8 (1929): 18–22.

"Quand la politique faisait rêver." Special Report of *L'Orient-Express* no. 1 (November 1995).

Rabbath, Edmond. *La Constitution libanaise: Origines, textes et commentaires.* Beirut: Université Libanaise, 1982.

———. *La formation historique du Liban constitutionnel et politique.* 2nd ed. Beirut: Publications de l'Université Libanaise, 1986.

Rafeq, Abdul-Karim. *The Province of Damascus, 1723–1783.* Beirut: Khayats, 1970.

———. "Les provinces arabes (XVIe siècle–XVIIIe siècle)." In Mantran, ed., *Histoire de l'Empire Ottoman,* 341–420.

Raymond, André, ed. *La Syrie, d'aujourd'hui.* Paris: Éditions du CNRS, 1980.

Reclus, Élisée. *L'homme et la terre . . .* 6 vols. Paris: Librairie Universelle, 1905–8.

Riachi, Georges. "The City of Beirut, Its Origin and Evolution." In Berger, ed., *The New Metropolis in the Arab World,* 103–14.

Riad, Mahmoud. "Au coeur du conflit." Interview in *Revue d'études palestiniennes* 19 (Spring 1986): 7–16.

Rodinson, Maxime. *Israël et le refus arabe: 75 ans d'histoire.* Paris: Éditions du Seuil, 1968.

———. *L'Islam: Politique et croyance.* Paris: Fayard, 1993.

Rondot, Philippe. *Le Proche-Orient à la recherche de la paix, 1973–1982.* Paris: Presses Universitaires de France, 1982.

———. "Beyrouth 1930." In Beyhum, ed., *Reconstruire Beyrouth,* 69–74.

Roussel, Pierre. "Laodicée de Phénicie." *Bulletin de correspondance hellénique* 35 (1911): 433–40.

Rouvier, Jules. "Une métropole phénicienne oubliée, Laodicée métropole de Canaan." *Al-Mashriq* 1 (1898): 17–20.

Rowe, Peter G., and Hashim Sarkis, eds. *Projecting Beirut: Episodes in the Construction and Reconstruction of a Modern City.* Munich and New York: Prestel Verlag, 1998.

Ruppert, Helmut. "Beyrouth, une ville d'Orient marquée par l'Occident." Translated and edited by Éric Verdeil and Laurent Combes. *Les Cahiers du Cermoc* 21 (1999): 1–169.

Rustom, Assad. "Idārat al-Shām, rūhuha wa haykaluha wa atharuha." In al-Jam'iyyah al-

Misrīyyah lil-Dirāsāt al-Tārīkhīyyah, ed., *Dhikrā al-batal al-fātih Ibrahim Pasha, 1848–1948*. Reprint, Cairo: Madbuli, 1990.

Sabry, Muhammad. *L'Empire égyptien sous Mohamed-Ali et la question d'Orient, 1811–1849: Égypte, Arabie, Soudan, Morée, Crète, Syrie, Palestine*. Paris: Paul Geuthner, 1930.

Sachar, Howard M. *Europe Leaves the Middle East, 1936–1954*. New York: Alfred A. Knopf, 1972.

Sader, Helen. "Ancient Beirut: Urban Growth in the Light of Recent Excavations." In Rowe and Sarkis, eds., *Projecting Beirut*, 23–40.

Saʿdūn, Fawwaz. *Al-Haraka al-islāhiyya fī Bayrūt fī awākhir al-ʿasr al-ʿuthmānī*. Beirut: Dār an-Nahār, 1994.

al-Saʿīd, Nāsir. *Tārīkh āl Saʿūd*. Beirut: [no publisher indicated], 1978.

Salām, Nawaf. "L'insurrection de 1958 au Liban." Doctoral thesis in history, Université de Paris-IV (Sorbonne), 1979.

———. *Mythe et politique au Liban: Trois essais*. Beirut: Éditions FMA, 1987.

———. "The Institution of the Presidency in Elections in Lebanon." In Shehadi and Harney, eds., *Politics and the Economy in Lebanon*, 69–74.

———. *La condition libanaise: Des communautés, du citoyen et de l'état*. Beirut: Dār an-Nahār, 1998.

Salamé, Ghassan. *Le théâtre politique au Liban (1968–1973): Approche idéologique et esthétique*. Beirut: Dār el-Mashriq, 1974.

Salibi, Kamal S. *The Modern History of Lebanon*. New York: Praeger, 1965.

———. *Cross Roads to Civil War: Lebanon, 1958–1976*. Delmar, N.Y.: Caravan Books, 1976.

———. "Beirut under the Young Turks as Depicted in the Political Memoirs of Salīm ʿAlī Salām." In Jacques Berque and Dominique Chevallier, eds., *Les Arabes par leurs archives: XVIe–XXe siècles*, 193–215. Paris: Éditions du CNRS, 1976.

———. *A House of Many Mansions: The History of Lebanon Reconsidered*. Berkeley: University of California Press; London: I. B. Tauris, 1988.

Sālim, Latīfa Muhammad. *Al-Hukm al-masrī fī-l-Shām, 1831–1841*. 2nd ed. Cairo: Madbuli, 1990.

Sartre, Maurice. *L'Orient romain: Provinces et sociétés en Méditerranée orientale d'Auguste aux Sévères (31 avant J.-C.–235 après J.-C.)*. Paris: Éditions du Seuil, 1991.

———. *D'Alexandre à Zénobie: Histoire de Levant antique, IVe siècle av. J.-C.–IIIe siècle ap. J.-C.* Paris: Fayard, 2001.

———. *The Middle East under Rome*. Translated by Catherine Porter and Elizabeth Rawlings with Jeannine Routier-Pucci. Cambridge, Mass.: Belknap Press of Harvard University Press, 2005.

Saydah, Roger. "The Prehistory of Beirut." In *Beirut—Crossroads of Cultures*. Beirut: Salwa Nassar Foundation for Lebanese Studies/Librairie du Liban, 1970.

Sayigh, Rosemary. *Palestinians: From Peasants to Revolutionaries*. London: Zed Press, 1979.

Schölch, Alexander. "Le développement économique de la Palestine, 1856–1882." *Revue d'études palestiniennes*, no. 10 (Winter 1984): 93–113.

Sehnaoui, Nada. *L'Occidentalisation de la vie quotidienne à Beyrouth, 1860–1914*. Beirut: Dār an-Nahār, 2002.

Seikaly, May. *Haifa: Transformation of an Arab Society, 1918–1939*. London: I. B. Tauris, 2002.

Sharāra, Waddāh. *Al-Silm al-ahlī al-bārid, Lubnān, al-mujtama' wa-l-dawla, 1964–1967.* Beirut: Dār an-Nahār, 1980.

Shehadi, Nadim, and Bridget Harney, eds. *Politics and the Economy in Lebanon.* Oxford: Centre for Lebanese Studies, 1989.

Sinno, Chadia. "Évolution des structures urbaines du centre-ville de Beyrouth." Master's thesis in urban studies, Université de Paris-VIII, 1986.

Stoakes, Frank. "The Supervigilantes: The Lebanese Kataeb Party as a Builder, Surrogate, and Defender of the State." *Middle Eastern Studies* 11, no. 3 (October 1975): 215–236.

Suwayd, Muhammad. *Ya fu'ādī.* Beirut: Dār an-Nahār, 1994.

Tabet, Jade. "La ville imparfaite: Le concept de centralité urbaine dans les projets d'aménagement et de reconstruction de Beyrouth." In Beyhum, ed., *Reconstruire Beyrouth,* 85–120.

——. "From Colonial Style to Regional Revivalism: Modern Architecture in Lebanon and the Problem of Cultural Identity." In Rowe and Sarkis, eds. *Projecting Beirut,* 83–106.

——. *Beyrouth.* Paris: Institut Français d'Architecture, 2001.

Terrasse, Michel. "Écochard." In *Dictionnaire des architectes.* Paris: Encyclopaedia Universalis/Albin Michel, 1999.

Thobie, Jacques. *Intérêts et impérialisme français dans l'Empire ottoman, 1895–1914.* Paris: Imprimerie Nationale, 1977.

Tibawi, Abdul-Latif. *American Interests in Syria, 1800–1901: A Study of Educational, Literary and Religious Work.* Oxford: Clarendon Press, 1966.

——. "The Genesis and Early History of the Syrian Protestant College." *Middle East Journal* 21, nos. 1 and 2 (1967): 1–15 and 199–212.

Touma, Toufic. *Paysans et institutions féodales chez les druzes et les maronites du Liban du XVIIe siècle à 1914.* 2 vols. Beirut: Publications de l'Université Libanaise, 1972.

Traboulsi, Fawaz. "Identités et solidarités croisées dans les conflits du Liban contemporaine." Doctoral thesis in history, Université de Paris-VIII, 1993.

——. "Ahmad Farès al-Chidyaq, de la modernité en tant que femme." *L'Orient-Express,* no. 5 (April 1996).

——. "Un amour de soie." *L'Orient-Express,* no. 6 (May 1996).

——. "Le pas de deux de l'émir Abdel-Kader et de Youssef bey Karam." *L'Orient-Express,* no. 11 (October 1996).

Winslow, Charles. *Lebanon: War and Politics in a Fragmented Society.* New York: Routledge, 1996.

Zamir, Meir. *The Formation of Modern Lebanon.* Ithaca, N.Y.: Cornell University Press, 1988.

Zisser, Eyal. *Lebanon: The Challenge of Independence.* London: I. B. Tauris, 2000.

Ziyadé, Khaled. "Riad al-Solh, l'enfant des villes, l'homme des mutations." *L'Orient-Express,* no. 1 (Novemember 1995).

PHOTOGRAPHIC CREDITS

Abbudi, Saïd	Figures 102a–c
Arab Image Foundation	Figure 55
Ayad, Sami	Figure 98
Beirut, Ministry of Tourism, photo archive	Figures 1, 108
Beirut, National Archives	Figure 37
Chami, Joseph G., *Le Mémorial du Liban* (Beirut: Joseph G. Chami, 2002)	Figures 62, 71, 73a–b, 75, 83, 91
Debbas, Fouad, collection	Figures 19, 21, 30, 33, 34, 68, 70
Farrukh, Hani, collection	Figures 36, 74
al-Hajj, Badr, collection	Figure 54
Kassatly, Houda	Figures 88, 103, 109, 110
Kassir, Maïsa	Figures 2, 4, 5, 6, 7, 8, 9, 11, 12, 13, 93
Kassir, Sleiman	Figure 105
MAPS Geosystems, Beirut-Munich	Figures 3, 104, 106
An-Nahār archives	Figure 77
Nicolas Sursock Museum	Figure 72
L'Orient-Express archives	Figures 80, 81, 84, 85, 86, 89, 90, 94, 95, 96, 97, 99, 100, 101, 107
L'Orient–Le Jour archives	Figures 76, 87, 92
Salam, Nawaf, collection	Figures 10, 14, 15, 17, 18, 20, 22, 23, 24, 25a–b, 26, 27, 28, 29, 31, 32, 35, 41, 43, 44, 45, 46, 47, 48, 49, 52, 53, 56, 57, 59, 60, 61, 63, 64, 65, 67, 69
Salam, Nawaf, and Farès Sassine, *Liban, le siècle en images* (Beirut: Dār an-Nahār, 2000)	Figures 50, 55, 78, 79, 98
Sassine, Farès, and Ghassan Tuéni, *El Bourj, place de la liberté et porte du Levant* (Beirut: Dār an-Nahār, 2000)	Figures 16, 38
Sehnaoui Ziadé, Leila, collection	Figures 39, 40a–b, 42

INDEX

Page numbers in italic indicate illustrations.

COMPOSITOR
Integrated Composition Systems

TEXT
10/12.5 Minion Pro

DISPLAY
Minion Pro

INDEXER
Barbara Roos

CPSIA information can be obtained
at www.ICGtesting.com
Printed in the USA
LVOW12s0223090217

523458LV00006B/40/P